ULTIMATE COMICS

DIVIDED WE FALL

UNITED WE STAND

★ ★ ★

Collection Editor: **Jennifer Grünwald**   Assistant Editors: **Alex Starbuck** & **Nelson Ribeiro**
Editor, Special Projects: **Mark D. Beazley**   Senior Editor, Special Projects: **Jeff Youngquist**
Senior Vice President of Sales: **David Gabriel**   SVP of Brand Planning & Communications: **Michael Pasciullo**
Book Designer: **Rodolfo Muraguchi**

Editor in Chief: **Axel Alonso**   Chief Creative Officer: **Joe Quesada**
Publisher: **Dan Buckley**   Executive Producer: **Alan Fine**

★ ★ ★

ULTIMATE COMICS DIVIDED WE FALL, UNITED WE STAND. Contains material originally published in magazine form as ULTIMATE COMICS X-MEN #13-18, ULTIMATE COMICS ULTIMATES #13-18 and ULTIMATE COMICS SPIDER-MAN #13-17. First printing 2013. ISBN# 978-0-7851-6781-5. Published by MARVEL WORLDWIDE, INC., a subsidiary of MARVEL ENTERTAINMENT, LLC. OFFICE OF PUBLICATION: 135 West 50th Street, New York, NY 10020. Copyright © 2012 and 2013 Marvel Characters, Inc. All rights reserved. All characters featured in this issue and the distinctive names and likenesses thereof, and all related indicia are trademarks of Marvel Characters, Inc. No similarity between any of the names, characters, persons, and/or institutions in this magazine with those of any living or dead person or institution is intended, and any such similarity which may exist is purely coincidental. **Printed in the U.S.A.** ALAN FINE, EVP - Office of the President, Marvel Worldwide, Inc. and EVP & CMO Marvel Characters B.V.; DAN BUCKLEY, Publisher & President - Print, Animation & Digital Divisions; JOE QUESADA, Chief Creative Officer; TOM BREVOORT, SVP of Publishing; DAVID BOGART, SVP of Operations & Procurement, Publishing; RUWAN JAYATILLEKE, SVP & Associate Publisher, Publishing; C.B. CEBULSKI, SVP of Creator & Content Development; DAVID GABRIEL, SVP of Publishing Sales & Circulation; MICHAEL PASCIULLO, SVP of Brand Planning & Communications; JIM O'KEEFE, VP of Operations & Logistics; DAN CARR, Executive Director of Publishing Technology; SUSAN CRESPI, Editorial Operations Manager; ALEX MORALES, Publishing Operations Manager; STAN LEE, Chairman Emeritus. For information regarding advertising in Marvel Comics or on Marvel.com, please contact Niza Disla, Director of Marvel Partnerships, at ndisla@marvel.com. For Marvel subscription inquiries, please call 800-217-9158. **Manufactured between 12/3/2012 and 1/14/2013 by R.R. DONNELLEY, INC., SALEM, VA, USA.**

10 9 8 7 6 5 4 3 2 1

DIVIDED WE FALL

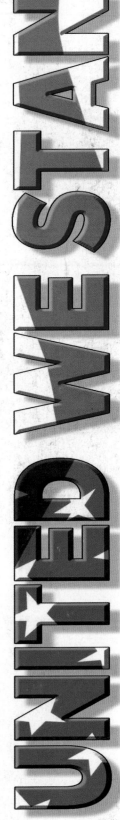

ULTIMATE COMICS ULTIMATES #13-18

WRITER: **SAM HUMPHRIES**
PENCILERS: **BILLY TAN** (#13-15)
& **LUKE ROSS** (#16-18)
WITH **TIMOTHY GREEN II** (#14)
INKERS: **TERRY PALLOT** (#13-15)
& **LUKE ROSS** (#16-18)
COLORISTS: **MATT MILLA** (#13 & #15-18) &
IFANSYAH NOOR (#14-15) WITH **ANDRES MOSSA** & **JESUS ABURTOV** (#15)
LETTERER: **VC'S CLAYTON COWLES**
COVER ART: **MICHAEL KOMARCK**

★

ULTIMATE COMICS X-MEN #13-18

WRITER: **BRIAN WOOD**
PENCILERS: **PACO MEDINA** (#13-16),
REILLY BROWN (#13-14),
CARLO BARBERI (#16-18)
& **AGUSTIN PADILLA** (#18)
INKERS: **JUAN VLASCO** (#13-18)
& **TERRY PALLOT** (#13-14)
COLORIST: **MARTE GRACIA**
LETTERER: **VC'S JOE SABINO**
COVER ART: **KAARE ANDREWS** (#13),
DAVE JOHNSON (#14 & #16-18)
& **PHIL NOTO** (#15)

★

ULTIMATE COMICS SPIDER-MAN #13-18

WRITER: **BRIAN MICHAEL BENDIS**
ARTISTS: **DAVID MARQUEZ** (#13-15 & #18)
& **PEPE LARRAZ** (#16-17)
COLOR ARTIST: **JUSTIN PONSOR**
LETTERER: **VC'S CORY PETIT**
COVER ART: **JORGE MOLINA** (#13-15),
DAVID MARQUEZ & **RAINIER BEREDO** (#16 & #18) AND **SARA PICHELLI** & **RAINIER BEREDO** (#17)

★

ASSISTANT EDITORS:
JON MOISAN & **EMILY SHAW**
ASSOCIATE EDITOR: **SANA AMANAT**
EDITOR: **MARK PANICCIA**

UNITED WE STAND

1

★

ULTIMATE COMICS **ULTIMATES** #13

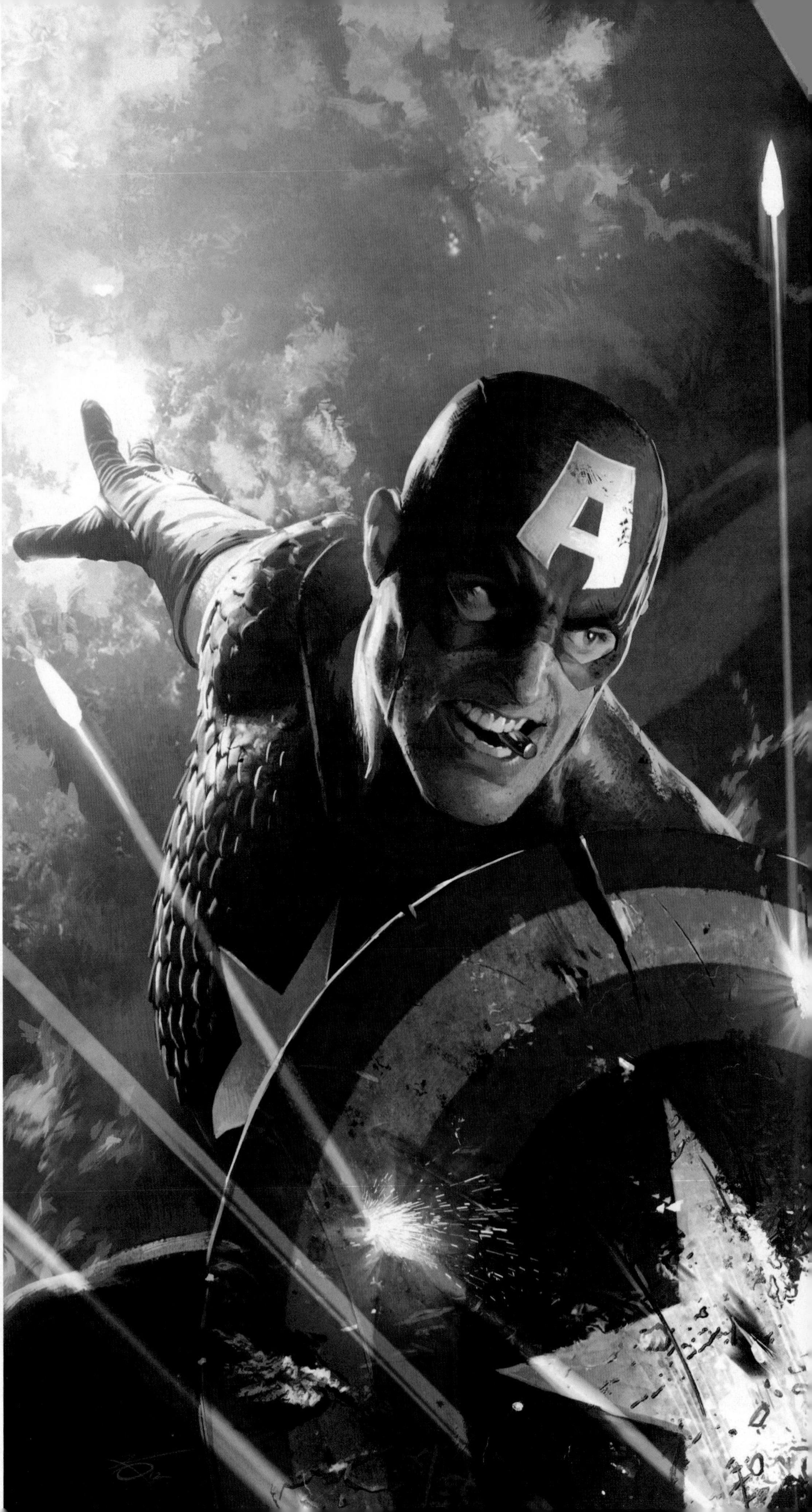

AN ELITE GOVERNMENT-SPONSORED META-HUMAN TASK FORCE, THEY FACE ANY AND ALL GLOBAL THREATS. LED BY GENERAL NICK FURY, THEY ARE...

ULTIMATE COMICS THE ULTIMATES

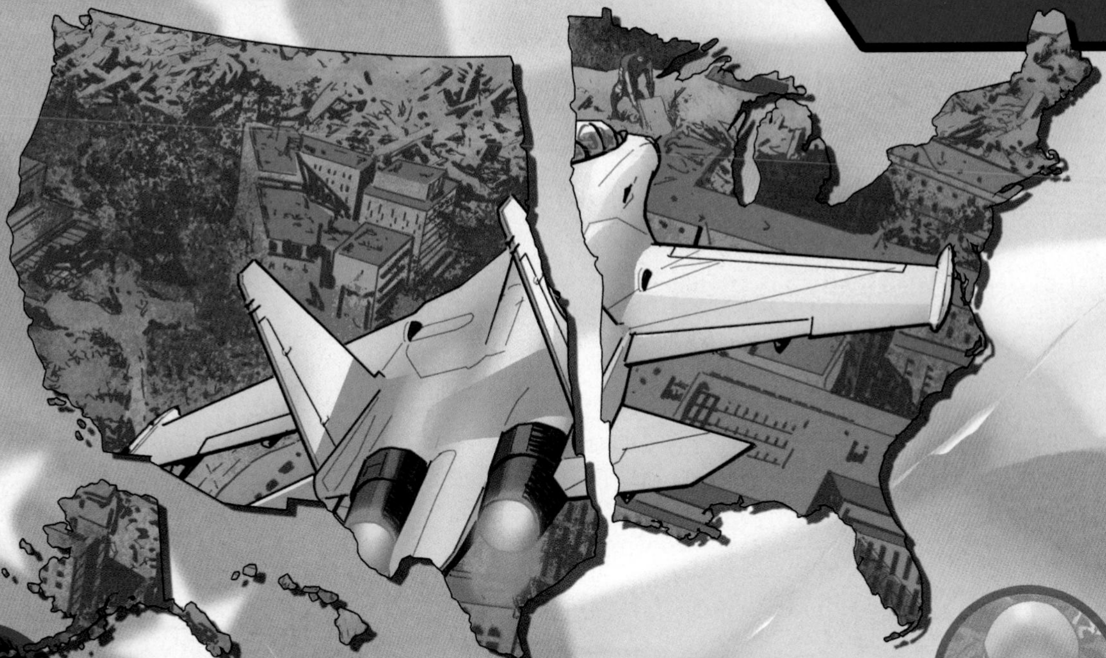

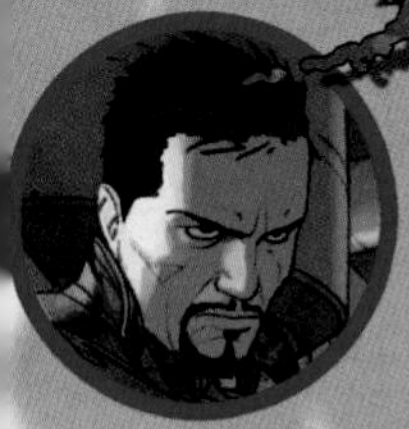

IRON MAN

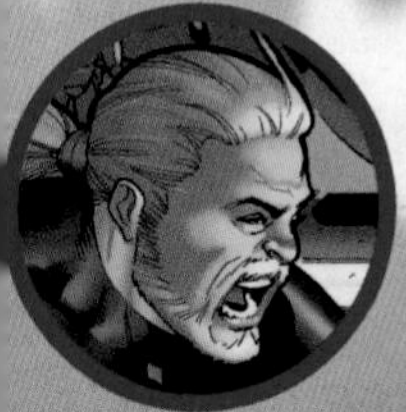

THOR

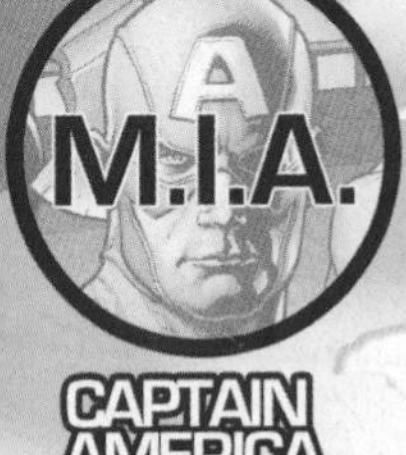
M.I.A.

CAPTAIN AMERICA

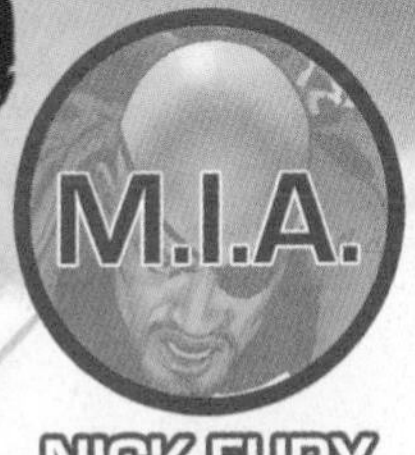
M.I.A.

NICK FURY

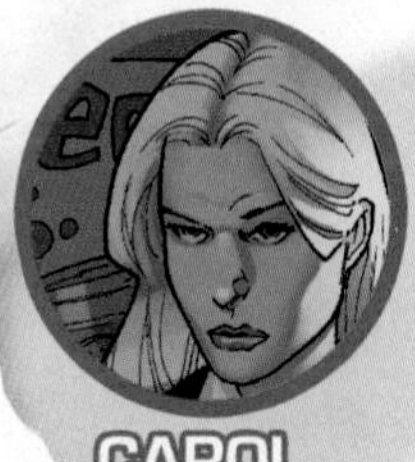

CAROL DANVERS

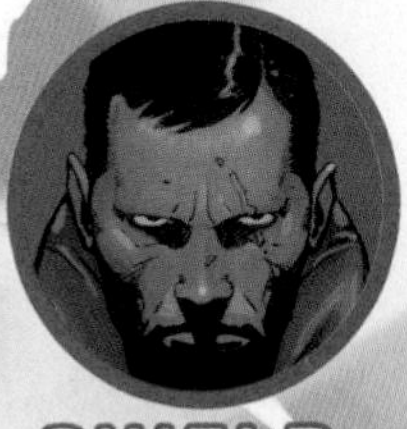

S.H.I.E.L.D. DIRECTOR FLUMM

The Ultimates are scattered.

Washington is decimated.

The government is a mess.

The Southwest is in chaos.

States are seceding from the union.

America is falling apart.

When you see this: AR, open up the MARVEL AR APP (available on applicable Apple ® iOS or Android TM devices) and use your camera-enabled device to unlock extra-special exclusive features!

S.H.I.E.L.D. SITUATION MAP:

[Anti-government militia hot spots]

Montana, N.Dakota
S.Dakota, Wyoming
Arizona, New Mexico
N.Carolina, S.Carolina
Georgia

[Eastern seaboard control zone]

New England,
New York,
New Jersey,
Delaware,
Washington, D.C.,
Maryland,
Virginia

secured by
National Guard
under emergency
powers
committee

[the West Coast]

California, Oregon
Washington
status unknown

[Great Lakes states]

Minnesota,
Wisconsin,
Michigan,
Illinois,
Indiana, Ohio
status unknown

ANTI-MATTER
NO FLY
ZONE

SENTINEL
PUSH

SOUTHERN
CALIFORNIA
REFUGEE ZONE

NUCLEAR-ARMED
NATION

DALLAS:
CAPITAL CITY OF
THE NEW REPUBLIC
OF TEXAS

Classified Position

Camp Hutton, secure
location of the President
of the United States

[Sentinel-controlled no man's land]

New Mexico, Arizona
Utah, Oklahoma
abandoned by the
US government

[The New Republic of Texas]

Texas
declared state
independence

ALL STATES
SHOWN IN WHITE
ARE U.S. GOVERNMENT
CONTROLLED ZONES

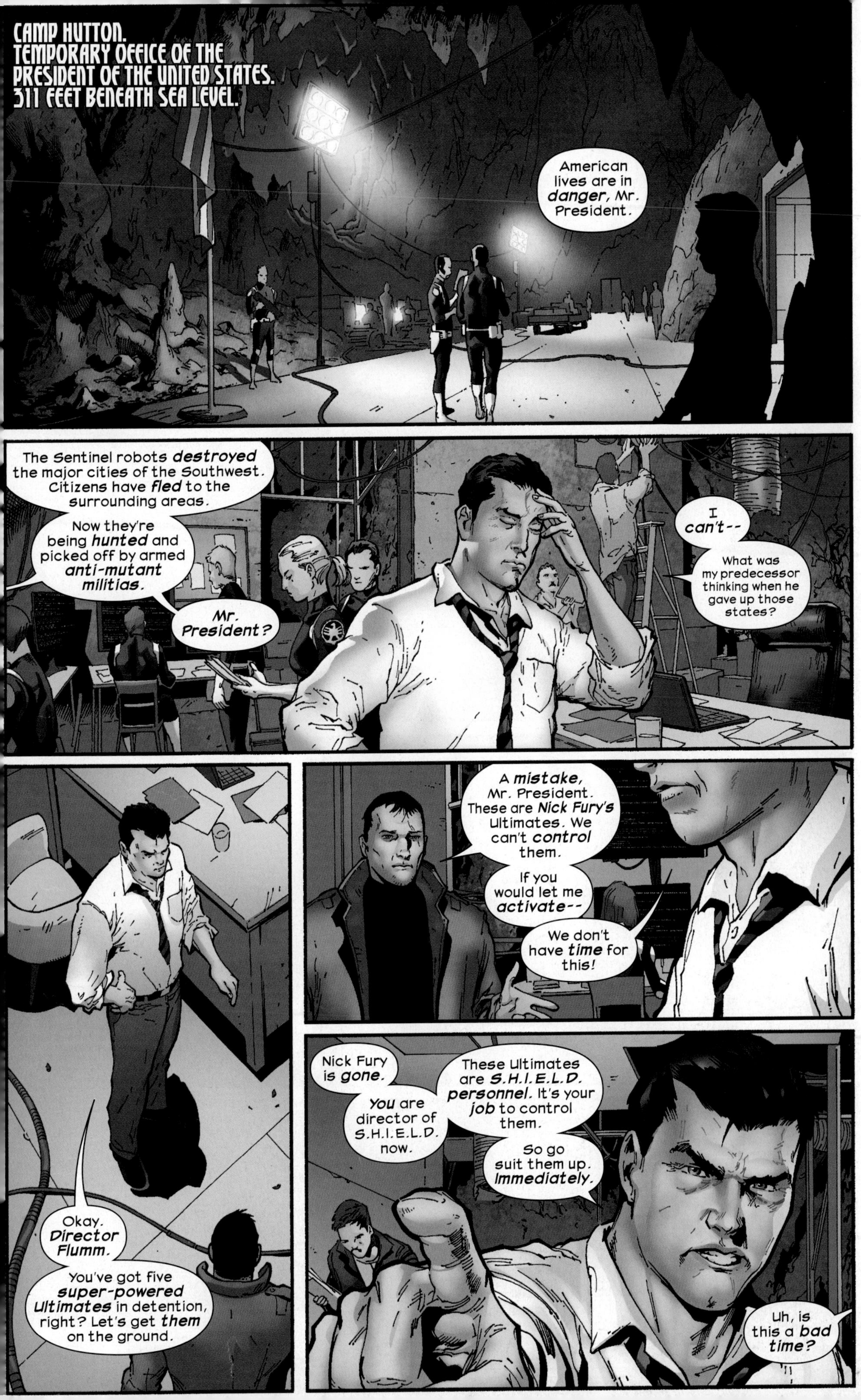
CAMP HUTTON.
TEMPORARY OFFICE OF THE PRESIDENT OF THE UNITED STATES.
311 FEET BENEATH SEA LEVEL.
American lives are in danger, Mr. President.
The Sentinel robots destroyed the major cities of the Southwest. Citizens have fled to the surrounding areas.
Now they're being hunted and picked off by armed anti-mutant militias.
Mr. President?
I can't--
What was my predecessor thinking when he gave up those states?
A mistake, Mr. President. These are Nick Fury's Ultimates. We can't control them.
If you would let me activate--
We don't have time for this!
Okay. Director Flumm.
You've got five super-powered Ultimates in detention, right? Let's get them on the ground.
Nick Fury is gone.
You are director of S.H.I.E.L.D. now.
These Ultimates are S.H.I.E.L.D. personnel. It's your job to control them.
So go suit them up. Immediately.
Uh, is this a bad time?

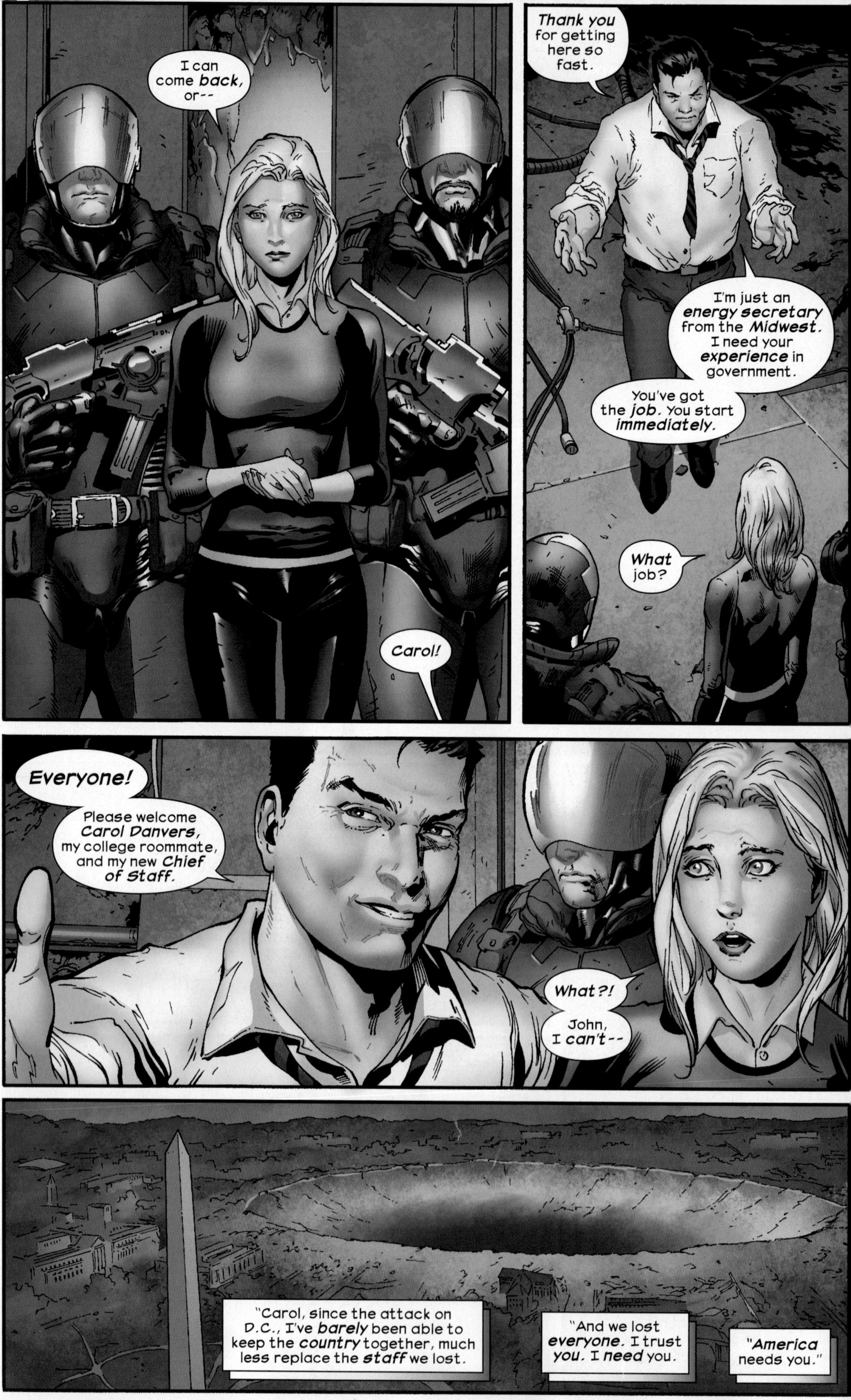
I can come *back*, or--
Carol!
Thank you for getting here so fast.
I'm just an *energy secretary* from the *Midwest*. I need your *experience* in government.
You've got the *job*. You start *immediately*.
What job?
Everyone!
Please welcome *Carol Danvers*, my college roommate, and my new *Chief of Staff*.
What?!
John, I *can't*--
"Carol, since the attack on D.C., I've *barely* been able to keep the *country* together, much less replace the *staff* we lost.
"And we lost *everyone*. I trust *you*. I *need* you.
"*America* needs you."

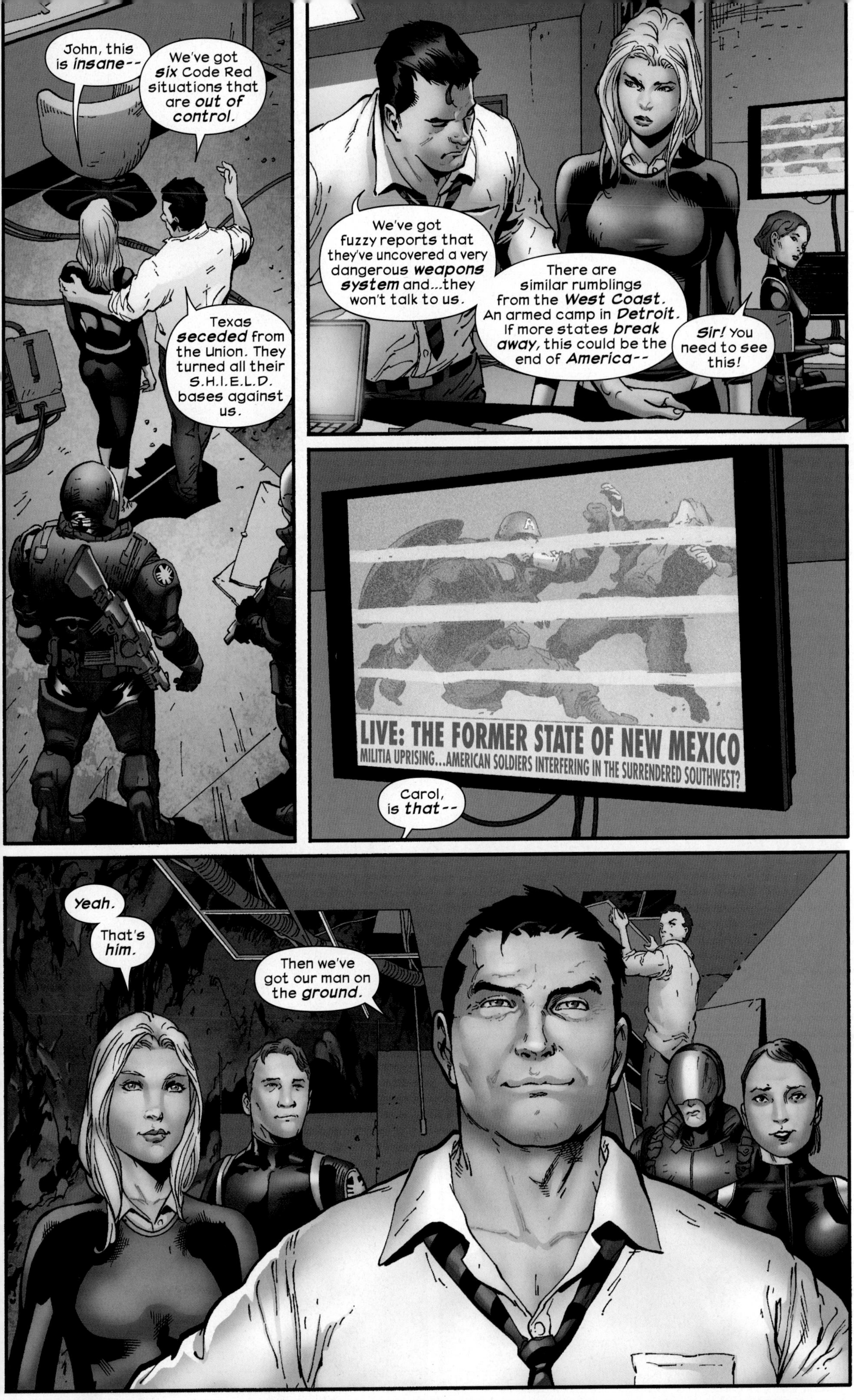
John, this is insane--
We've got six Code Red situations that are out of control.
Texas seceded from the Union. They turned all their S.H.I.E.L.D. bases against us.
We've got fuzzy reports that they've uncovered a very dangerous weapons system and...they won't talk to us.
There are similar rumblings from the West Coast. An armed camp in Detroit. If more states break away, this could be the end of America--
Sir! You need to see this!
LIVE: THE FORMER STATE OF NEW MEXICO
MILITIA UPRISING...AMERICAN SOLDIERS INTERFERING IN THE SURRENDERED SOUTHWEST?
Carol, is that--
Yeah.
That's him.
Then we've got our man on the ground.

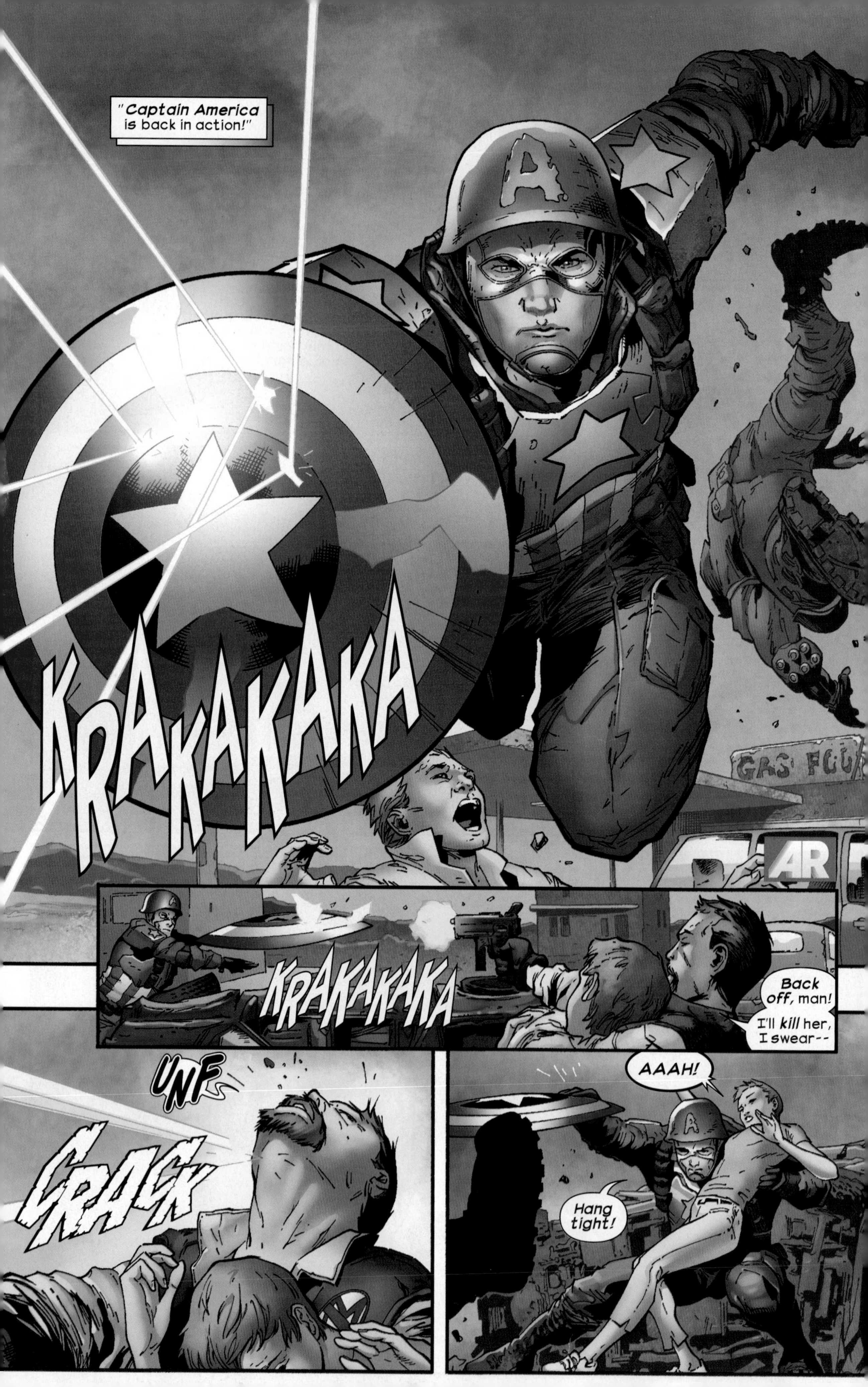
"Captain America is back in action!"
KRAKAKAKA
KRAKAKAKA
Back off, man!
I'll kill her, I swear--
UNF
CRACK
AAAH!
Hang tight!

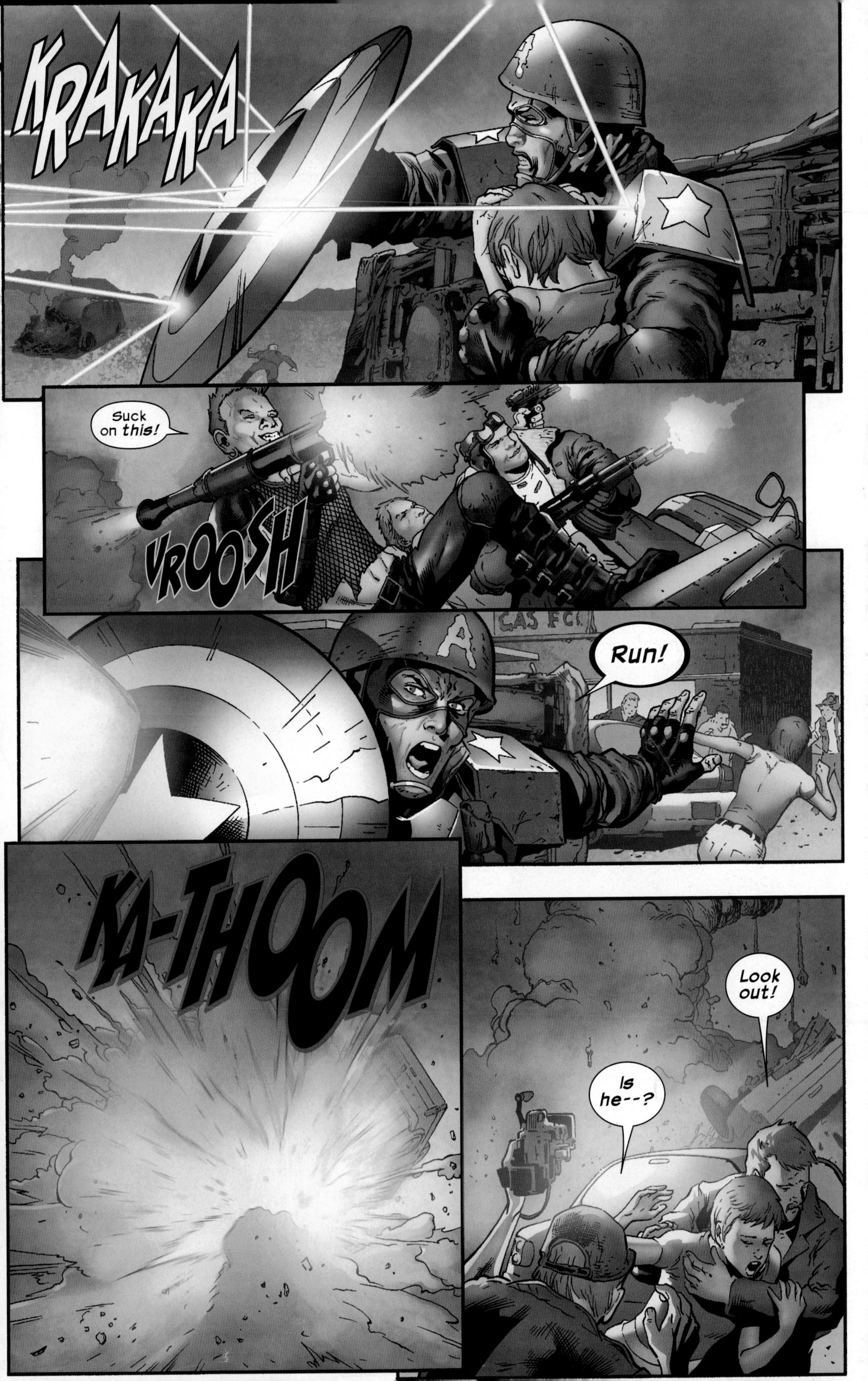
KRAKAKA
Suck on this!
VROOSH
Run!
KA-THOOM
Look out!
Is he--?

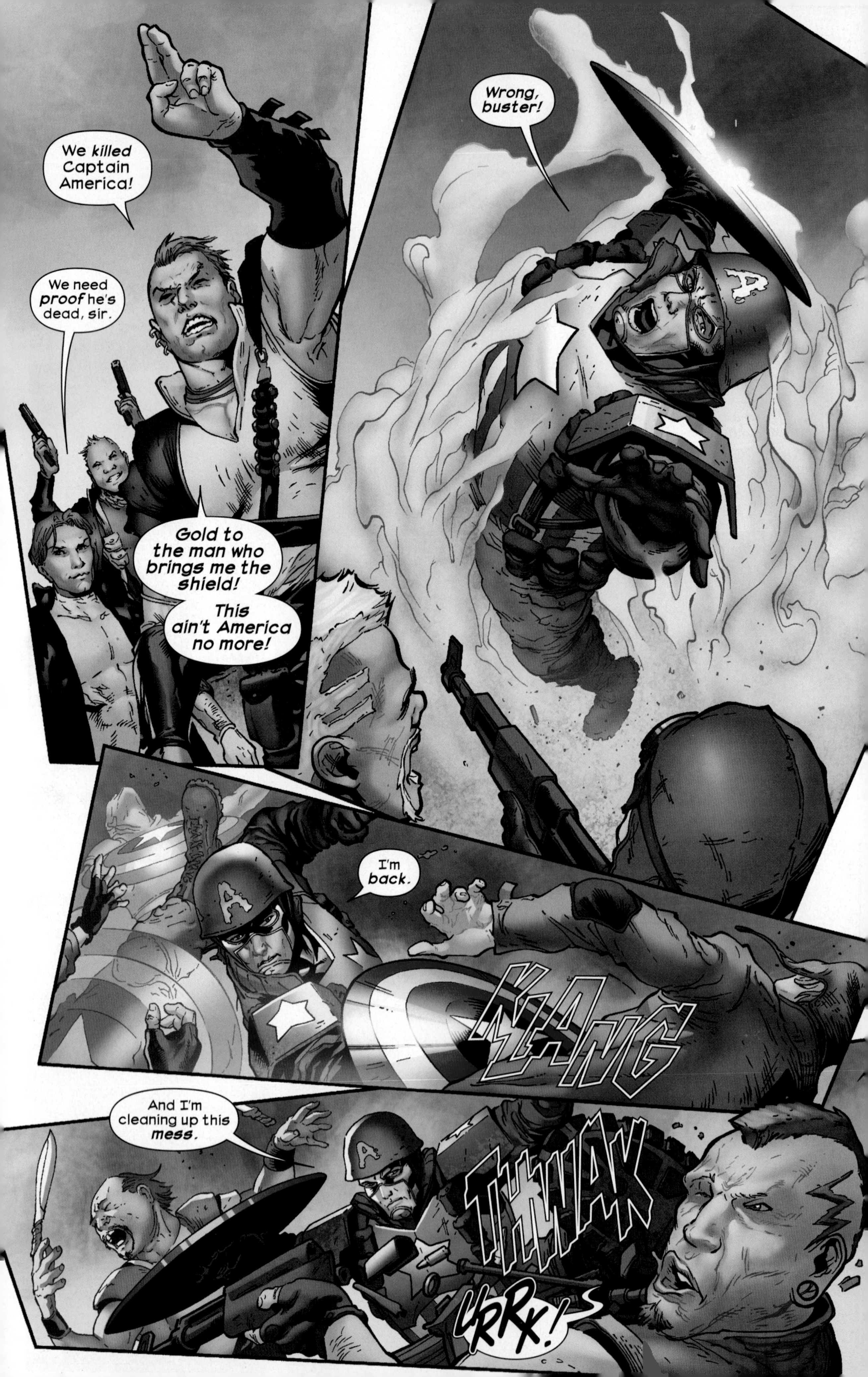
We killed Captain America!
We need proof he's dead, sir.
Gold to the man who brings me the shield!
This ain't America no more!
Wrong, buster!
I'm back.
KLANG
And I'm cleaning up this mess.
THWAK
URRK!

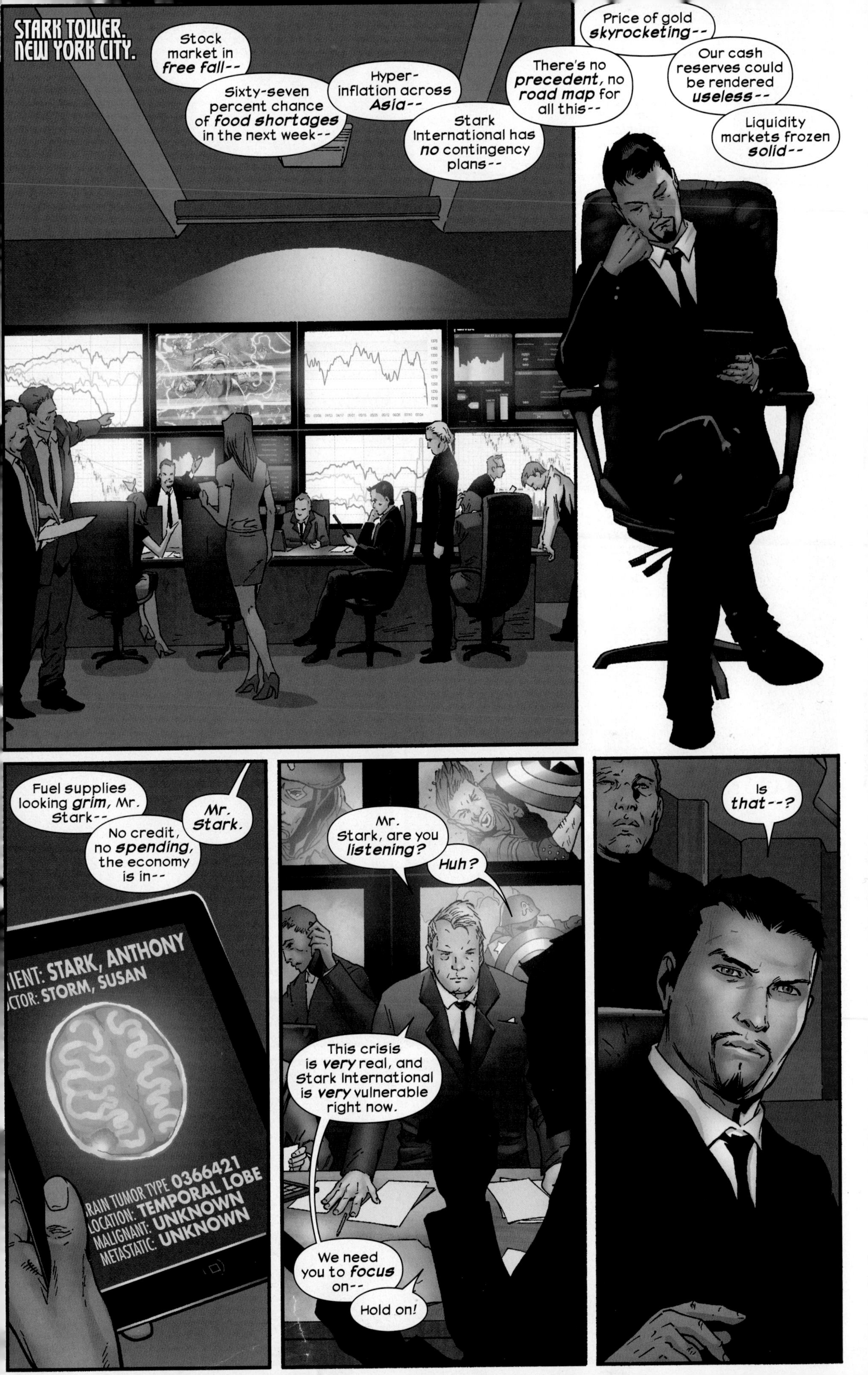
STARK TOWER. NEW YORK CITY.
Stock market in free fall--
Sixty-seven percent chance of food shortages in the next week--
Hyper-inflation across Asia--
Stark International has no contingency plans--
There's no precedent, no road map for all this--
Price of gold skyrocketing--
Our cash reserves could be rendered useless--
Liquidity markets frozen solid--
Fuel supplies looking grim, Mr. Stark--
No credit, no spending, the economy is in--
Mr. Stark.
TIENT: STARK, ANTHONY
OCTOR: STORM, SUSAN
RAIN TUMOR TYPE 0366421
LOCATION: TEMPORAL LOBE
MALIGNANT: UNKNOWN
METASTATIC: UNKNOWN
Mr. Stark, are you listening?
Huh?
This crisis is very real, and Stark International is very vulnerable right now.
We need you to focus on--
Hold on!
Is that--?

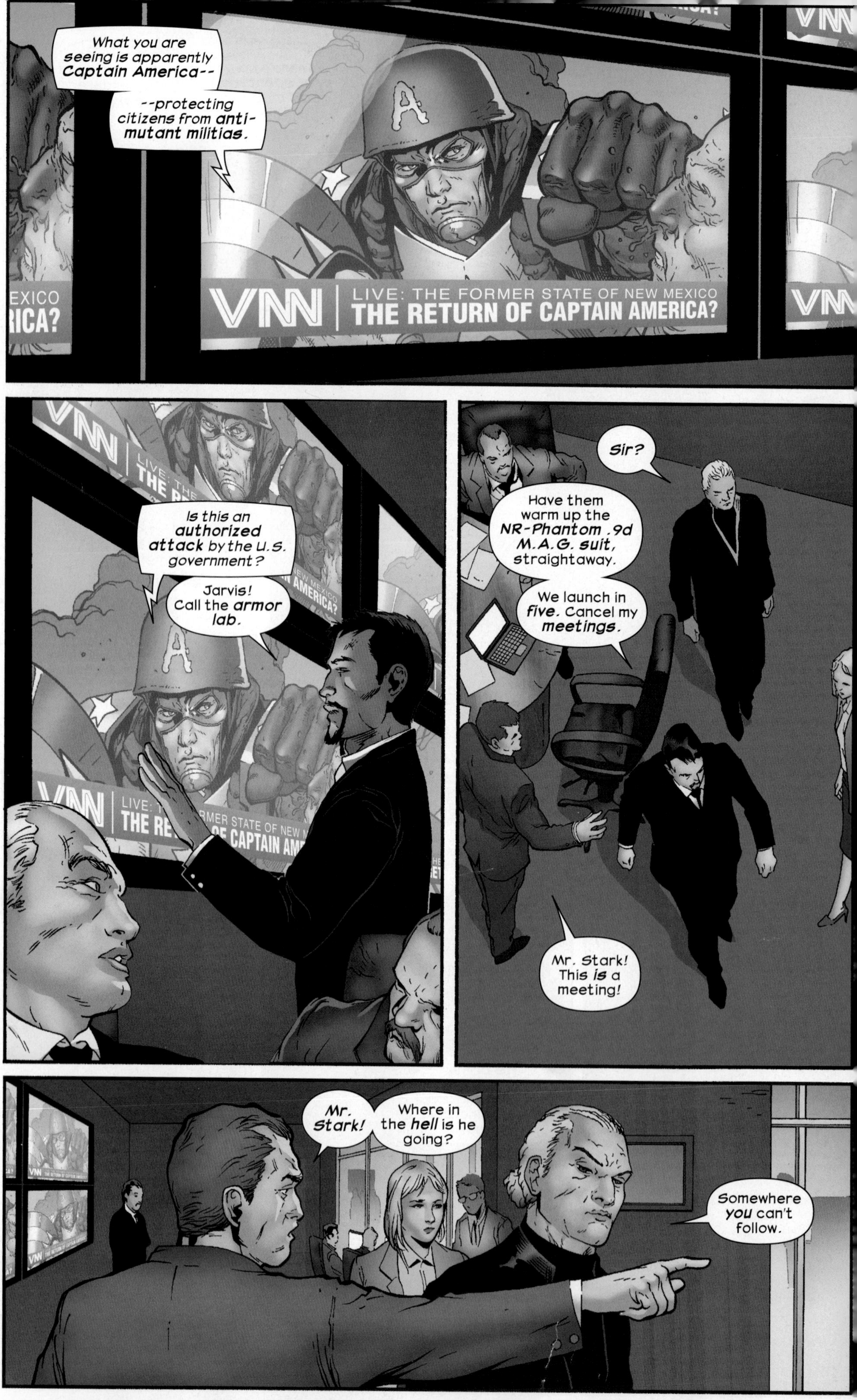
What you are seeing is apparently Captain America--
--protecting citizens from anti-mutant militias.
VNN
LIVE: THE FORMER STATE OF NEW MEXICO
THE RETURN OF CAPTAIN AMERICA?
Is this an authorized attack by the U.S. government?
Jarvis! Call the armor lab.
Sir?
Have them warm up the NR-Phantom .9d M.A.G. suit, straightaway.
We launch in five. Cancel my meetings.
Mr. Stark! This is a meeting!
Mr. Stark!
Where in the hell is he going?
Somewhere you can't follow.

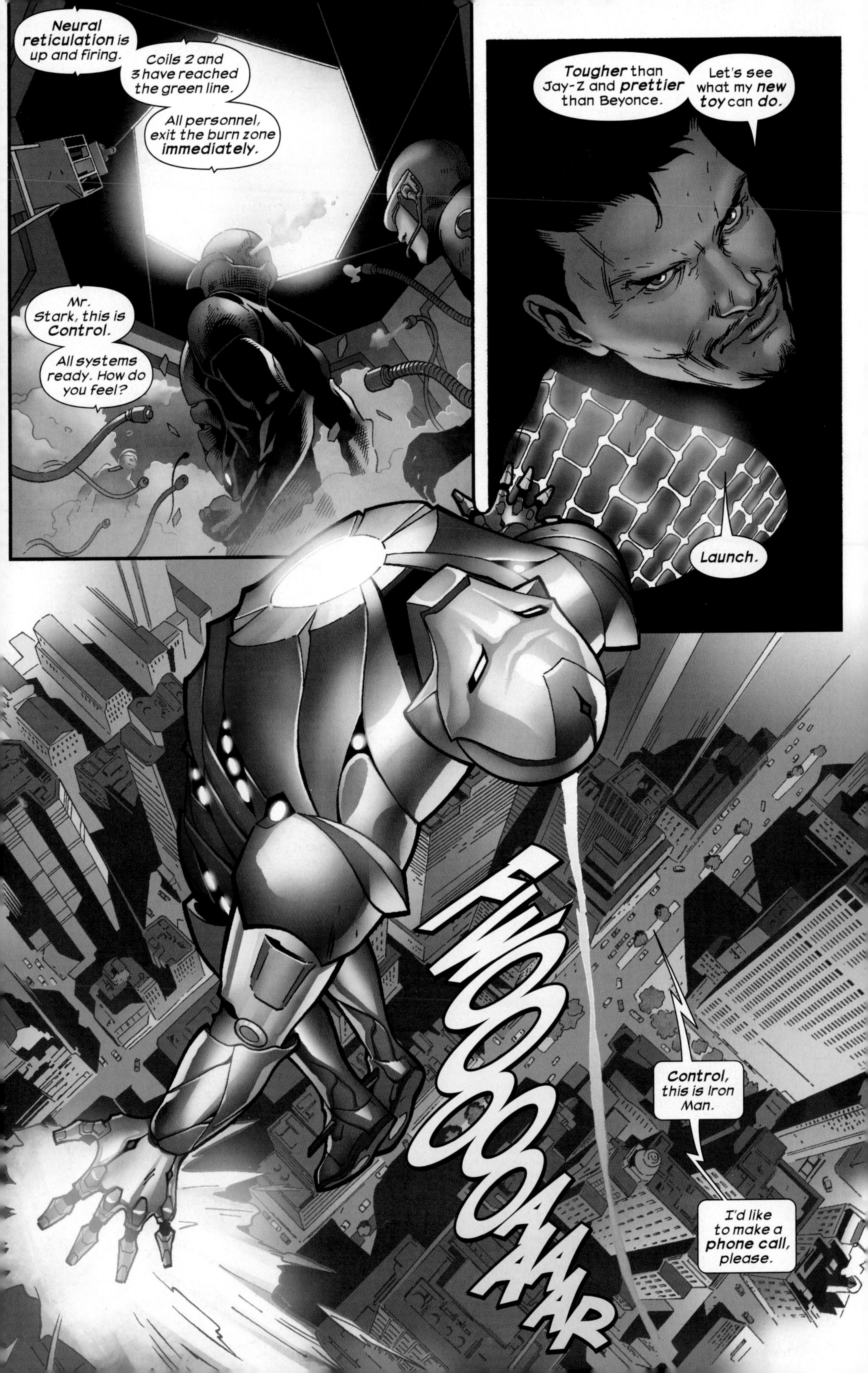
Neural reticulation is up and firing.
Coils 2 and 3 have reached the green line.
All personnel, exit the burn zone immediately.
Mr. Stark, this is Control.
All systems ready. How do you feel?
Tougher than Jay-Z and prettier than Beyonce.
Let's see what my new toy can do.
Launch.
FWOOOOOOAAAAR
Control, this is Iron Man.
I'd like to make a phone call, please.

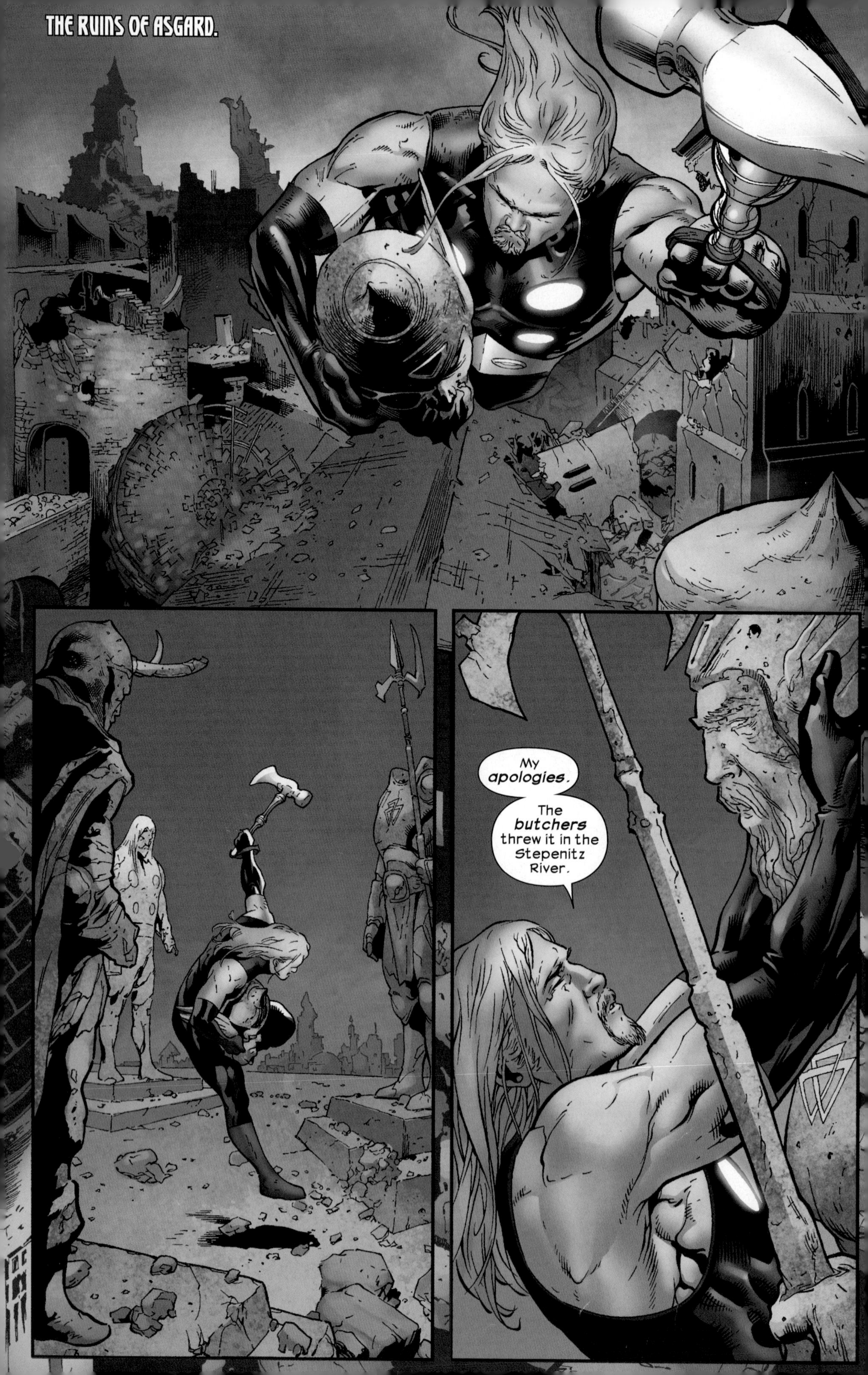
THE RUINS OF ASGARD.
My *apologies.*
The *butchers* threw it in the Stepenitz River.

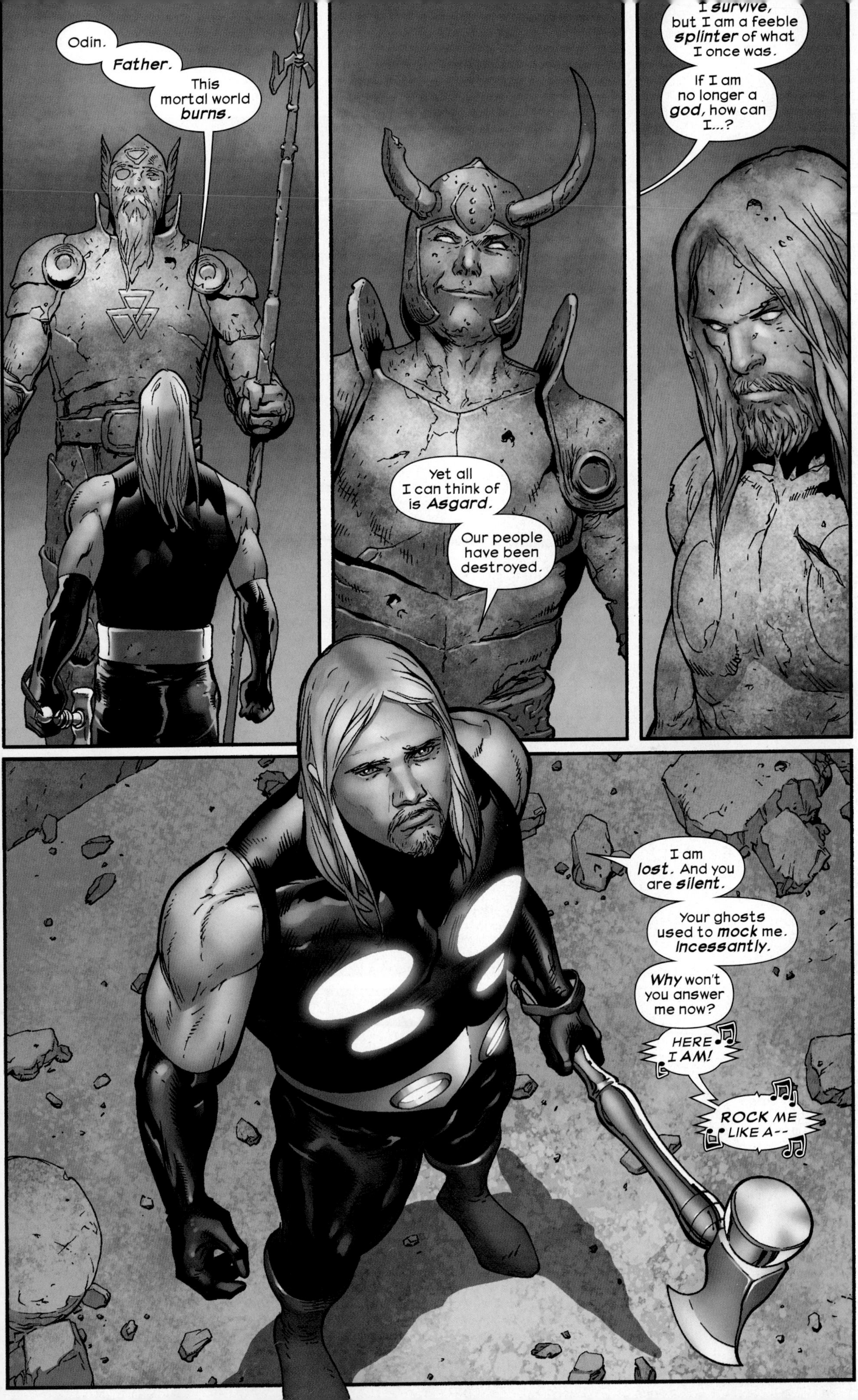
Odin.
Father.
This mortal world burns.
Yet all I can think of is Asgard.
Our people have been destroyed.
I survive, but I am a feeble splinter of what I once was.
If I am no longer a god, how can I...?
I am lost. And you are silent.
Your ghosts used to mock me. Incessantly.
Why won't you answer me now?
HERE I AM!
ROCK ME LIKE A--

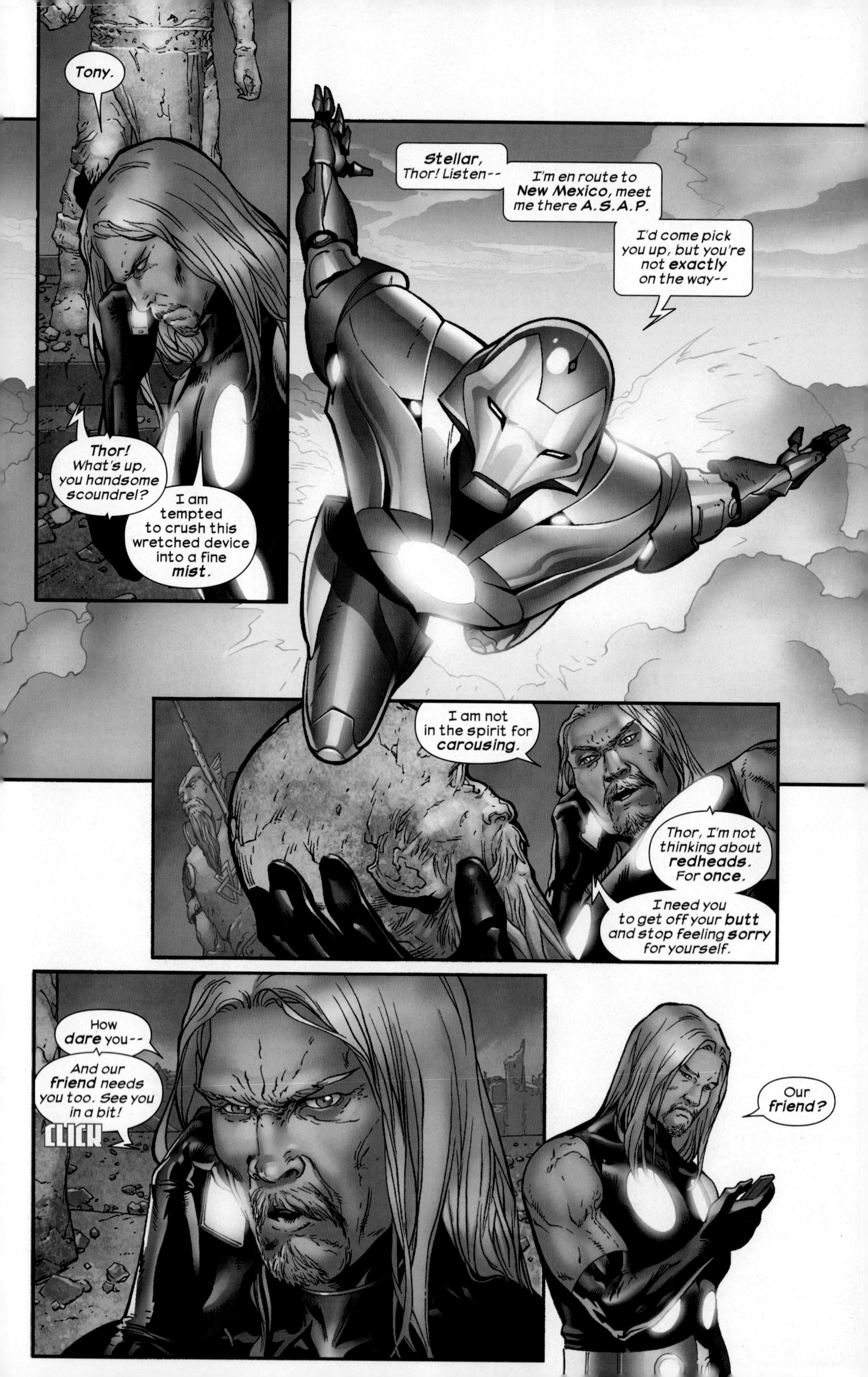
Tony.
Stellar, Thor! Listen--
I'm en route to New Mexico, meet me there A.S.A.P.
I'd come pick you up, but you're not exactly on the way--
Thor! What's up, you handsome scoundrel?
I am tempted to crush this wretched device into a fine mist.
I am not in the spirit for carousing.
Thor, I'm not thinking about redheads. For once.
I need you to get off your butt and stop feeling sorry for yourself.
How dare you--
And our friend needs you too. See you in a bit!
CLICK
Our friend?

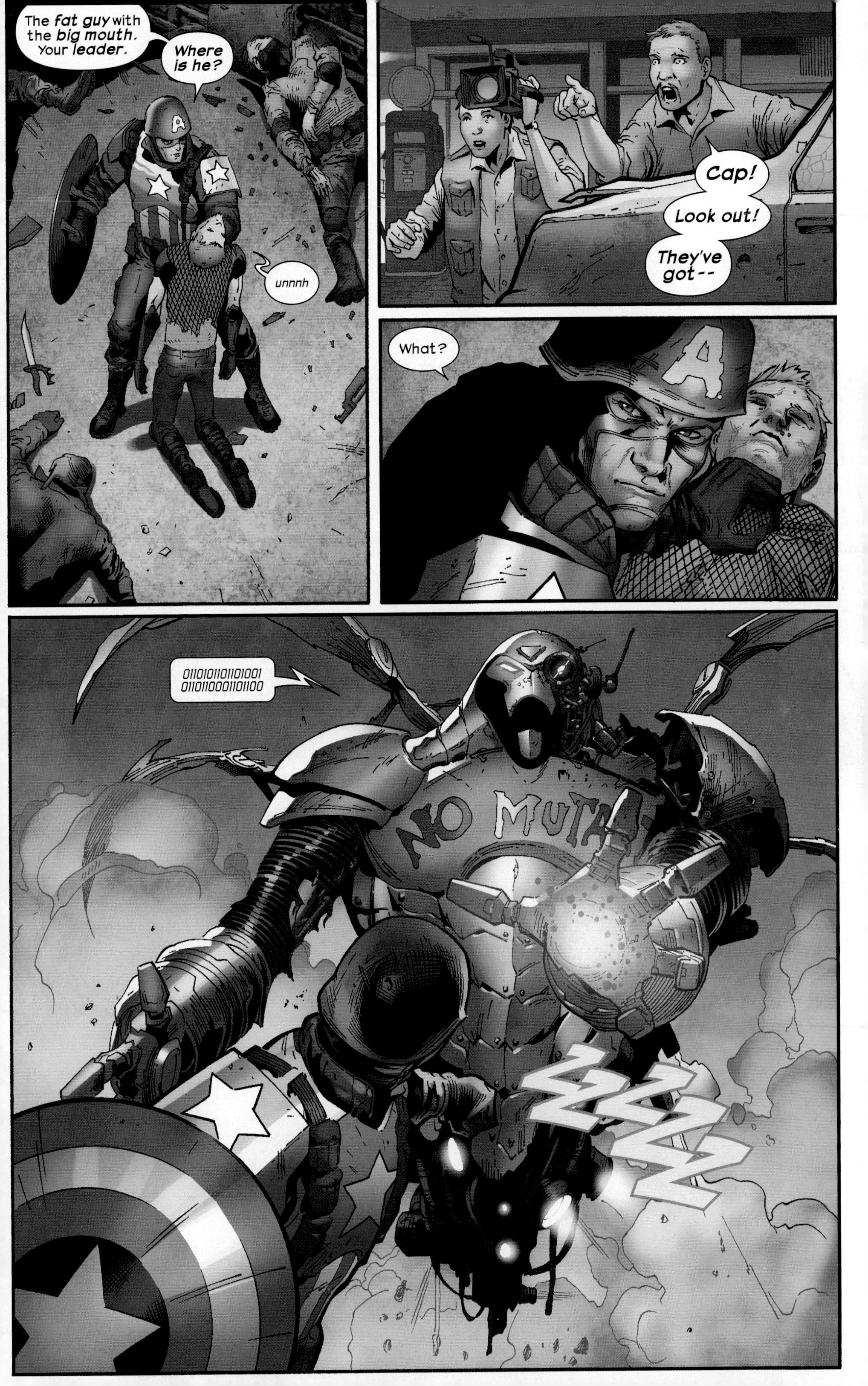

The fat guy with the big mouth. Your leader.
Where is he?
unnnh
Cap!
Look out!
They've got--
What?
0101011011010001 0110110001101100
ZZZZ
NO MUTA

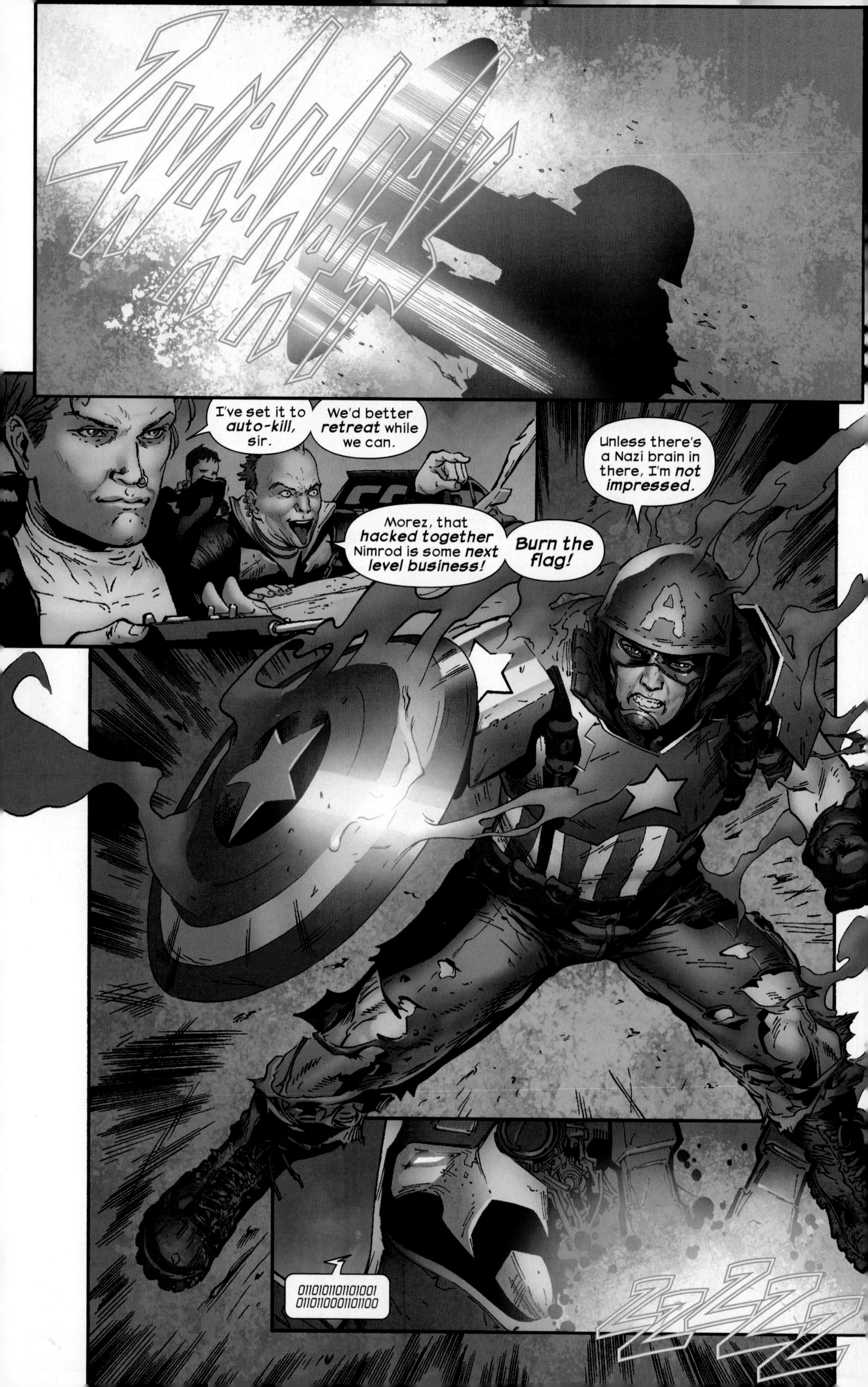
I've set it to auto-kill, sir.
We'd better retreat while we can.
Unless there's a Nazi brain in there, I'm not impressed.
Morez, that hacked together Nimrod is some next level business!
Burn the flag!
0110101101101001 0110110001101100

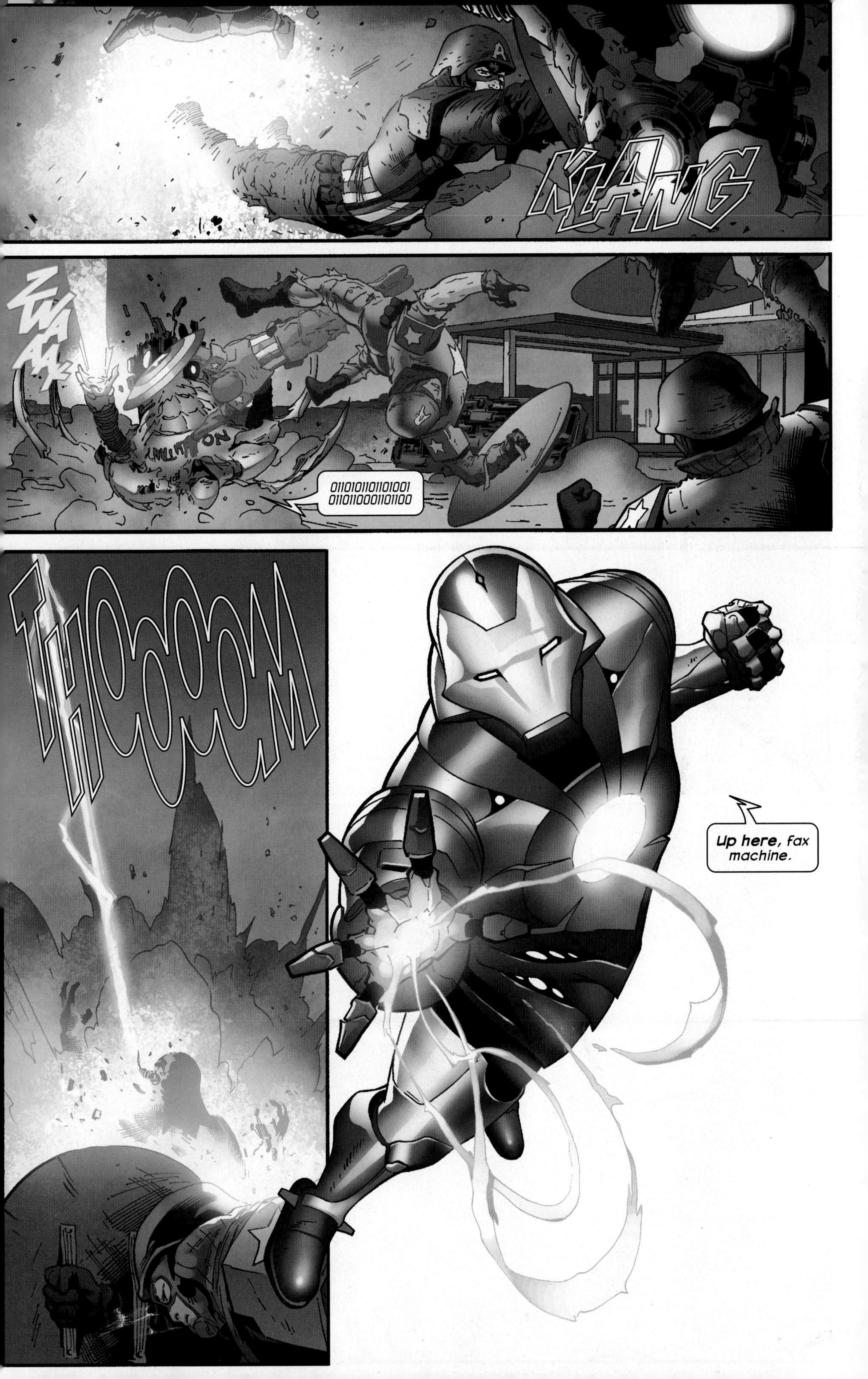
KLANG
ZWAAK
01101011011010010
01101100011011000
THOOOOM
Up here, fax machine.

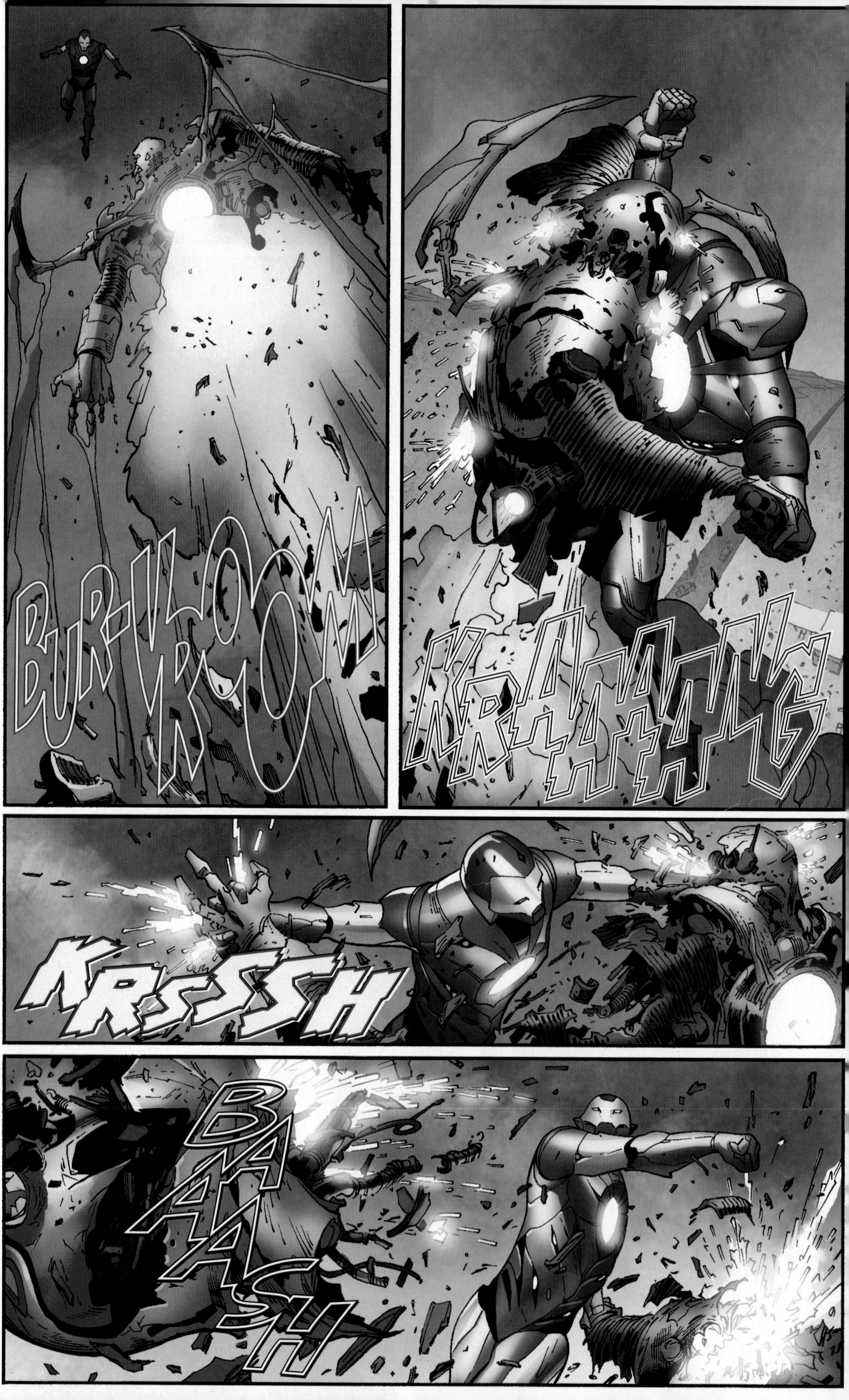
BUR-VROOM
KRANNNNG
KR-SSSH
BAAAASH

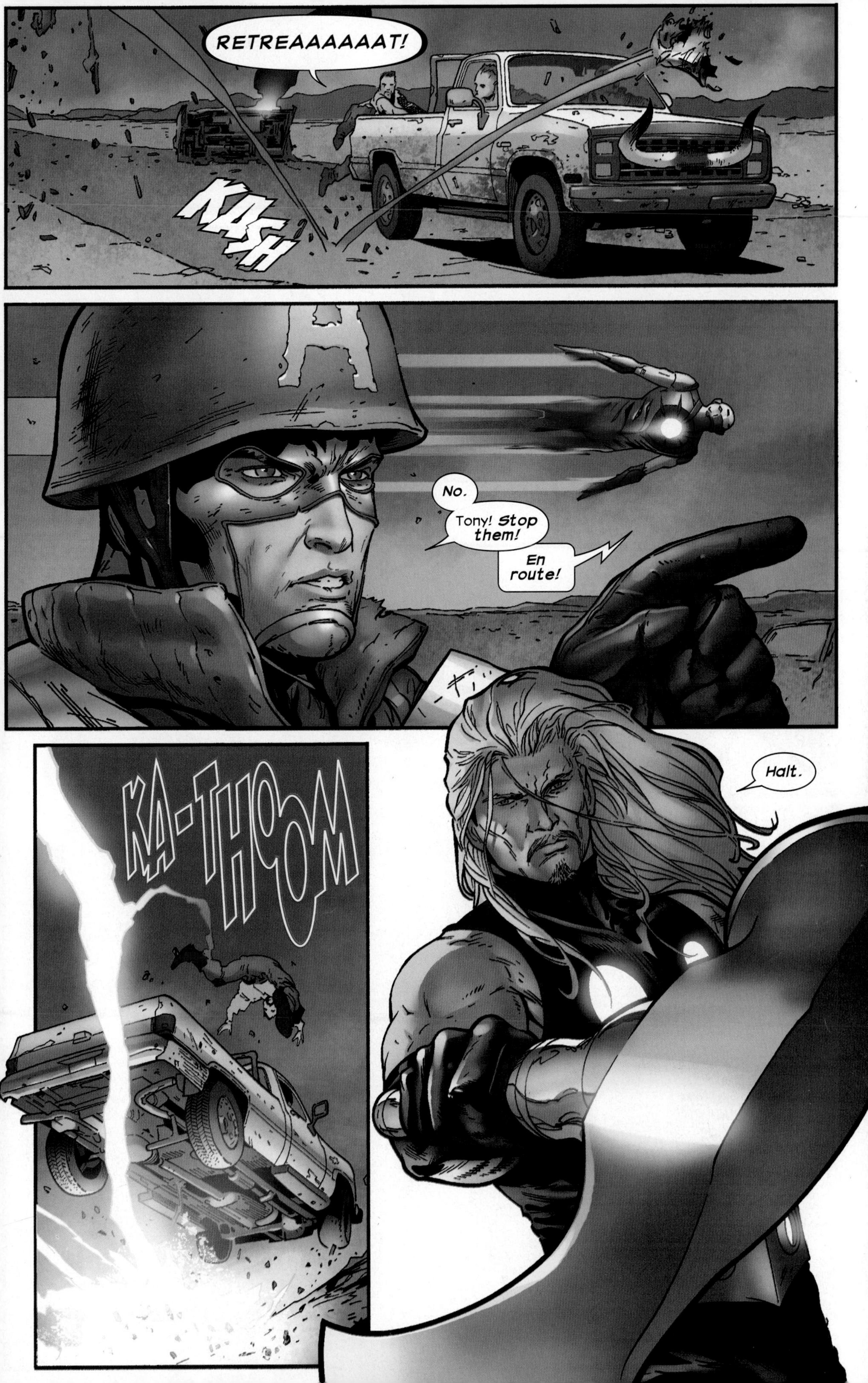
RETREAAAAAAT!
KASH
No.
Tony! Stop them!
En route!
KA-THOOM
Halt.

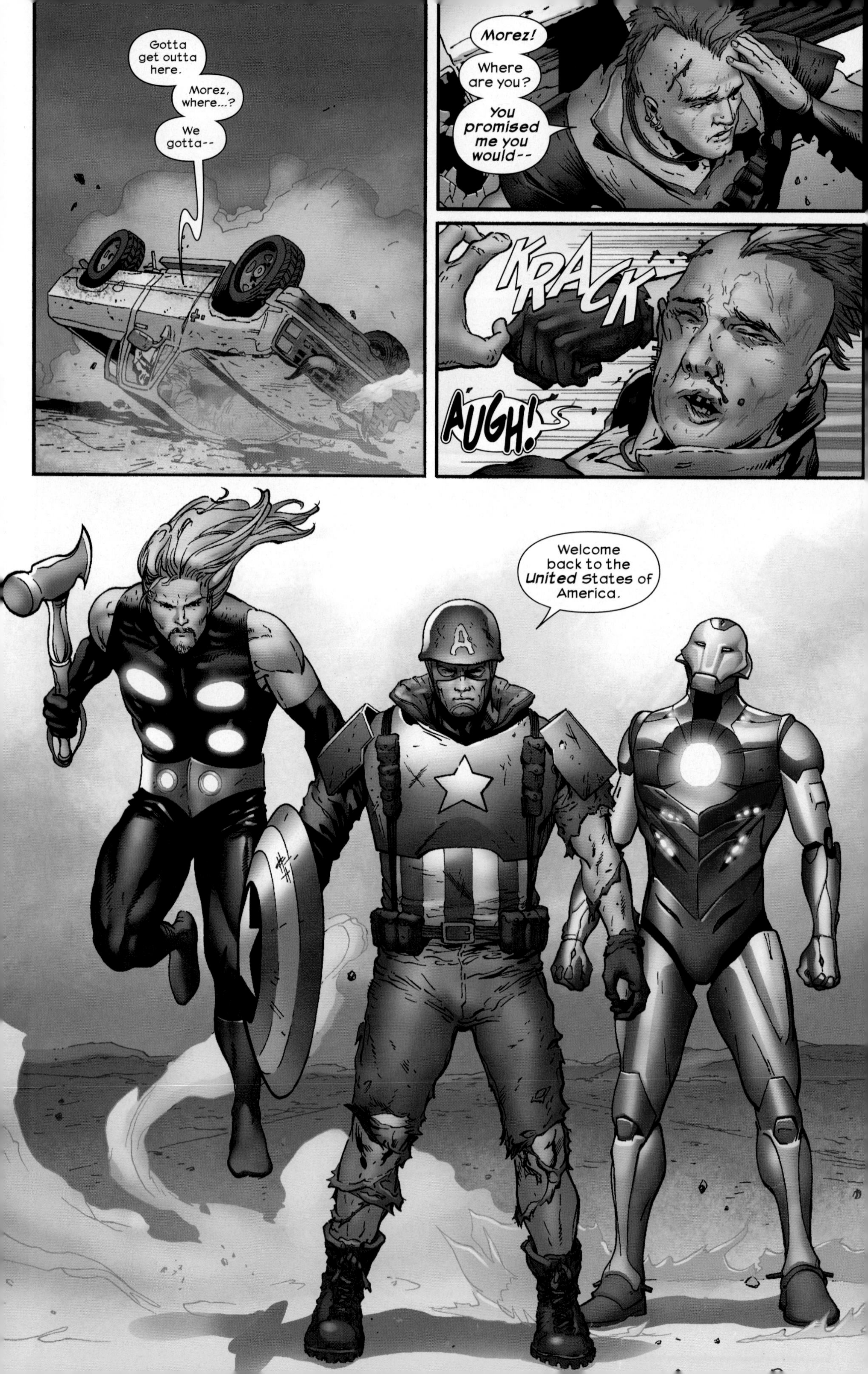

Gotta get outta here.
Morez, where...?
We gotta--
Morez!
Where are you?
You promised me you would--
KRACK
AUGH!
Welcome back to the United States of America.

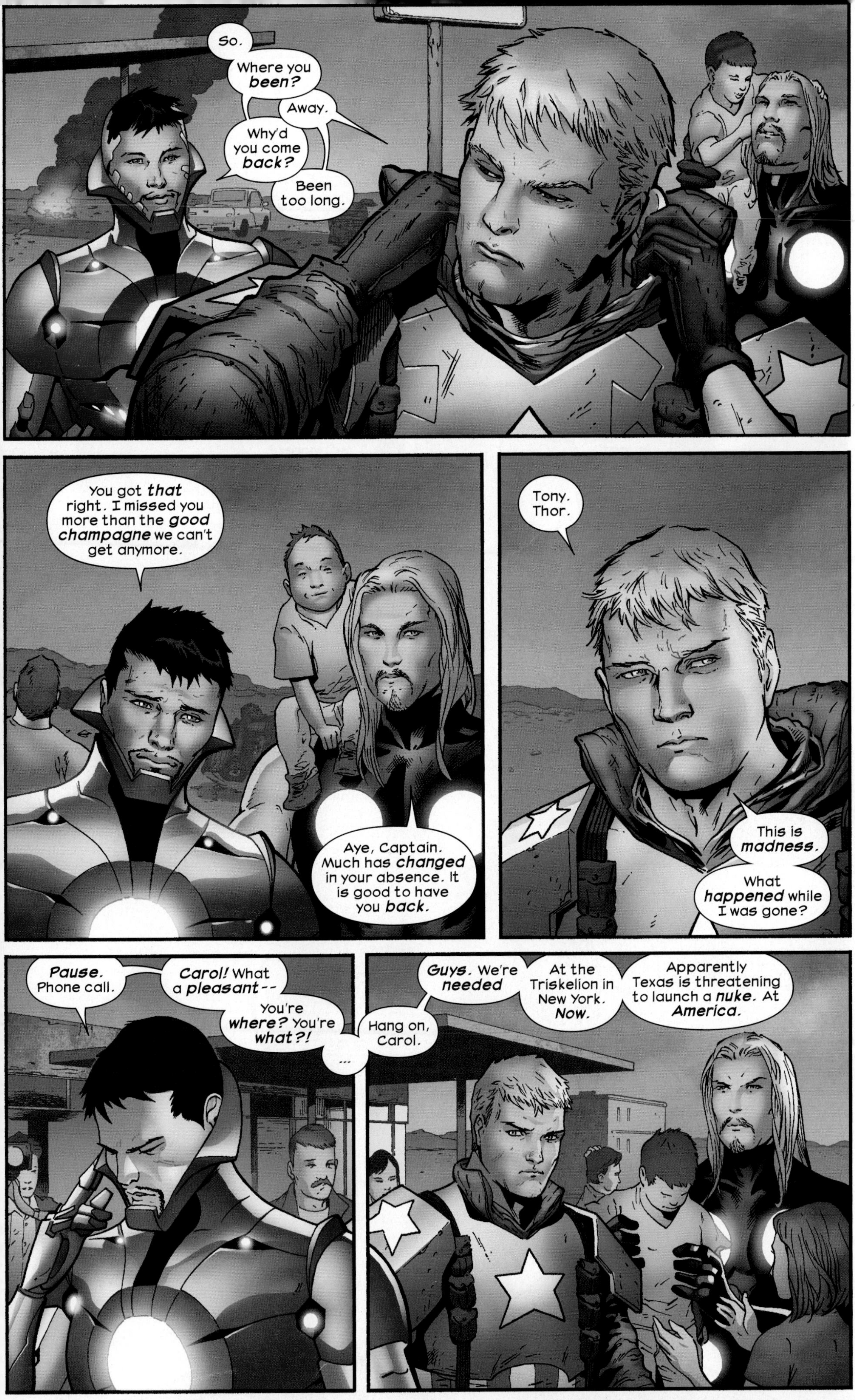
So.
Where you been?
Away.
Why'd you come back?
Been too long.
You got that right. I missed you more than the good champagne we can't get anymore.
Aye, Captain. Much has changed in your absence. It is good to have you back.
Tony. Thor.
This is madness.
What happened while I was gone?
Pause. Phone call.
Carol! What a pleasant--
You're where? You're what?!
...
Hang on, Carol.
Guys. We're needed
At the Triskelion in New York. Now.
Apparently Texas is threatening to launch a nuke. At America.

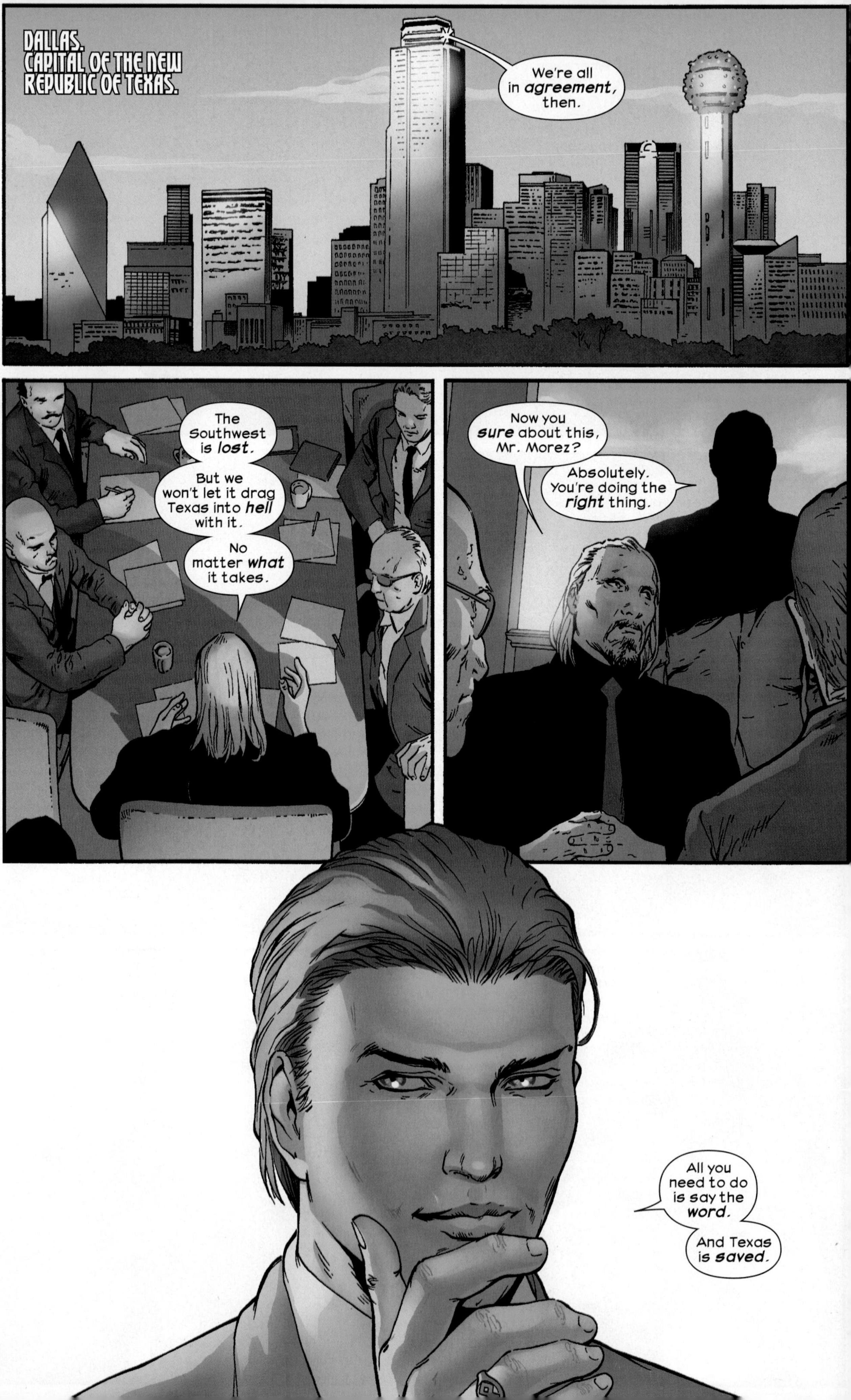
DALLAS. CAPITAL OF THE NEW REPUBLIC OF TEXAS.
We're all in *agreement*, then.
The Southwest is *lost*.
But we won't let it drag Texas into *hell* with it.
No matter *what* it takes.
Now you *sure* about this, Mr. Morez?
Absolutely. You're doing the *right* thing.
All you need to do is say the *word*.
And Texas is *saved*.

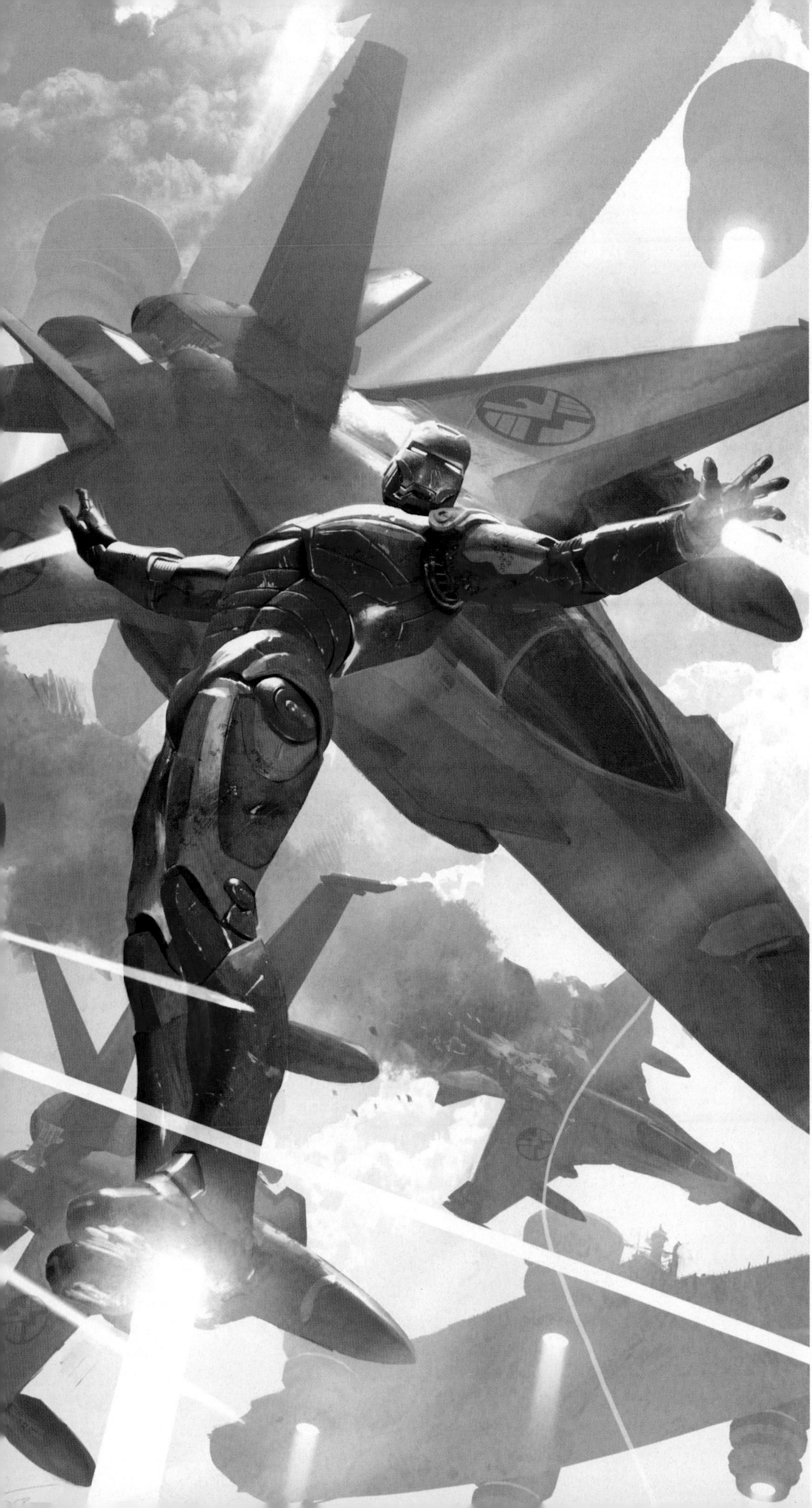

2

★

ULTIMATE COMICS **ULTIMATES** #14

S.H.I.E.L.D. SITUATION MAP:

[Anti-government militia hot spots]

Montana, N.Dakota
S.Dakota, Wyoming
Arizona, New Mexico
N.Carolina, S.Carolina
Georgia

[Eastern seaboard control zone]

New England,
New York,
New Jersey,
Delaware,
Washington, D.C.,
Maryland,
Virginia

secured by
National Guard
under emergency
powers
committee

[the West Coast]

California, Oregon
Washington
status unknown

[Great Lakes states]

Minnesota,
Wisconsin,
Michigan,
Illinois,
Indiana, Ohio
status unknown

ANTI-MATTER
NO FLY
ZONE

SENTINEL
PUSH

SOUTHERN
CALIFORNIA
REFUGEE ZONE

NUCLEAR-ARMED
NATION

DALLAS:
CAPITAL CITY OF
THE NEW REPUBLIC
OF TEXAS

Classified Position

Camp Hutton, secure
location of the President
of the United States

[Sentinel-controlled no man's land]

New Mexico, Arizona
Utah, Oklahoma
abandoned by the
US government

[The New Republic of Texas]

Texas
declared state
independence

ALL STATES
SHOWN IN WHITE
ARE U.S. GOVERNMENT
CONTROLLED ZONES

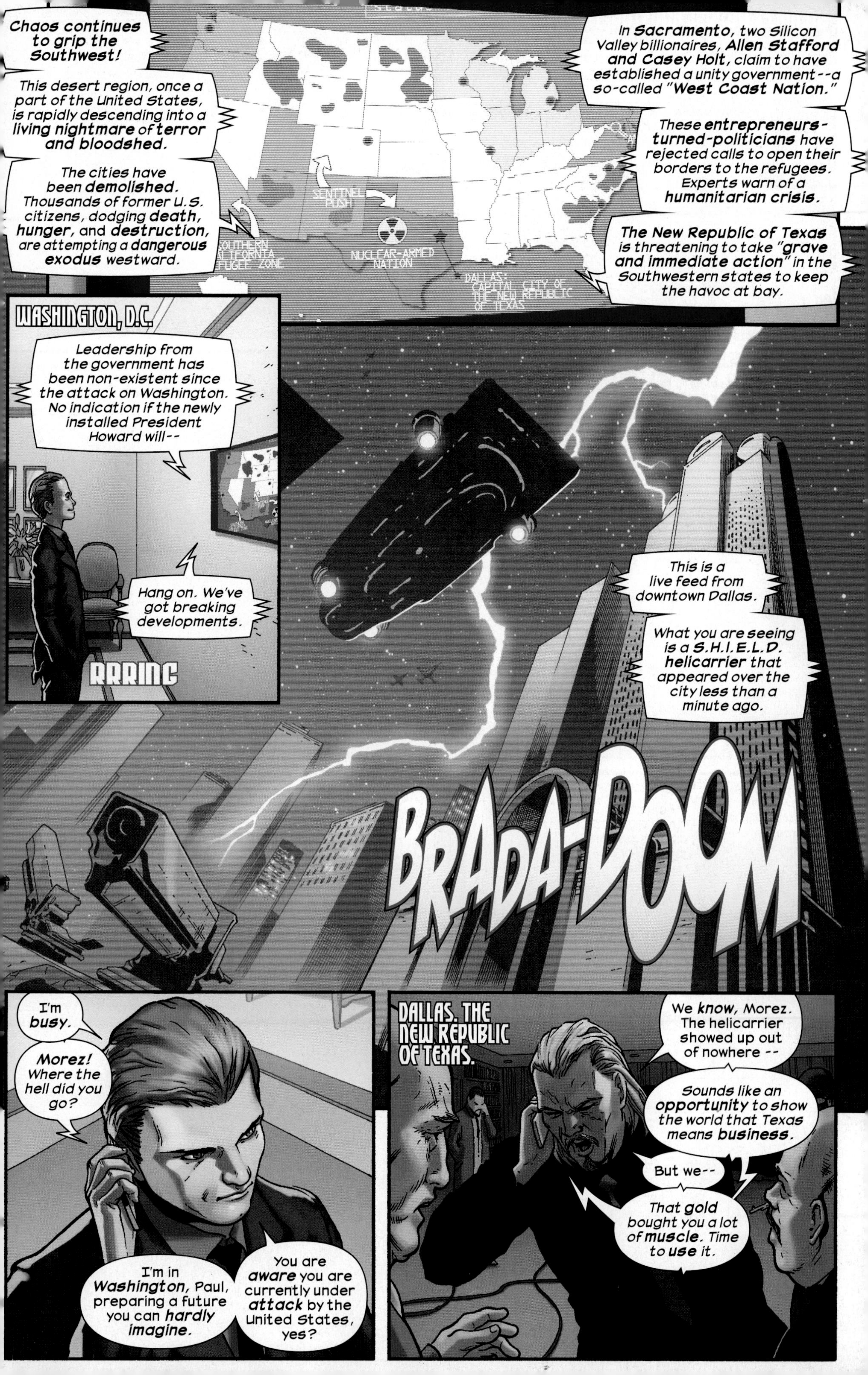

Chaos continues to grip the Southwest!
This desert region, once a part of the United States, is rapidly descending into a living nightmare of terror and bloodshed.
The cities have been demolished. Thousands of former U.S. citizens, dodging death, hunger, and destruction, are attempting a dangerous exodus westward.
SENTINEL PUSH
NUCLEAR-ARMED NATION
DALLAS: CAPITAL CITY OF THE NEW REPUBLIC OF TEXAS
In Sacramento, two Silicon Valley billionaires, Allen Stafford and Casey Holt, claim to have established a unity government--a so-called "West Coast Nation."
These entrepreneurs-turned-politicians have rejected calls to open their borders to the refugees. Experts warn of a humanitarian crisis.
The New Republic of Texas is threatening to take "grave and immediate action" in the Southwestern states to keep the havoc at bay.
WASHINGTON, D.C.
Leadership from the government has been non-existent since the attack on Washington. No indication if the newly installed President Howard will--
Hang on. We've got breaking developments.
RRRING
This is a live feed from downtown Dallas.
What you are seeing is a S.H.I.E.L.D. helicarrier that appeared over the city less than a minute ago.
BRADA-DOOM
I'm busy.
Morez! Where the hell did you go?
I'm in Washington, Paul, preparing a future you can hardly imagine.
You are aware you are currently under attack by the United States, yes?
DALLAS. THE NEW REPUBLIC OF TEXAS.
We know, Morez. The helicarrier showed up out of nowhere --
Sounds like an opportunity to show the world that Texas means business.
But we--
That gold bought you a lot of muscle. Time to use it.

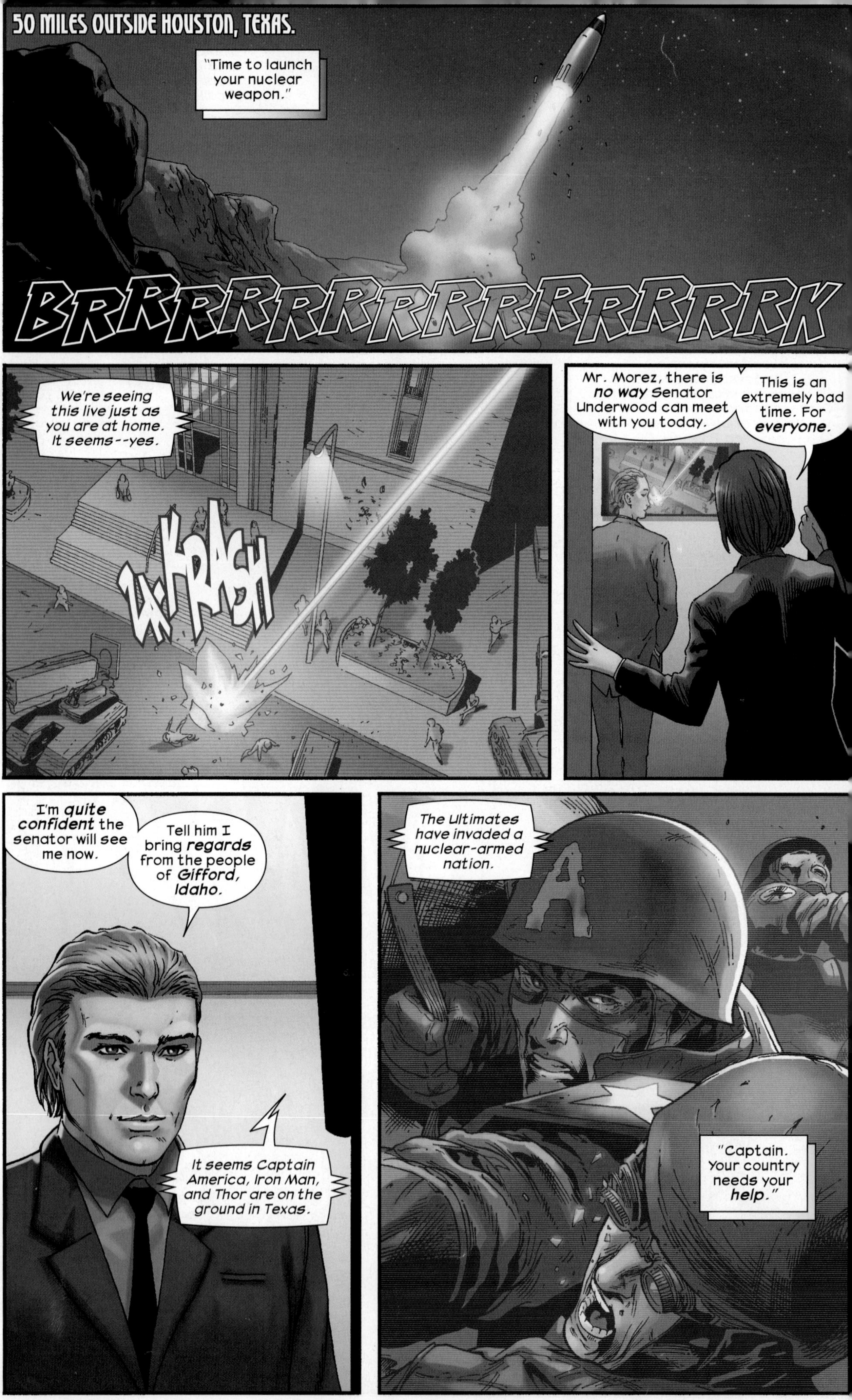
50 MILES OUTSIDE HOUSTON, TEXAS.
"Time to launch your nuclear weapon."
BRRRRRRRRRRRRRRK
We're seeing this live just as you are at home. It seems--yes.
ZA-KRASH
Mr. Morez, there is no way Senator Underwood can meet with you today.
This is an extremely bad time. For everyone.
I'm quite confident the senator will see me now.
Tell him I bring regards from the people of Gifford, Idaho.
It seems Captain America, Iron Man, and Thor are on the ground in Texas.
The Ultimates have invaded a nuclear-armed nation.
"Captain. Your country needs your help."

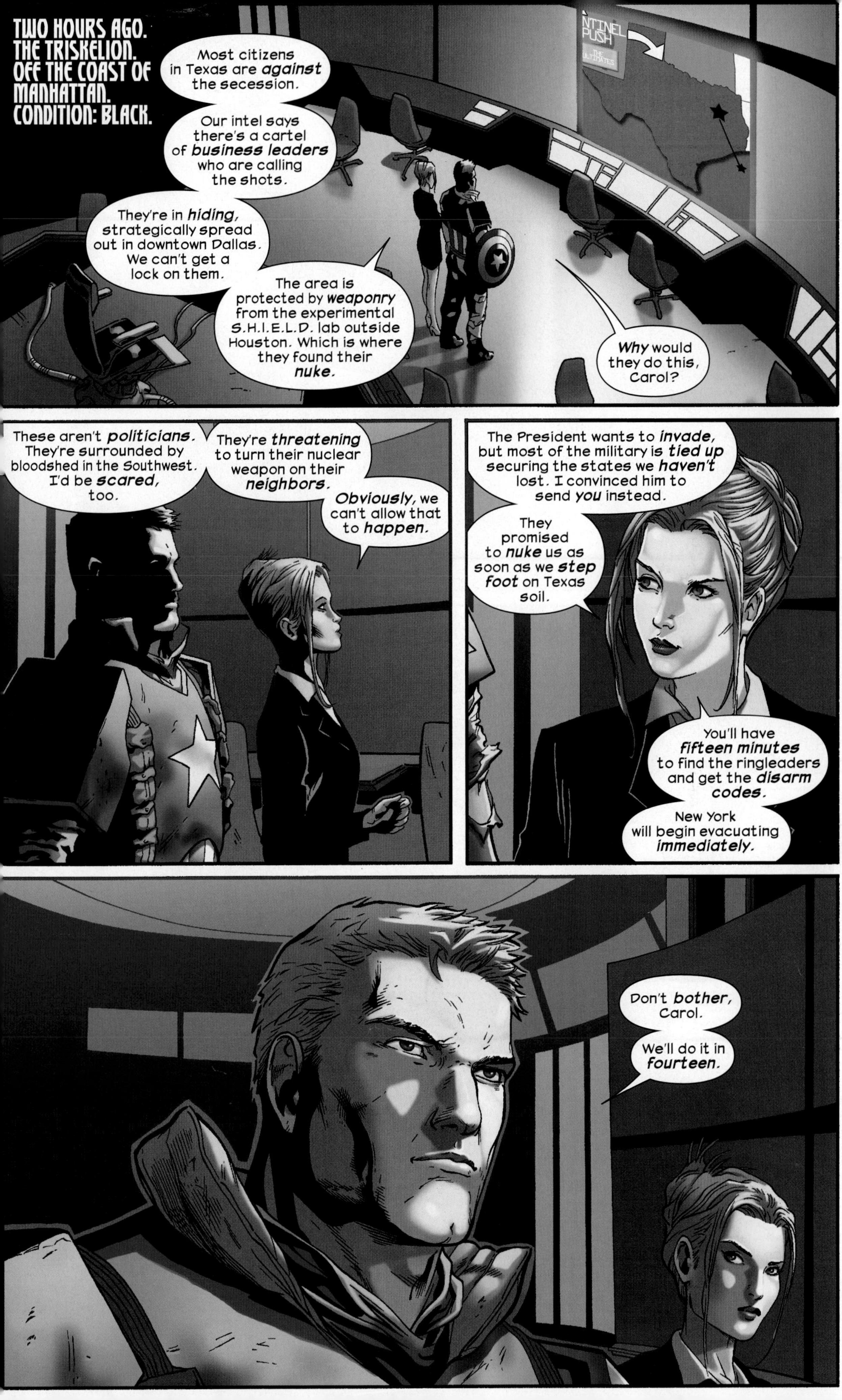
TWO HOURS AGO. THE TRISKELION. OFF THE COAST OF MANHATTAN. CONDITION: BLACK.
NTINEL PUSH
THE ULTIMATES
Most citizens in Texas are *against* the secession.
Our intel says there's a cartel of *business leaders* who are calling the shots.
They're in *hiding*, strategically spread out in downtown Dallas. We can't get a lock on them.
The area is protected by *weaponry* from the experimental S.H.I.E.L.D. lab outside Houston. Which is where they found their *nuke*.
Why would they do this, Carol?
These aren't *politicians*. They're surrounded by bloodshed in the Southwest. I'd be *scared*, too.
They're *threatening* to turn their nuclear weapon on their *neighbors*.
Obviously, we can't allow that to *happen*.
The President wants to *invade*, but most of the military is *tied up* securing the states we *haven't* lost. I convinced him to send *you* instead.
They promised to *nuke* us as soon as we *step foot* on Texas soil.
You'll have *fifteen minutes* to find the ringleaders and get the *disarm codes*.
New York will begin evacuating *immediately*.
Don't *bother*, Carol.
We'll do it in *fourteen*.

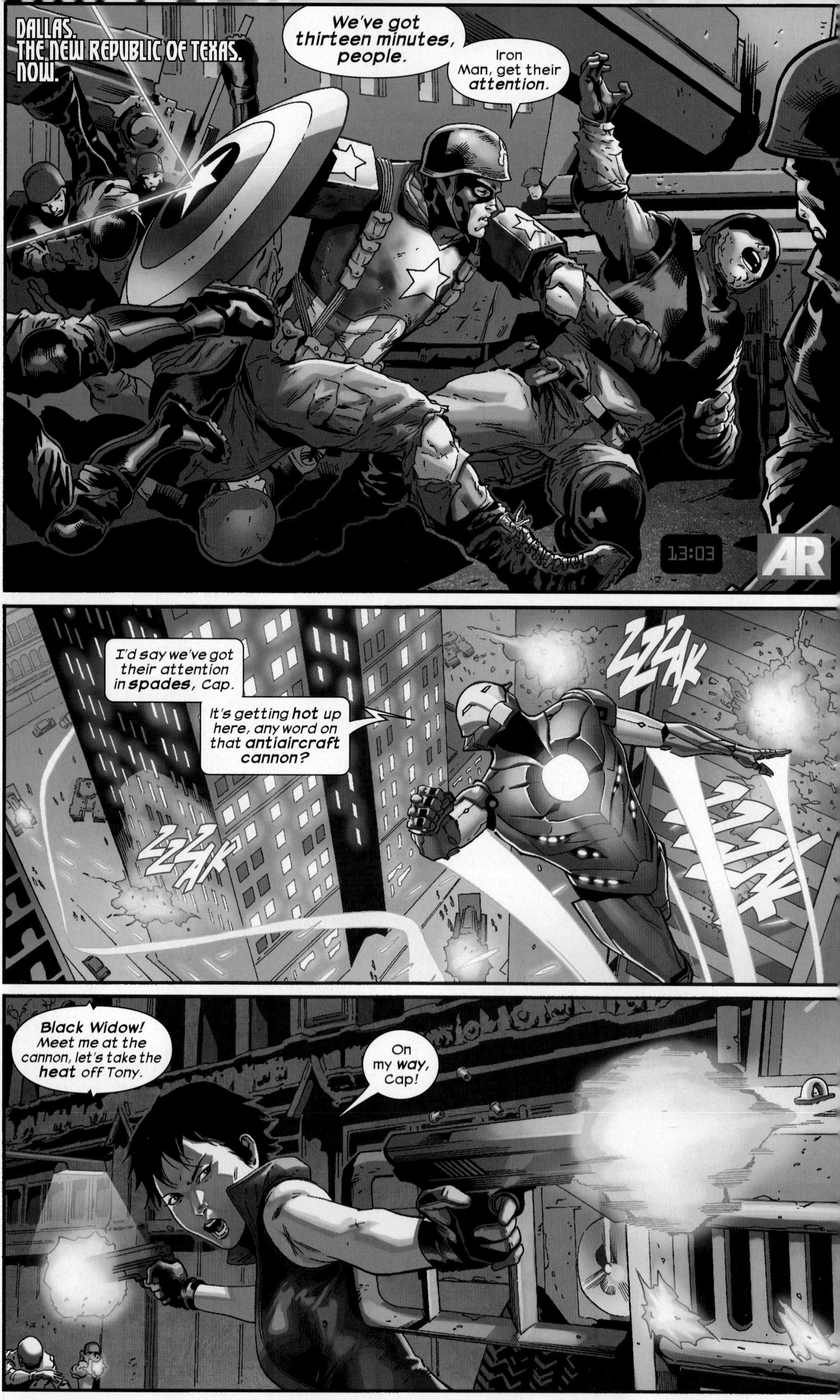
DALLAS.
THE NEW REPUBLIC OF TEXAS.
NOW.
We've got thirteen minutes, people.
Iron Man, get their attention.
13:03
AR
I'd say we've got their attention in spades, Cap.
It's getting hot up here, any word on that antiaircraft cannon?
ZZZAK
ZZZAK
ZZZAK
Black Widow! Meet me at the cannon, let's take the heat off Tony.
On my way, Cap!

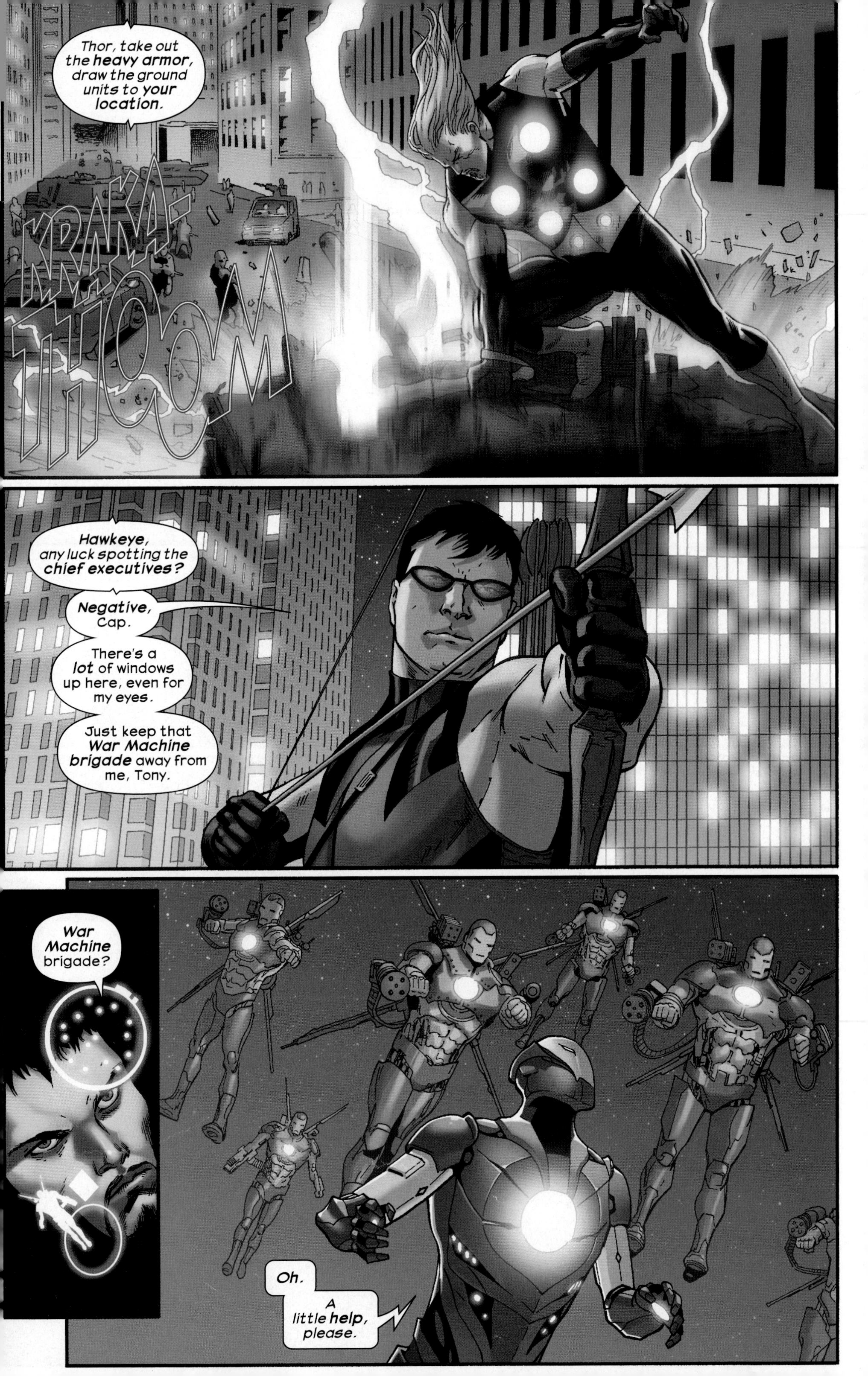

Thor, take out the heavy armor, draw the ground units to your location.
KRAKA-THOOM
Hawkeye, any luck spotting the chief executives?
Negative, Cap.
There's a lot of windows up here, even for my eyes.
Just keep that War Machine brigade away from me, Tony.
War Machine brigade?
Oh.
A little help, please.

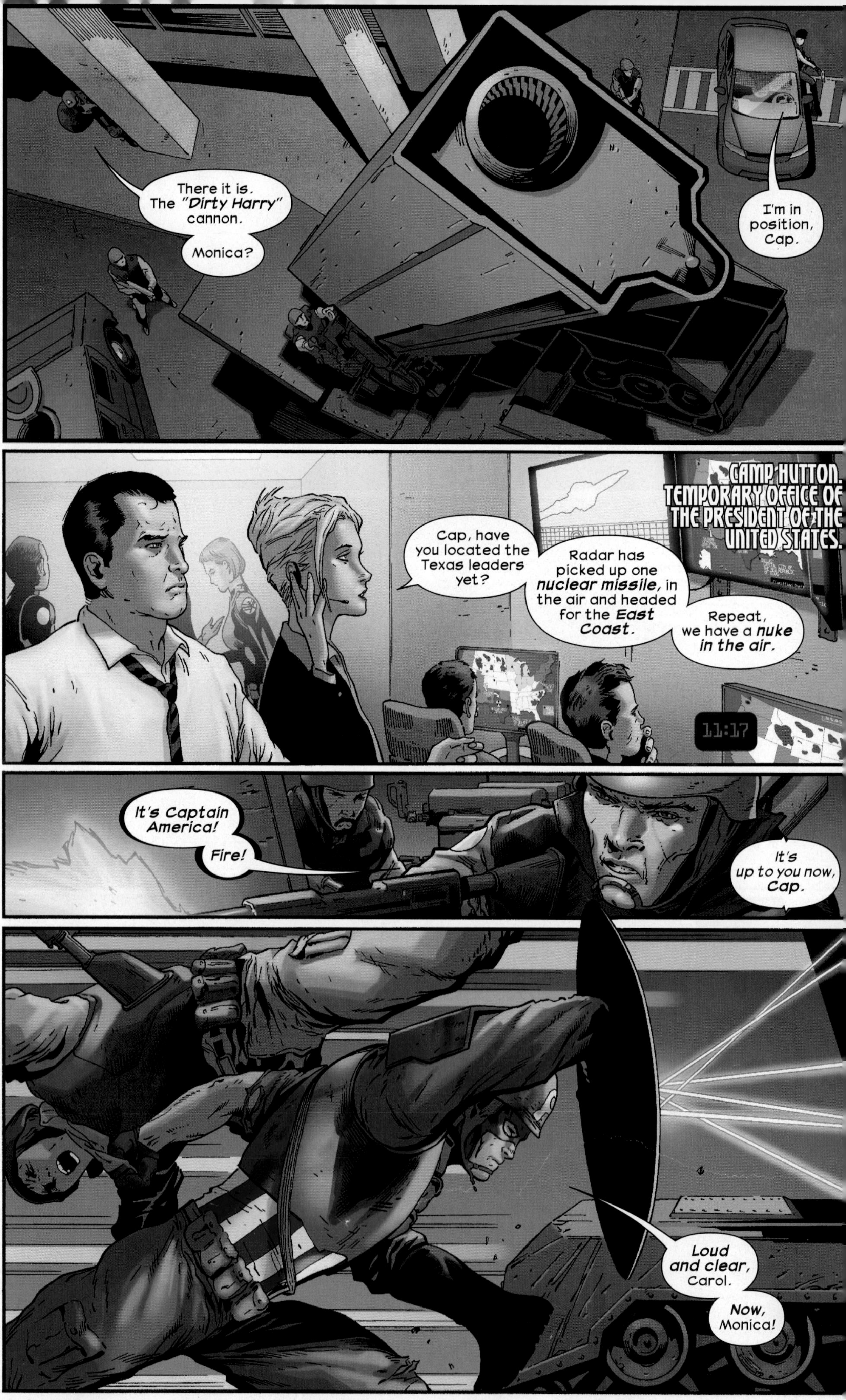
There it is. The "Dirty Harry" cannon.
Monica?
I'm in position, Cap.
CAMP HUTTON. TEMPORARY OFFICE OF THE PRESIDENT OF THE UNITED STATES.
Cap, have you located the Texas leaders yet?
Radar has picked up one nuclear missile, in the air and headed for the East Coast.
Repeat, we have a nuke in the air.
11:17
It's Captain America!
Fire!
It's up to you now, Cap.
Loud and clear, Carol.
Now, Monica!

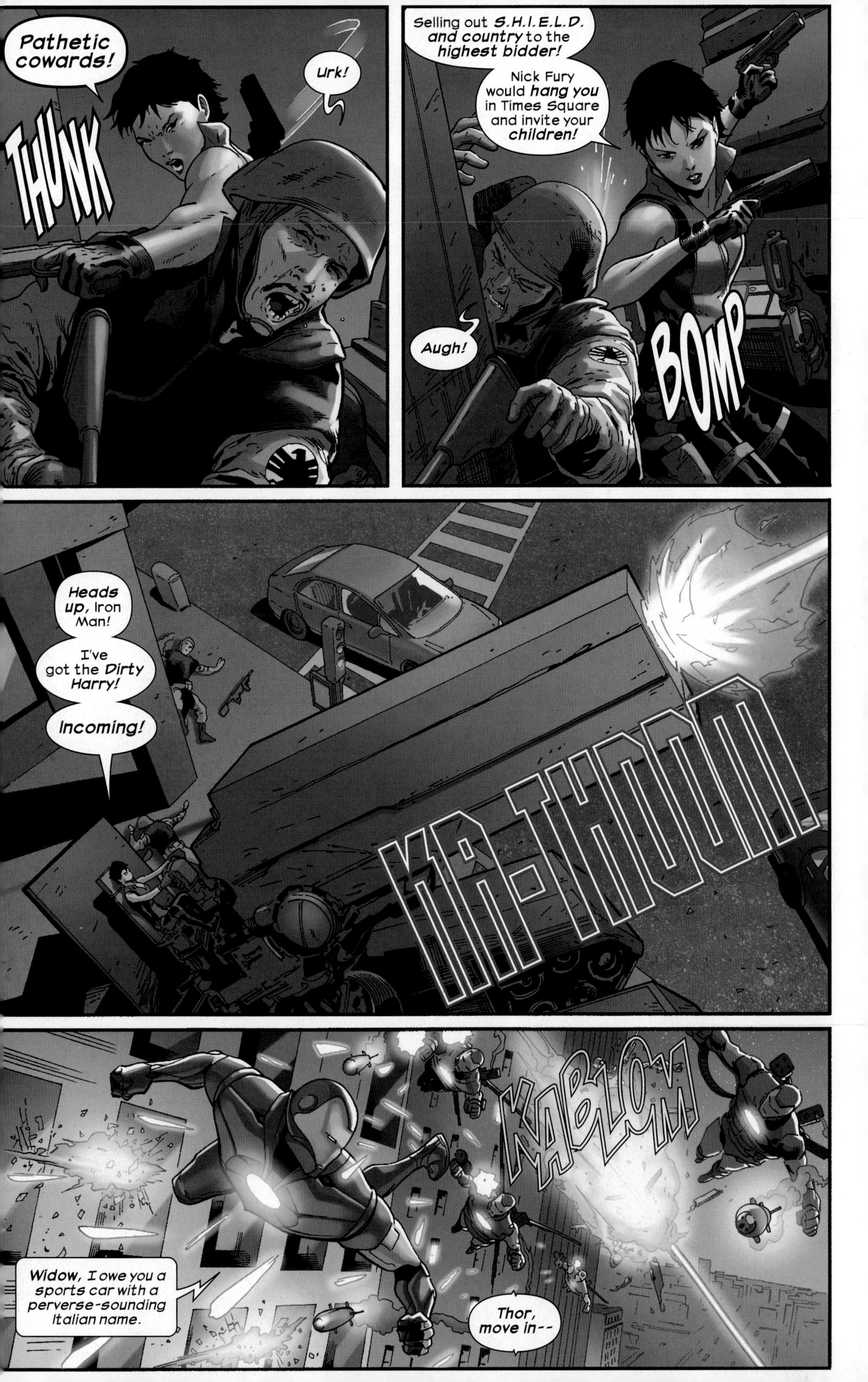
Pathetic cowards!
THUNK
Urk!
Selling out S.H.I.E.L.D. and country to the highest bidder!
Nick Fury would hang you in Times Square and invite your children!
Augh!
BOMP
Heads up, Iron Man!
I've got the Dirty Harry!
Incoming!
KA-THOOM
KABLOOM
Widow, I owe you a sports car with a perverse-sounding Italian name.
Thor, move in--

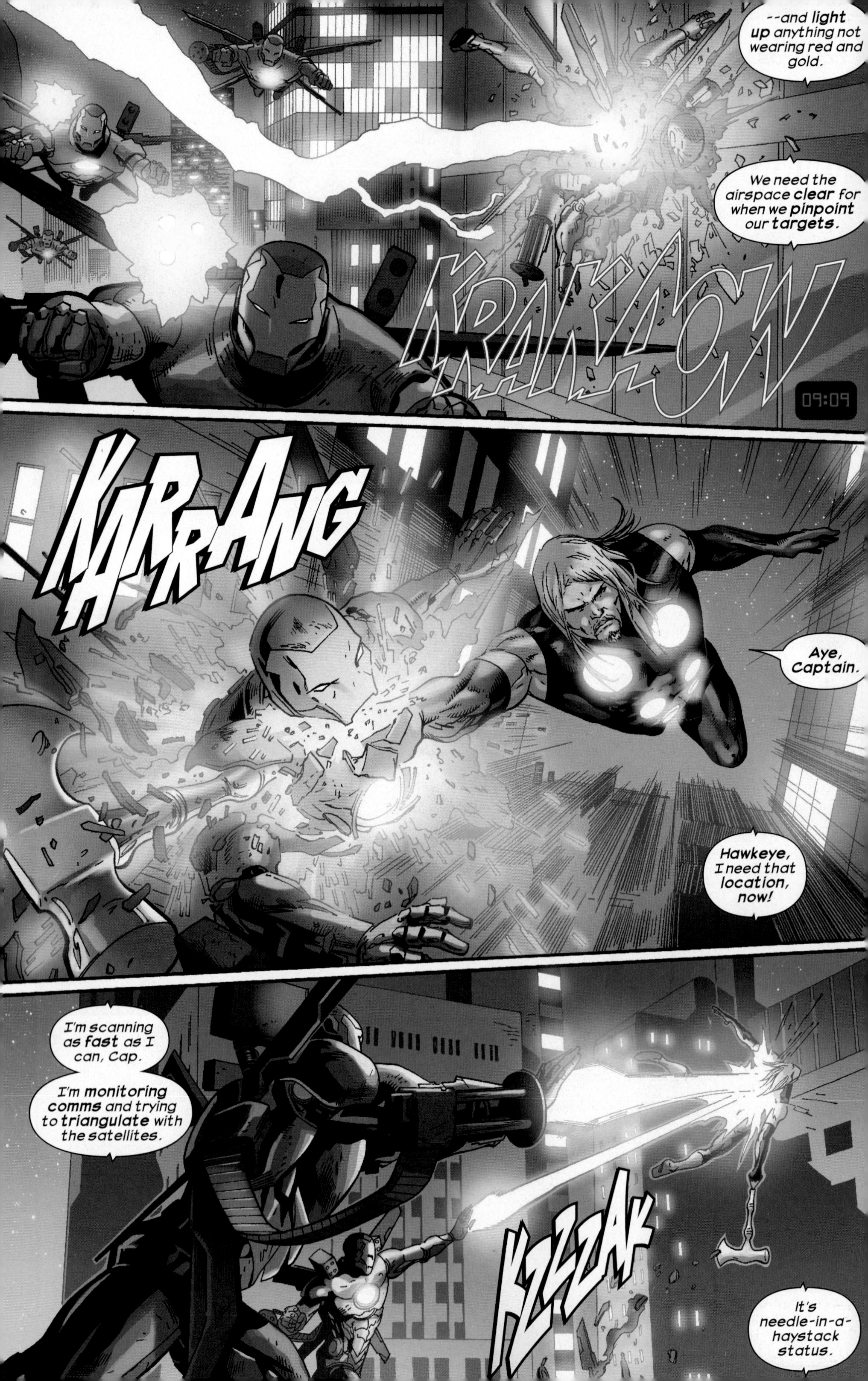
--and light up anything not wearing red and gold.
We need the airspace clear for when we pinpoint our targets.
KRAKAKOW
09:09
KARRANG
Aye, Captain.
Hawkeye, I need that location, now!
I'm scanning as fast as I can, Cap.
I'm monitoring comms and trying to triangulate with the satellites.
KZZZAK
It's needle-in-a-haystack status.

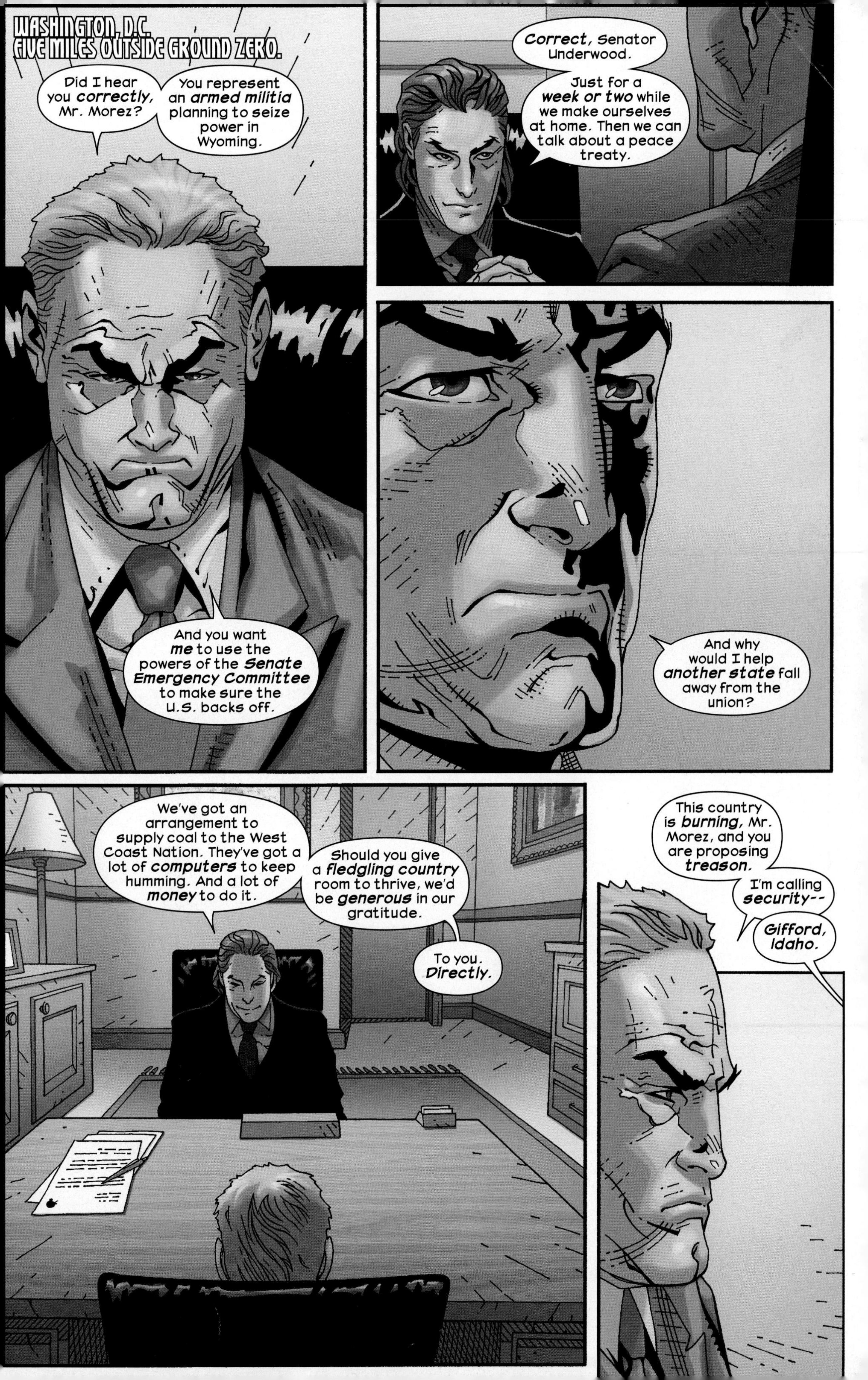

WASHINGTON, D.C.
FIVE MILES OUTSIDE GROUND ZERO.
Did I hear you correctly, Mr. Morez?
You represent an armed militia planning to seize power in Wyoming.
And you want me to use the powers of the Senate Emergency Committee to make sure the U.S. backs off.
Correct, Senator Underwood.
Just for a week or two while we make ourselves at home. Then we can talk about a peace treaty.
And why would I help another state fall away from the union?
We've got an arrangement to supply coal to the West Coast Nation. They've got a lot of computers to keep humming. And a lot of money to do it.
Should you give a fledgling country room to thrive, we'd be generous in our gratitude.
To you. Directly.
This country is burning, Mr. Morez, and you are proposing treason.
I'm calling security--
Gifford, Idaho.

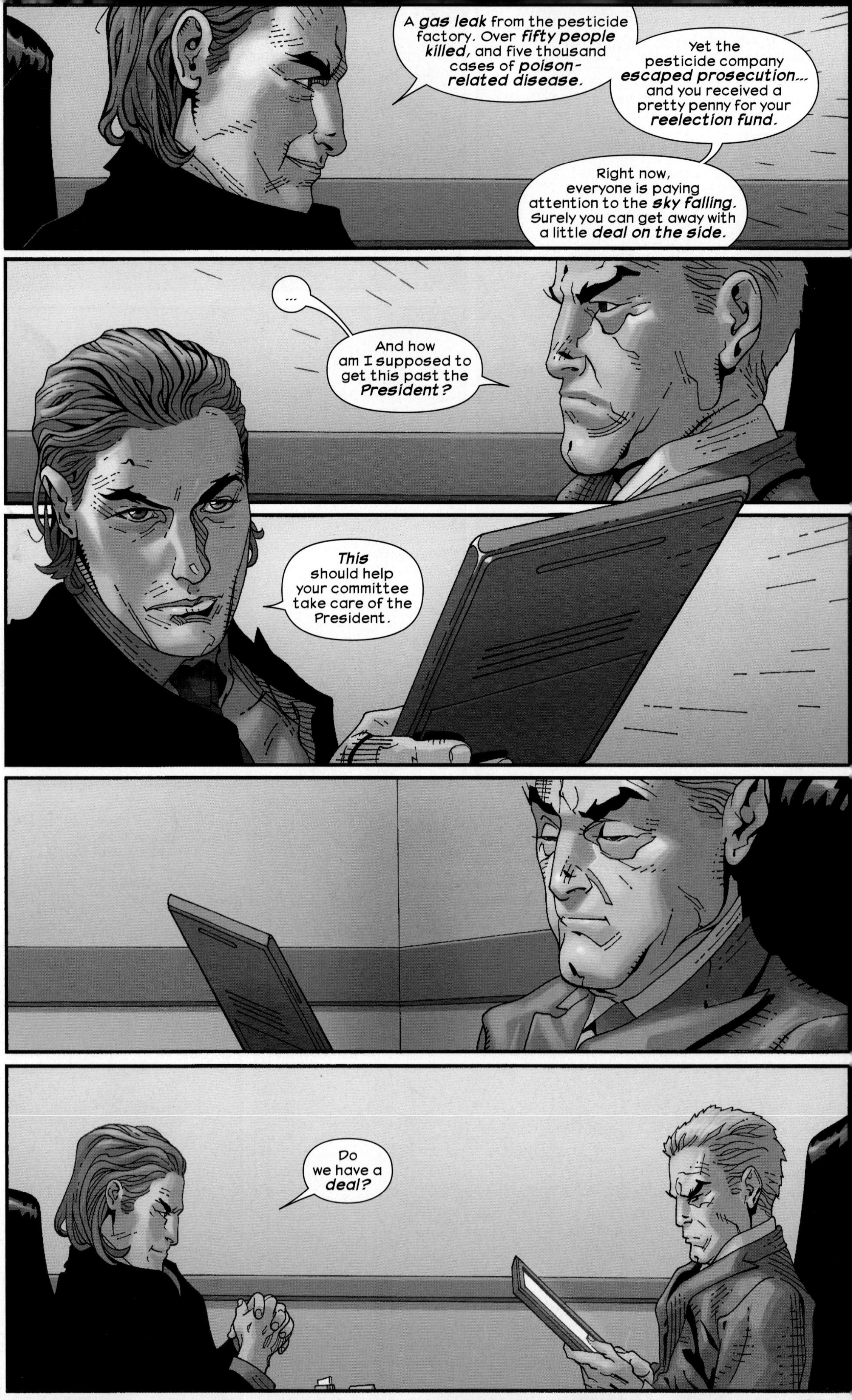
A gas leak from the pesticide factory. Over fifty people killed, and five thousand cases of poison-related disease.
Yet the pesticide company escaped prosecution... and you received a pretty penny for your reelection fund.
Right now, everyone is paying attention to the sky falling. Surely you can get away with a little deal on the side.
...
And how am I supposed to get this past the President?
This should help your committee take care of the President.
Do we have a deal?

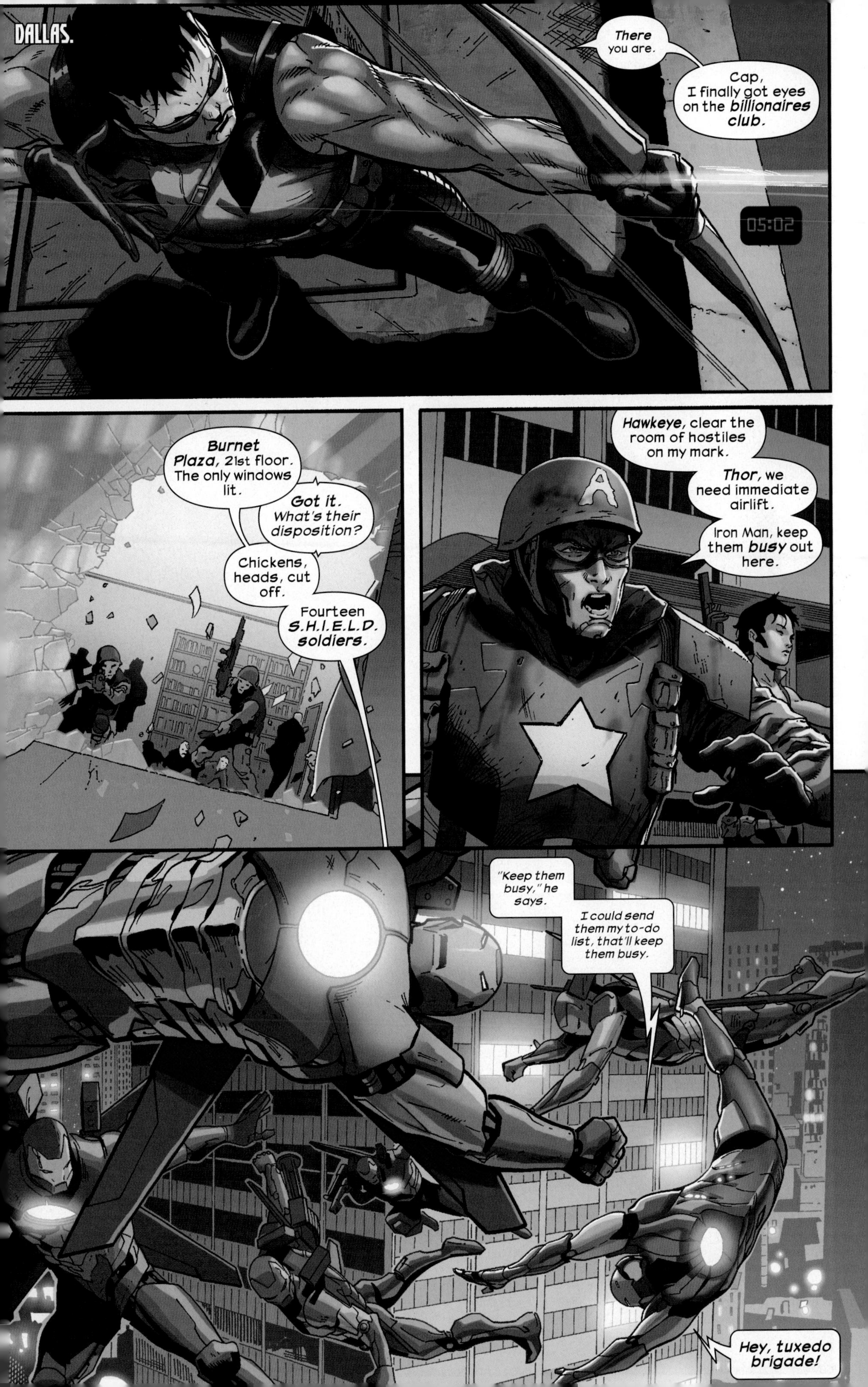
DALLAS.
There you are.
Cap, I finally got eyes on the billionaires club.
05:02
Burnet Plaza, 21st floor. The only windows lit.
Got it. What's their disposition?
Chickens, heads, cut off.
Fourteen S.H.I.E.L.D. soldiers.
Hawkeye, clear the room of hostiles on my mark.
Thor, we need immediate airlift.
Iron Man, keep them busy out here.
"Keep them busy," he says.
I could send them my to-do list, that'll keep them busy.
Hey, tuxedo brigade!

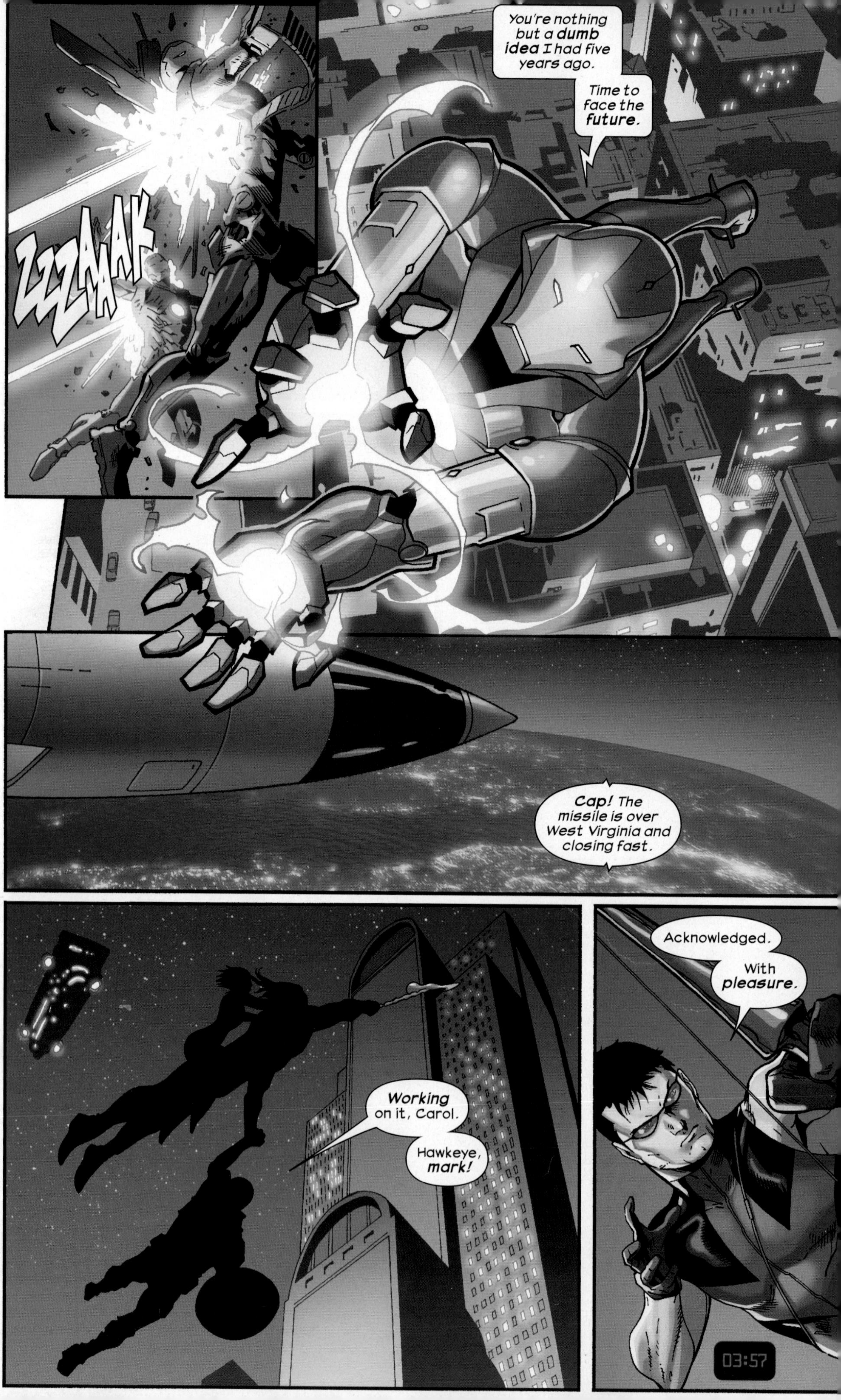
ZZZAAAAK
You're nothing but a dumb idea I had five years ago.
Time to face the future.
Cap! The missile is over West Virginia and closing fast.
Working on it, Carol.
Hawkeye, mark!
Acknowledged.
With pleasure.
03:57

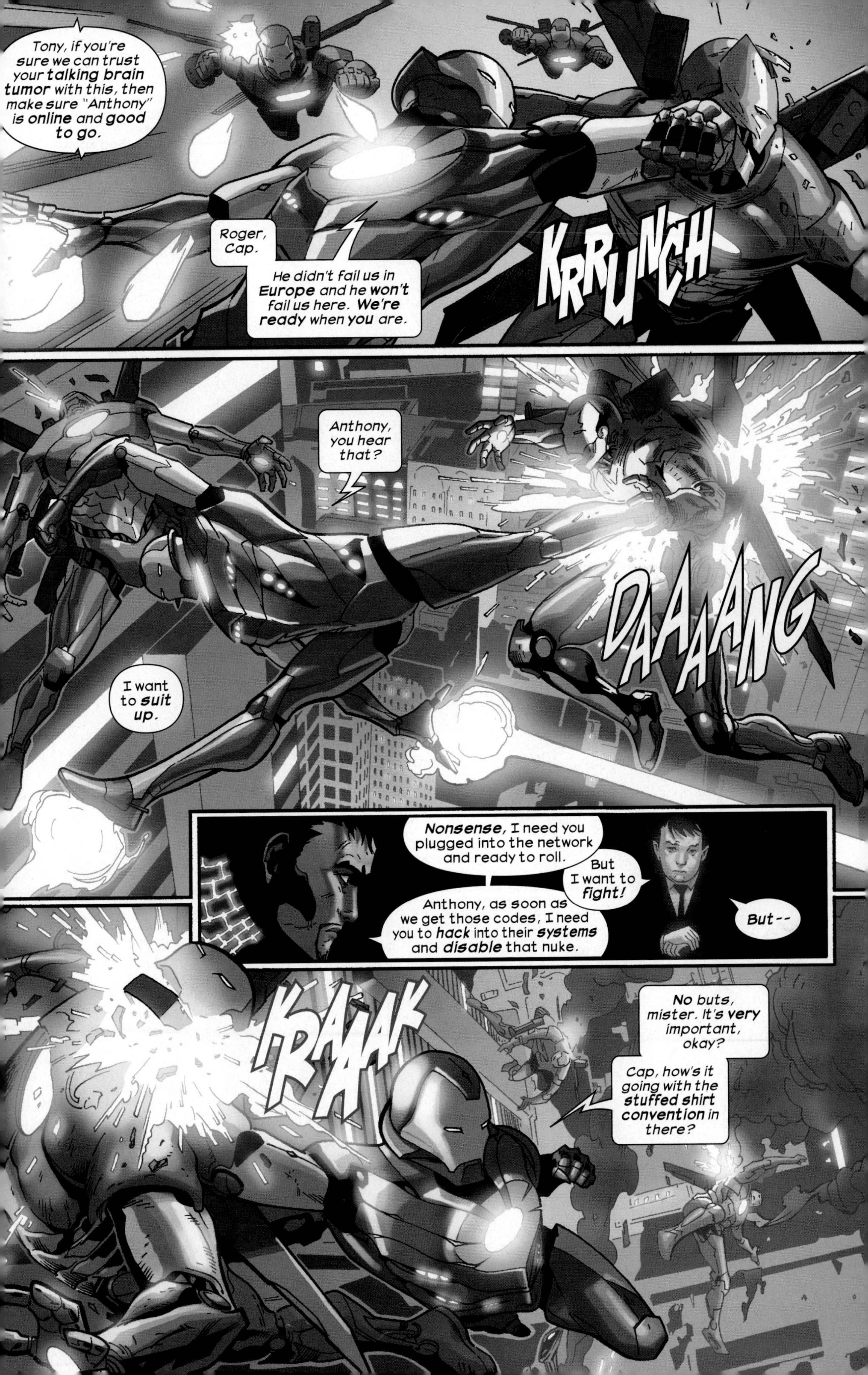
Tony, if you're sure we can trust your **talking brain tumor** with this, then make sure "Anthony" is **online** and **good to go.**
Roger, Cap.
He didn't fail us in **Europe** and he **won't** fail us here. **We're ready** when **you** are.
KRRUNCH
Anthony, you hear that?
DAAAANG
I want to **suit up.**
Nonsense, I need you plugged into the network and ready to roll.
But I want to ***fight!***
Anthony, as soon as we get those codes, I need you to ***hack*** into their ***systems*** and ***disable*** that nuke.
But--
KRAAAK
No buts, mister. It's **very** important, okay?
Cap, how's it going with the **stuffed shirt convention** in there?

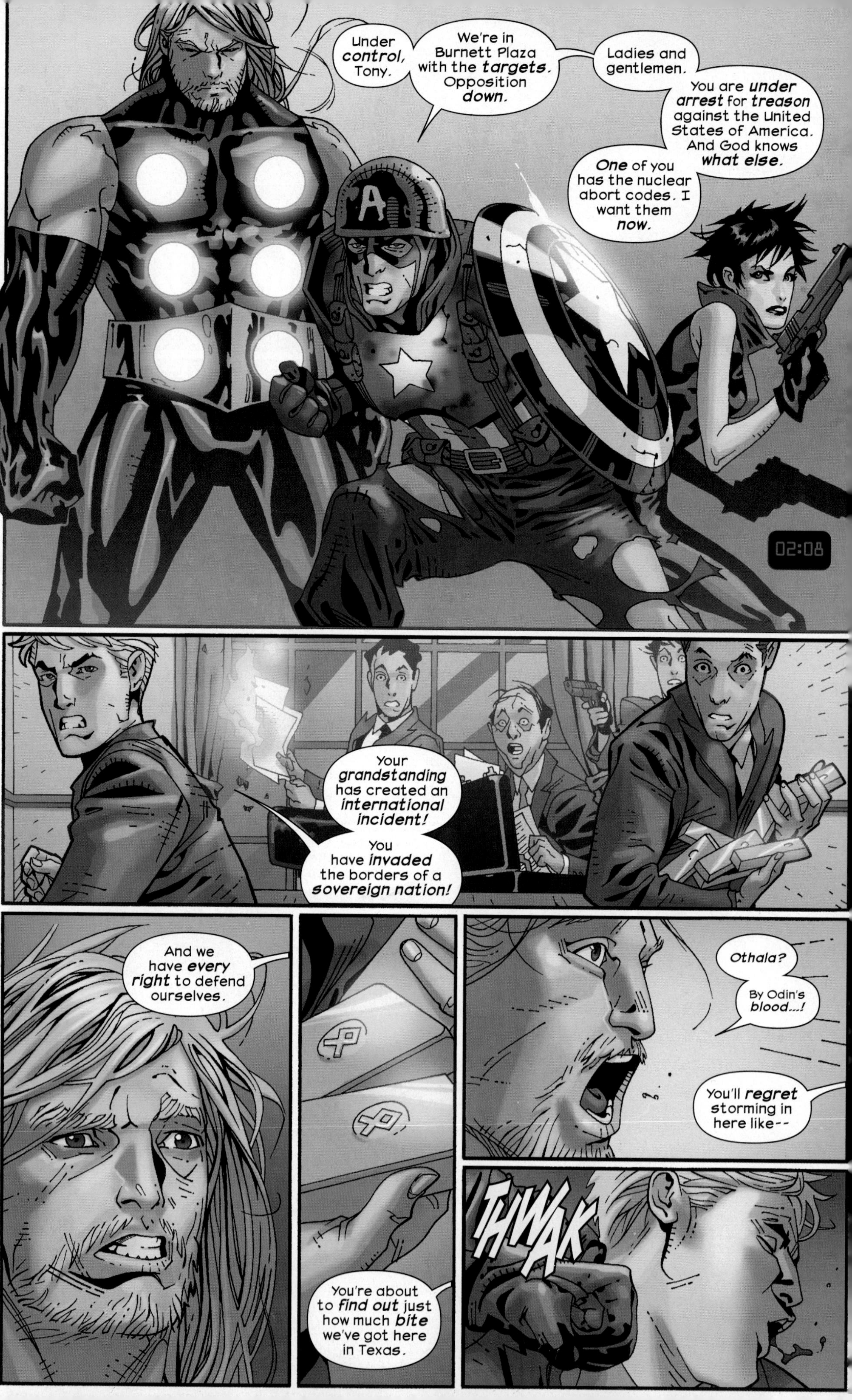
Under control, Tony.
We're in Burnett Plaza with the targets. Opposition down.
Ladies and gentlemen.
You are under arrest for treason against the United States of America. And God knows what else.
One of you has the nuclear abort codes. I want them now.
02:08
Your grandstanding has created an international incident!
You have invaded the borders of a sovereign nation!
And we have every right to defend ourselves.
You're about to find out just how much bite we've got here in Texas.
Othala?
By Odin's blood...!
You'll regret storming in here like--
THWAK

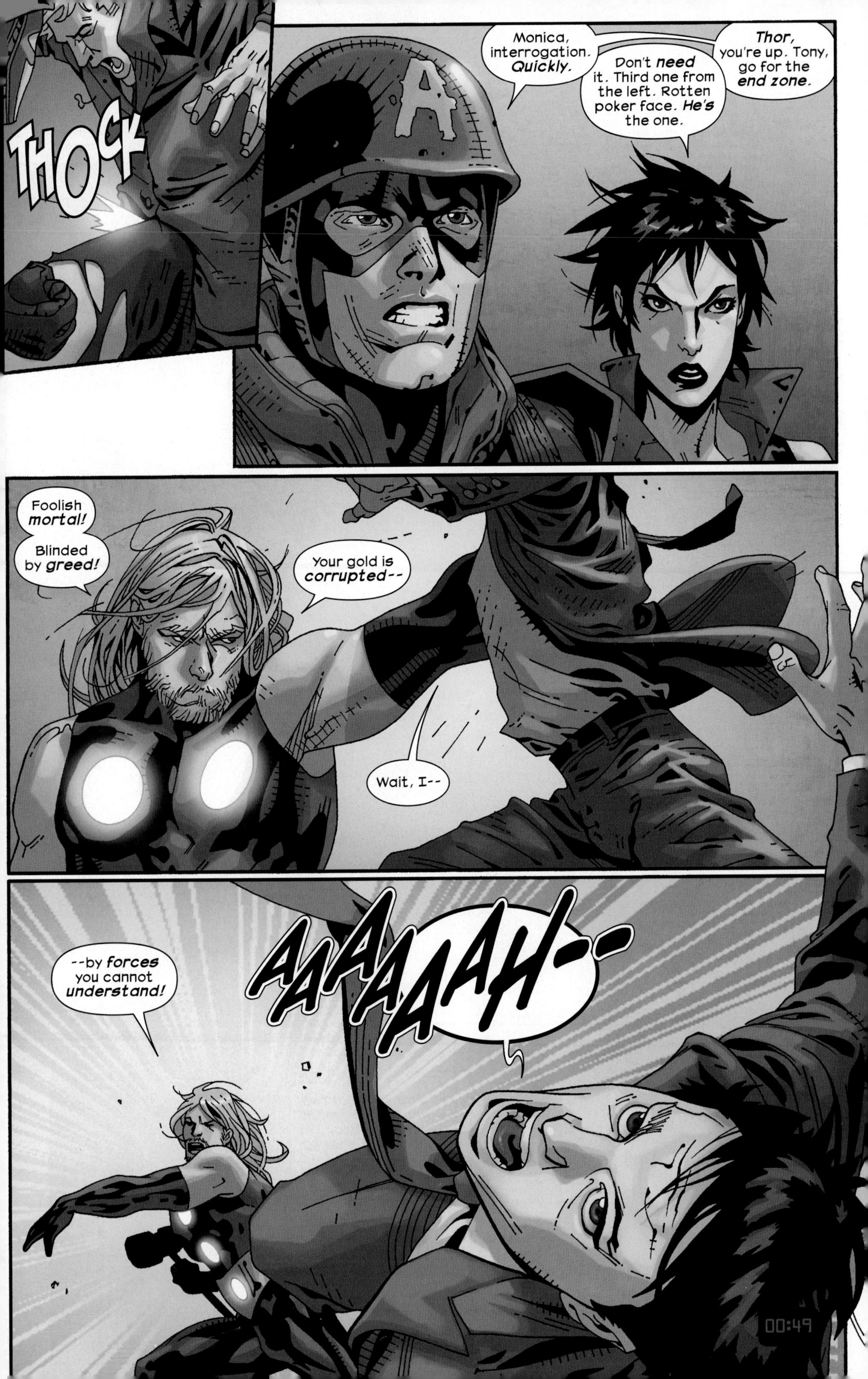
THOCK
Monica, interrogation. Quickly.
Thor, you're up. Tony, go for the end zone.
Don't need it. Third one from the left. Rotten poker face. He's the one.
Foolish mortal!
Blinded by greed!
Your gold is corrupted--
Wait, I--
--by forces you cannot understand!
AAAAAAH--
00:49

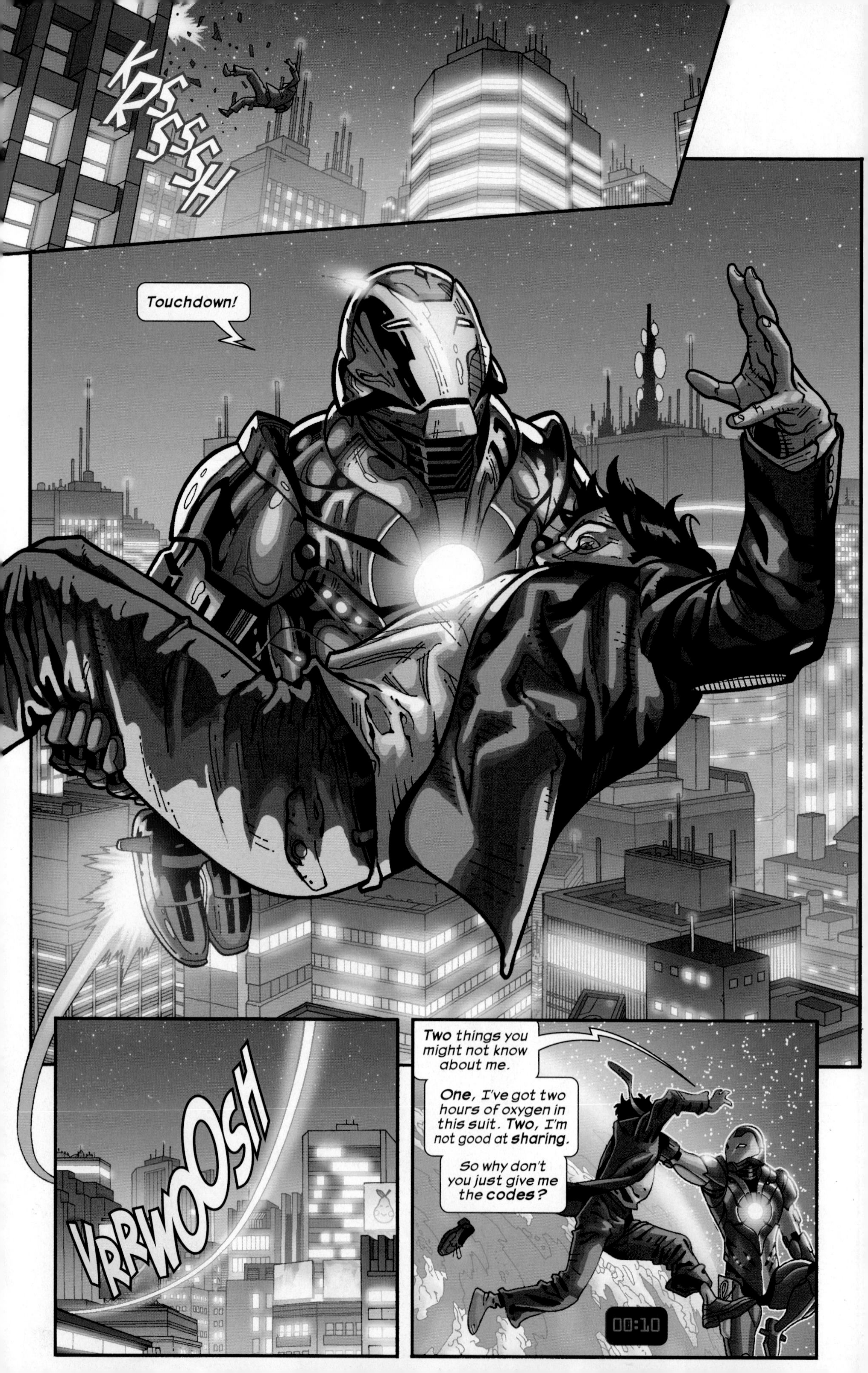
KRSSSH
Touchdown!
VRRWOOSH
Two things you might not know about me.
One, I've got two hours of oxygen in this suit. Two, I'm not good at sharing.
So why don't you just give me the codes?
00:10

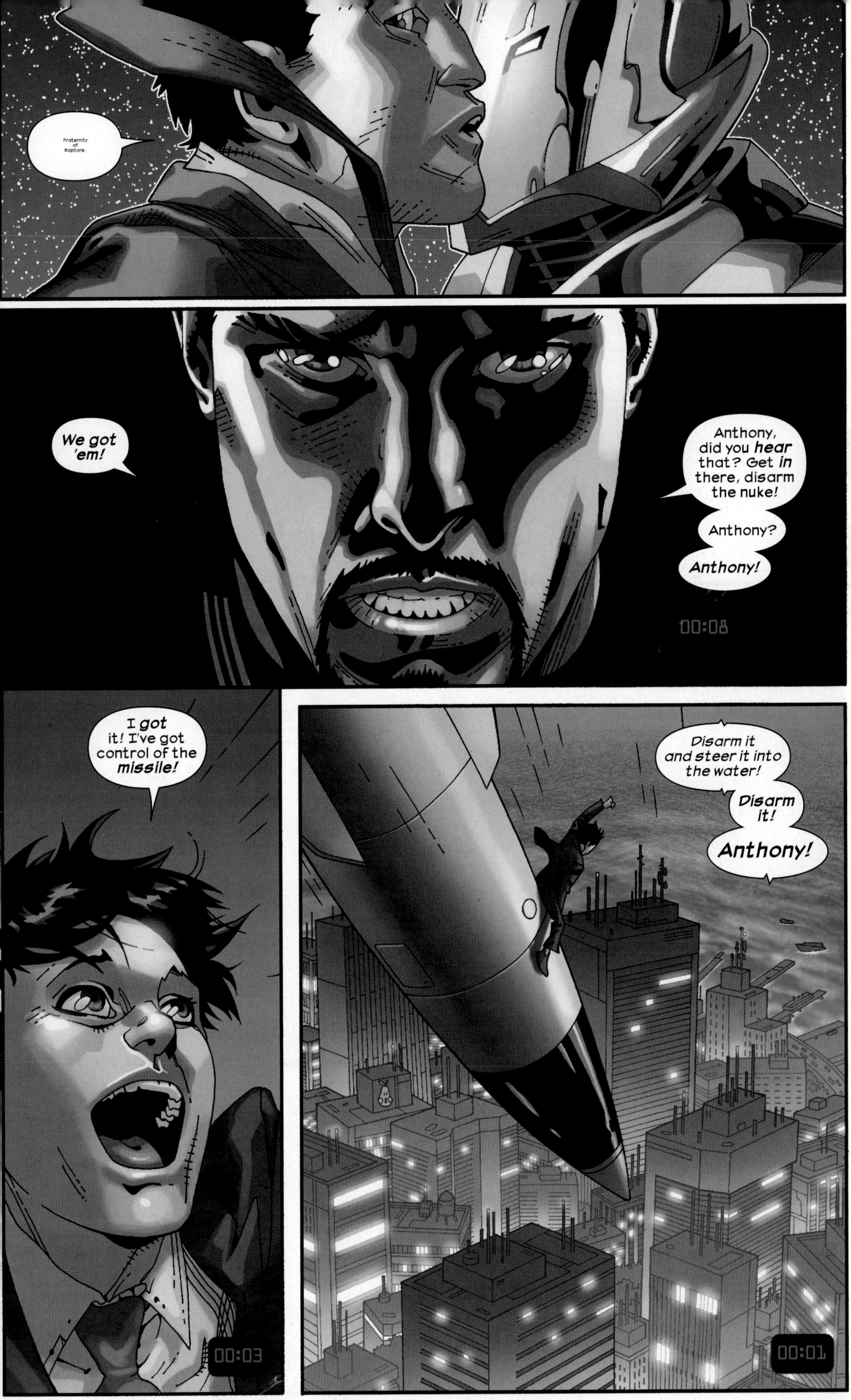
Fraternity of Raptors.
We got 'em!
Anthony, did you hear that? Get in there, disarm the nuke!
Anthony?
Anthony!
00:08
I got it! I've got control of the missile!
00:03
Disarm it and steer it into the water!
Disarm it!
Anthony!
00:01

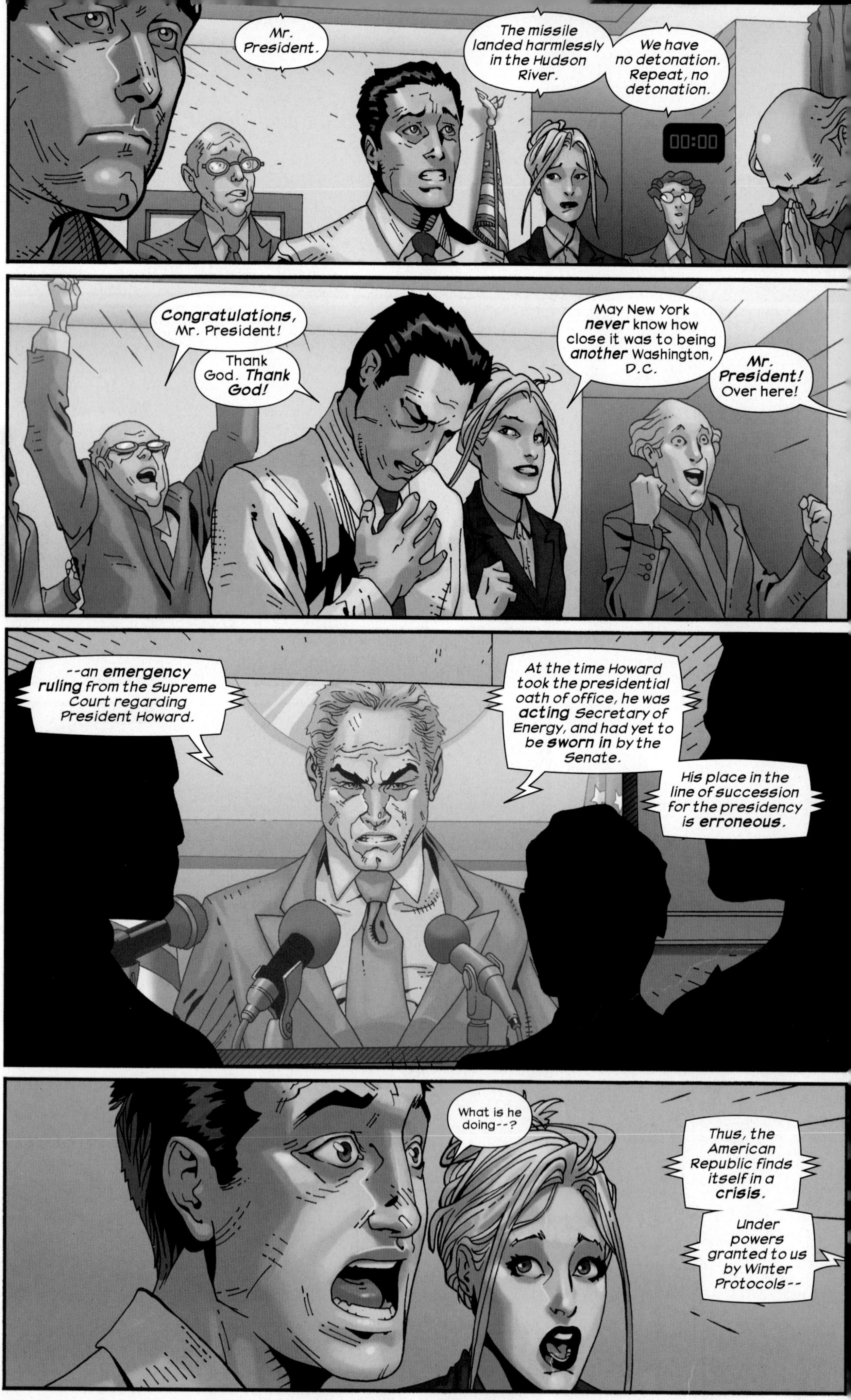
Mr. President.
The missile landed harmlessly in the Hudson River.
We have no detonation. Repeat, no detonation.
00:00
Congratulations, Mr. President!
Thank God. Thank God!
May New York never know how close it was to being another Washington, D.C.
Mr. President! Over here!
--an emergency ruling from the Supreme Court regarding President Howard.
At the time Howard took the presidential oath of office, he was acting Secretary of Energy, and had yet to be sworn in by the Senate.
His place in the line of succession for the presidency is erroneous.
What is he doing--?
Thus, the American Republic finds itself in a crisis.
Under powers granted to us by Winter Protocols--

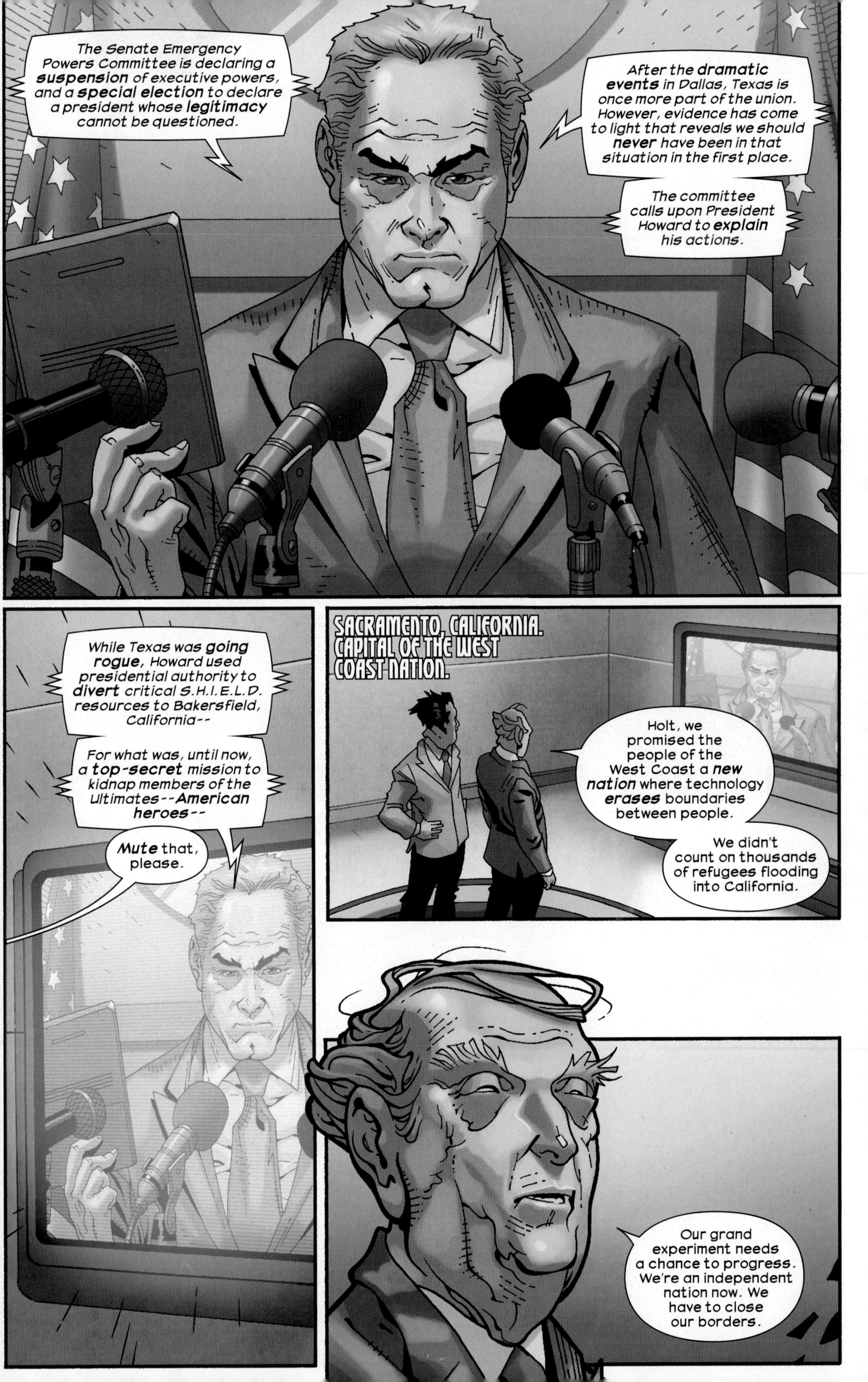

The Senate Emergency Powers Committee is declaring a suspension of executive powers, and a special election to declare a president whose legitimacy cannot be questioned.
After the dramatic events in Dallas, Texas is once more part of the union. However, evidence has come to light that reveals we should never have been in that situation in the first place.
The committee calls upon President Howard to explain his actions.
While Texas was going rogue, Howard used presidential authority to divert critical S.H.I.E.L.D. resources to Bakersfield, California--
For what was, until now, a top-secret mission to kidnap members of the Ultimates--American heroes--
Mute that, please.
SACRAMENTO, CALIFORNIA. CAPITAL OF THE WEST COAST NATION.
Holt, we promised the people of the West Coast a new nation where technology erases boundaries between people.
We didn't count on thousands of refugees flooding into California.
Our grand experiment needs a chance to progress. We're an independent nation now. We have to close our borders.

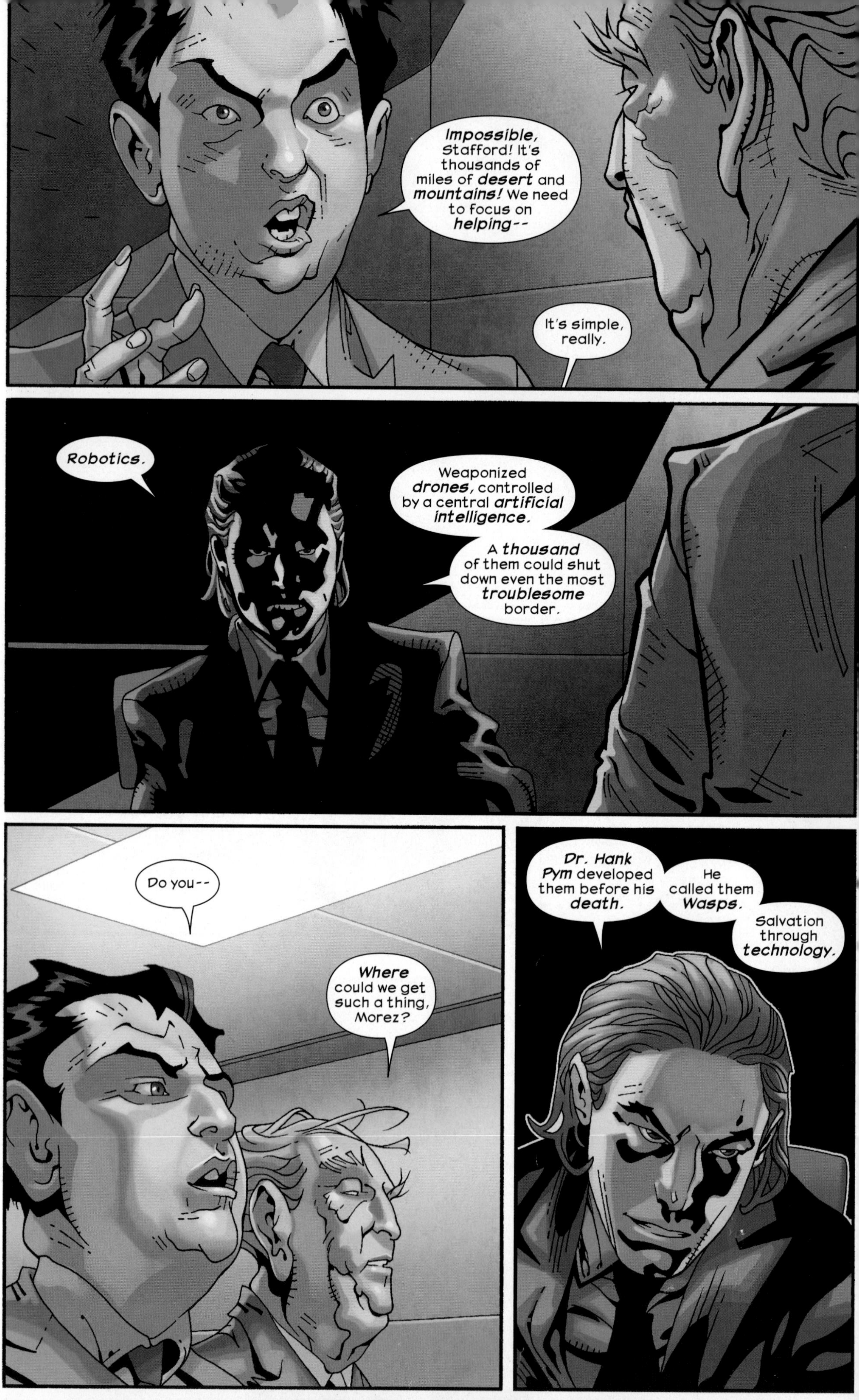
Impossible, Stafford! It's thousands of miles of desert and mountains! We need to focus on helping--
It's simple, really.
Robotics.
Weaponized drones, controlled by a central artificial intelligence.
A thousand of them could shut down even the most troublesome border.
Do you--
Where could we get such a thing, Morez?
Dr. Hank Pym developed them before his death.
He called them Wasps.
Salvation through technology.

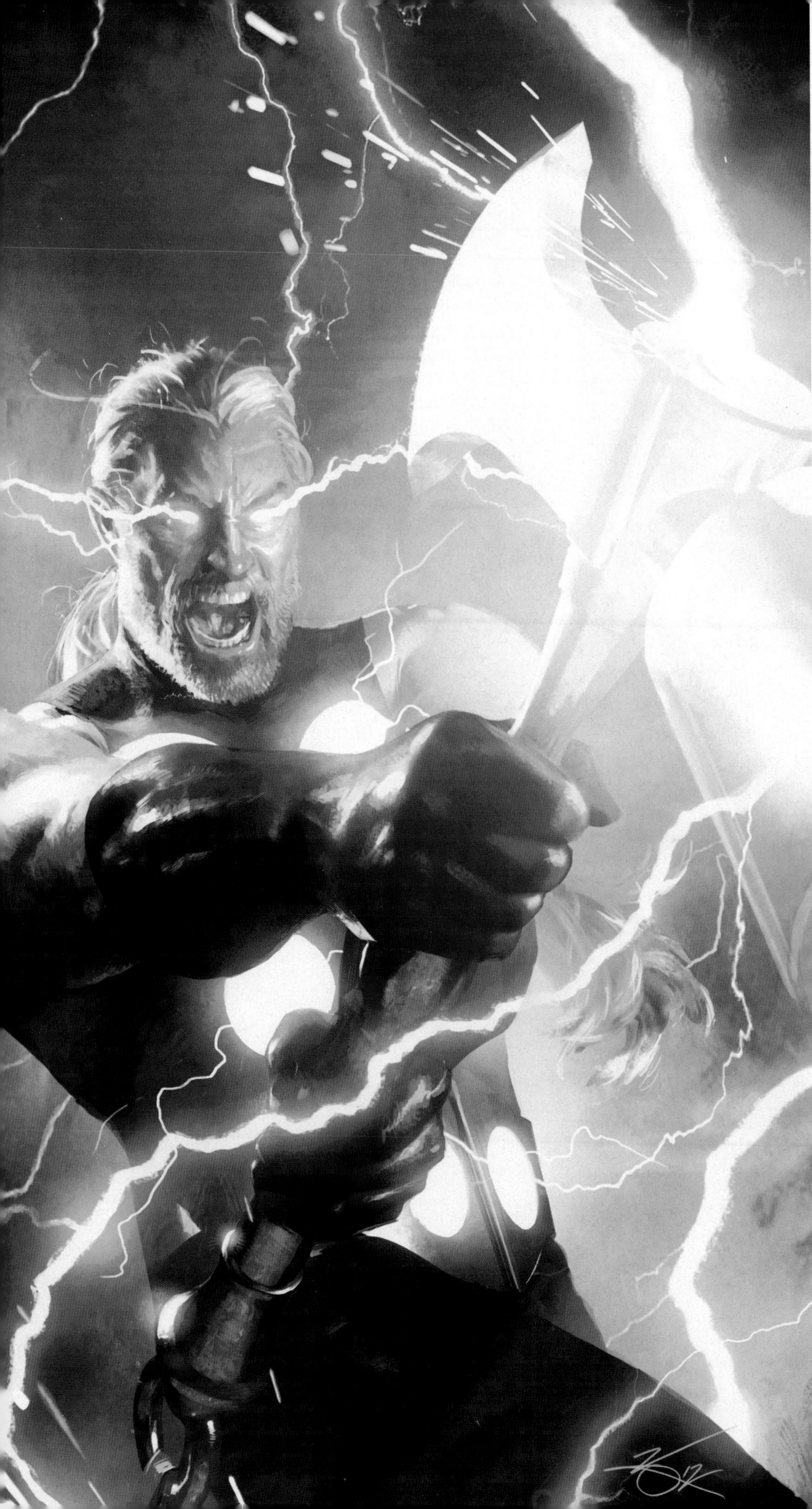

3

ULTIMATE COMICS **ULTIMATES** #15

S.H.I.E.L.D. SITUATION MAP:

[Anti-government militia hot spots]

Idaho, Montana,
N.Dakota, S.Dakota,
Wyoming, Arizona,
New Mexico, N.Carolina,
S.Carolina, Georgia

[Eastern seaboard control zone]

New England,
New York,
New Jersey,
Delaware,
Washington D.C.,
Maryland,
Pennsylvania,
Virginia

secured by
National Guard
under emergency
powers
committee

[the West Coast]

California, Oregon,
Washington
status unknown

[Great Lakes states]

Minnesota,
Wisconsin,
Michigan,
Illinois,
Indiana, Ohio
status unknown

ANTI-MATTER
NO FLY
ZONE

SENTINEL
PUSH

AREA OF
URBAN
UNREST

SOUTHERN
CALIFORNIA
REFUGEE ZONE

[Sentinel-controlled no-man's-land]

New Mexico, Arizona,
Utah, Oklahoma
abandoned by the
U.S. government

Classified Position

Camp Hutton, secure
location of the President
of the United States

ALL STATES
SHOWN IN WHITE
ARE U.S. GOVERNMENT-
CONTROLLED ZONES

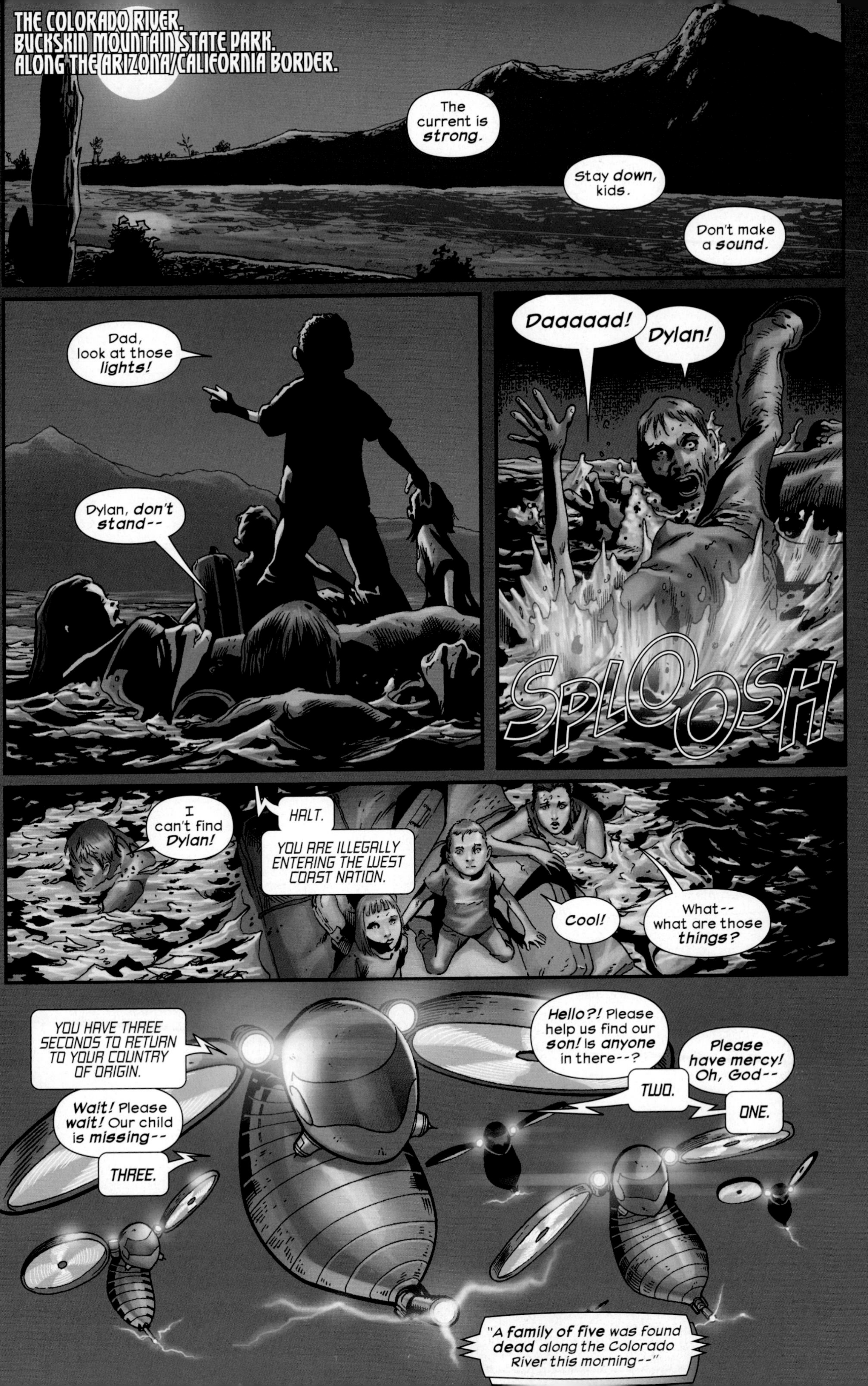

THE COLORADO RIVER.
BUCKSKIN MOUNTAIN STATE PARK.
ALONG THE ARIZONA/CALIFORNIA BORDER.
The current is strong.
Stay down, kids.
Don't make a sound.
Dad, look at those lights!
Dylan, don't stand--
Daaaaad!
Dylan!
SPLOOSH
I can't find Dylan!
HALT.
YOU ARE ILLEGALLY ENTERING THE WEST COAST NATION.
Cool!
What-- what are those things?
YOU HAVE THREE SECONDS TO RETURN TO YOUR COUNTRY OF ORIGIN.
Wait! Please wait! Our child is missing--
THREE.
Hello?! Please help us find our son! Is anyone in there--?
TWO.
Please have mercy! Oh, God--
ONE.
"A family of five was found dead along the Colorado River this morning--"

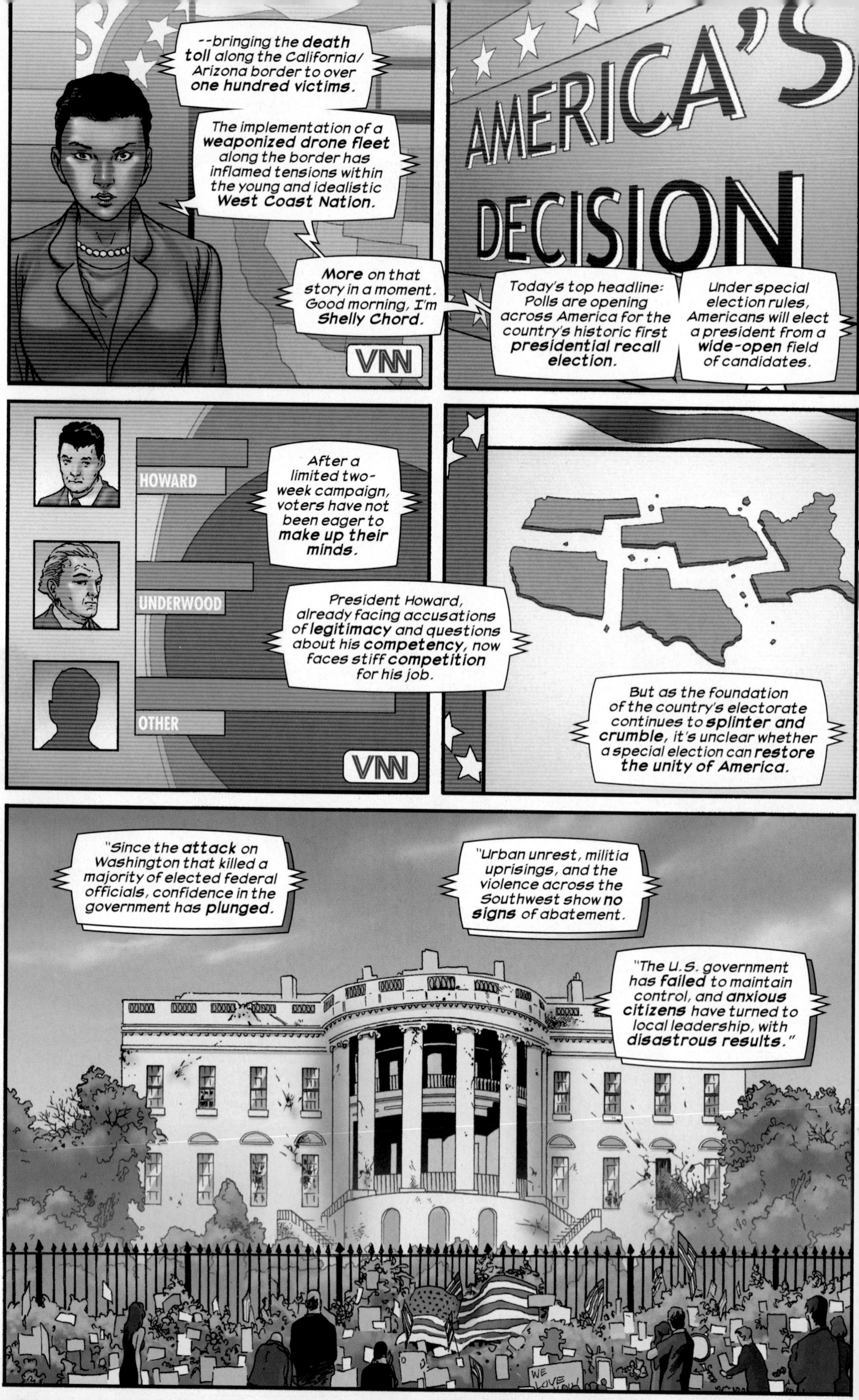

--bringing the death toll along the California/ Arizona border to over one hundred victims.
The implementation of a weaponized drone fleet along the border has inflamed tensions within the young and idealistic West Coast Nation.
More on that story in a moment. Good morning, I'm Shelly Chord.
VNN
AMERICA'S DECISION
Today's top headline: Polls are opening across America for the country's historic first presidential recall election.
Under special election rules, Americans will elect a president from a wide-open field of candidates.
HOWARD
UNDERWOOD
OTHER
After a limited two-week campaign, voters have not been eager to make up their minds.
President Howard, already facing accusations of legitimacy and questions about his competency, now faces stiff competition for his job.
VNN
But as the foundation of the country's electorate continues to splinter and crumble, it's unclear whether a special election can restore the unity of America.
"Since the attack on Washington that killed a majority of elected federal officials, confidence in the government has plunged.
"Urban unrest, militia uprisings, and the violence across the Southwest show no signs of abatement.
"The U.S. government has failed to maintain control, and anxious citizens have turned to local leadership, with disastrous results."

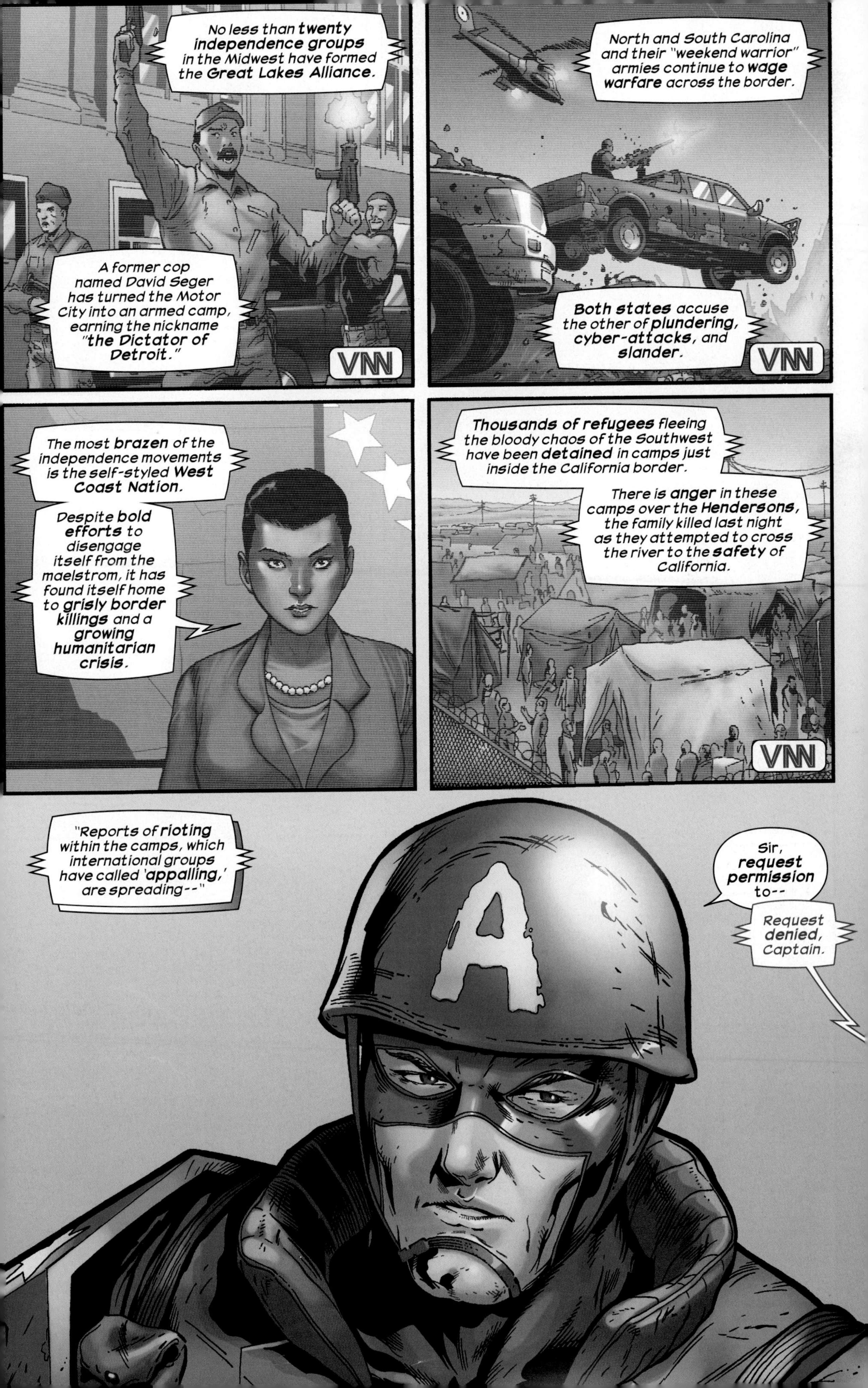

No less than twenty independence groups in the Midwest have formed the Great Lakes Alliance.
A former cop named David Seger has turned the Motor City into an armed camp, earning the nickname "the Dictator of Detroit."
VNN
North and South Carolina and their "weekend warrior" armies continue to wage warfare across the border.
Both states accuse the other of plundering, cyber-attacks, and slander.
VNN
The most brazen of the independence movements is the self-styled West Coast Nation.
Despite bold efforts to disengage itself from the maelstrom, it has found itself home to grisly border killings and a growing humanitarian crisis.
Thousands of refugees fleeing the bloody chaos of the Southwest have been detained in camps just inside the California border.
There is anger in these camps over the Hendersons, the family killed last night as they attempted to cross the river to the safety of California.
VNN
"Reports of rioting within the camps, which international groups have called 'appalling,' are spreading--"
Sir, request permission to--
Request denied, Captain.

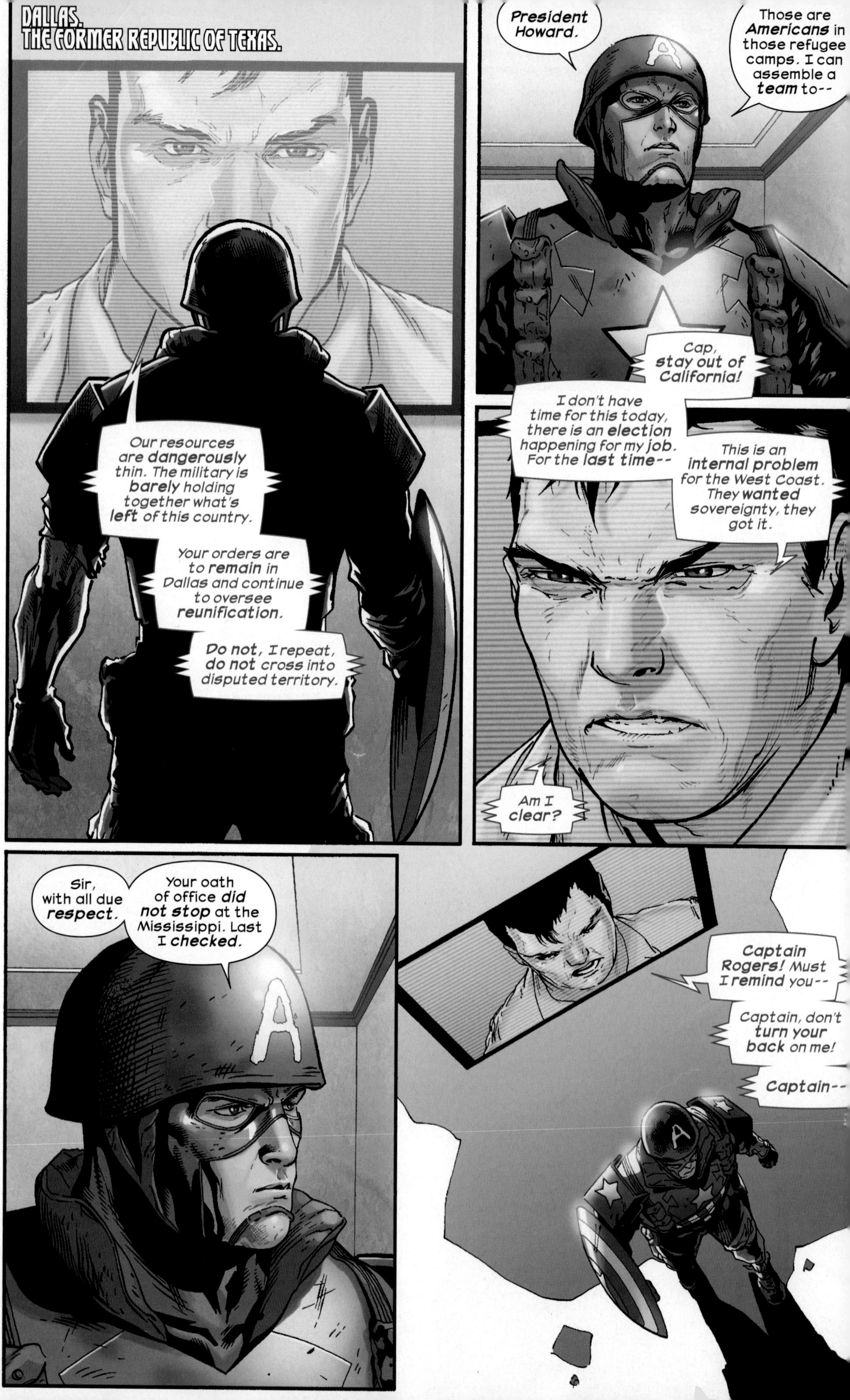
DALLAS.
THE FORMER REPUBLIC OF TEXAS.
Our resources are dangerously thin. The military is barely holding together what's left of this country.
Your orders are to remain in Dallas and continue to oversee reunification.
Do not, I repeat, do not cross into disputed territory.
President Howard.
Those are Americans in those refugee camps. I can assemble a team to--
Cap, stay out of California!
I don't have time for this today, there is an election happening for my job. For the last time--
This is an internal problem for the West Coast. They wanted sovereignty, they got it.
Am I clear?
Sir, with all due respect.
Your oath of office did not stop at the Mississippi. Last I checked.
Captain Rogers! Must I remind you--
Captain, don't turn your back on me!
Captain--

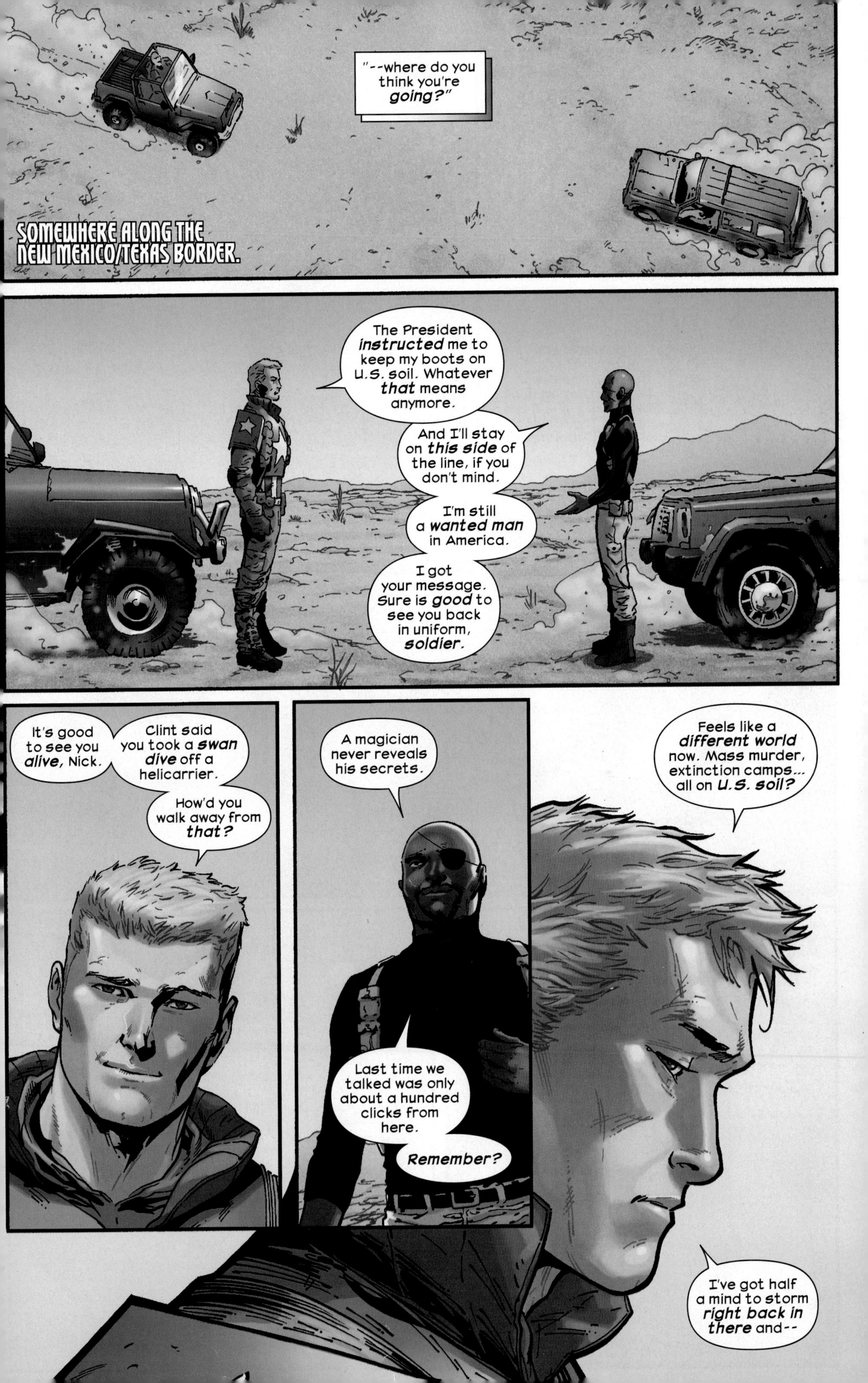
"--where do you think you're *going?*"
SOMEWHERE ALONG THE NEW MEXICO/TEXAS BORDER.
The President *instructed* me to keep my boots on U.S. soil. Whatever *that* means anymore.
And I'll stay on *this side* of the line, if you don't mind.
I'm still a *wanted man* in America.
I got your message. Sure is *good* to see you back in uniform, *soldier.*
It's good to see you *alive,* Nick.
Clint said you took a *swan dive* off a helicarrier.
How'd you walk away from *that?*
A magician never reveals his secrets.
Last time we talked was only about a hundred clicks from here.
Remember?
Feels like a *different world* now. Mass murder, extinction camps... all on *U.S. soil?*
I've got half a mind to storm *right back in there* and--

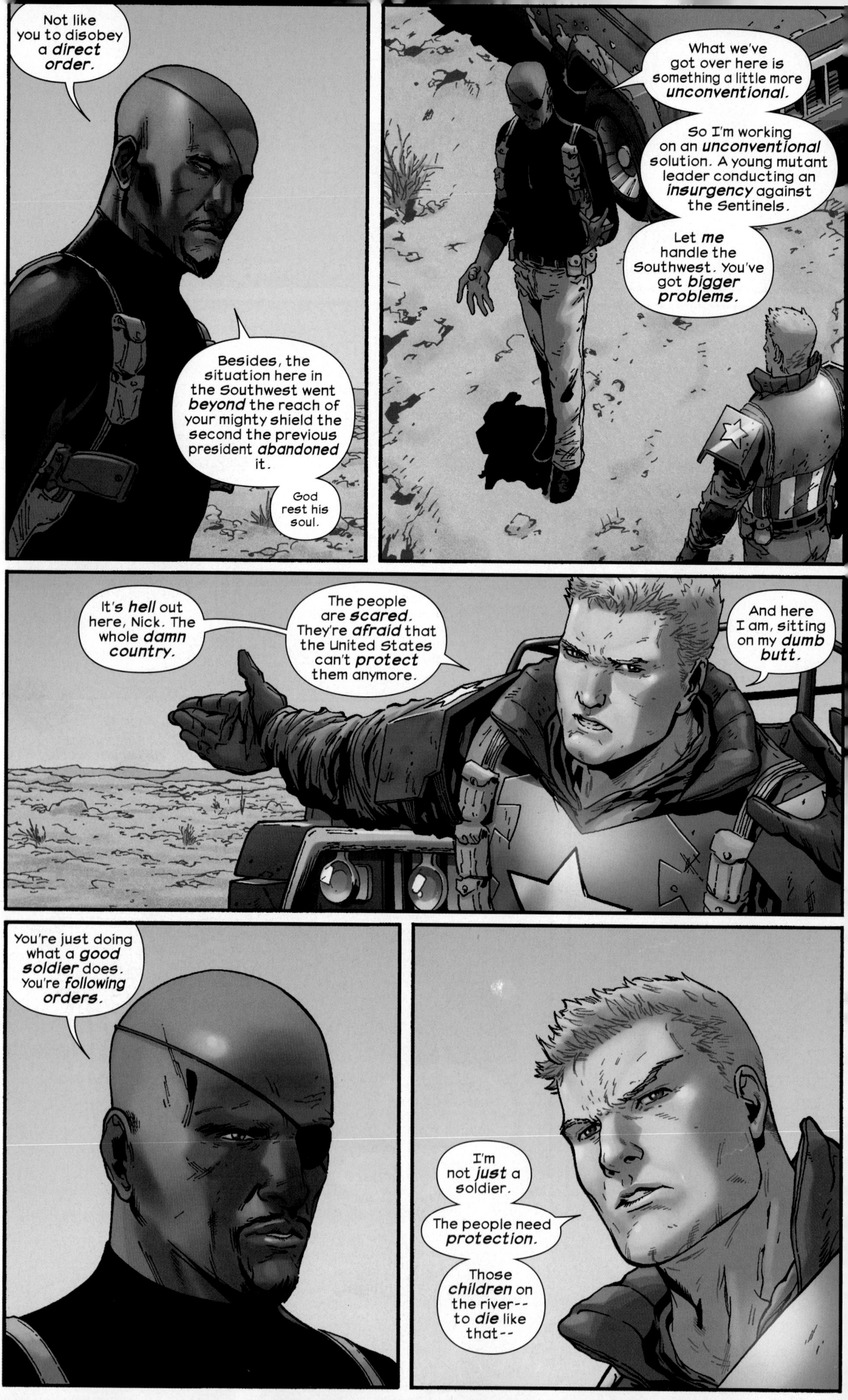
Not like you to disobey a *direct order.*
Besides, the situation here in the Southwest went *beyond* the reach of your mighty shield the second the previous president *abandoned* it.
God rest his soul.
What we've got over here is something a little more *unconventional.*
So I'm working on an *unconventional* solution. A young mutant leader conducting an *insurgency* against the Sentinels.
Let *me* handle the Southwest. You've got *bigger problems.*
It's *hell* out here, Nick. The whole *damn country.*
The people are *scared.* They're *afraid* that the United States can't *protect* them anymore.
And here I am, sitting on my *dumb butt.*
You're just doing what a *good soldier* does. You're *following orders.*
I'm not *just* a soldier.
The people need *protection.*
Those *children* on the river-- to *die* like that--

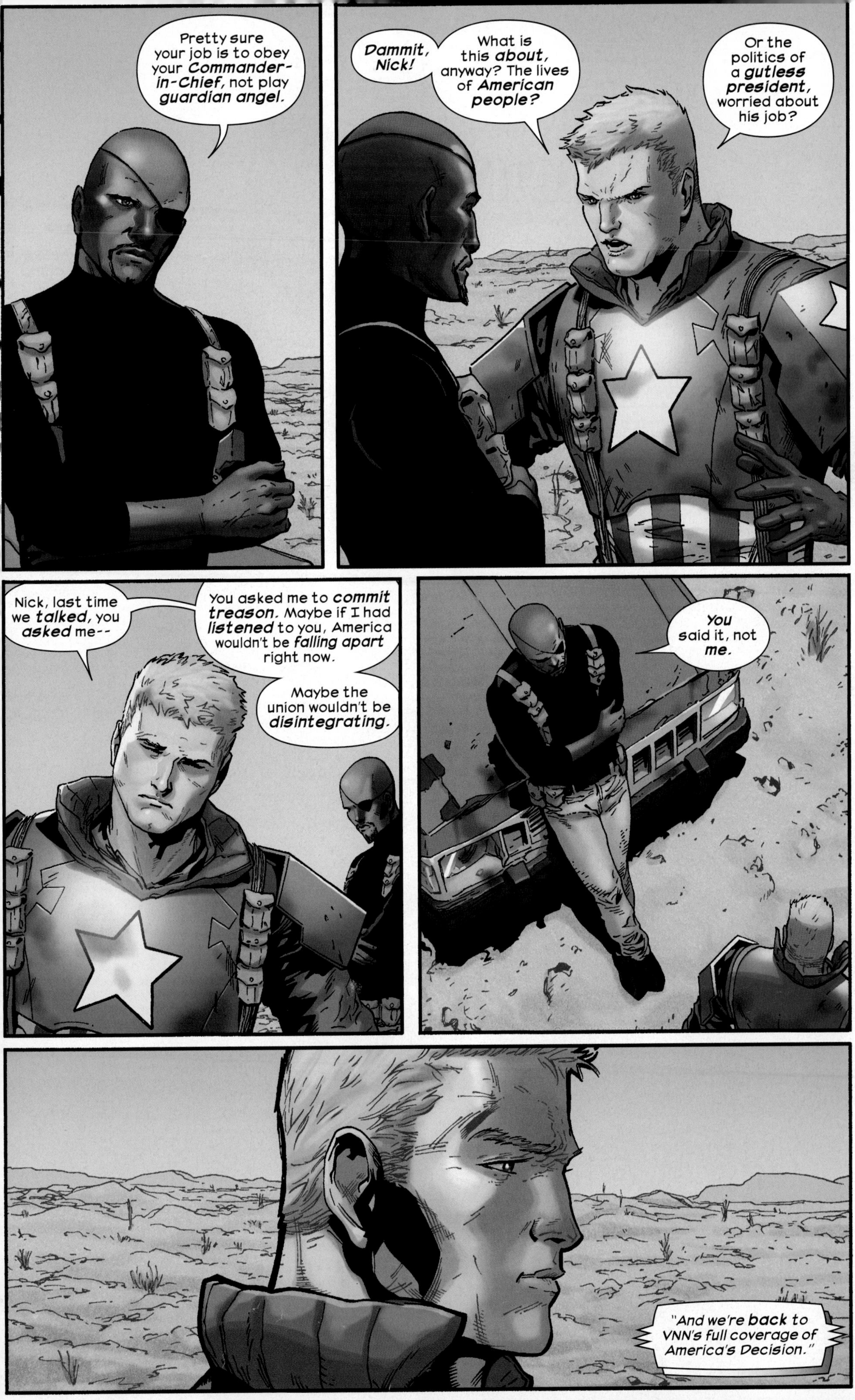
Pretty sure your job is to obey your Commander-in-Chief, not play guardian angel.
Dammit, Nick!
What is this about, anyway? The lives of American people?
Or the politics of a gutless president, worried about his job?
Nick, last time we talked, you asked me--
You asked me to commit treason. Maybe if I had listened to you, America wouldn't be falling apart right now.
Maybe the union wouldn't be disintegrating.
You said it, not me.
"And we're back to VNN's full coverage of America's Decision."

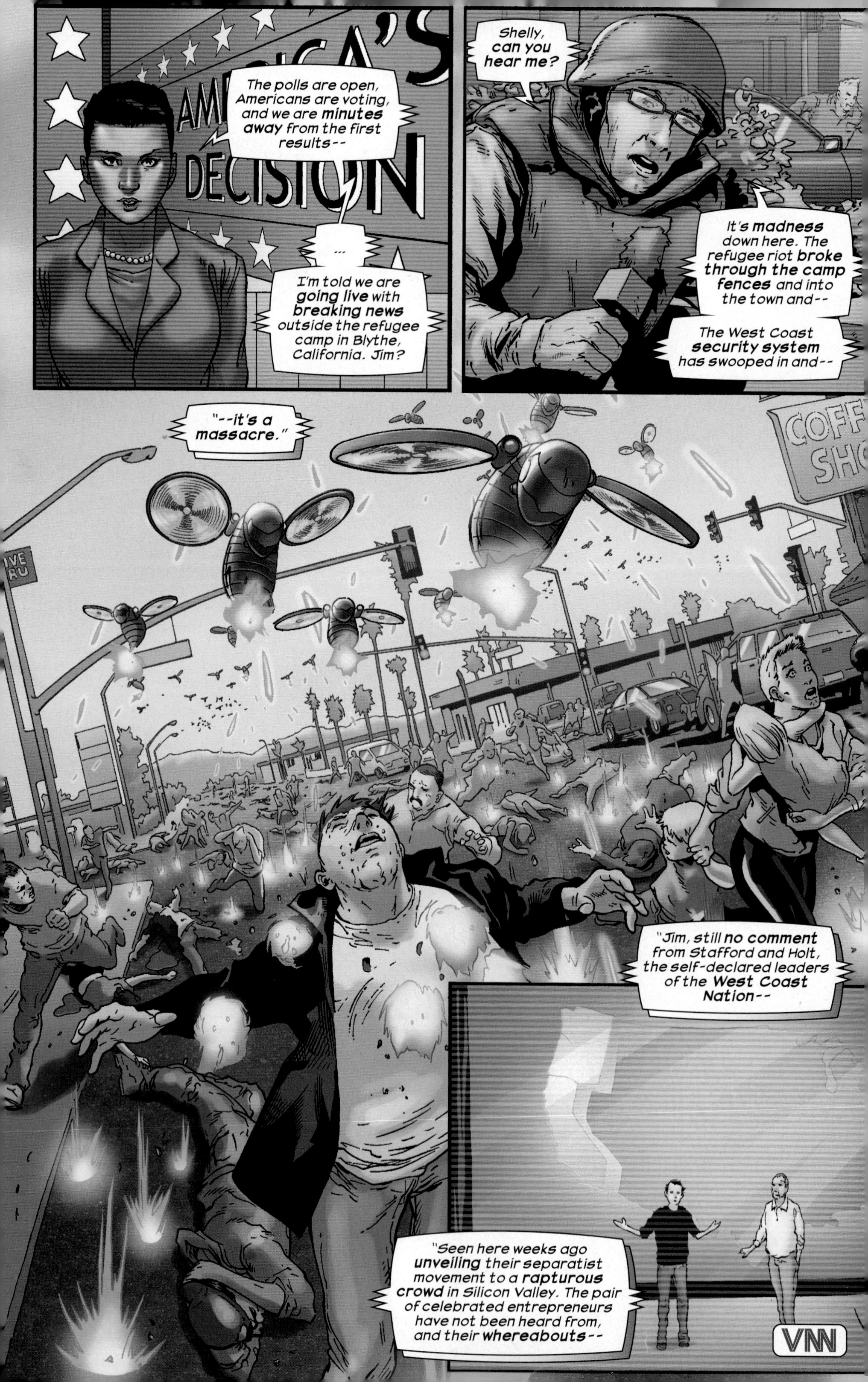
AMERICA'S DECISION
The polls are open, Americans are voting, and we are minutes away from the first results--
...
I'm told we are going live with breaking news outside the refugee camp in Blythe, California. Jim?
Shelly, can you hear me?
It's madness down here. The refugee riot broke through the camp fences and into the town and--
The West Coast security system has swooped in and--
"--it's a massacre."
"Jim, still no comment from Stafford and Holt, the self-declared leaders of the West Coast Nation--
"Seen here weeks ago unveiling their separatist movement to a rapturous crowd in Silicon Valley. The pair of celebrated entrepreneurs have not been heard from, and their whereabouts--
VNN

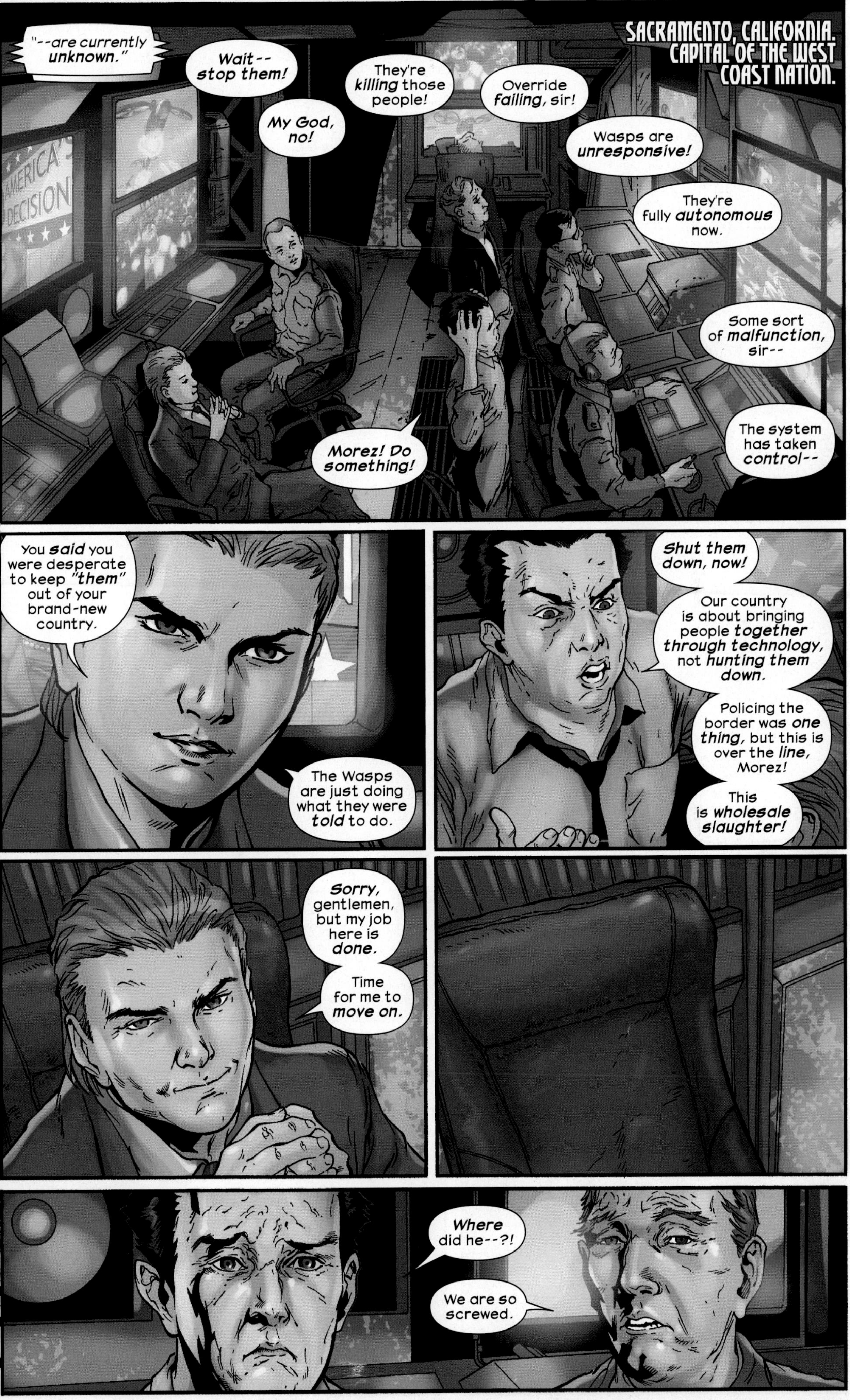
"--are currently unknown."
Wait-- stop them!
My God, no!
They're killing those people!
Override failing, sir!
Wasps are unresponsive!
They're fully autonomous now.
SACRAMENTO, CALIFORNIA. CAPITAL OF THE WEST COAST NATION.
AMERICA'S DECISION
Some sort of malfunction, sir--
The system has taken control--
Morez! Do something!
You said you were desperate to keep "them" out of your brand-new country.
The Wasps are just doing what they were told to do.
Shut them down, now!
Our country is about bringing people together through technology, not hunting them down.
Policing the border was one thing, but this is over the line, Morez!
This is wholesale slaughter!
Sorry, gentlemen, but my job here is done.
Time for me to move on.
Where did he--?!
We are so screwed.

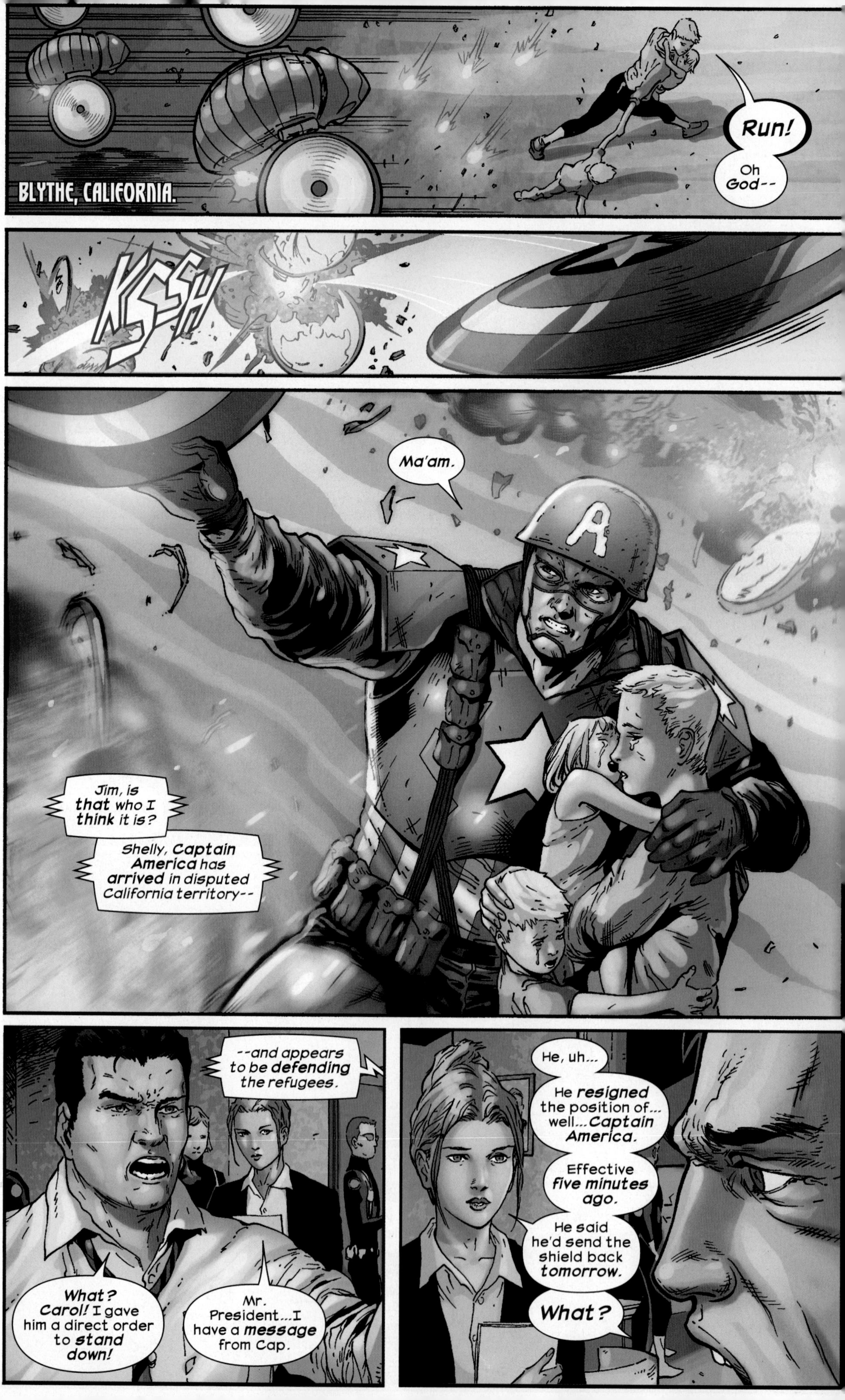
BLYTHE, CALIFORNIA.
Run!
Oh God--
KSSH
Ma'am.
Jim, is that who I think it is?
Shelly, Captain America has arrived in disputed California territory--
--and appears to be defending the refugees.
What? Carol! I gave him a direct order to stand down!
Mr. President...I have a message from Cap.
He, uh...
He resigned the position of... well...Captain America.
Effective five minutes ago.
He said he'd send the shield back tomorrow.
What?

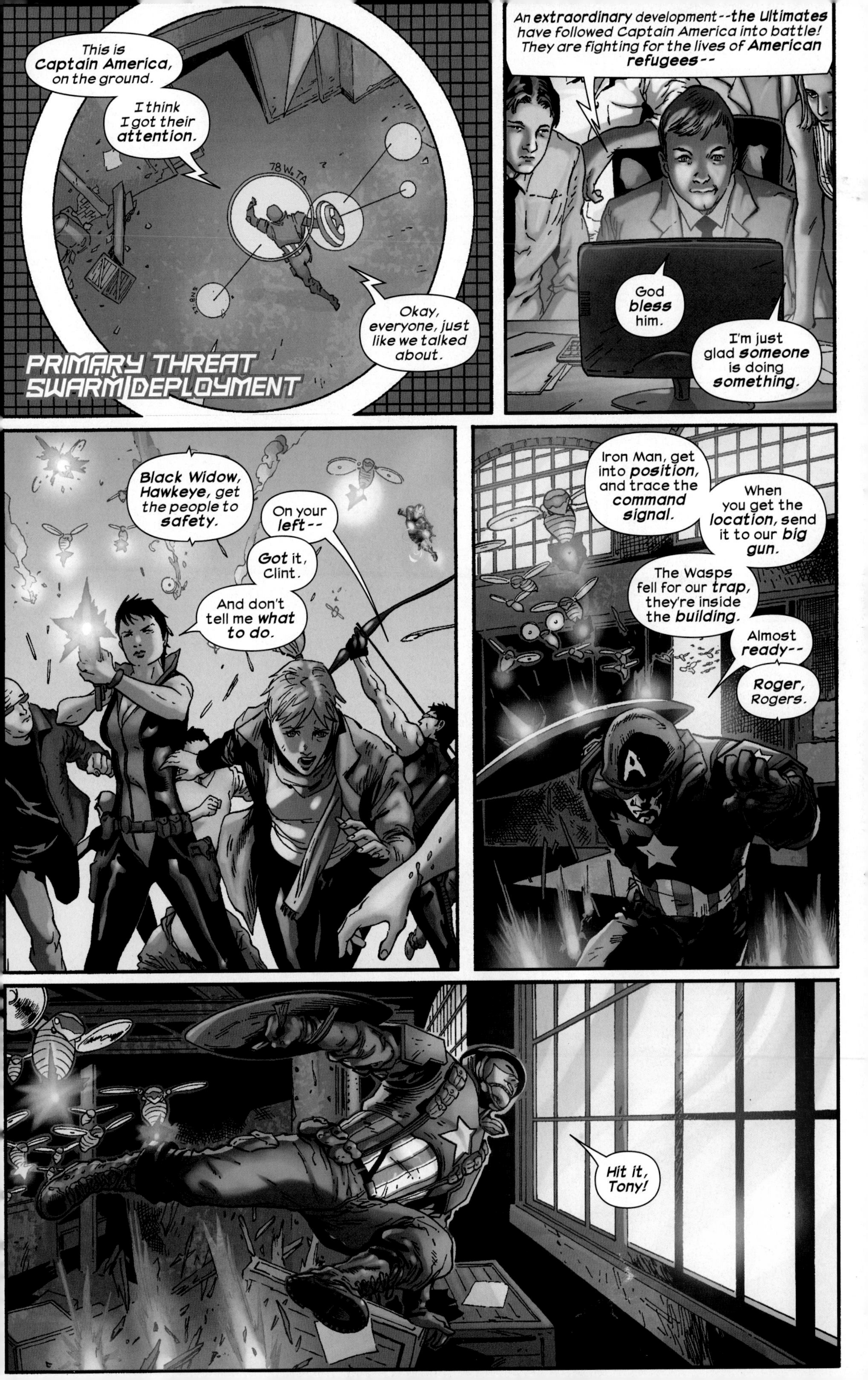
This is Captain America, on the ground.
I think I got their attention.
78 W. TA
Okay, everyone, just like we talked about.
PRIMARY THREAT
SWARM DEPLOYMENT
An extraordinary development--the Ultimates have followed Captain America into battle! They are fighting for the lives of American refugees--
God bless him.
I'm just glad someone is doing something.
Black Widow, Hawkeye, get the people to safety.
On your left--
Got it, Clint.
And don't tell me what to do.
Iron Man, get into position, and trace the command signal.
When you get the location, send it to our big gun.
The Wasps fell for our trap, they're inside the building.
Almost ready--
Roger, Rogers.
Hit it, Tony!

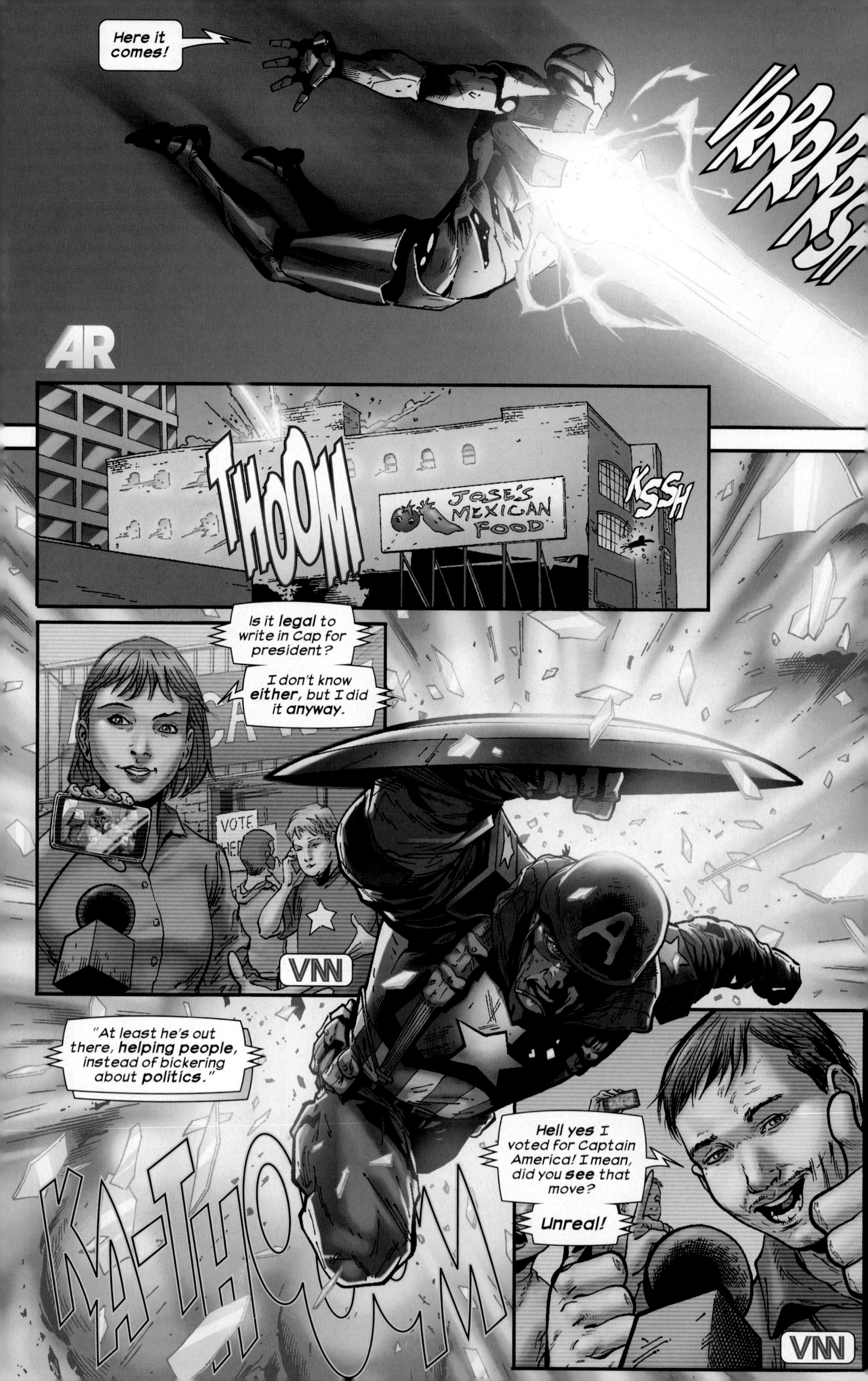

Here it comes!
VRRRRSHH
AR
THOOM
JOSE'S MEXICAN FOOD
KSSH
Is it legal to write in Cap for president?
I don't know either, but I did it anyway.
VOTE
VNN
"At least he's out there, helping people, instead of bickering about politics."
KA-THOOOM
Hell yes I voted for Captain America! I mean, did you see that move?
Unreal!
VNN

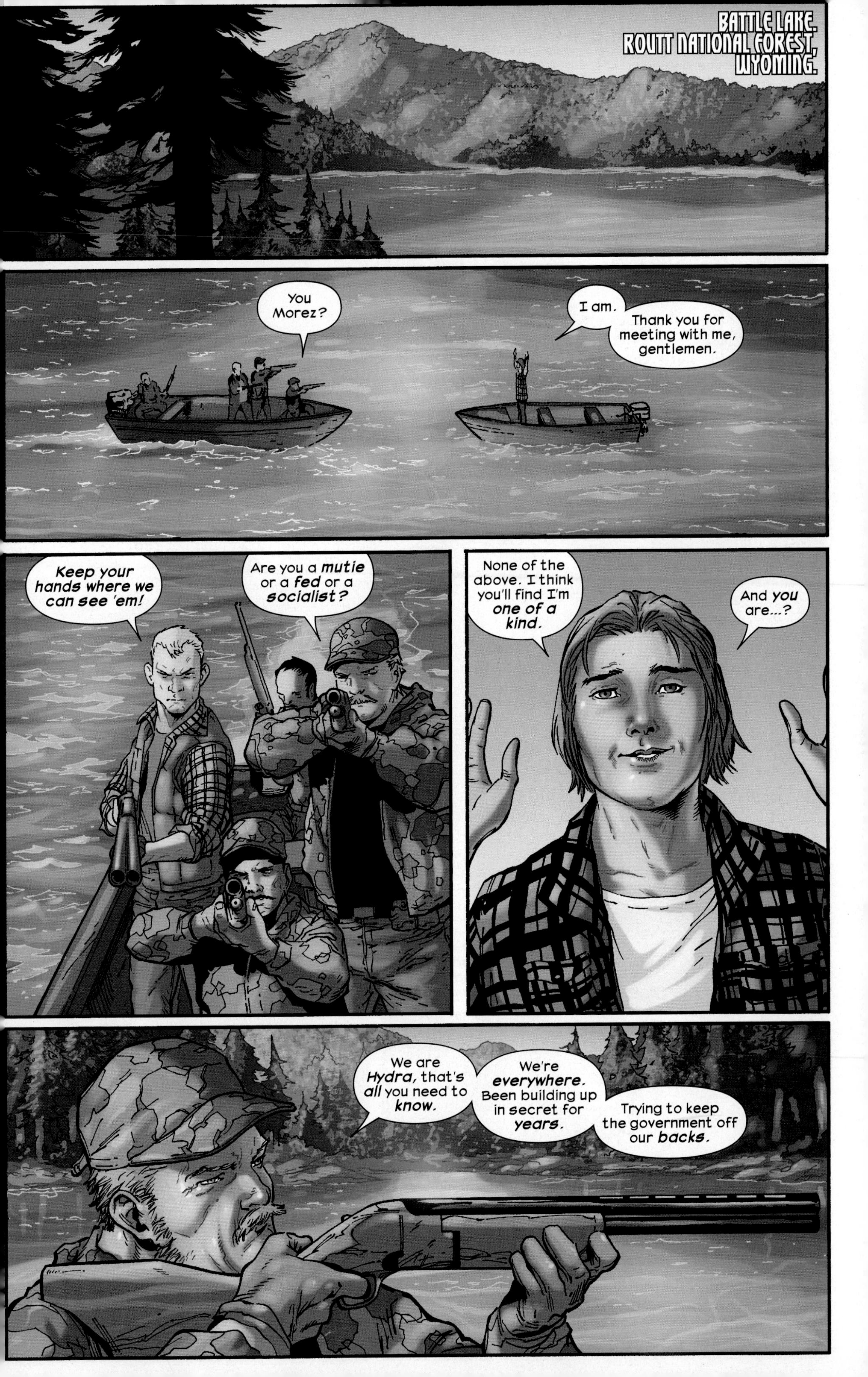
BATTLE LAKE. ROUTT NATIONAL FOREST, WYOMING.
You Morez?
I am.
Thank you for meeting with me, gentlemen.
Keep your hands where we can see 'em!
Are you a mutie or a fed or a socialist?
None of the above. I think you'll find I'm one of a kind.
And you are...?
We are Hydra, that's all you need to know.
We're everywhere. Been building up in secret for years.
Trying to keep the government off our backs.

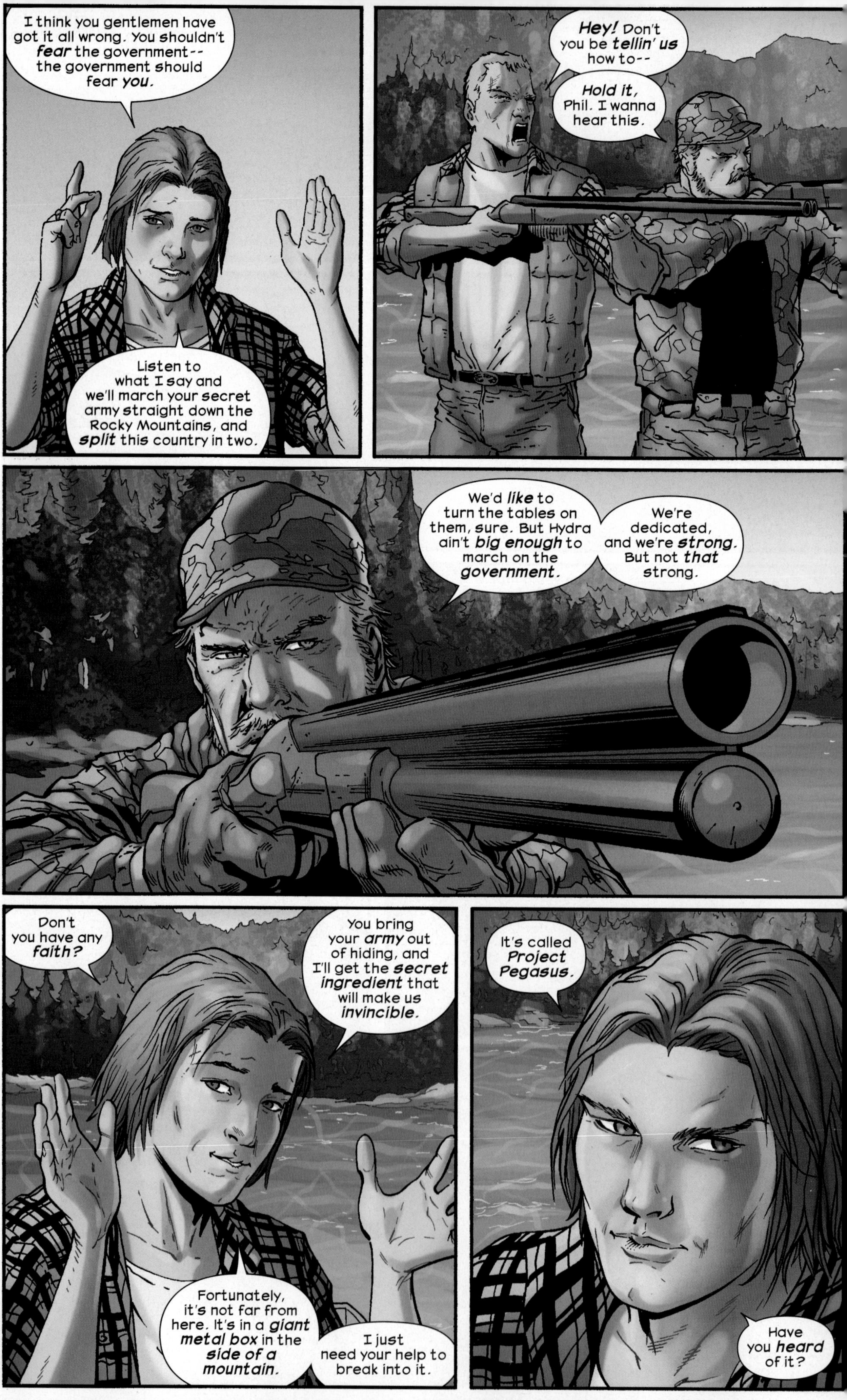

I think you gentlemen have got it all wrong. You shouldn't *fear* the government-- the government should fear *you.*
Listen to what I say and we'll march your secret army straight down the Rocky Mountains, and *split* this country in two.
Hey! Don't you be *tellin' us* how to--
Hold it, Phil. I wanna hear this.
We'd *like* to turn the tables on them, sure. But Hydra ain't *big enough* to march on the *government.*
We're dedicated, and we're *strong.* But not *that* strong.
Don't you have any *faith?*
You bring your *army* out of hiding, and I'll get the *secret ingredient* that will make us *invincible.*
Fortunately, it's not far from here. It's in a *giant metal box* in the *side of a mountain.*
I just need your help to break into it.
It's called *Project Pegasus.*
Have you *heard* of it?

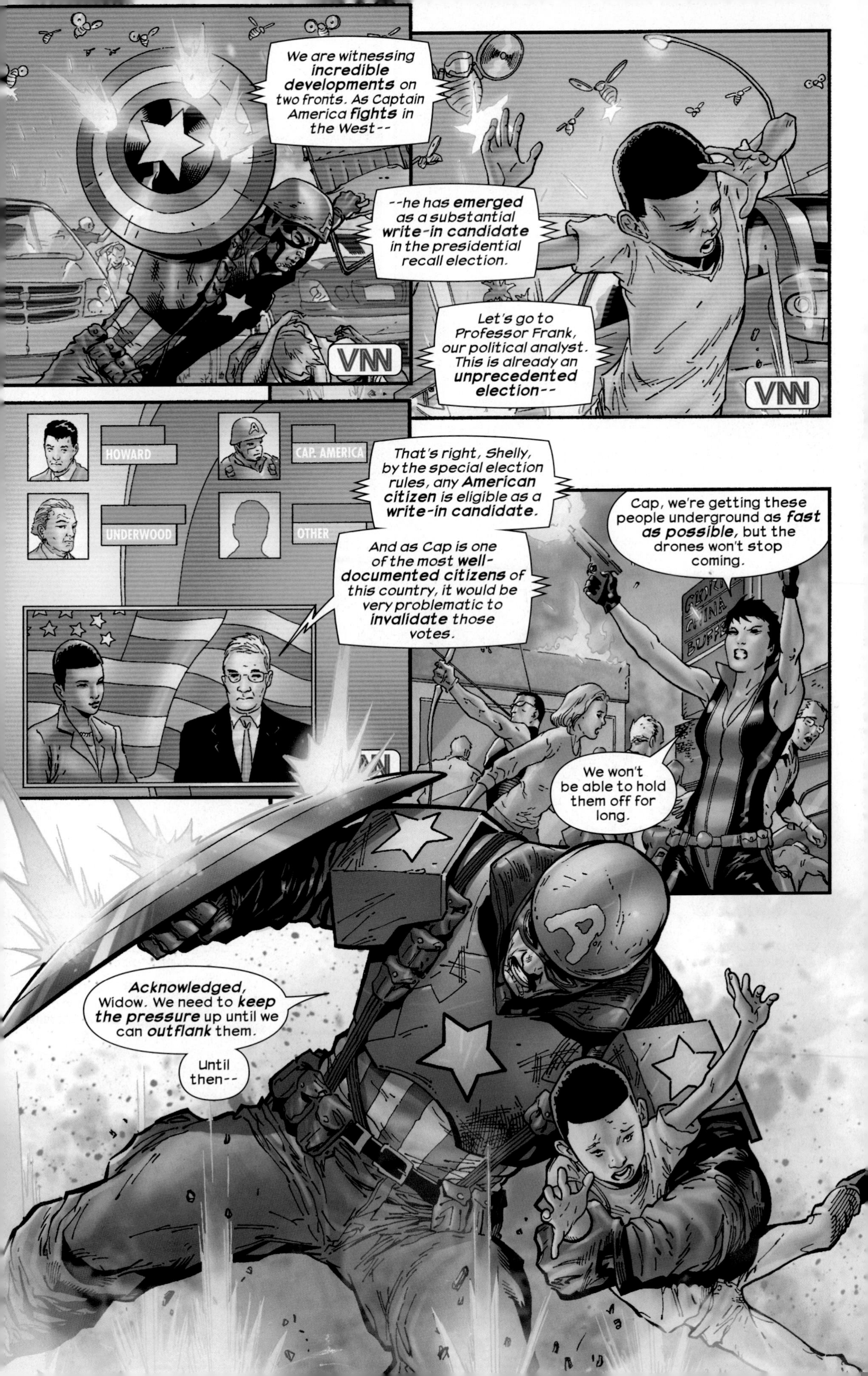
We are witnessing incredible developments on two fronts. As Captain America fights in the West--
--he has emerged as a substantial write-in candidate in the presidential recall election.
VNN
Let's go to Professor Frank, our political analyst. This is already an unprecedented election--
VNN
HOWARD
CAP. AMERICA
UNDERWOOD
OTHER
That's right, Shelly, by the special election rules, any American citizen is eligible as a write-in candidate.
And as Cap is one of the most well-documented citizens of this country, it would be very problematic to invalidate those votes.
Cap, we're getting these people underground as fast as possible, but the drones won't stop coming.
We won't be able to hold them off for long.
Acknowledged, Widow. We need to keep the pressure up until we can outflank them.
Until then--

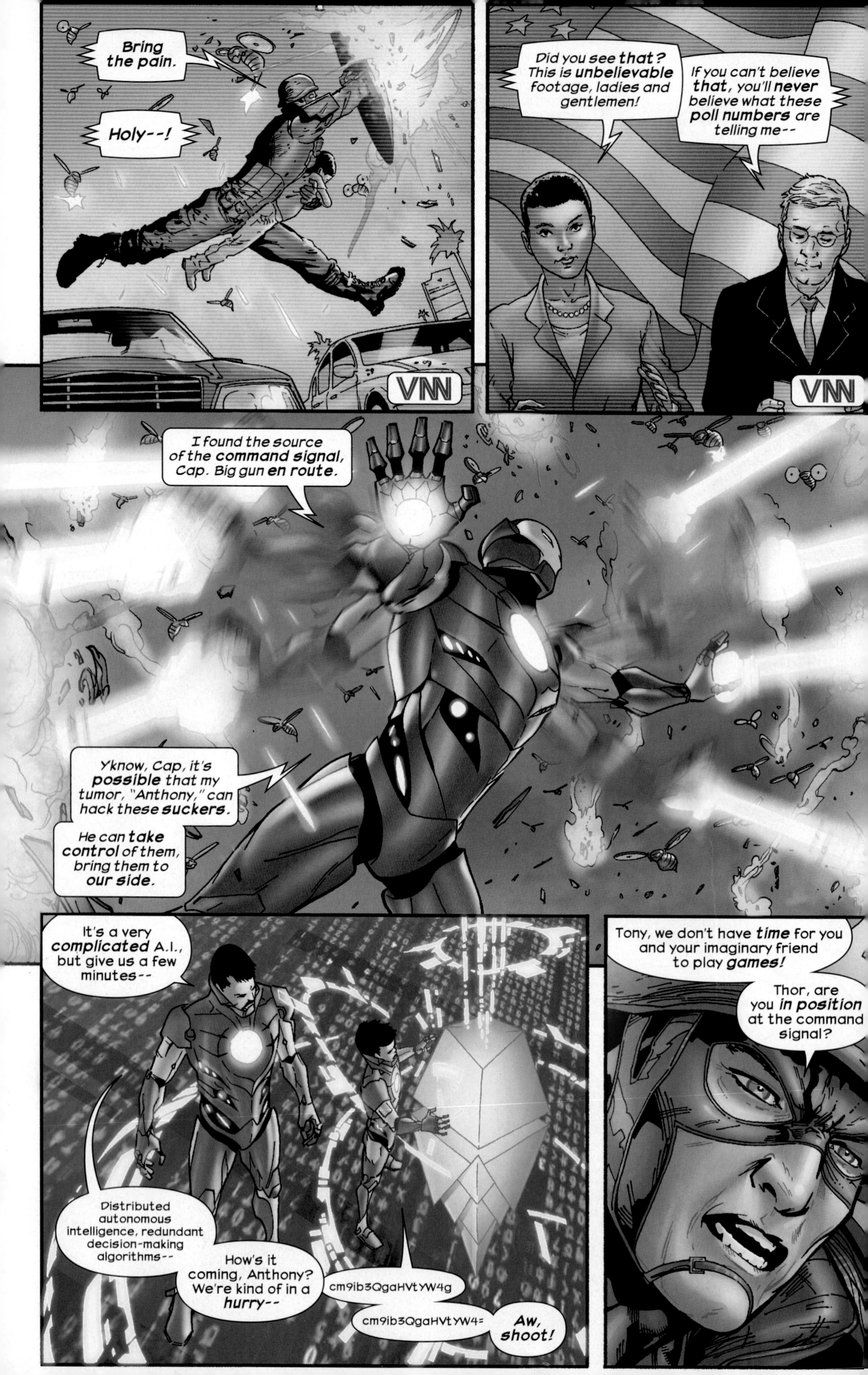
Bring the pain.
Holy--!
VNN
Did you see that? This is unbelievable footage, ladies and gentlemen!
If you can't believe that, you'll never believe what these poll numbers are telling me--
VNN
I found the source of the command signal, Cap. Big gun en route.
Yknow, Cap, it's possible that my tumor, "Anthony," can hack these suckers.
He can take control of them, bring them to our side.
It's a very complicated A.I., but give us a few minutes--
Distributed autonomous intelligence, redundant decision-making algorithms--
How's it coming, Anthony? We're kind of in a hurry--
cm9ib3QgaHVtYW4g
cm9ib3QgaHVtYW4=
Aw, shoot!
Tony, we don't have time for you and your imaginary friend to play games!
Thor, are you in position at the command signal?

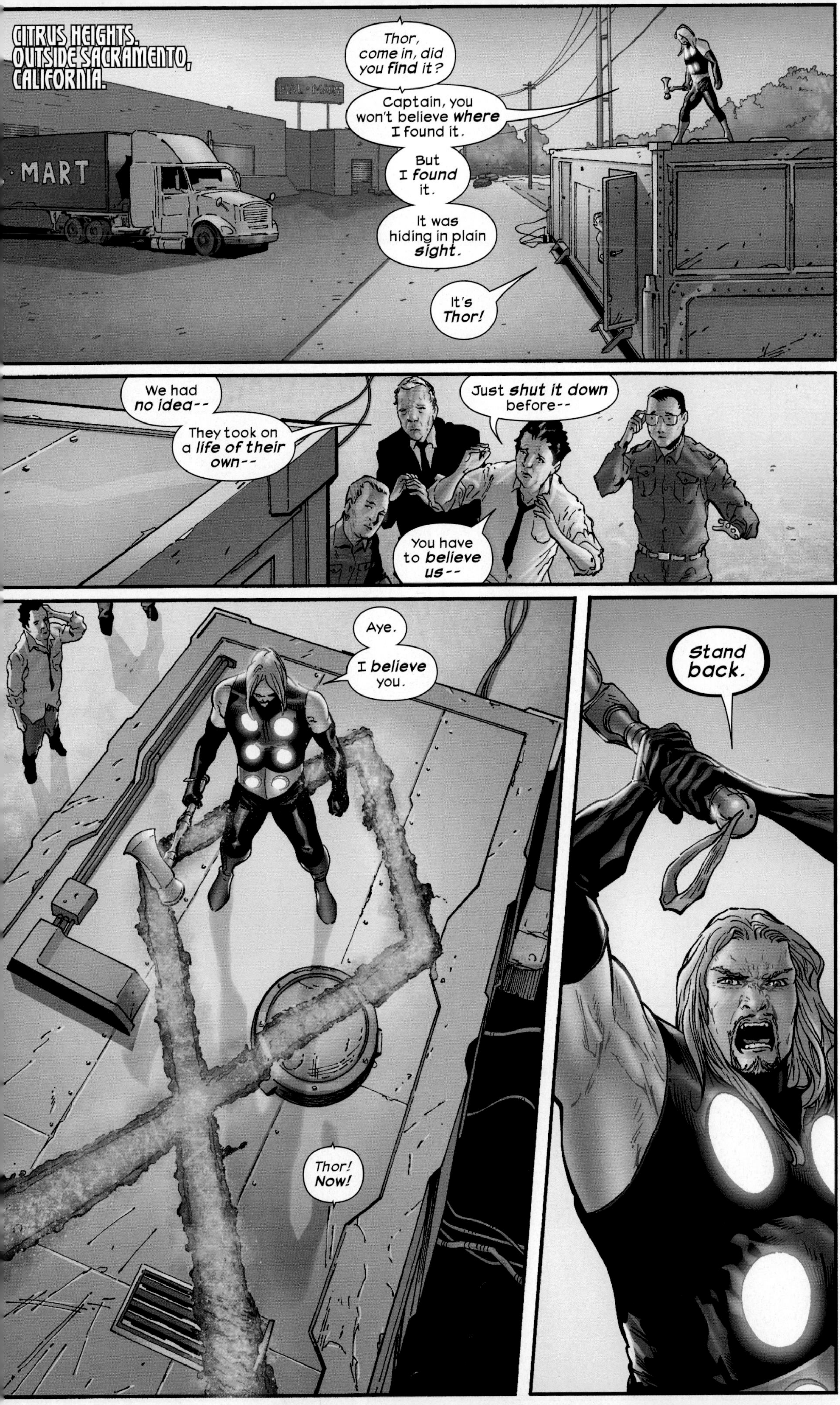
CITRUS HEIGHTS. OUTSIDE SACRAMENTO, CALIFORNIA.
Thor, come in, did you *find* it?
Captain, you won't believe *where* I found it.
But I *found* it.
It was hiding in plain *sight*.
It's *Thor!*
We had *no idea*--
They took on a *life of their own*--
Just *shut it down* before--
You have to *believe us*--
Aye.
I *believe* you.
Thor! Now!
Stand back.

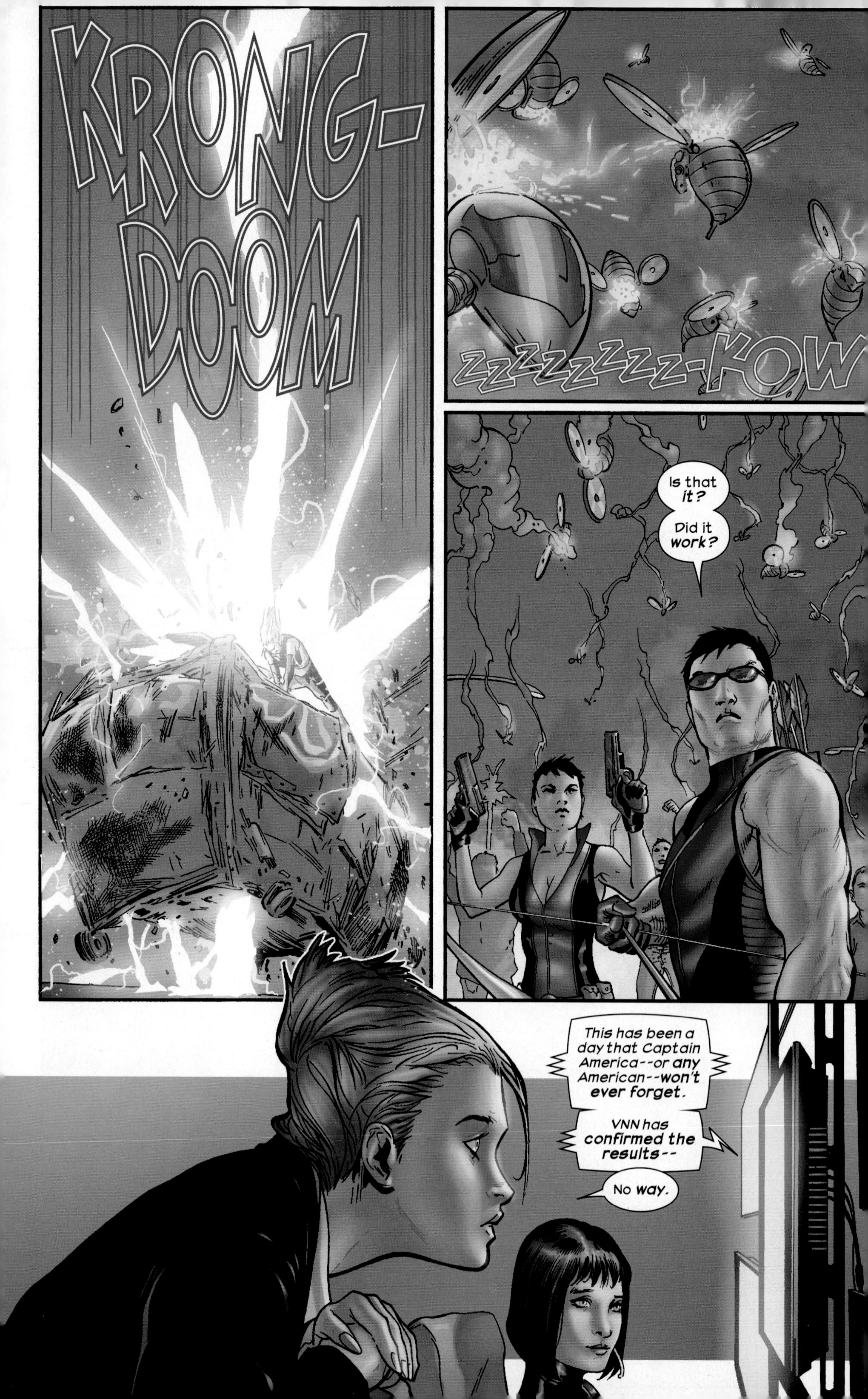
KRONG-DOOM
ZZZZZZZZZ-KOW
Is that it?
Did it work?
This has been a day that Captain America--or any American--won't ever forget.
VNN has confirmed the results--
No way.

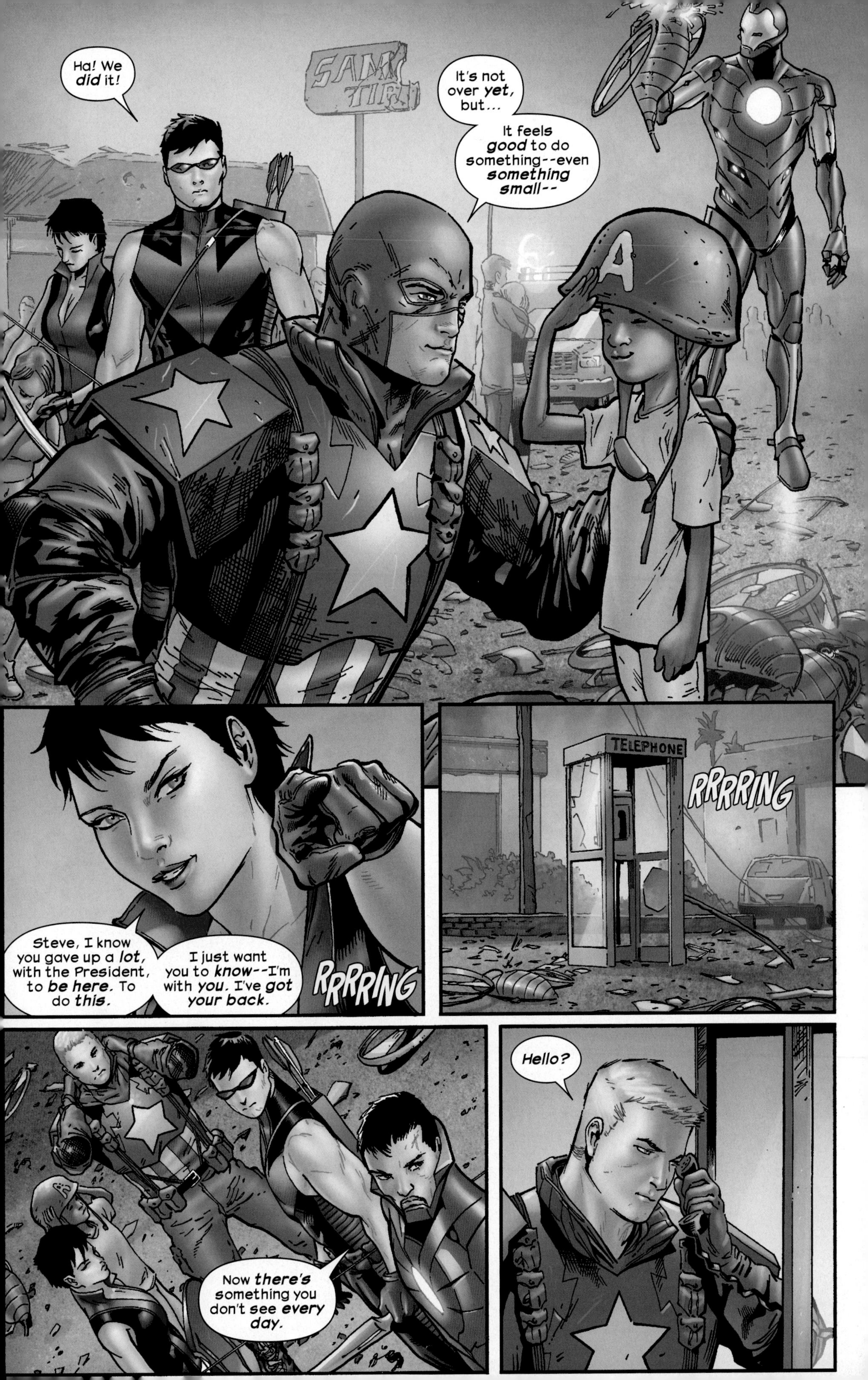

Ha! We *did* it!
SAM TIR
It's not over *yet*, but...
It feels *good* to do something--even *something small*--
TELEPHONE
RRRRING
Steve, I know you gave up a *lot*, with the President, to *be here*. To do *this*.
I just want you to *know*--I'm with *you*. I've *got your back*.
RRRRING
Now *there's* something you don't see *every day*.
Hello?

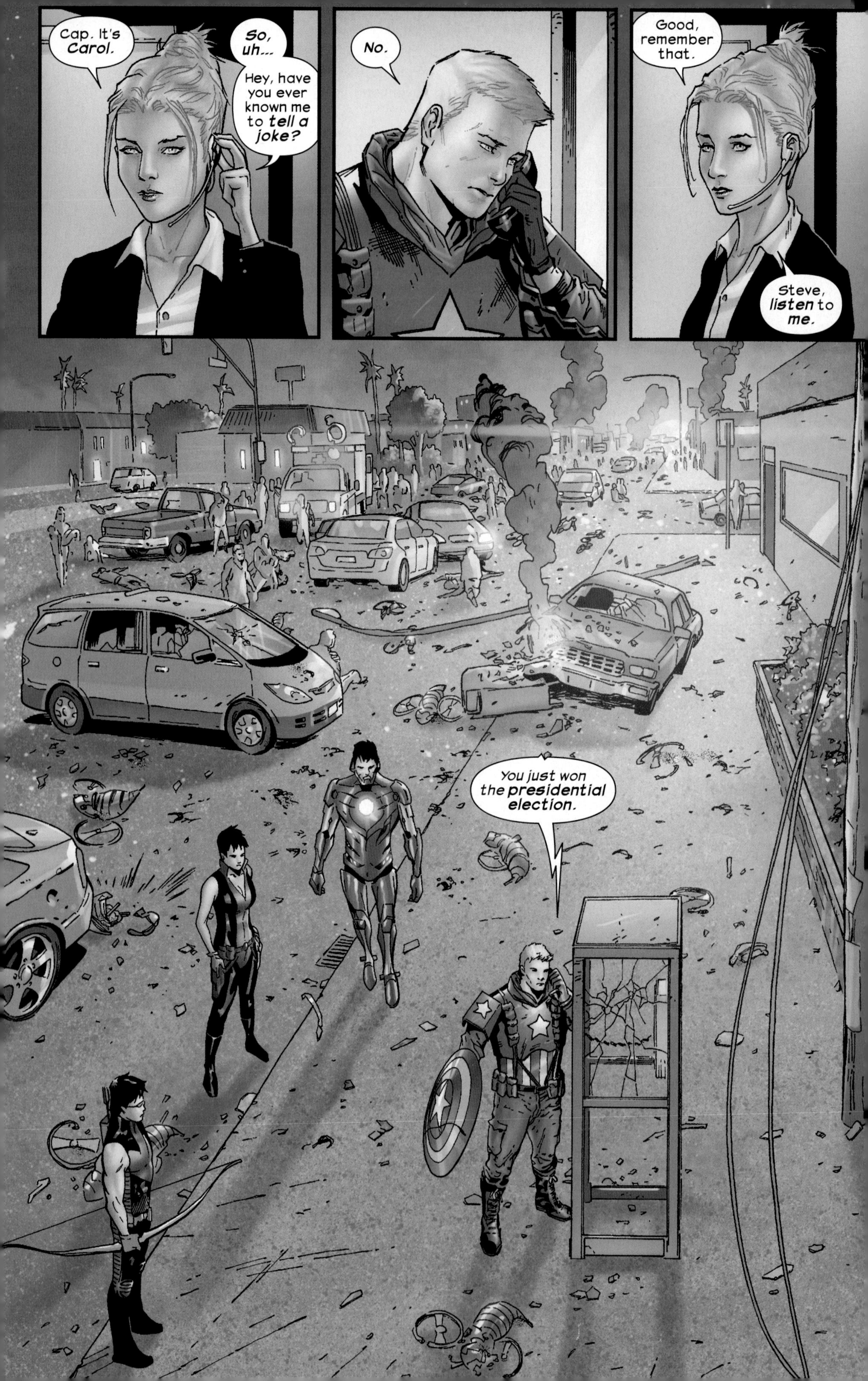
Cap. It's Carol.
So, uh...
Hey, have you ever known me to tell a joke?
No.
Good, remember that.
Steve, listen to me.
You just won the presidential election.

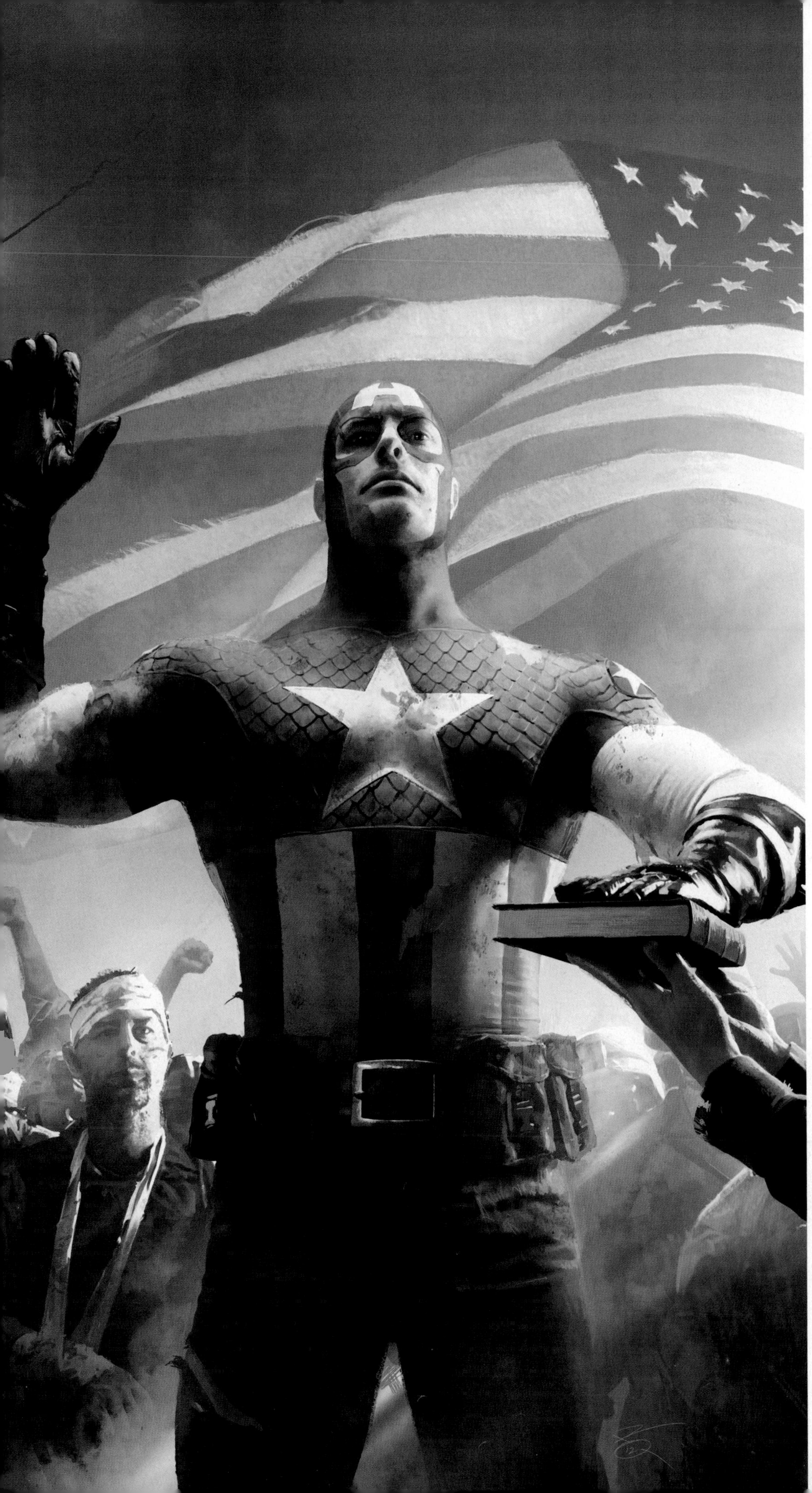

4

★

ULTIMATE COMICS **ULTIMATES** #16

S.H.I.E.L.D. SITUATION MAP:

[Anti-government militia hot spots]

Idaho, Montana, N. Dakota, S. Dakota, Arizona, New Mexico, N. Carolina, S. Carolina, Georgia

[Eastern seaboard control zone]

New England, New York, New Jersey, Delaware, Washington, D.C., Maryland, Pennsylvania, Virginia

secured by National Guard under emergency powers committee

[The West Coast Nation]

California, Oregon, Washington

Independent nation

Wyoming

status unknown

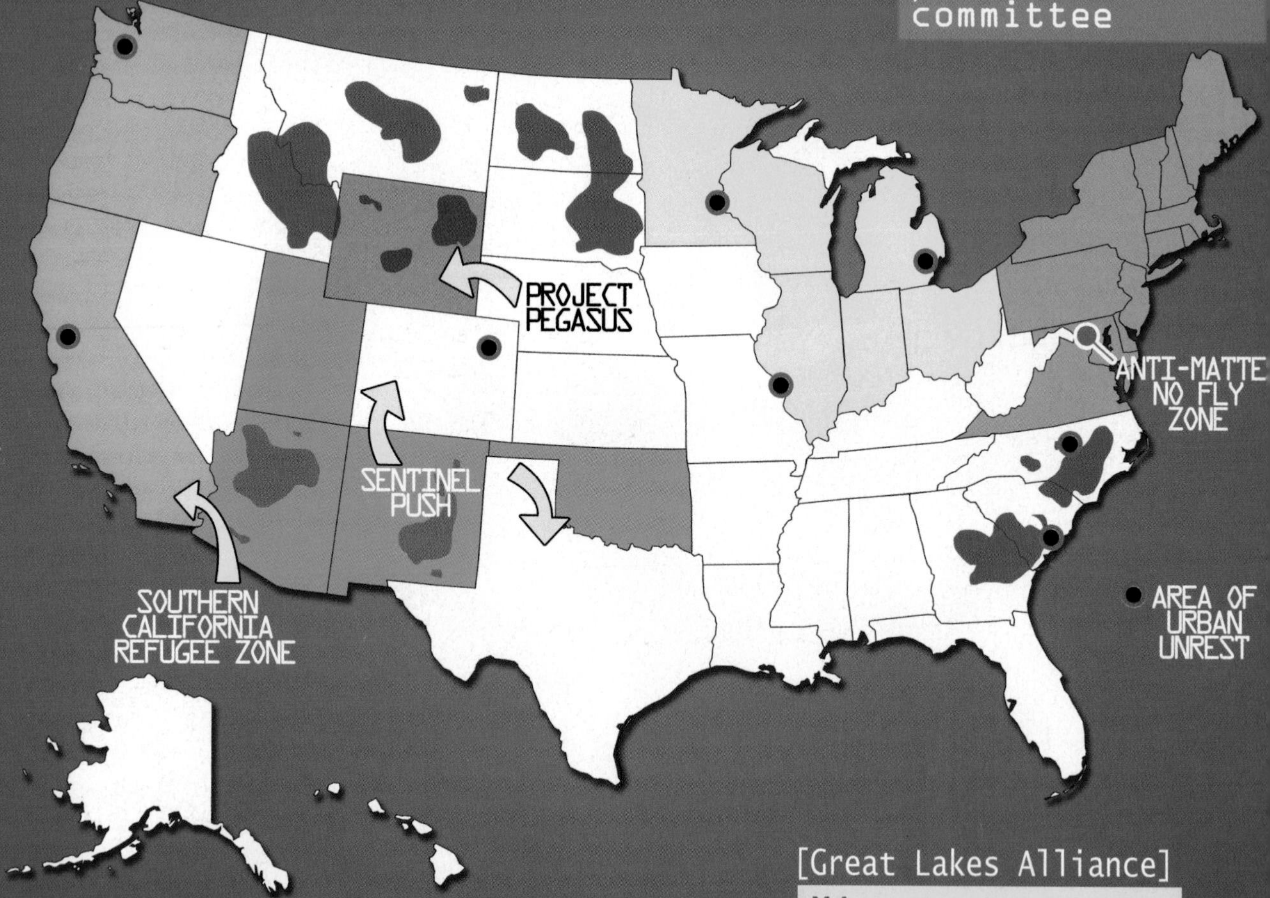

PROJECT PEGASUS
SENTINEL PUSH
SOUTHERN CALIFORNIA REFUGEE ZONE
ANTI-MATTE NO FLY ZONE
AREA OF URBAN UNREST

[Sentinel-controlled no-man's-land]

New Mexico, Arizona, Utah, Oklahoma

abandoned by the U.S. government

[Great Lakes Alliance]

Minnesota, Wisconsin, Michigan, Illinois, Indiana, Ohio

Independent nation

ALL STATES SHOWN IN WHITE ARE U.S. GOVERNMENT-CONTROLLED ZONES

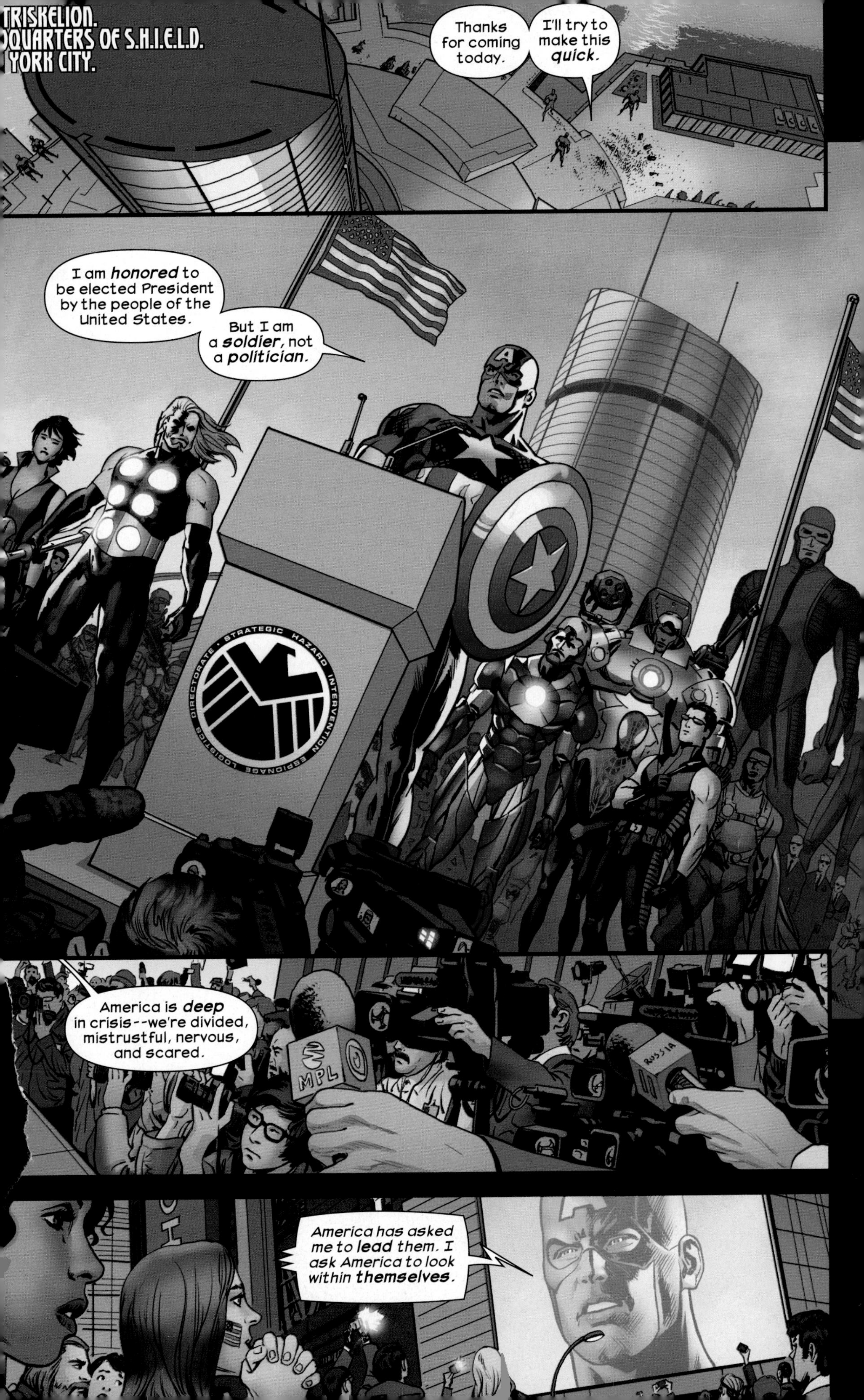
TRISKELION.
QUARTERS OF S.H.I.E.L.D.
YORK CITY.
Thanks for coming today.
I'll try to make this *quick*.
I am *honored* to be elected President by the people of the United States.
But I am a *soldier*, not a *politician*.
STRATEGIC HAZARD INTERVENTION ESPIONAGE LOGISTICS DIRECTORATE
America is *deep* in crisis--we're divided, mistrustful, nervous, and scared.
MPL
RUSSIA
America has asked me to *lead* them. I ask America to look within *themselves*.

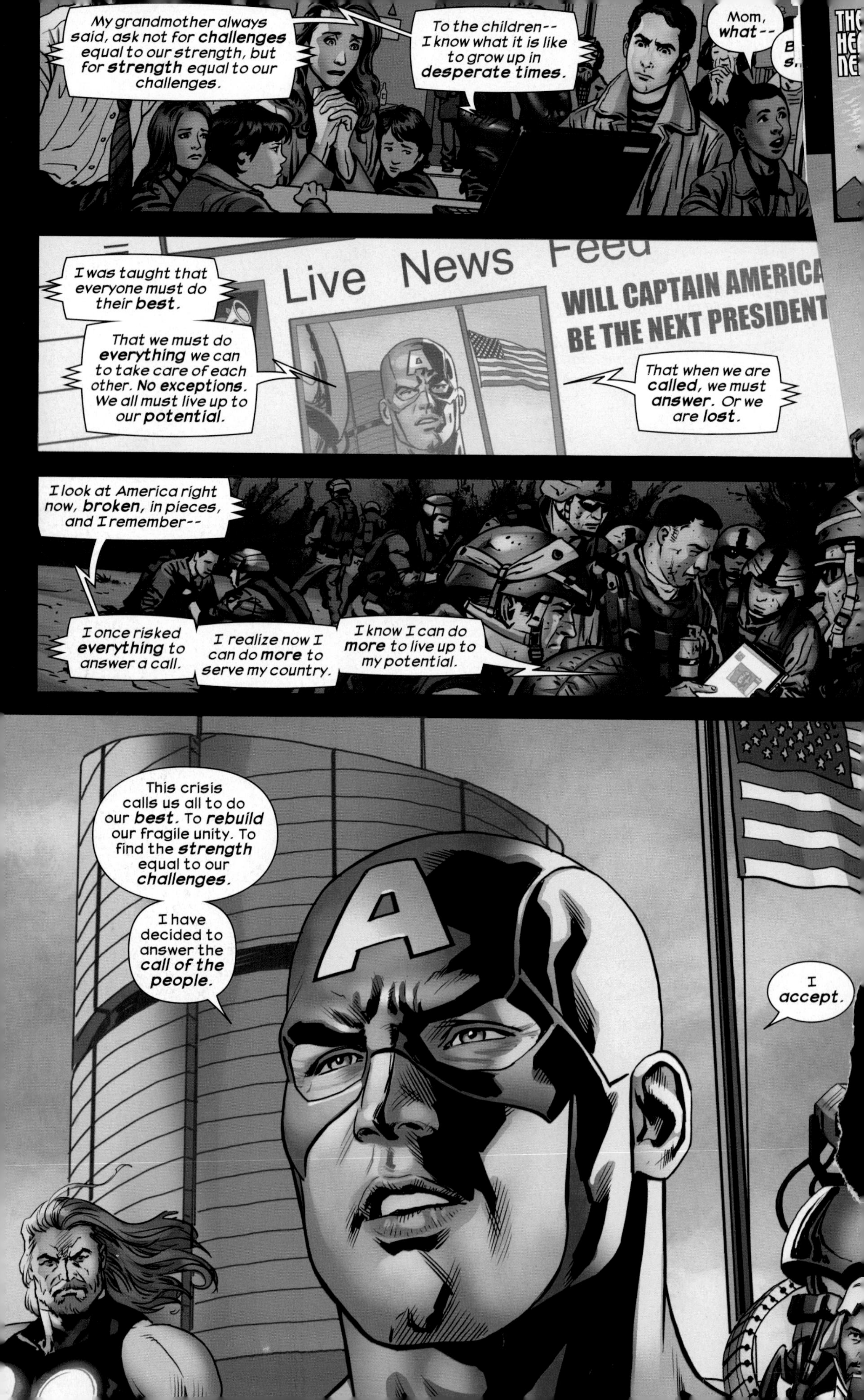

My grandmother always said, ask not for challenges equal to our strength, but for strength equal to our challenges.
To the children-- I know what it is like to grow up in desperate times.
Mom, what--
Live News Feed
WILL CAPTAIN AMERICA BE THE NEXT PRESIDENT
I was taught that everyone must do their best.
That we must do everything we can to take care of each other. No exceptions. We all must live up to our potential.
That when we are called, we must answer. Or we are lost.
I look at America right now, broken, in pieces, and I remember--
I once risked everything to answer a call.
I realize now I can do more to serve my country.
I know I can do more to live up to my potential.
This crisis calls us all to do our best. To rebuild our fragile unity. To find the strength equal to our challenges.
I have decided to answer the call of the people.
I accept.

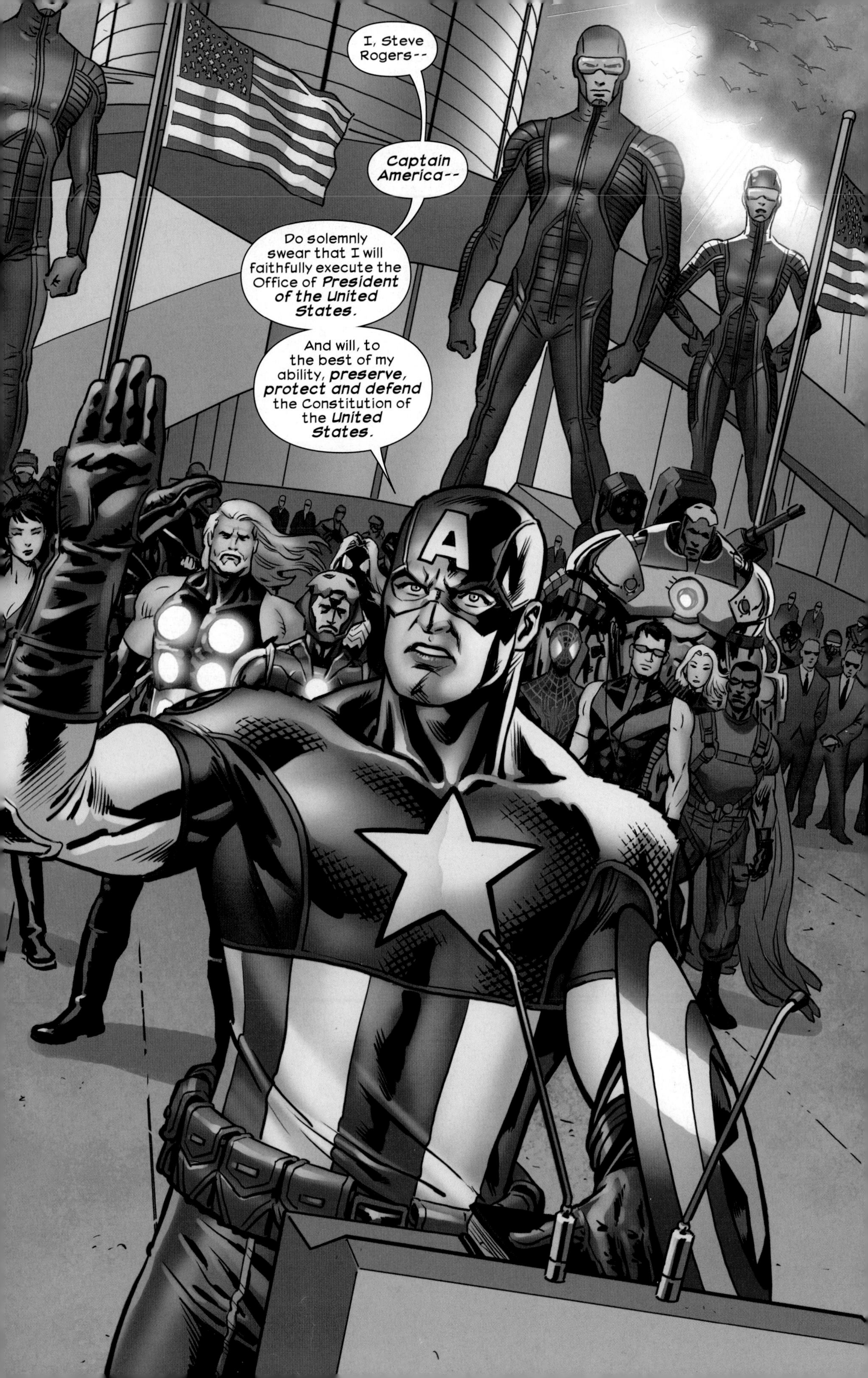
I, Steve Rogers--
Captain America--
Do solemnly swear that I will faithfully execute the Office of *President of the United States.*
And will, to the best of my ability, ***preserve, protect and defend*** the Constitution of the *United States.*

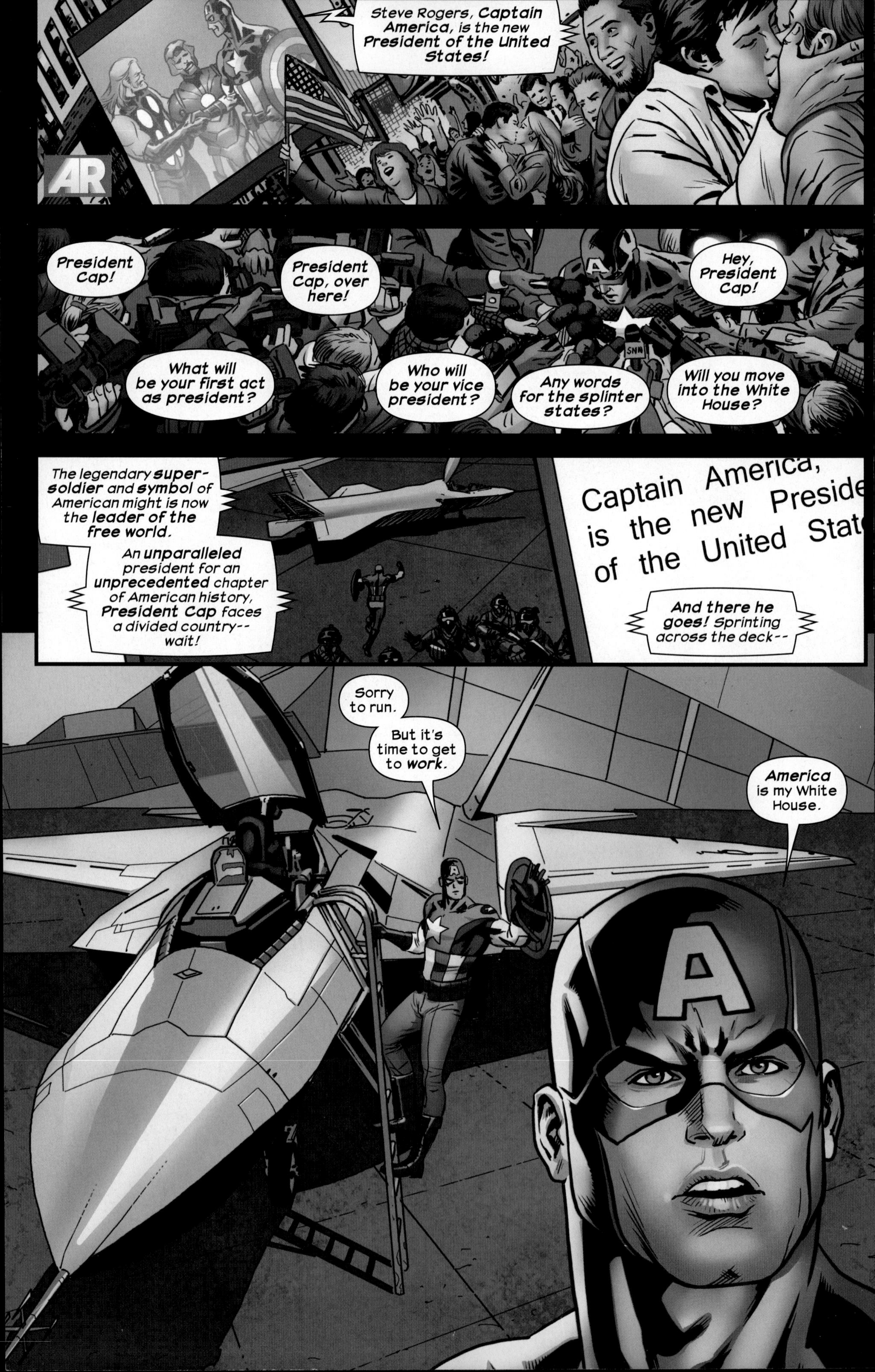
Steve Rogers, Captain America, is the new President of the United States!
AR
President Cap!
President Cap, over here!
Hey, President Cap!
What will be your first act as president?
Who will be your vice president?
Any words for the splinter states?
Will you move into the White House?
SNN
The legendary super-soldier and symbol of American might is now the leader of the free world.
An unparalleled president for an unprecedented chapter of American history, President Cap faces a divided country-- wait!
Captain America, is the new Preside of the United Stat
And there he goes! Sprinting across the deck--
Sorry to run.
But it's time to get to work.
America is my White House.

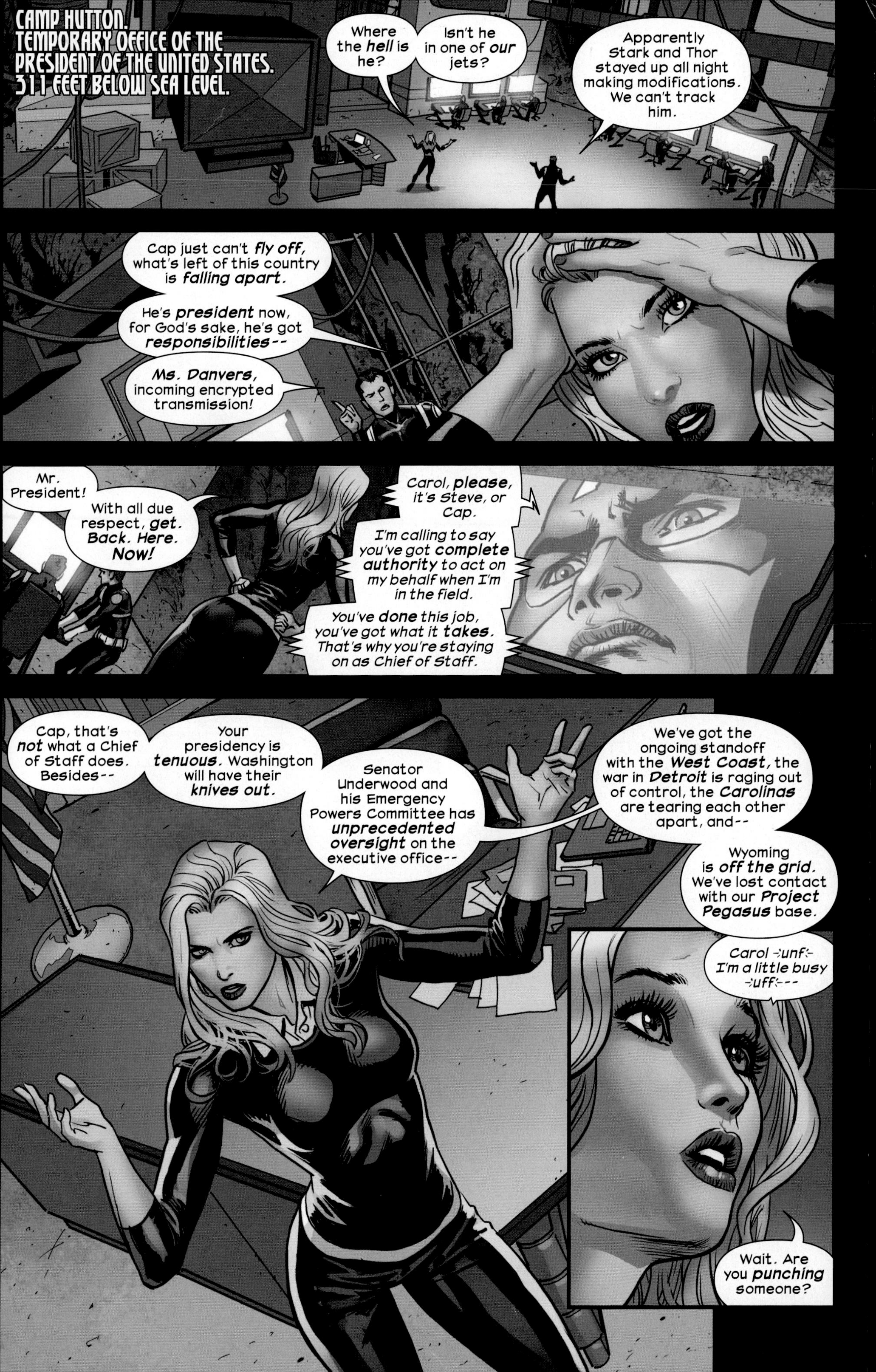
CAMP HUTTON.
TEMPORARY OFFICE OF THE PRESIDENT OF THE UNITED STATES.
311 FEET BELOW SEA LEVEL.
Where the hell is he?
Isn't he in one of our jets?
Apparently Stark and Thor stayed up all night making modifications. We can't track him.
Cap just can't fly off, what's left of this country is falling apart.
He's president now, for God's sake, he's got responsibilities--
Ms. Danvers, incoming encrypted transmission!
Mr. President!
With all due respect, get. Back. Here. Now!
Carol, please, it's Steve, or Cap.
I'm calling to say you've got complete authority to act on my behalf when I'm in the field.
You've done this job, you've got what it takes. That's why you're staying on as Chief of Staff.
Cap, that's not what a Chief of Staff does. Besides--
Your presidency is tenuous. Washington will have their knives out.
Senator Underwood and his Emergency Powers Committee has unprecedented oversight on the executive office--
We've got the ongoing standoff with the West Coast, the war in Detroit is raging out of control, the Carolinas are tearing each other apart, and--
Wyoming is off the grid. We've lost contact with our Project Pegasus base.
Carol -unf- I'm a little busy -uff---
Wait. Are you punching someone?

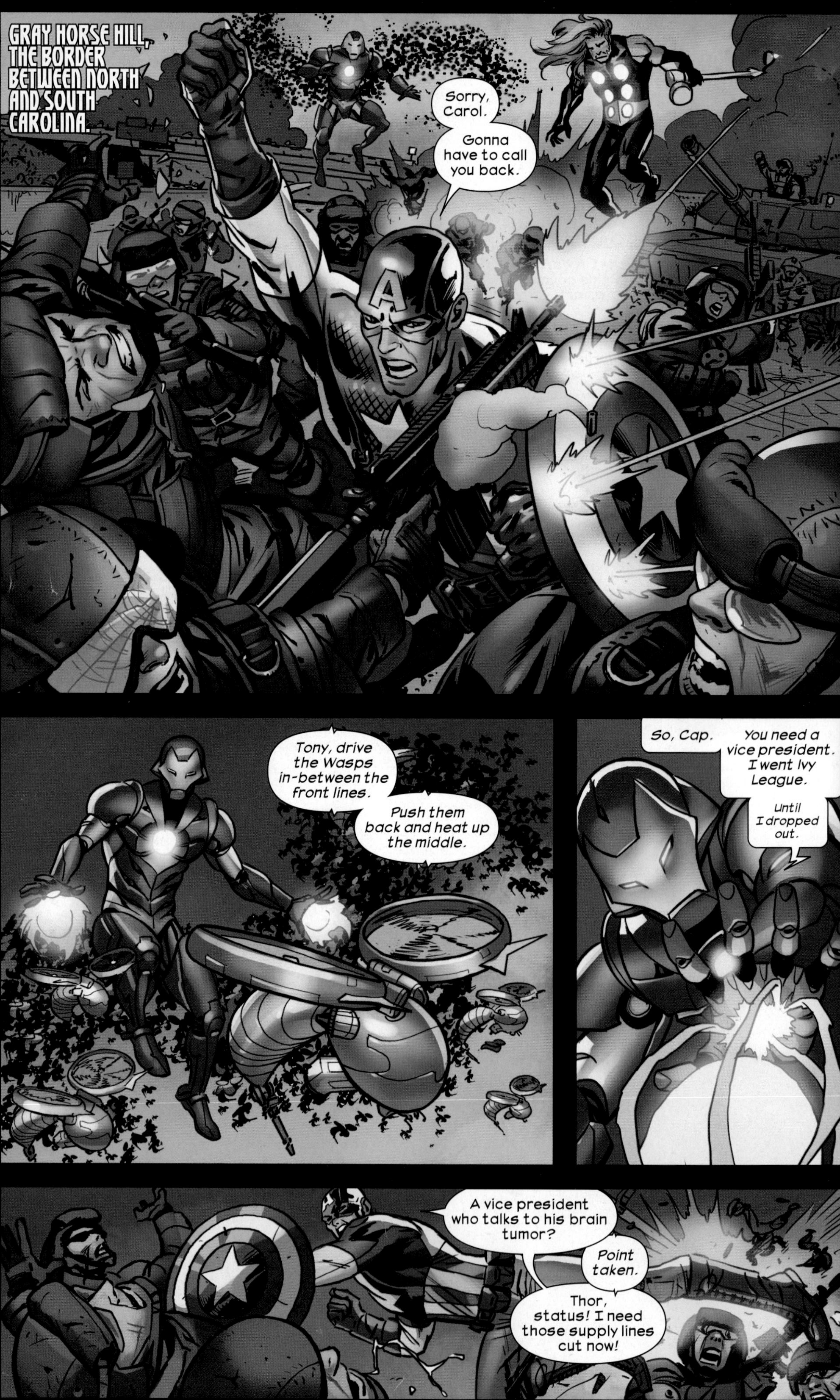
GRAY HORSE HILL, THE BORDER BETWEEN NORTH AND SOUTH CAROLINA.
Sorry, Carol.
Gonna have to call you back.
Tony, drive the Wasps in-between the front lines.
Push them back and heat up the middle.
So, Cap.
You need a vice president. I went Ivy League.
Until I dropped out.
A vice president who talks to his brain tumor?
Point taken.
Thor, status! I need those supply lines cut now!

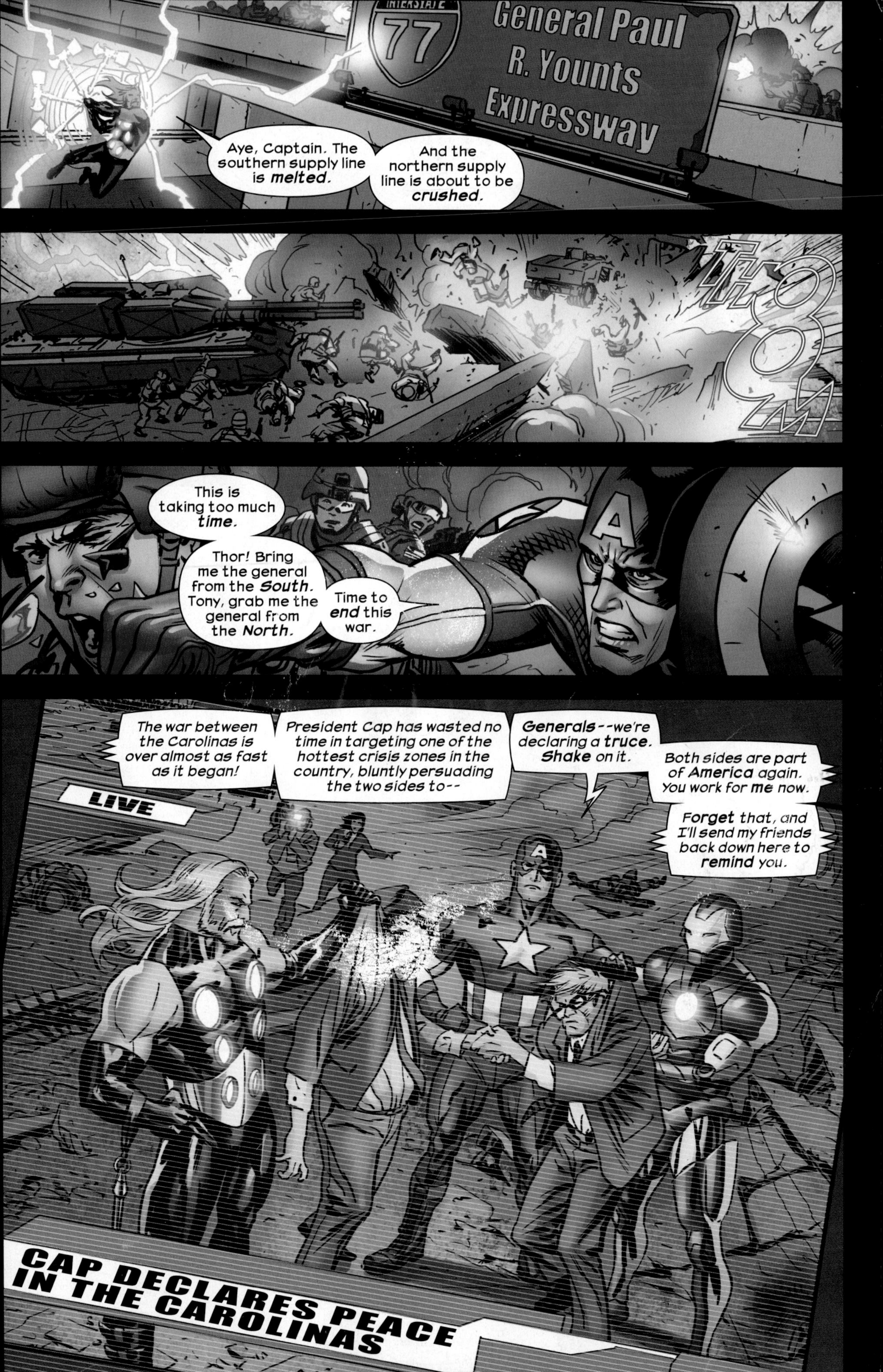

INTERSTATE
77
General Paul R. Younts Expressway
Aye, Captain. The southern supply line is melted.
And the northern supply line is about to be crushed.
THOOM
This is taking too much time.
Thor! Bring me the general from the South. Tony, grab me the general from the North.
Time to end this war.
The war between the Carolinas is over almost as fast as it began!
President Cap has wasted no time in targeting one of the hottest crisis zones in the country, bluntly persuading the two sides to--
Generals--we're declaring a truce. Shake on it.
Both sides are part of America again. You work for me now.
Forget that, and I'll send my friends back down here to remind you.
LIVE
CAP DECLARES PEACE IN THE CAROLINAS

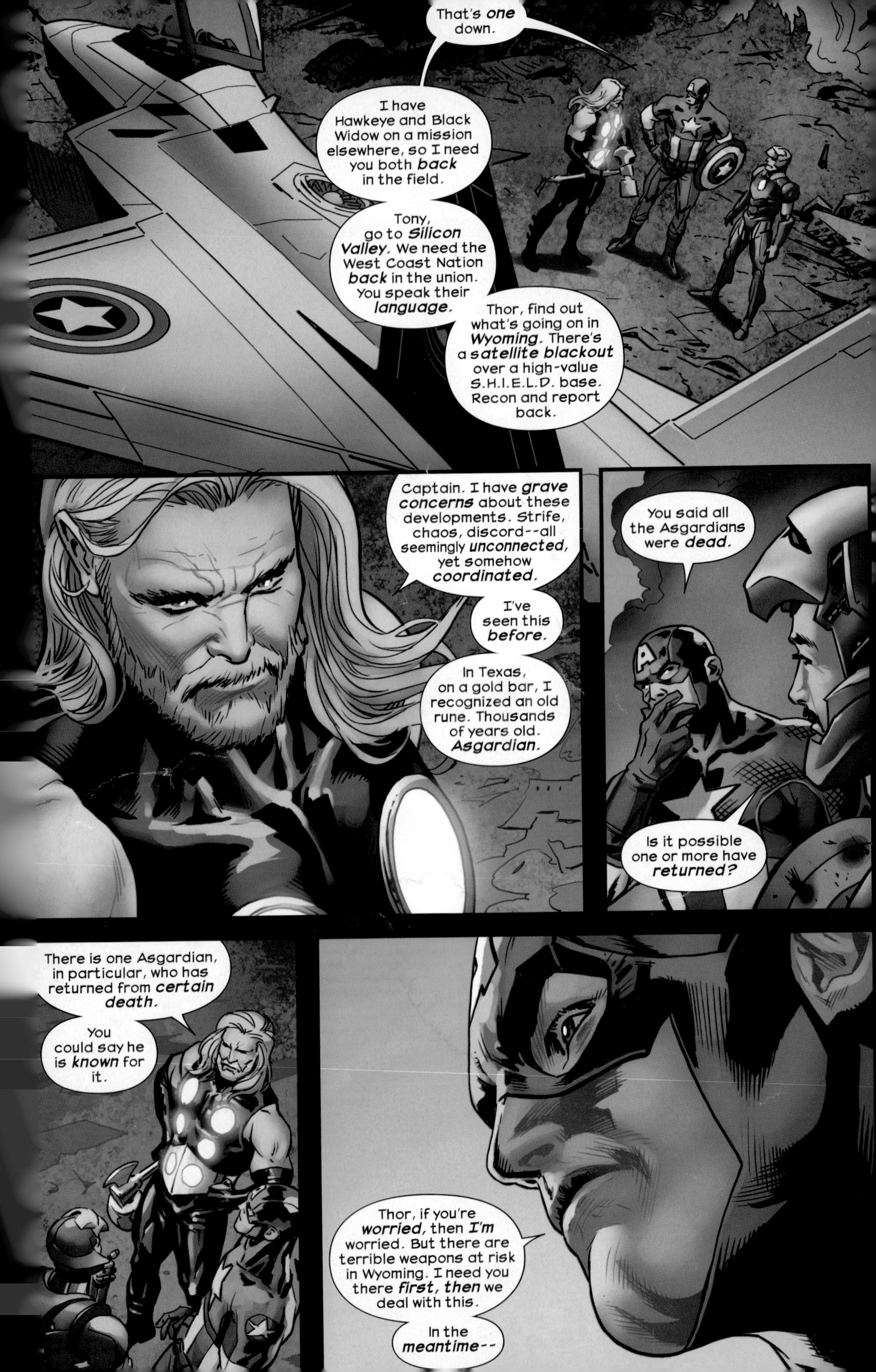

That's one down.
I have Hawkeye and Black Widow on a mission elsewhere, so I need you both back in the field.
Tony, go to Silicon Valley. We need the West Coast Nation back in the union. You speak their language.
Thor, find out what's going on in Wyoming. There's a satellite blackout over a high-value S.H.I.E.L.D. base. Recon and report back.
Captain. I have grave concerns about these developments. Strife, chaos, discord--all seemingly unconnected, yet somehow coordinated.
I've seen this before.
In Texas, on a gold bar, I recognized an old rune. Thousands of years old. Asgardian.
You said all the Asgardians were dead.
Is it possible one or more have returned?
There is one Asgardian, in particular, who has returned from certain death.
You could say he is known for it.
Thor, if you're worried, then I'm worried. But there are terrible weapons at risk in Wyoming. I need you there first, then we deal with this.
In the meantime--

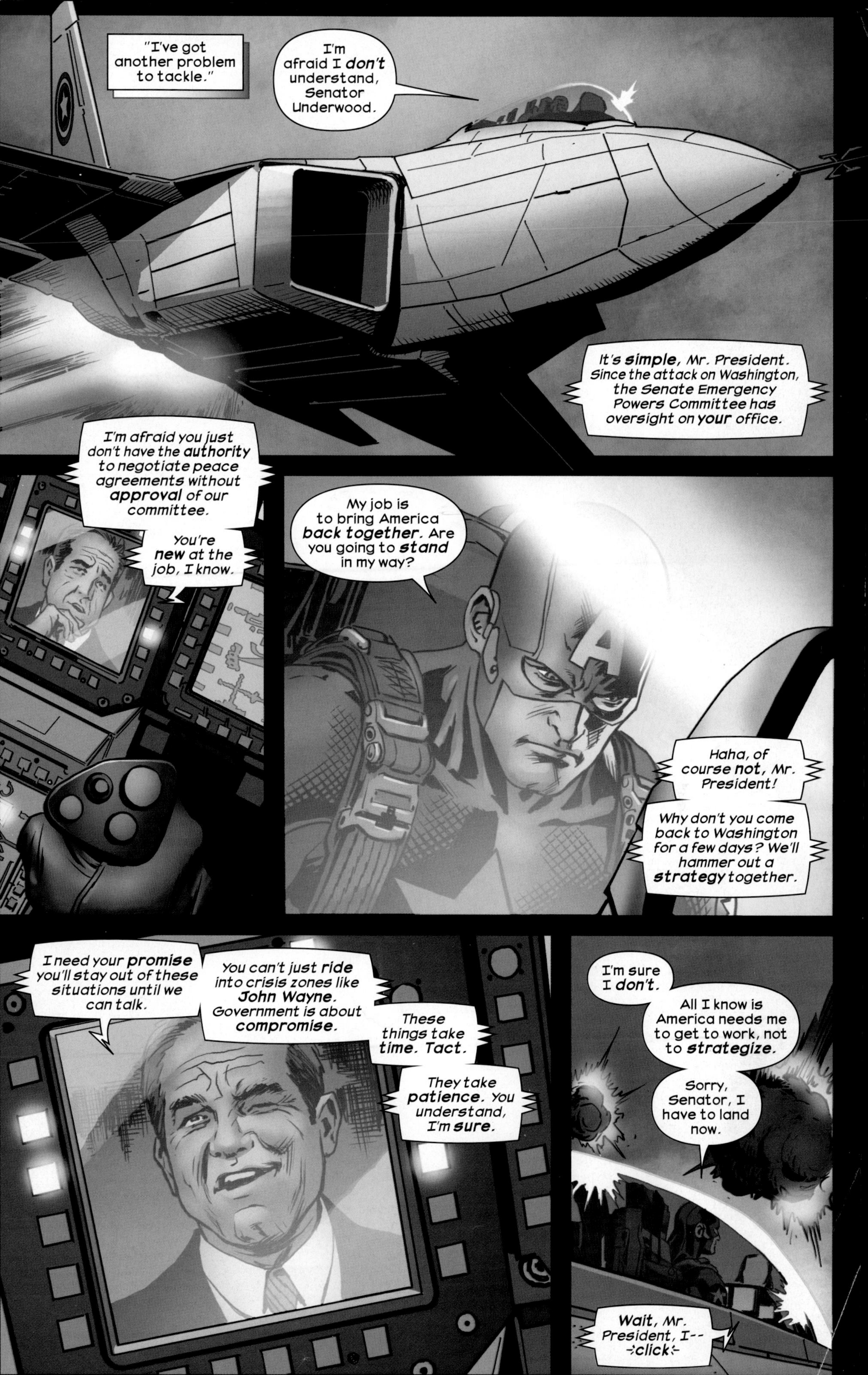
"I've got another problem to tackle."
I'm afraid I don't understand, Senator Underwood.
It's simple, Mr. President. Since the attack on Washington, the Senate Emergency Powers Committee has oversight on your office.
I'm afraid you just don't have the authority to negotiate peace agreements without approval of our committee.
You're new at the job, I know.
My job is to bring America back together. Are you going to stand in my way?
Haha, of course not, Mr. President!
Why don't you come back to Washington for a few days? We'll hammer out a strategy together.
I need your promise you'll stay out of these situations until we can talk.
You can't just ride into crisis zones like John Wayne. Government is about compromise.
These things take time. Tact.
They take patience. You understand, I'm sure.
I'm sure I don't.
All I know is America needs me to get to work, not to strategize.
Sorry, Senator, I have to land now.
Wait, Mr. President, I-- -click-

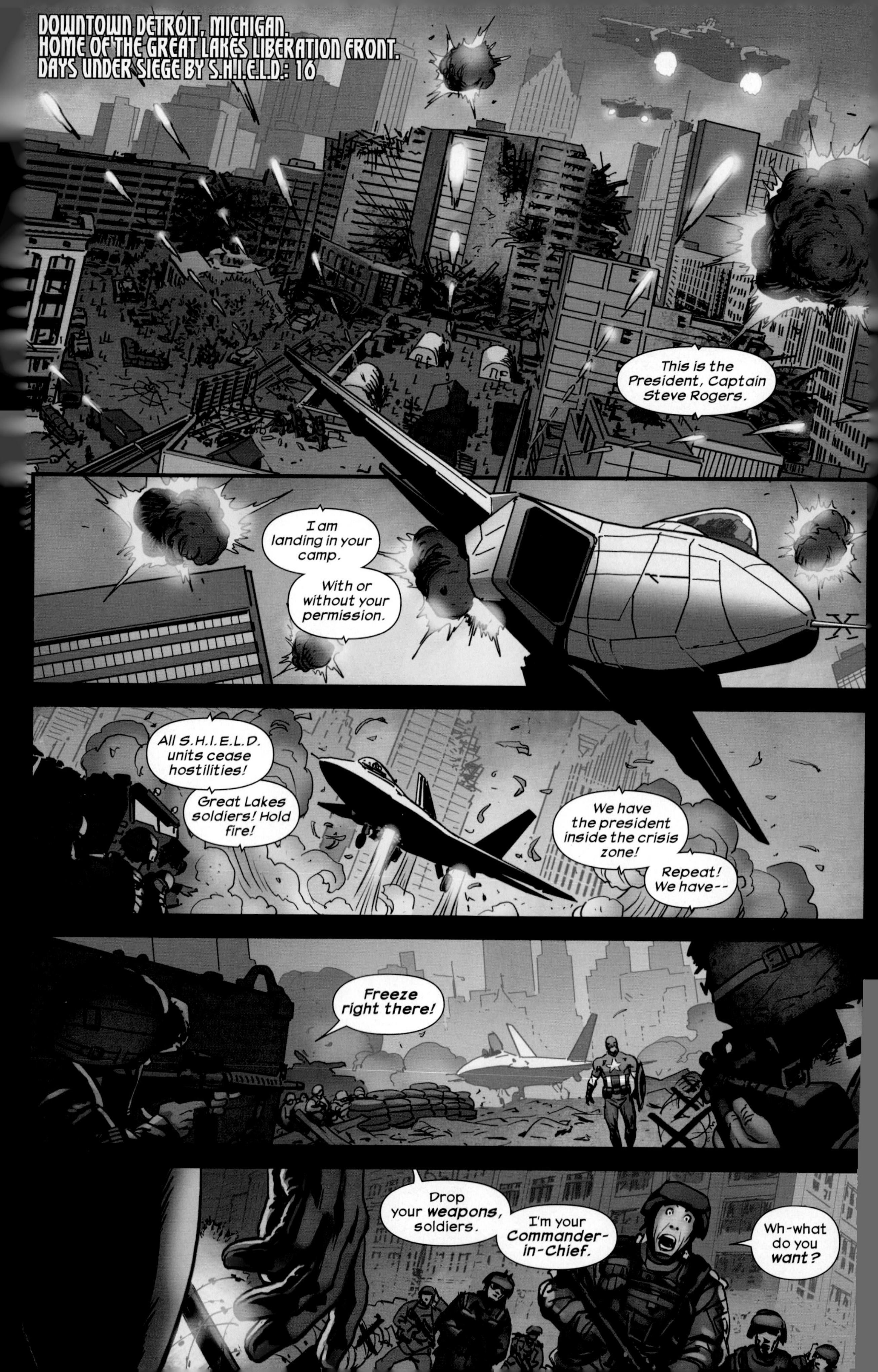
DOWNTOWN DETROIT, MICHIGAN.
HOME OF THE GREAT LAKES LIBERATION FRONT.
DAYS UNDER SIEGE BY S.H.I.E.L.D.: 16
This is the President, Captain Steve Rogers.
I am landing in your camp.
With or without your permission.
All S.H.I.E.L.D. units cease hostilities!
Great Lakes soldiers! Hold fire!
We have the president inside the crisis zone!
Repeat! We have--
Freeze right there!
Drop your weapons, soldiers.
I'm your Commander-in-Chief.
Wh-what do you want?

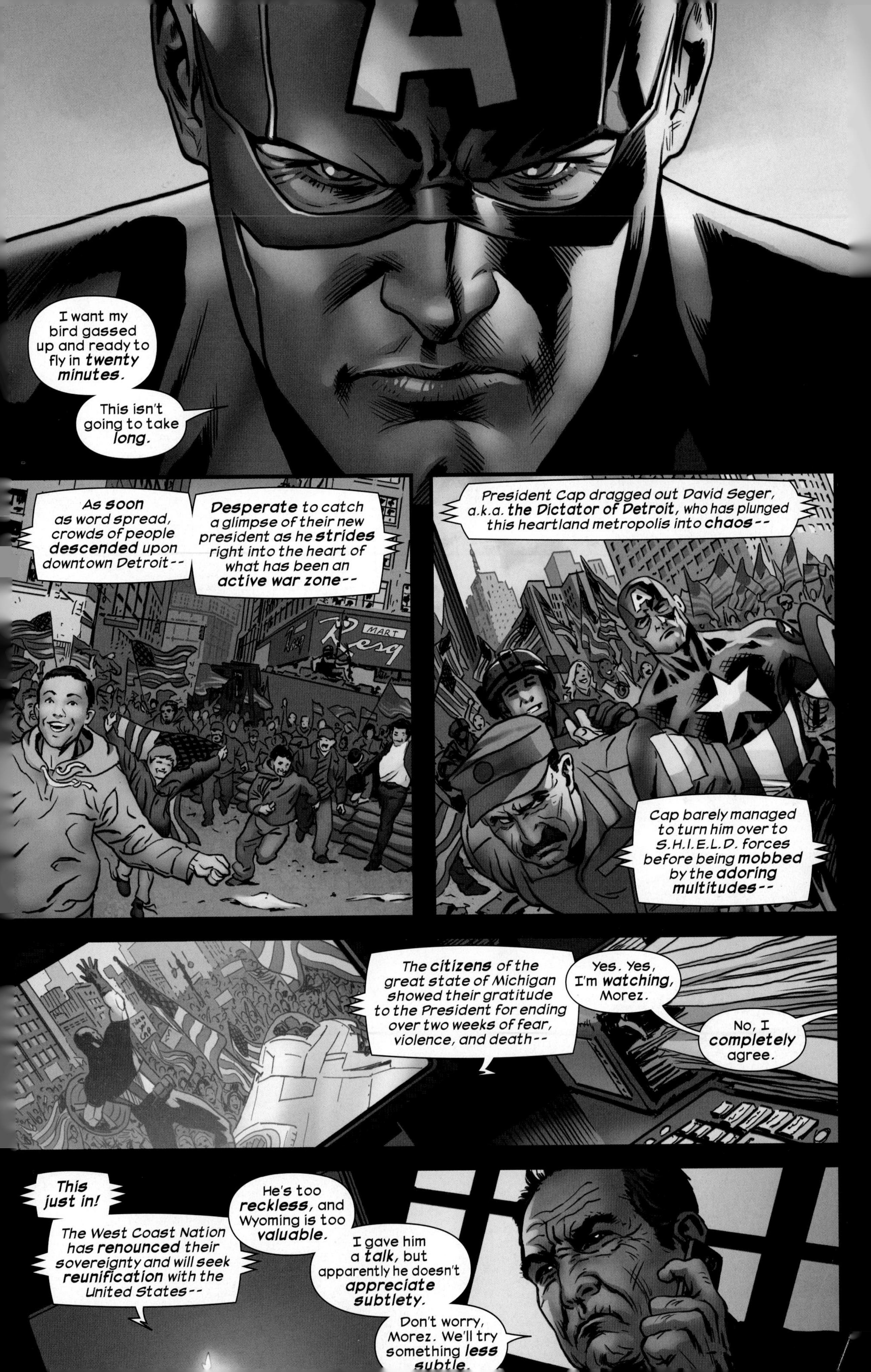

I want my bird gassed up and ready to fly in twenty minutes.
This isn't going to take long.
As soon as word spread, crowds of people descended upon downtown Detroit--
Desperate to catch a glimpse of their new president as he strides right into the heart of what has been an active war zone--
President Cap dragged out David Seger, a.k.a. the Dictator of Detroit, who has plunged this heartland metropolis into chaos--
Cap barely managed to turn him over to S.H.I.E.L.D. forces before being mobbed by the adoring multitudes--
The citizens of the great state of Michigan showed their gratitude to the President for ending over two weeks of fear, violence, and death--
Yes. Yes, I'm watching, Morez.
No, I completely agree.
This just in!
The West Coast Nation has renounced their sovereignty and will seek reunification with the United States--
He's too reckless, and Wyoming is too valuable.
I gave him a talk, but apparently he doesn't appreciate subtlety.
Don't worry, Morez. We'll try something less subtle.

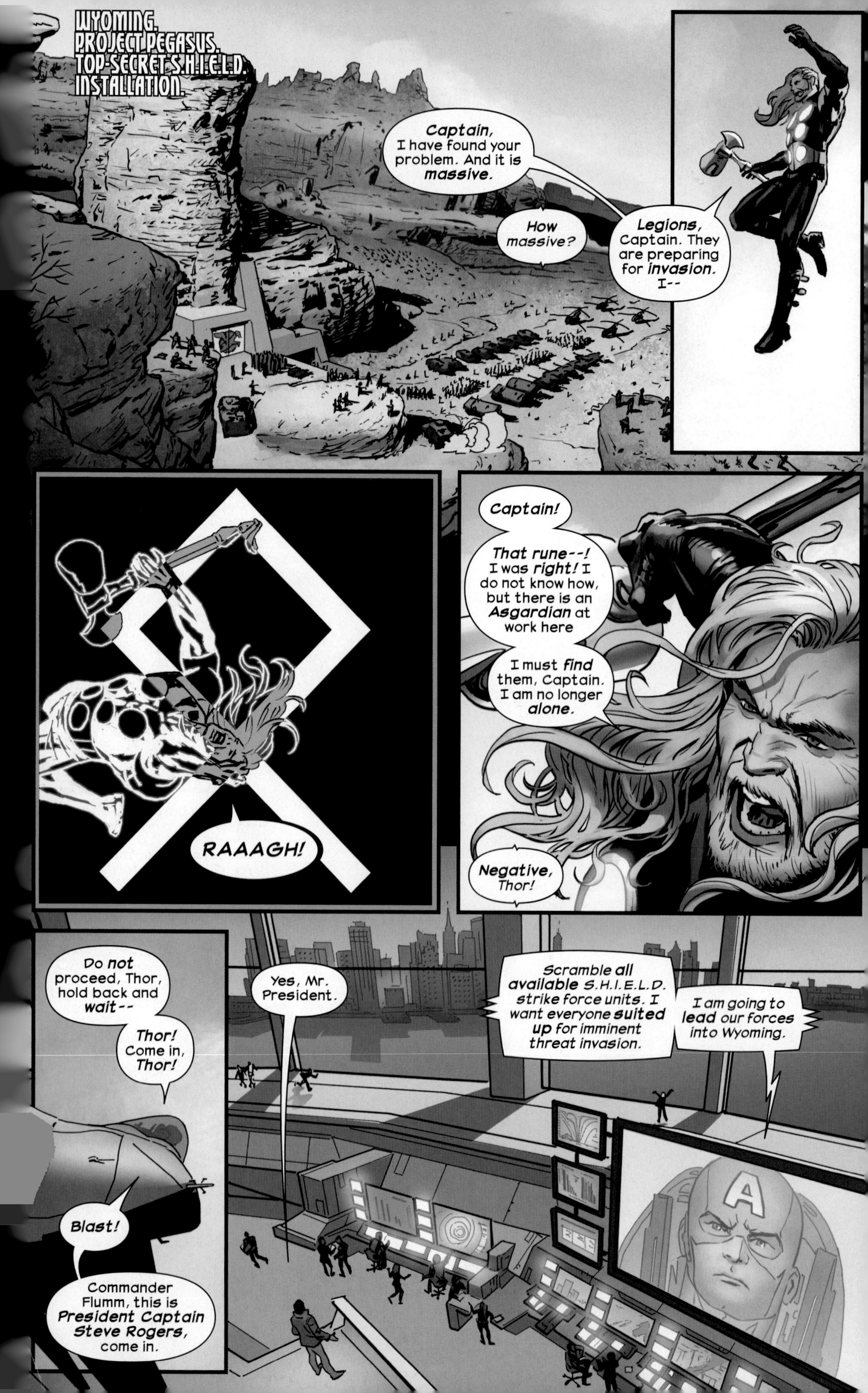
WYOMING.
PROJECT PEGASUS.
TOP-SECRET S.H.I.E.L.D. INSTALLATION.
Captain, I have found your problem. And it is massive.
How massive?
Legions, Captain. They are preparing for invasion. I--
RAAAGH!
Captain!
That rune--! I was right! I do not know how, but there is an Asgardian at work here
I must find them, Captain. I am no longer alone.
Negative, Thor!
Do not proceed, Thor, hold back and wait--
Thor! Come in, Thor!
Blast!
Commander Flumm, this is President Captain Steve Rogers, come in.
Yes, Mr. President.
Scramble all available S.H.I.E.L.D. strike force units. I want everyone suited up for imminent threat invasion.
I am going to lead our forces into Wyoming.

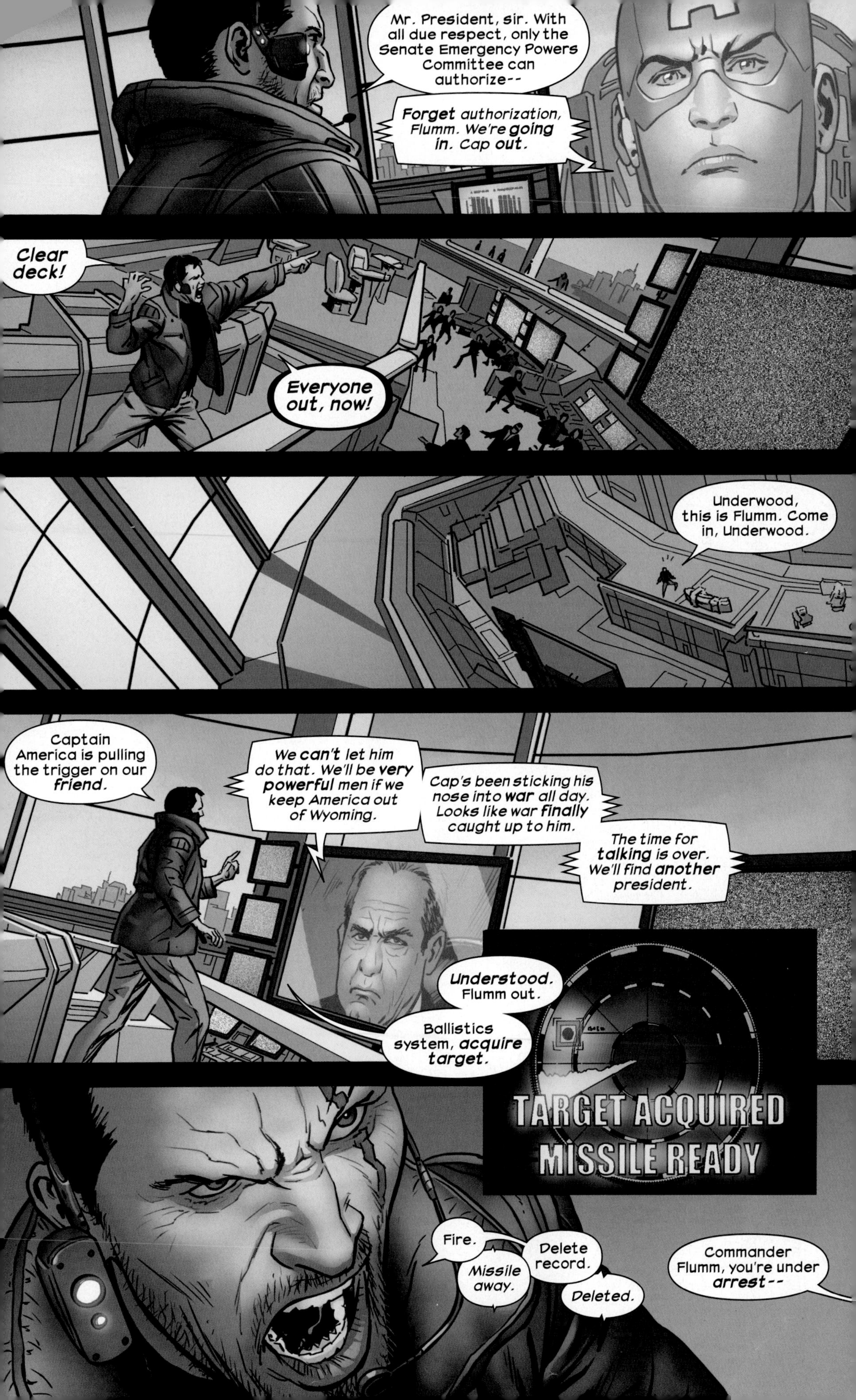
Mr. President, sir. With all due respect, only the Senate Emergency Powers Committee can authorize--
Forget authorization, Flumm. We're going in. Cap out.
Clear deck!
Everyone out, now!
Underwood, this is Flumm. Come in, Underwood.
Captain America is pulling the trigger on our friend.
We can't let him do that. We'll be very powerful men if we keep America out of Wyoming.
Cap's been sticking his nose into war all day. Looks like war finally caught up to him.
The time for talking is over. We'll find another president.
Understood. Flumm out.
Ballistics system, acquire target.
TARGET ACQUIRED
MISSILE READY
Fire.
Missile away.
Delete record.
Deleted.
Commander Flumm, you're under arrest--

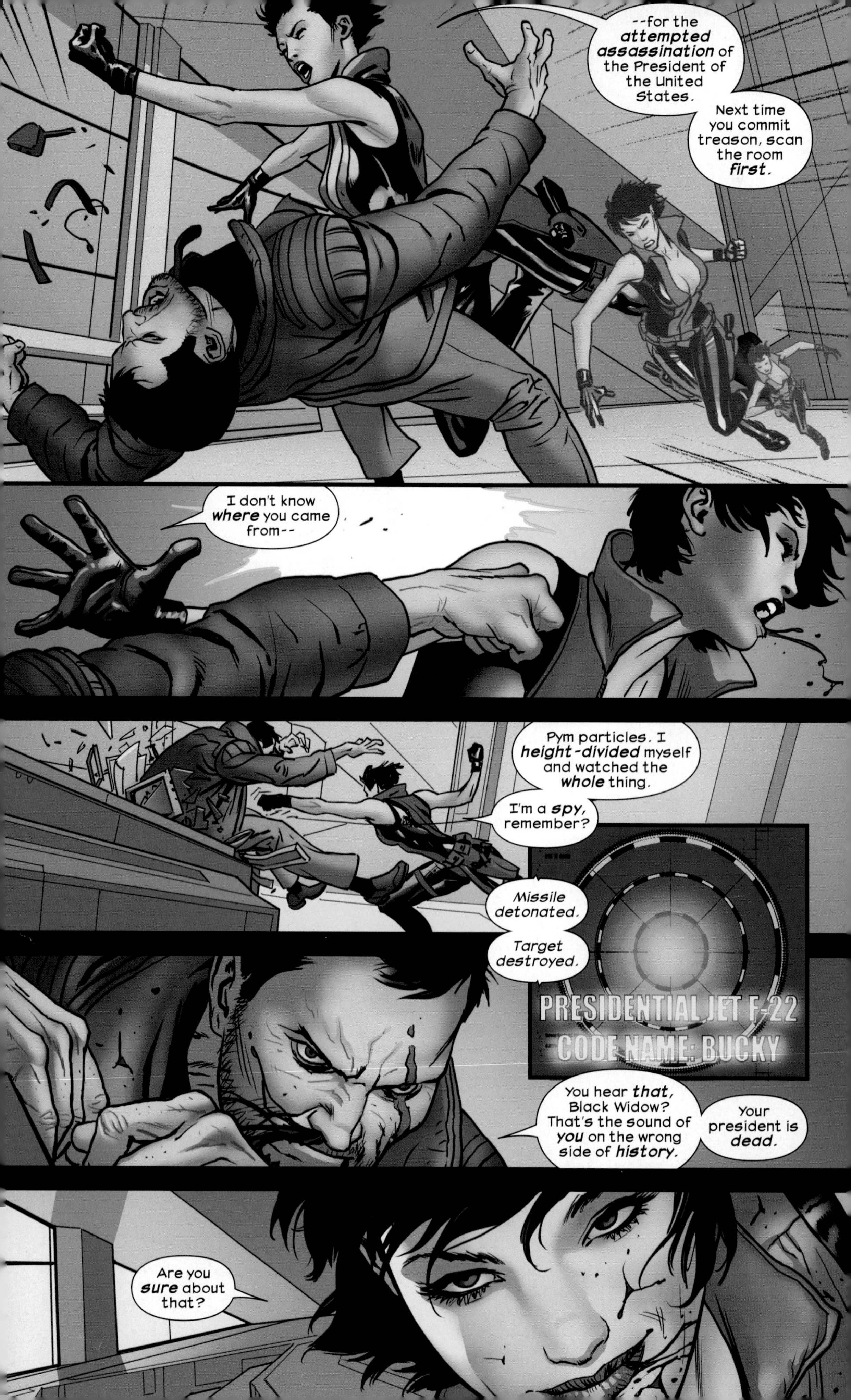
--for the attempted assassination of the President of the United States.
Next time you commit treason, scan the room first.
I don't know where you came from--
Pym particles. I height-divided myself and watched the whole thing.
I'm a spy, remember?
Missile detonated.
Target destroyed.
PRESIDENTIAL JET F-22
CODE NAME: BUCKY
You hear that, Black Widow? That's the sound of you on the wrong side of history.
Your president is dead.
Are you sure about that?

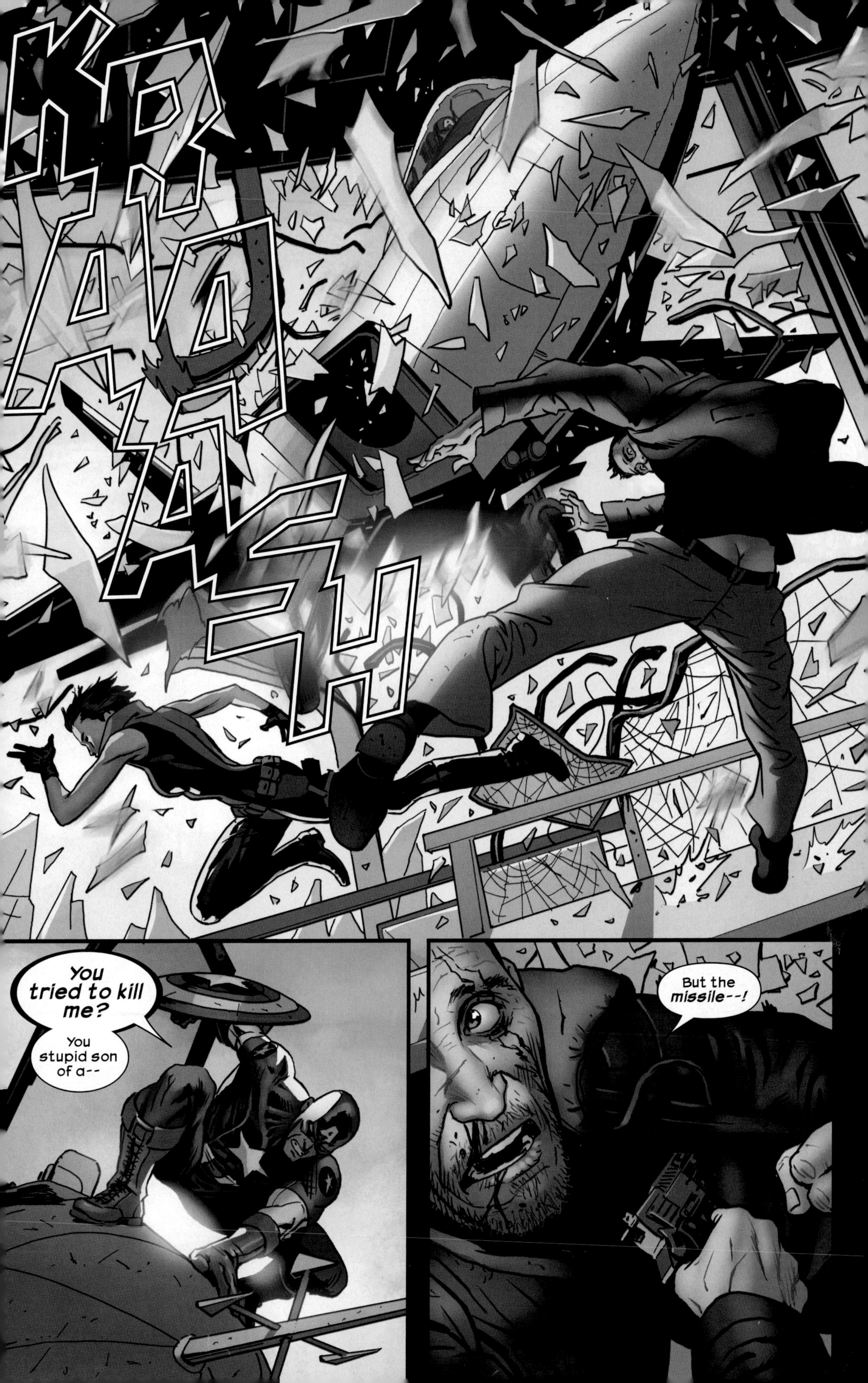
KRAAASH
You tried to kill me?
You stupid son of a--
But the *missile*--!

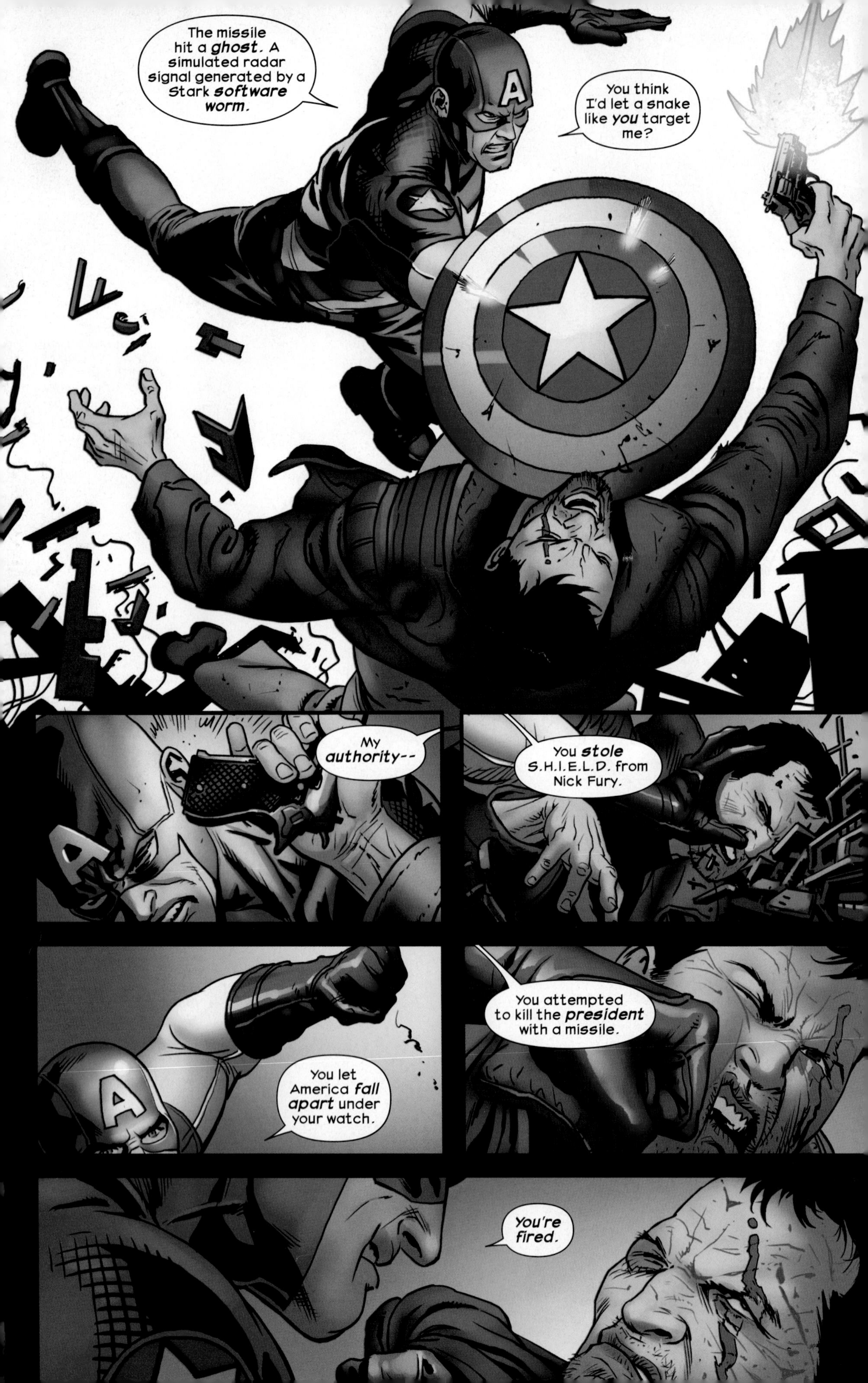
The missile hit a ghost. A simulated radar signal generated by a Stark software worm.
You think I'd let a snake like you target me?
My authority--
You stole S.H.I.E.L.D. from Nick Fury.
You let America fall apart under your watch.
You attempted to kill the president with a missile.
You're fired.

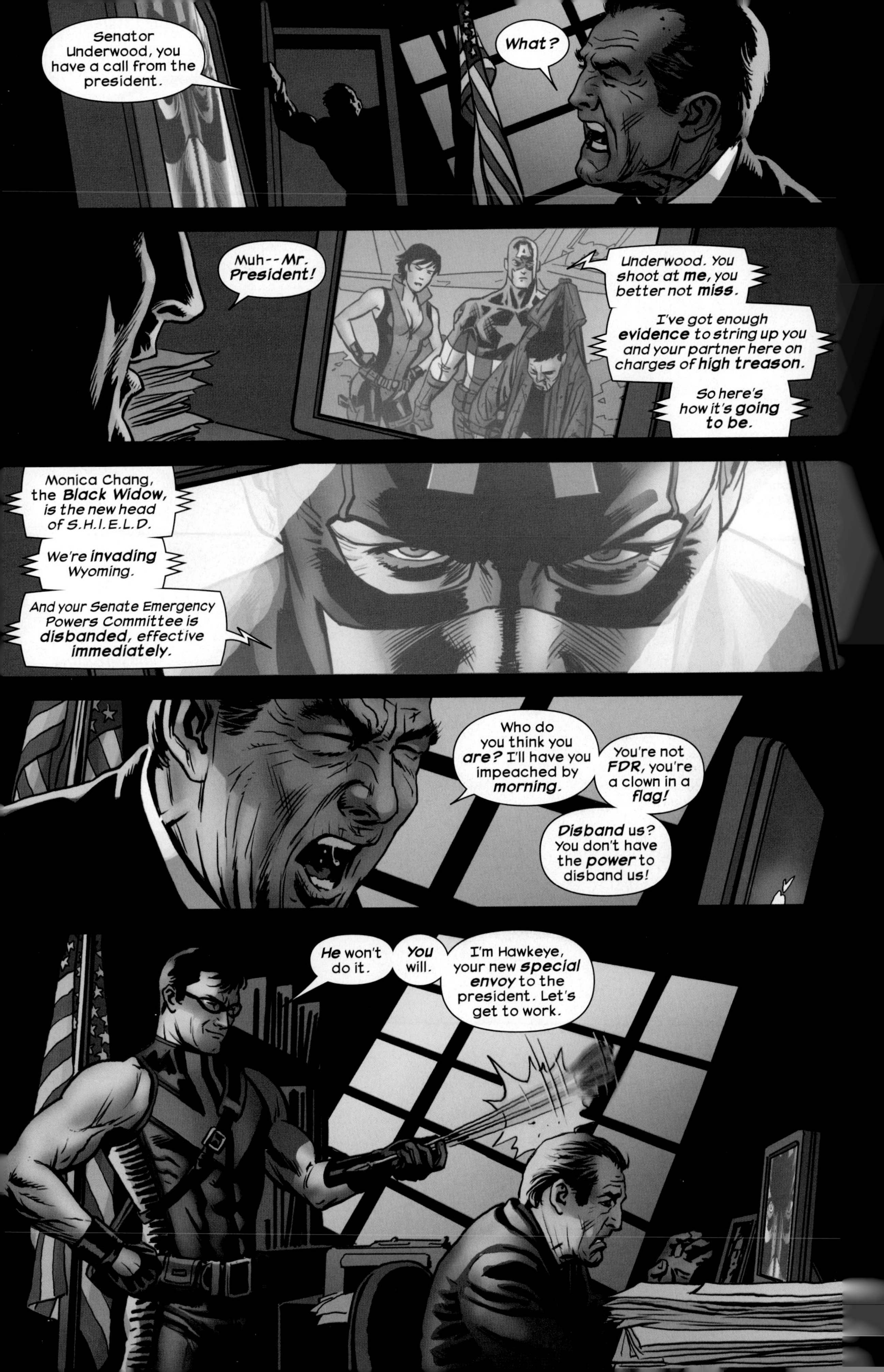
Senator Underwood, you have a call from the president.
What?
Muh--Mr. President!
Underwood. You shoot at me, you better not miss.
I've got enough evidence to string up you and your partner here on charges of high treason.
So here's how it's going to be.
Monica Chang, the Black Widow, is the new head of S.H.I.E.L.D.
We're invading Wyoming.
And your Senate Emergency Powers Committee is disbanded, effective immediately.
Who do you think you are? I'll have you impeached by morning.
You're not FDR, you're a clown in a flag!
Disband us? You don't have the power to disband us!
He won't do it.
You will.
I'm Hawkeye, your new special envoy to the president. Let's get to work.

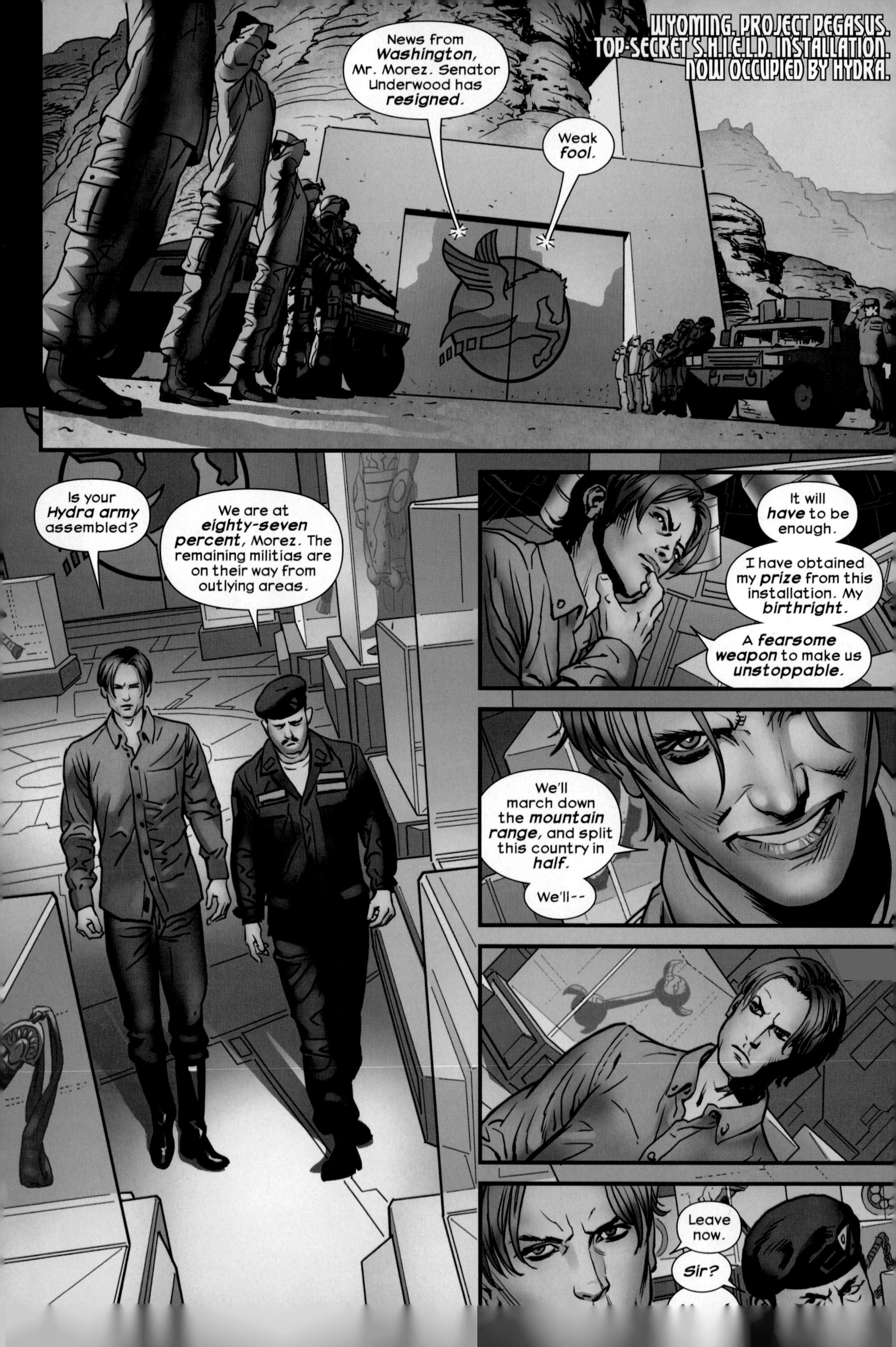
WYOMING. PROJECT PEGASUS. TOP-SECRET S.H.I.E.L.D. INSTALLATION. NOW OCCUPIED BY HYDRA.
News from *Washington*, Mr. Morez. Senator Underwood has *resigned*.
Weak *fool*.
Is your *Hydra army* assembled?
We are at *eighty-seven percent*, Morez. The remaining militias are on their way from outlying areas.
It will *have* to be enough.
I have obtained my *prize* from this installation. My *birthright*.
A *fearsome weapon* to make us *unstoppable*.
We'll march down the *mountain range*, and split this country in *half*.
We'll--
Leave now.
Sir?

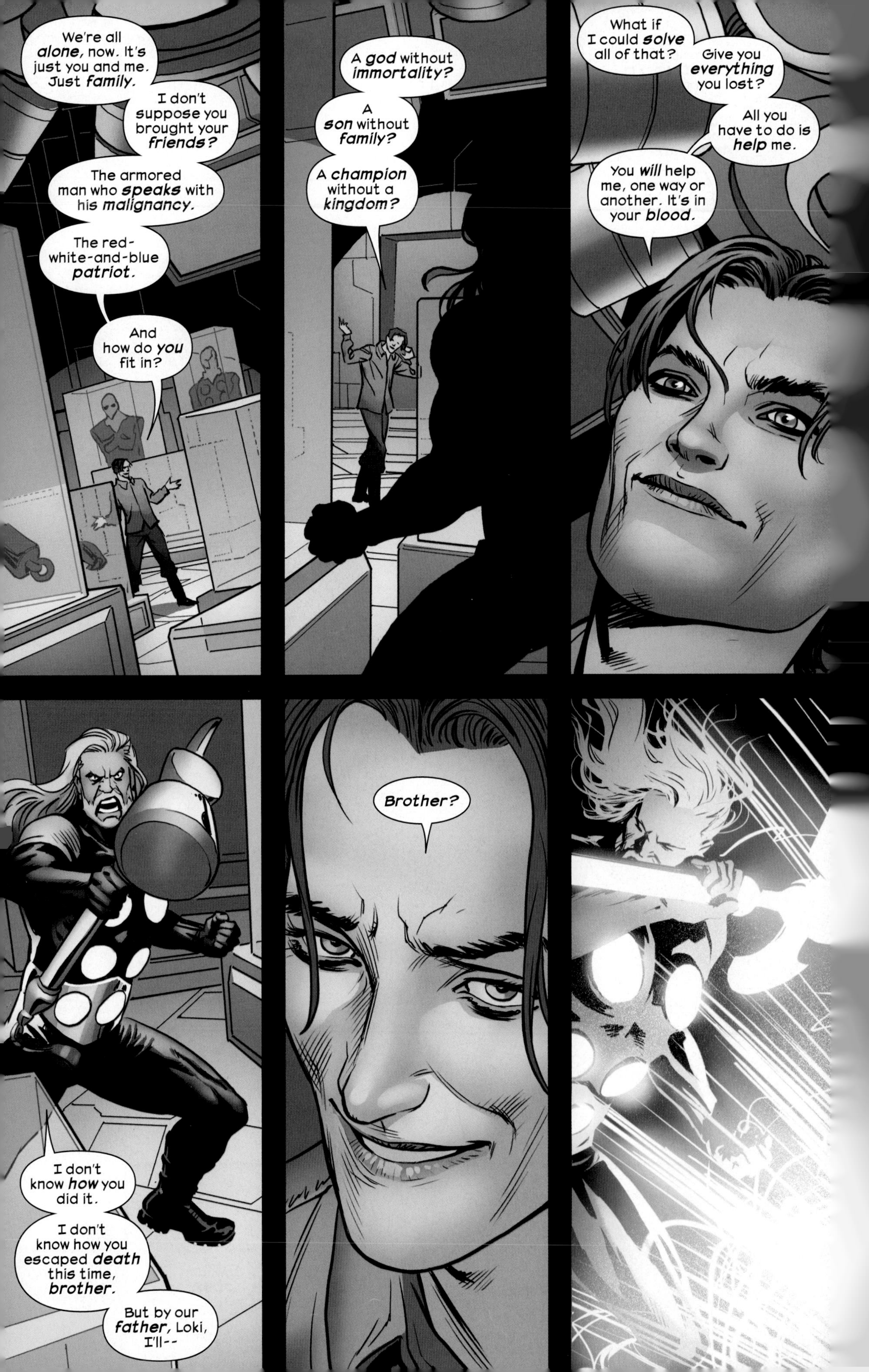
We're all *alone*, now. It's just you and me. Just *family*.
I don't suppose you brought your *friends?*
The armored man who *speaks* with his *malignancy*.
The red-white-and-blue *patriot*.
And how do *you* fit in?
A *god* without *immortality?*
A *son* without *family?*
A *champion* without a *kingdom?*
What if I could *solve* all of that?
Give you *everything* you lost?
All you have to do is *help* me.
You *will* help me, one way or another. It's in your *blood*.
I don't know *how* you did it.
I don't know how you escaped *death* this time, *brother*.
But by our *father*, Loki, I'll--
Brother?

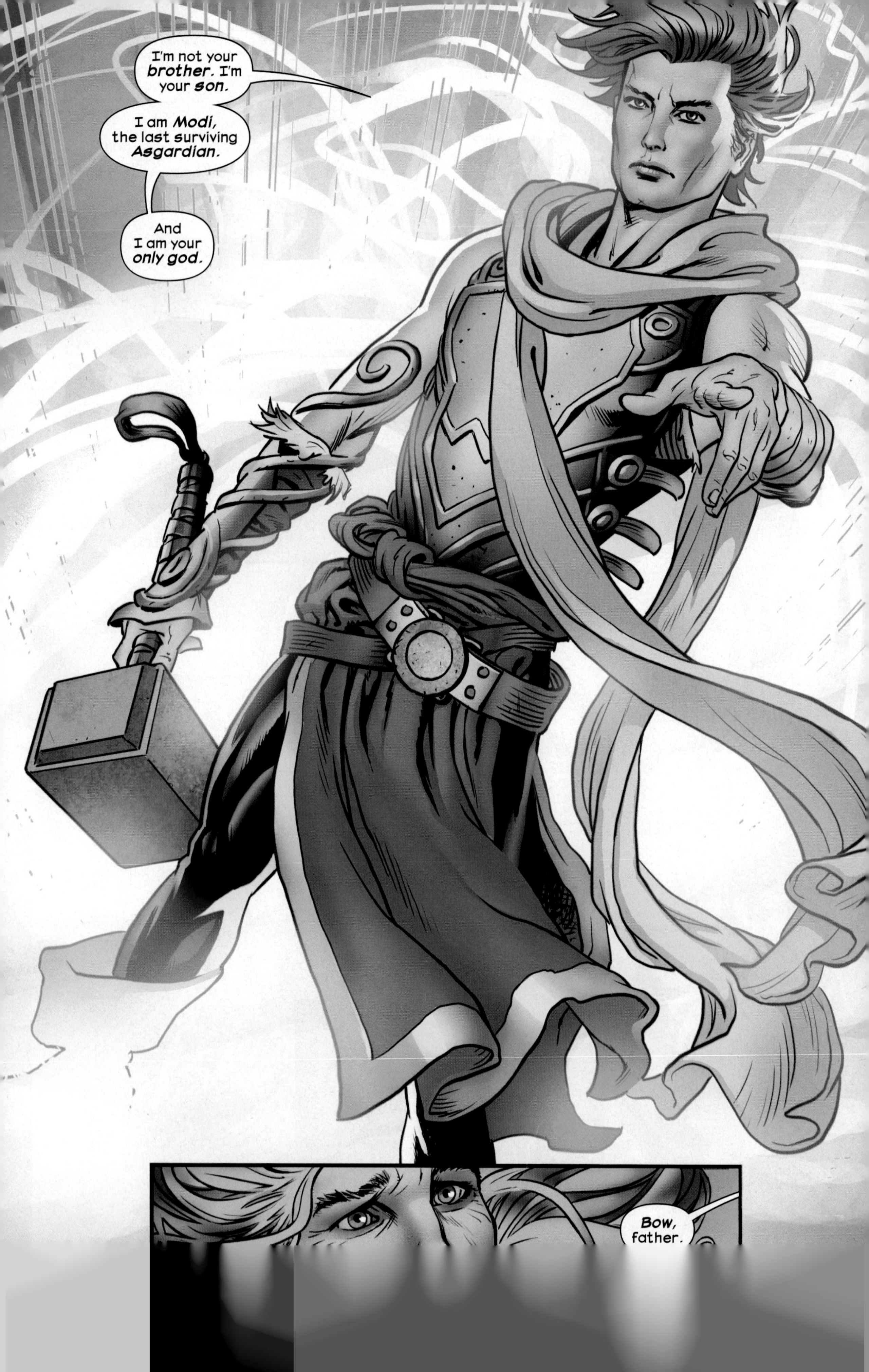
I'm not your brother. I'm your son.
I am Modi, the last surviving Asgardian.
And I am your only god.
Bow, father.

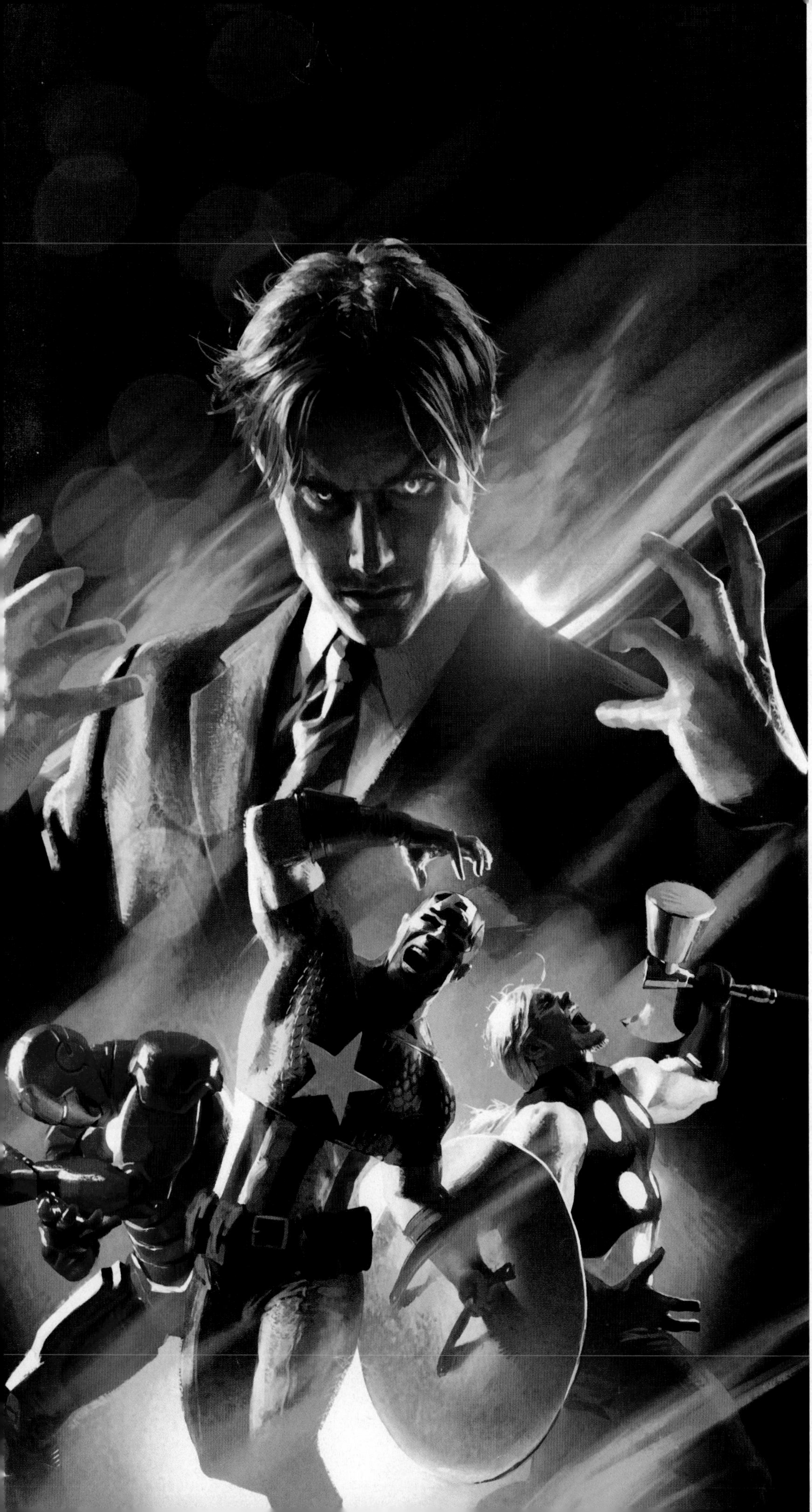

5

ULTIMATE COMICS **ULTIMATES** #17

S.H.I.E.L.D. SITUATION MAP:

[Anti-government militia hot spots]

Idaho, Montana, N. Dakota, S. Dakota, Arizona, New Mexico, Wyoming

Wyoming

status unknown

[Eastern seaboard control zone]

New England, New York, New Jersey, Delaware, Washington, D.C., Maryland, Pennsylvania, Virginia

secured by National Guard under emergency powers committee

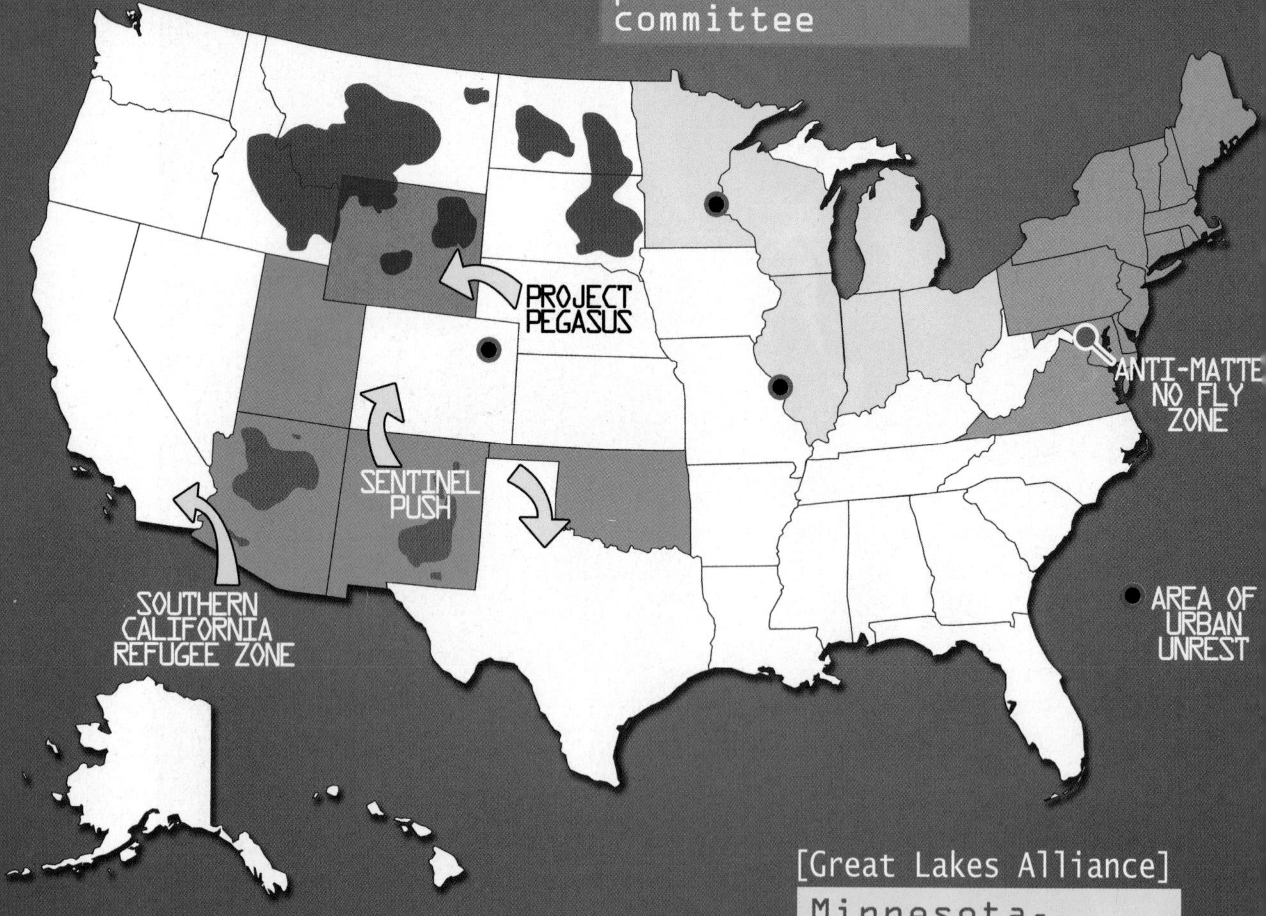

PROJECT PEGASUS
ANTI-MATTE NO FLY ZONE
SENTINEL PUSH
SOUTHERN CALIFORNIA REFUGEE ZONE
AREA OF URBAN UNREST

[Great Lakes Alliance]

Minnesota, Wisconsin, Michigan, Illinois, Indiana, Ohio

Independent nation

[Sentinel-controlled no-man's-land]

New Mexico, Arizona, Utah, Oklahoma

abandoned by the U.S. government

ALL STATES SHOWN IN WHITE ARE U.S. GOVERNMENT-CONTROLLED ZONES

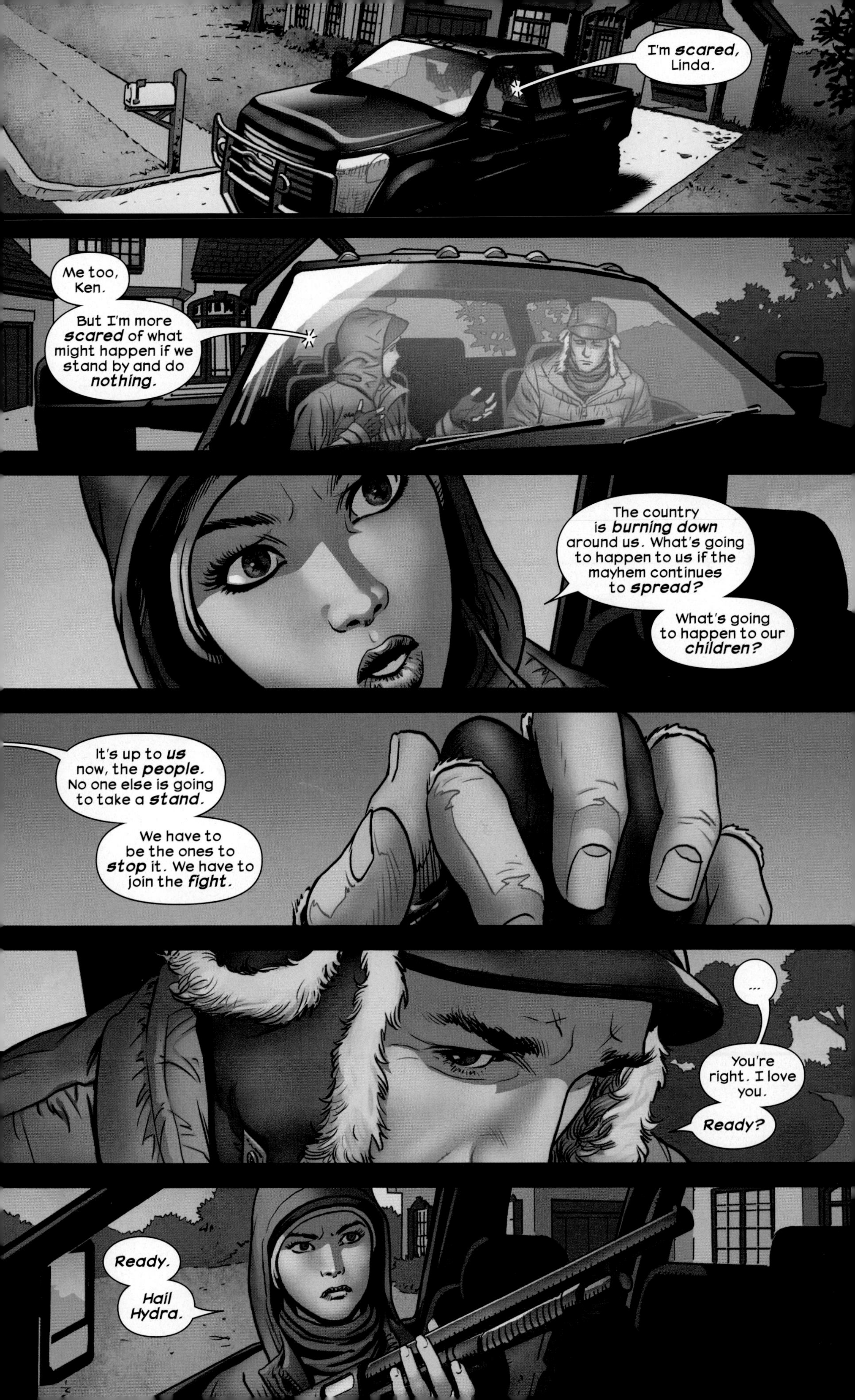
I'm scared, Linda.
Me too, Ken.
But I'm more scared of what might happen if we stand by and do nothing.
The country is burning down around us. What's going to happen to us if the mayhem continues to spread?
What's going to happen to our children?
It's up to us now, the people. No one else is going to take a stand.
We have to be the ones to stop it. We have to join the fight.
...
You're right. I love you.
Ready?
Ready.
Hail Hydra.

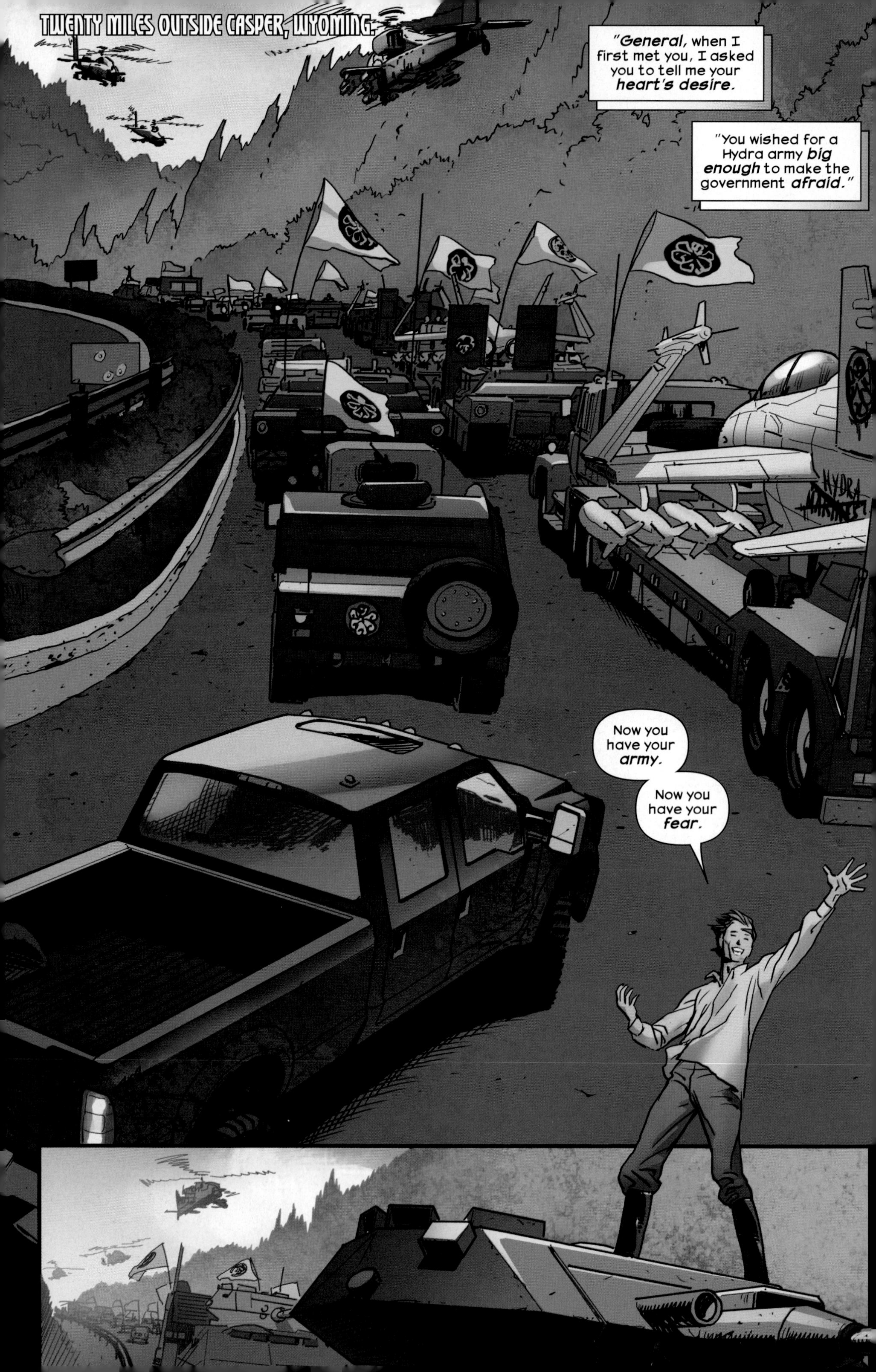

TWENTY MILES OUTSIDE CASPER, WYOMING.
"General, when I first met you, I asked you to tell me your heart's desire.
"You wished for a Hydra army big enough to make the government afraid."
Now you have your army.
Now you have your fear.

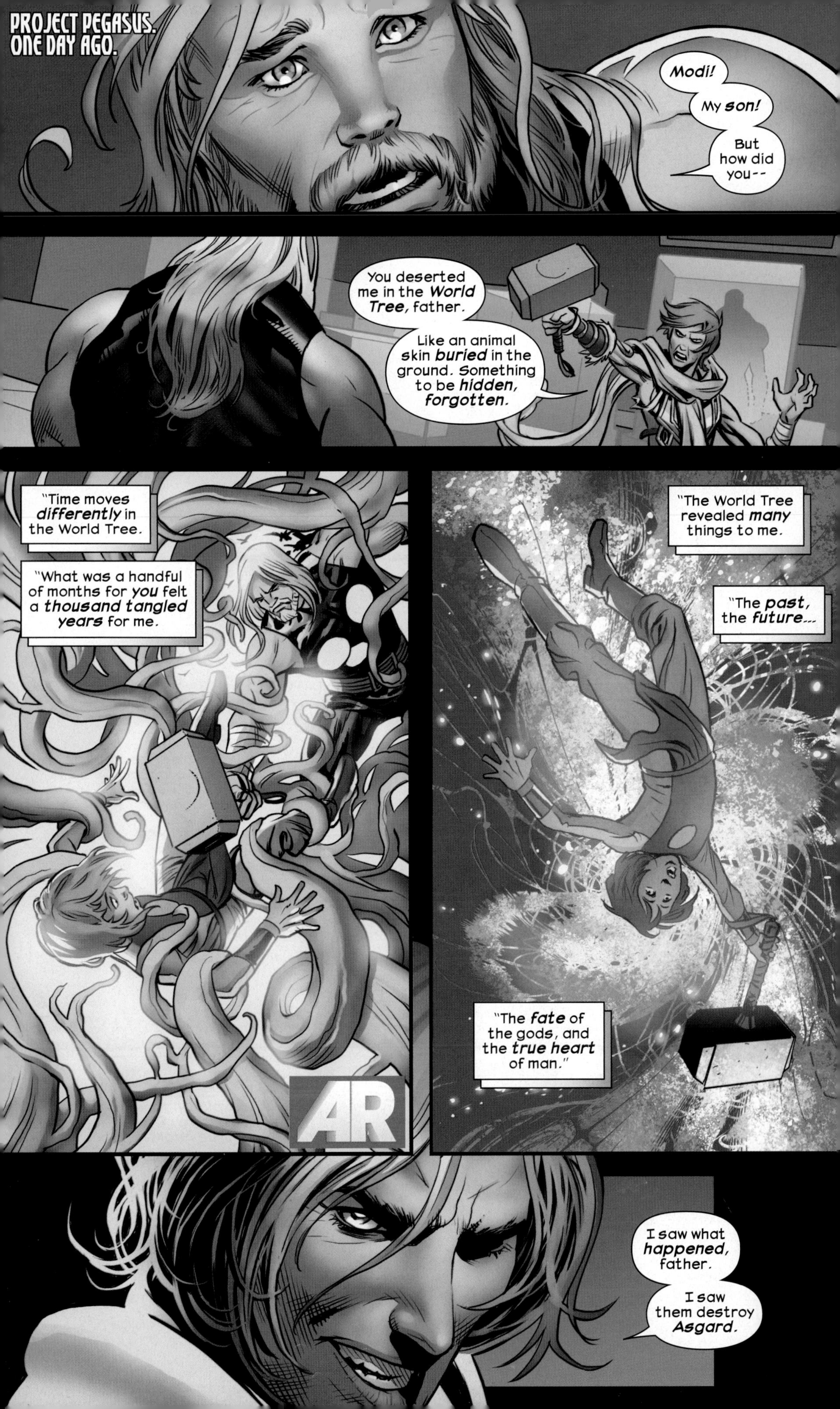
PROJECT PEGASUS. ONE DAY AGO.
Modi!
My son!
But how did you--
You deserted me in the World Tree, father.
Like an animal skin buried in the ground. Something to be hidden, forgotten.
"Time moves differently in the World Tree.
"What was a handful of months for you felt a thousand tangled years for me.
"The World Tree revealed many things to me.
"The past, the future...
"The fate of the gods, and the true heart of man."
I saw what happened, father.
I saw them destroy Asgard.

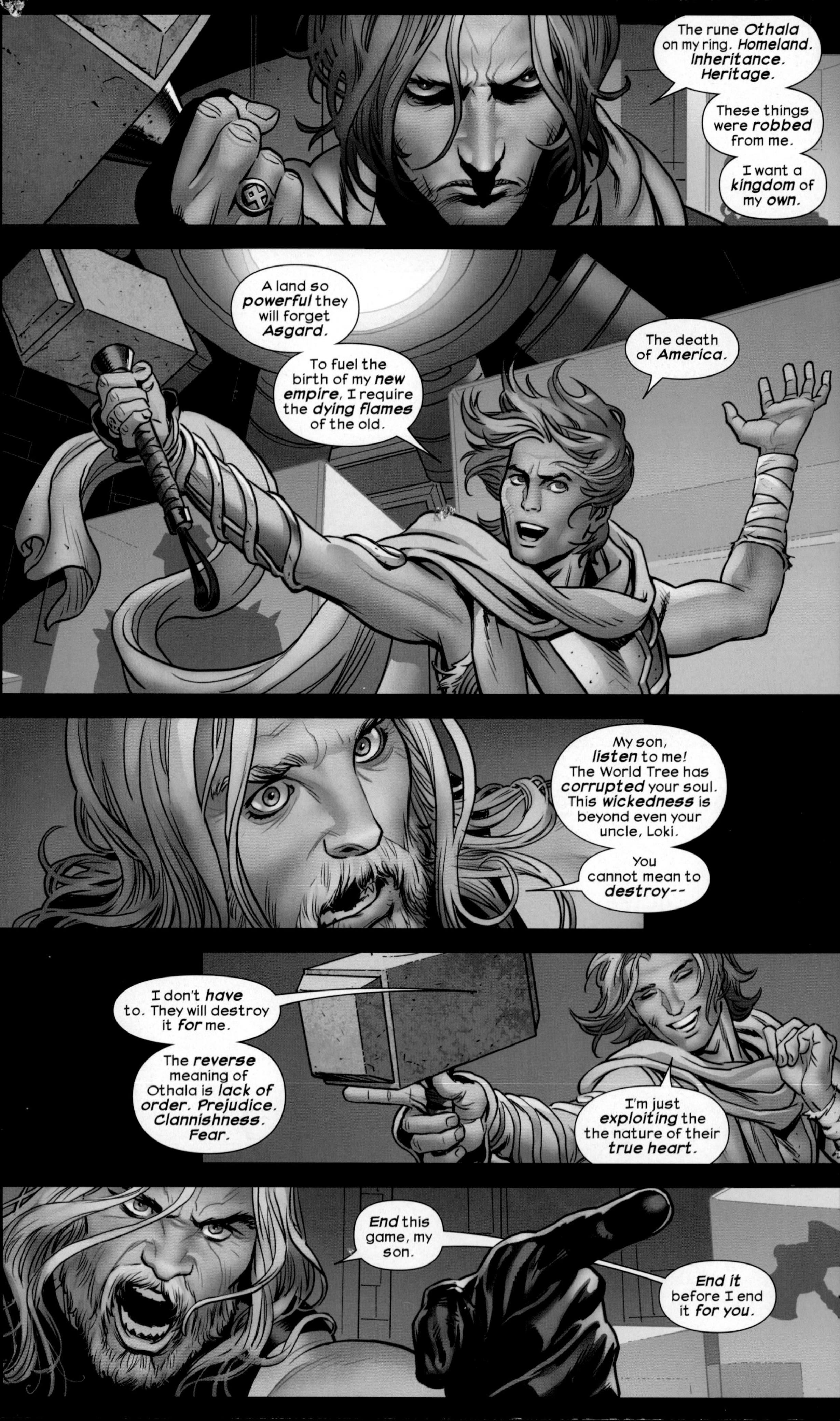
The rune Othala on my ring. Homeland. Inheritance. Heritage.
These things were robbed from me.
I want a kingdom of my own.
A land so powerful they will forget Asgard.
To fuel the birth of my new empire, I require the dying flames of the old.
The death of America.
My son, listen to me! The World Tree has corrupted your soul. This wickedness is beyond even your uncle, Loki.
You cannot mean to destroy--
I don't have to. They will destroy it for me.
The reverse meaning of Othala is lack of order. Prejudice. Clannishness. Fear.
I'm just exploiting the the nature of their true heart.
End this game, my son.
End it before I end it for you.

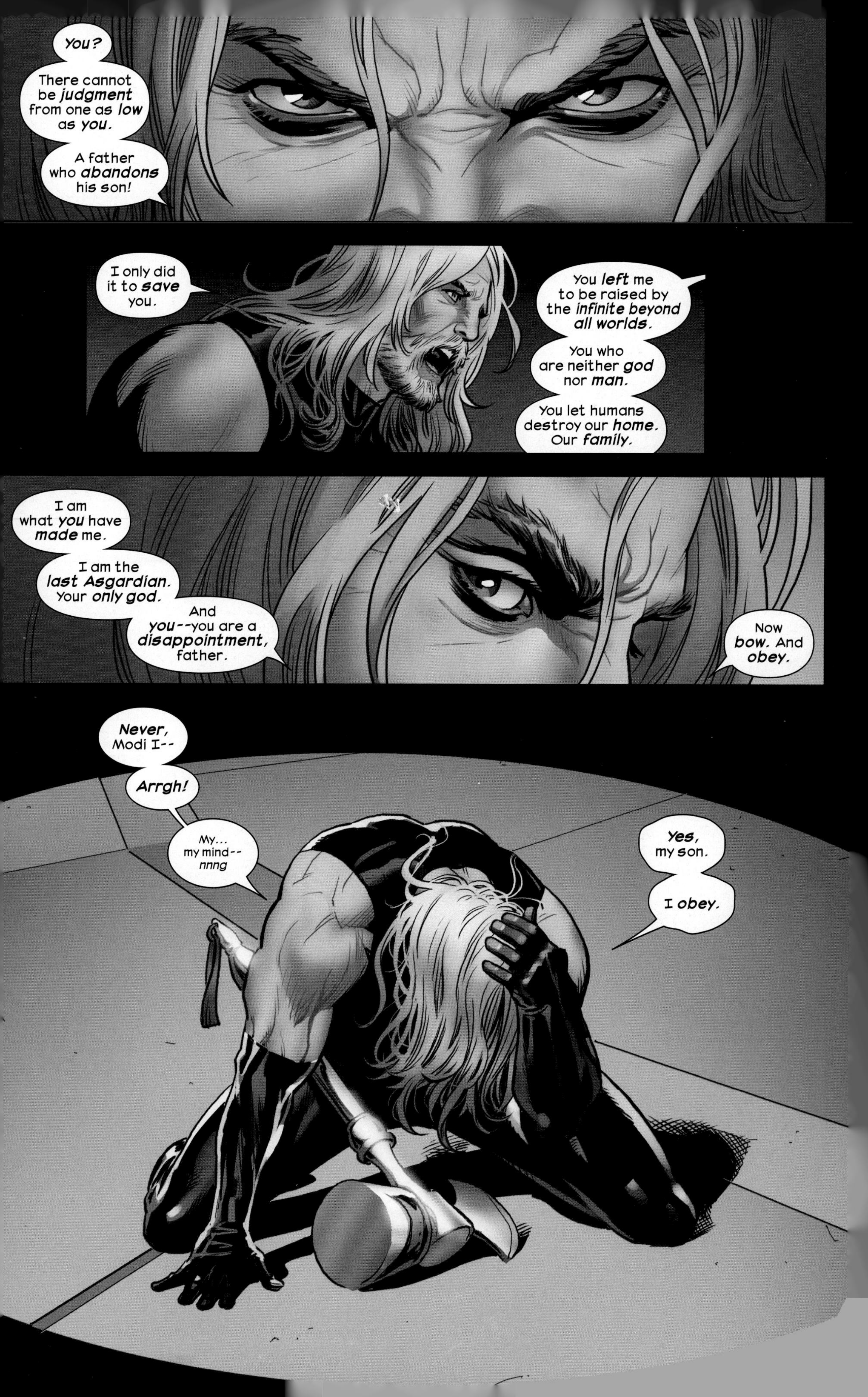
You?
There cannot be judgment from one as low as you.
A father who abandons his son!
I only did it to save you.
You left me to be raised by the infinite beyond all worlds.
You who are neither god nor man.
You let humans destroy our home. Our family.
I am what you have made me.
I am the last Asgardian. Your only god.
And you--you are a disappointment, father.
Now bow. And obey.
Never, Modi I--
Arrgh!
My... my mind--nnng
Yes, my son.
I obey.

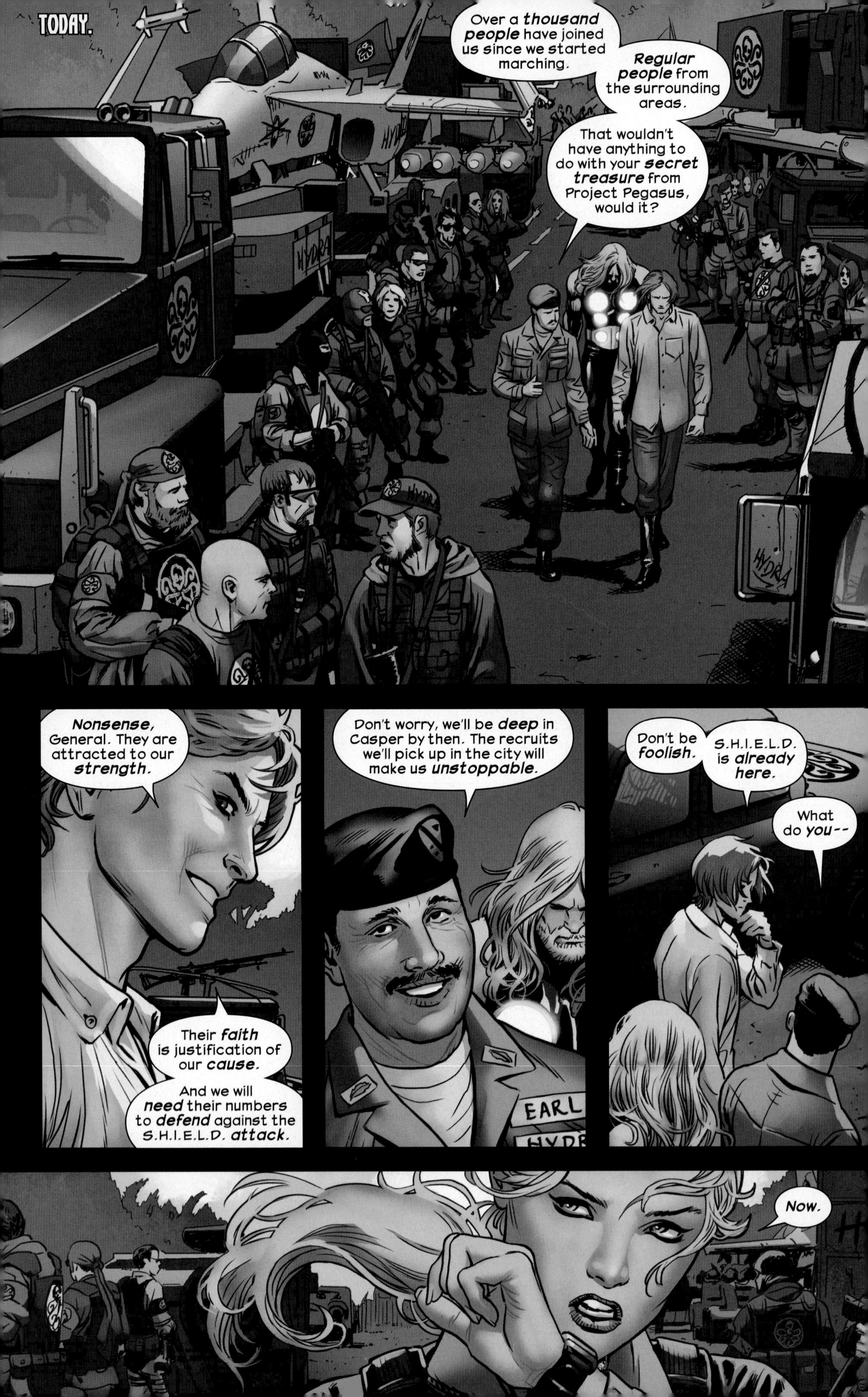

TODAY.
Over a *thousand* *people* have joined us since we started marching.
Regular *people* from the surrounding areas.
That wouldn't have anything to do with your *secret* *treasure* from Project Pegasus, would it?
Nonsense, General. They are attracted to our *strength.*
Their *faith* is justification of our *cause.*
And we will *need* their numbers to *defend* against the S.H.I.E.L.D. *attack.*
Don't worry, we'll be *deep* in Casper by then. The recruits we'll pick up in the city will make us *unstoppable.*
EARL
Don't be *foolish.*
S.H.I.E.L.D. is *already* *here.*
What do *you--*
Now.

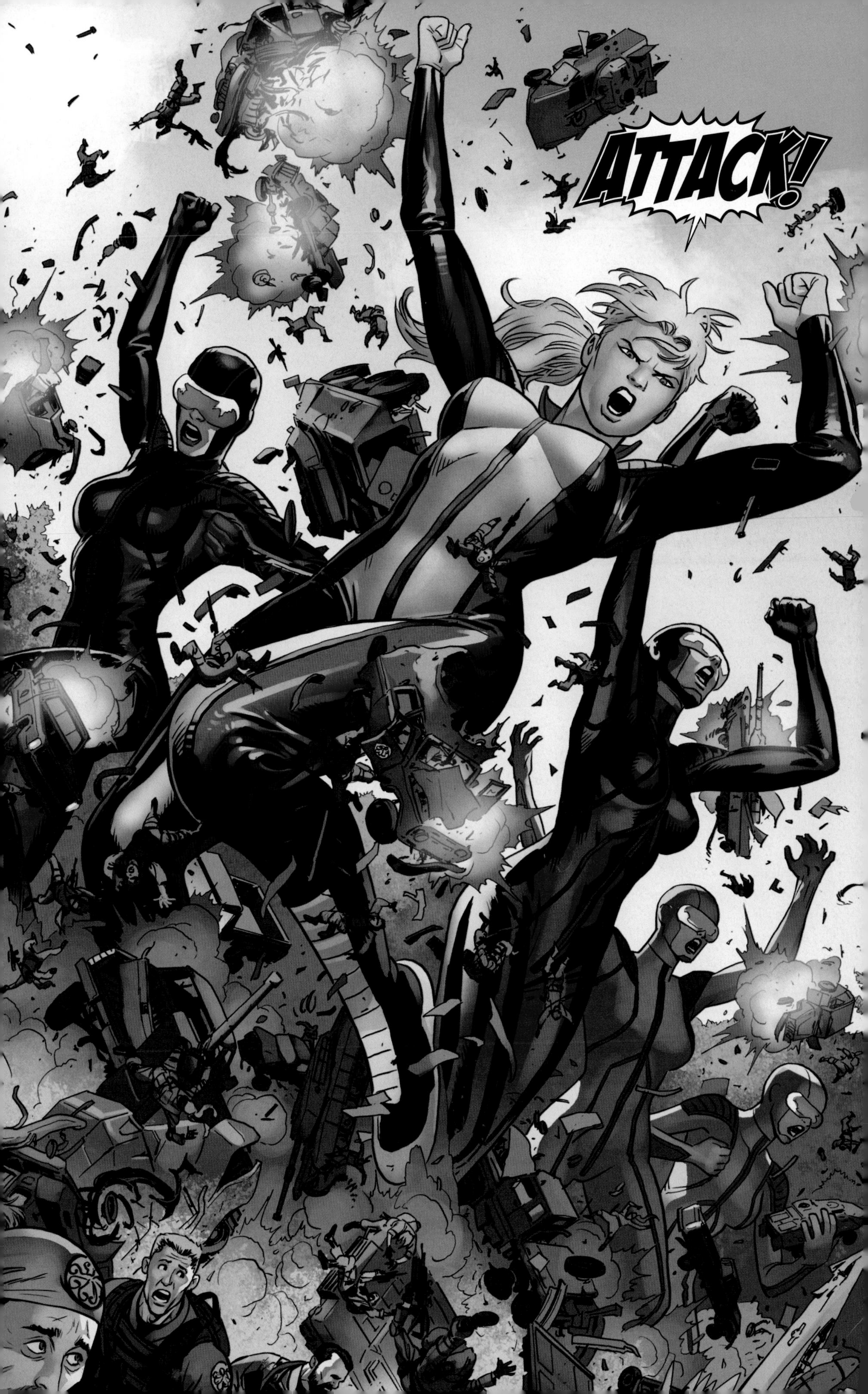
ATTACK!

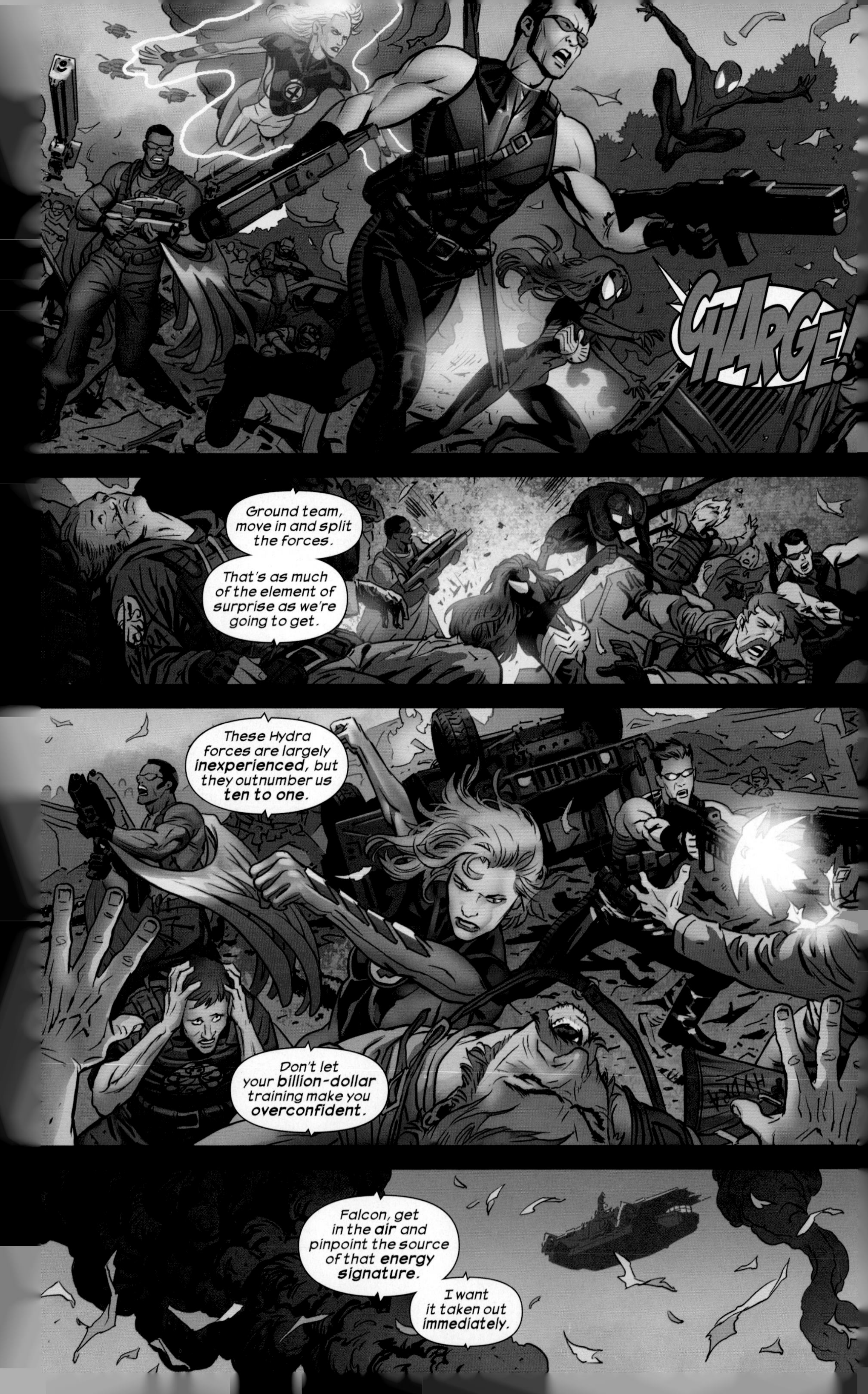
CHARGE!
Ground team, move in and split the forces.
That's as much of the element of surprise as we're going to get.
These Hydra forces are largely **inexperienced**, but they outnumber us **ten to one**.
Don't let your **billion-dollar** training make you **overconfident**.
Falcon, get in the **air** and pinpoint the source of that **energy signature**.
I want it taken out **immediately**.

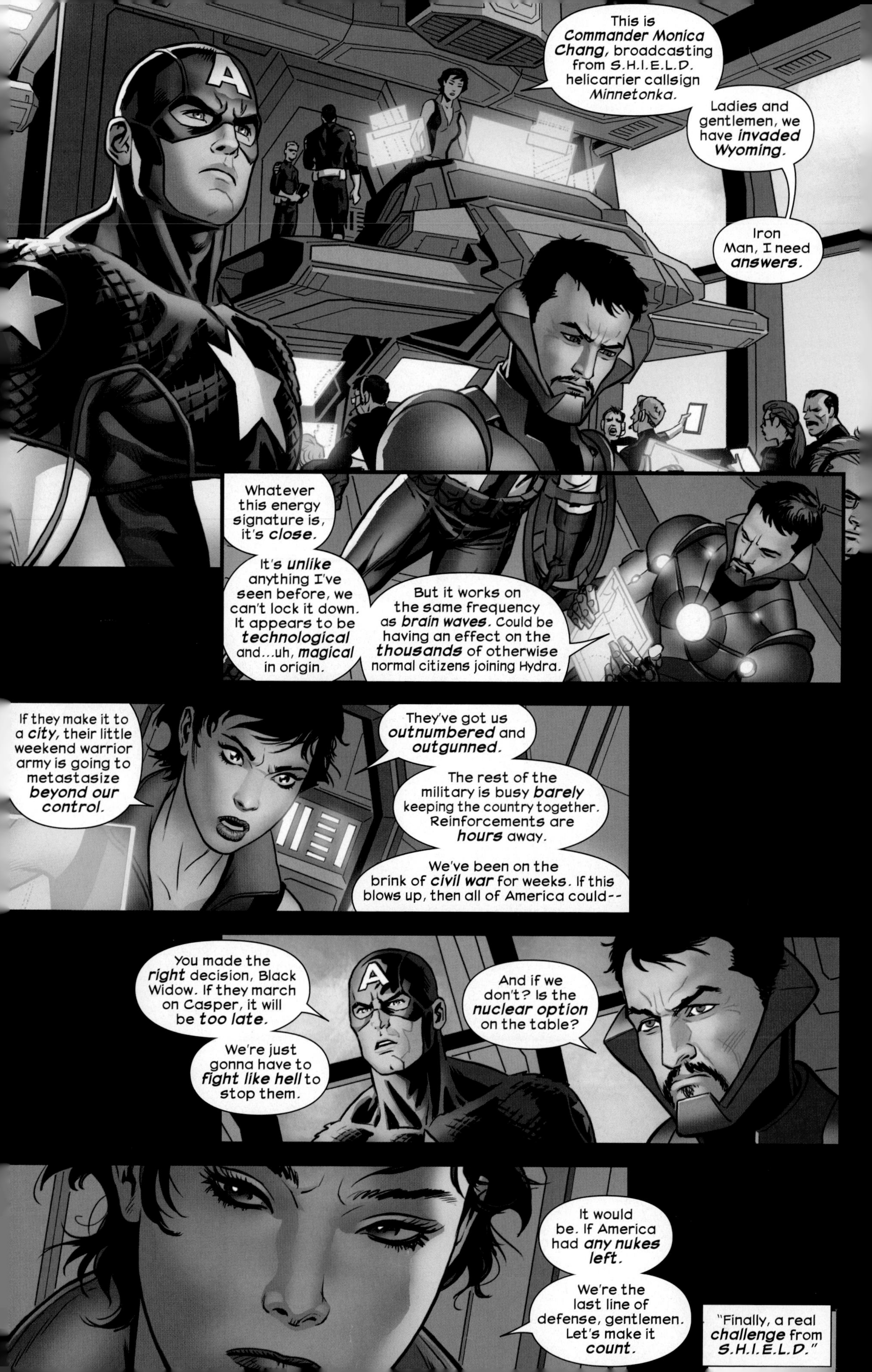
This is Commander Monica Chang, broadcasting from S.H.I.E.L.D. helicarrier callsign Minnetonka.
Ladies and gentlemen, we have invaded Wyoming.
Iron Man, I need answers.
Whatever this energy signature is, it's close.
It's unlike anything I've seen before, we can't lock it down. It appears to be technological and...uh, magical in origin.
But it works on the same frequency as brain waves. Could be having an effect on the thousands of otherwise normal citizens joining Hydra.
If they make it to a city, their little weekend warrior army is going to metastasize beyond our control.
They've got us outnumbered and outgunned.
The rest of the military is busy barely keeping the country together. Reinforcements are hours away.
We've been on the brink of civil war for weeks. If this blows up, then all of America could--
You made the right decision, Black Widow. If they march on Casper, it will be too late.
We're just gonna have to fight like hell to stop them.
And if we don't? Is the nuclear option on the table?
It would be. If America had any nukes left.
We're the last line of defense, gentlemen. Let's make it count.
"Finally, a real challenge from S.H.I.E.L.D."

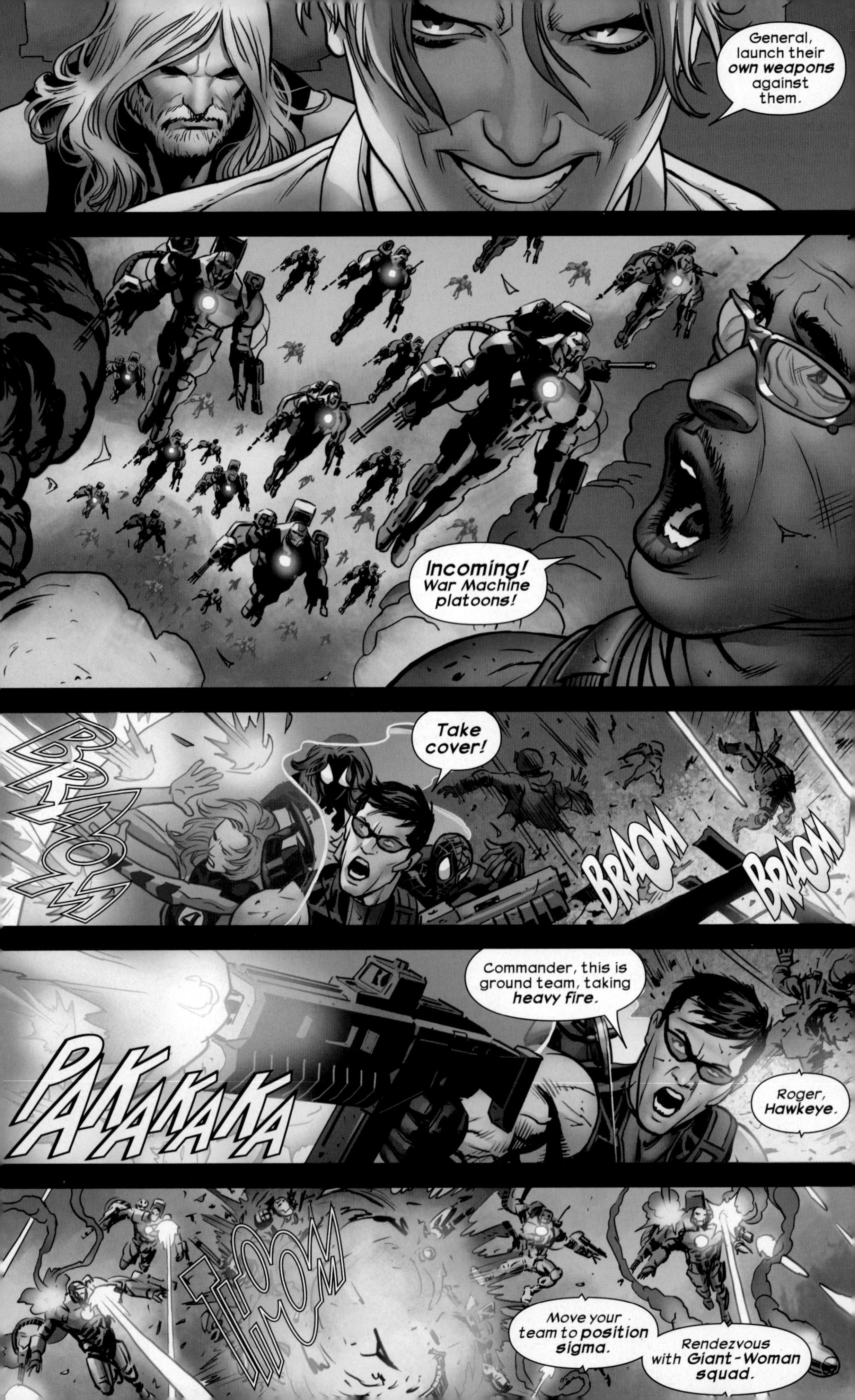
General, launch their own weapons against them.
Incoming! War Machine platoons!
BRAOOM
Take cover!
BRAOM
BRAOM
Commander, this is ground team, taking heavy fire.
PAKAKAKA
Roger, Hawkeye.
TFOOM
Move your team to position sigma.
Rendezvous with Giant-Woman squad.

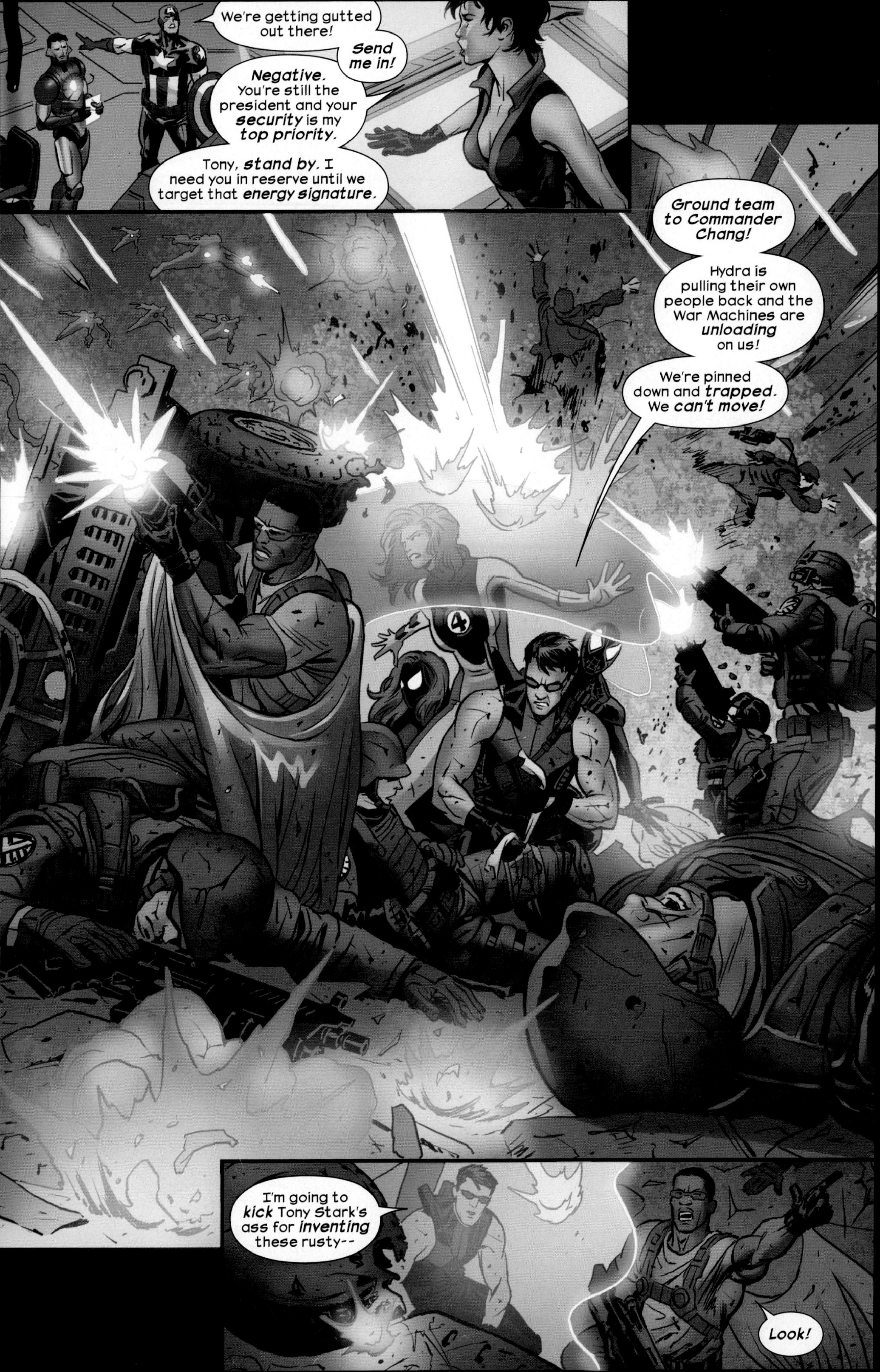
We're getting gutted out there!
Send me in!
Negative. You're still the president and your security is my top priority.
Tony, stand by. I need you in reserve until we target that energy signature.
Ground team to Commander Chang!
Hydra is pulling their own people back and the War Machines are unloading on us!
We're pinned down and trapped. We can't move!
I'm going to kick Tony Stark's ass for inventing these rusty--
Look!

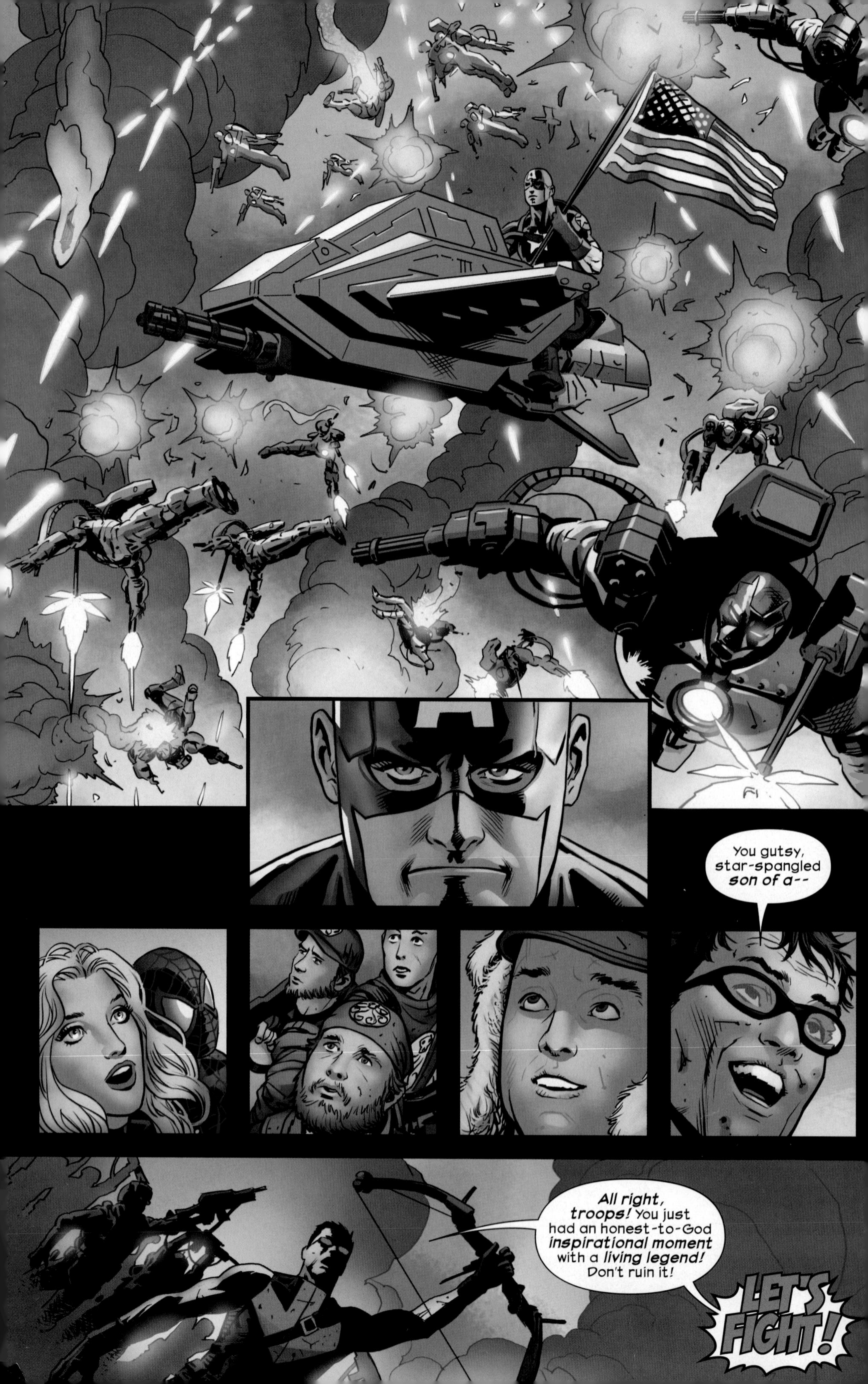

You gutsy, star-spangled son of a--
All right, troops! You just had an honest-to-God inspirational moment with a living legend! Don't ruin it!
LET'S FIGHT!

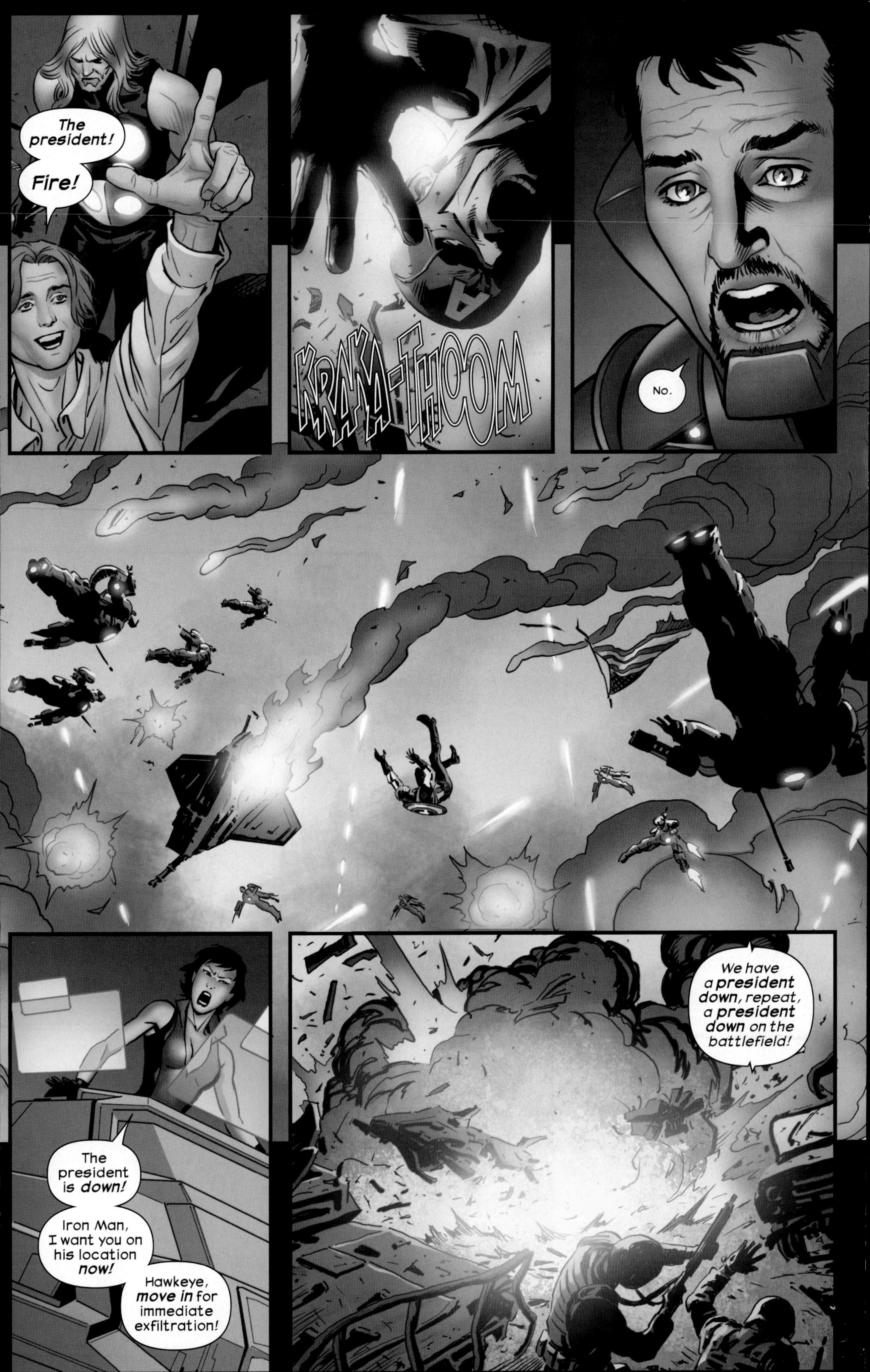
The president!
Fire!
KRAKA-THOOM
No.
The president is down!
Iron Man, I want you on his location now!
Hawkeye, move in for immediate exfiltration!
We have a president down, repeat, a president down on the battlefield!

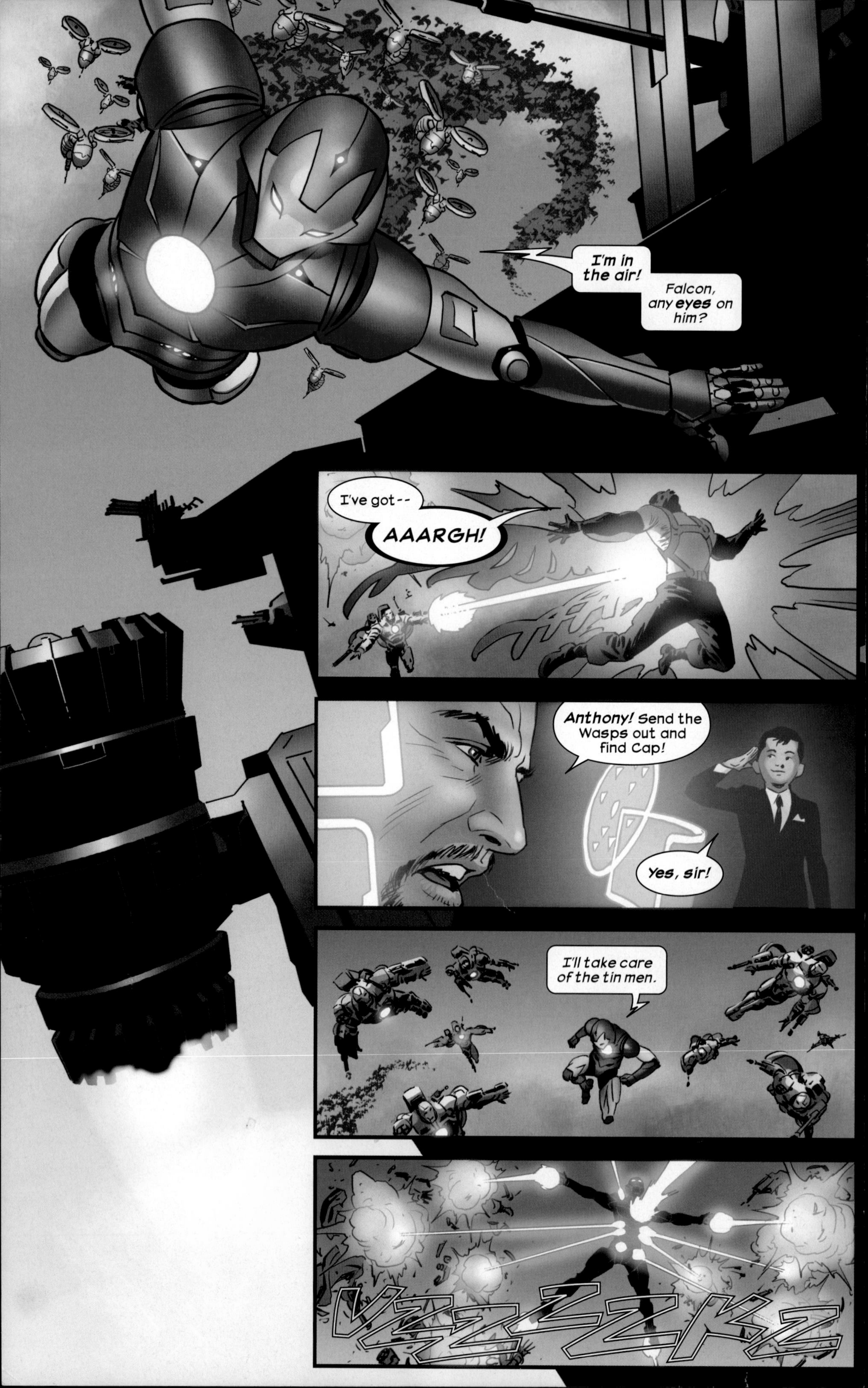
I'm in the air!
Falcon, any eyes on him?
I've got--
AAARGH!
Anthony! Send the Wasps out and find Cap!
Yes, sir!
I'll take care of the tin men.
VZZZZKZ

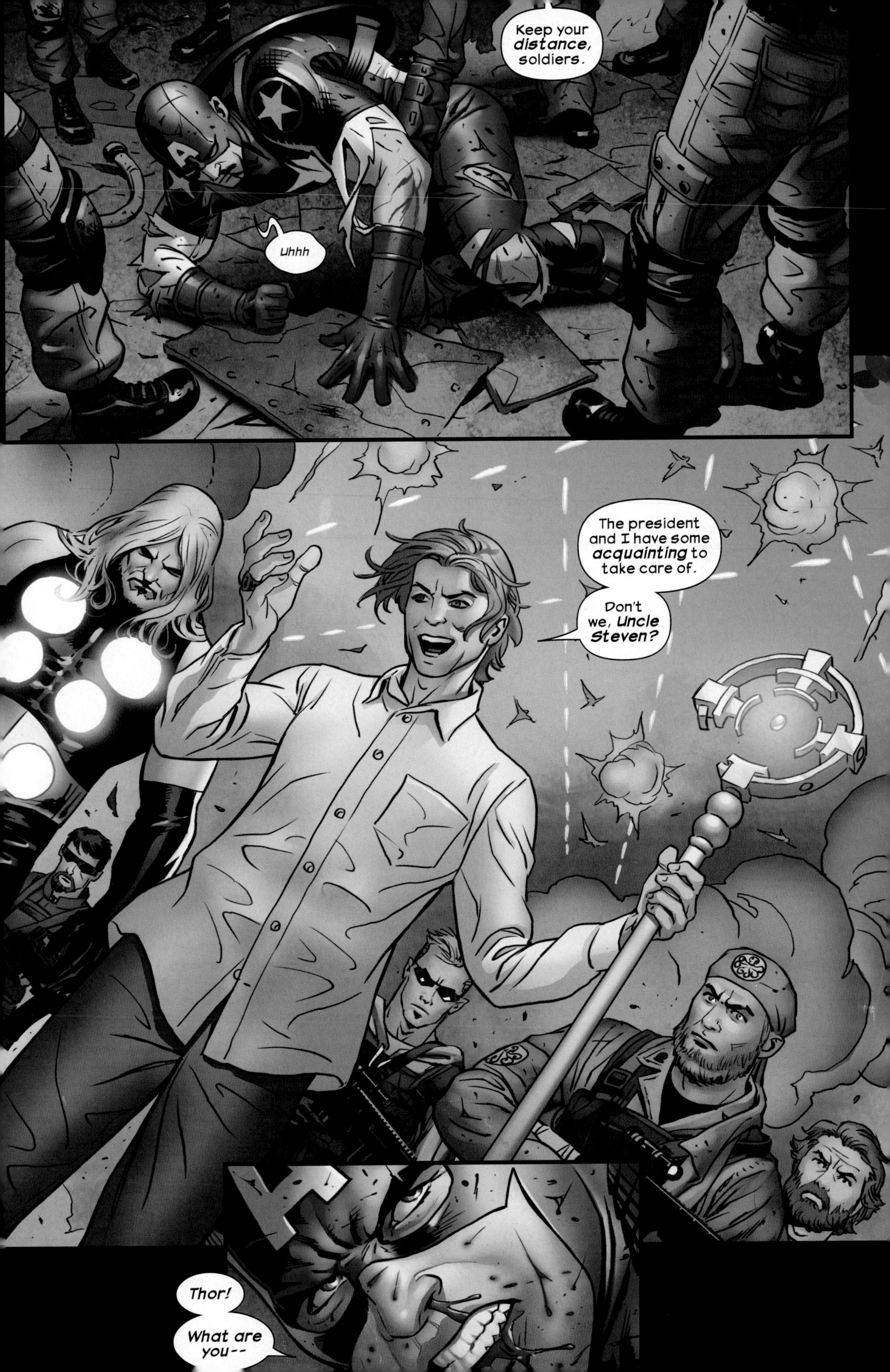
Keep your *distance*, soldiers.
Uhhh
The president and I have some *acquainting* to take care of.
Don't we, *Uncle Steven?*
Thor!
What are you--

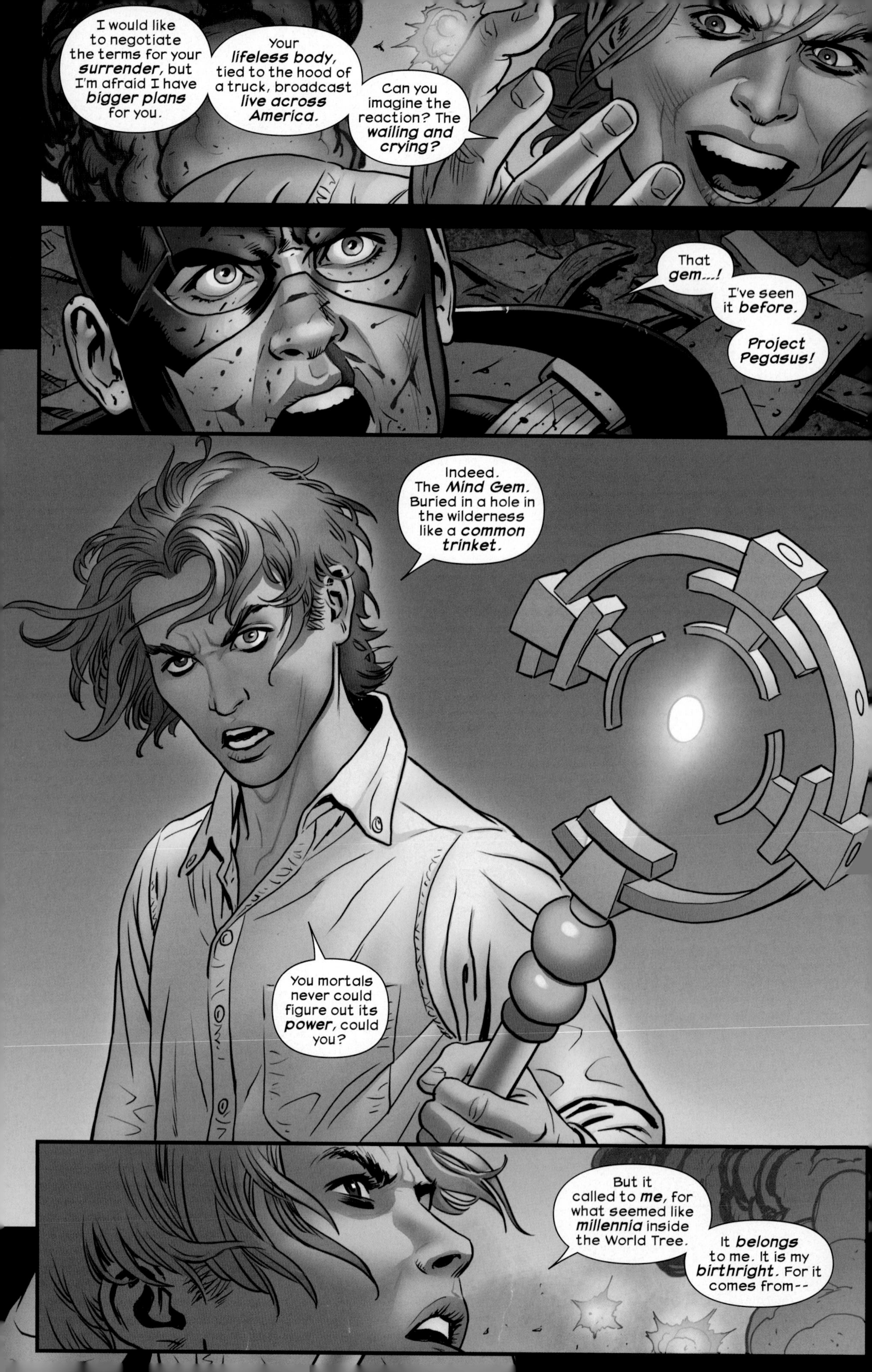
I would like to negotiate the terms for your surrender, but I'm afraid I have bigger plans for you.
Your lifeless body, tied to the hood of a truck, broadcast live across America.
Can you imagine the reaction? The wailing and crying?
That gem...!
I've seen it before.
Project Pegasus!
Indeed. The Mind Gem. Buried in a hole in the wilderness like a common trinket.
You mortals never could figure out its power, could you?
But it called to me, for what seemed like millennia inside the World Tree.
It belongs to me. It is my birthright. For it comes from--

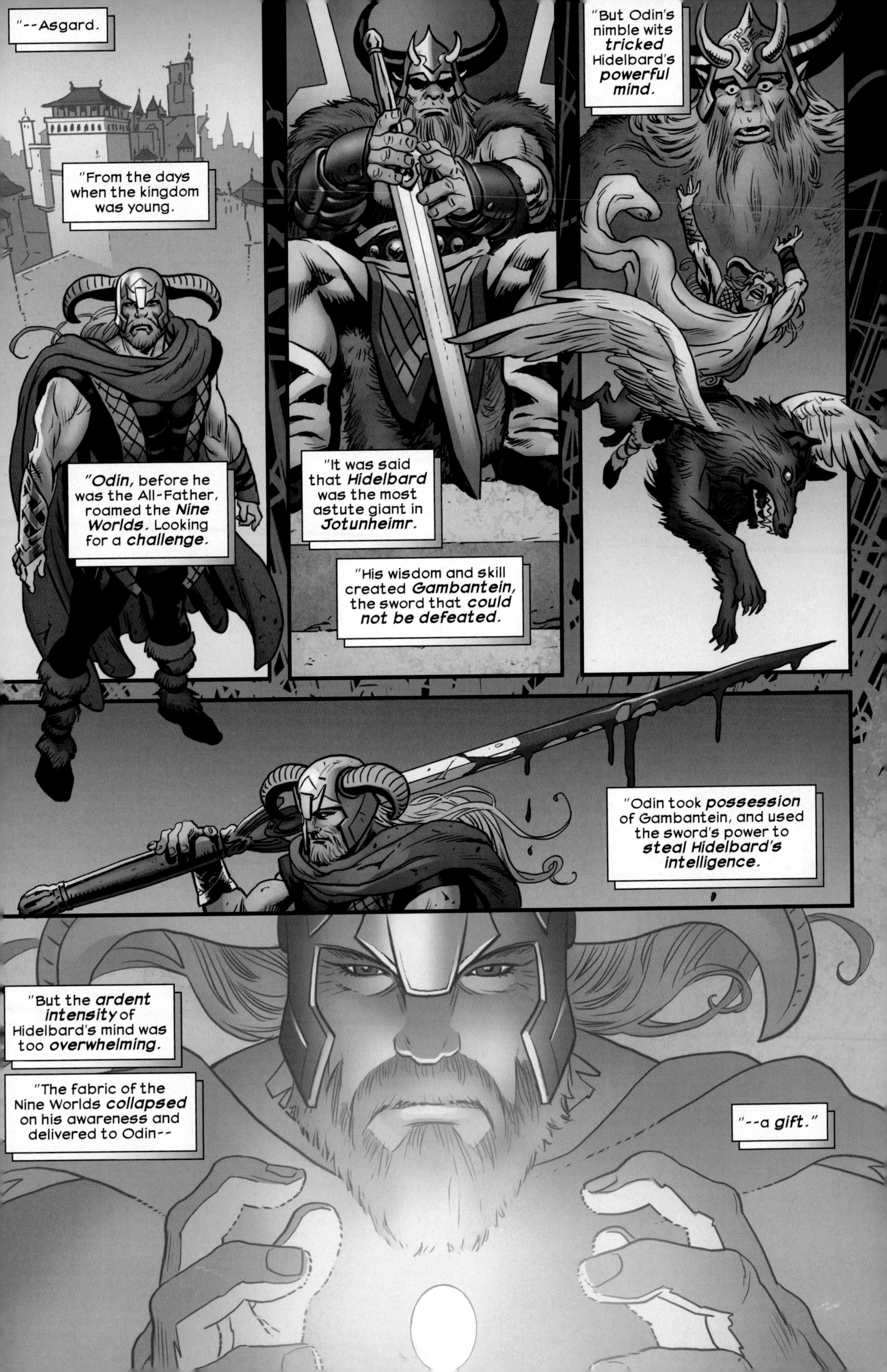
"--Asgard.
"From the days when the kingdom was young.
"*Odin,* before he was the All-Father, roamed the *Nine Worlds.* Looking for a *challenge.*
"It was said that *Hidelbard* was the most astute giant in *Jotunheimr.*
"His wisdom and skill created *Gambantein,* the sword that *could not be defeated.*
"But Odin's nimble wits *tricked* Hidelbard's *powerful mind.*
"Odin took *possession* of Gambantein, and used the sword's power to *steal Hidelbard's intelligence.*
"But the *ardent intensity* of Hidelbard's mind was too *overwhelming.*
"The fabric of the Nine Worlds *collapsed* on his awareness and delivered to Odin--
"--a *gift.*"

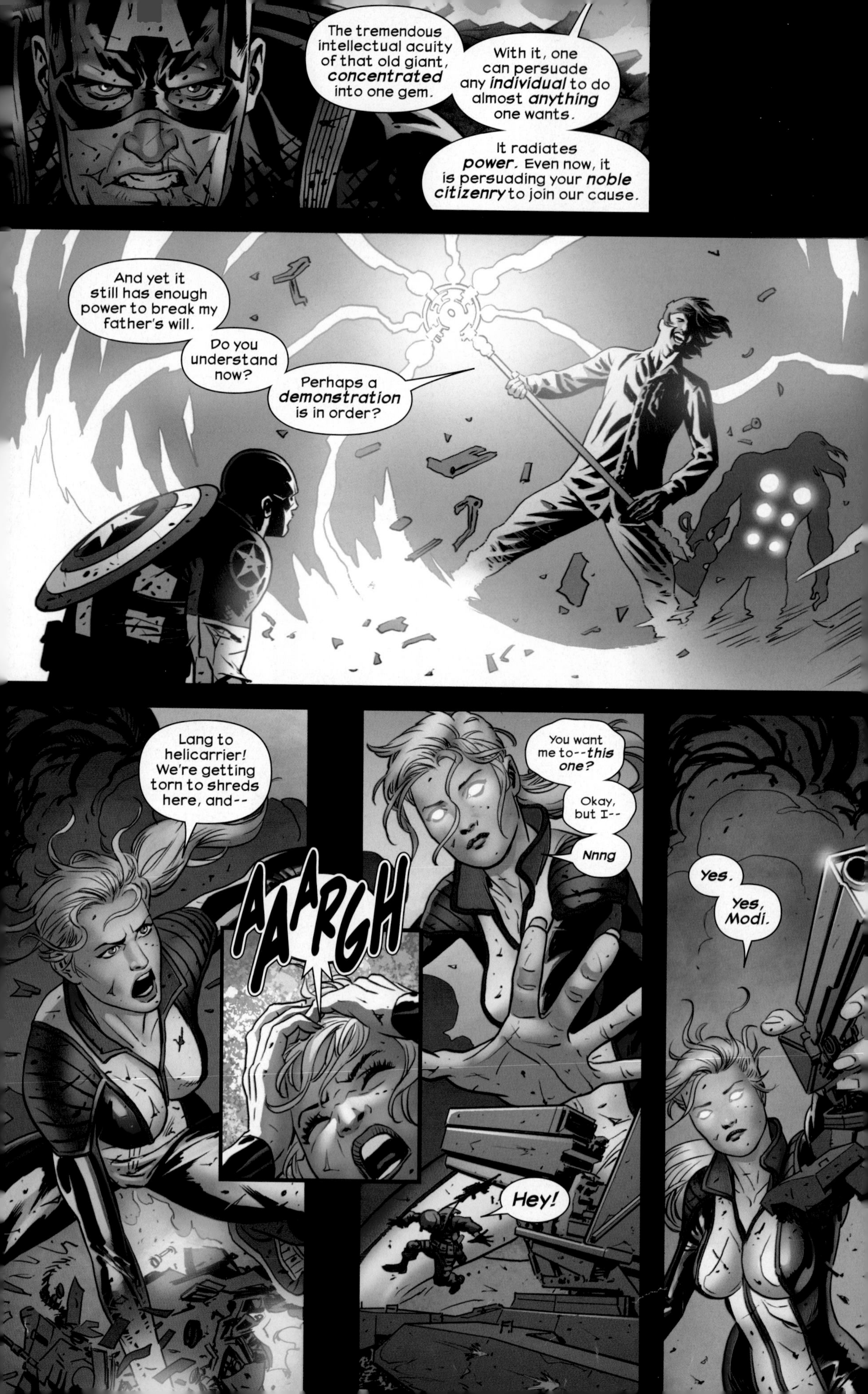
The tremendous intellectual acuity of that old giant, **concentrated** into one gem.
With it, one can persuade any **individual** to do almost **anything** one wants.
It radiates **power.** Even now, it is persuading your **noble citizenry** to join our cause.
And yet it still has enough power to break my father's will.
Do you understand now?
Perhaps a **demonstration** is in order?
Lang to helicarrier! We're getting torn to shreds here, and--
AAARGH
You want me to--**this one?**
Okay, but I--
Nnng
Hey!
Yes.
Yes, Modi.

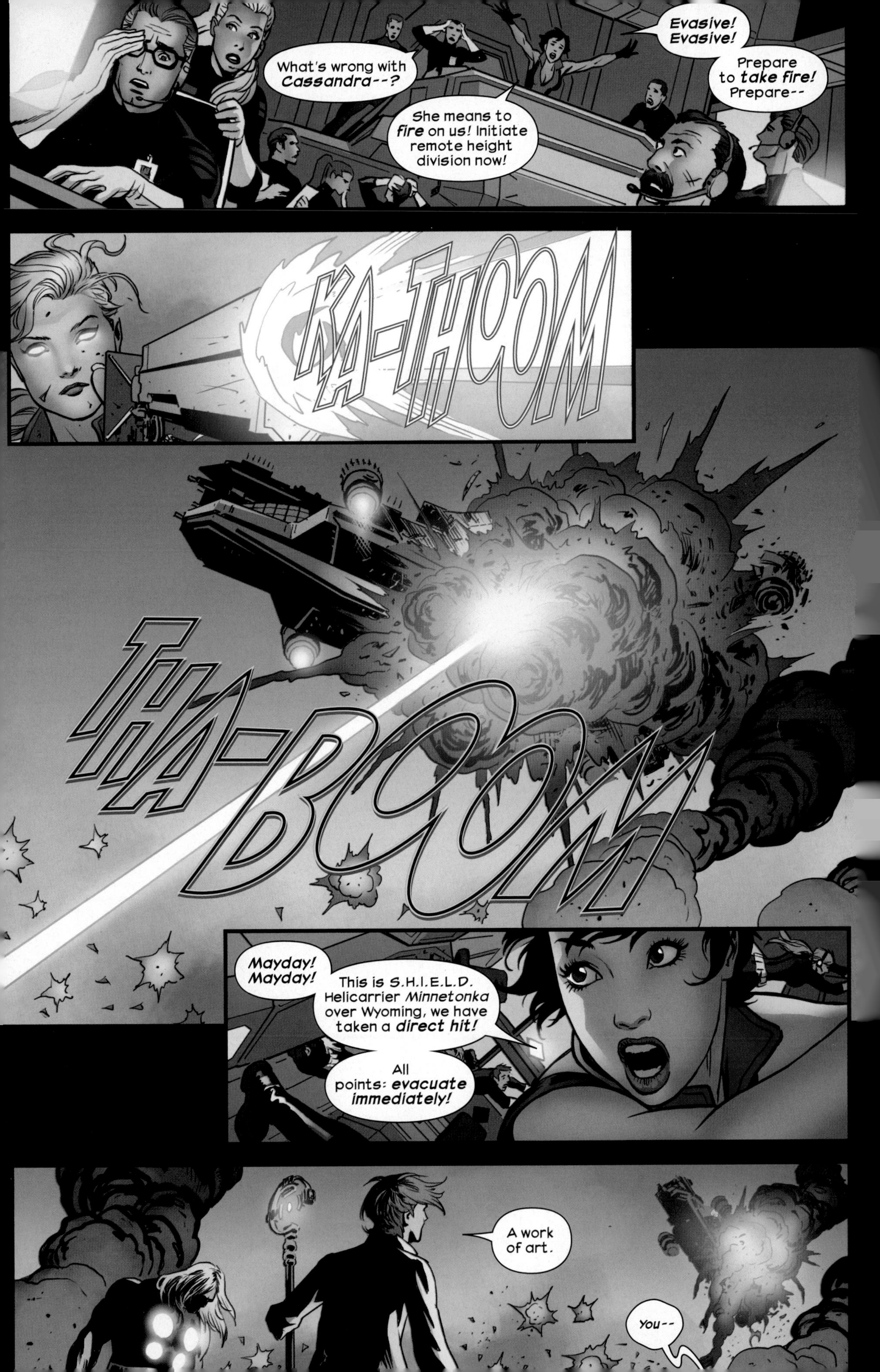
What's wrong with Cassandra--?
She means to fire on us! Initiate remote height division now!
Evasive! Evasive!
Prepare to take fire! Prepare--
KA-THOOM
THA-BOOOM
Mayday! Mayday!
This is S.H.I.E.L.D. Helicarrier Minnetonka over Wyoming, we have taken a direct hit!
All points: evacuate immediately!
A work of art.
You--

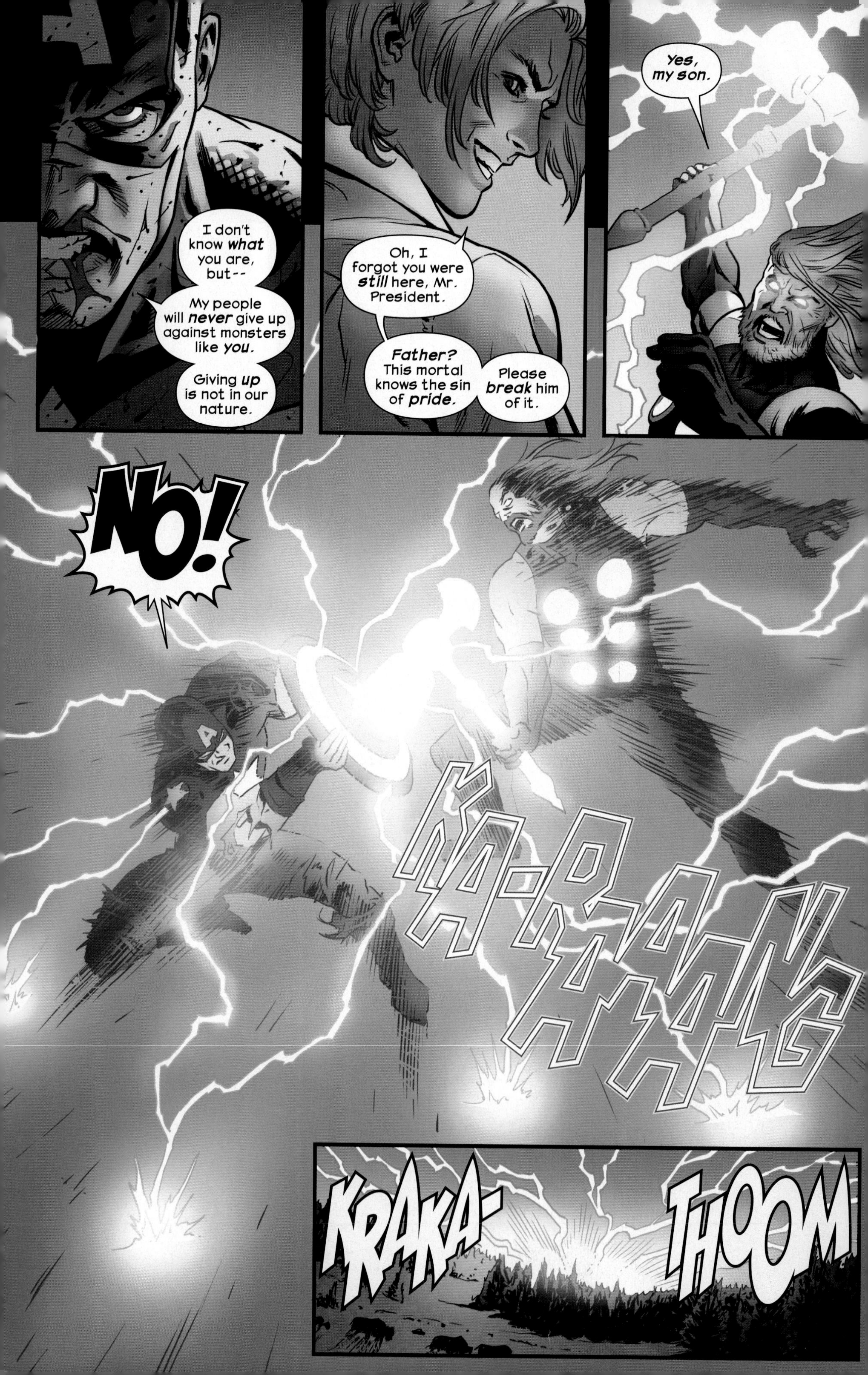

I don't know what you are, but--
My people will never give up against monsters like you.
Giving up is not in our nature.
Oh, I forgot you were still here, Mr. President.
Father? This mortal knows the sin of pride.
Please break him of it.
Yes, my son.
NO!
KA-RAAANNNG
KRAKA-
THOOM

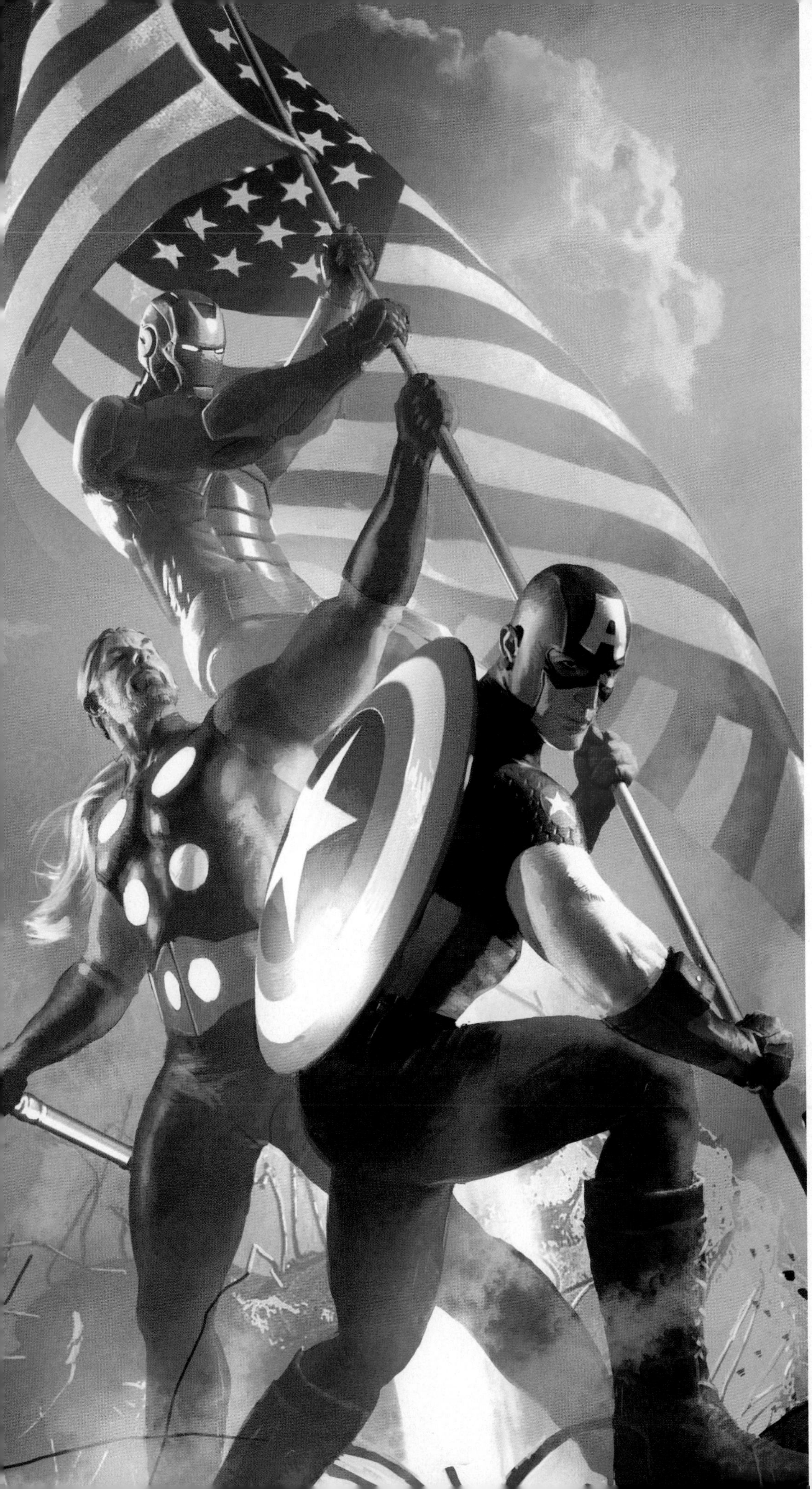

6

ULTIMATE COMICS **ULTIMATES** #18

S.H.I.E.L.D. SITUATION MAP:

[Anti-government militia hot spots]

Idaho, Montana,
N. Dakota, S. Dakota,
Wyoming

Wyoming
status unknown

[Eastern seaboard control zone]

New England,
New York,
New Jersey,
Delaware,
Washington, D.C.,
Maryland,
Pennsylvania,
Virginia

secured by
National Guard
under emergency
powers
committee

PROJECT
PEGASUS

ANTI-MATTER
NO FLY
ZONE

AREA OF
URBAN
UNREST

[Great Lakes Alliance]

Minnesota,
Wisconsin,
Michigan,
Illinois,
Indiana, Ohio

Independent
nation

ALL STATES
SHOWN IN WHITE
ARE U.S. GOVERNMENT-
CONTROLLED ZONES

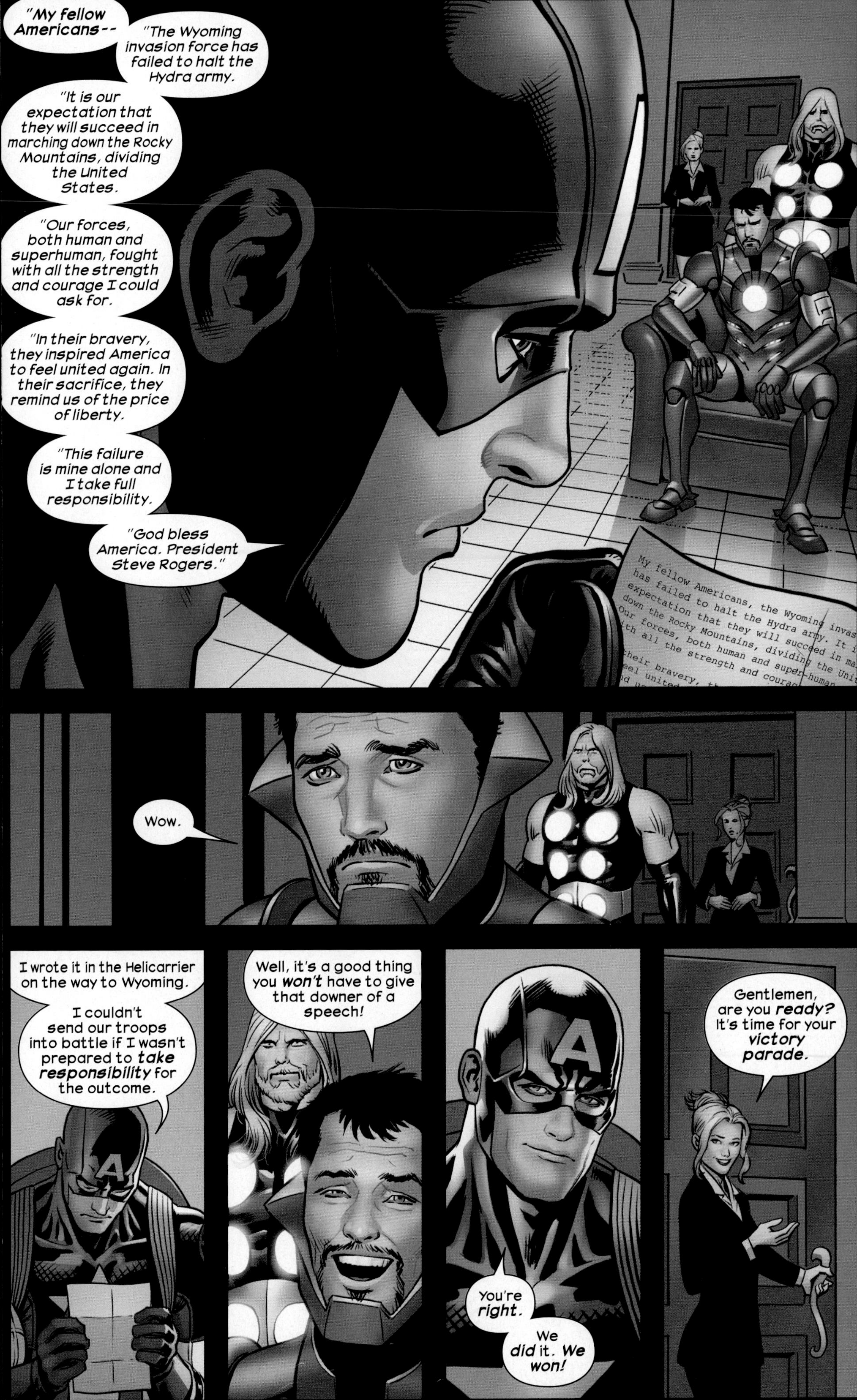
"My fellow Americans--
"The Wyoming invasion force has failed to halt the Hydra army.
"It is our expectation that they will succeed in marching down the Rocky Mountains, dividing the United States.
"Our forces, both human and superhuman, fought with all the strength and courage I could ask for.
"In their bravery, they inspired America to feel united again. In their sacrifice, they remind us of the price of liberty.
"This failure is mine alone and I take full responsibility.
"God bless America. President Steve Rogers."
My fellow Americans, the Wyoming
has failed to halt the Hydra
expectation that they will
down the Rocky Mountains, dividing the
Our forces, both human and
all the strength and
Wow.
I wrote it in the Helicarrier on the way to Wyoming.
I couldn't send our troops into battle if I wasn't prepared to take responsibility for the outcome.
Well, it's a good thing you won't have to give that downer of a speech!
You're right.
We did it. We won!
Gentlemen, are you ready? It's time for your victory parade.

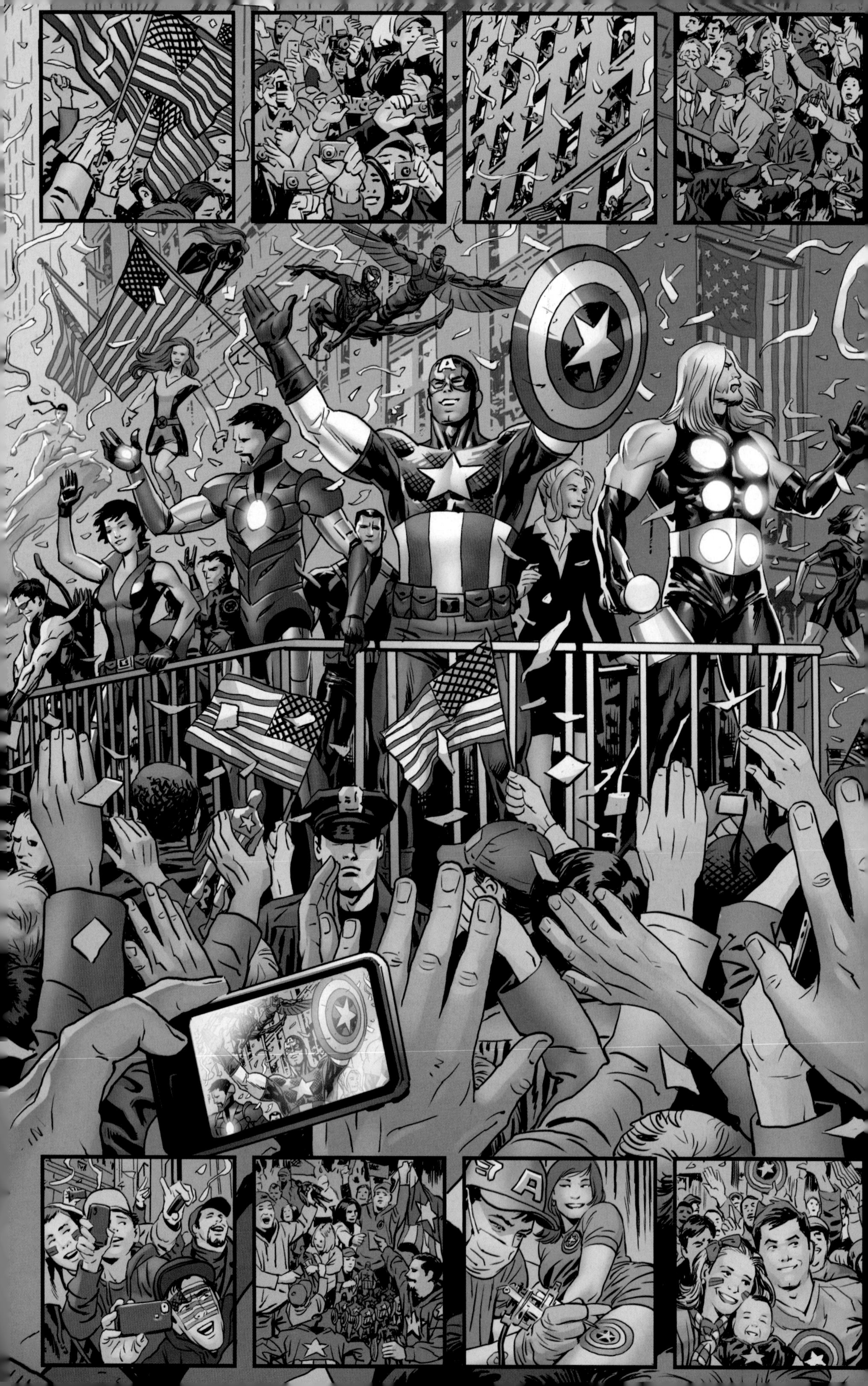

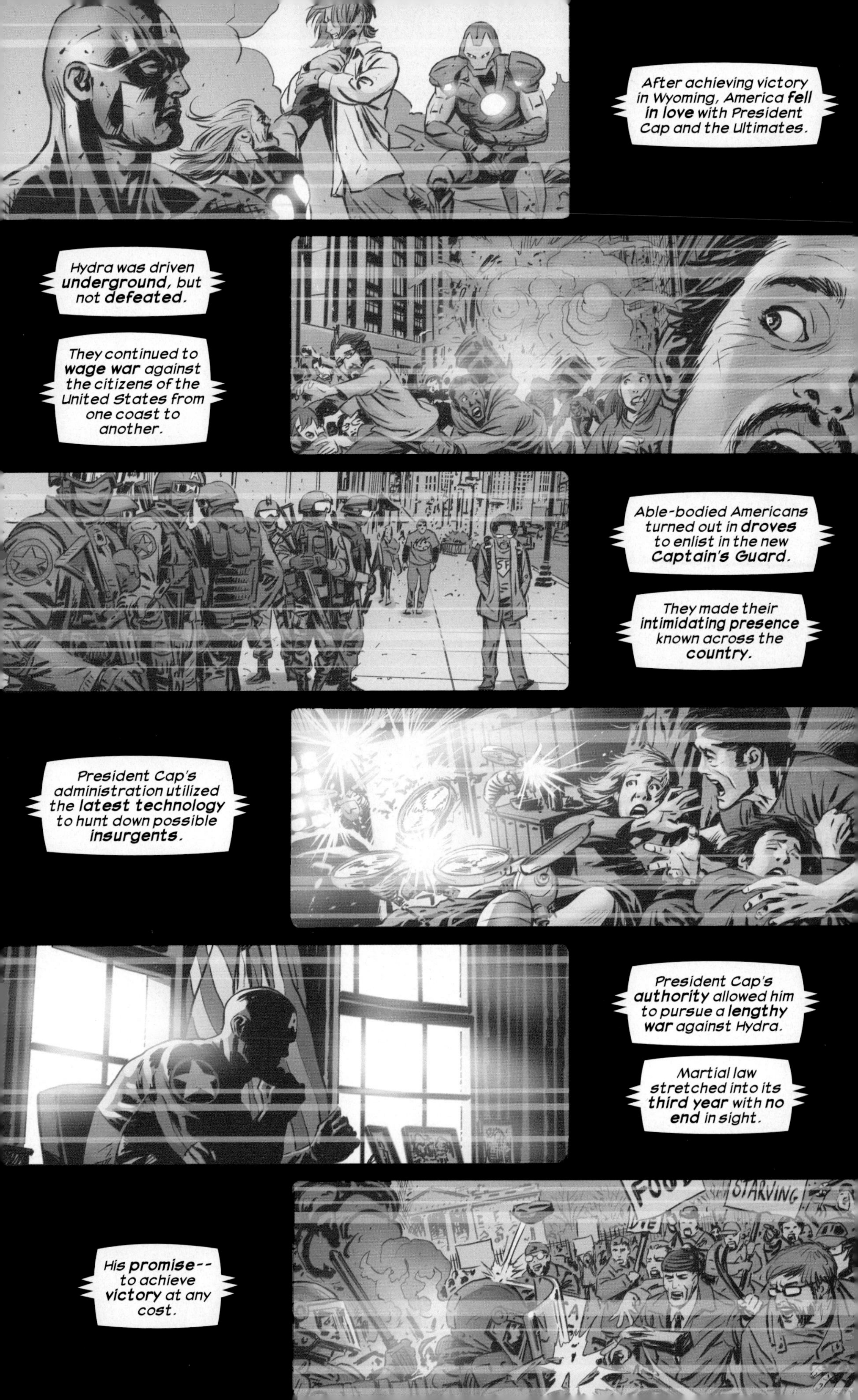
After achieving victory in Wyoming, America **fell in love** with President Cap and the Ultimates.
Hydra was driven **underground**, but not **defeated**.
They continued to **wage war** against the citizens of the United States from one coast to another.
Able-bodied Americans turned out in **droves** to enlist in the new ***Captain's Guard***.
They made their ***intimidating presence*** known across the **country**.
President Cap's administration utilized the ***latest technology*** to hunt down possible ***insurgents***.
President Cap's ***authority*** allowed him to pursue a ***lengthy war*** against Hydra.
Martial law stretched into its ***third year*** with ***no end*** in sight.
His ***promise***--to achieve ***victory*** at any cost.
FOO
STARVING

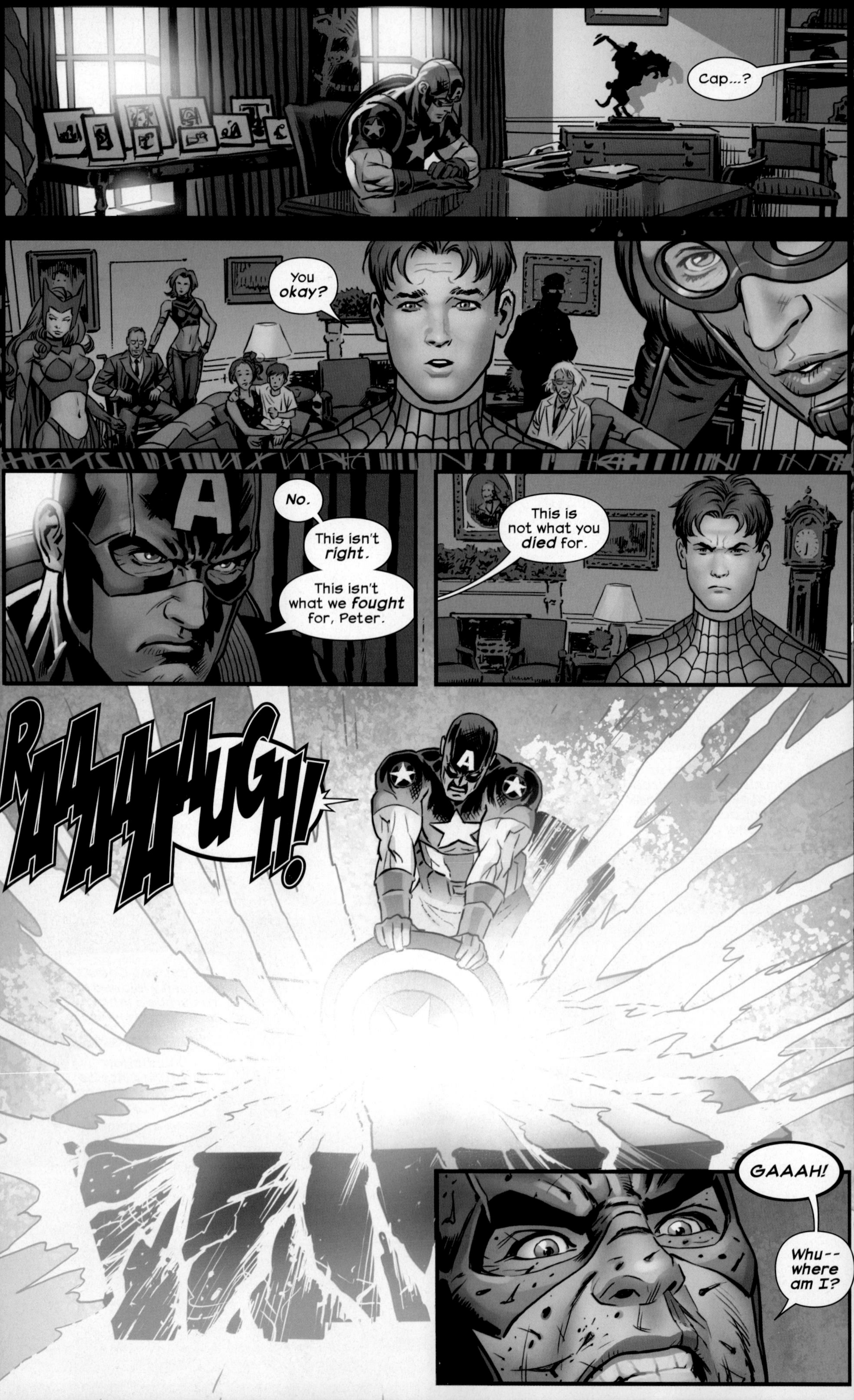
Cap...?
You okay?
No.
This isn't right.
This isn't what we fought for, Peter.
This is not what you died for.
RAAAAAUGH!
GAAAH!
Whu-- where am I?

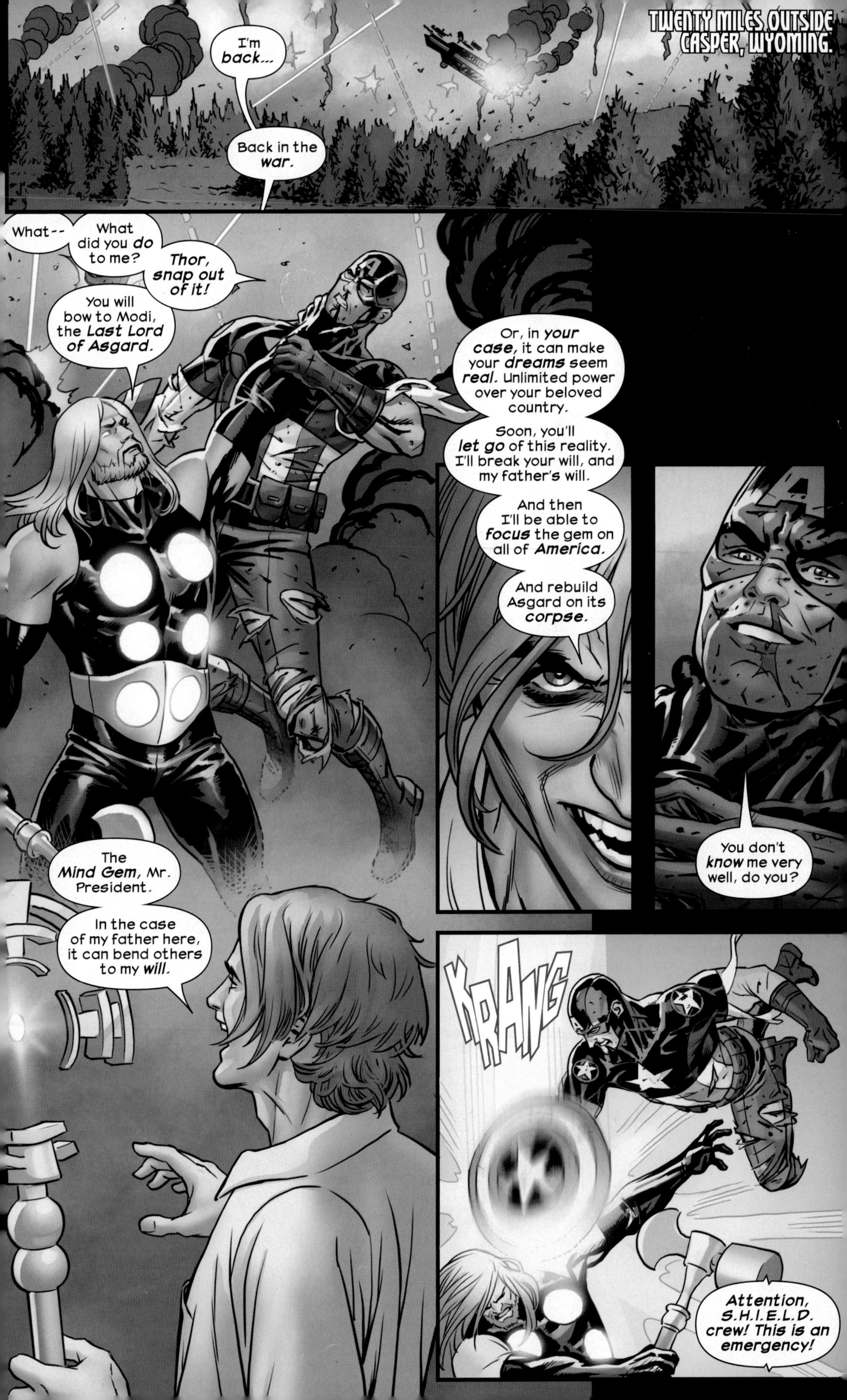

TWENTY MILES OUTSIDE CASPER, WYOMING.
I'm back...
Back in the war.
What--
What did you do to me?
Thor, snap out of it!
You will bow to Modi, the Last Lord of Asgard.
The Mind Gem, Mr. President.
In the case of my father here, it can bend others to my will.
Or, in your case, it can make your dreams seem real. Unlimited power over your beloved country.
Soon, you'll let go of this reality. I'll break your will, and my father's will.
And then I'll be able to focus the gem on all of America.
And rebuild Asgard on its corpse.
You don't know me very well, do you?
KRANG
Attention, S.H.I.E.L.D. crew! This is an emergency!

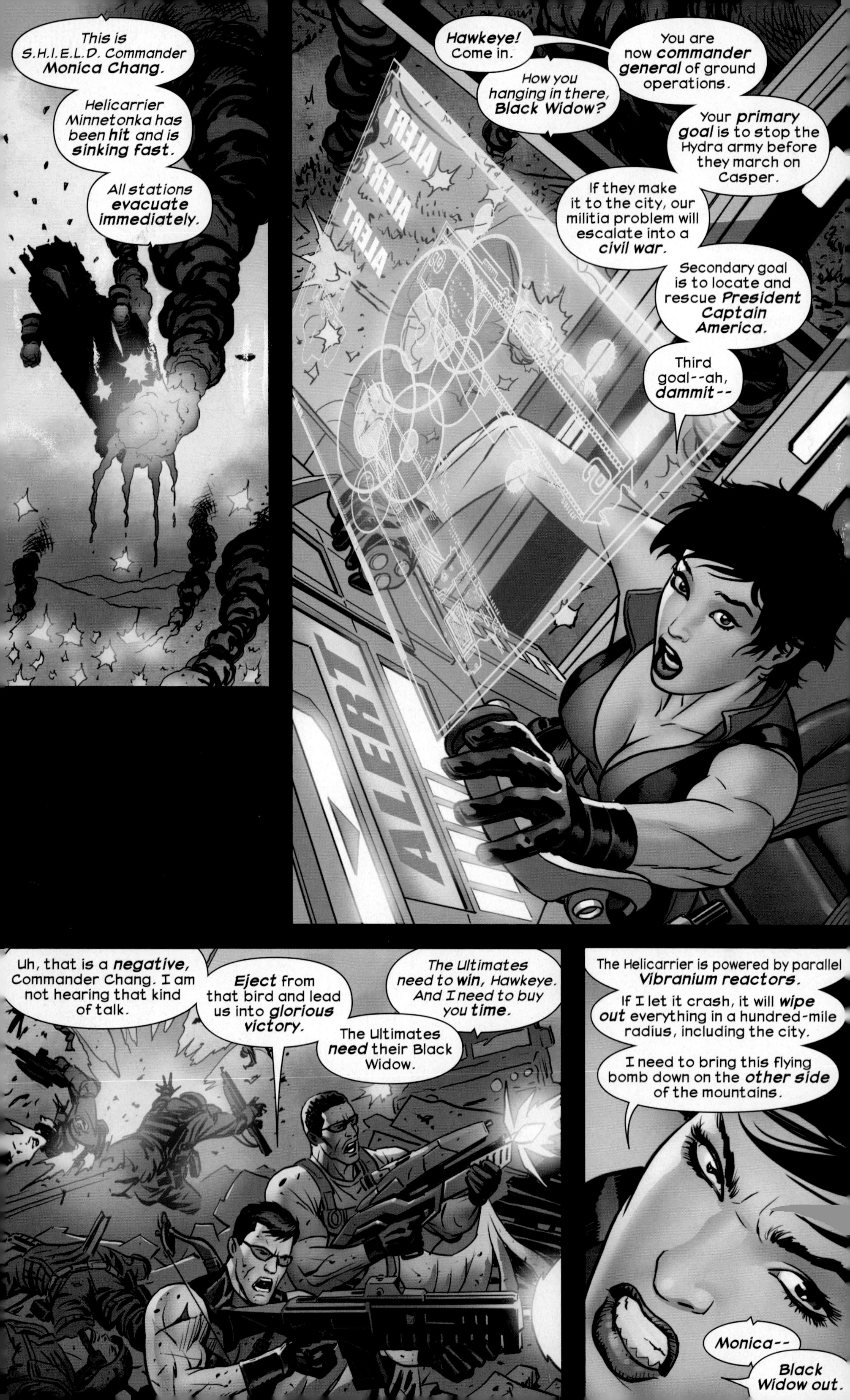
This is S.H.I.E.L.D. Commander Monica Chang.
Helicarrier Minnetonka has been hit and is sinking fast.
All stations evacuate immediately.
Hawkeye! Come in.
How you hanging in there, Black Widow?
You are now commander general of ground operations.
Your primary goal is to stop the Hydra army before they march on Casper.
If they make it to the city, our militia problem will escalate into a civil war.
Secondary goal is to locate and rescue President Captain America.
Third goal--ah, dammit--
ALERT
ALERT
ALERT
ALERT
Uh, that is a negative, Commander Chang. I am not hearing that kind of talk.
Eject from that bird and lead us into glorious victory.
The Ultimates need to win, Hawkeye. And I need to buy you time.
The Ultimates need their Black Widow.
The Helicarrier is powered by parallel Vibranium reactors.
If I let it crash, it will wipe out everything in a hundred-mile radius, including the city.
I need to bring this flying bomb down on the other side of the mountains.
Monica--
Black Widow out.

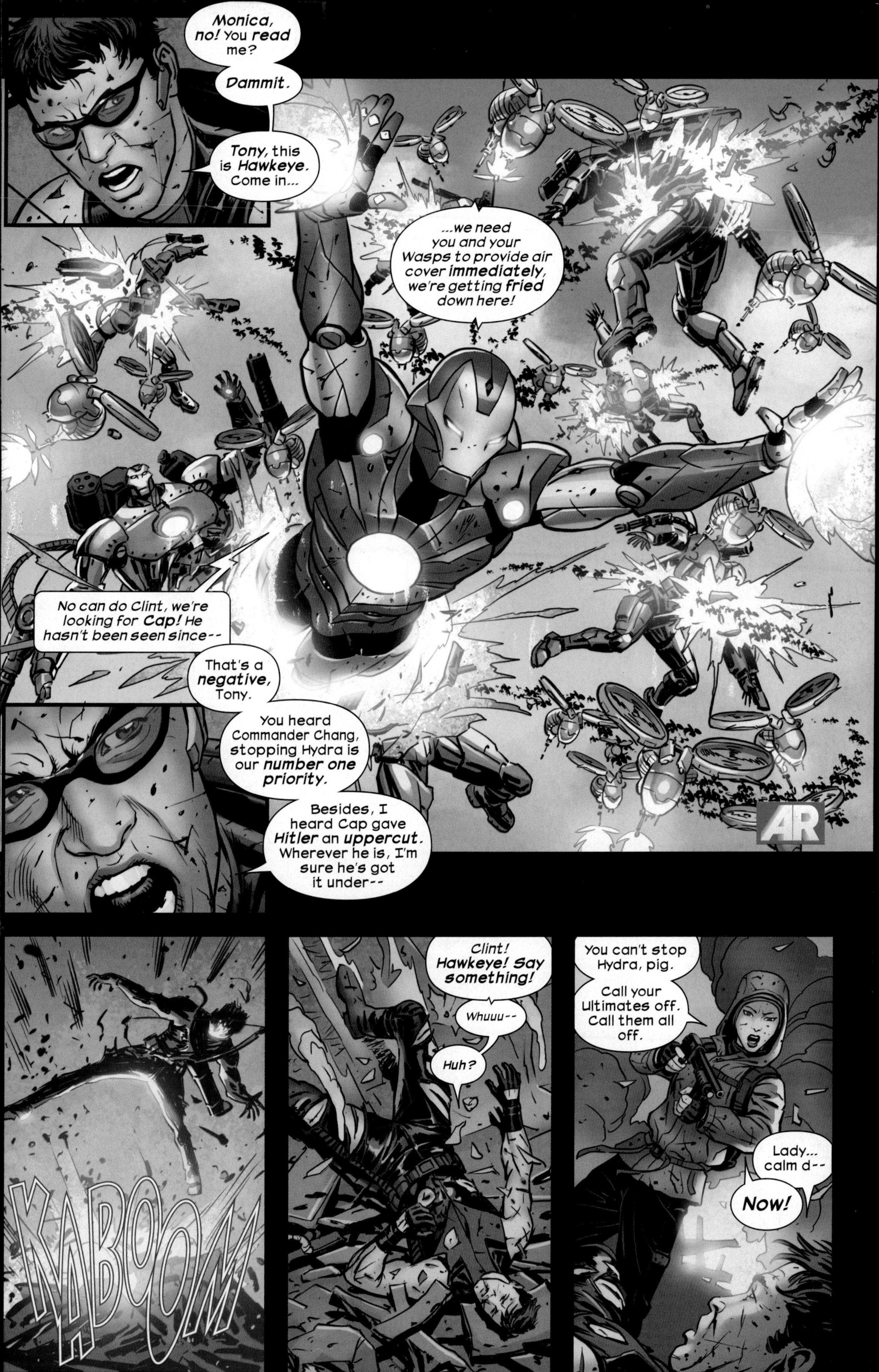

Monica, no! You read me?
Dammit.
Tony, this is Hawkeye. Come in...
...we need you and your Wasps to provide air cover immediately, we're getting fried down here!
No can do Clint, we're looking for Cap! He hasn't been seen since--
That's a negative, Tony.
You heard Commander Chang, stopping Hydra is our number one priority.
Besides, I heard Cap gave Hitler an uppercut. Wherever he is, I'm sure he's got it under--
KABOOOM
Clint! Hawkeye! Say something!
Whuuu--
Huh?
You can't stop Hydra, pig.
Call your Ultimates off. Call them all off.
Lady... calm d--
Now!

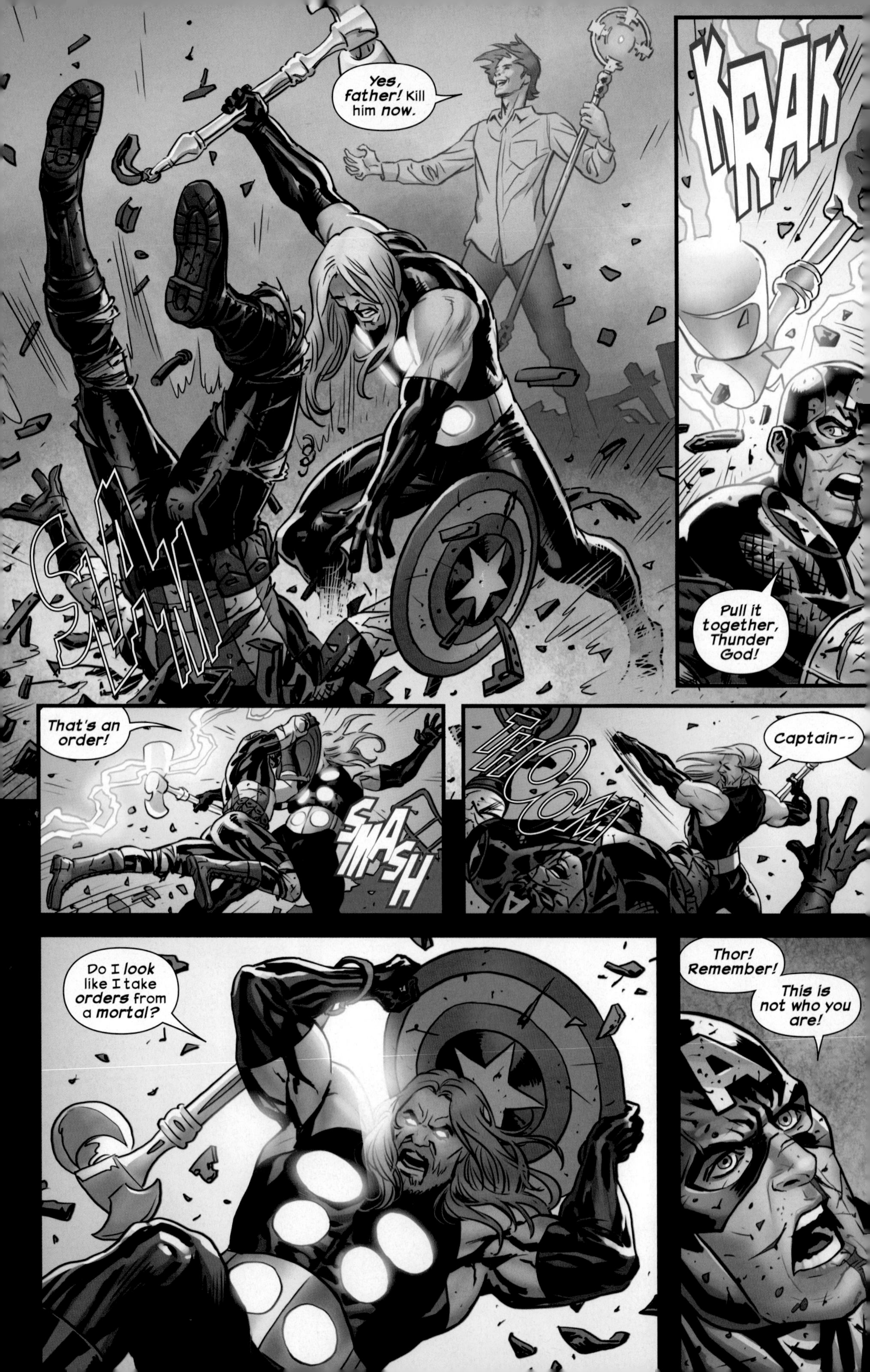
Yes, father! Kill him now.
KRAK
SLAM
Pull it together, Thunder God!
That's an order!
SMASH
THOOM
Captain--
Do I look like I take orders from a mortal?
Thor! Remember!
This is not who you are!

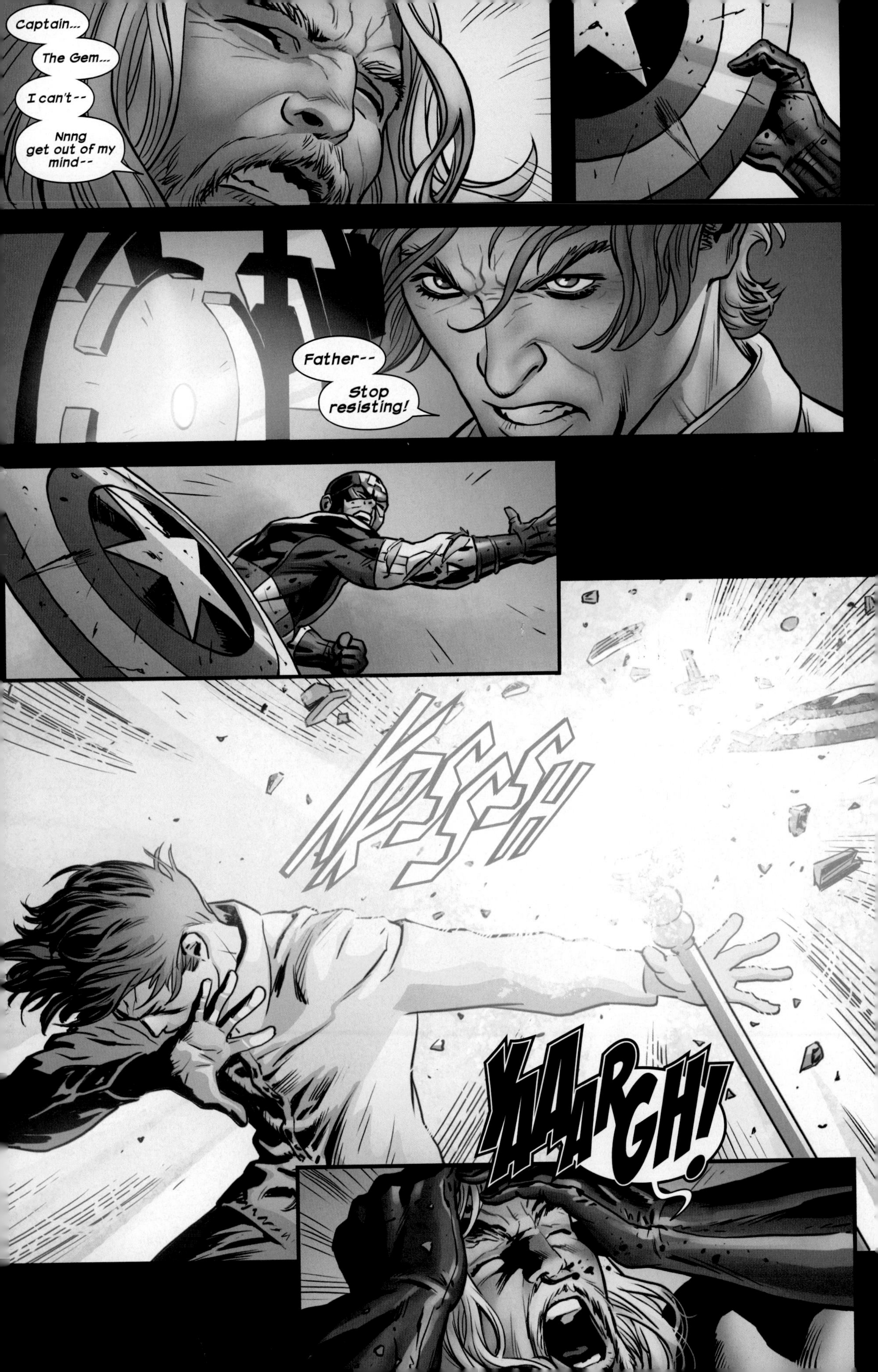
Captain...
The Gem...
I can't--
Nnng get out of my mind--
Father--
Stop resisting!
KRSSH
KYAARGH!

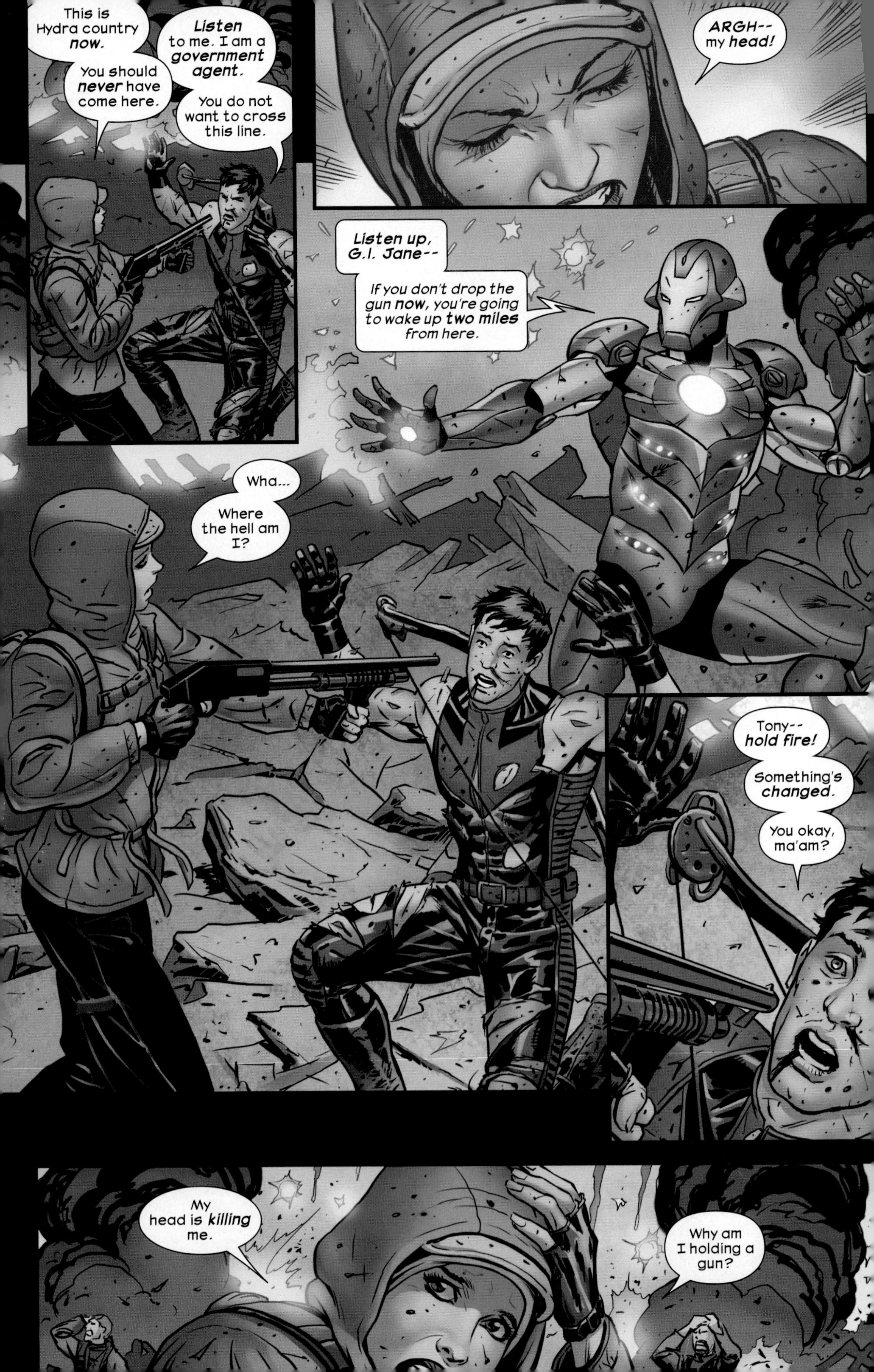

This is Hydra country now.
You should never have come here.
Listen to me. I am a government agent.
You do not want to cross this line.
ARGH-- my head!
Listen up, G.I. Jane--
If you don't drop the gun now, you're going to wake up two miles from here.
Wha...
Where the hell am I?
Tony-- hold fire!
Something's changed.
You okay, ma'am?
My head is killing me.
Why am I holding a gun?

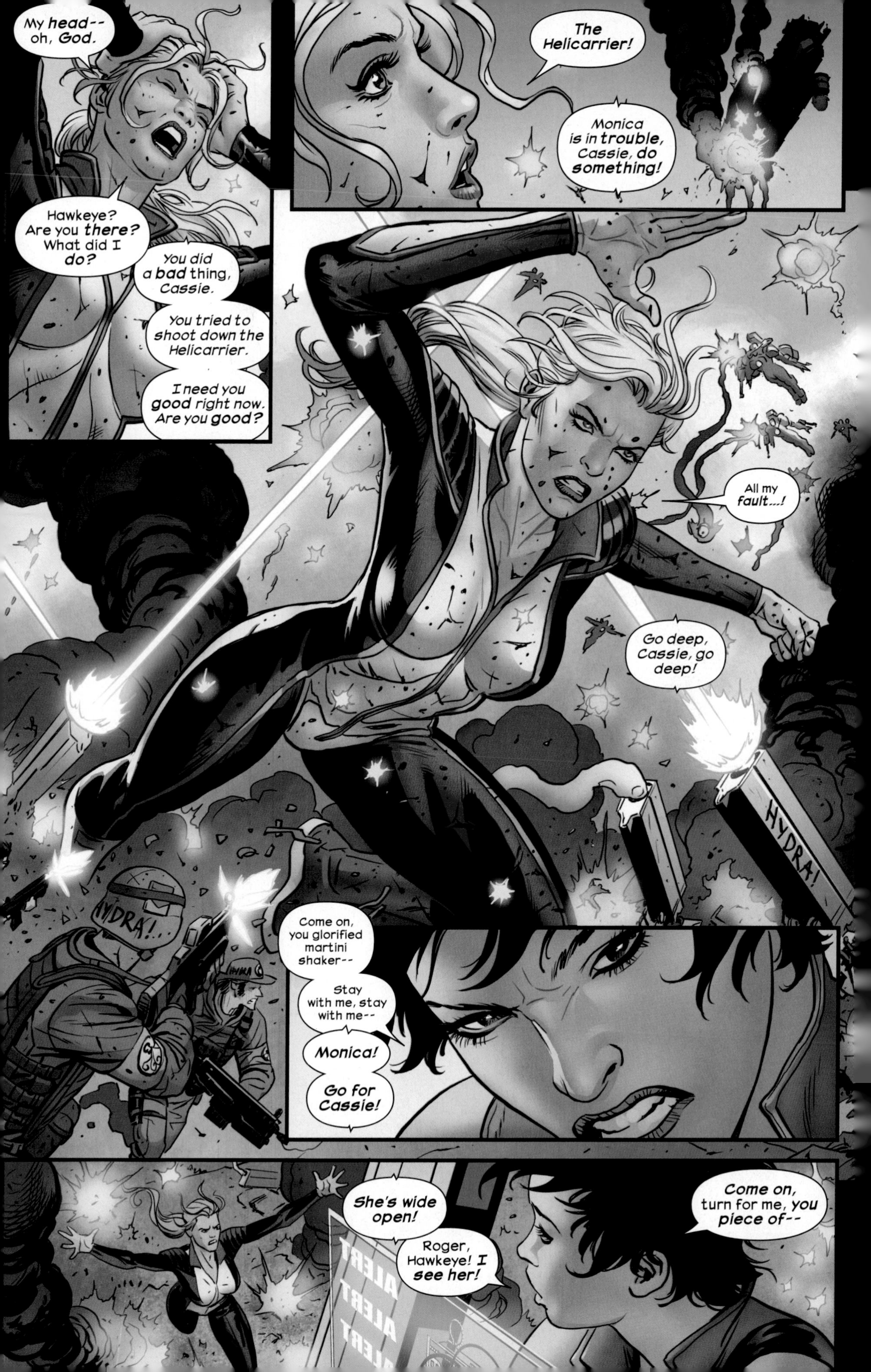
My head--
oh, God.
The Helicarrier!
Monica is in trouble, Cassie, do something!
Hawkeye? Are you there? What did I do?
You did a bad thing, Cassie.
You tried to shoot down the Helicarrier.
I need you good right now. Are you good?
All my fault...!
Go deep, Cassie, go deep!
HYDRA!
HYDRA!
Come on, you glorified martini shaker--
Stay with me, stay with me--
Monica!
Go for Cassie!
She's wide open!
Roger, Hawkeye! I see her!
Come on, turn for me, you piece of--
ALERT
ALERT
ALERT

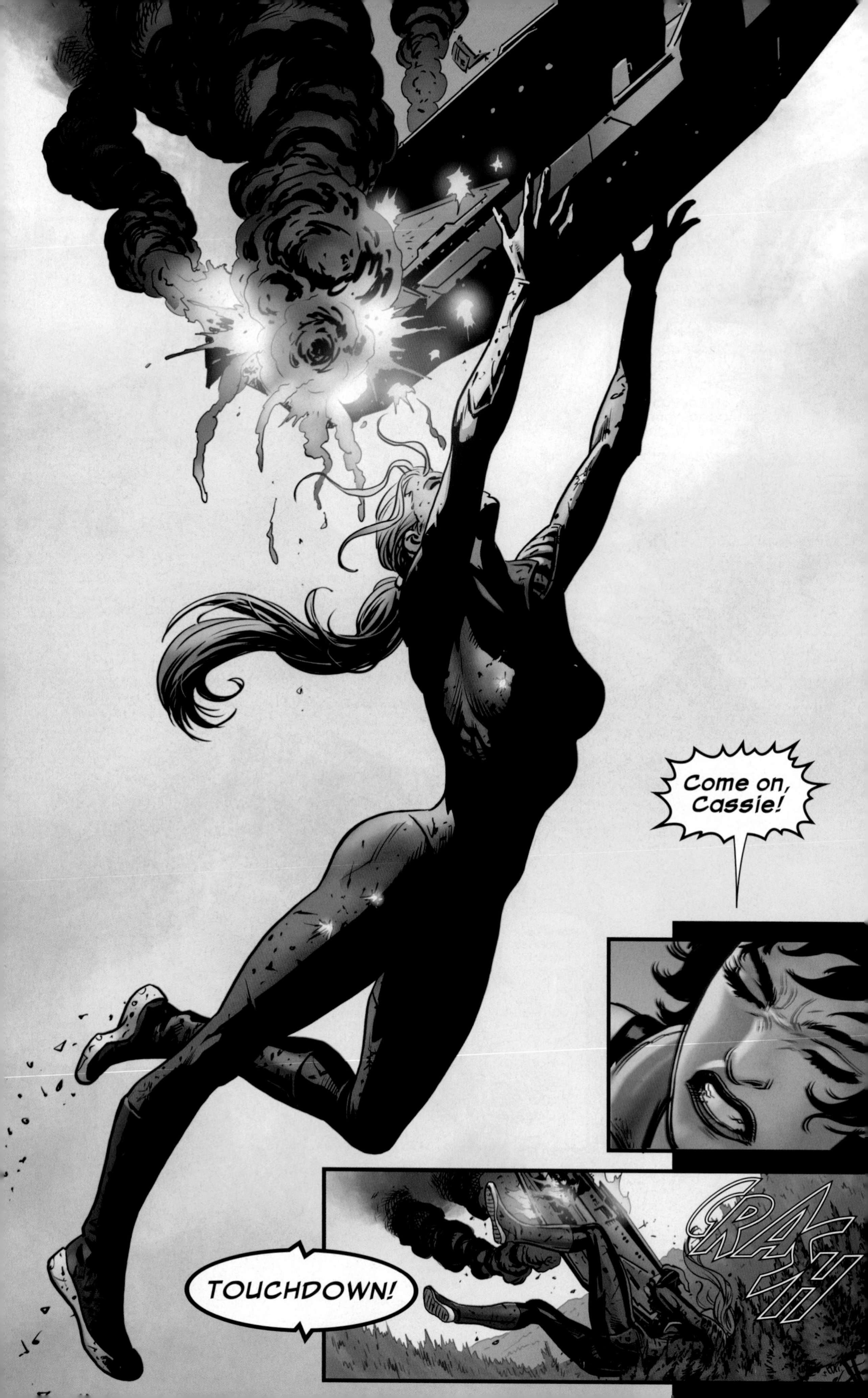
Come on, Cassie!
TOUCHDOWN!
CRAASH

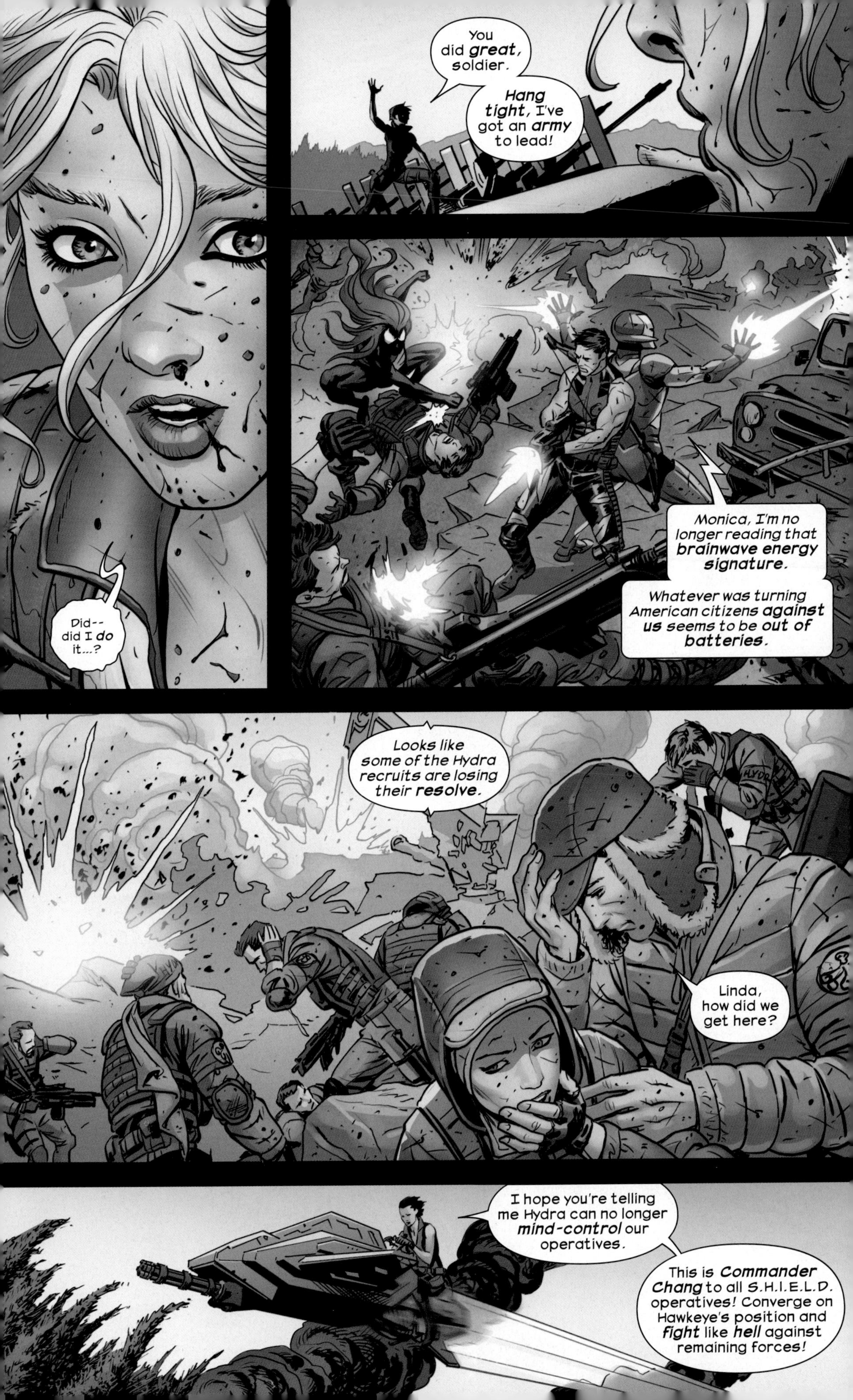
You did great, soldier.
Hang tight, I've got an army to lead!
Did-- did I do it...?
Monica, I'm no longer reading that brainwave energy signature.
Whatever was turning American citizens against us seems to be out of batteries.
Looks like some of the Hydra recruits are losing their resolve.
Linda, how did we get here?
I hope you're telling me Hydra can no longer mind-control our operatives.
This is Commander Chang to all S.H.I.E.L.D. operatives! Converge on Hawkeye's position and fight like hell against remaining forces!

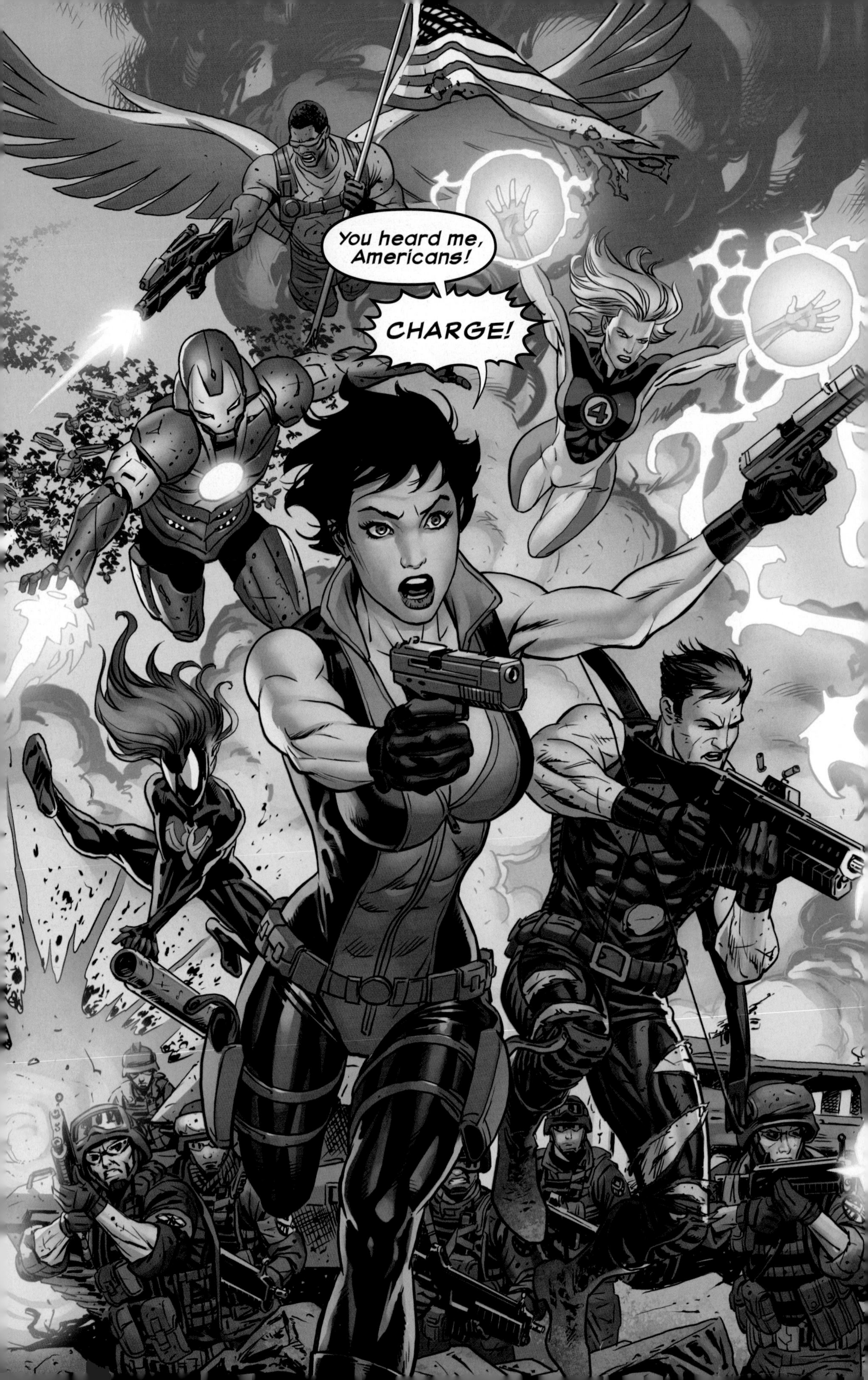
You heard me, Americans!
CHARGE!

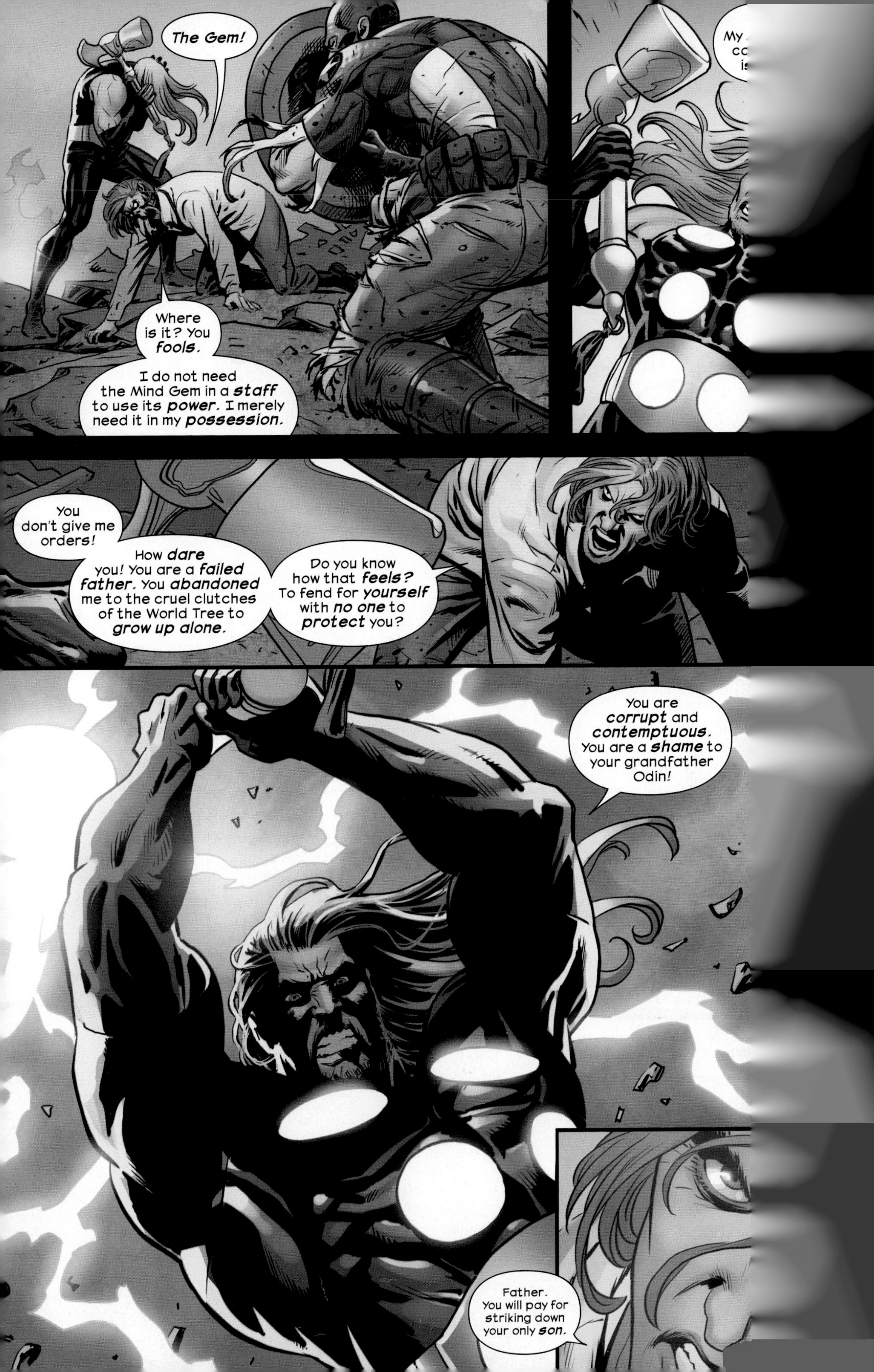
The Gem!
Where is it? You fools.
I do not need the Mind Gem in a staff to use its power. I merely need it in my possession.
You don't give me orders!
How dare you! You are a failed father. You abandoned me to the cruel clutches of the World Tree to grow up alone.
Do you know how that feels? To fend for yourself with no one to protect you?
You are corrupt and contemptuous. You are a shame to your grandfather Odin!
Father. You will pay for striking down your only son.

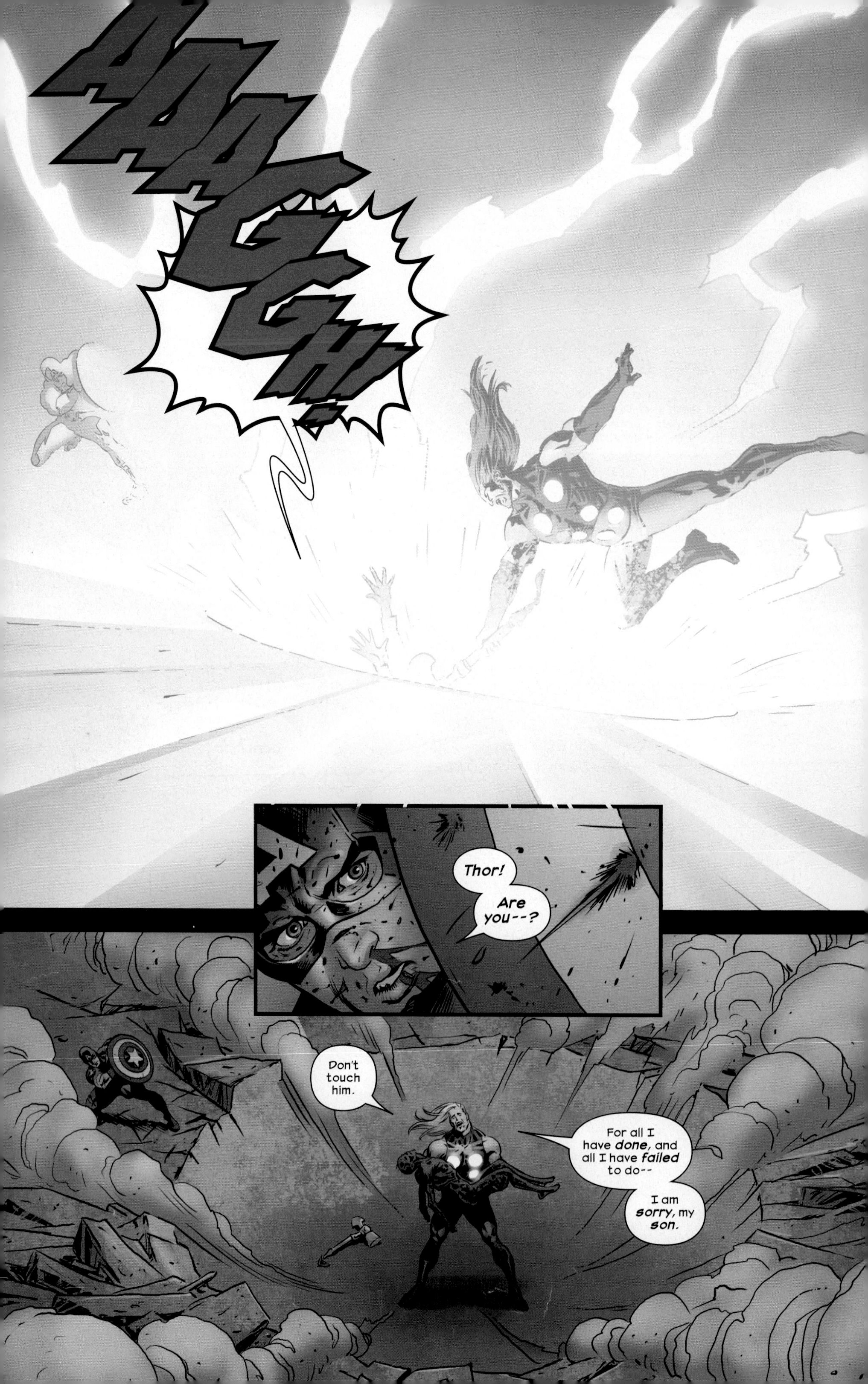
AAAGGH!!
Thor!
Are you--?
Don't touch him.
For all I have done, and all I have failed to do--
I am sorry, my son.

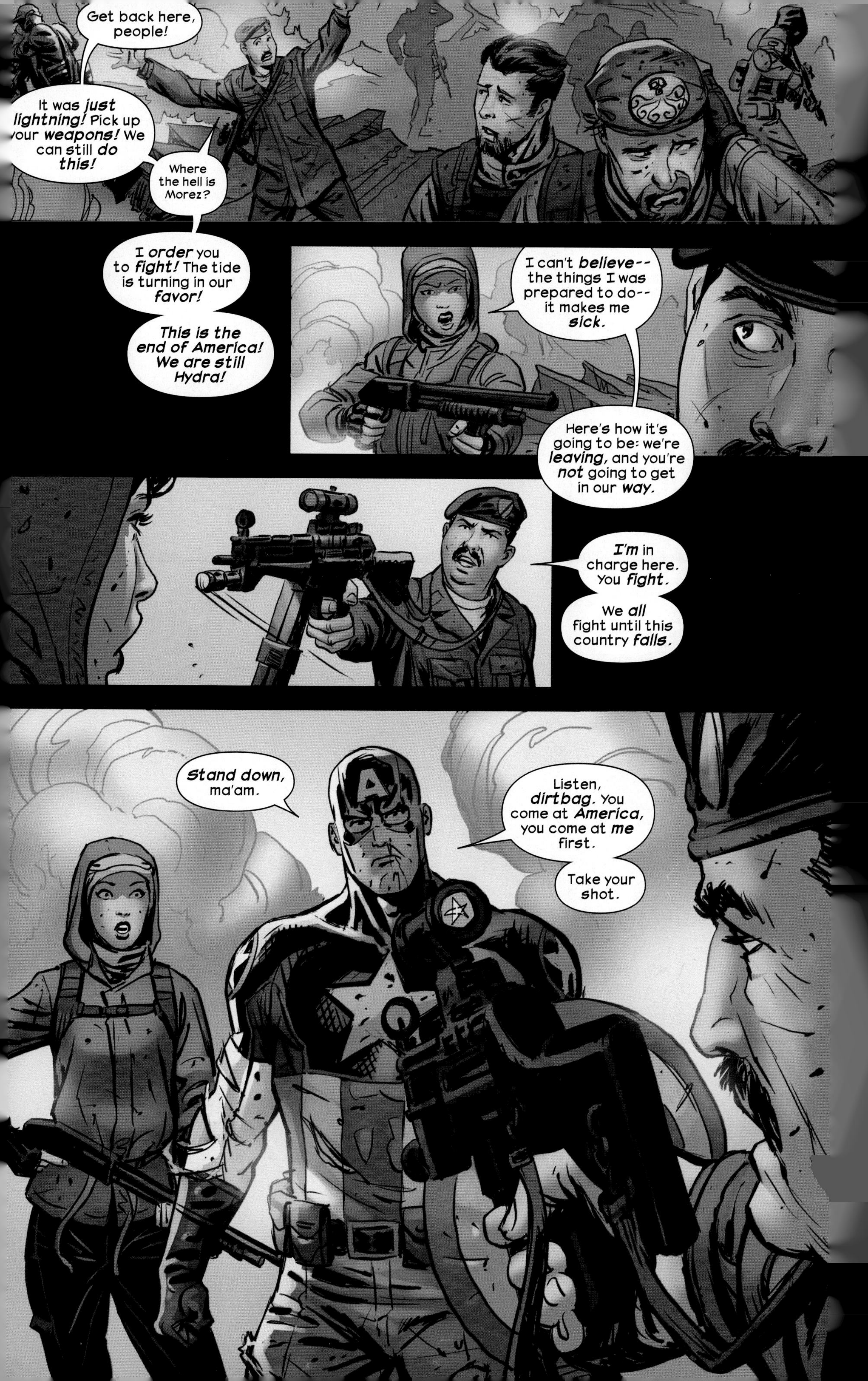
Get back here, people!
It was just lightning! Pick up your weapons! We can still do this!
Where the hell is Morez?
I order you to fight! The tide is turning in our favor!
This is the end of America! We are still Hydra!
I can't believe-- the things I was prepared to do-- it makes me sick.
Here's how it's going to be: we're leaving, and you're not going to get in our way.
I'm in charge here. You fight.
We all fight until this country falls.
Stand down, ma'am.
Listen, dirtbag. You come at America, you come at me first.
Take your shot.

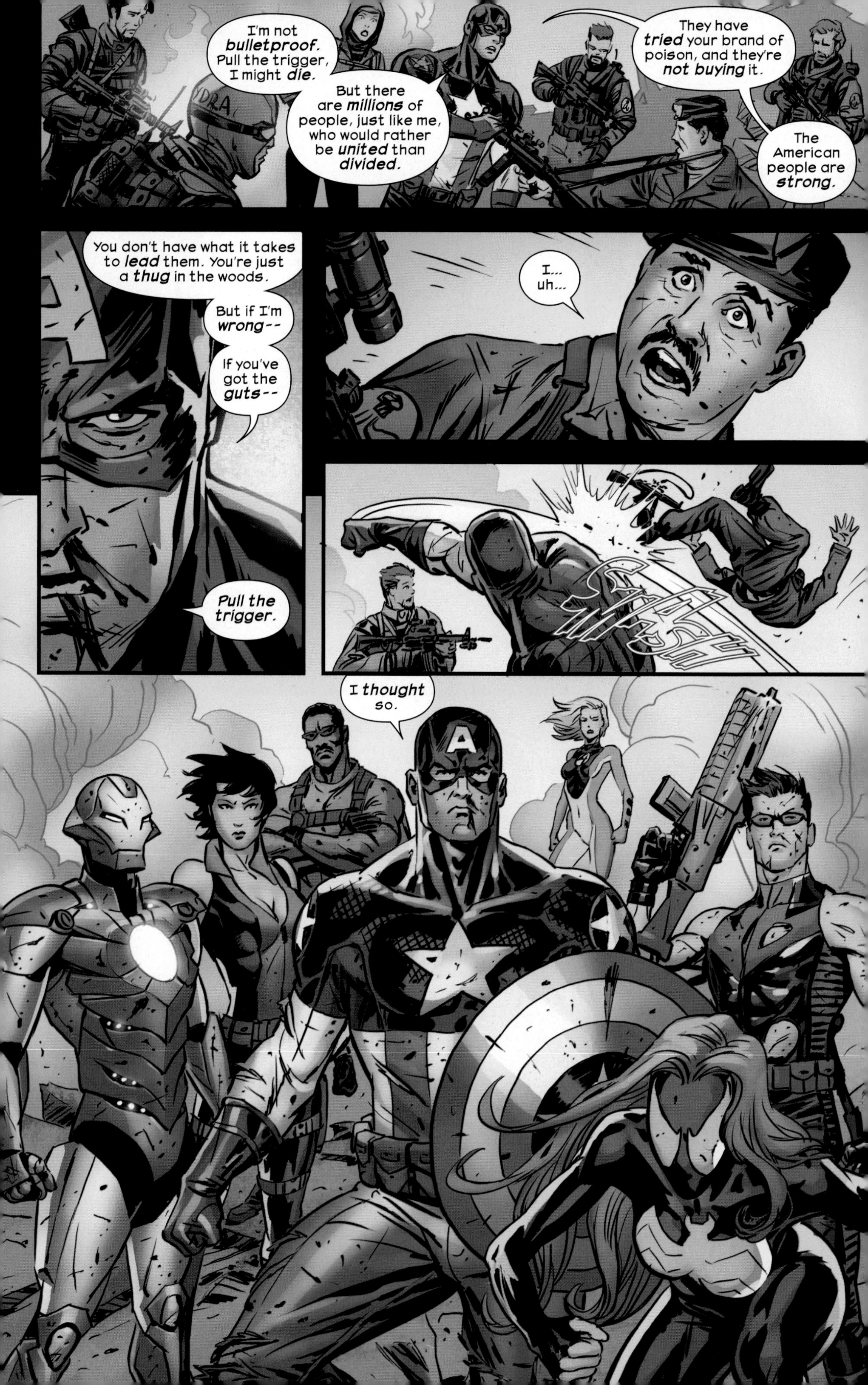
I'm not bulletproof. Pull the trigger, I might die.
But there are millions of people, just like me, who would rather be united than divided.
They have tried your brand of poison, and they're not buying it.
The American people are strong.
You don't have what it takes to lead them. You're just a thug in the woods.
But if I'm wrong--
If you've got the guts--
Pull the trigger.
I... uh...
I thought so.

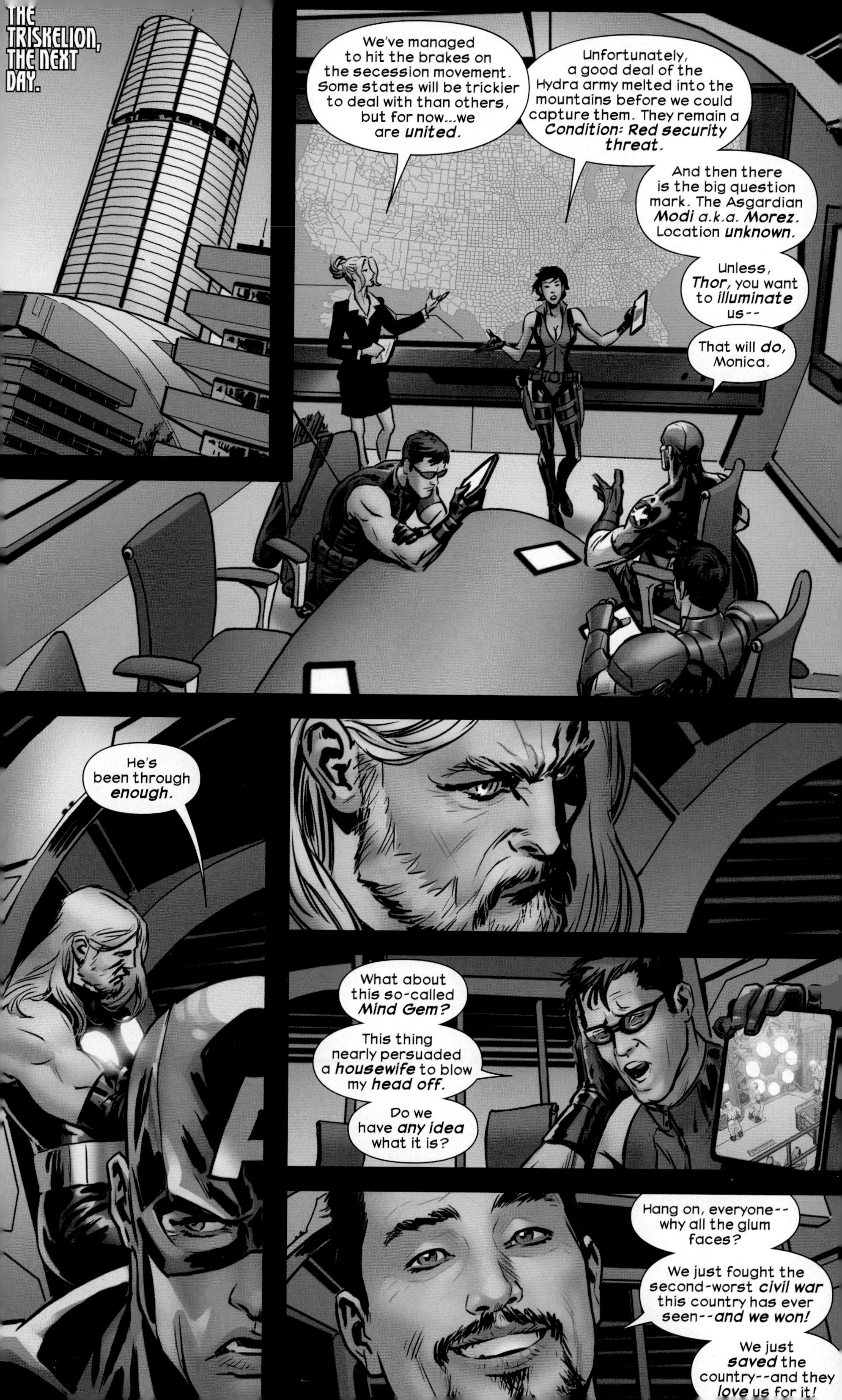
THE TRISKELION, THE NEXT DAY.
We've managed to hit the brakes on the secession movement. Some states will be trickier to deal with than others, but for now...we are united.
Unfortunately, a good deal of the Hydra army melted into the mountains before we could capture them. They remain a Condition: Red security threat.
And then there is the big question mark. The Asgardian Modi a.k.a. Morez. Location unknown.
Unless, Thor, you want to illuminate us--
That will do, Monica.
He's been through enough.
What about this so-called Mind Gem?
This thing nearly persuaded a housewife to blow my head off.
Do we have any idea what it is?
Hang on, everyone--why all the glum faces?
We just fought the second-worst civil war this country has ever seen--and we won!
We just saved the country--and they love us for it!

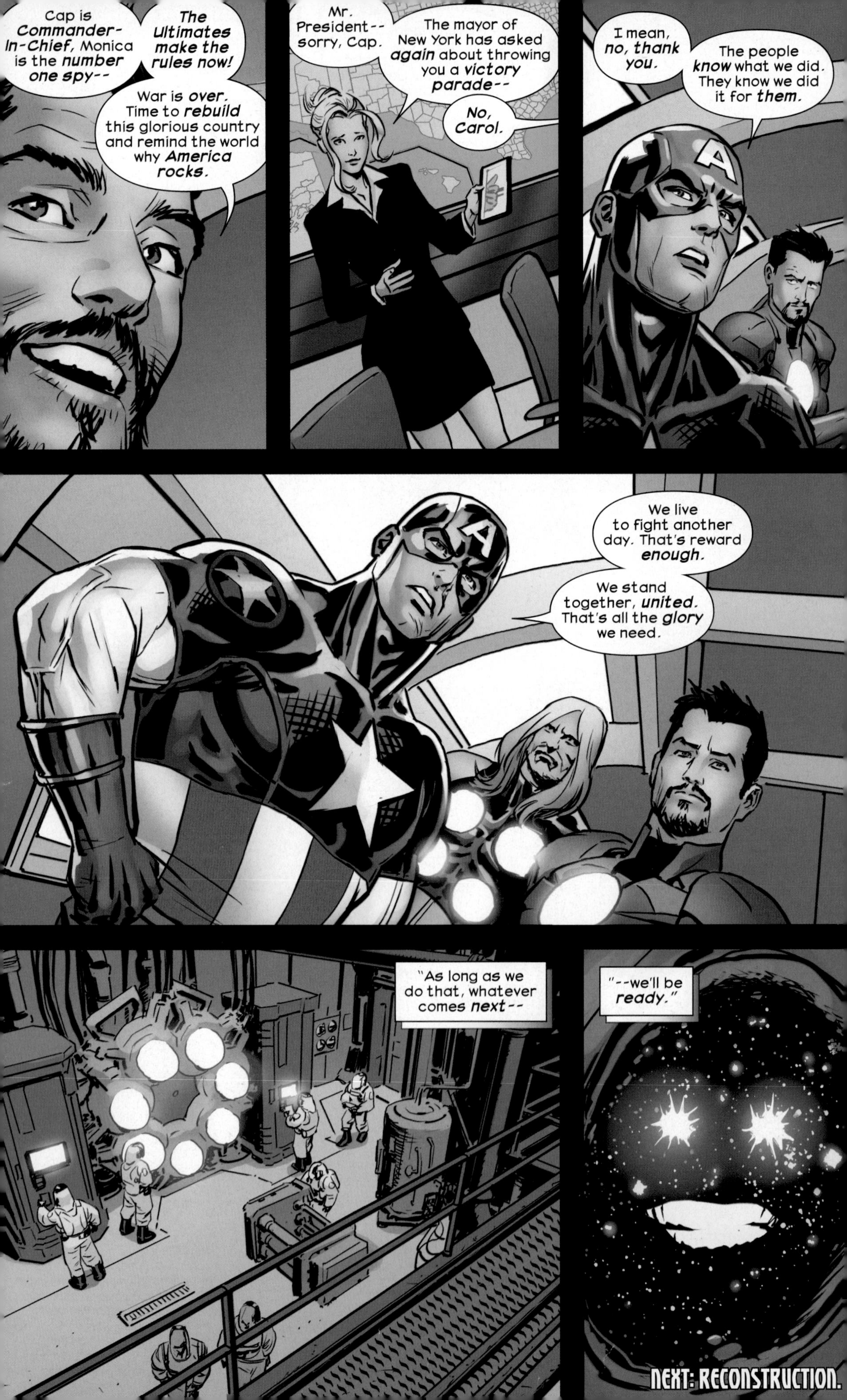

Cap is Commander-In-Chief, Monica is the number one spy--
The Ultimates make the rules now!
War is over. Time to rebuild this glorious country and remind the world why America rocks.
Mr. President--sorry, Cap.
The mayor of New York has asked again about throwing you a victory parade--
No, Carol.
I mean, no, thank you.
The people know what we did. They know we did it for them.
We live to fight another day. That's reward enough.
We stand together, united. That's all the glory we need.
"As long as we do that, whatever comes next--
"--we'll be ready."
NEXT: RECONSTRUCTION.

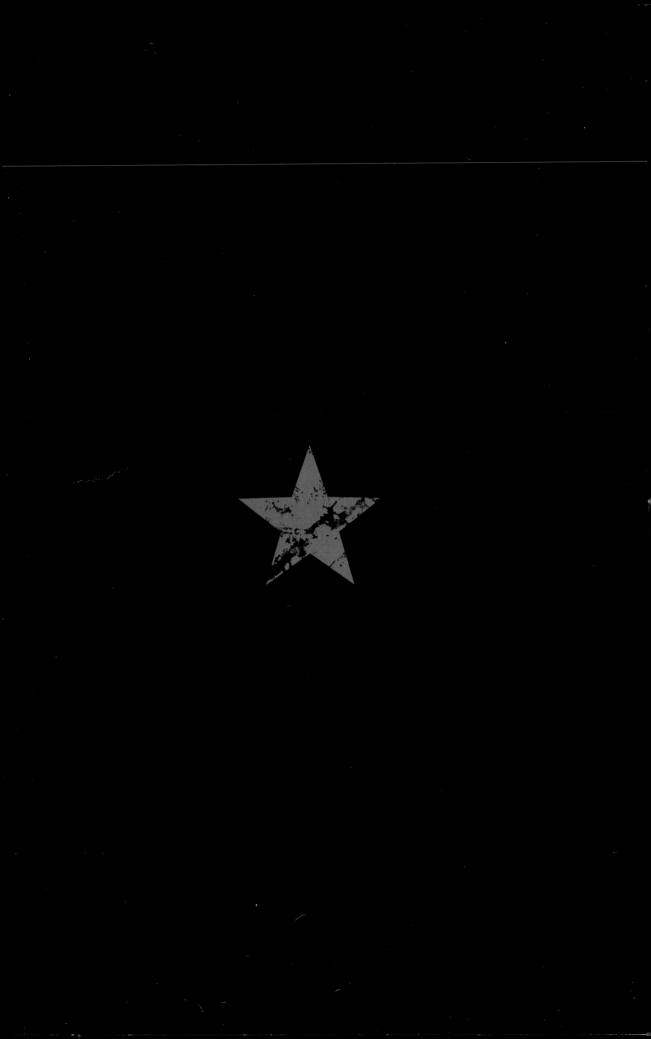

7

★

ULTIMATE COMICS **X-MEN** #13

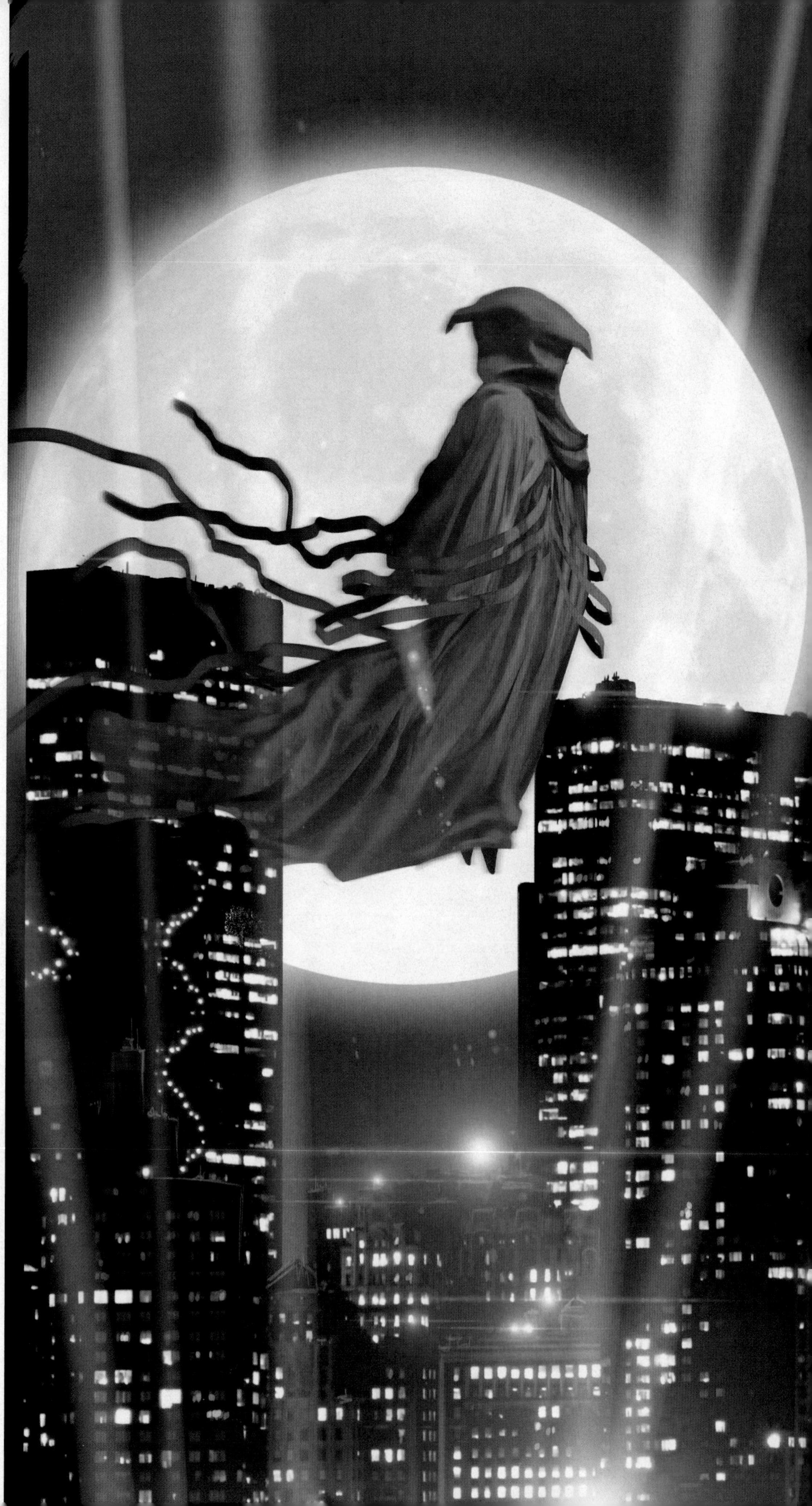

HATED AND FEARED MORE THAN EVER, ONE GROUP OF YOUNG HEROES HAS BANDED TOGETHER TO FIGHT BACK.

X-MEN

OKLAHOMA CITY, OKLAHOMA

ALBUQUERQUE, NEW MEXICO

PHOENIX, ARIZONA

LAS VEGAS, NEVADA

PREVIOUSLY:

After Magneto's Ultimatum Wave caused worldwide calamity, Executive Order 3144 was put into action, allowing mutants to be shot on sight if they refused to turn themselves over to authorities.

William Stryker Jr. (a powerful leader of the anti-mutant movement in America) "died" and transferred his consciousness into the government-sanctioned Nimrod Sentinel army. These killing machines have unleashed a campaign of hate and violence against mutantkind. Focusing their attention on the mutant containment camps in the Southwestern states, the Sentinels' murderous mission has forced the already-taxed government into defeat.

In a press conference to the nation, the President reveals that the country had no choice but to give up the Southwestern states to the Sentinels, advising everyone to seek shelter from the deadly automatons. With martial law in effect and Sentinels bringing mutants closer and closer to extinction, who can rise up to save the nation from the edge of destruction?

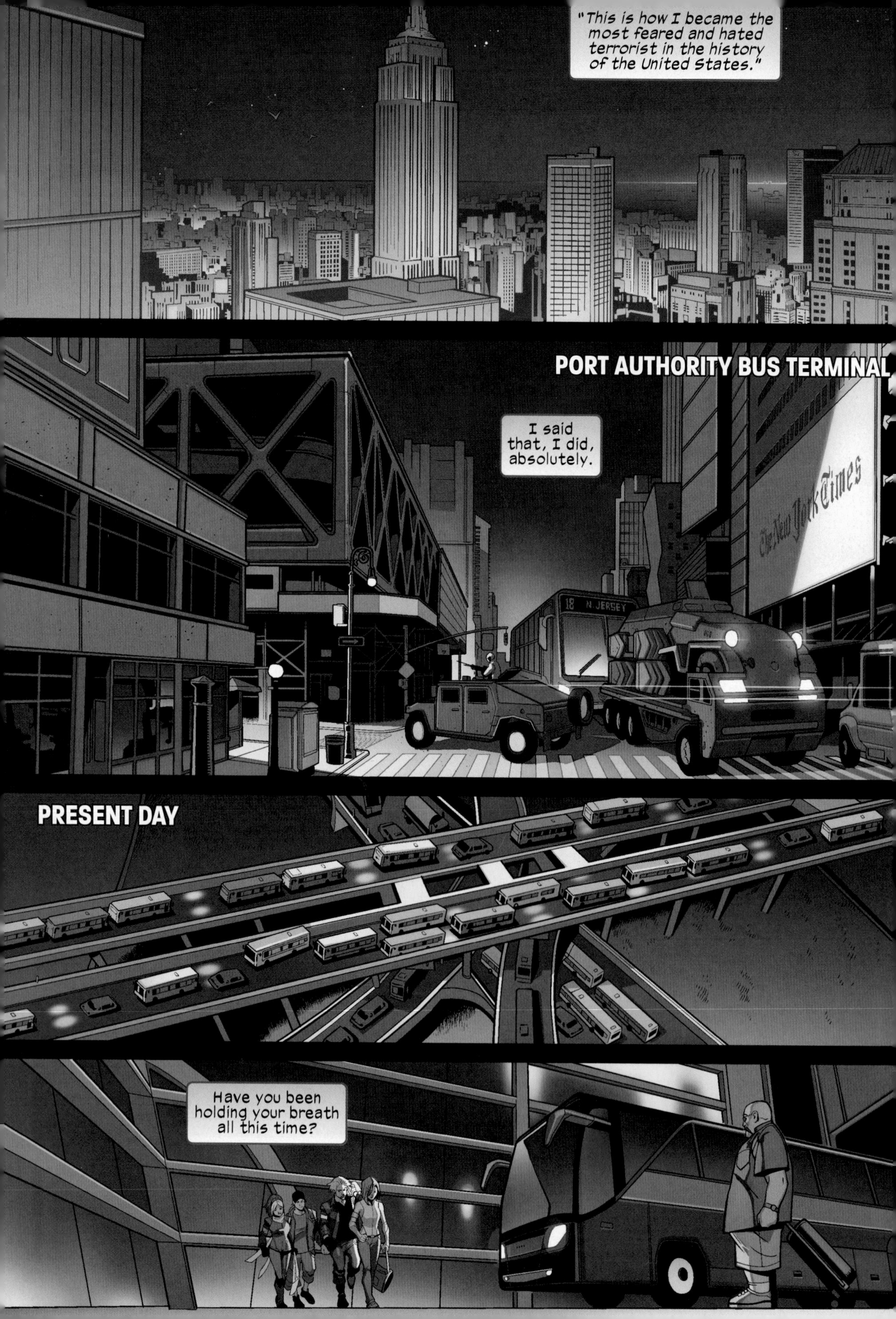
"This is how I became the most feared and hated terrorist in the history of the United States."
PORT AUTHORITY BUS TERMINAL
I said that, I did, absolutely.
18 N. JERSEY
The New York Times
PRESENT DAY
Have you been holding your breath all this time?

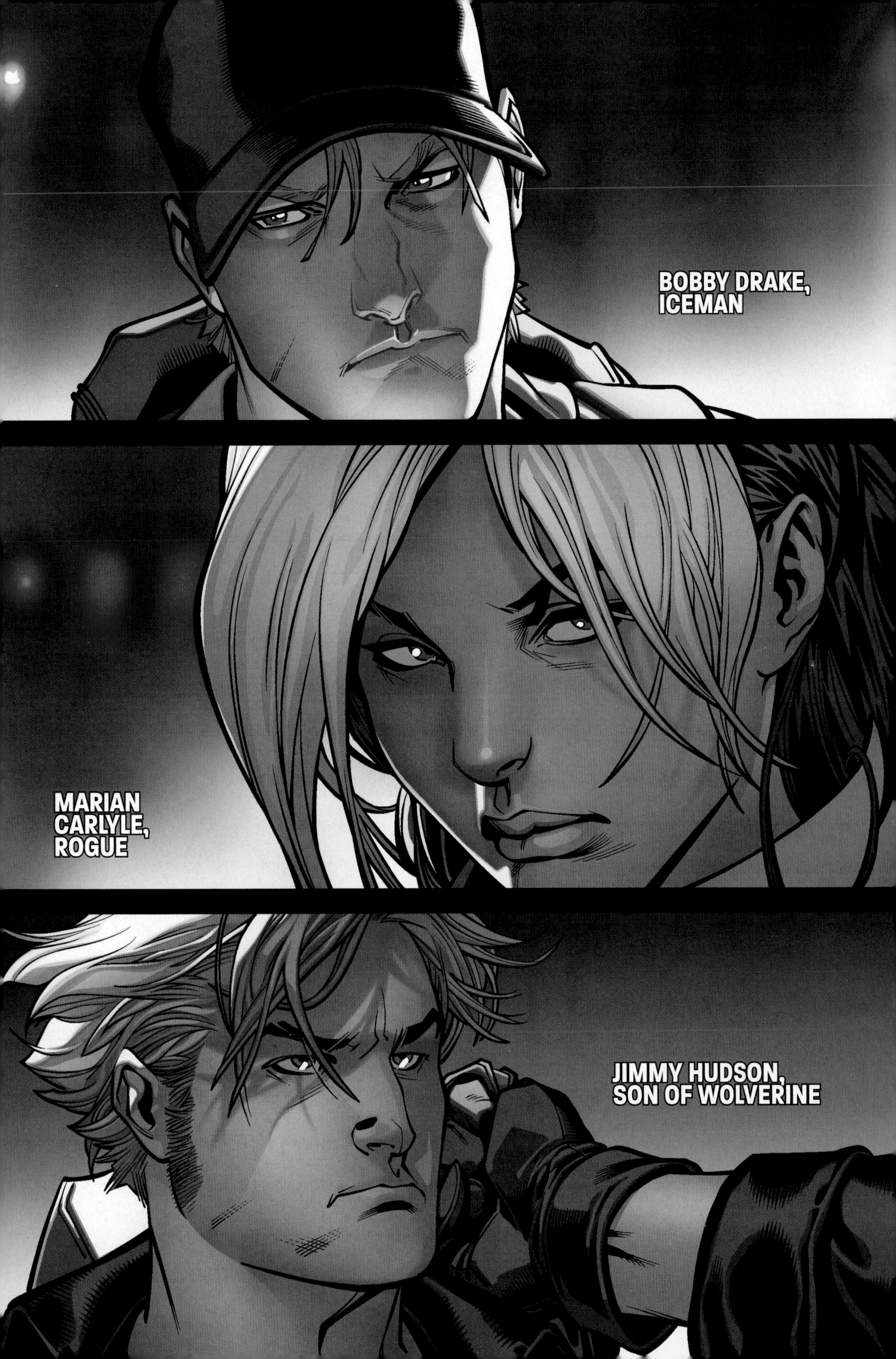
BOBBY DRAKE,
ICEMAN
MARIAN
CARLYLE,
ROGUE
JIMMY HUDSON,
SON OF WOLVERINE

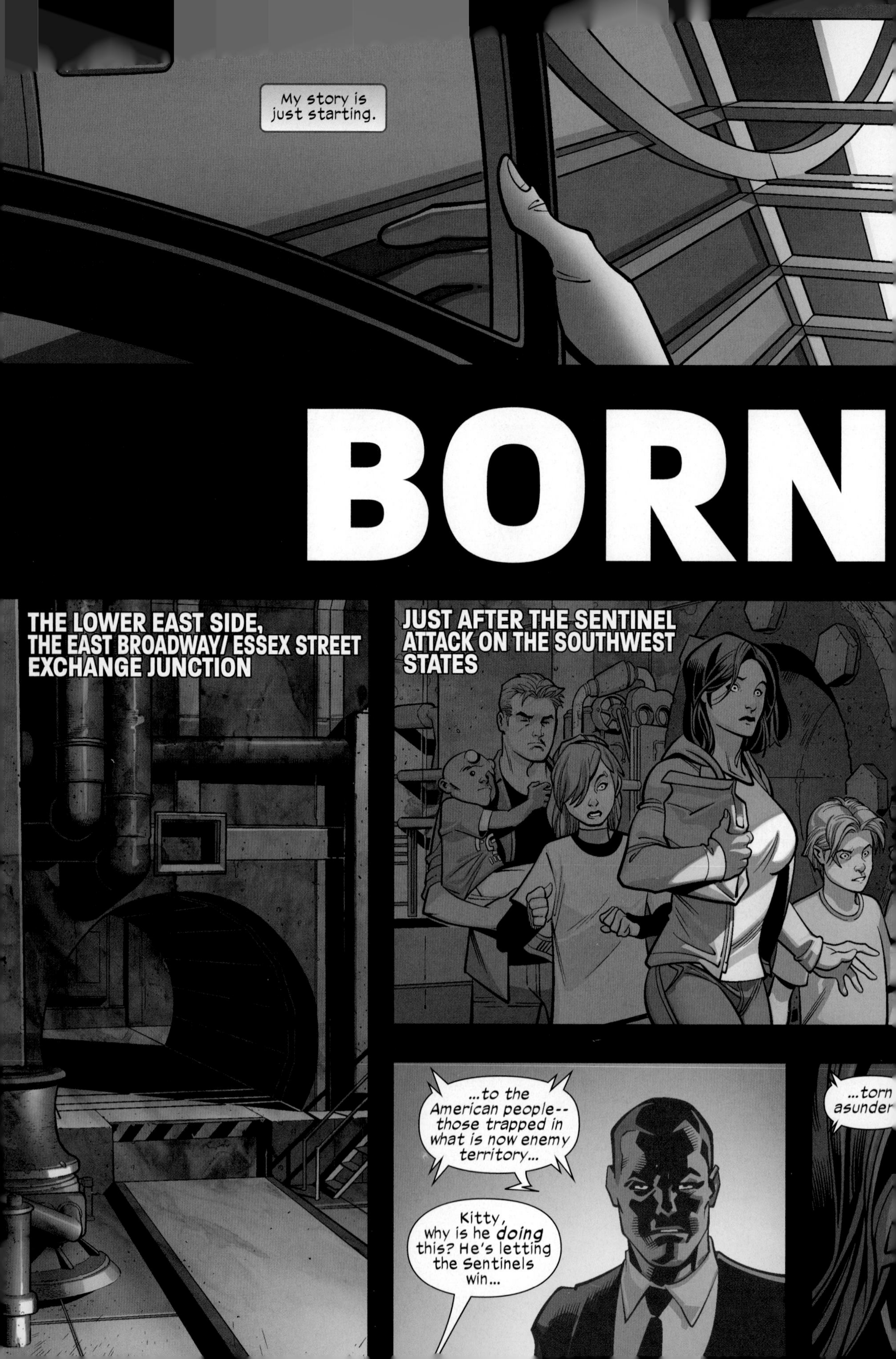

My story is just starting.

BORN

**THE LOWER EAST SIDE,
THE EAST BROADWAY/ ESSEX STREET
EXCHANGE JUNCTION**

**JUST AFTER THE SENTINEL
ATTACK ON THE SOUTHWEST
STATES**

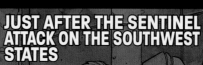

...to the American people-- those trapped in what is now enemy territory...

Kitty, why is he *doing* this? He's letting the Sentinels win...

...torn asunder

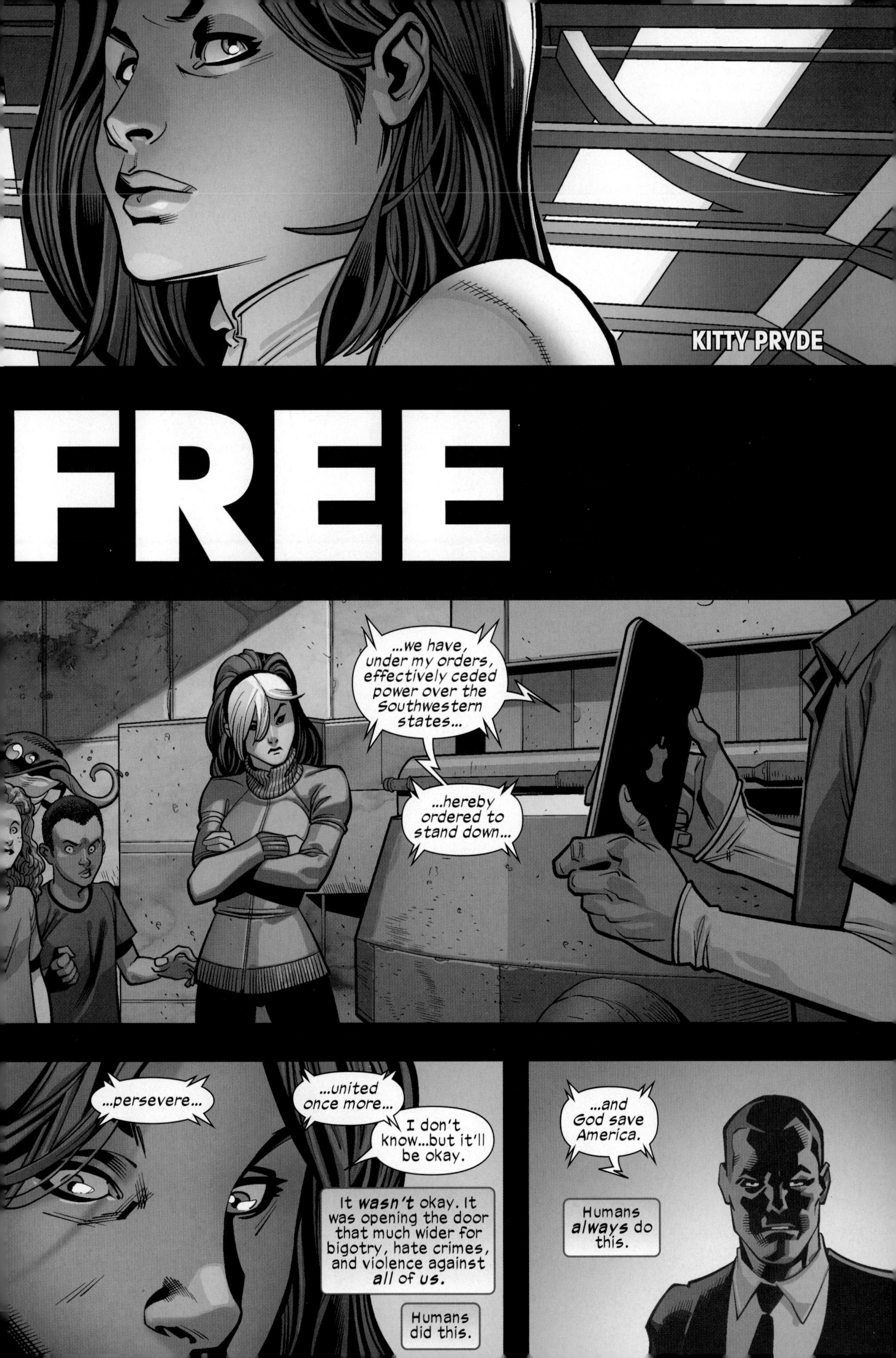
KITTY PRYDE
FREE
...we have, under my orders, effectively ceded power over the Southwestern states...
...hereby ordered to stand down...
...persevere...
...united once more...
I don't know...but it'll be okay.
It wasn't okay. It was opening the door that much wider for bigotry, hate crimes, and violence against all of us.
Humans did this.
...and God save America.
Humans always do this.

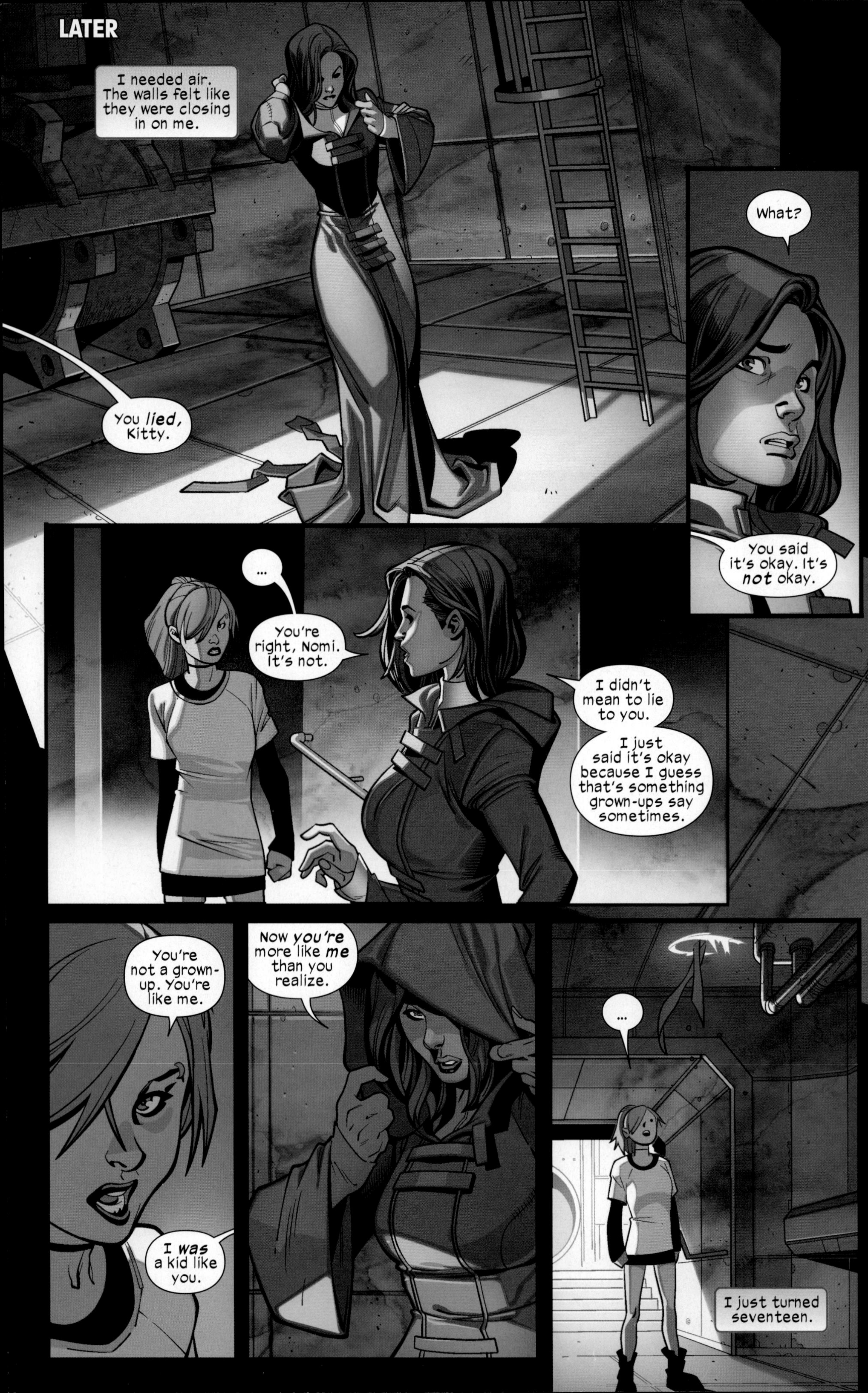

LATER
I needed air. The walls felt like they were closing in on me.
You lied, Kitty.
What?
You said it's okay. It's not okay.
...
You're right, Nomi. It's not.
I didn't mean to lie to you.
I just said it's okay because I guess that's something grown-ups say sometimes.
You're not a grown-up. You're like me.
I was a kid like you.
Now you're more like me than you realize.
...
I just turned seventeen.

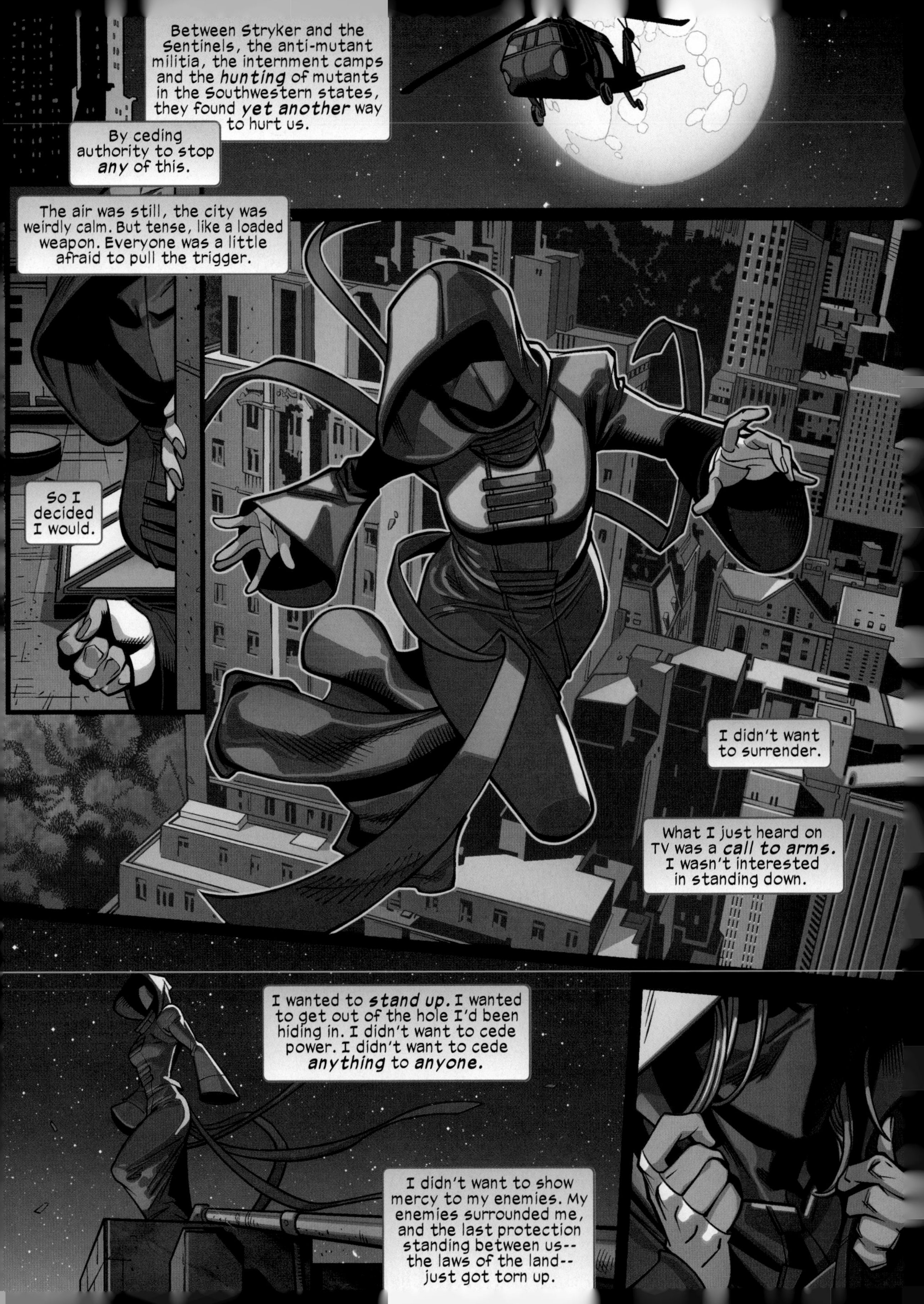
Between Stryker and the Sentinels, the anti-mutant militia, the internment camps and the *hunting* of mutants in the Southwestern states, they found *yet another* way to hurt us.
By ceding authority to stop *any* of this.
The air was still, the city was weirdly calm. But tense, like a loaded weapon. Everyone was a little afraid to pull the trigger.
So I decided I would.
I didn't want to surrender.
What I just heard on TV was a *call to arms.* I wasn't interested in standing down.
I wanted to *stand up.* I wanted to get out of the hole I'd been hiding in. I didn't want to cede power. I didn't want to cede *anything* to *anyone.*
I didn't want to show mercy to my enemies. My enemies surrounded me, and the last protection standing between us-- the laws of the land-- just got torn up.

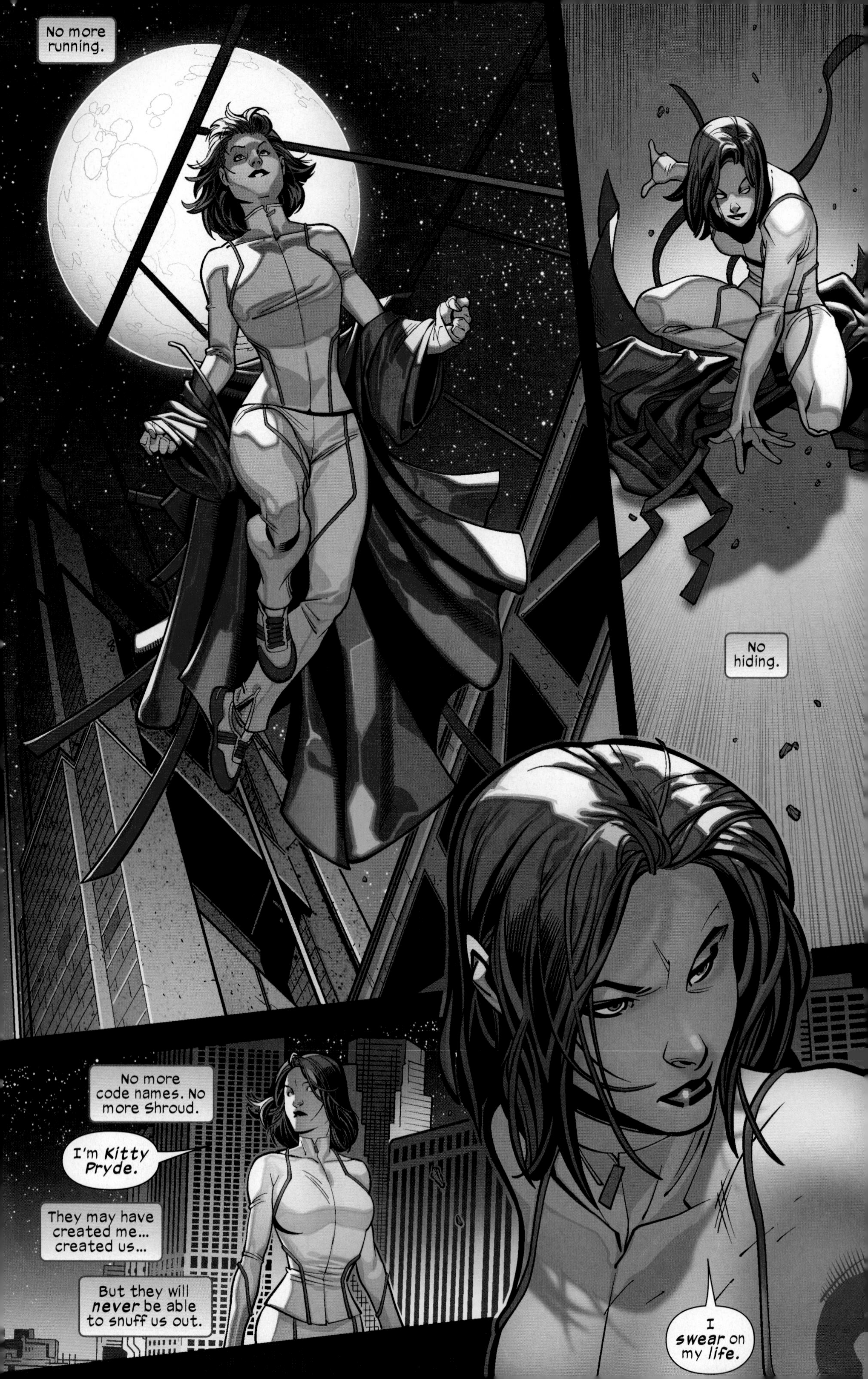
No more running.
No hiding.
No more code names. No more Shroud.
I'm Kitty Pryde.
They may have created me... created us...
But they will never be able to snuff us out.
I swear on my life.

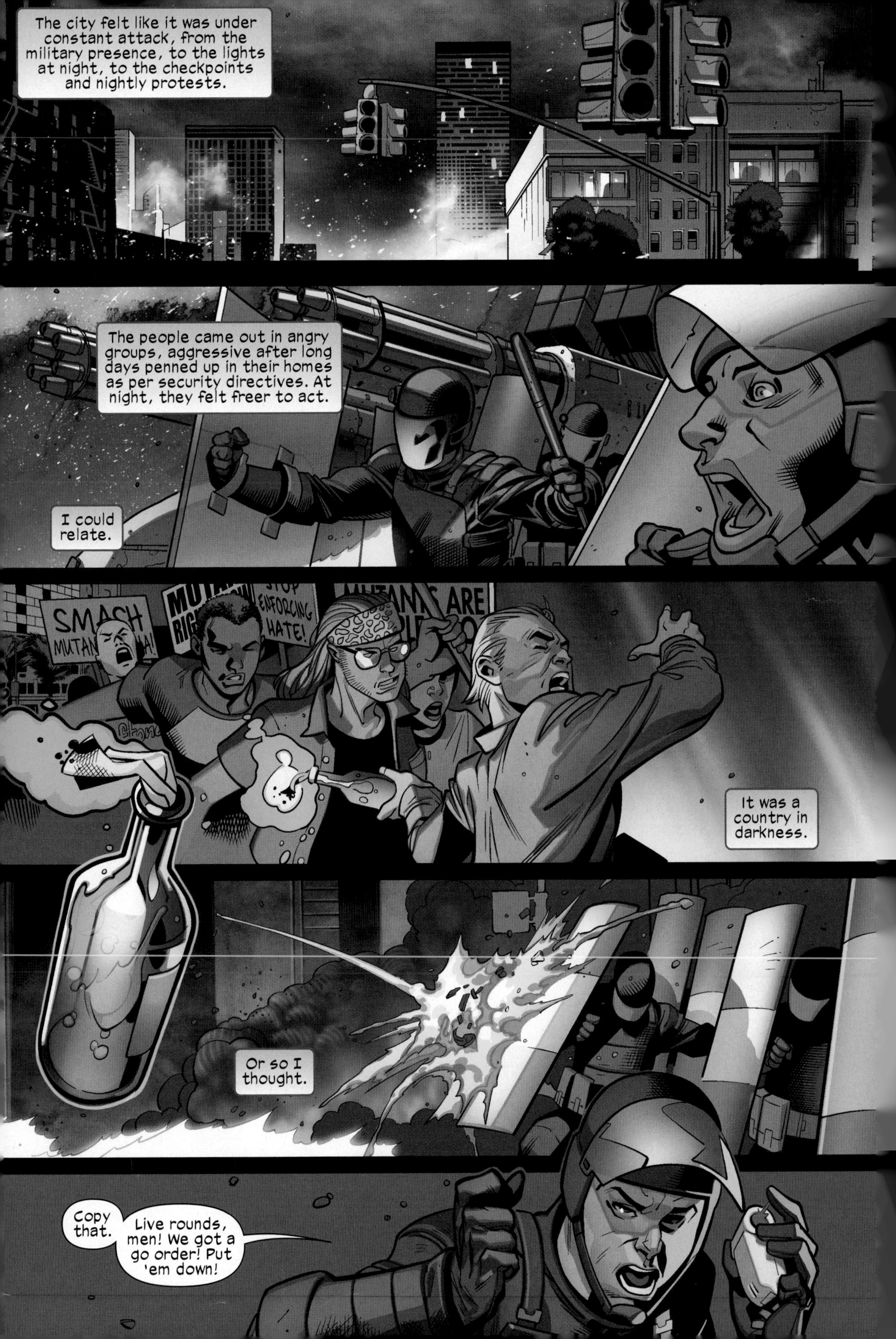

The city felt like it was under constant attack, from the military presence, to the lights at night, to the checkpoints and nightly protests.
The people came out in angry groups, aggressive after long days penned up in their homes as per security directives. At night, they felt freer to act.
I could relate.
SMASH
STOP ENFORCING HATE!
It was a country in darkness.
Or so I thought.
Copy that.
Live rounds, men! We got a go order! Put 'em down!

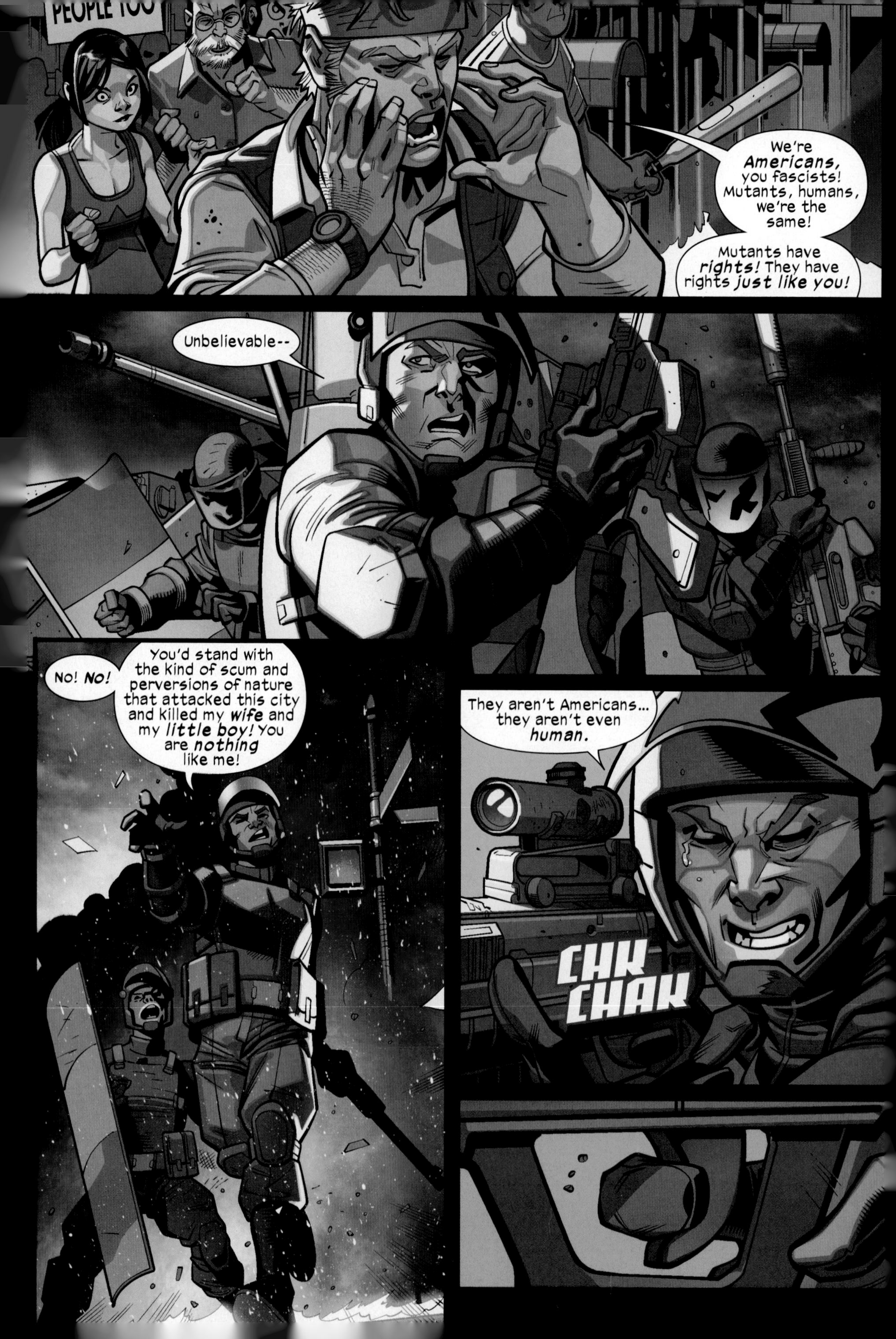
PEOPLE TOO
We're Americans, you fascists! Mutants, humans, we're the same!
Mutants have rights! They have rights just like you!
Unbelievable--
No! NO!
You'd stand with the kind of scum and perversions of nature that attacked this city and killed my wife and my little boy! You are nothing like me!
They aren't Americans... they aren't even human.
CHK CHAK

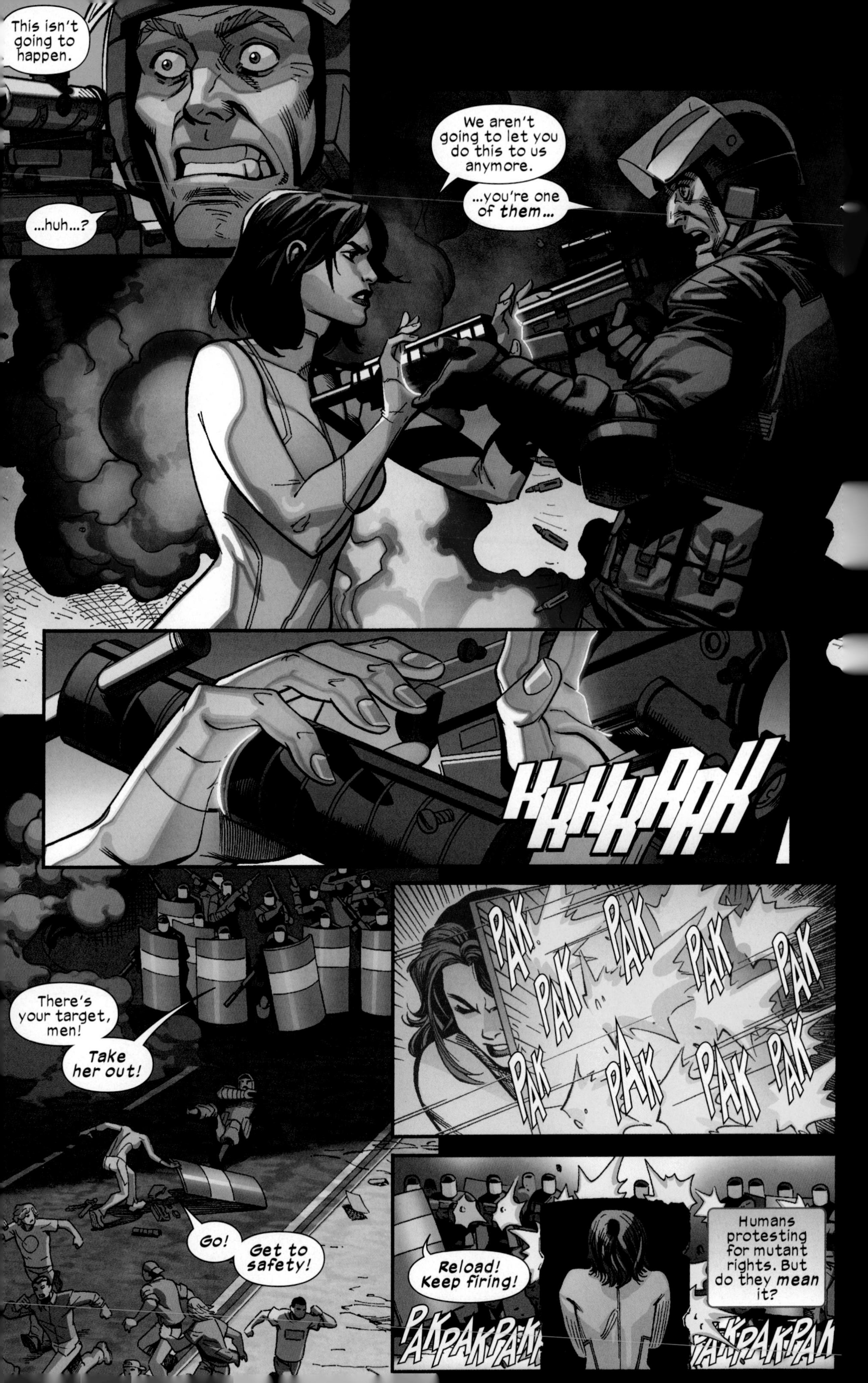
This isn't going to happen.
...huh...?
We aren't going to let you do this to us anymore.
...you're one of *them*...
KKKKRAK
There's your target, men!
Take her out!
PAK PAK PAK PAK PAK PAK PAK PAK PAK PAK
Go!
Get to safety!
Reload! Keep firing!
Humans protesting for mutant rights. But do they *mean* it?
PAKPAKPAK
PAKPAKPAK

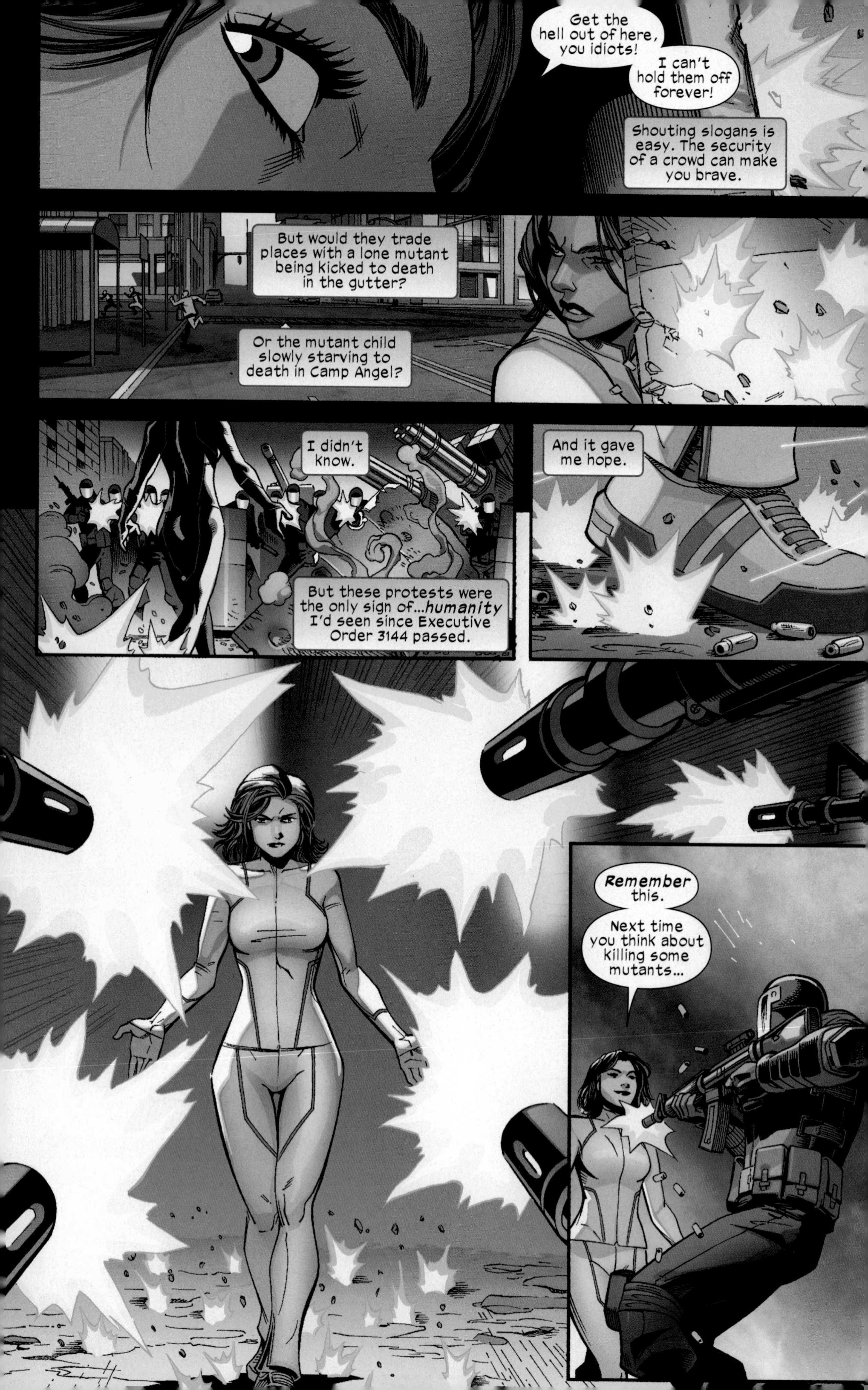
Get the hell out of here, you idiots!
I can't hold them off forever!
Shouting slogans is easy. The security of a crowd can make you brave.
But would they trade places with a lone mutant being kicked to death in the gutter?
Or the mutant child slowly starving to death in Camp Angel?
I didn't know.
But these protests were the only sign of...*humanity* I'd seen since Executive Order 3144 passed.
And it gave me hope.
Remember this.
Next time you think about killing some mutants...

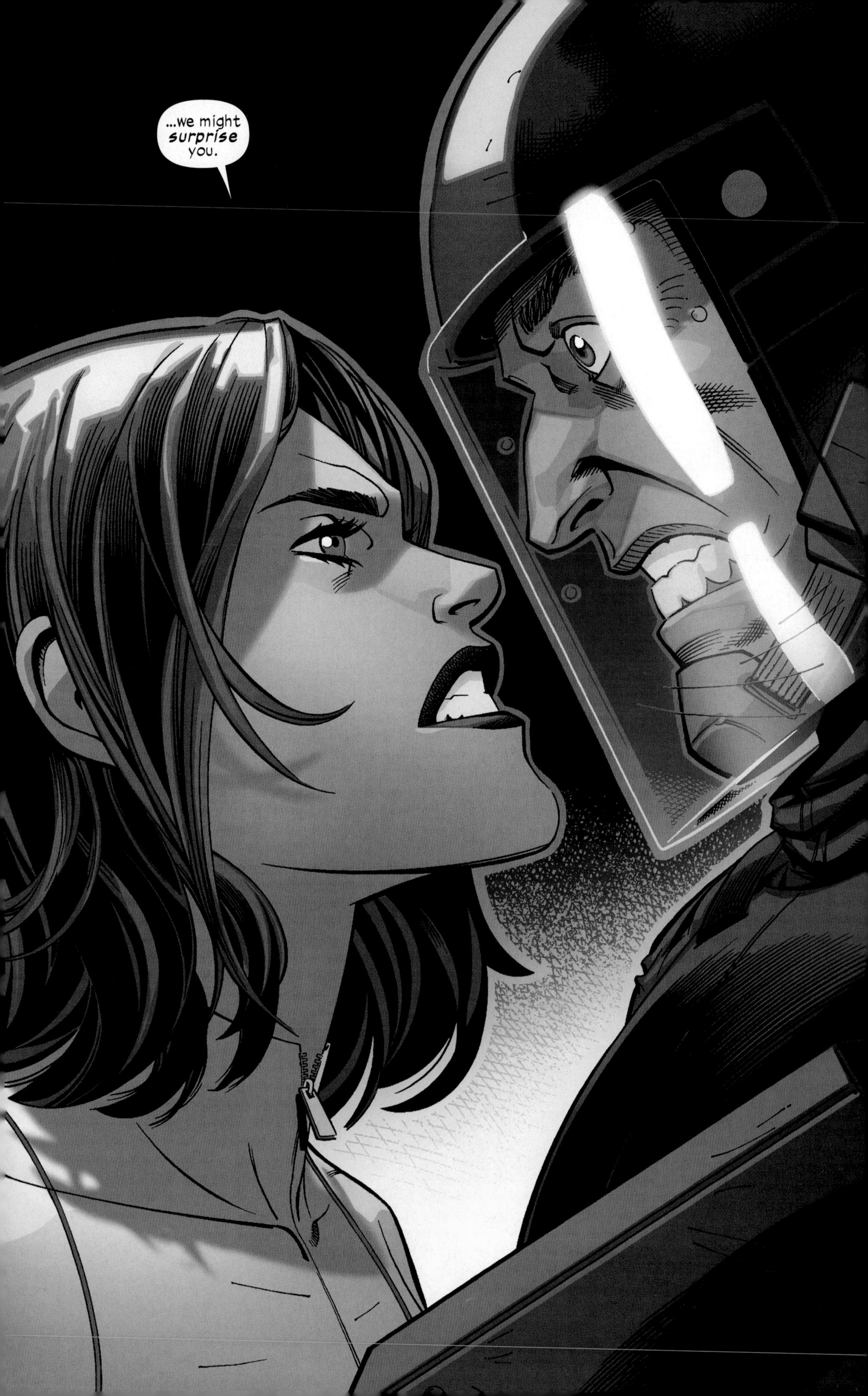
...we might *surprise* you.

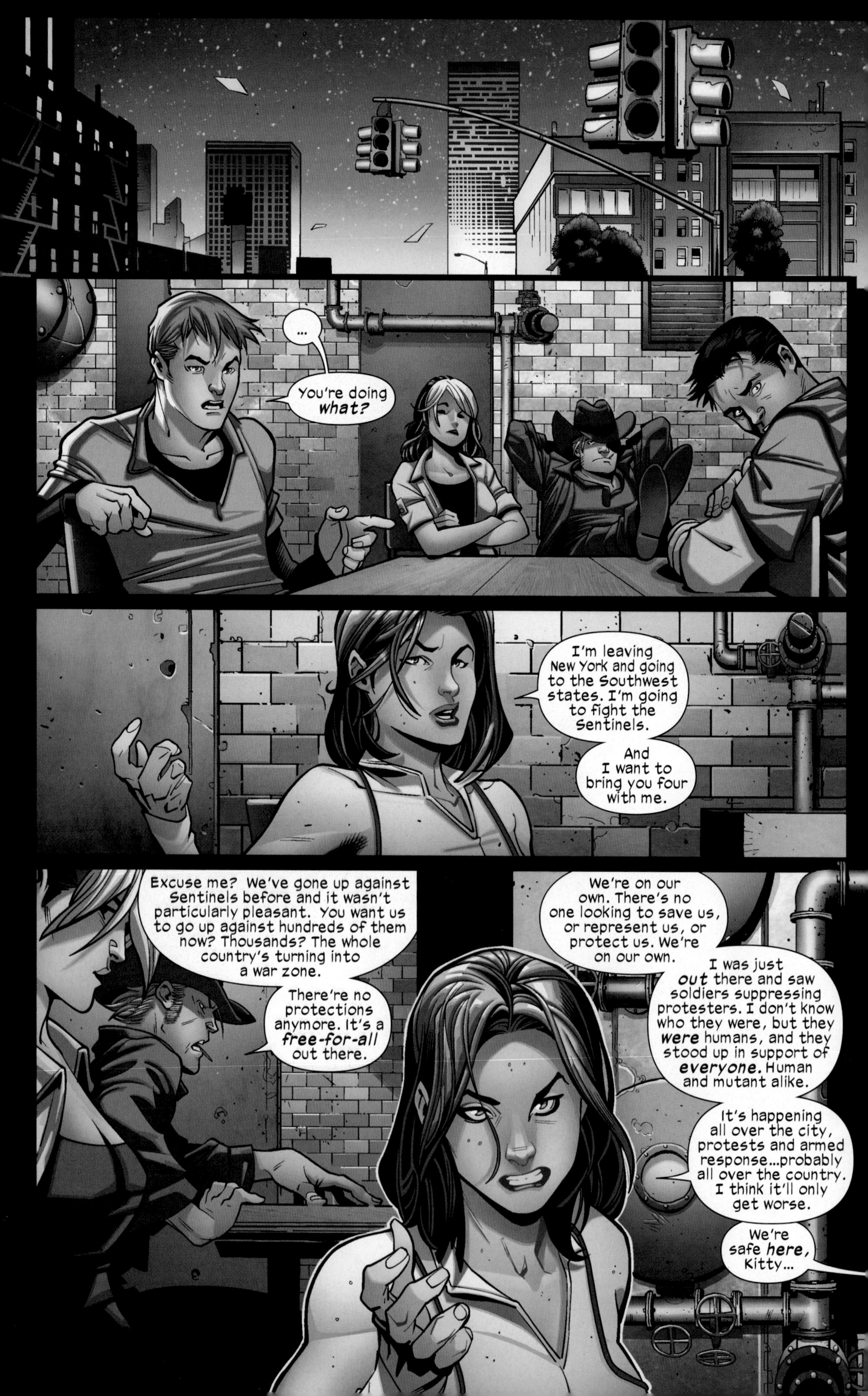
...
You're doing *what?*
I'm leaving New York and going to the Southwest states. I'm going to fight the Sentinels.
And I want to bring you four with me.
Excuse me? We've gone up against Sentinels before and it wasn't particularly pleasant. You want us to go up against hundreds of them now? Thousands? The whole country's turning into a war zone.
There're no protections anymore. It's a *free-for-all* out there.
We're on our own. There's no one looking to save us, or represent us, or protect us. We're on our own.
I was just *out* there and saw soldiers suppressing protesters. I don't know who they were, but they *were* humans, and they stood up in support of *everyone.* Human and mutant alike.
It's happening all over the city, protests and armed response...probably all over the country. I think it'll only get worse.
We're safe *here,* Kitty...

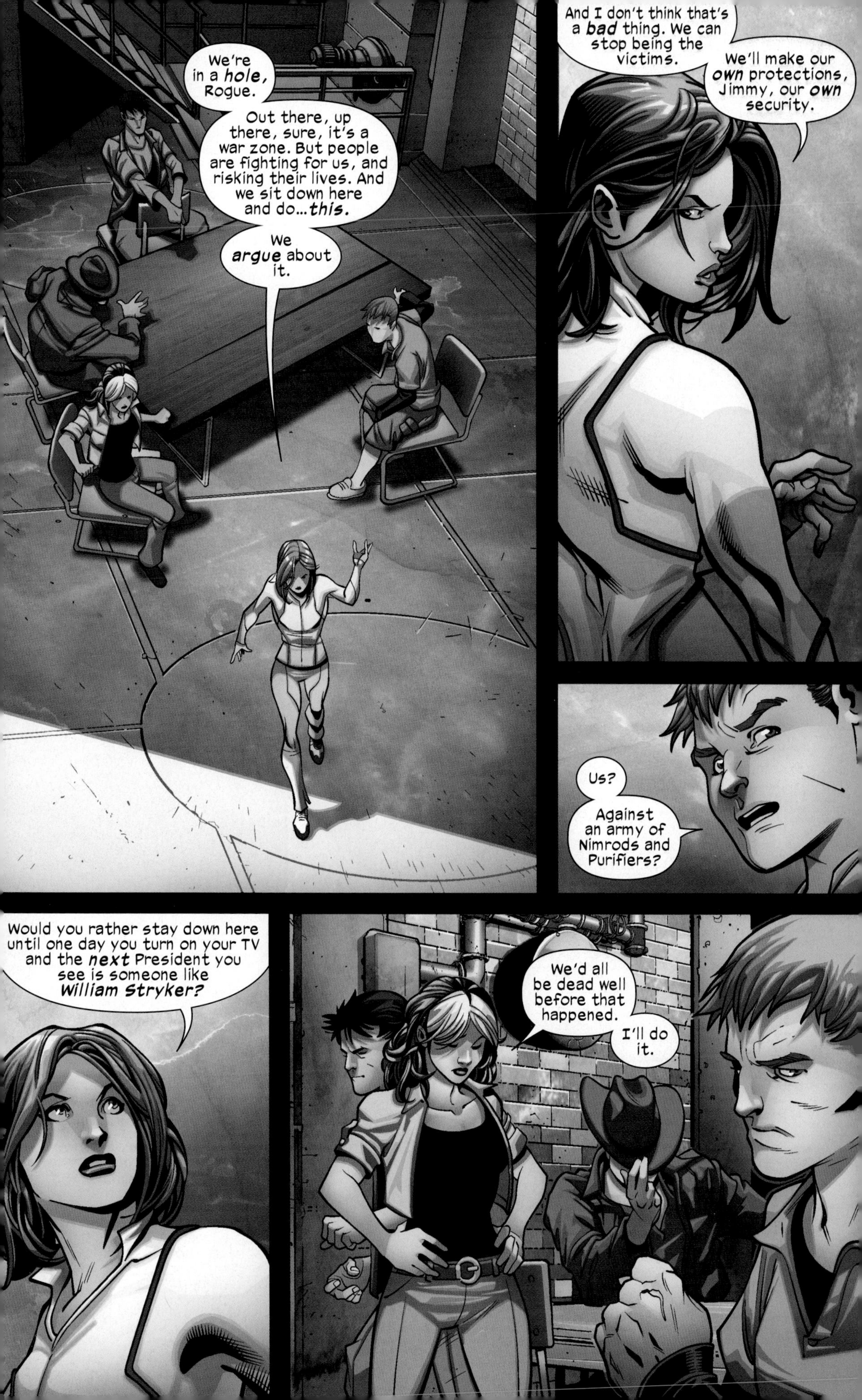
We're in a *hole,* Rogue.
Out there, up there, sure, it's a war zone. But people are fighting for us, and risking their lives. And we sit down here and do... *this.*
We *argue* about it.
And I don't think that's a *bad* thing. We can stop being the victims.
We'll make our *own* protections, Jimmy, our *own* security.
Us?
Against an army of Nimrods and Purifiers?
Would you rather stay down here until one day you turn on your TV and the *next* President you see is someone like *William Stryker?*
We'd all be dead well before that happened.
I'll do it.

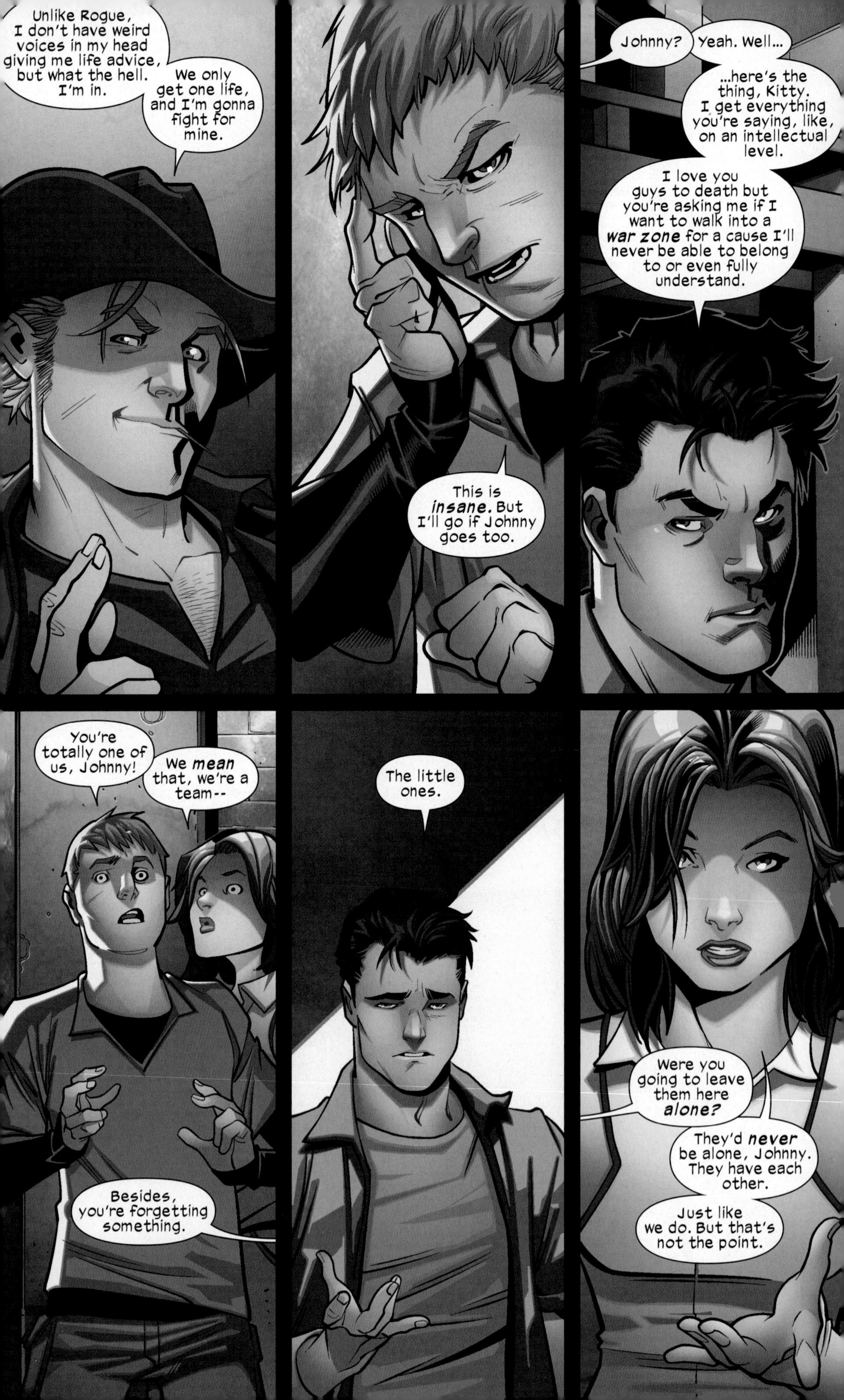
Unlike Rogue, I don't have weird voices in my head giving me life advice, but what the hell. I'm in.
We only get one life, and I'm gonna fight for mine.
This is *insane.* But I'll go if Johnny goes too.
Johnny?
Yeah. Well...
...here's the thing, Kitty. I get everything you're saying, like, on an intellectual level.
I love you guys to death but you're asking me if I want to walk into a *war zone* for a cause I'll never be able to belong to or even fully understand.
You're totally one of us, Johnny!
We *mean* that, we're a team--
Besides, you're forgetting something.
The little ones.
Were you going to leave them here *alone?*
They'd *never* be alone, Johnny. They have each other.
Just like we do. But that's not the point.

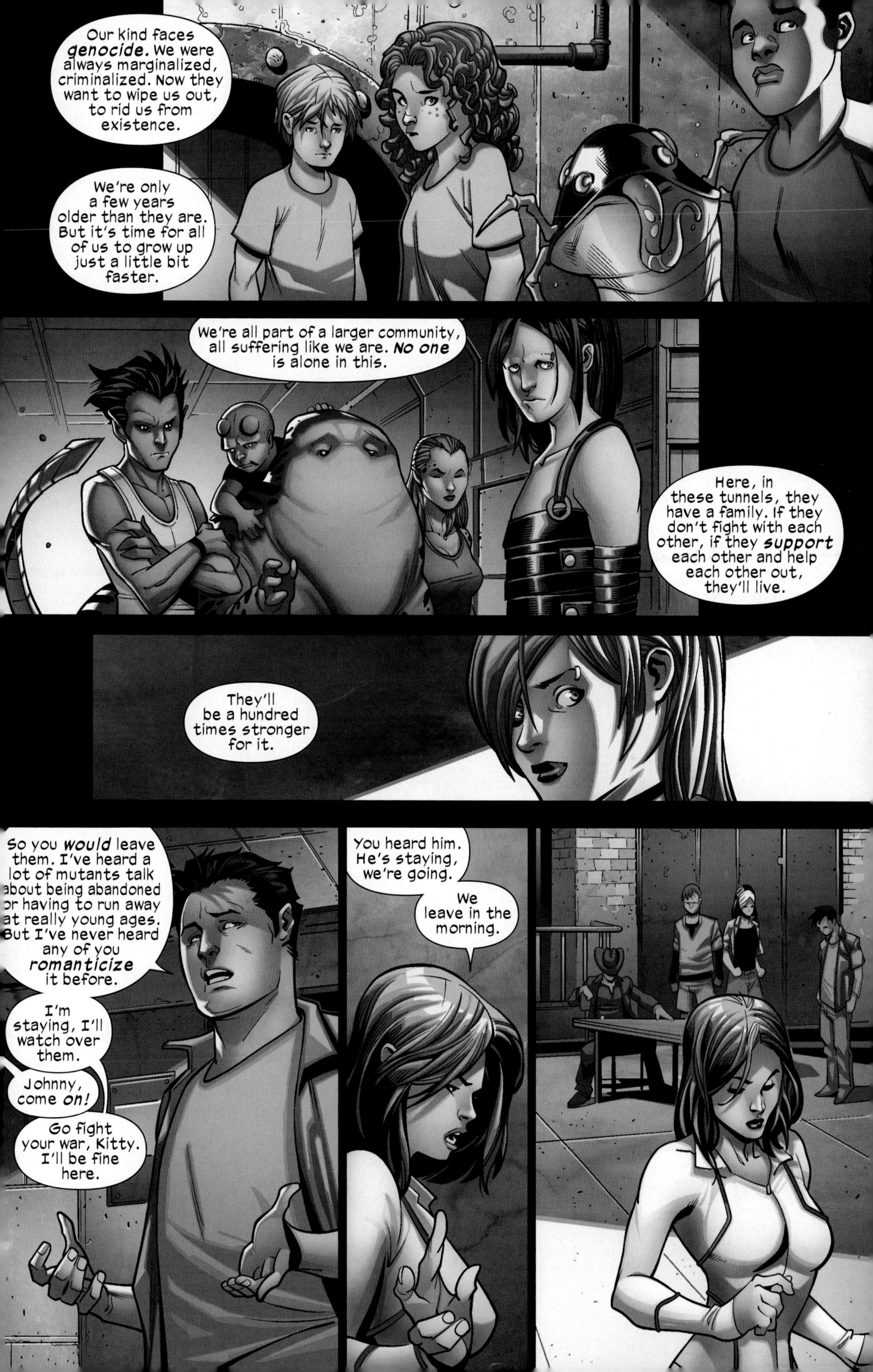

Our kind faces *genocide.* We were always marginalized, criminalized. Now they want to wipe us out, to rid us from existence.
We're only a few years older than they are. But it's time for all of us to grow up just a little bit faster.
We're all part of a larger community, all suffering like we are. *No one* is alone in this.
Here, in these tunnels, they have a family. If they don't fight with each other, if they *support* each other and help each other out, they'll live.
They'll be a hundred times stronger for it.
So you *would* leave them. I've heard a lot of mutants talk about being abandoned or having to run away at really young ages. But I've never heard any of you *romanticize* it before.
I'm staying, I'll watch over them.
Johnny, come *on!*
Go fight your war, Kitty. I'll be fine here.
You heard him. He's staying, we're going.
We leave in the morning.

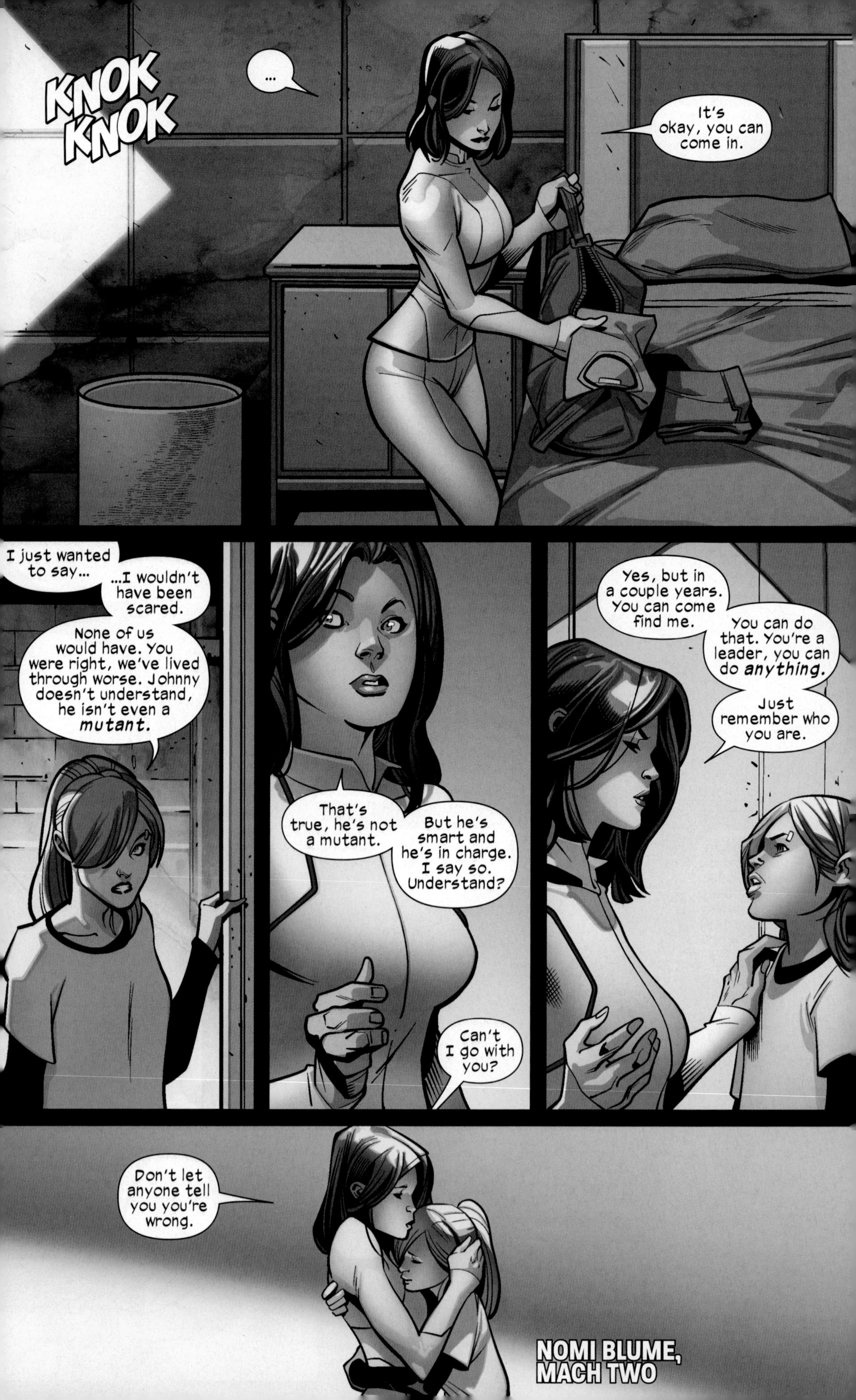
KNOK KNOK
...
It's okay, you can come in.
I just wanted to say...
...I wouldn't have been scared.
None of us would have. You were right, we've lived through worse. Johnny doesn't understand, he isn't even a *mutant.*
That's true, he's not a mutant.
But he's smart and he's in charge. I say so. Understand?
Can't I go with you?
Yes, but in a couple years. You can come find me.
You can do that. You're a leader, you can do *anything.*
Just remember who you are.
Don't let anyone tell you you're wrong.
NOMI BLUME, MACH TWO

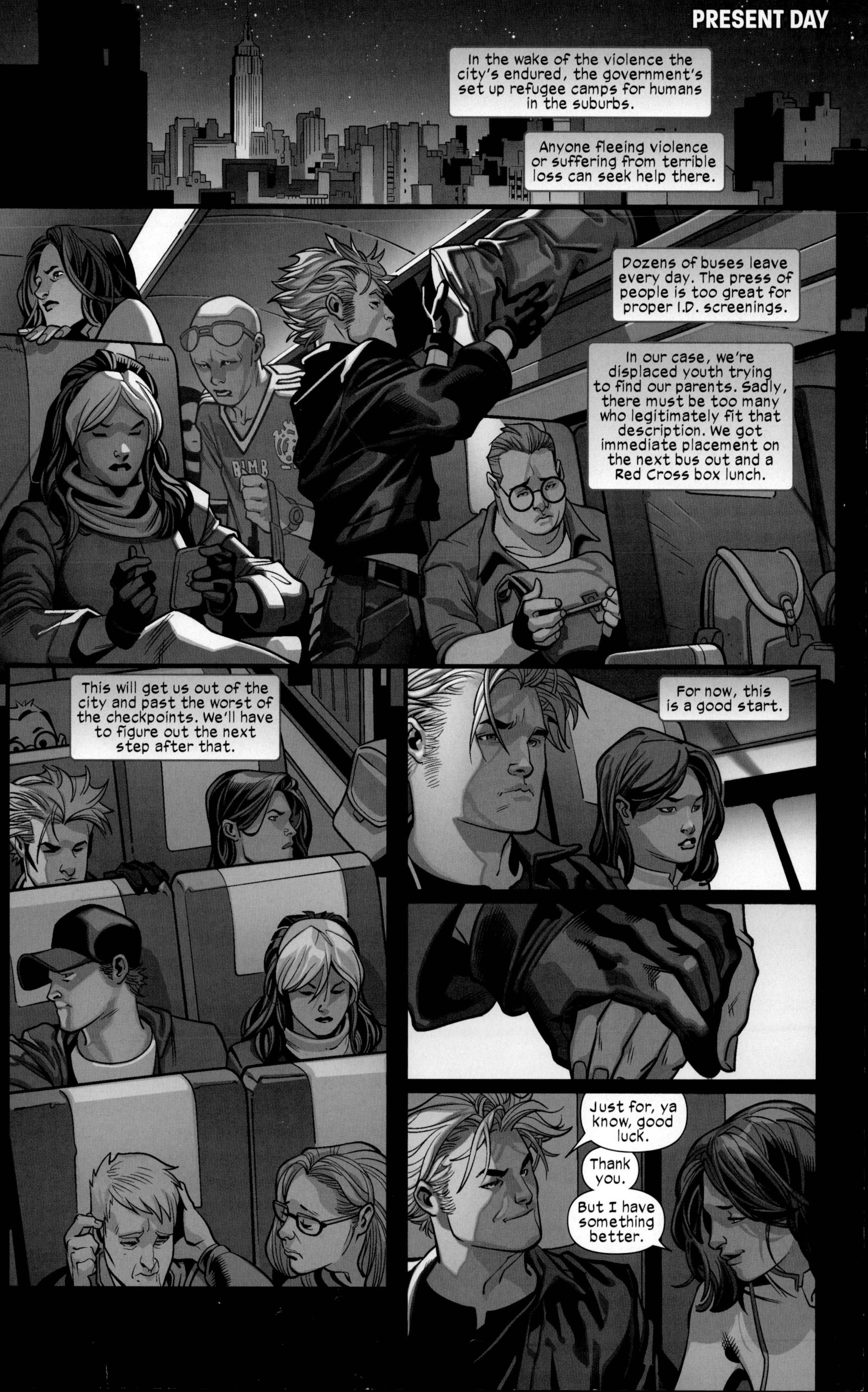
PRESENT DAY
In the wake of the violence the city's endured, the government's set up refugee camps for humans in the suburbs.
Anyone fleeing violence or suffering from terrible loss can seek help there.
Dozens of buses leave every day. The press of people is too great for proper I.D. screenings.
In our case, we're displaced youth trying to find our parents. Sadly, there must be too many who legitimately fit that description. We got immediate placement on the next bus out and a Red Cross box lunch.
This will get us out of the city and past the worst of the checkpoints. We'll have to figure out the next step after that.
For now, this is a good start.
Just for, ya know, good luck.
Thank you.
But I have something better.

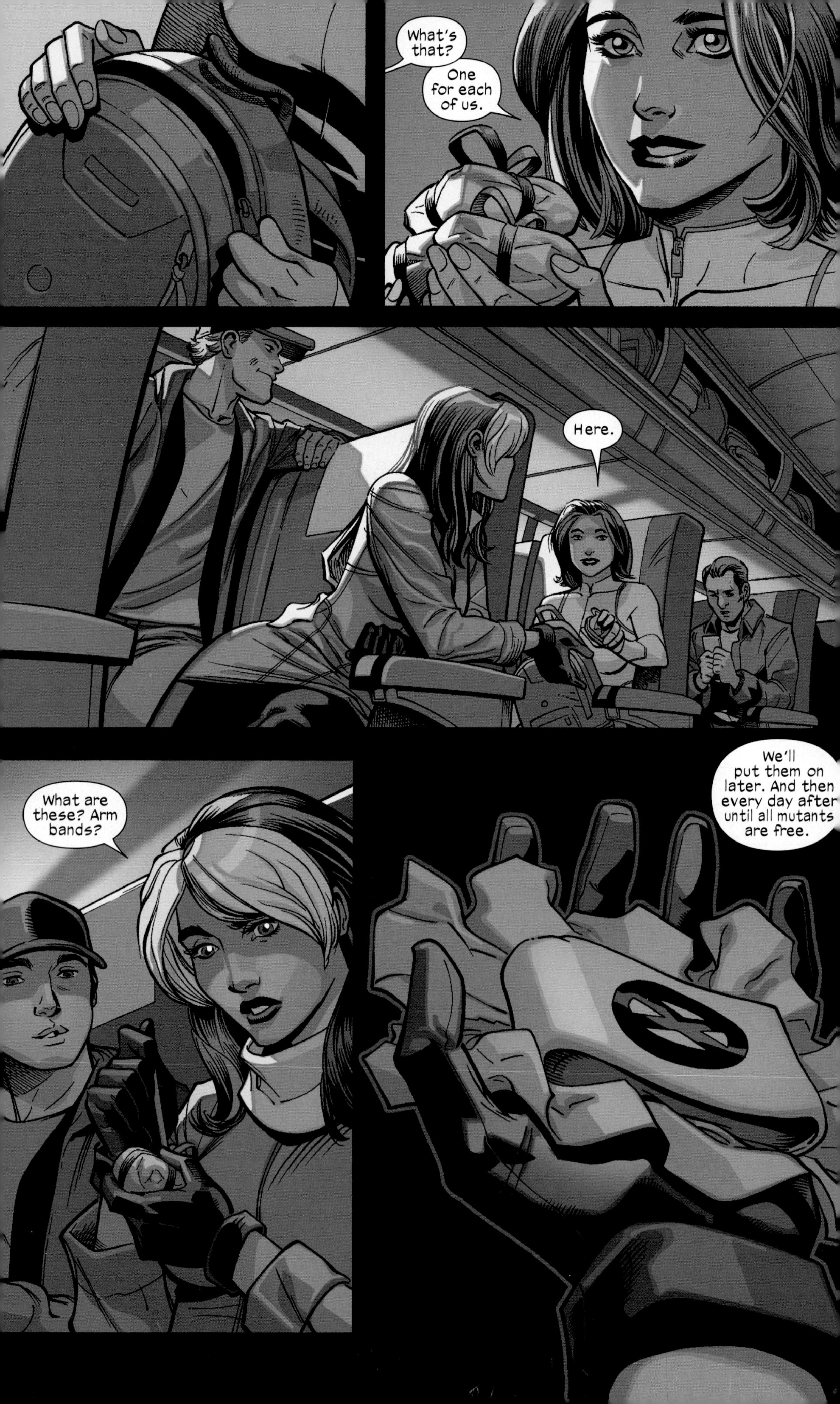
What's that?
One for each of us.
Here.
What are these? Arm bands?
We'll put them on later. And then every day after until all mutants are free.

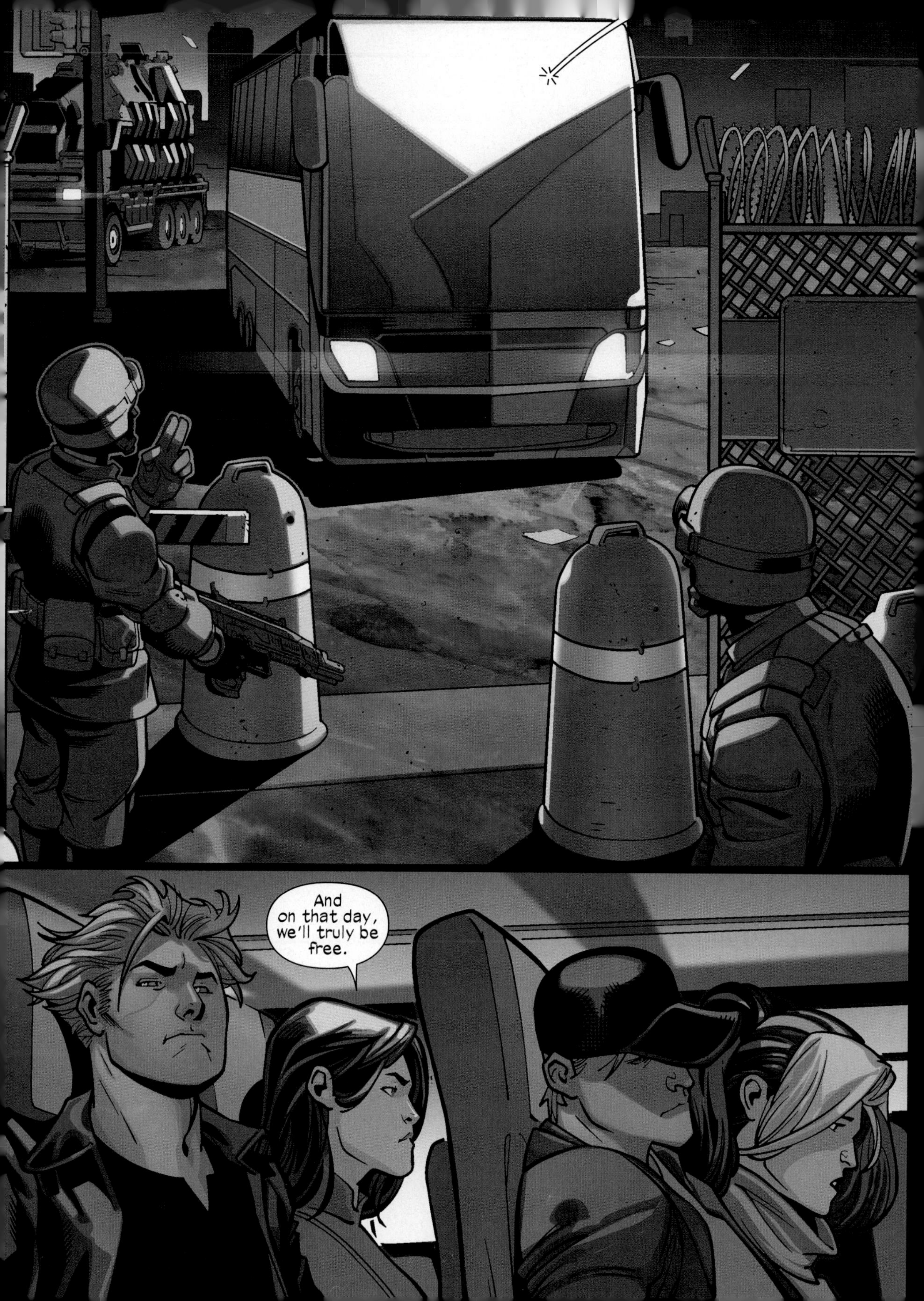
And on that day, we'll truly be free.

8

ULTIMATE COMICS **X-MEN** #14

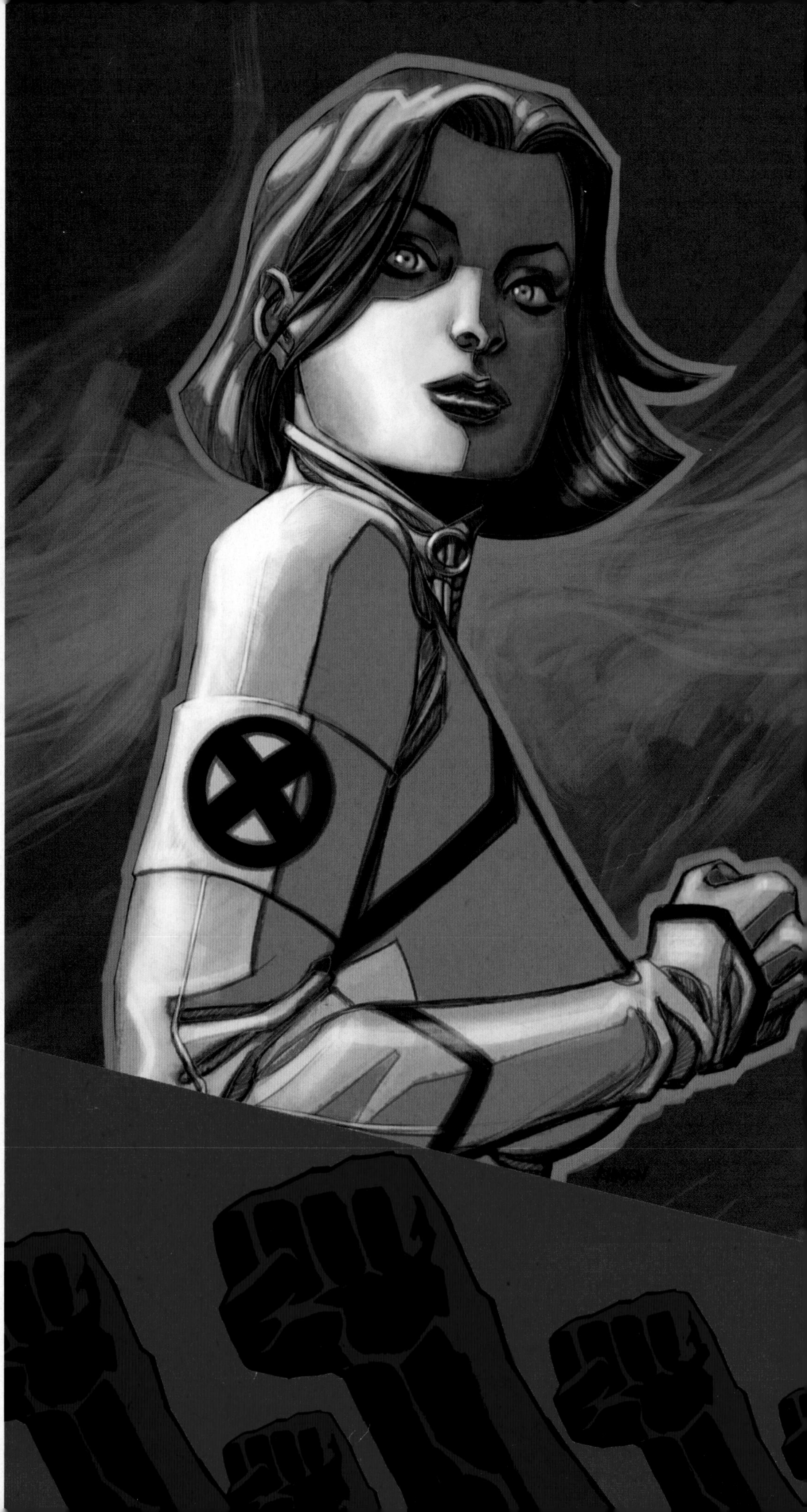

S.H.I.E.L.D. SITUATION MAP:

[Anti-government militia hot spots]

Montana, N. Dakota
S. Dakota, Wyoming
Arizona, New Mexico
N. Carolina, S. Carolina
Georgia

[Eastern seaboard control zone]

New England,
New York,
New Jersey,
Delaware,
Washington, D.C.,
Maryland,
Virginia

secured by
National Guard
under emergency
powers
committee

the West Coast]

California, Oregon
Washington
status unknown

[Great Lakes states]

Minnesota,
Wisconsin,
Michigan,
Illinois,
Indiana, Ohio
status unknown

ANTI-MATTER
NO FLY
ZONE

SENTINEL
PUSH

SOUTHERN
CALIFORNIA
REFUGEE ZONE

NUCLEAR-ARMED
NATION

DALLAS:
CAPITAL CITY OF
THE NEW REPUBLIC
OF TEXAS

Classified Position

Camp Hutton, secure
location of the President
of the United States

[Sentinel-controlled no man's land]

New Mexico, Arizona
Utah, Oklahoma
abandoned by the
US government

[The New Republic of Texas]

Texas
declared state
independence

ALL STATES
SHOWN IN WHITE
ARE U.S. GOVERNMENT
CONTROLLED ZONES

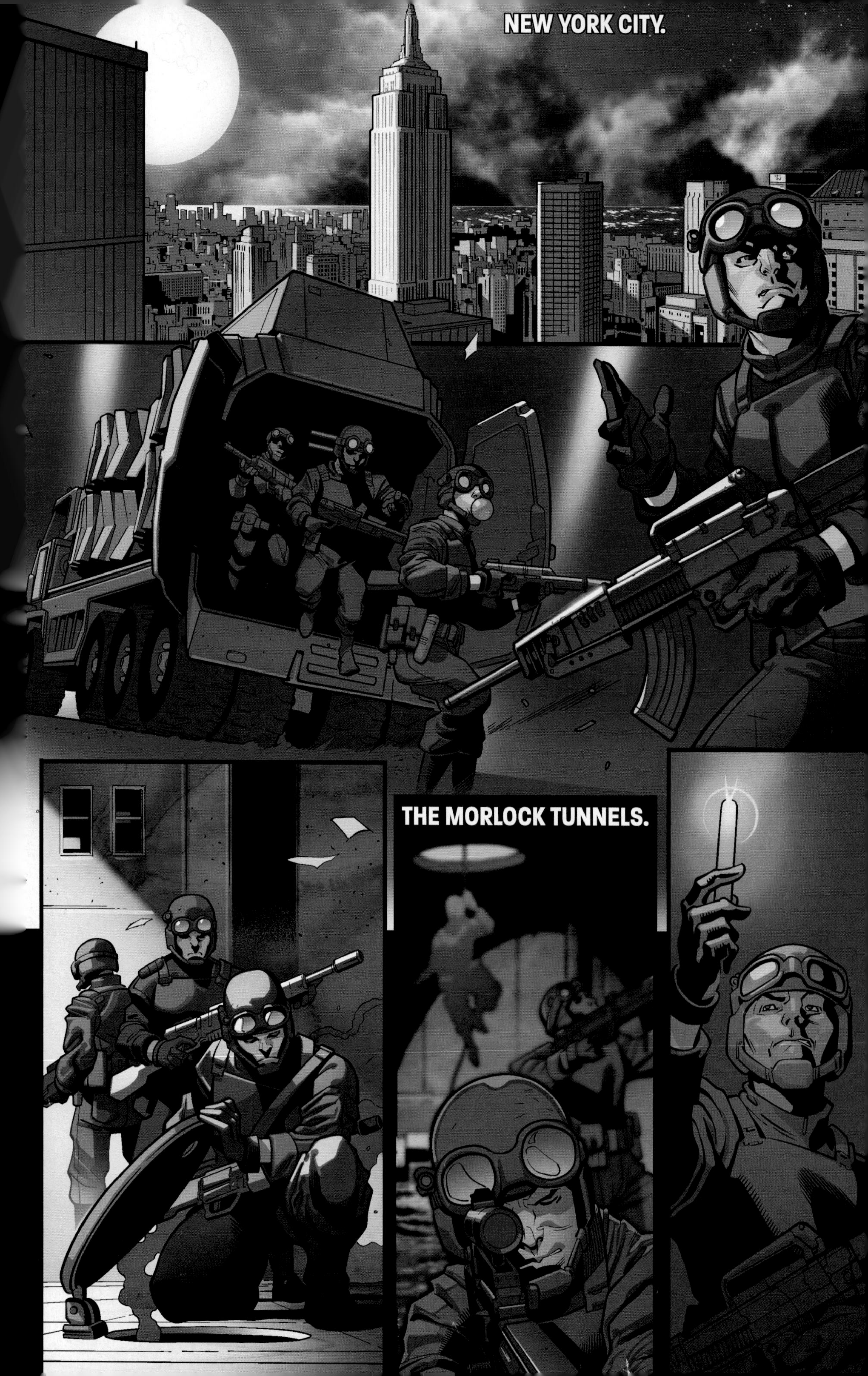
NEW YORK CITY.
THE MORLOCK TUNNELS.

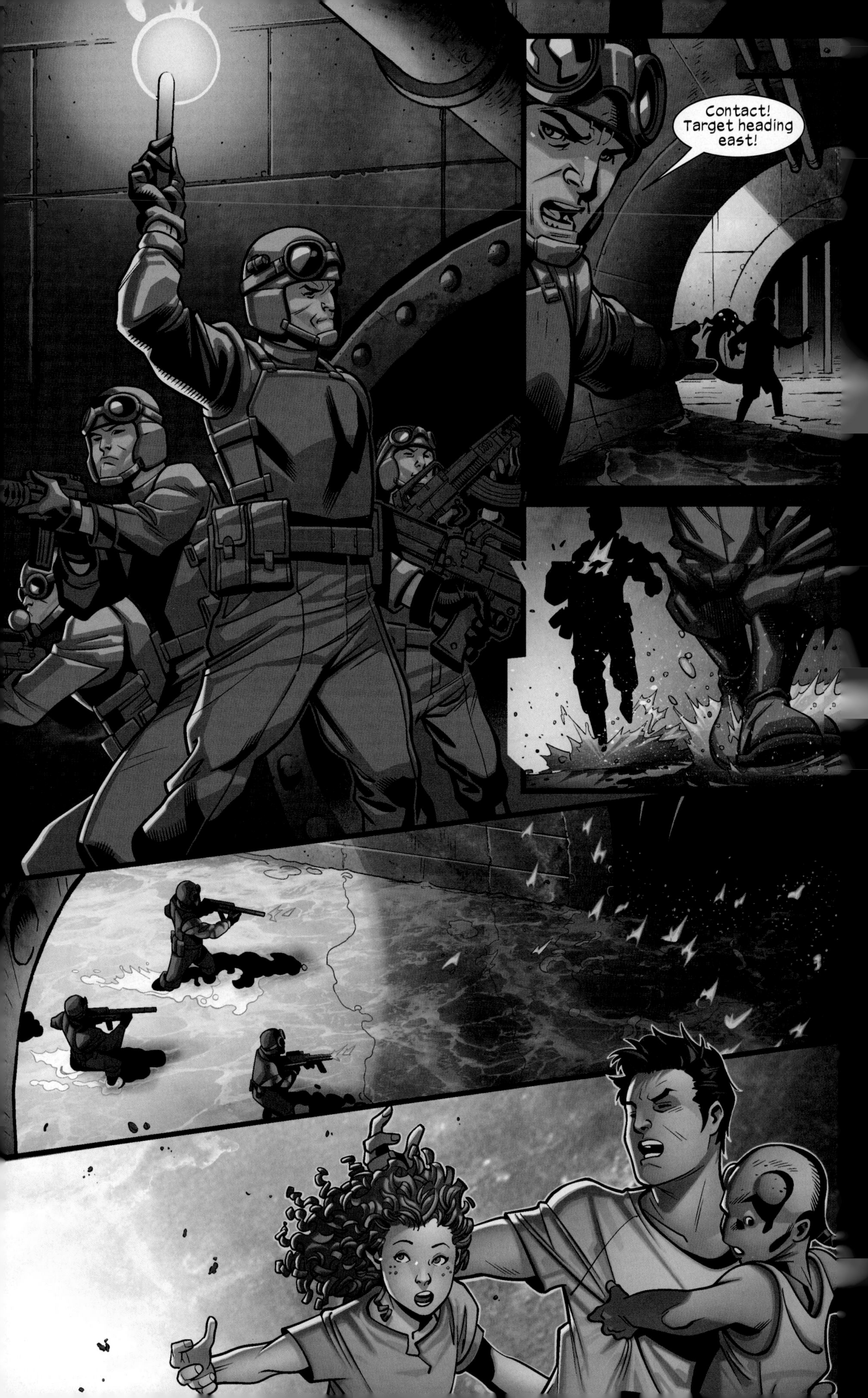
Contact! Target heading east!

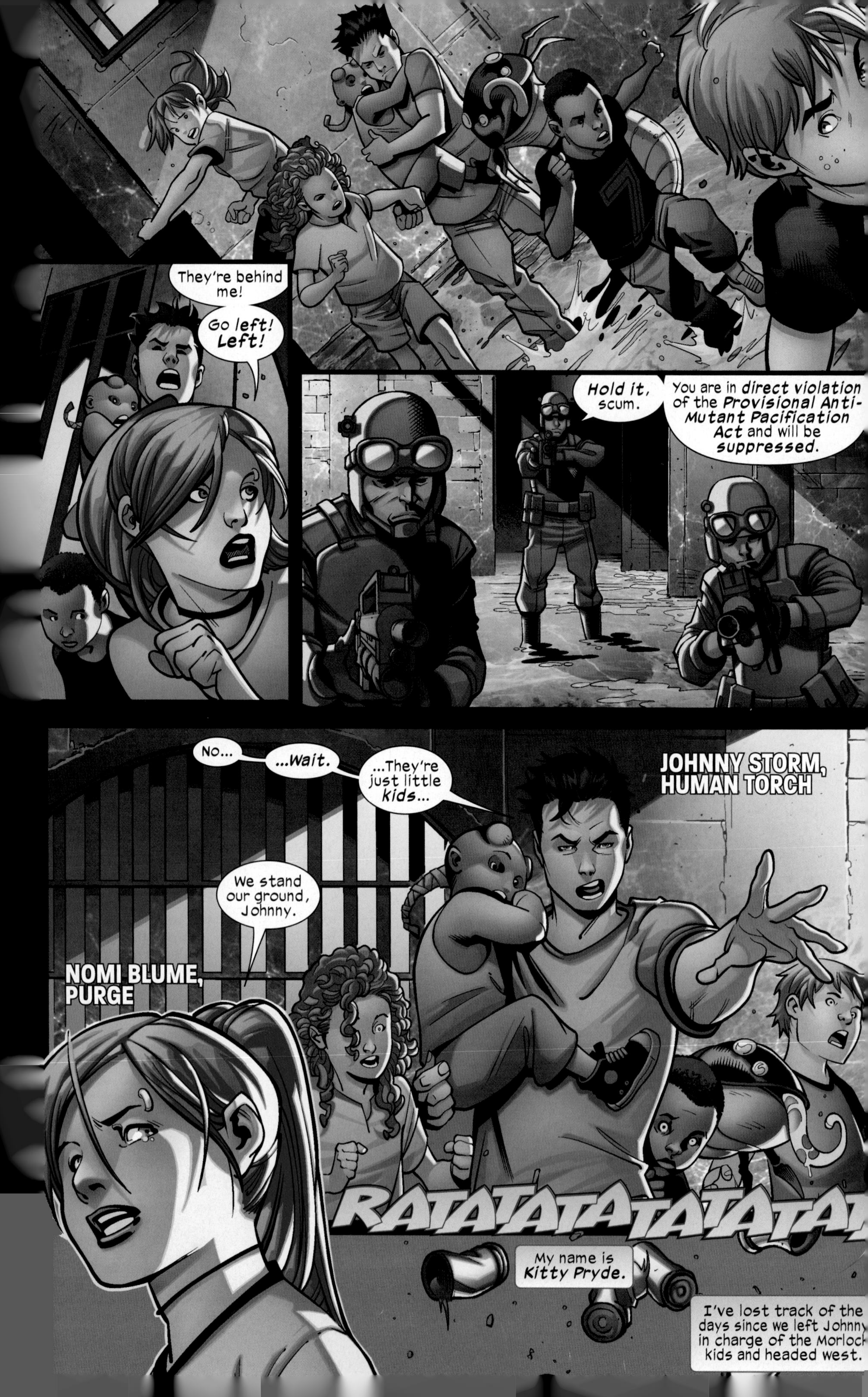
They're behind me!
Go left! Left!
Hold it, scum.
You are in direct violation of the Provisional Anti-Mutant Pacification Act and will be suppressed.
No...
...Wait.
...They're just little kids...
JOHNNY STORM, HUMAN TORCH
We stand our ground, Johnny.
NOMI BLUME, PURGE
RATATATATATATATAT
My name is Kitty Pryde.
I've lost track of the days since we left Johnny in charge of the Morlock kids and headed west.

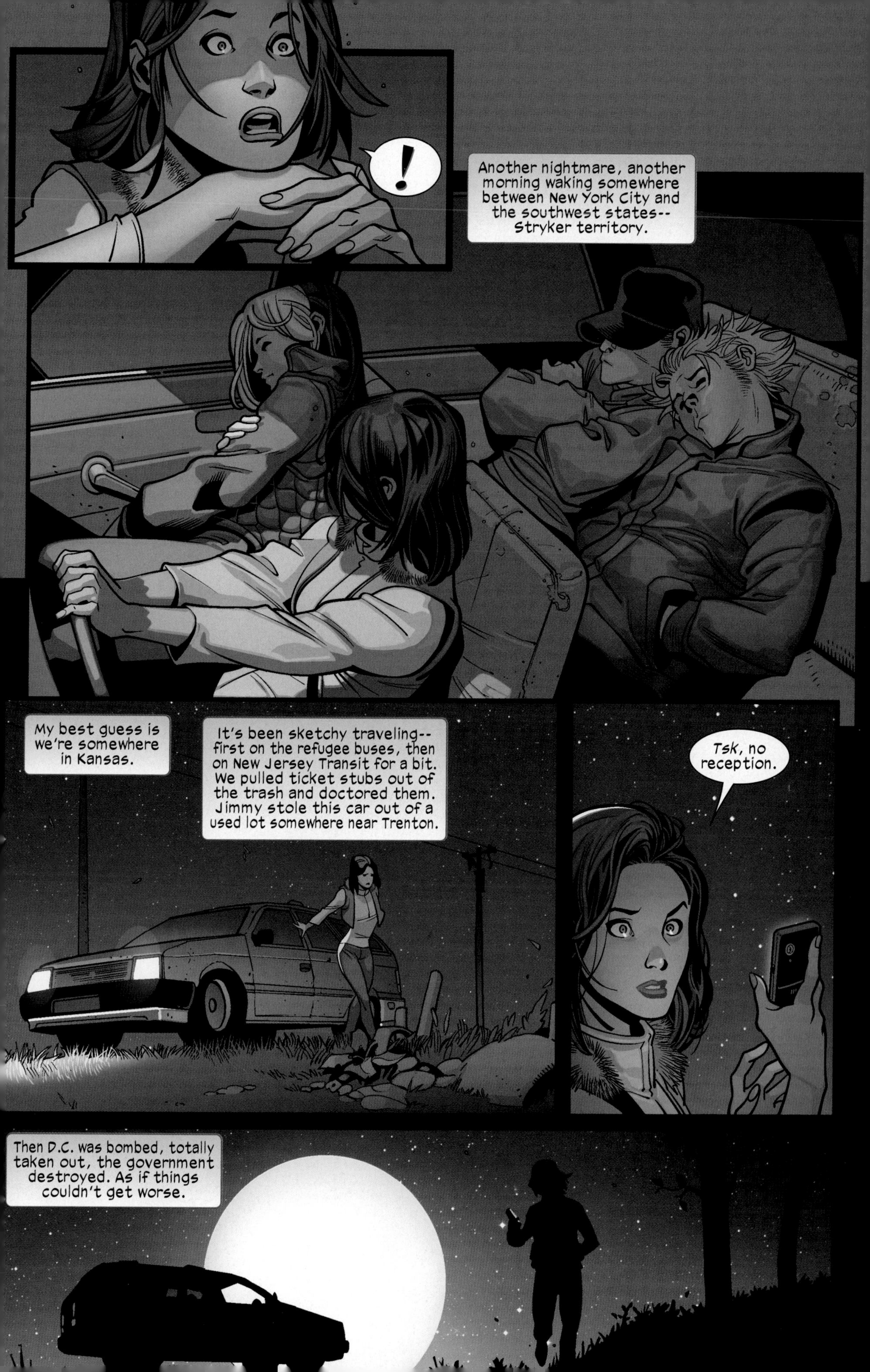
!
Another nightmare, another morning waking somewhere between New York City and the southwest states-- Stryker territory.
My best guess is we're somewhere in Kansas.
It's been sketchy traveling-- first on the refugee buses, then on New Jersey Transit for a bit. We pulled ticket stubs out of the trash and doctored them. Jimmy stole this car out of a used lot somewhere near Trenton.
Tsk, no reception.
Then D.C. was bombed, totally taken out, the government destroyed. As if things couldn't get worse.

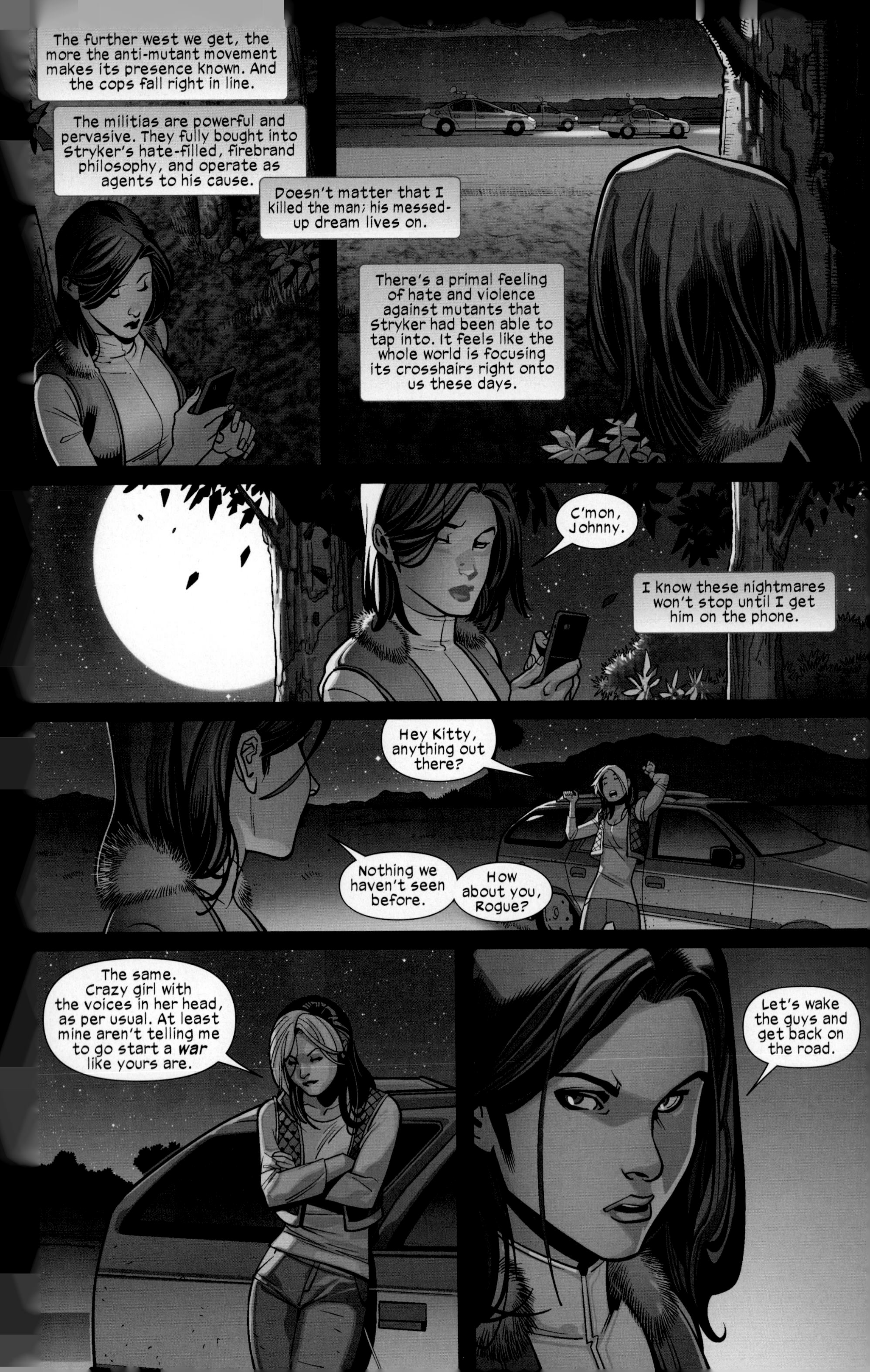

The further west we get, the more the anti-mutant movement makes its presence known. And the cops fall right in line.
The militias are powerful and pervasive. They fully bought into Stryker's hate-filled, firebrand philosophy, and operate as agents to his cause.
Doesn't matter that I killed the man; his messed-up dream lives on.
There's a primal feeling of hate and violence against mutants that Stryker had been able to tap into. It feels like the whole world is focusing its crosshairs right onto us these days.
C'mon, Johnny.
I know these nightmares won't stop until I get him on the phone.
Hey Kitty, anything out there?
Nothing we haven't seen before.
How about you, Rogue?
The same. Crazy girl with the voices in her head, as per usual. At least mine aren't telling me to go start a *war* like yours are.
Let's wake the guys and get back on the road.

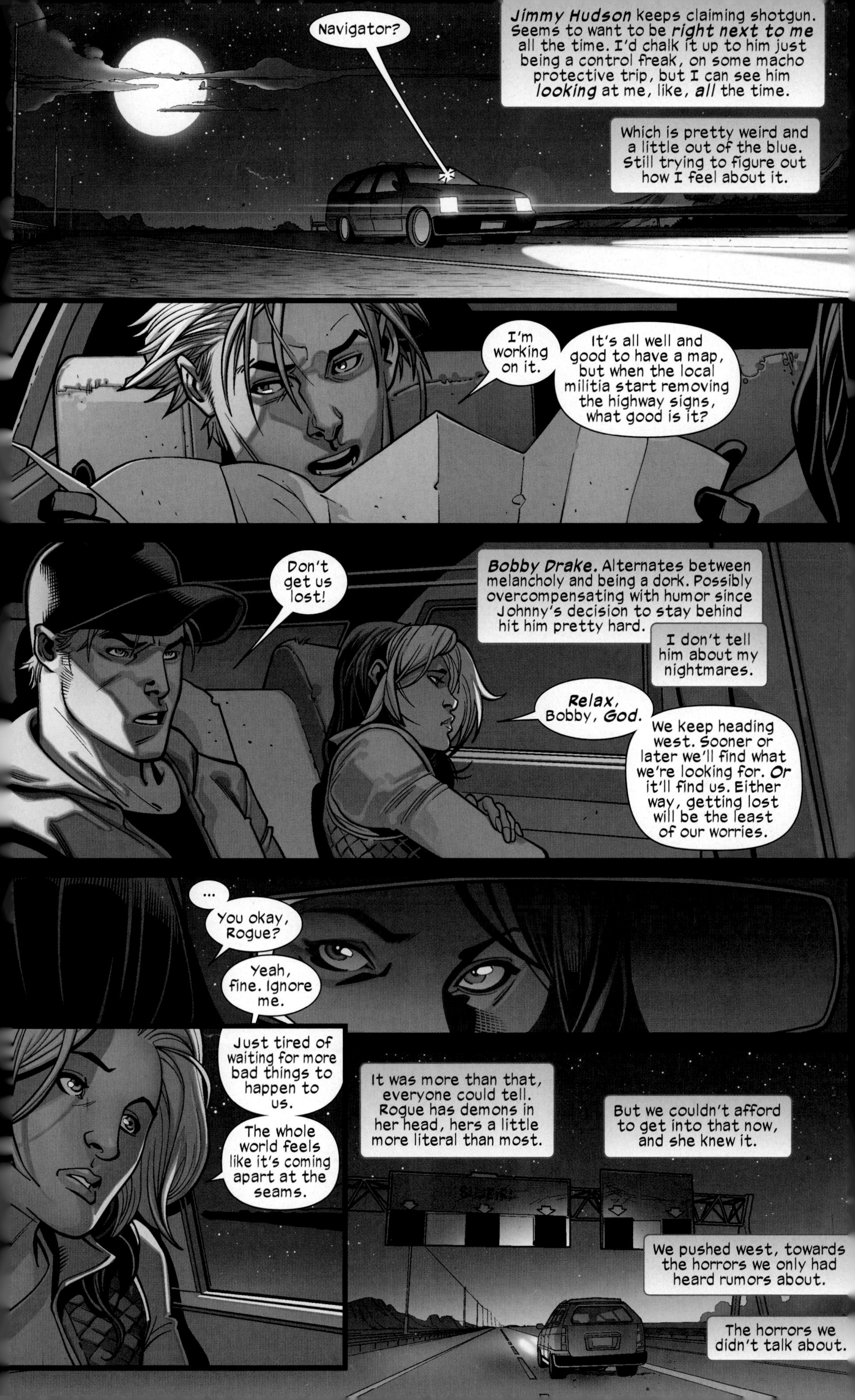
Jimmy Hudson keeps claiming shotgun. Seems to want to be right next to me all the time. I'd chalk it up to him just being a control freak, on some macho protective trip, but I can see him looking at me, like, all the time.
Navigator?
Which is pretty weird and a little out of the blue. Still trying to figure out how I feel about it.
I'm working on it.
It's all well and good to have a map, but when the local militia start removing the highway signs, what good is it?
Bobby Drake. Alternates between melancholy and being a dork. Possibly overcompensating with humor since Johnny's decision to stay behind hit him pretty hard.
Don't get us lost!
I don't tell him about my nightmares.
Relax, Bobby, God.
We keep heading west. Sooner or later we'll find what we're looking for. Or it'll find us. Either way, getting lost will be the least of our worries.
...
You okay, Rogue?
Yeah, fine. Ignore me.
Just tired of waiting for more bad things to happen to us.
The whole world feels like it's coming apart at the seams.
It was more than that, everyone could tell. Rogue has demons in her head, hers a little more literal than most.
But we couldn't afford to get into that now, and she knew it.
We pushed west, towards the horrors we only had heard rumors about.
The horrors we didn't talk about.

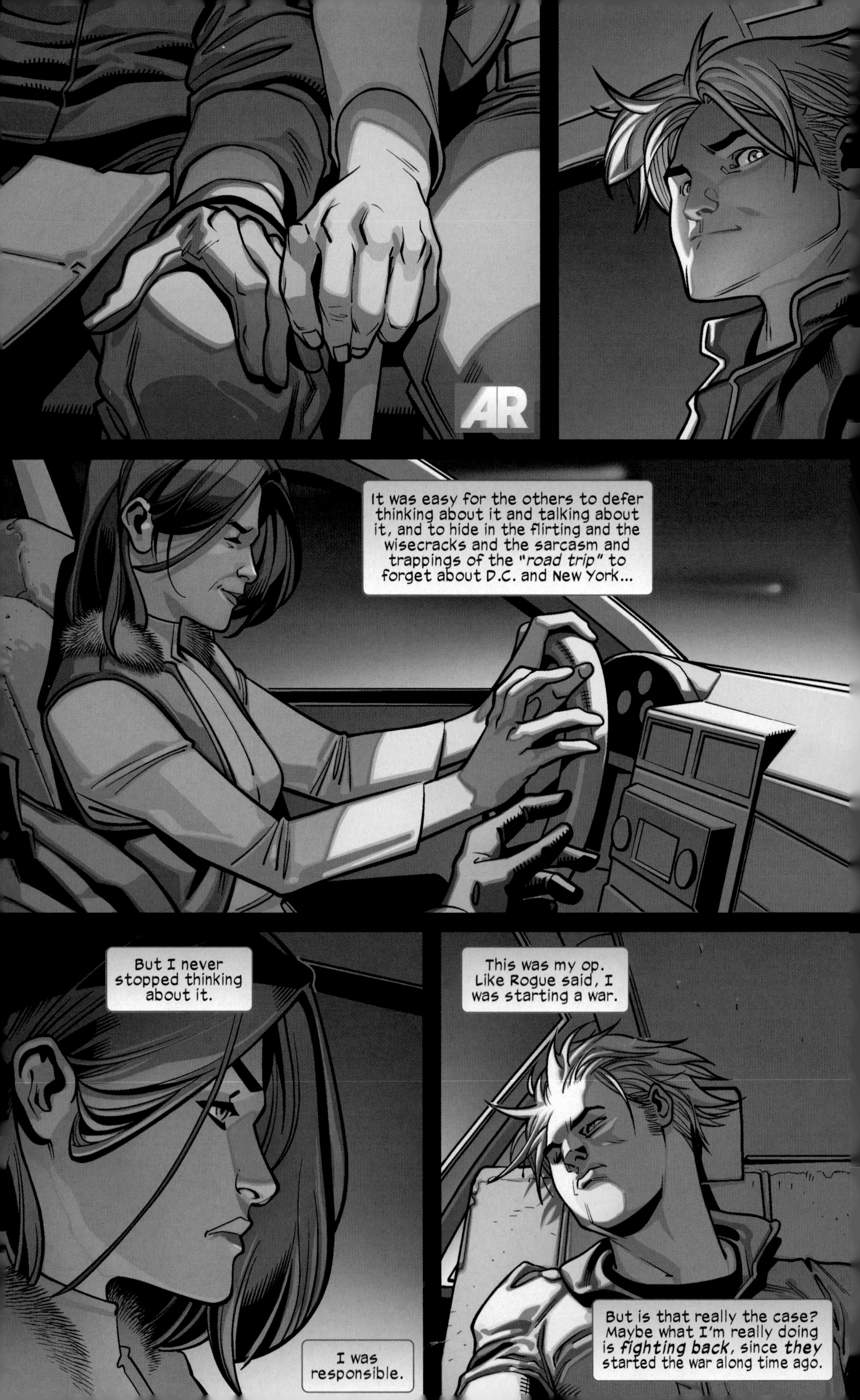
AR
It was easy for the others to defer thinking about it and talking about it, and to hide in the flirting and the wisecracks and the sarcasm and trappings of the "road trip" to forget about D.C. and New York...
But I never stopped thinking about it.
I was responsible.
This was my op. Like Rogue said, I was starting a war.
But is that really the case? Maybe what I'm really doing is fighting back, since they started the war along time ago.

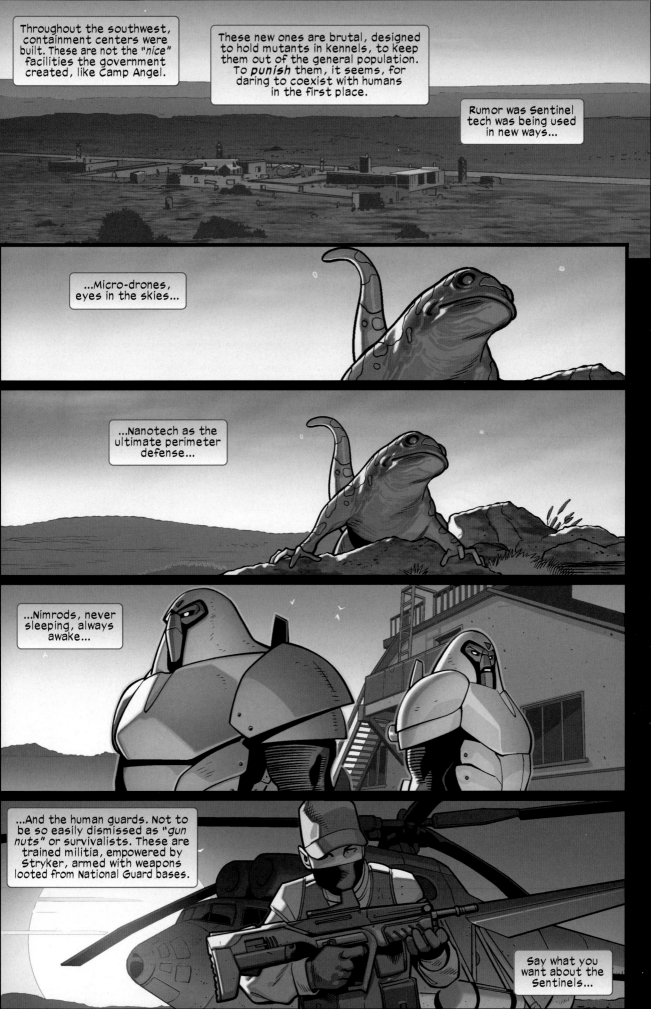

Throughout the southwest, containment centers were built. These are not the "nice" facilities the government created, like Camp Angel.

These new ones are brutal, designed to hold mutants in kennels, to keep them out of the general population. To *punish* them, it seems, for daring to coexist with humans in the first place.

Rumor was Sentinel tech was being used in new ways...

...Micro-drones, eyes in the skies...

...Nanotech as the ultimate perimeter defense...

...Nimrods, never sleeping, always awake...

...And the human guards. Not to be so easily dismissed as "*gun nuts*" or survivalists. These are trained militia, empowered by Stryker, armed with weapons looted from National Guard bases.

Say what you want about the Sentinels...

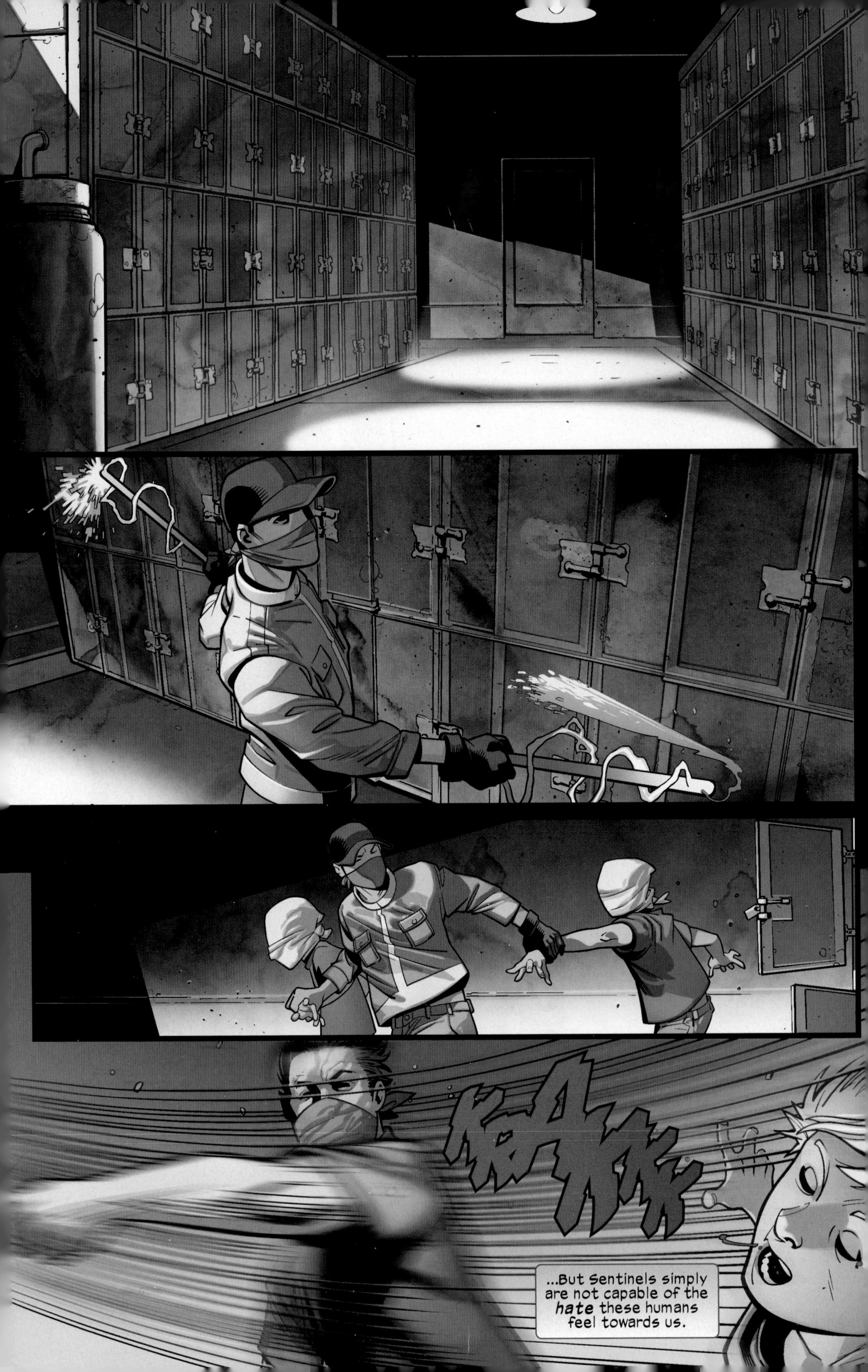

KRAKK
...But Sentinels simply are not capable of the *hate* these humans feel towards us.

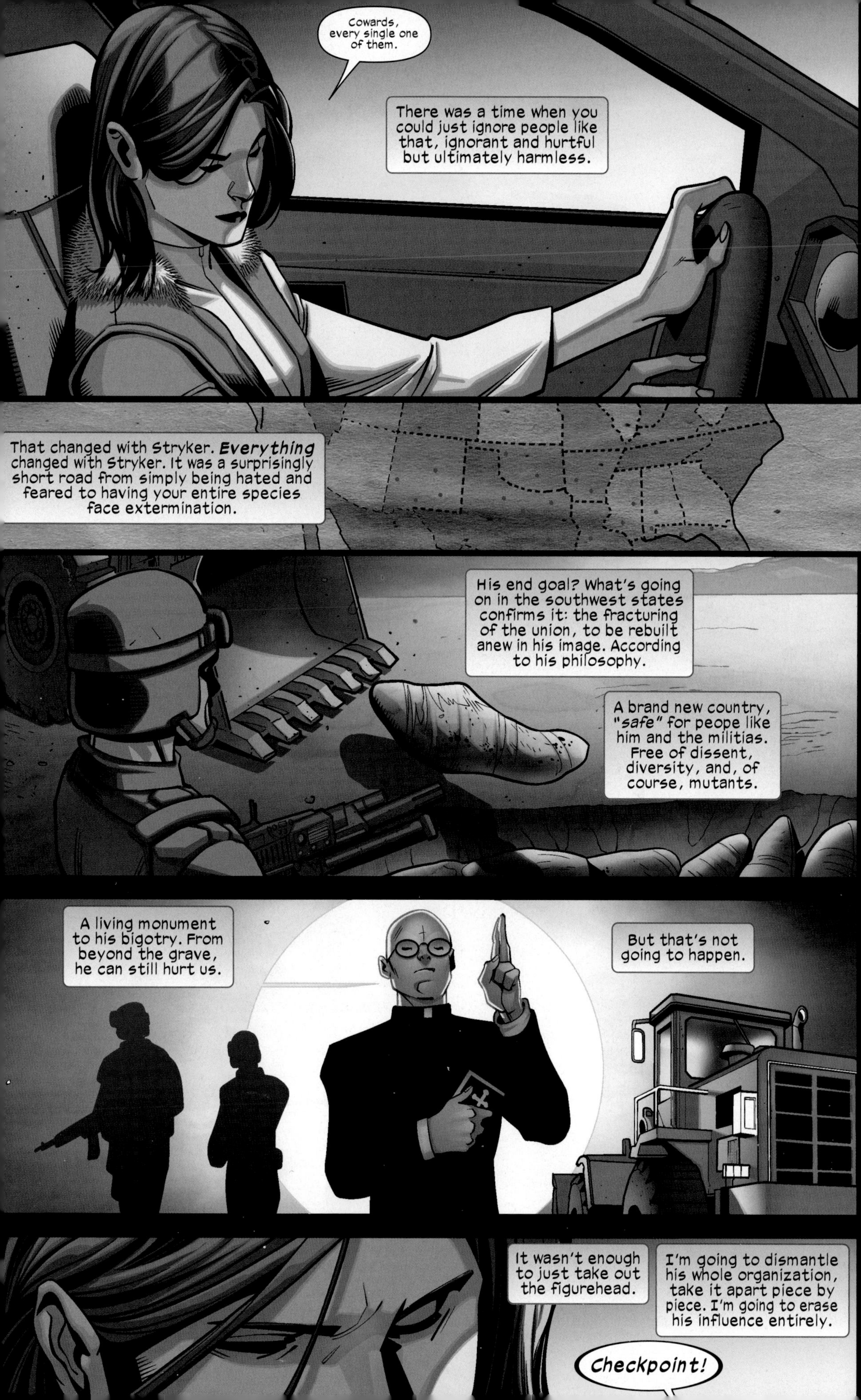

Cowards, every single one of them.
There was a time when you could just ignore people like that, ignorant and hurtful but ultimately harmless.
That changed with Stryker. *Everything* changed with Stryker. It was a surprisingly short road from simply being hated and feared to having your entire species face extermination.
His end goal? What's going on in the southwest states confirms it: the fracturing of the union, to be rebuilt anew in his image. According to his philosophy.
A brand new country, "*safe*" for peope like him and the militias. Free of dissent, diversity, and, of course, mutants.
A living monument to his bigotry. From beyond the grave, he can still hurt us.
But that's not going to happen.
It wasn't enough to just take out the figurehead.
I'm going to dismantle his whole organization, take it apart piece by piece. I'm going to erase his influence entirely.
Checkpoint!

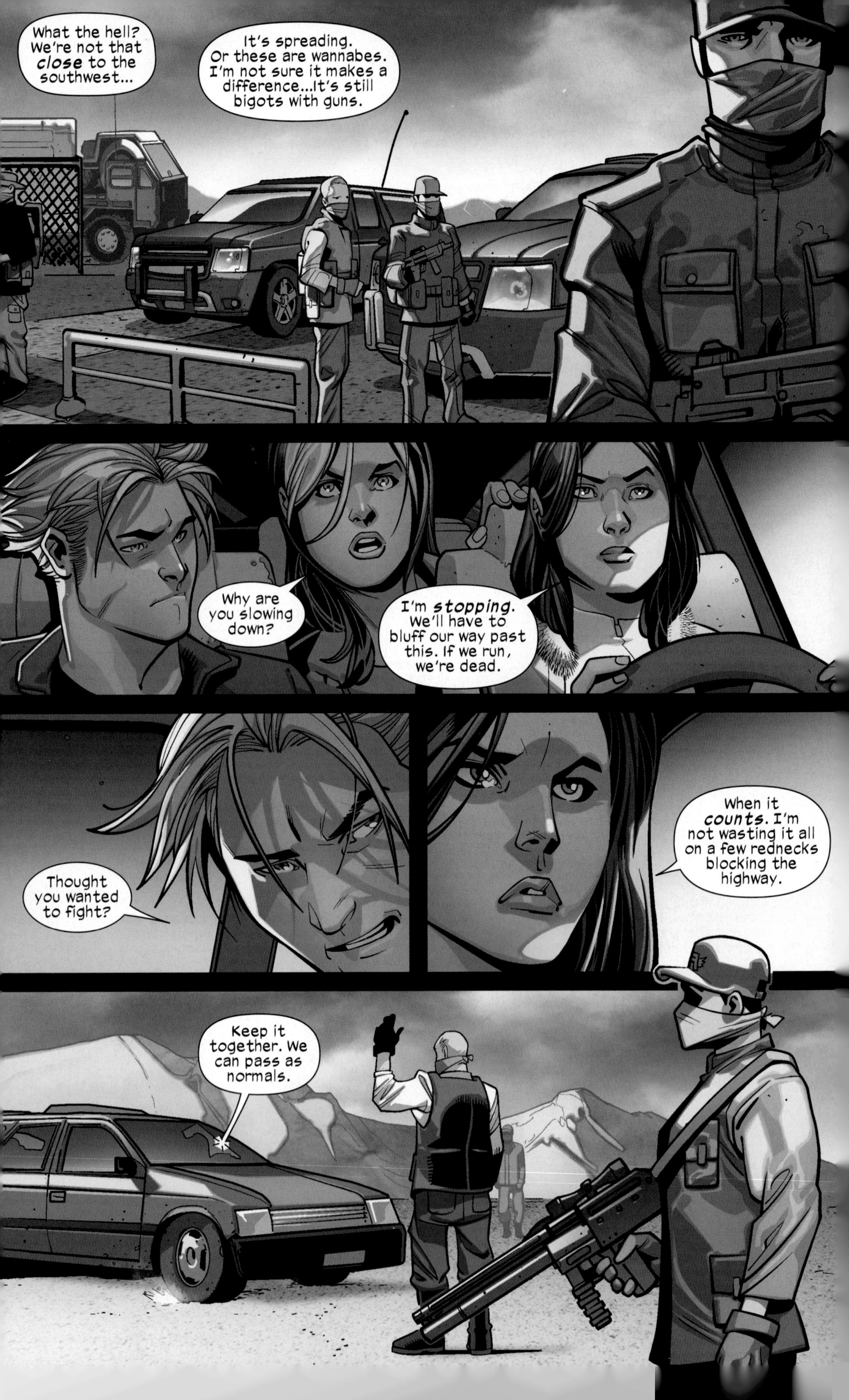
What the hell? We're not that close to the southwest...
It's spreading. Or these are wannabes. I'm not sure it makes a difference...It's still bigots with guns.
Why are you slowing down?
I'm stopping. We'll have to bluff our way past this. If we run, we're dead.
Thought you wanted to fight?
When it counts. I'm not wasting it all on a few rednecks blocking the highway.
Keep it together. We can pass as normals.

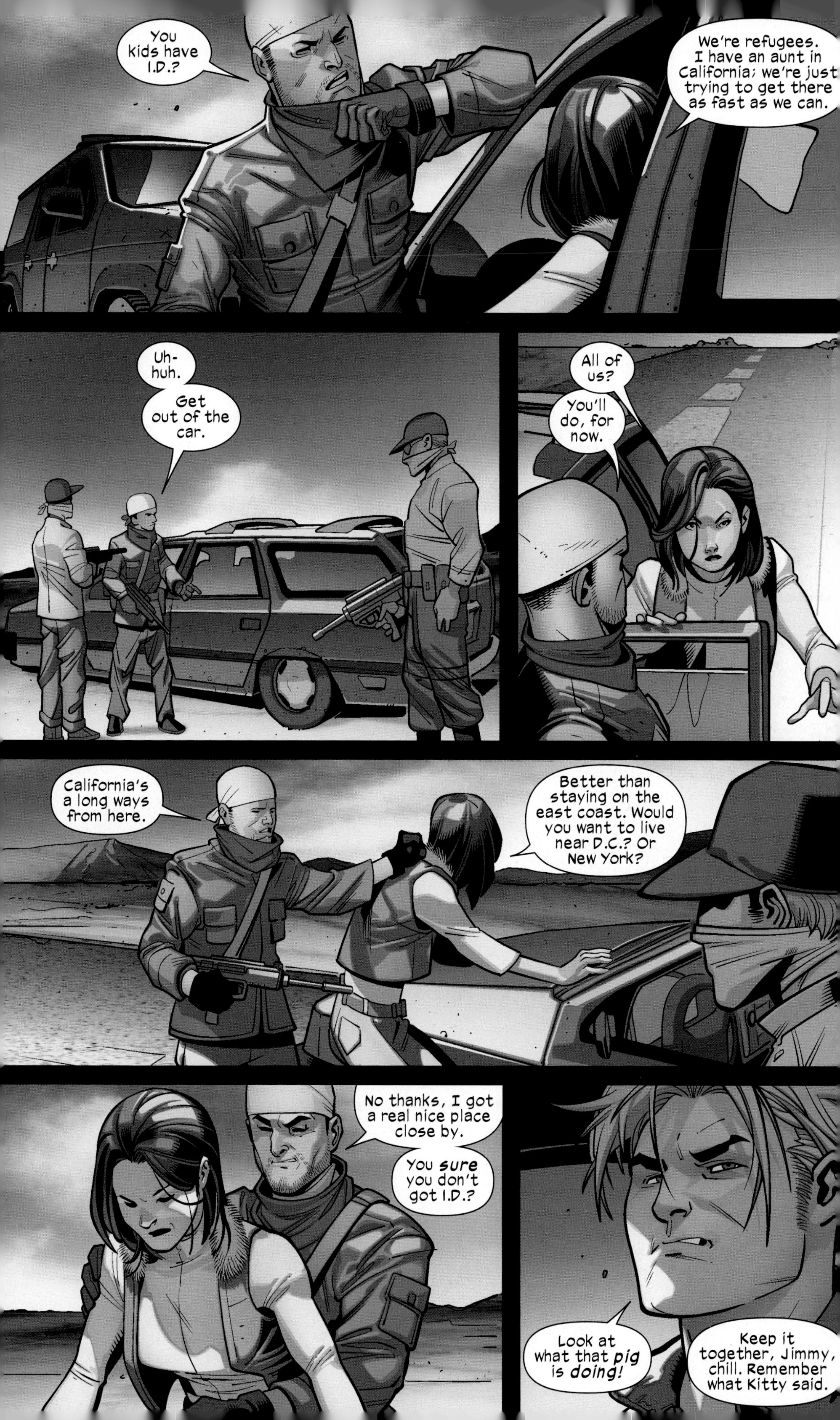
You kids have I.D.?
We're refugees. I have an aunt in California; we're just trying to get there as fast as we can.
Uh-huh.
Get out of the car.
All of us?
You'll do, for now.
California's a long ways from here.
Better than staying on the east coast. Would you want to live near D.C.? Or New York?
No thanks, I got a real nice place close by.
You *sure* you don't got I.D.?
Look at what that *pig* is *doing!*
Keep it together, Jimmy, chill. Remember what Kitty said.

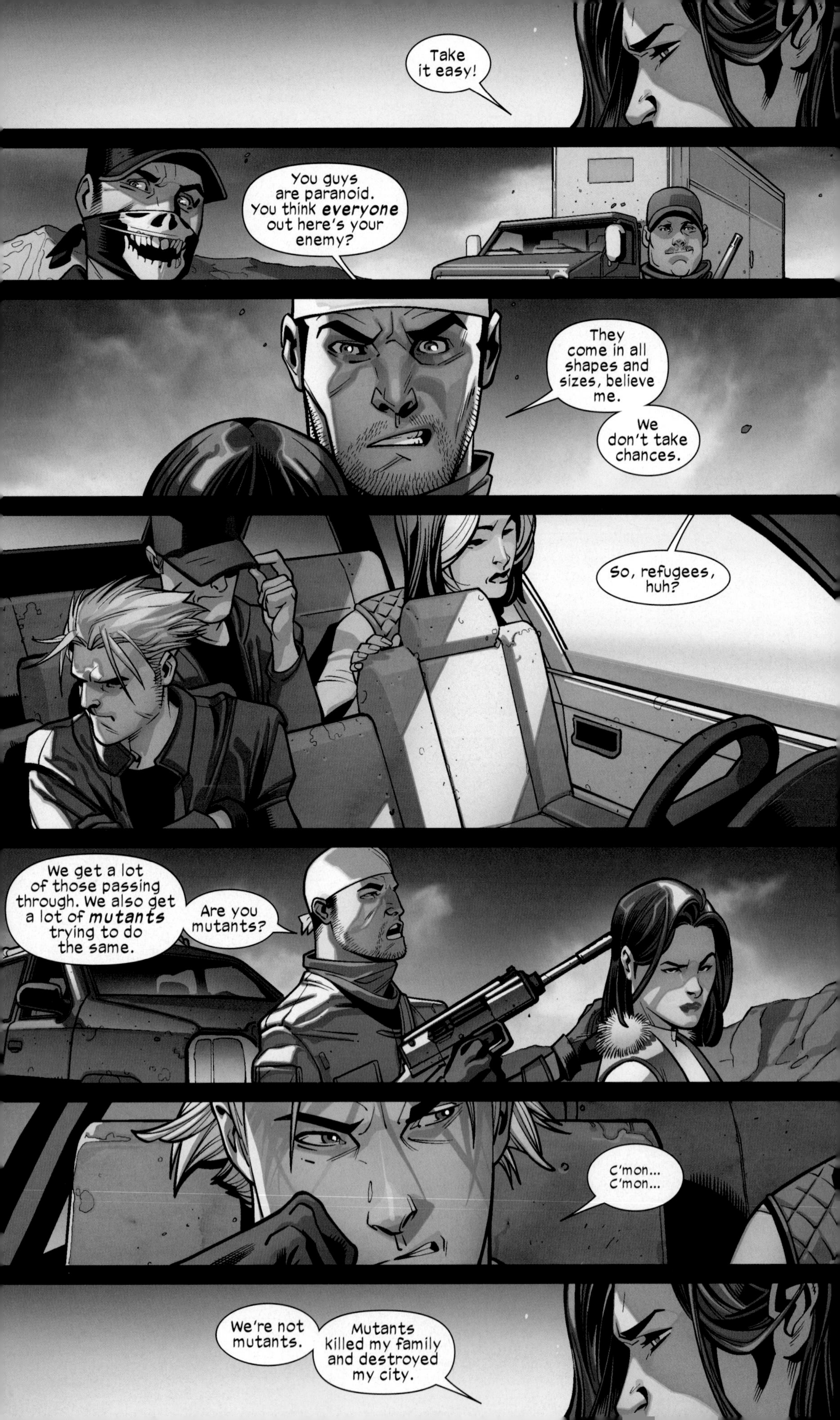

Take it easy!
You guys are paranoid. You think *everyone* out here's your enemy?
They come in all shapes and sizes, believe me.
We don't take chances.
So, refugees, huh?
We get a lot of those passing through. We also get a lot of *mutants* trying to do the same.
Are you mutants?
C'mon... C'mon...
We're not mutants.
Mutants killed my family and destroyed my city.

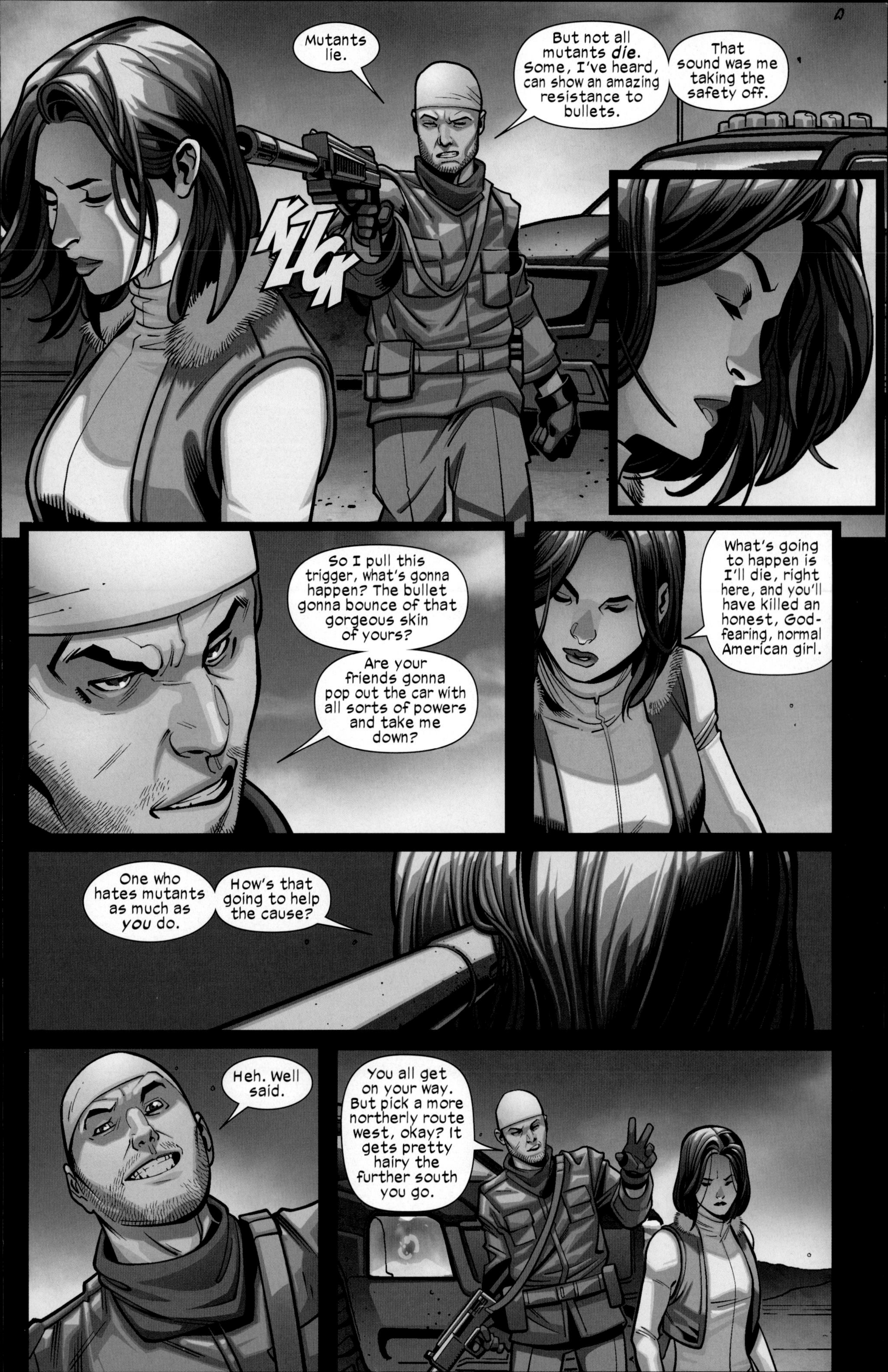
Mutants lie.
But not all mutants *die*. Some, I've heard, can show an amazing resistance to bullets.
That sound was me taking the safety off.
KLIK
So I pull this trigger, what's gonna happen? The bullet gonna bounce of that gorgeous skin of yours?
Are your friends gonna pop out the car with all sorts of powers and take me down?
What's going to happen is I'll die, right here, and you'll have killed an honest, God-fearing, normal American girl.
One who hates mutants as much as *you* do.
How's that going to help the cause?
Heh. Well said.
You all get on your way. But pick a more northerly route west, okay? It gets pretty hairy the further south you go.

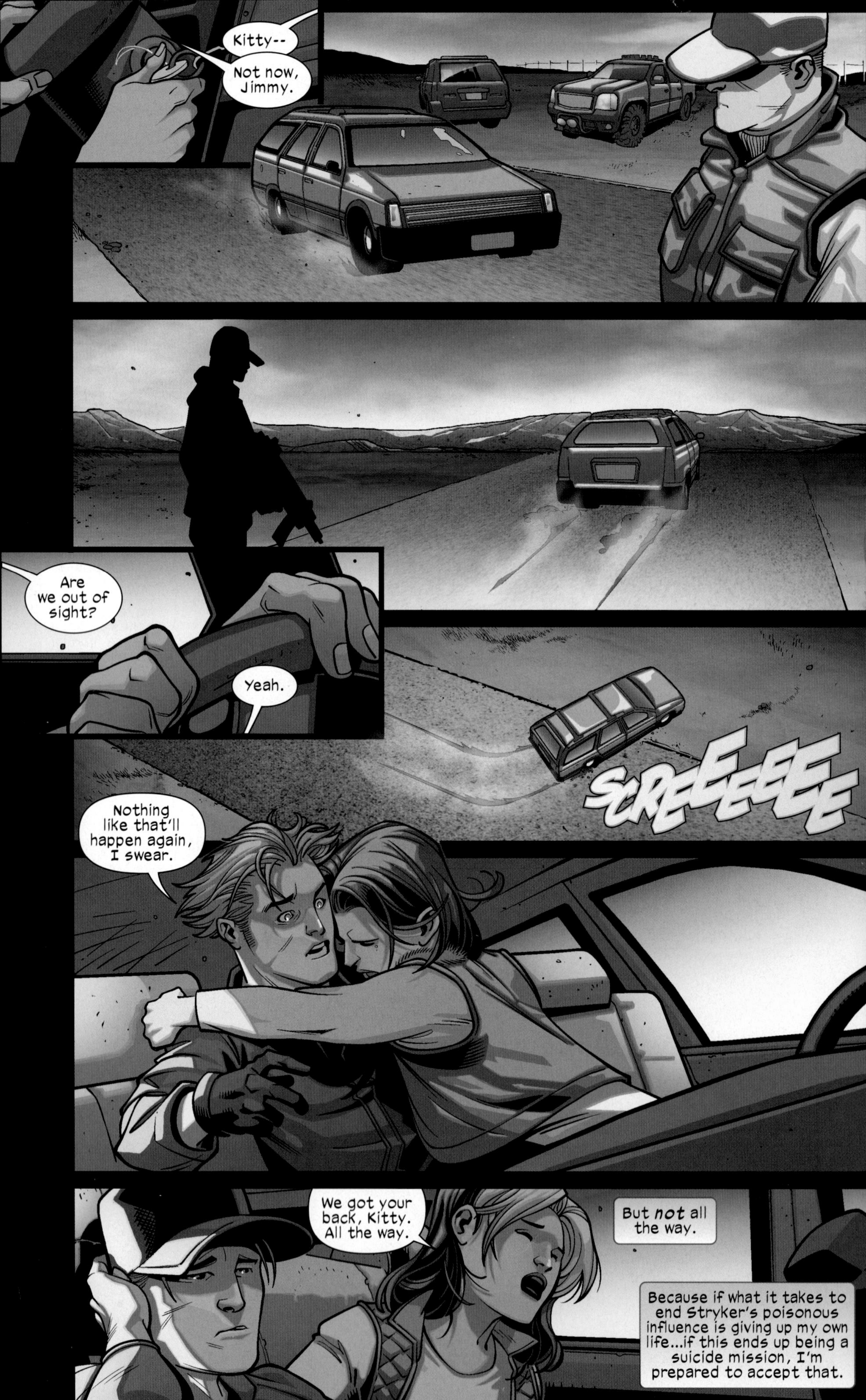

Kitty--
Not now, Jimmy.
Are we out of sight?
Yeah.
SCREEEEEEE
Nothing like that'll happen again, I swear.
We got your back, Kitty. All the way.
But *not* all the way.
Because if what it takes to end Stryker's poisonous influence is giving up my own life...if this ends up being a suicide mission, I'm prepared to accept that.

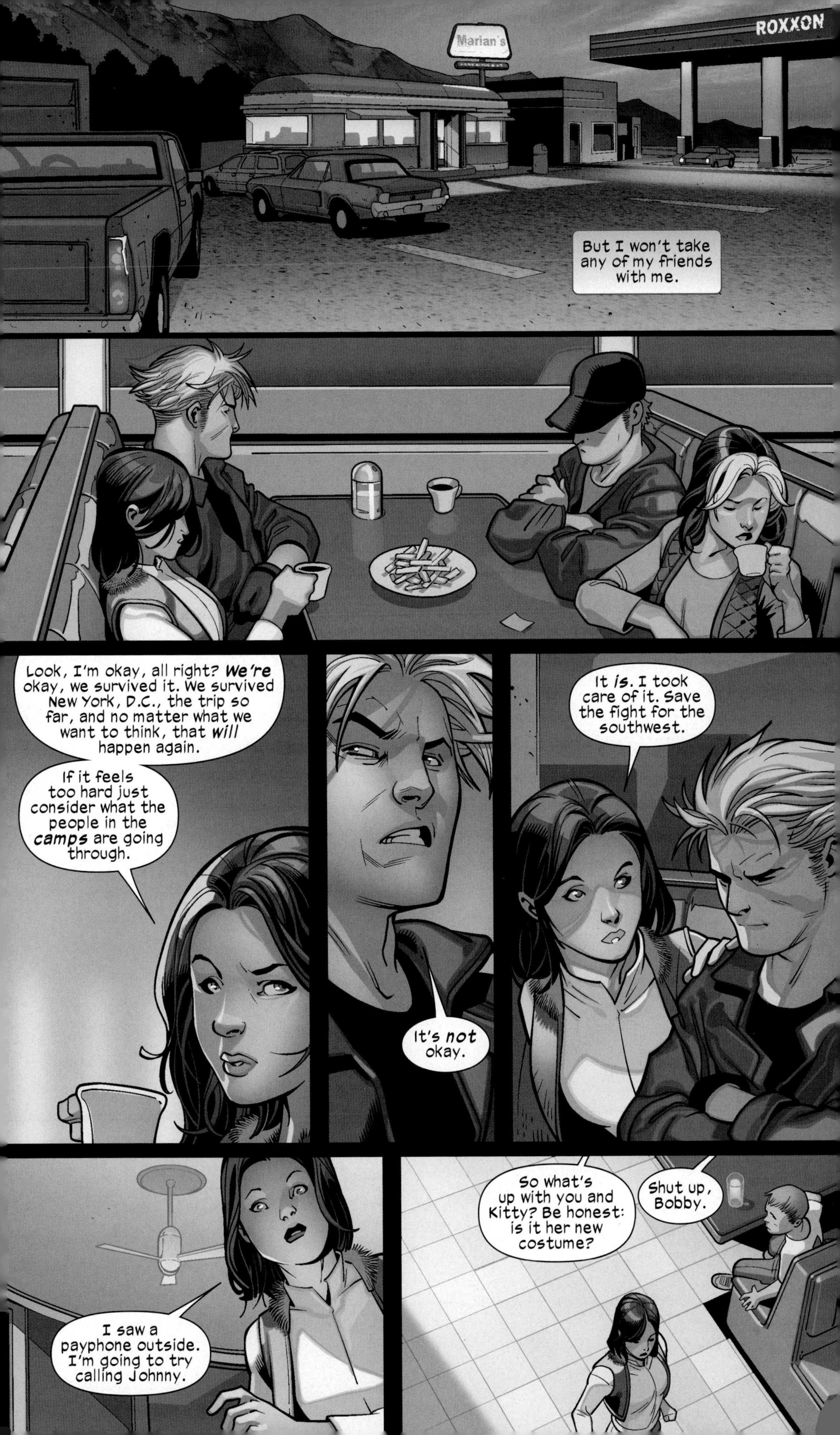
Marian's
ROXXON
But I won't take any of my friends with me.
Look, I'm okay, all right? We're okay, we survived it. We survived New York, D.C., the trip so far, and no matter what we want to think, that will happen again.
If it feels too hard just consider what the people in the camps are going through.
It's not okay.
It is. I took care of it. Save the fight for the southwest.
I saw a payphone outside. I'm going to try calling Johnny.
So what's up with you and Kitty? Be honest: is it her new costume?
Shut up, Bobby.

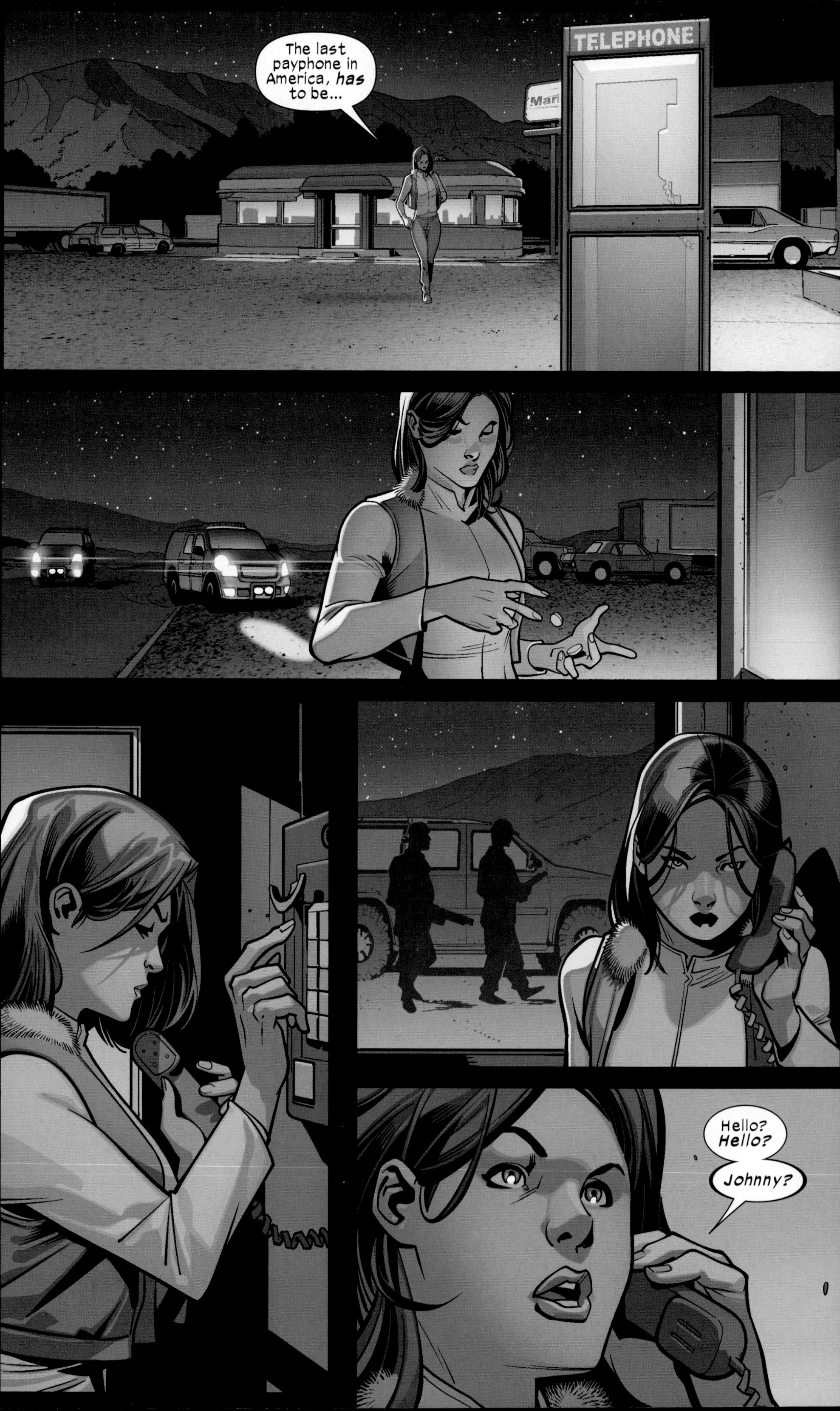
The last payphone in America, *has* to be...
TELEPHONE
Hello? *Hello?*
Johnny?

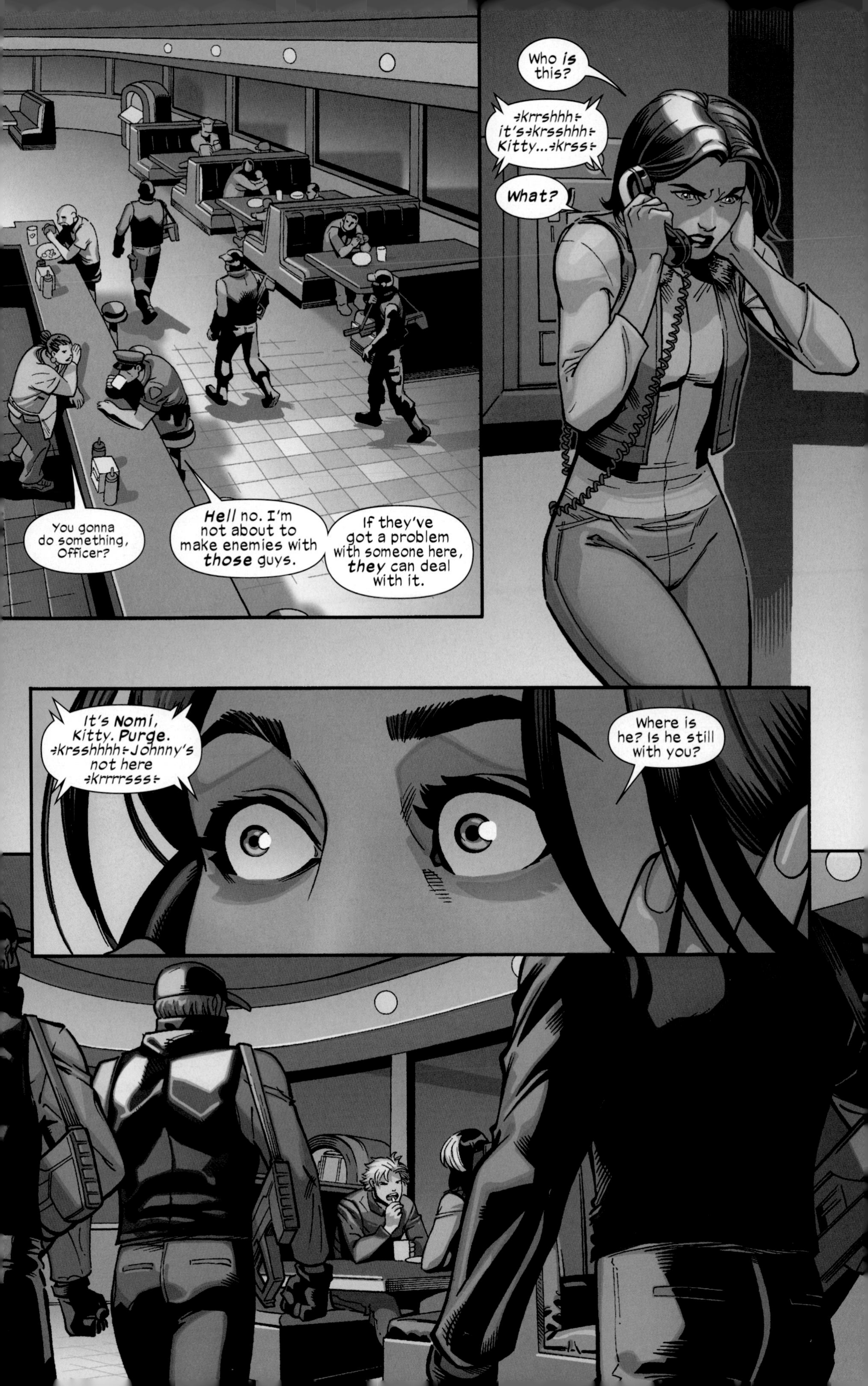

You gonna do something, Officer?
Hell no. I'm not about to make enemies with those guys.
If they've got a problem with someone here, they can deal with it.
Who is this?
-krrshhh- it's -krsshhh- Kitty... -krss-
What?
It's Nomi, Kitty. Purge. -krsshhhh- Johnny's not here -krrrrsss-
Where is he? Is he still with you?

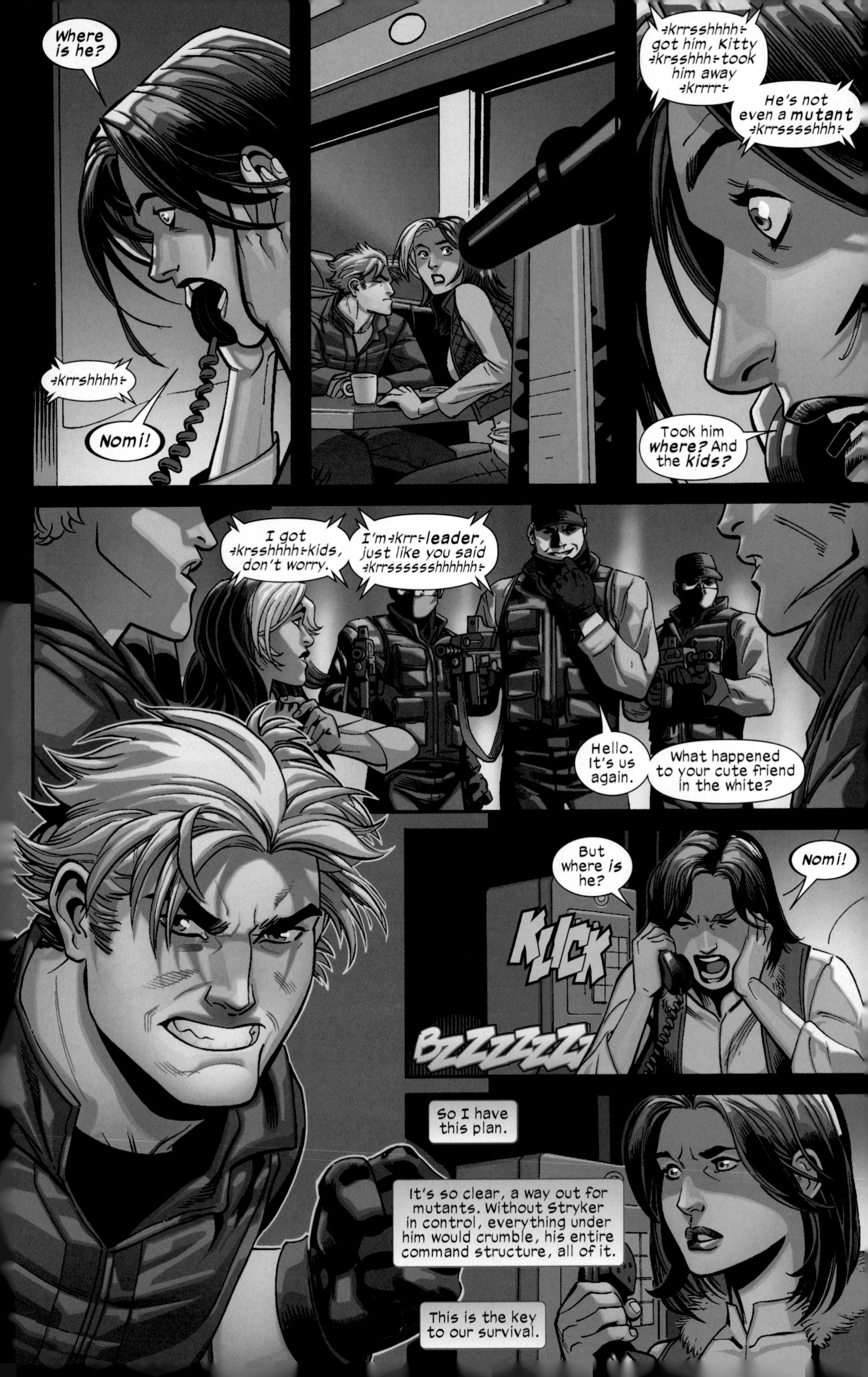

Where is he?
+krrshhhh+
Nomi!
+krrsshhhh+ got him, Kitty +krsshhh+ took him away +krrrr+
He's not even a mutant +krrssshhh+
Took him where? And the kids?
I got +krsshhhh+ kids, don't worry.
I'm +krr+ leader, just like you said +krrssssshhhhhh+
Hello. It's us again.
What happened to your cute friend in the white?
But where is he?
Nomi!
KLICK
BZZZZZZ
So I have this plan.
It's so clear, a way out for mutants. Without Stryker in control, everything under him would crumble, his entire command structure, all of it.
This is the key to our survival.

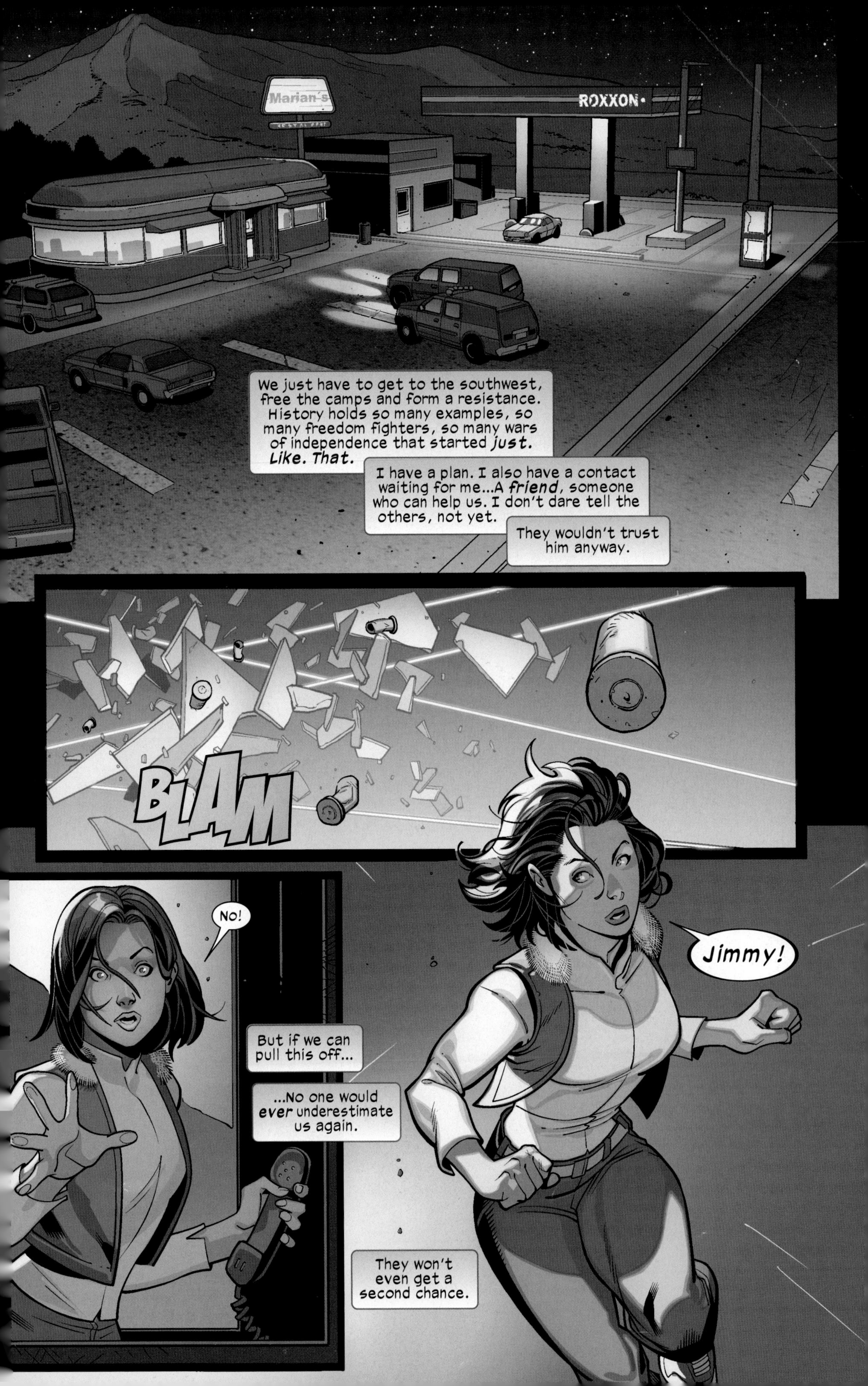
Marian's
ROXXON
We just have to get to the southwest, free the camps and form a resistance. History holds so many examples, so many freedom fighters, so many wars of independence that started *just. Like. That.*
I have a plan. I also have a contact waiting for me...A *friend*, someone who can help us. I don't dare tell the others, not yet.
They wouldn't trust him anyway.
BLAM
No!
Jimmy!
But if we can pull this off...
...No one would *ever* underestimate us again.
They won't even get a second chance.

9

ULTIMATE COMICS **X-MEN** #15

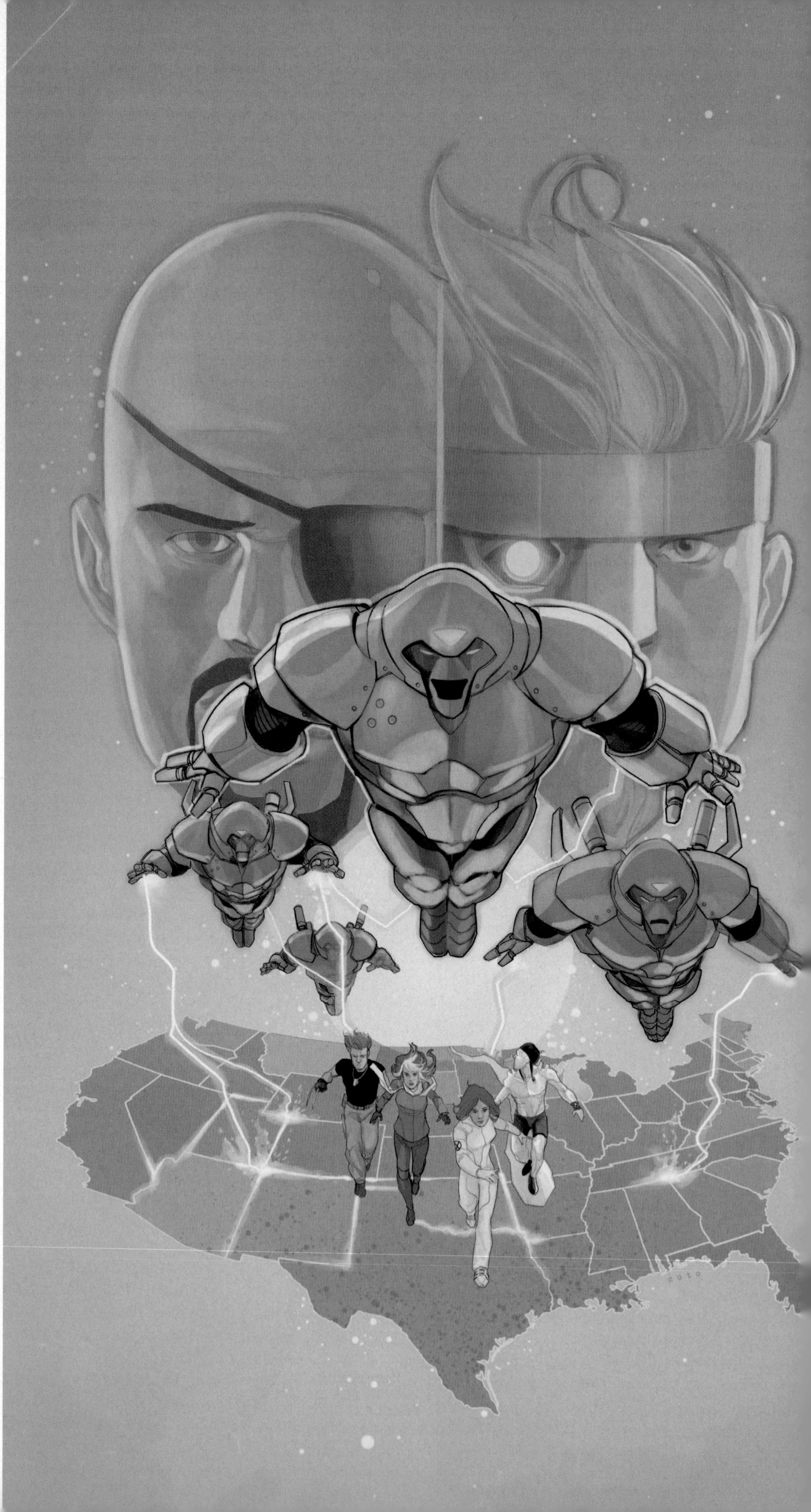

S.H.I.E.L.D. SITUATION MAP:

[Anti-government militia hot spots]

Montana, N.Dakota, S.Dakota, Wyoming, Arizona, New Mexico, N.Carolina, S.Carolina, Georgia

[Eastern seaboard control zone]

New England, New York, New Jersey, Delaware, Washington D.C., Maryland, Virginia

secured by National Guard under emergency powers committee

[the West Coast]

California, Oregon, Washington
 status unknown

[Great Lakes states]

Minnesota, Wisconsin, Michigan, Illinois, Indiana, Ohio
 status unknown

ANTI-MATTER NO FLY ZONE

SENTINEL PUSH

SOUTHERN CALIFORNIA REFUGEE ZONE

NUCLEAR-ARMED NATION

AREA OF URBAN UNREST

DALLAS: CAPITAL CITY OF THE NEW REPUBLIC OF TEXAS

Classified Position

Camp Hutton, secure location of the President of the United States

[The New Republic of Texas]

Texas

declared state independence

[Sentinel-controlled no-man's-land]

New Mexico, Arizona, Utah, Oklahoma
abandoned by the U.S. government

ALL STATES SHOWN IN WHITE ARE U.S. GOVERNMENT-CONTROLLED ZONES

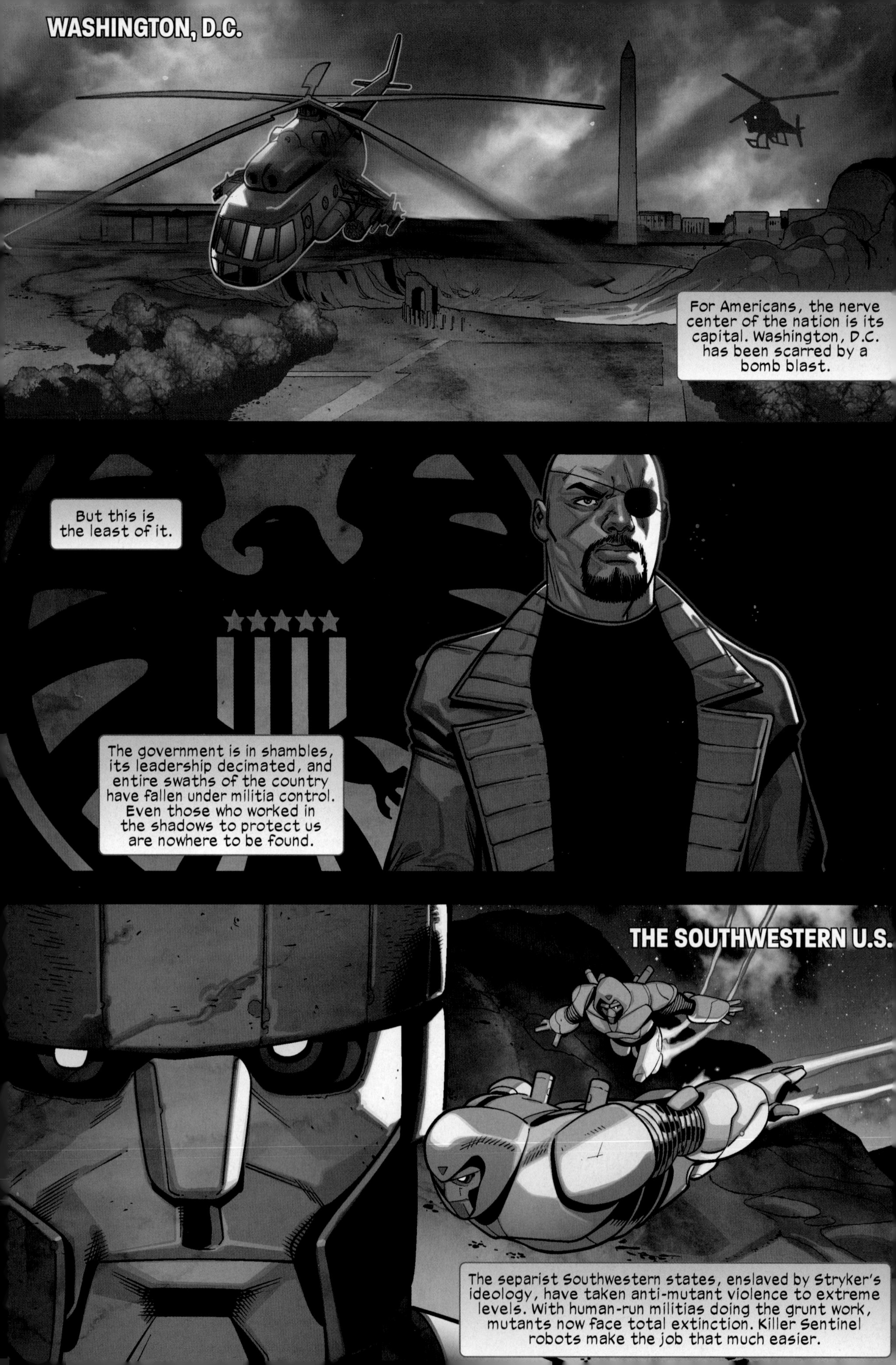
WASHINGTON, D.C.
For Americans, the nerve center of the nation is its capital. Washington, D.C. has been scarred by a bomb blast.
But this is the least of it.
The government is in shambles, its leadership decimated, and entire swaths of the country have fallen under militia control. Even those who worked in the shadows to protect us are nowhere to be found.
THE SOUTHWESTERN U.S.
The separist Southwestern states, enslaved by Stryker's ideology, have taken anti-mutant violence to extreme levels. With human-run militias doing the grunt work, mutants now face total extinction. Killer Sentinel robots make the job that much easier.

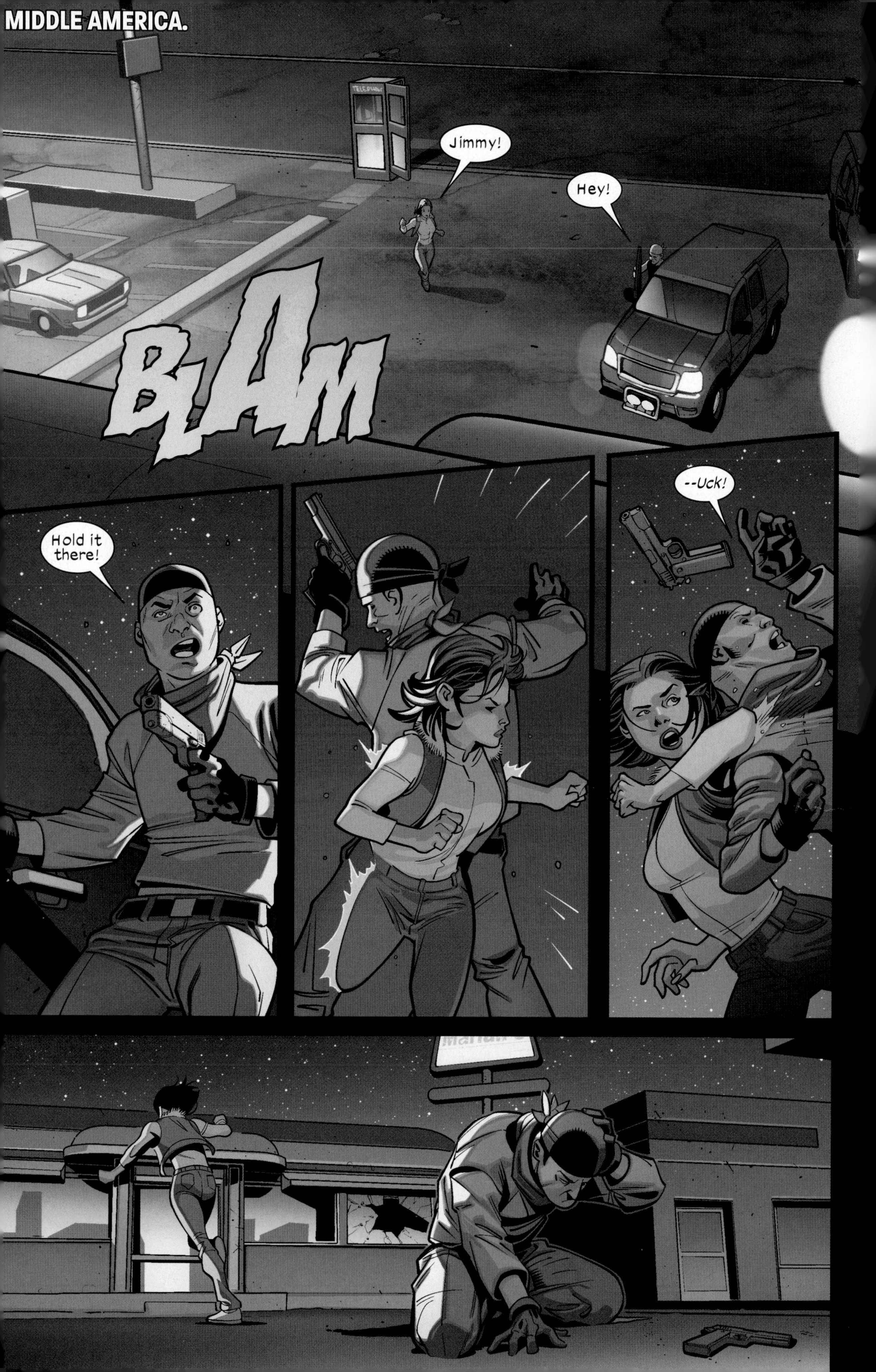
MIDDLE AMERICA.
Jimmy!
Hey!
BLAM
Hold it there!
--Uck!

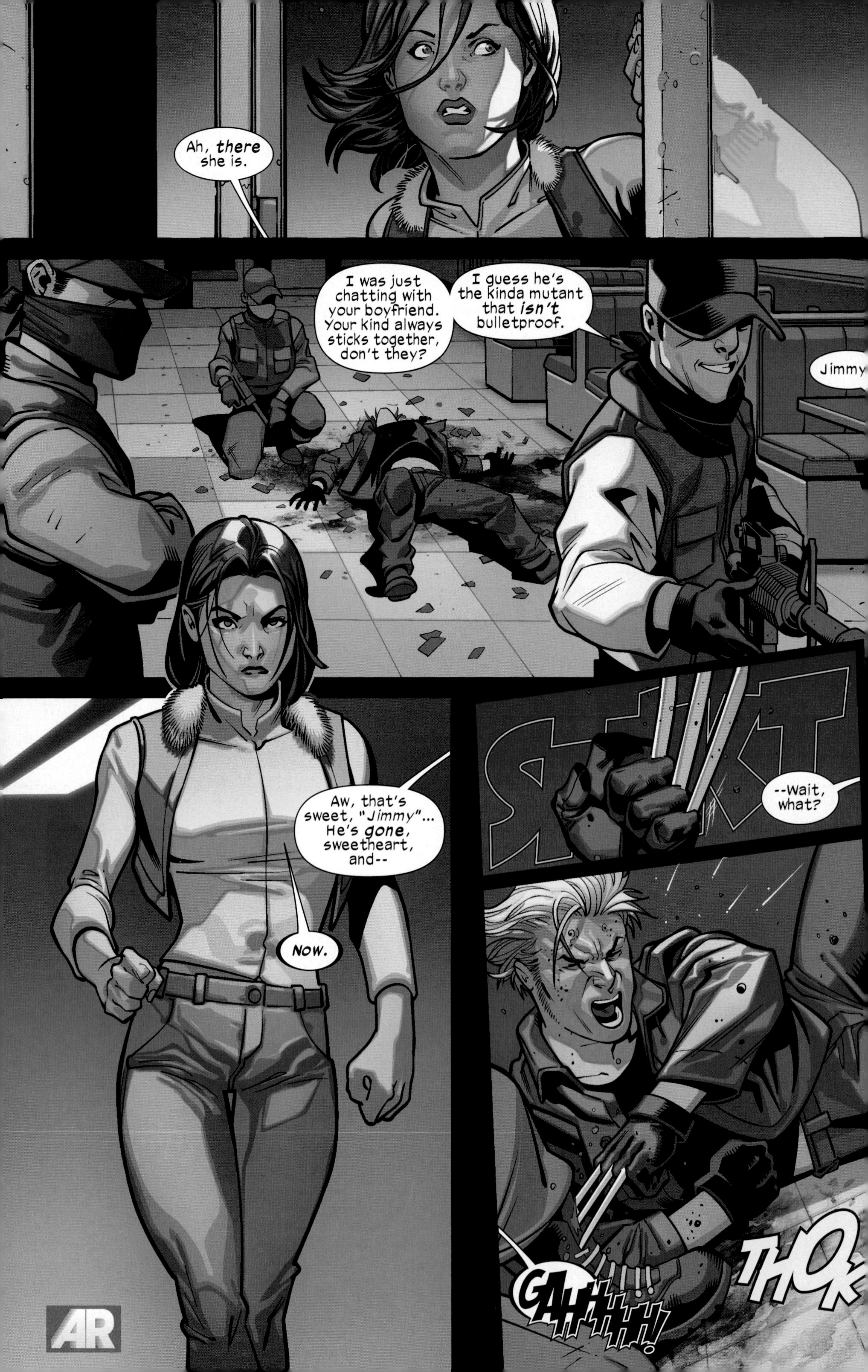

Ah, *there* she is.
I was just chatting with your boyfriend. Your kind always sticks together, don't they?
I guess he's the kinda mutant that *isn't* bulletproof.
Jimmy
Aw, that's sweet, "*Jimmy*"... He's *gone*, sweetheart, and--
NOW.
--Wait, what?
GAHHHHH!
THOK

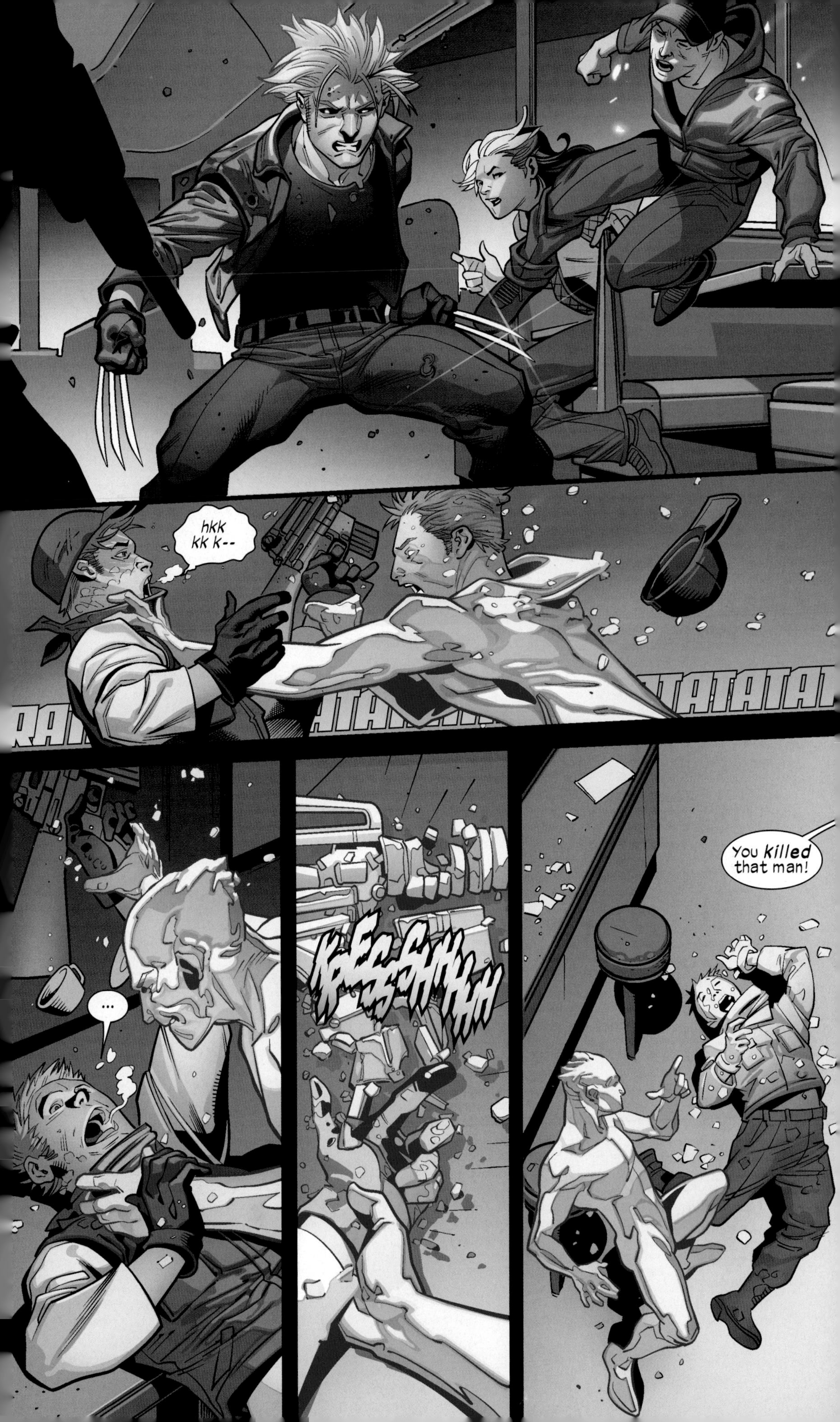
hkk kk k--
...
You killed that man!

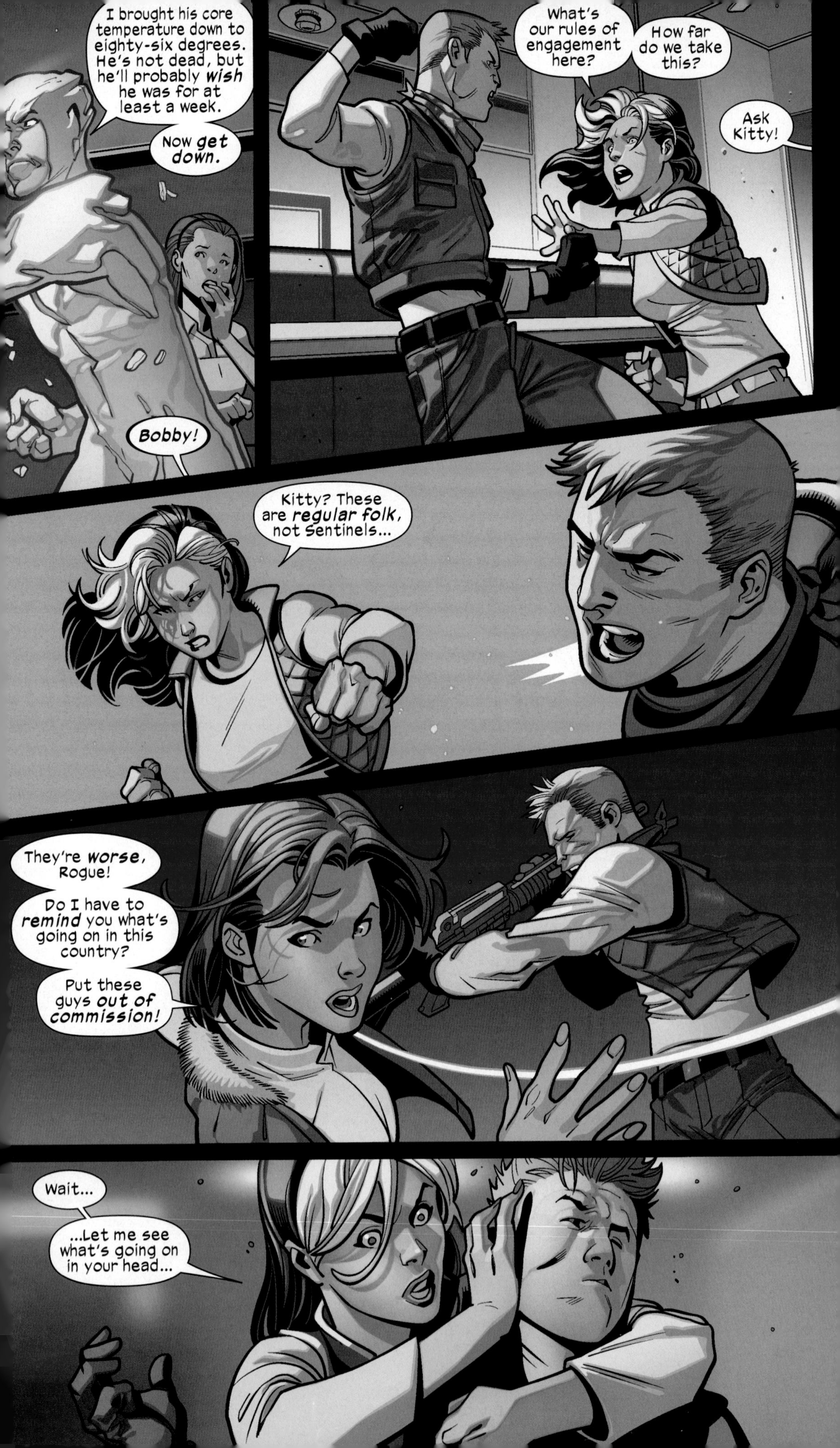
I brought his core temperature down to eighty-six degrees. He's not dead, but he'll probably wish he was for at least a week.
Now get down.
Bobby!
What's our rules of engagement here?
How far do we take this?
Ask Kitty!
Kitty? These are regular folk, not Sentinels...
They're worse, Rogue!
Do I have to remind you what's going on in this country?
Put these guys out of commission!
Wait...
...Let me see what's going on in your head...

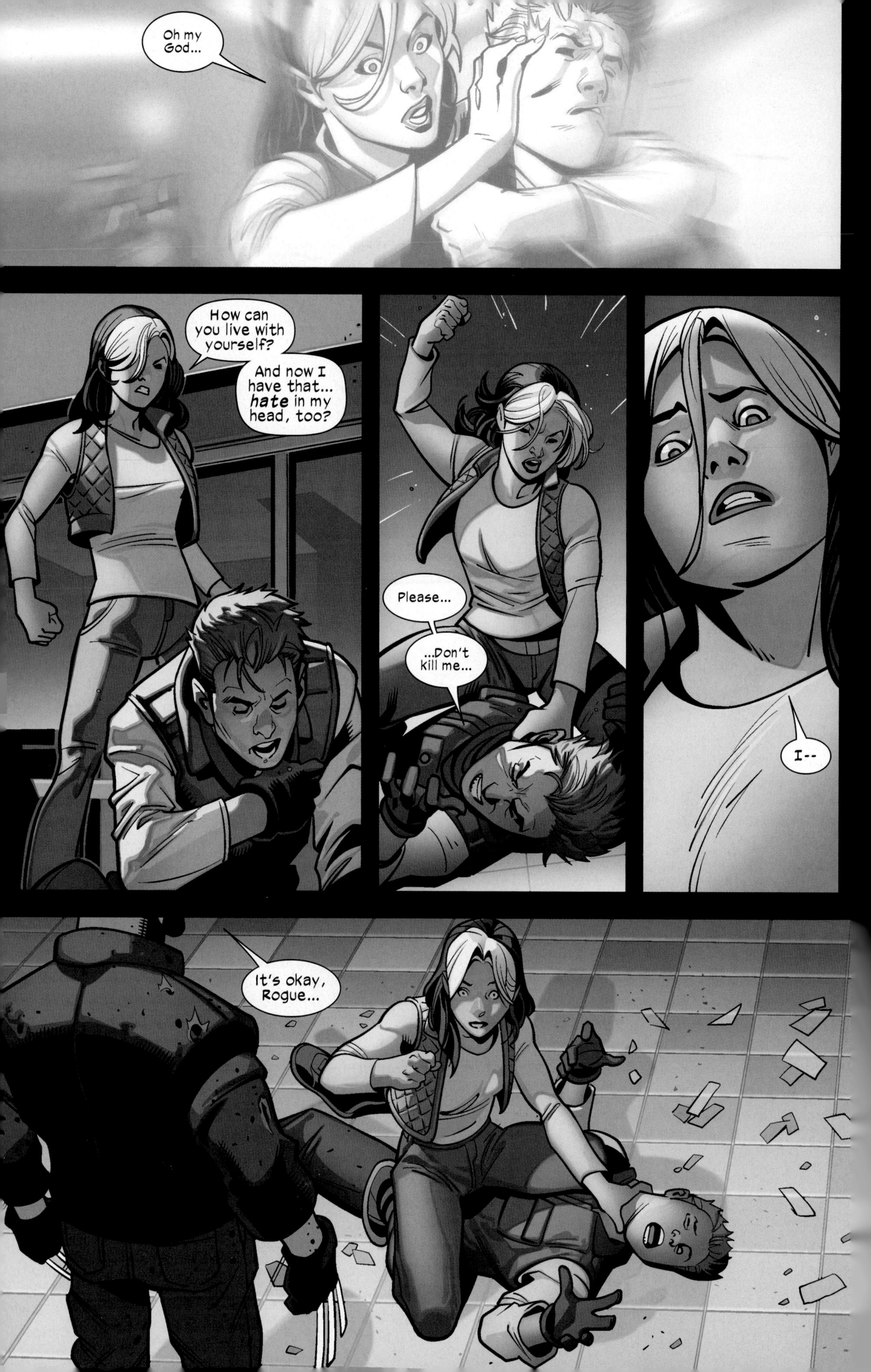
Oh my God...
How can you live with yourself?
And now I have that... *hate* in my head, too?
Please...
...Don't kill me...
I--
It's okay, Rogue...

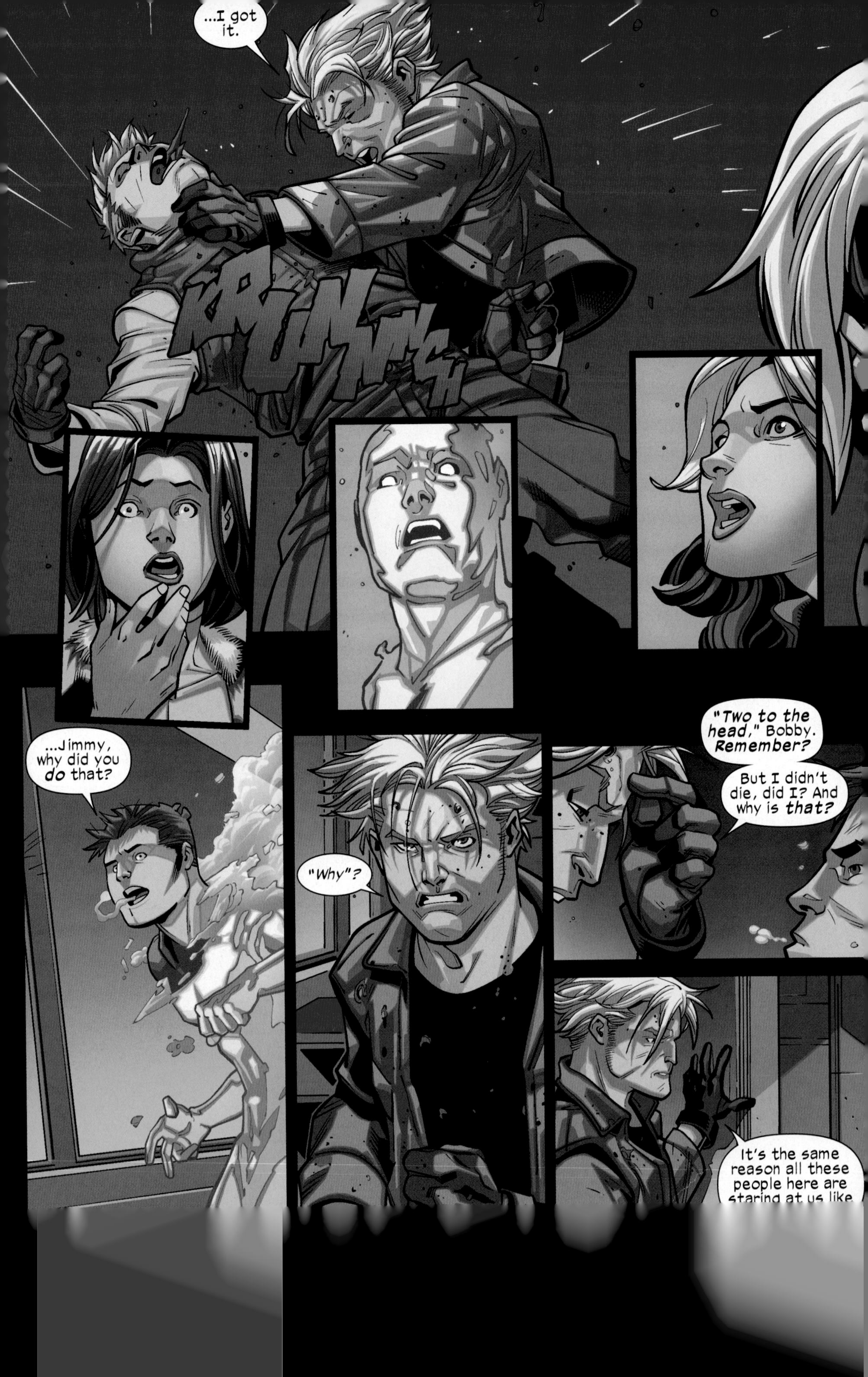

...I got it.
KRUNNCH
...Jimmy, why did you do that?
"Why"?
"Two to the head," Bobby. Remember?
But I didn't die, did I? And why is that?
It's the same reason all these people here are staring at us like

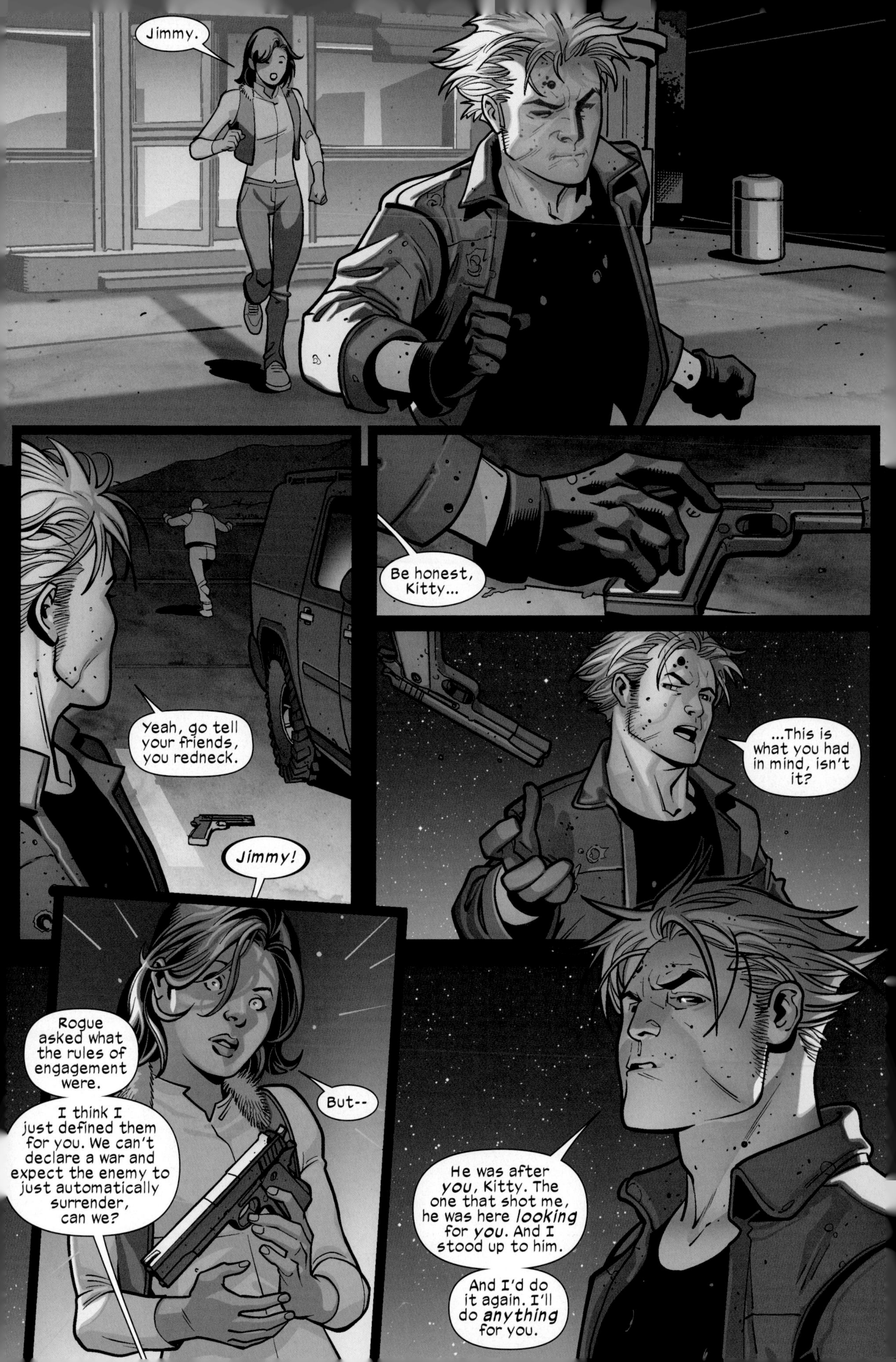
Jimmy.
Yeah, go tell your friends, you redneck.
Be honest, Kitty...
...This is what you had in mind, isn't it?
Jimmy!
Rogue asked what the rules of engagement were.
I think I just defined them for you. We can't declare a war and expect the enemy to just automatically surrender, can we?
But--
He was after *you*, Kitty. The one that shot me, he was here *looking* for *you*. And I stood up to him.
And I'd do it again. I'll do *anything* for you.

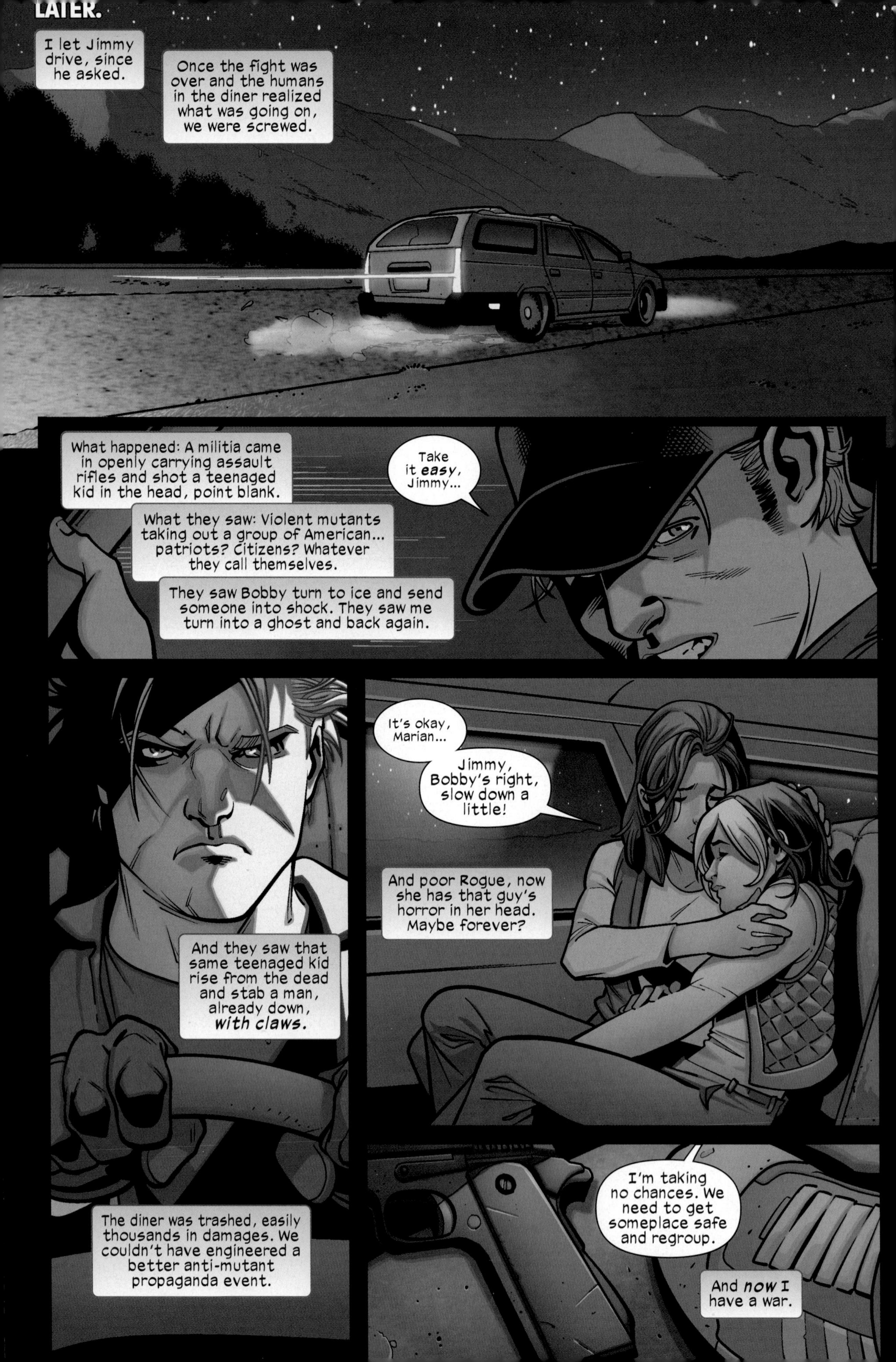
LATER.
I let Jimmy drive, since he asked.
Once the fight was over and the humans in the diner realized what was going on, we were screwed.
What happened: A militia came in openly carrying assault rifles and shot a teenaged kid in the head, point blank.
Take it *easy*, Jimmy...
What they saw: Violent mutants taking out a group of American... patriots? Citizens? Whatever they call themselves.
They saw Bobby turn to ice and send someone into shock. They saw me turn into a ghost and back again.
And they saw that same teenaged kid rise from the dead and stab a man, already down, *with claws.*
It's okay, Marian...
Jimmy, Bobby's right, slow down a little!
And poor Rogue, now she has that guy's horror in her head. Maybe forever?
The diner was trashed, easily thousands in damages. We couldn't have engineered a better anti-mutant propaganda event.
I'm taking no chances. We need to get someplace safe and regroup.
And *now* I have a war.

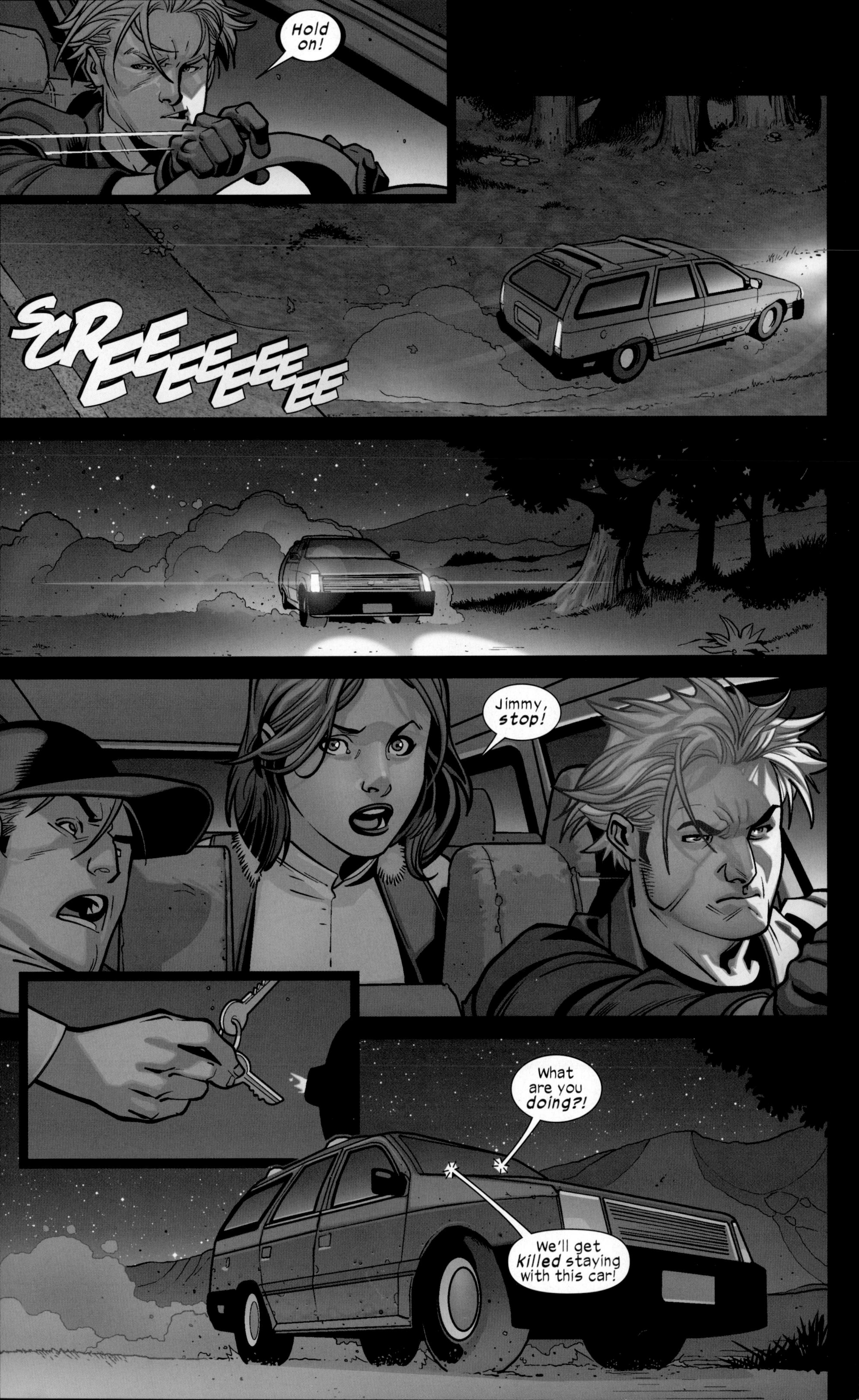
Hold on!
SCREEEEEEEEEEE
Jimmy, stop!
What are you doing?!
We'll get killed staying with this car!

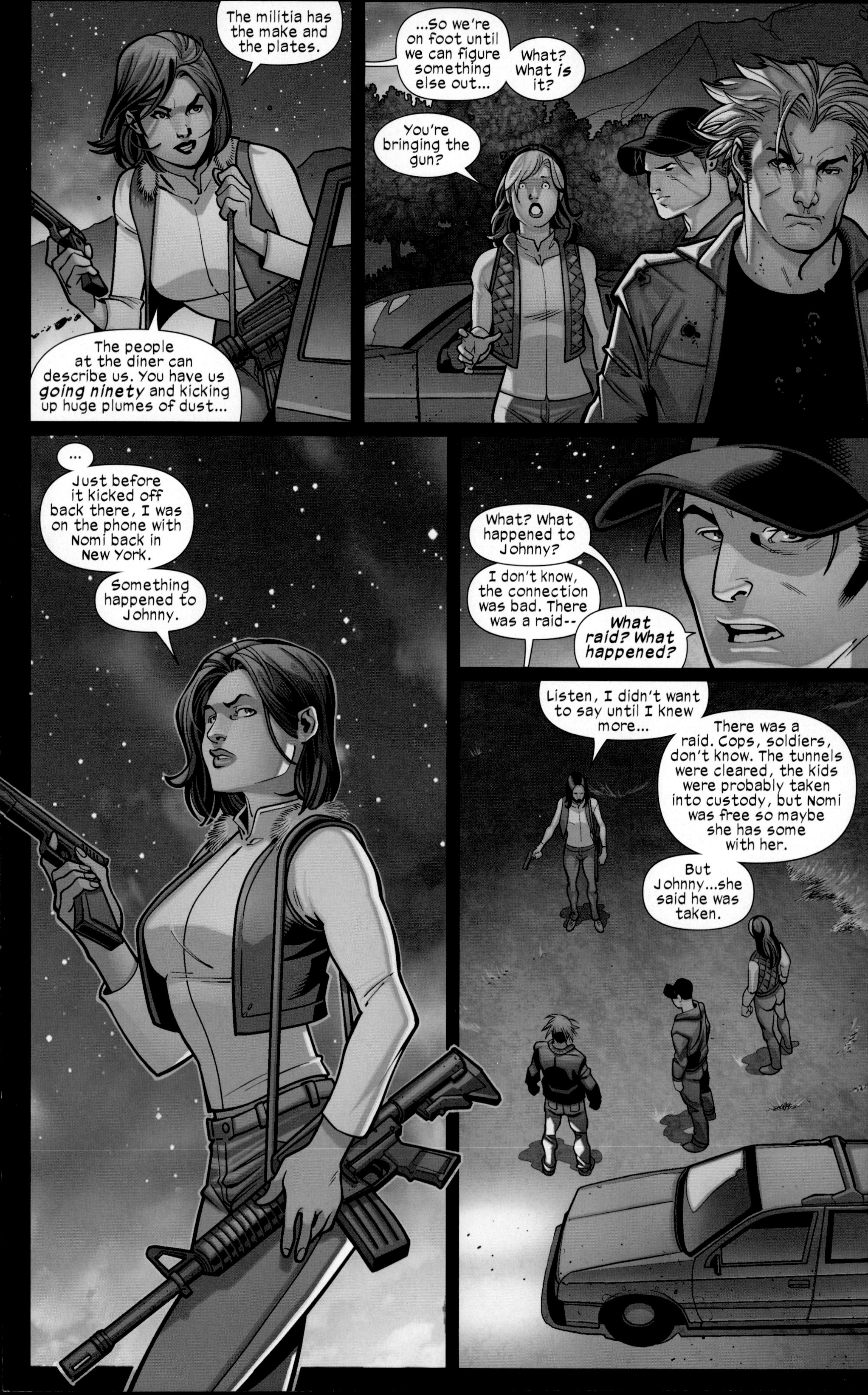
The militia has the make and the plates.
The people at the diner can describe us. You have us *going ninety* and kicking up huge plumes of dust...
...So we're on foot until we can figure something else out...
What? What *is* it?
You're bringing the gun?
...
Just before it kicked off back there, I was on the phone with Nomi back in New York.
Something happened to Johnny.
What? What happened to Johnny?
I don't know, the connection was bad. There was a raid--
What raid? What happened?
Listen, I didn't want to say until I knew more...
There was a raid. Cops, soldiers, don't know. The tunnels were cleared, the kids were probably taken into custody, but Nomi was free so maybe she has some with her.
But Johnny...she said he was taken.

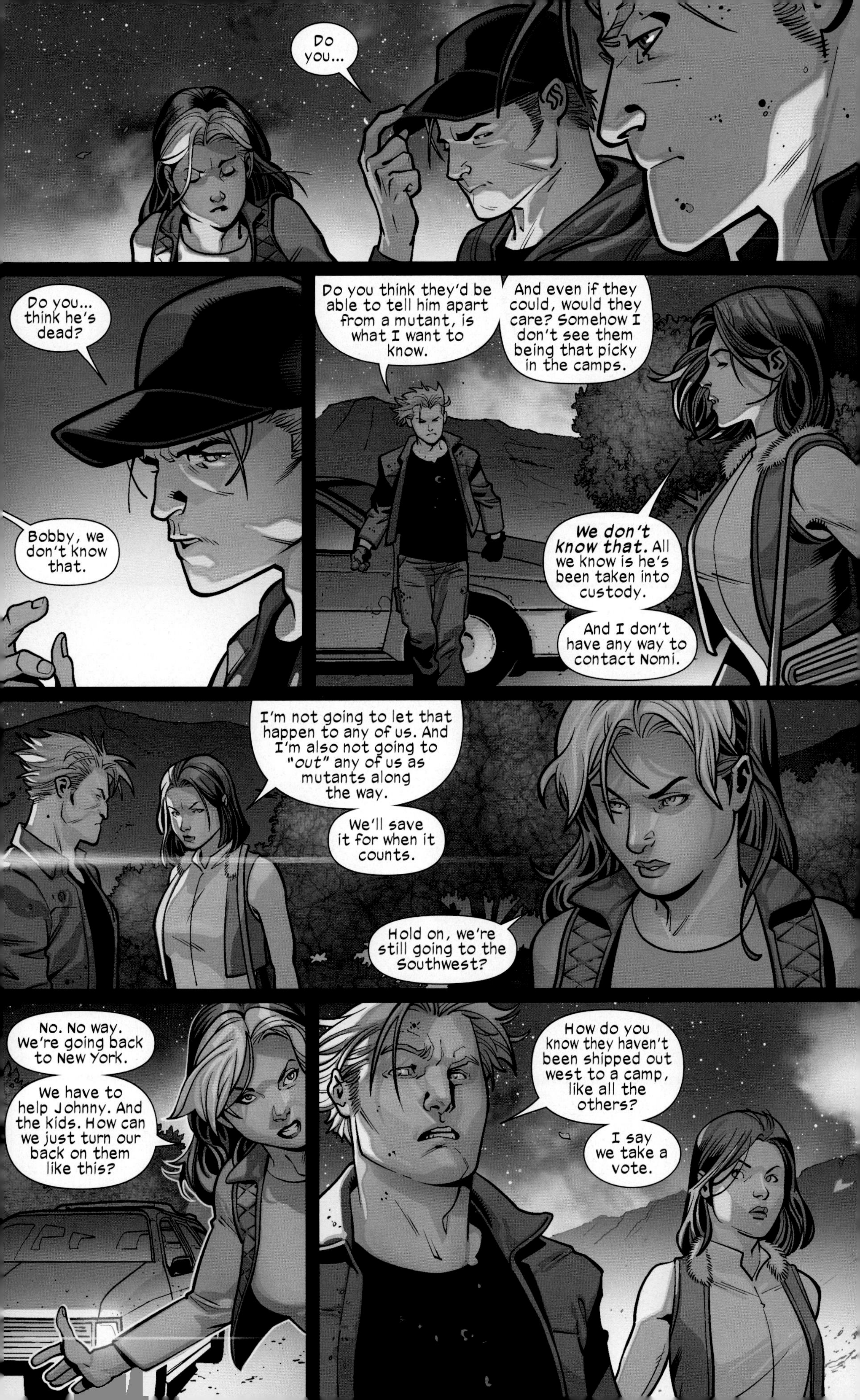
Do you...
Do you... think he's dead?
Bobby, we don't know that.
Do you think they'd be able to tell him apart from a mutant, is what I want to know.
And even if they could, would they care? Somehow I don't see them being that picky in the camps.
We don't know that. All we know is he's been taken into custody.
And I don't have any way to contact Nomi.
I'm not going to let that happen to any of us. And I'm also not going to "*out*" any of us as mutants along the way.
We'll save it for when it counts.
Hold on, we're still going to the Southwest?
No. No way. We're going back to New York.
We have to help Johnny. And the kids. How can we just turn our back on them like this?
How do you know they haven't been shipped out west to a camp, like all the others?
I say we take a vote.

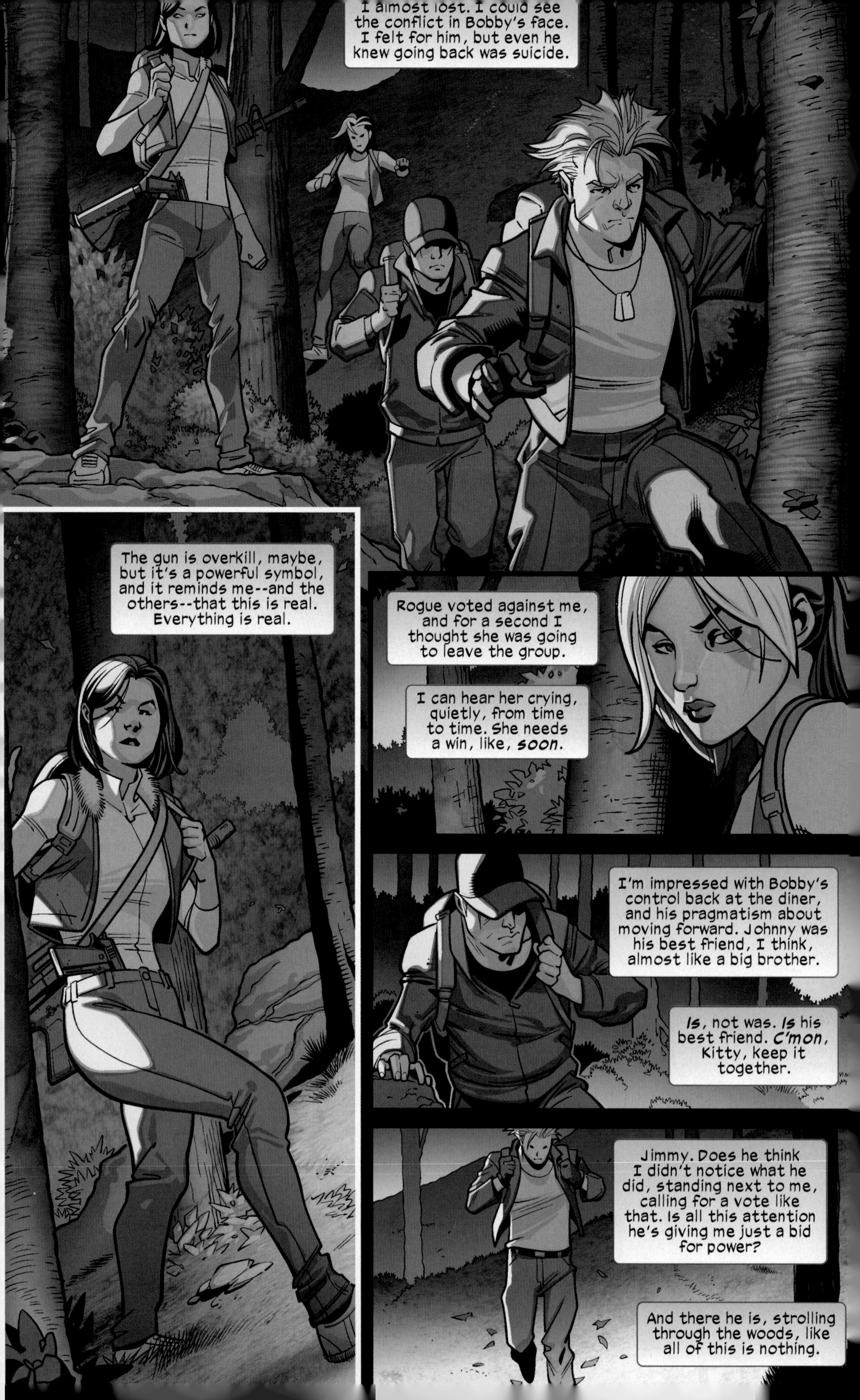
I almost lost. I could see the conflict in Bobby's face. I felt for him, but even he knew going back was suicide.
The gun is overkill, maybe, but it's a powerful symbol, and it reminds me--and the others--that this is real. Everything is real.
Rogue voted against me, and for a second I thought she was going to leave the group.
I can hear her crying, quietly, from time to time. She needs a win, like, *soon*.
I'm impressed with Bobby's control back at the diner, and his pragmatism about moving forward. Johnny was his best friend, I think, almost like a big brother.
Is, not was. *Is* his best friend. *C'mon*, Kitty, keep it together.
Jimmy. Does he think I didn't notice what he did, standing next to me, calling for a vote like that. Is all this attention he's giving me just a bid for power?
And there he is, strolling through the woods, like all of this is nothing.

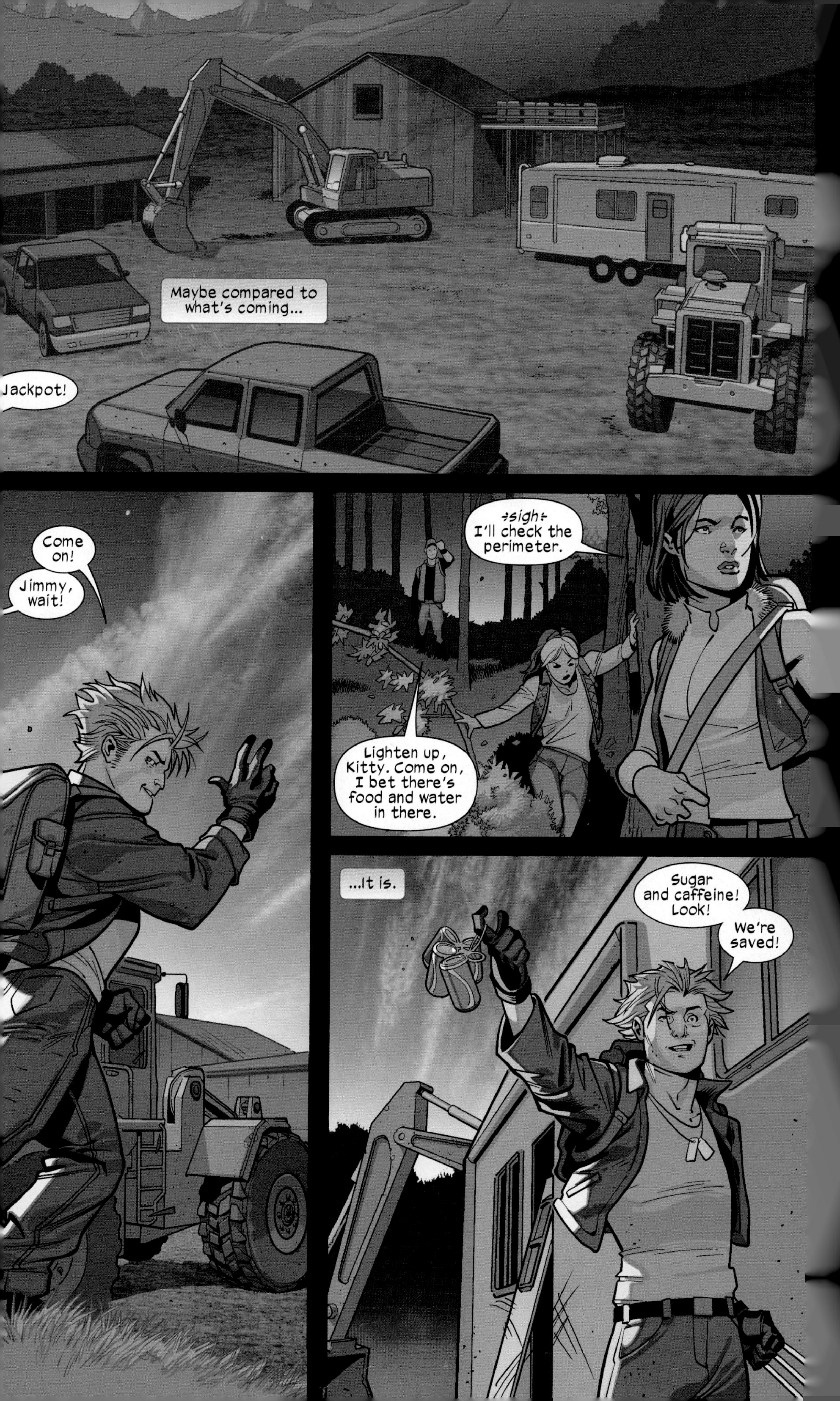
Maybe compared to what's coming...
Jackpot!
Come on!
Jimmy, wait!
≠sigh≠ I'll check the perimeter.
Lighten up, Kitty. Come on, I bet there's food and water in there.
...It is.
Sugar and caffeine! Look!
We're saved!

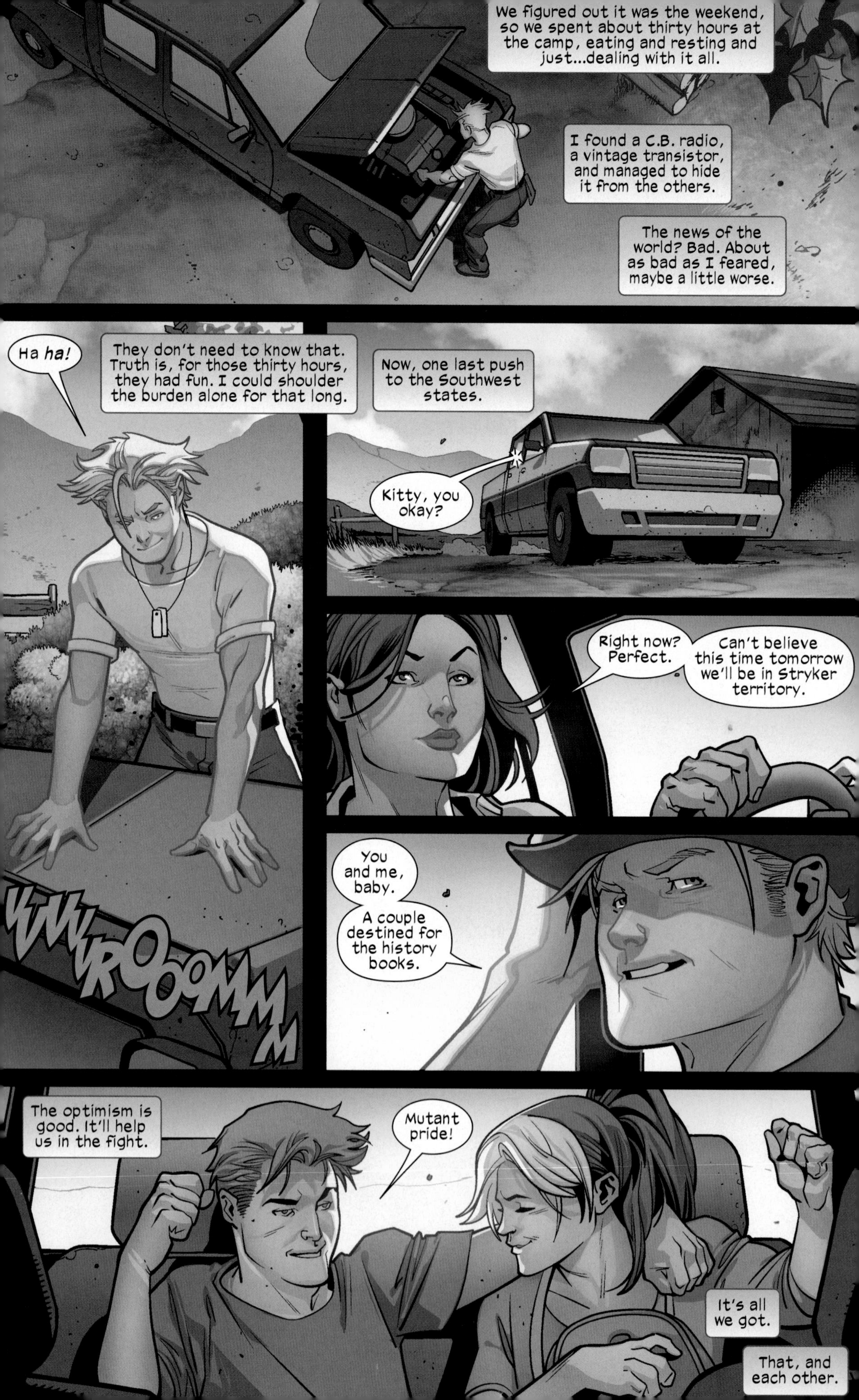
We figured out it was the weekend, so we spent about thirty hours at the camp, eating and resting and just...dealing with it all.
I found a C.B. radio, a vintage transistor, and managed to hide it from the others.
The news of the world? Bad. About as bad as I feared, maybe a little worse.
Ha *ha!*
They don't need to know that. Truth is, for those thirty hours, they had fun. I could shoulder the burden alone for that long.
VVVVROOOMMM
Now, one last push to the Southwest states.
Kitty, you okay?
Right now? Perfect.
Can't believe this time tomorrow we'll be in Stryker territory.
You and me, baby.
A couple destined for the history books.
The optimism is good. It'll help us in the fight.
Mutant pride!
It's all we got.
That, and each other.

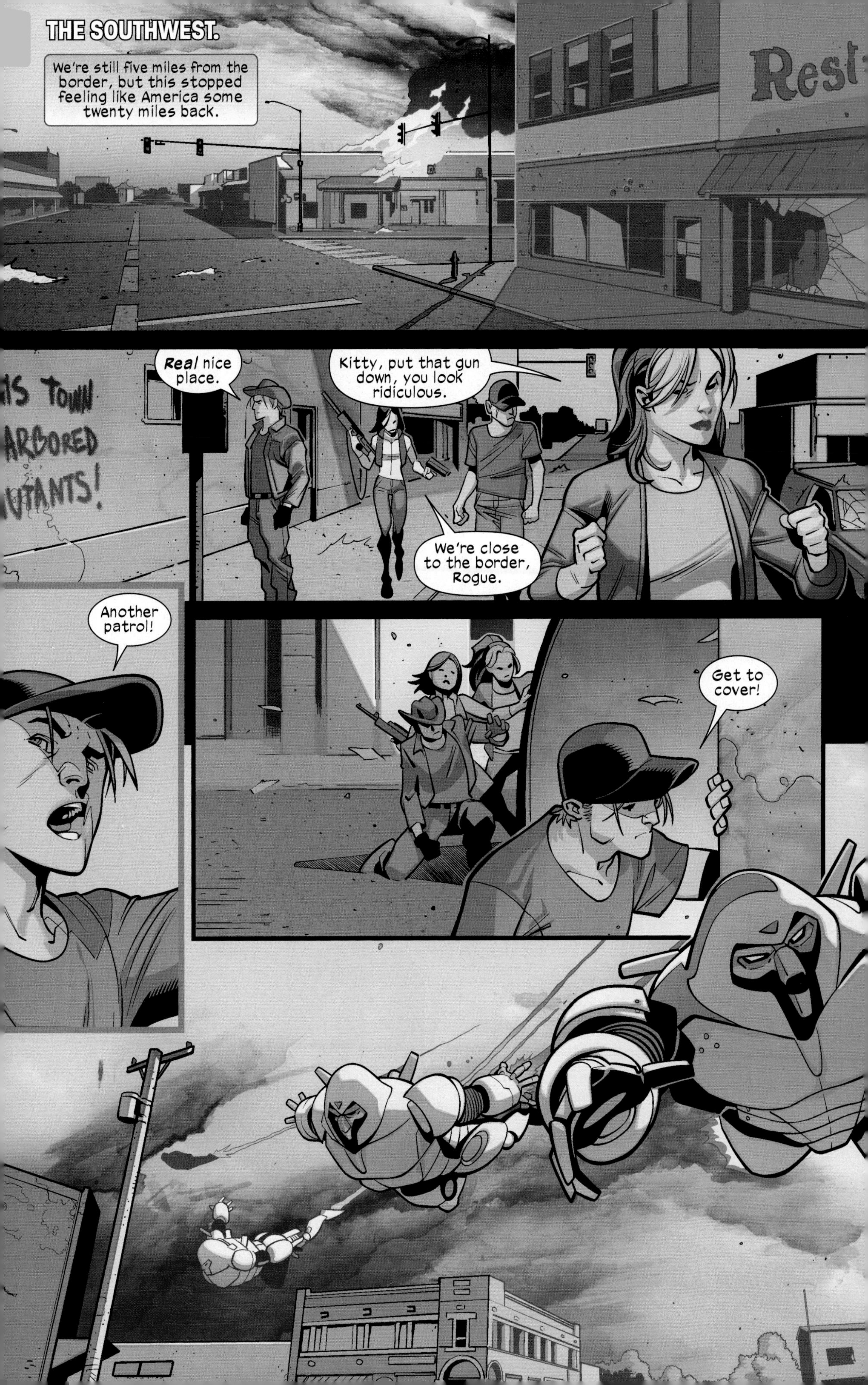
THE SOUTHWEST.
We're still five miles from the border, but this stopped feeling like America some twenty miles back.
Real nice place.
Kitty, put that gun down, you look ridiculous.
We're close to the border, Rogue.
Another patrol!
Get to cover!

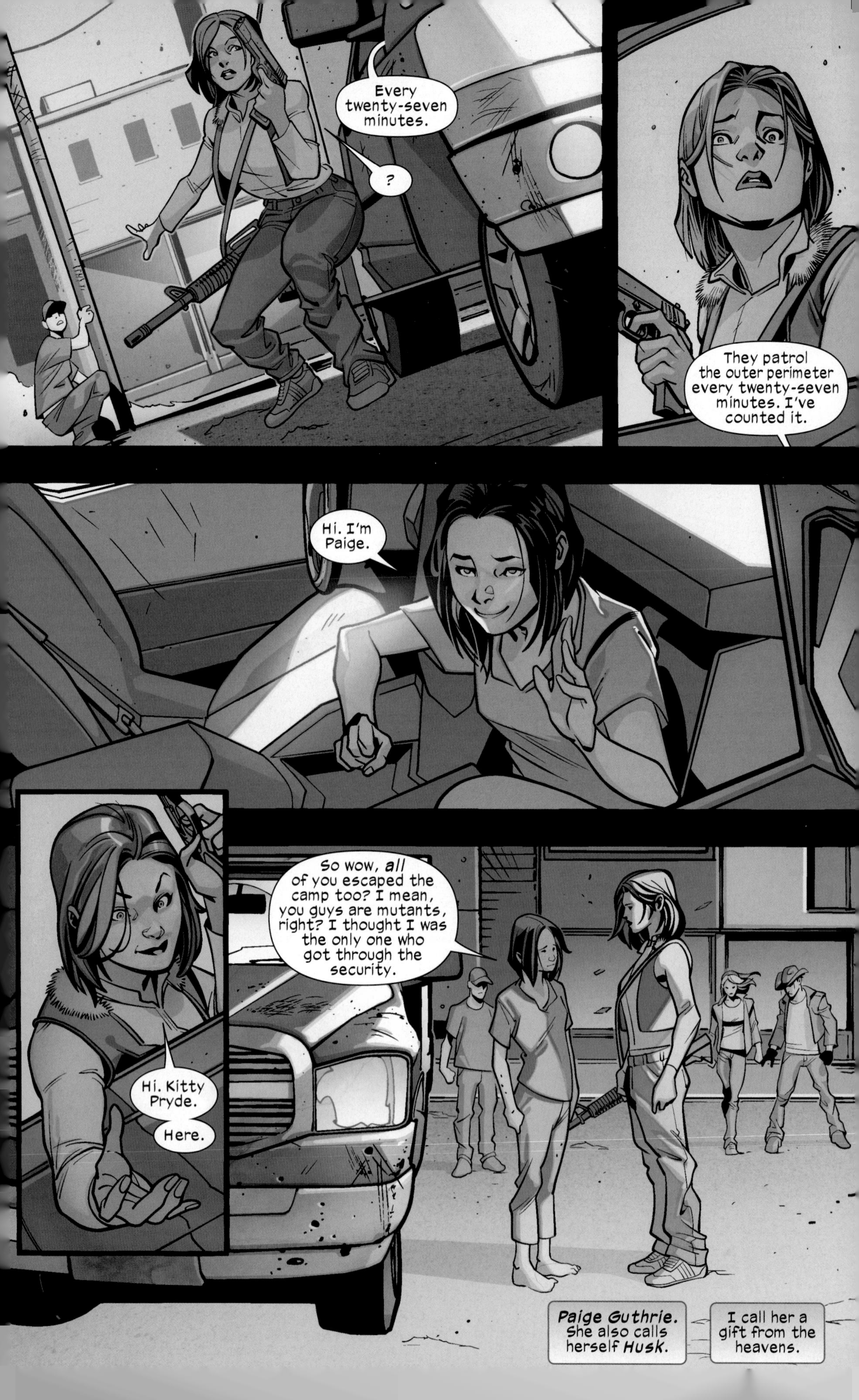
Every twenty-seven minutes.
?
They patrol the outer perimeter every twenty-seven minutes. I've counted it.
Hi. I'm Paige.
So wow, *all* of you escaped the camp too? I mean, you guys are mutants, right? I thought I was the only one who got through the security.
Hi. Kitty Pryde.
Here.
Paige Guthrie. She also calls herself *Husk.*
I call her a gift from the heavens.

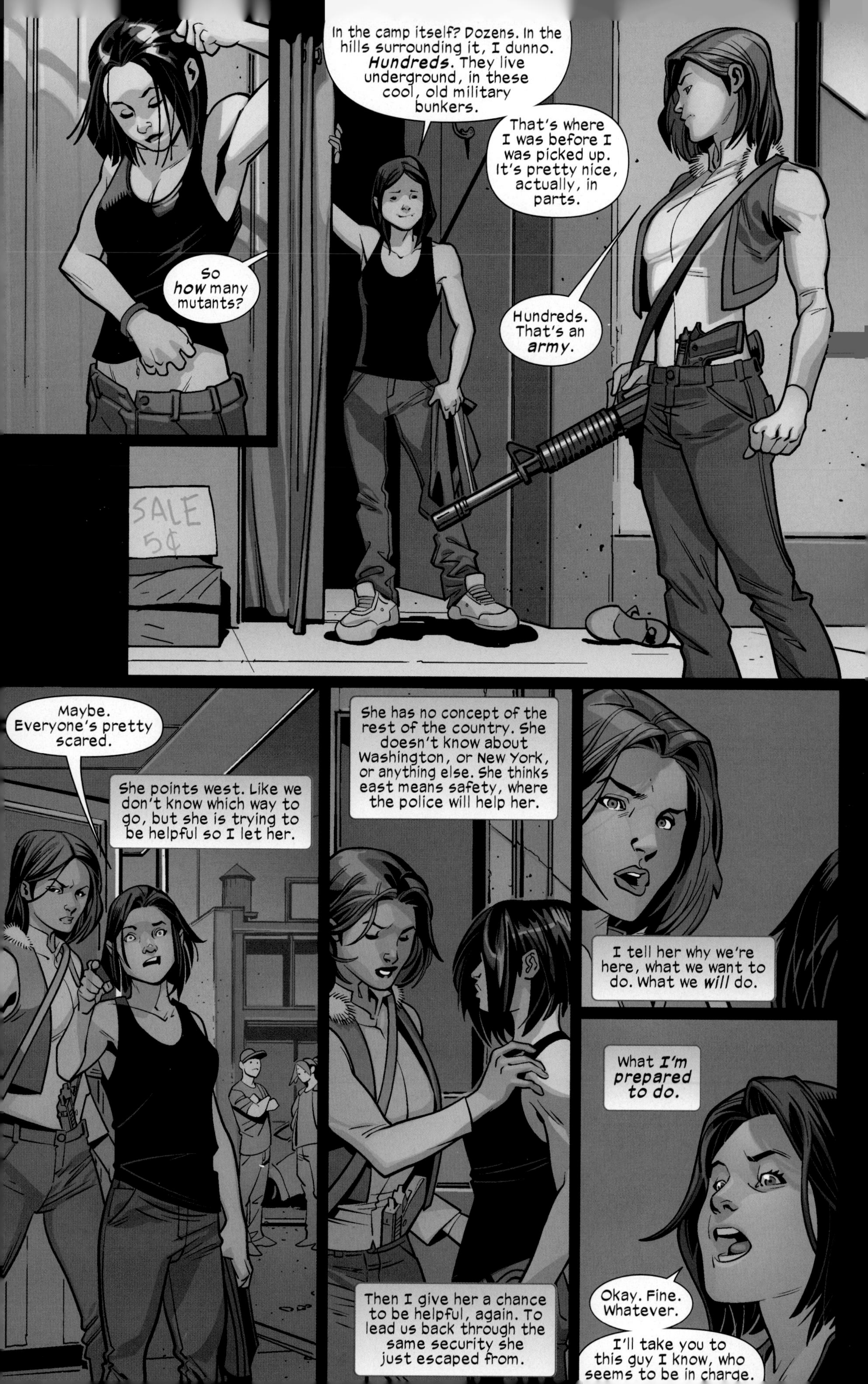
So how many mutants?
In the camp itself? Dozens. In the hills surrounding it, I dunno. Hundreds. They live underground, in these cool, old military bunkers.
That's where I was before I was picked up. It's pretty nice, actually, in parts.
Hundreds. That's an army.
SALE 5¢
Maybe. Everyone's pretty scared.
She points west. Like we don't know which way to go, but she is trying to be helpful so I let her.
She has no concept of the rest of the country. She doesn't know about Washington, or New York, or anything else. She thinks east means safety, where the police will help her.
Then I give her a chance to be helpful, again. To lead us back through the same security she just escaped from.
I tell her why we're here, what we want to do. What we will do.
What I'm prepared to do.
Okay. Fine. Whatever.
I'll take you to this guy I know, who seems to be in charge.

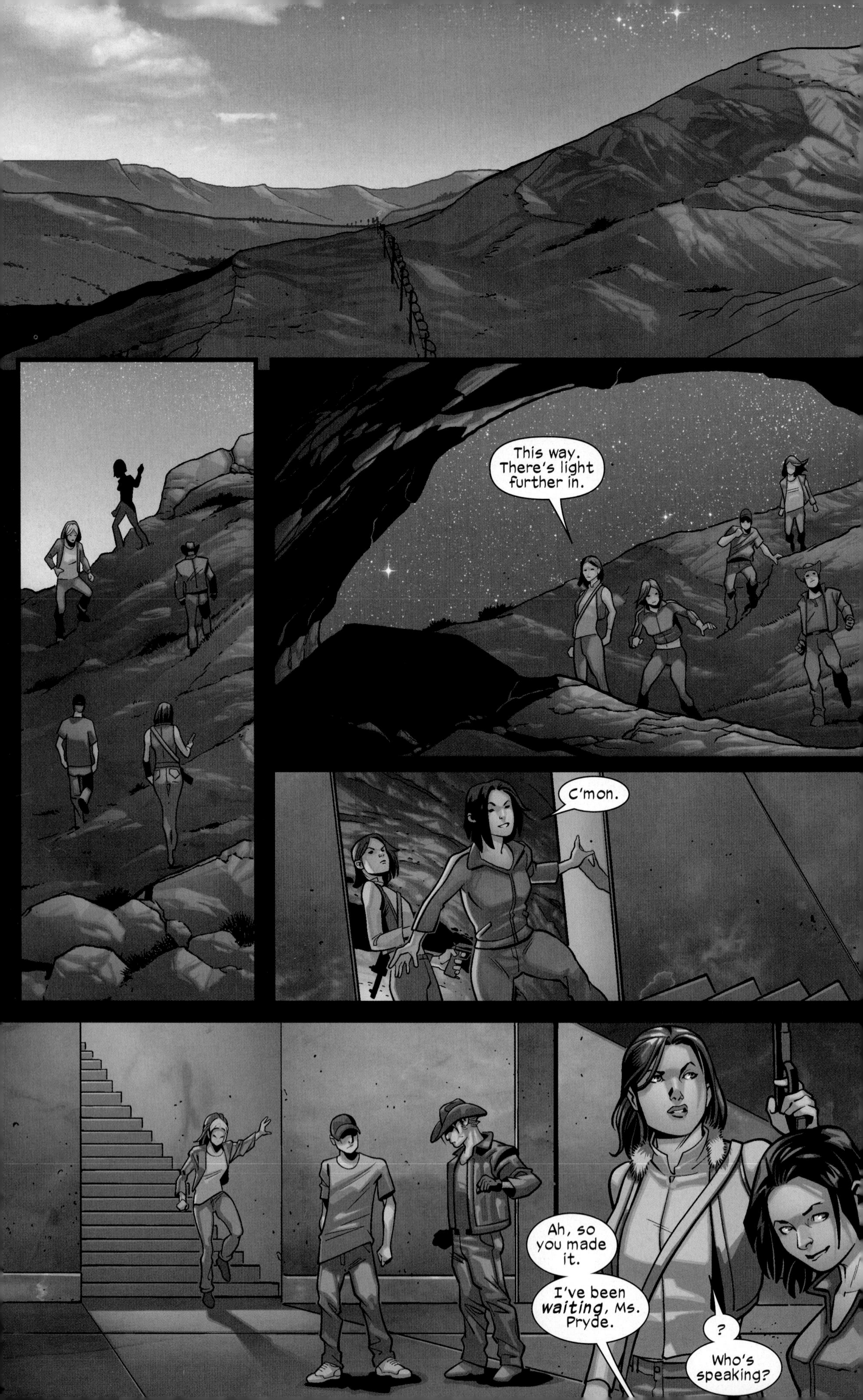
This way. There's light further in.
C'mon.
Ah, so you made it.
I've been *waiting*, Ms. Pryde.
?
Who's speaking?

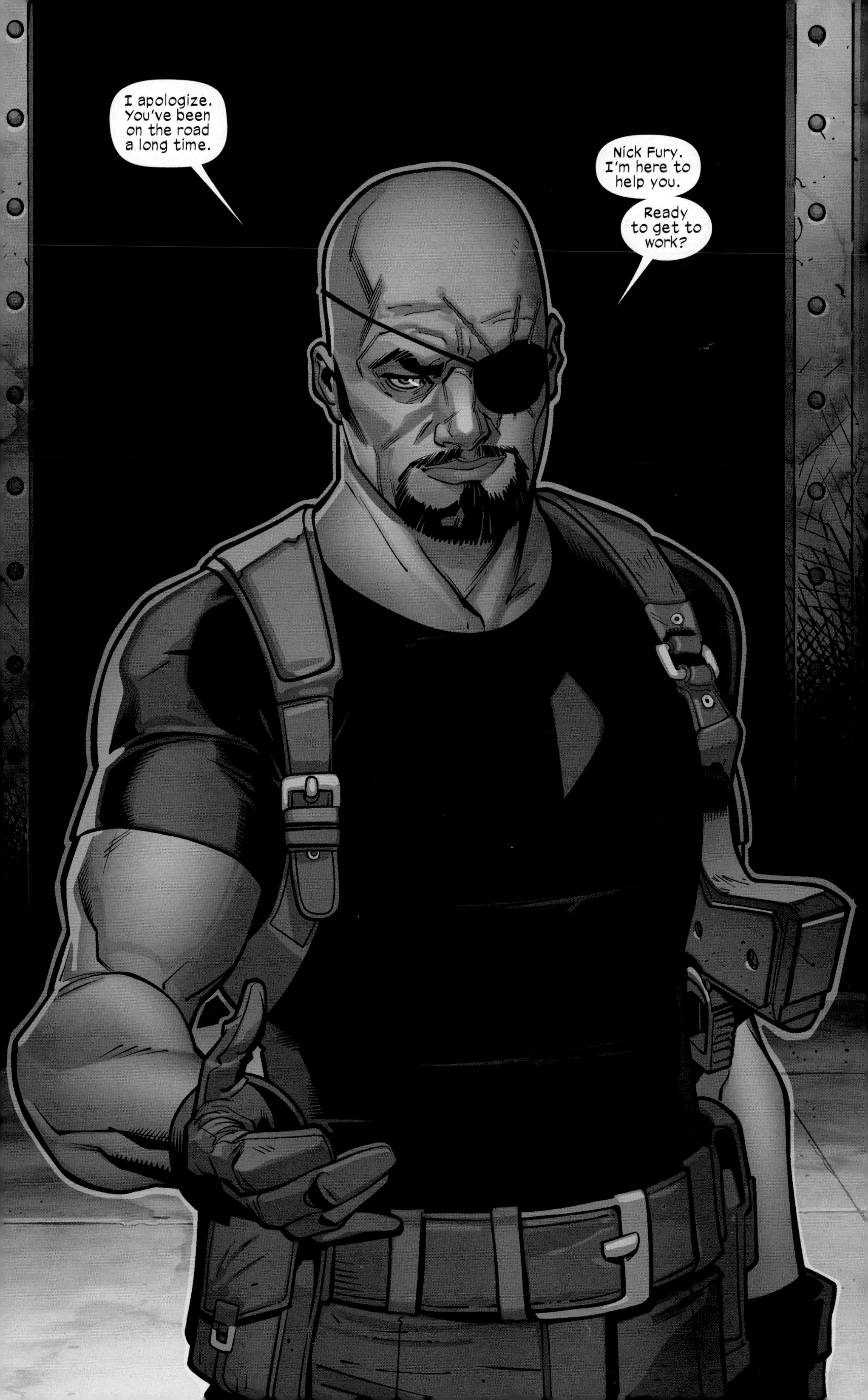
I apologize. You've been on the road a long time.
Nick Fury. I'm here to help you.
Ready to get to work?

10

ULTIMATE COMICS **X-MEN** #16

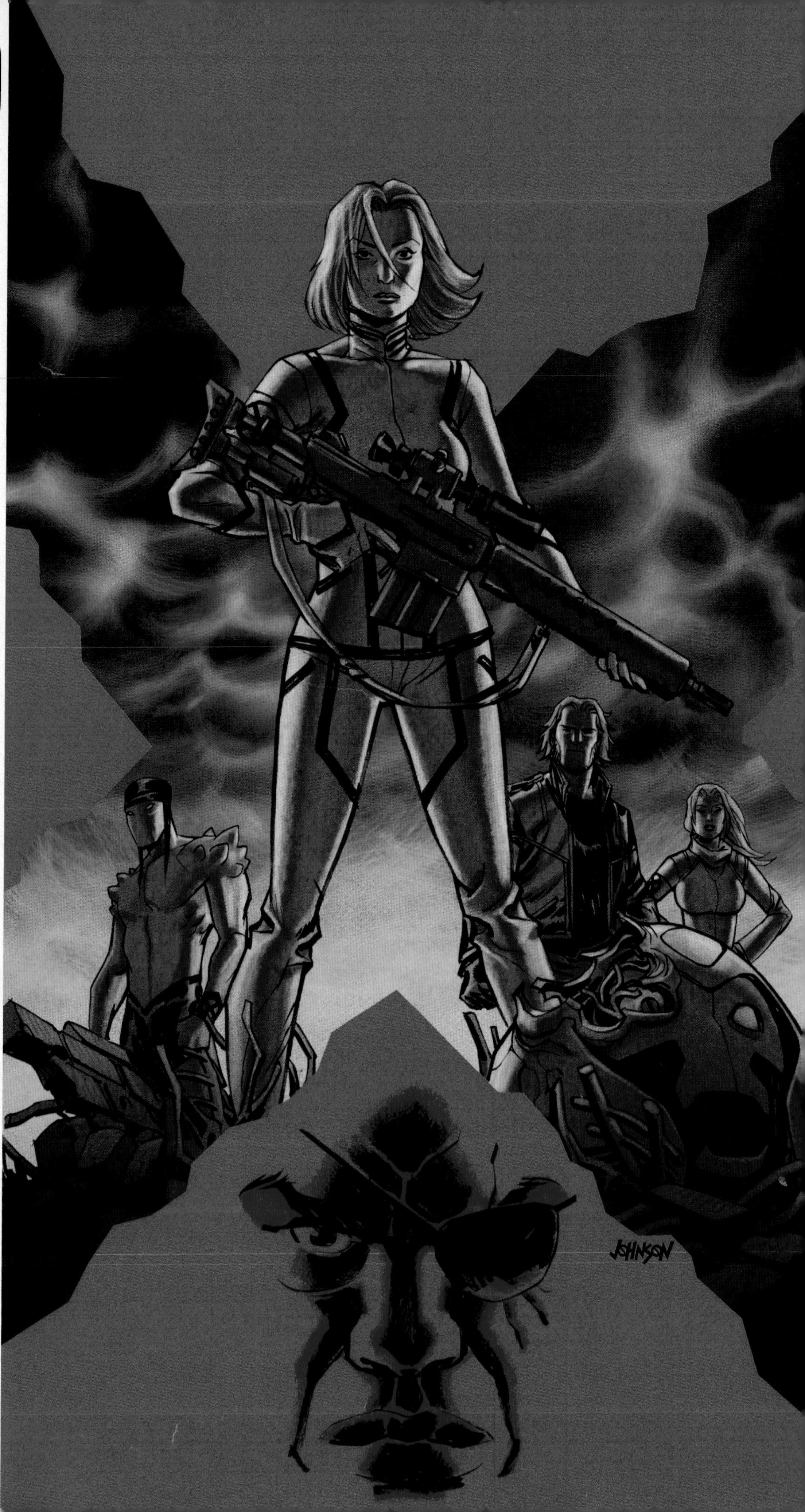
JOHNSON

S.H.I.E.L.D. SITUATION MAP:

Anti-government militia hot spots]

Montana,N.Dakota,
S.Dakota,Wyoming,
Idaho,Arizona,
New Mexico,N.Carolina,
S.Carolina,Georgia

[Eastern seaboard control zone]

New England,
New York,
Pennsylvania,
New Jersey,
Delaware,
Washington,D.C.,
Maryland,
Virginia

secured by
National Guard
under emergency
powers
committee

the West Coast]

California,Oregon,
Washington

declared
independent state

[Great Lakes states]

Minnesota,
Wisconsin,
Michigan,
Illinois,
Indiana,Ohio

status unknown

ANTI-MATTER
NO FLY
ZONE

SENTINEL
PUSH

AREA OF
URBAN
UNREST

SOUTHERN
CALIFORNIA
REFUGEE ZONE

Classified Position

Camp Hutton, secure
location of the President
of the United States

[Sentinel-controlled no-man's-land]

New Mexico,Arizona,
Utah,Oklahoma

abandoned by the
U.S. government

ALL STATES
SHOWN IN WHITE
ARE U.S. GOVERNMENT-
CONTROLLED ZONES

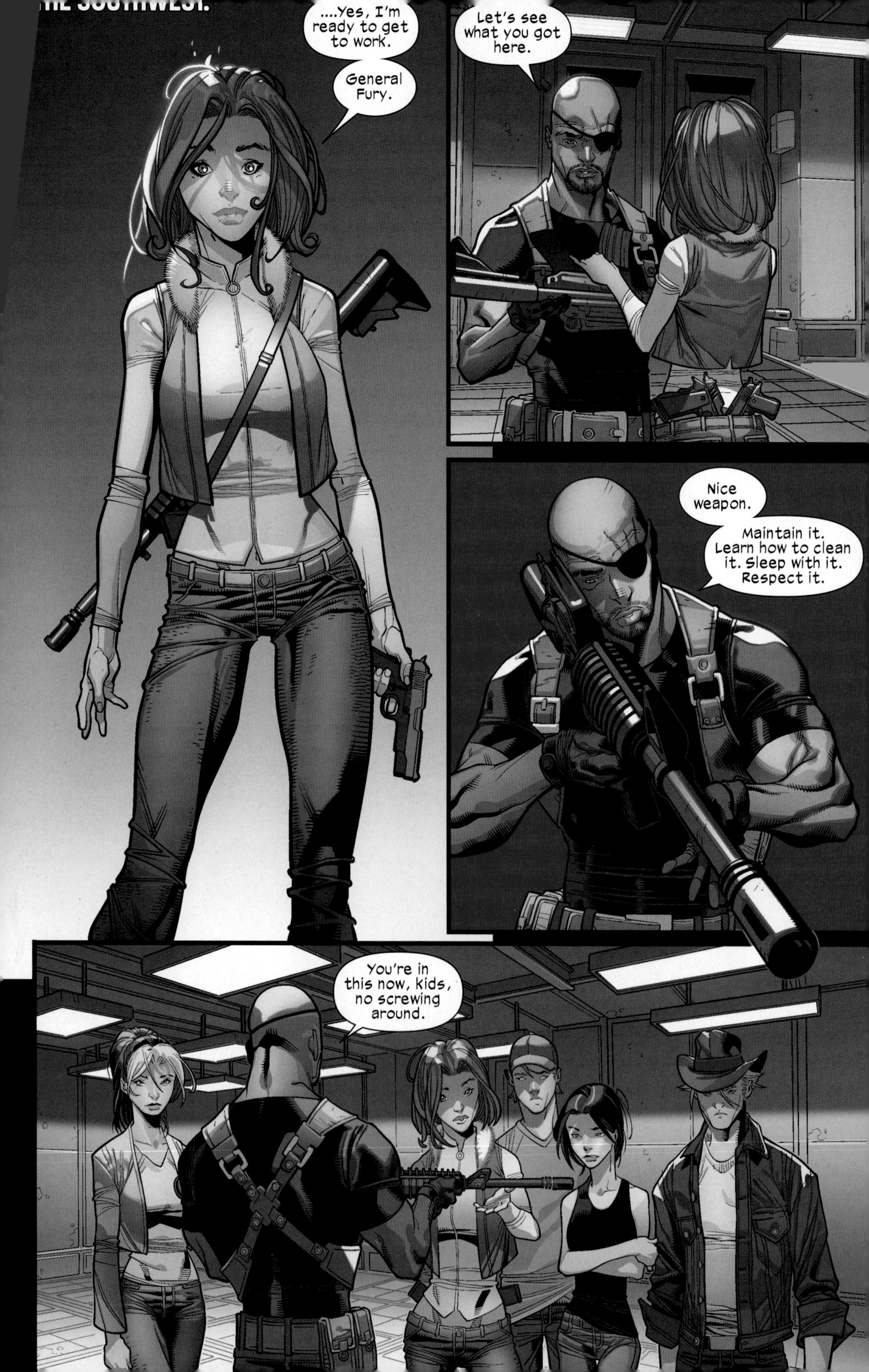
....Yes, I'm ready to get to work.
General Fury.
Let's see what you got here.
Nice weapon.
Maintain it. Learn how to clean it. Sleep with it. Respect it.
You're in this now, kids, no screwing around.

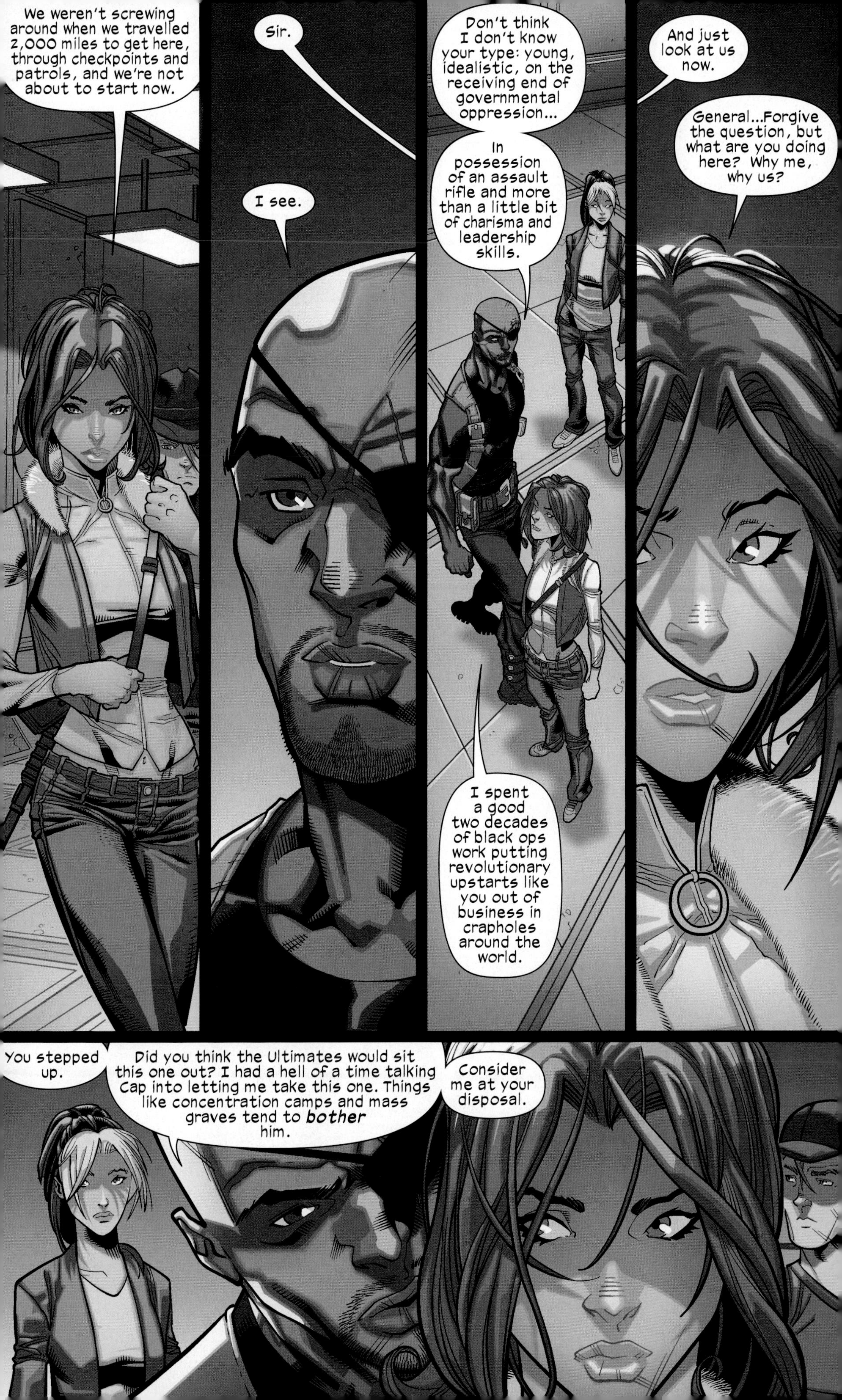
We weren't screwing around when we travelled 2,000 miles to get here, through checkpoints and patrols, and we're not about to start now.
Sir.
I see.
Don't think I don't know your type: young, idealistic, on the receiving end of governmental oppression...
In possession of an assault rifle and more than a little bit of charisma and leadership skills.
I spent a good two decades of black ops work putting revolutionary upstarts like you out of business in crapholes around the world.
And just look at us now.
General...Forgive the question, but what are you doing here? Why me, why us?
You stepped up.
Did you think the Ultimates would sit this one out? I had a hell of a time talking Cap into letting me take this one. Things like concentration camps and mass graves tend to *bother* him.
Consider me at your disposal.

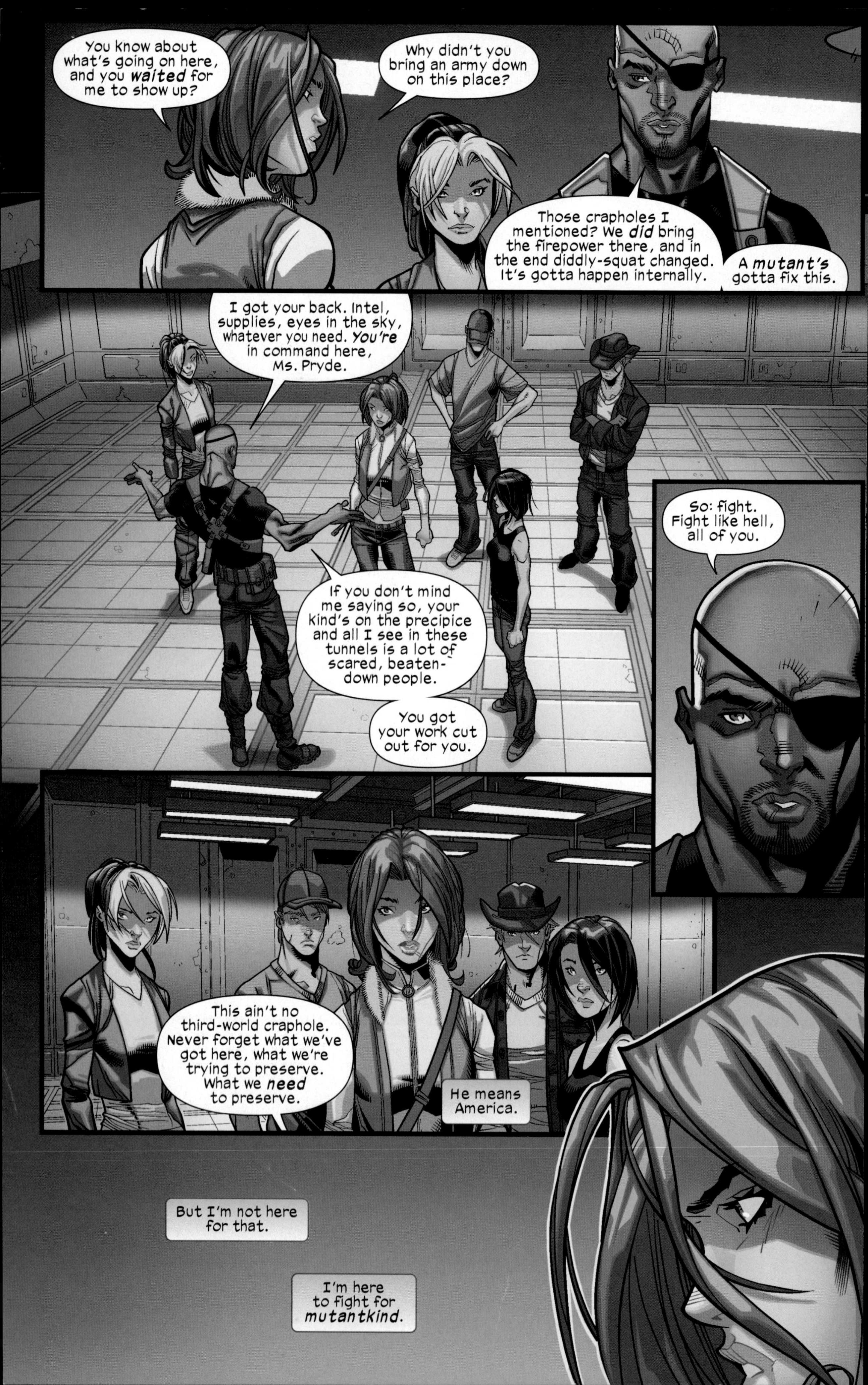

You know about what's going on here, and you *waited* for me to show up?
Why didn't you bring an army down on this place?
Those crapholes I mentioned? We *did* bring the firepower there, and in the end diddly-squat changed. It's gotta happen internally.
A *mutant's* gotta fix this.
I got your back. Intel, supplies, eyes in the sky, whatever you need. *You're* in command here, Ms. Pryde.
If you don't mind me saying so, your kind's on the precipice and all I see in these tunnels is a lot of scared, beaten-down people.
You got your work cut out for you.
So: fight. Fight like hell, all of you.
This ain't no third-world craphole. Never forget what we've got here, what we're trying to preserve. What we *need* to preserve.
He means America.
But I'm not here for that.
I'm here to fight for *mutantkind*.

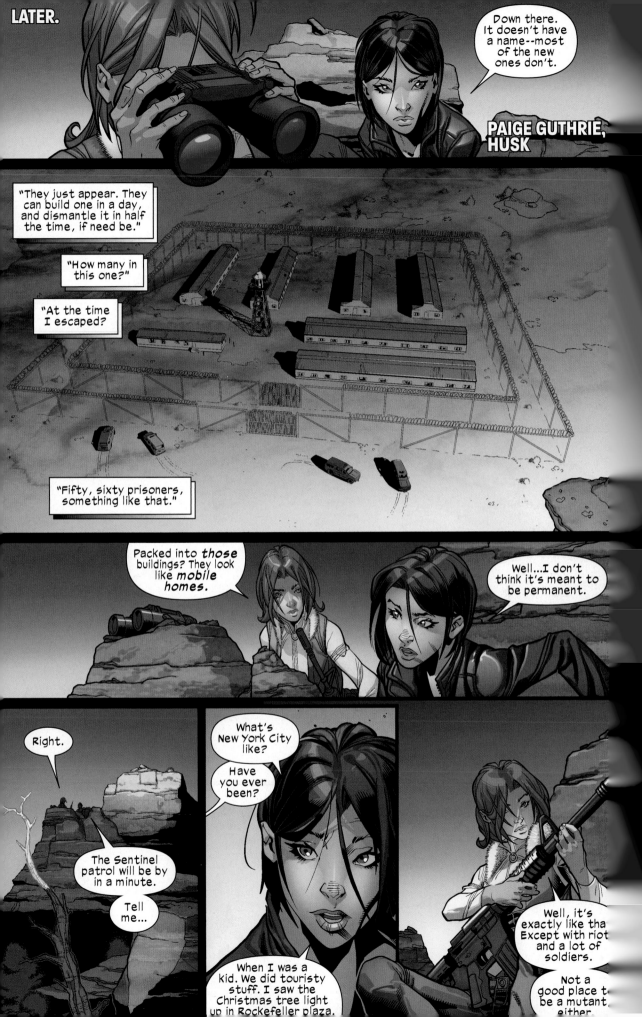

LATER.

Down there. It doesn't have a name--most of the new ones don't.

PAIGE GUTHRIE, HUSK

"They just appear. They can build one in a day, and dismantle it in half the time, if need be."

"How many in this one?"

"At the time I escaped?

"Fifty, sixty prisoners, something like that."

Packed into *those* buildings? They look like *mobile homes.*

Well...I don't think it's meant to be permanent.

Right.

The Sentinel patrol will be by in a minute.

Tell me...

What's New York City like?

Have you ever been?

When I was a kid. We did touristy stuff. I saw the Christmas tree light up in Rockefeller plaza.

Well, it's exactly like tha Except with riot and a lot of soldiers.

Not a good place t be a mutant. either.

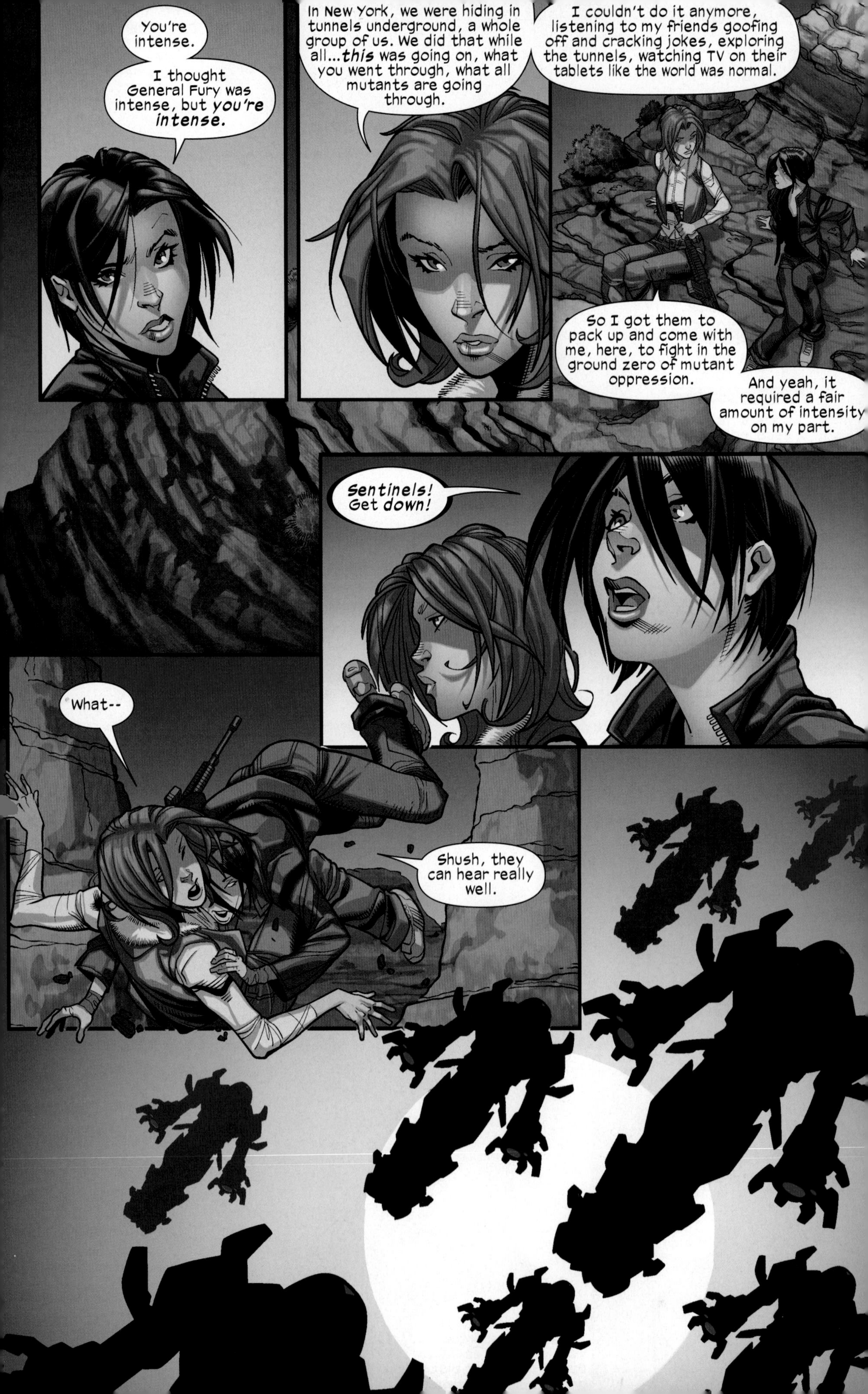
You're intense.
I thought General Fury was intense, but *you're intense.*
In New York, we were hiding in tunnels underground, a whole group of us. We did that while all...*this* was going on, what you went through, what all mutants are going through.
I couldn't do it anymore, listening to my friends goofing off and cracking jokes, exploring the tunnels, watching TV on their tablets like the world was normal.
So I got them to pack up and come with me, here, to fight in the ground zero of mutant oppression.
And yeah, it required a fair amount of intensity on my part.
Sentinels! Get down!
What--
Shush, they can hear really well.

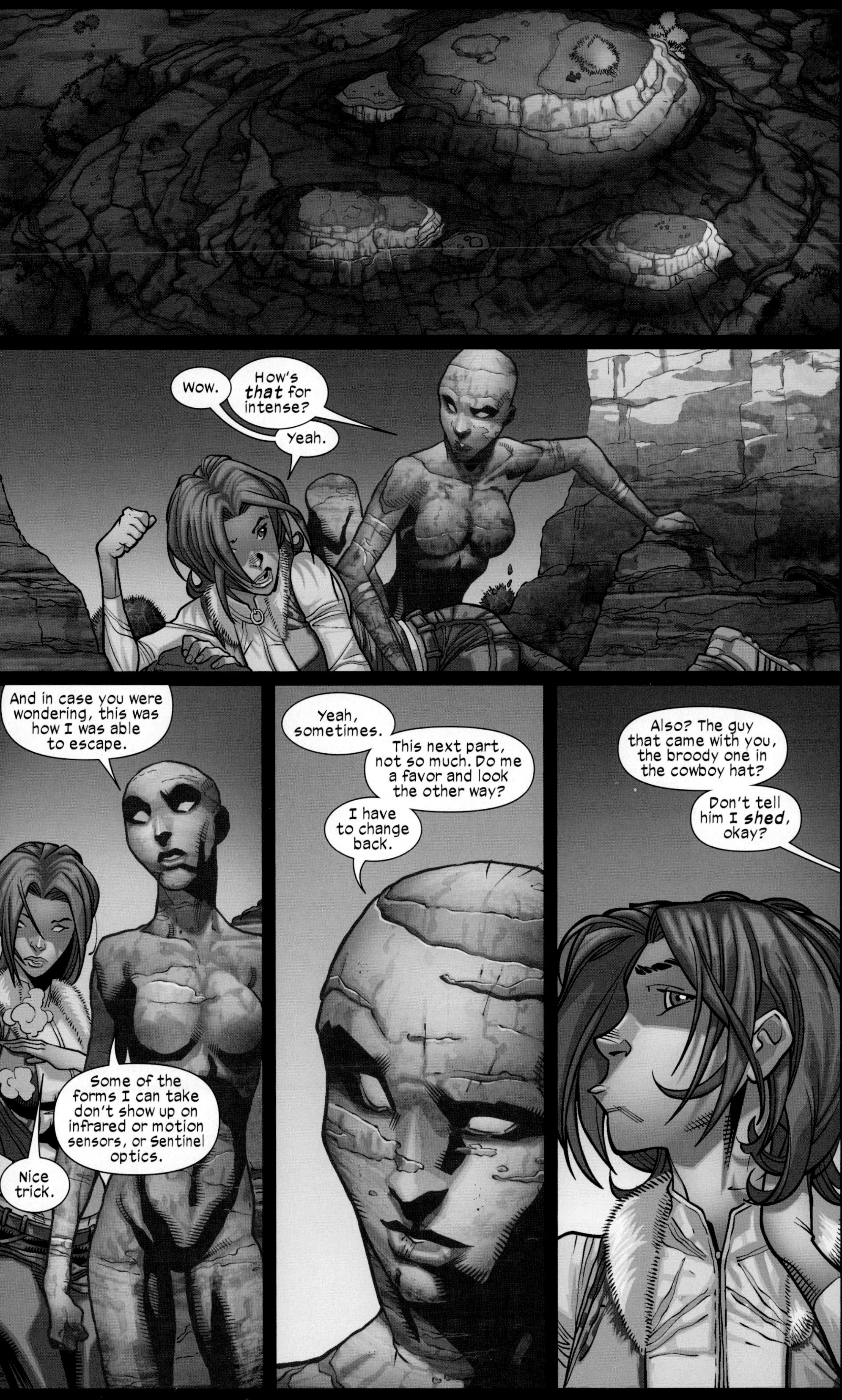
Wow.
How's *that* for intense?
Yeah.
And in case you were wondering, this was how I was able to escape.
Some of the forms I can take don't show up on infrared or motion sensors, or Sentinel optics.
Nice trick.
Yeah, sometimes.
This next part, not so much. Do me a favor and look the other way?
I have to change back.
Also? The guy that came with you, the broody one in the cowboy hat?
Don't tell him I *shed*, okay?

She took me around the whole area, hours of hiking and dozens of camps.

At first, all you see is endless landscape and wonder how it's possible that these states can be controlled as they are.

But then you see the intelligence behind it:

Natural choke points in the terrain, highways, rail lines, and rivers. And, of course, the Sentinel patrols.

I take notes. I draw maps. Husk answers every question I have, perfectly.

She's amazing.

Her own time in the camps...She's less free with that information but I get what I can. By the time the mutants arrive, they have already been beaten down, demoralized. Humiliated. And so they're herded like sheep.

"What about the executions and the mass graves?" I ask.

It comes, she says, when all attempts at intelligence-gathering have run their course. What intelligence, though?

What valuable information do mutants possibly possess? None, so they make it up.

The best liars live the longest...

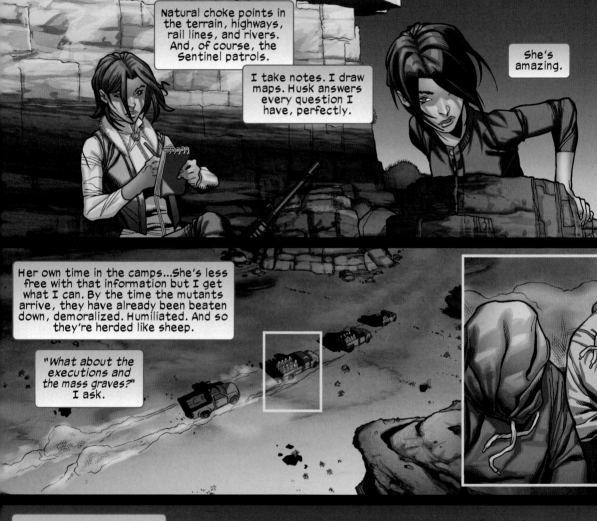

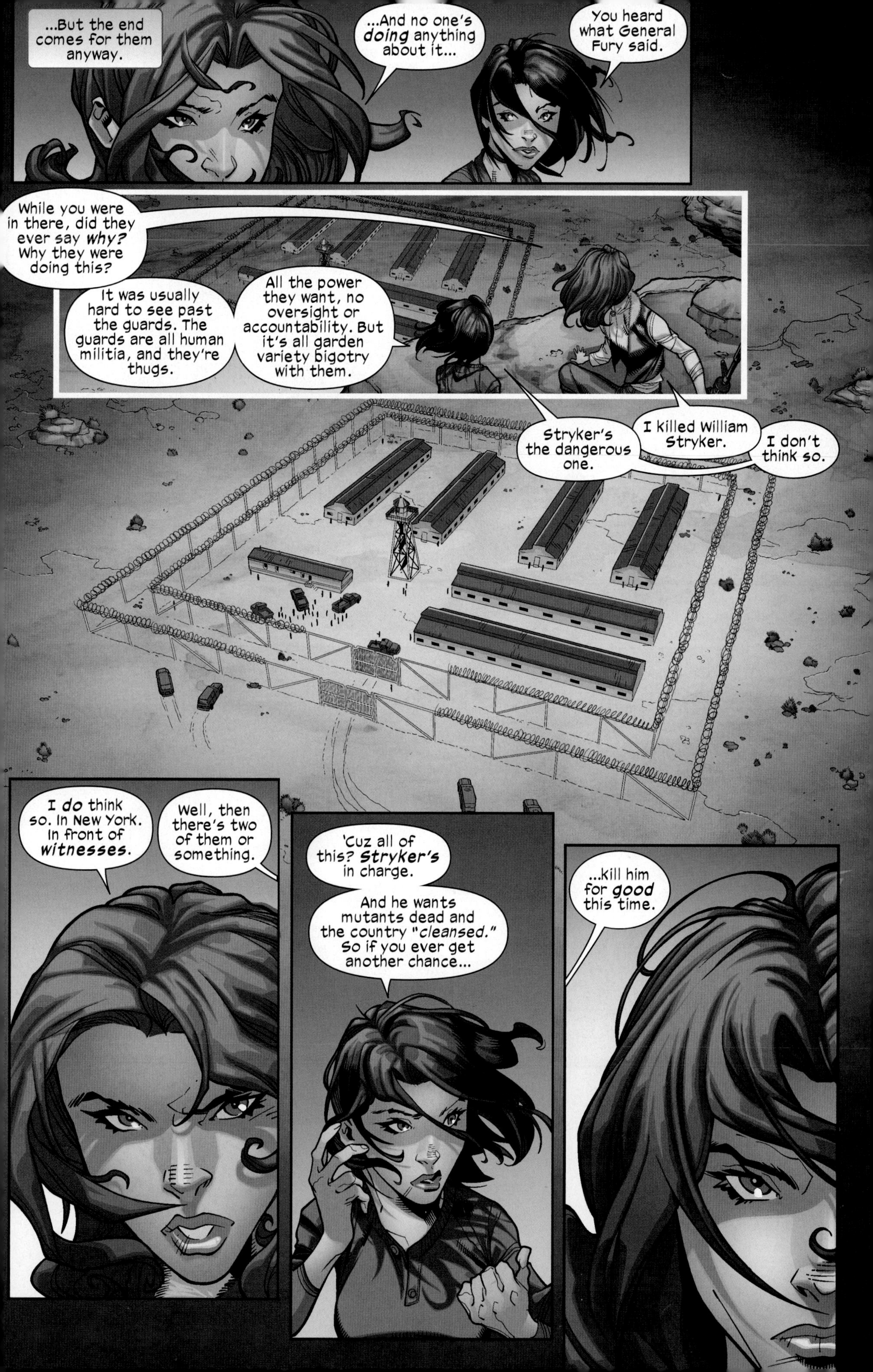

...But the end comes for them anyway.
...And no one's *doing* anything about it...
You heard what General Fury said.
While you were in there, did they ever say *why?* Why they were doing this?
It was usually hard to see past the guards. The guards are all human militia, and they're thugs.
All the power they want, no oversight or accountability. But it's all garden variety bigotry with them.
Stryker's the dangerous one.
I killed William Stryker.
I don't think so.
I *do* think so. In New York. In front of *witnesses*.
Well, then there's two of them or something.
'Cuz all of this? *Stryker's* in charge.
And he wants mutants dead and the country "*cleansed.*" So if you ever get another chance...
...kill him for *good* this time.

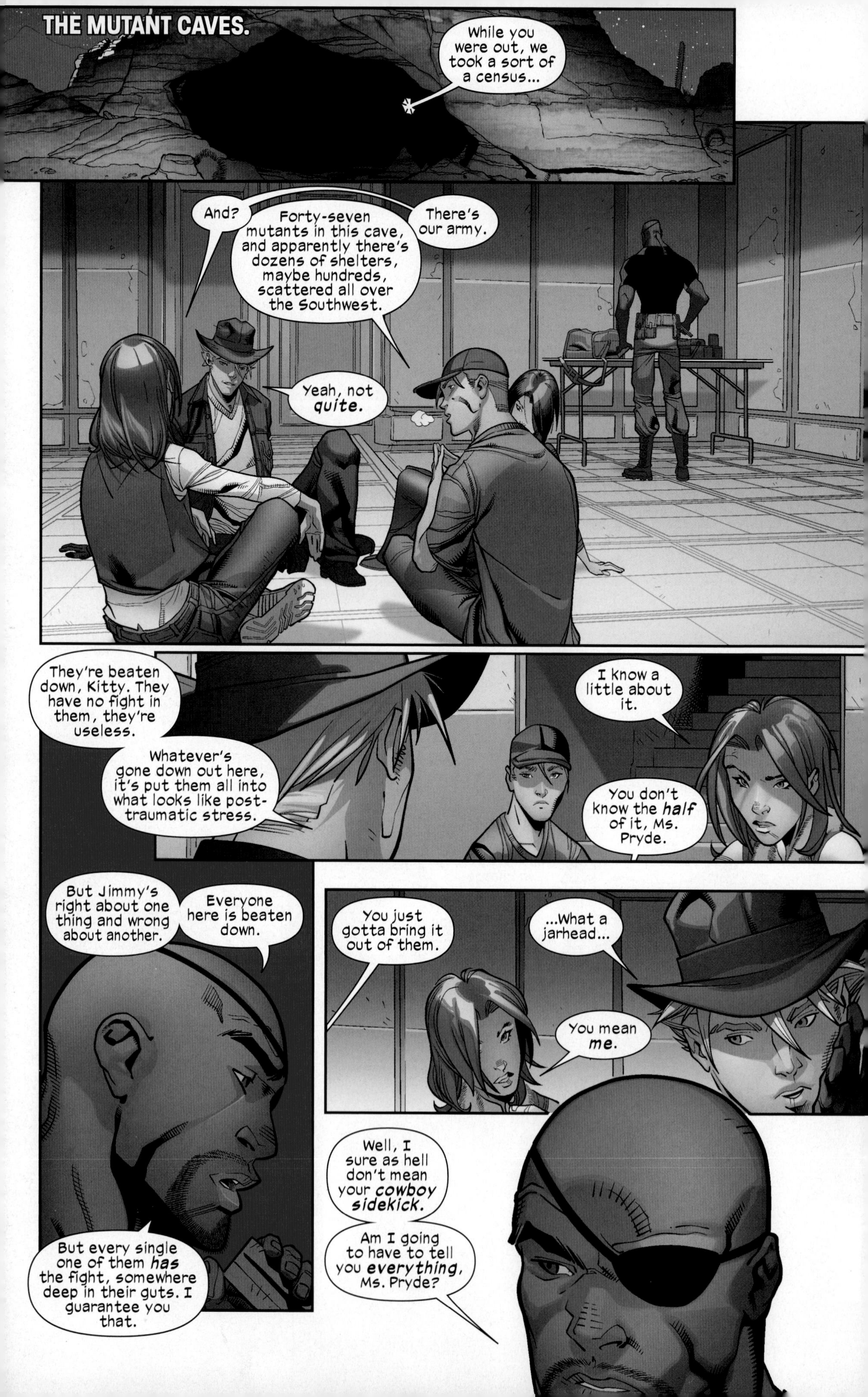
THE MUTANT CAVES.
While you were out, we took a sort of a census...
And?
Forty-seven mutants in this cave, and apparently there's dozens of shelters, maybe hundreds, scattered all over the Southwest.
There's our army.
Yeah, not *quite.*
They're beaten down, Kitty. They have no fight in them, they're useless.
Whatever's gone down out here, it's put them all into what looks like post-traumatic stress.
I know a little about it.
You don't know the *half* of it, Ms. Pryde.
But Jimmy's right about one thing and wrong about another.
Everyone here is beaten down.
But every single one of them *has* the fight, somewhere deep in their guts. I guarantee you that.
You just gotta bring it out of them.
...What a jarhead...
You mean *me.*
Well, I sure as hell don't mean your *cowboy sidekick.*
Am I going to have to tell you *everything,* Ms. Pryde?

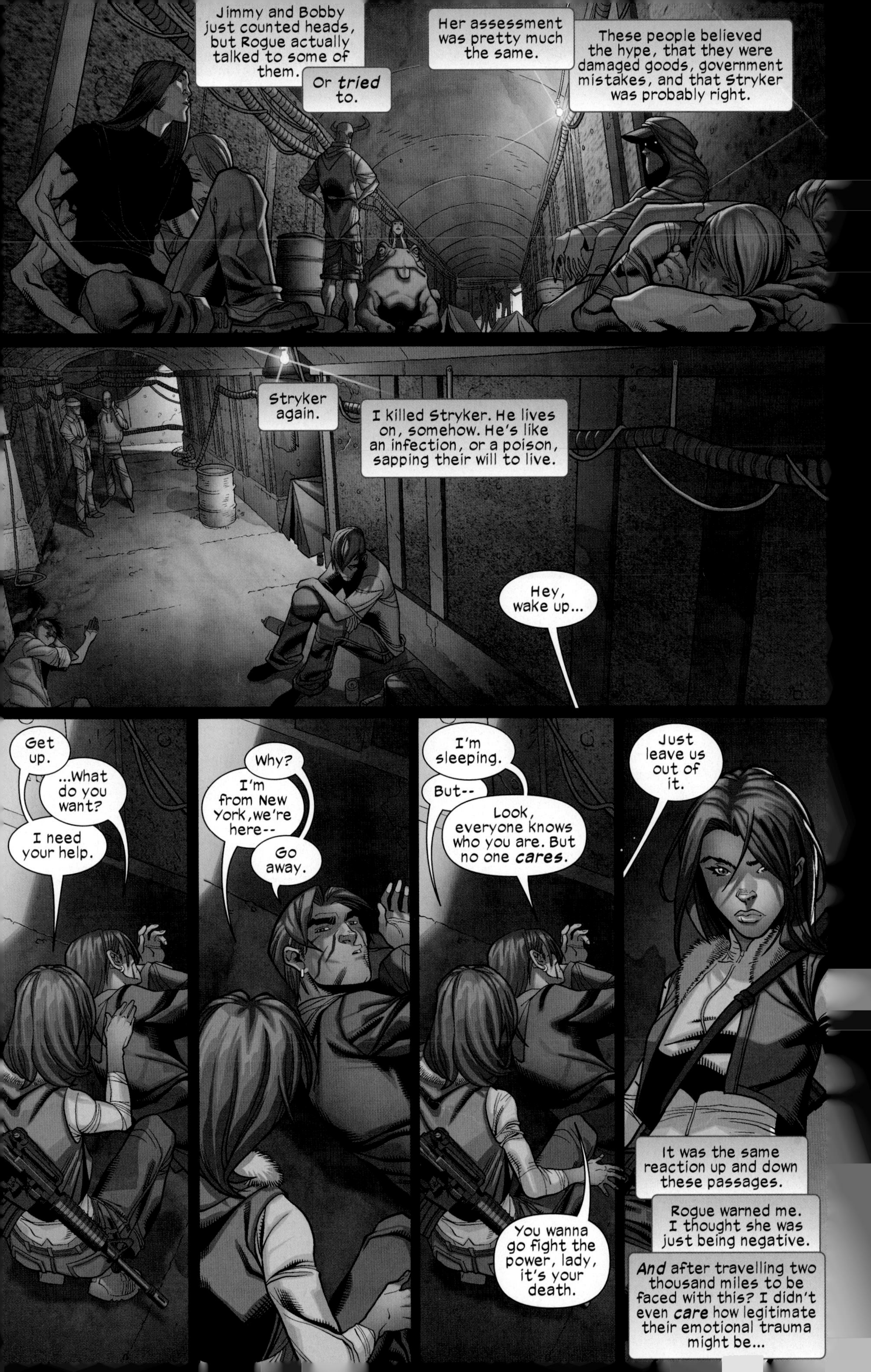

Jimmy and Bobby just counted heads, but Rogue actually talked to some of them.
Or *tried* to.
Her assessment was pretty much the same.
These people believed the hype, that they were damaged goods, government mistakes, and that Stryker was probably right.
Stryker again.
I killed Stryker. He lives on, somehow. He's like an infection, or a poison, sapping their will to live.
Hey, wake up...
Get up.
...What do you want?
I need your help.
Why?
I'm from New York, we're here--
Go away.
I'm sleeping.
But--
Look, everyone knows who you are. But no one *cares*.
You wanna go fight the power, lady, it's your death.
Just leave us out of it.
It was the same reaction up and down these passages.
Rogue warned me. I thought she was just being negative.
And after travelling two thousand miles to be faced with this? I didn't even *care* how legitimate their emotional trauma might be...

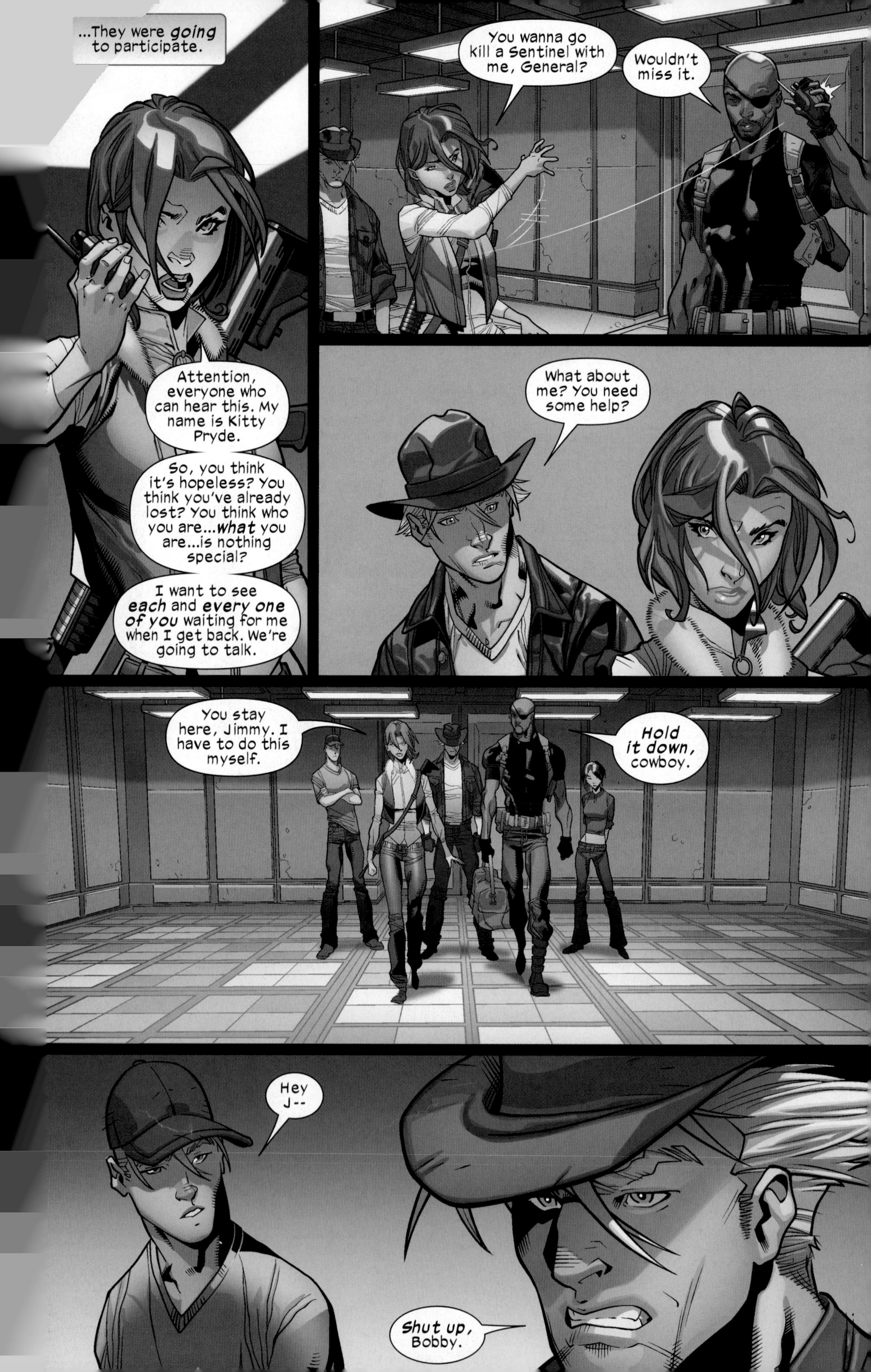
...They were *going* to participate.
Attention, everyone who can hear this. My name is Kitty Pryde.
So, you think it's hopeless? You think you've already lost? You think who you are...*what* you are...is nothing special?
I want to see *each* and *every one of you* waiting for me when I get back. We're going to talk.
You wanna go kill a Sentinel with me, General?
Wouldn't miss it.
What about me? You need some help?
You stay here, Jimmy. I have to do this myself.
Hold it down, cowboy.
Hey J--
Shut up, Bobby.

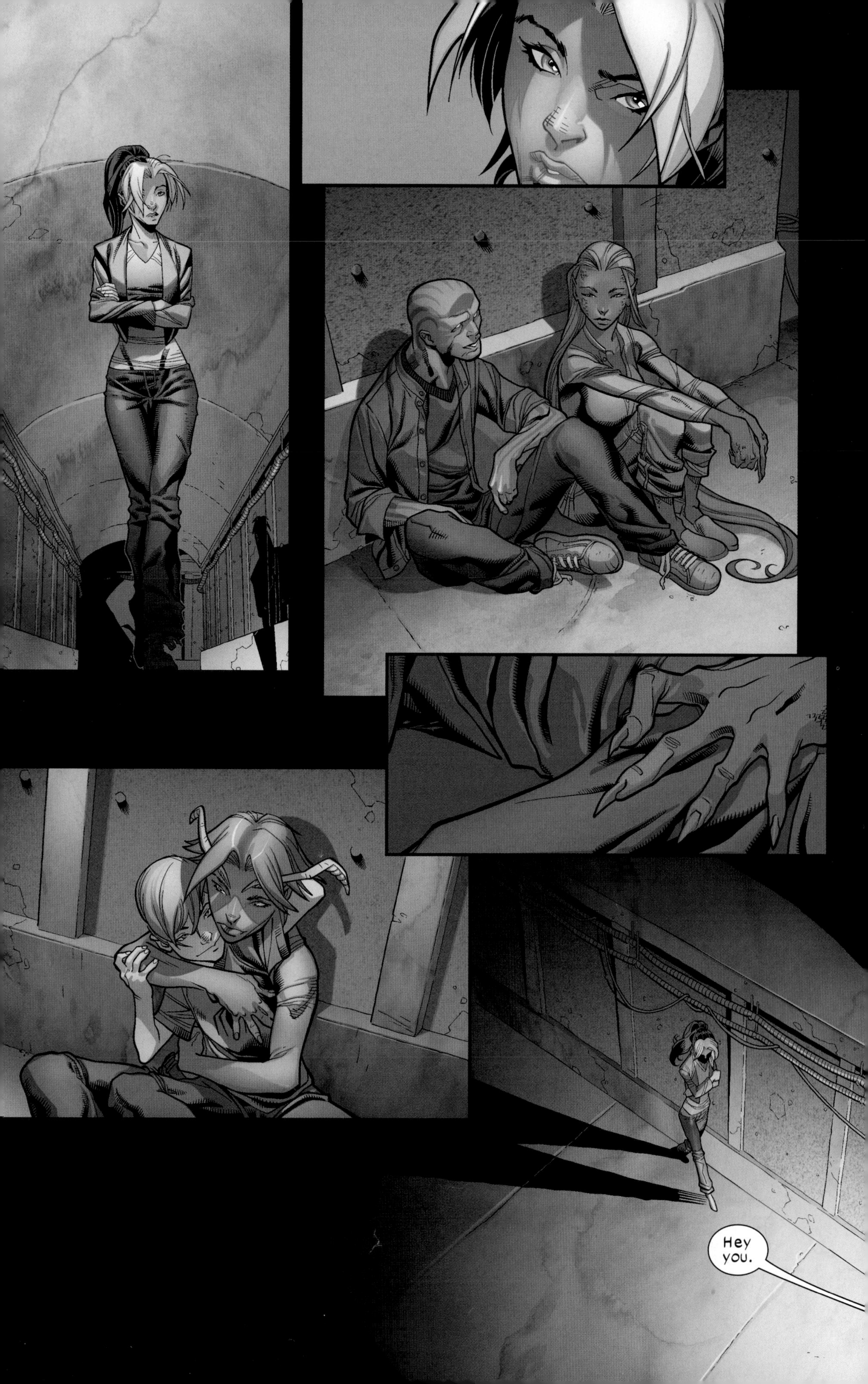
Hey you.

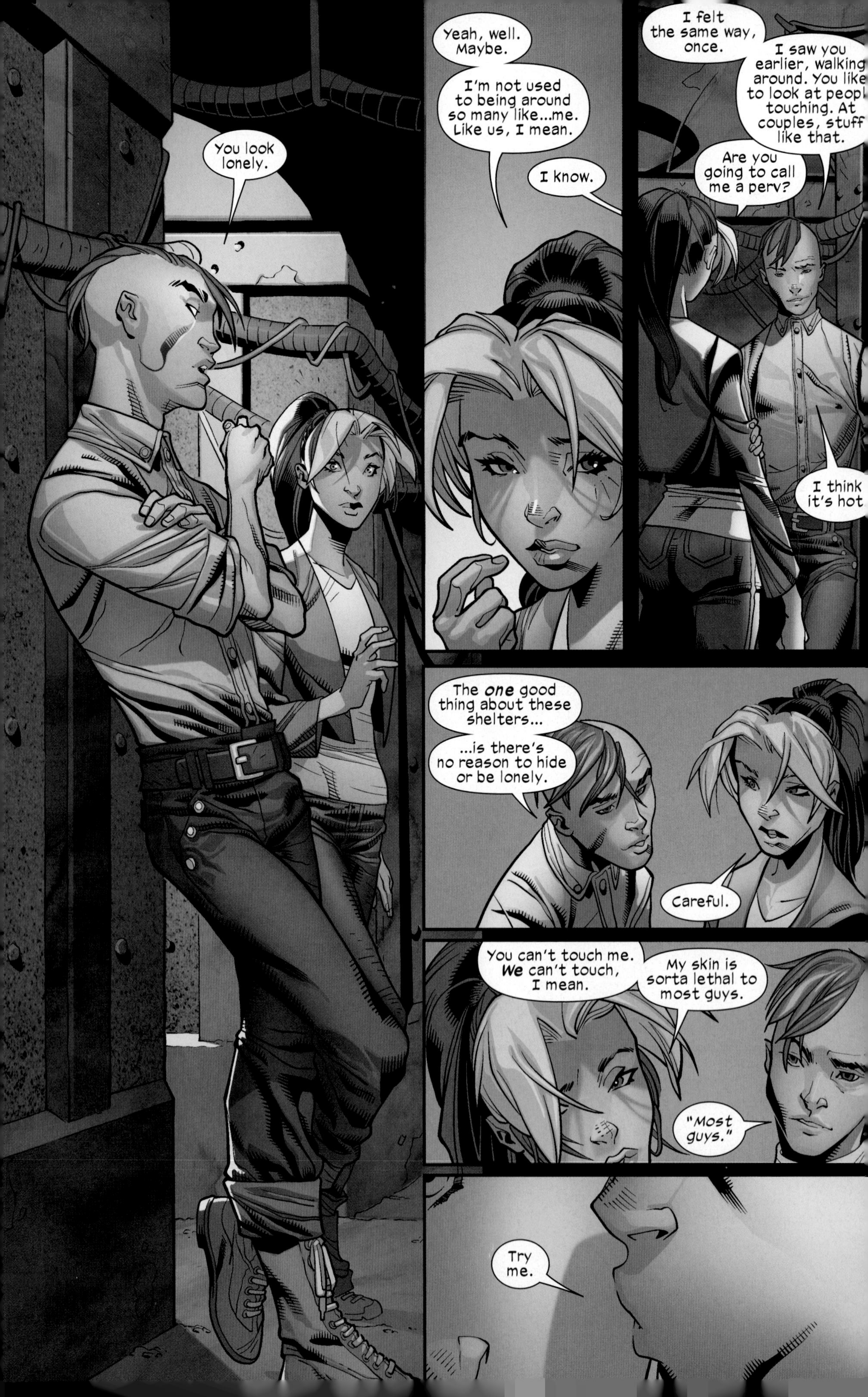
You look lonely.
Yeah, well. Maybe.
I'm not used to being around so many like...me. Like us, I mean.
I know.
I felt the same way, once.
I saw you earlier, walking around. You like to look at peopl touching. At couples, stuff like that.
Are you going to call me a perv?
I think it's hot
The *one* good thing about these shelters...
...is there's no reason to hide or be lonely.
Careful.
You can't touch me. **We** can't touch, I mean.
My skin is sorta lethal to most guys.
"Most guys."
Try me.

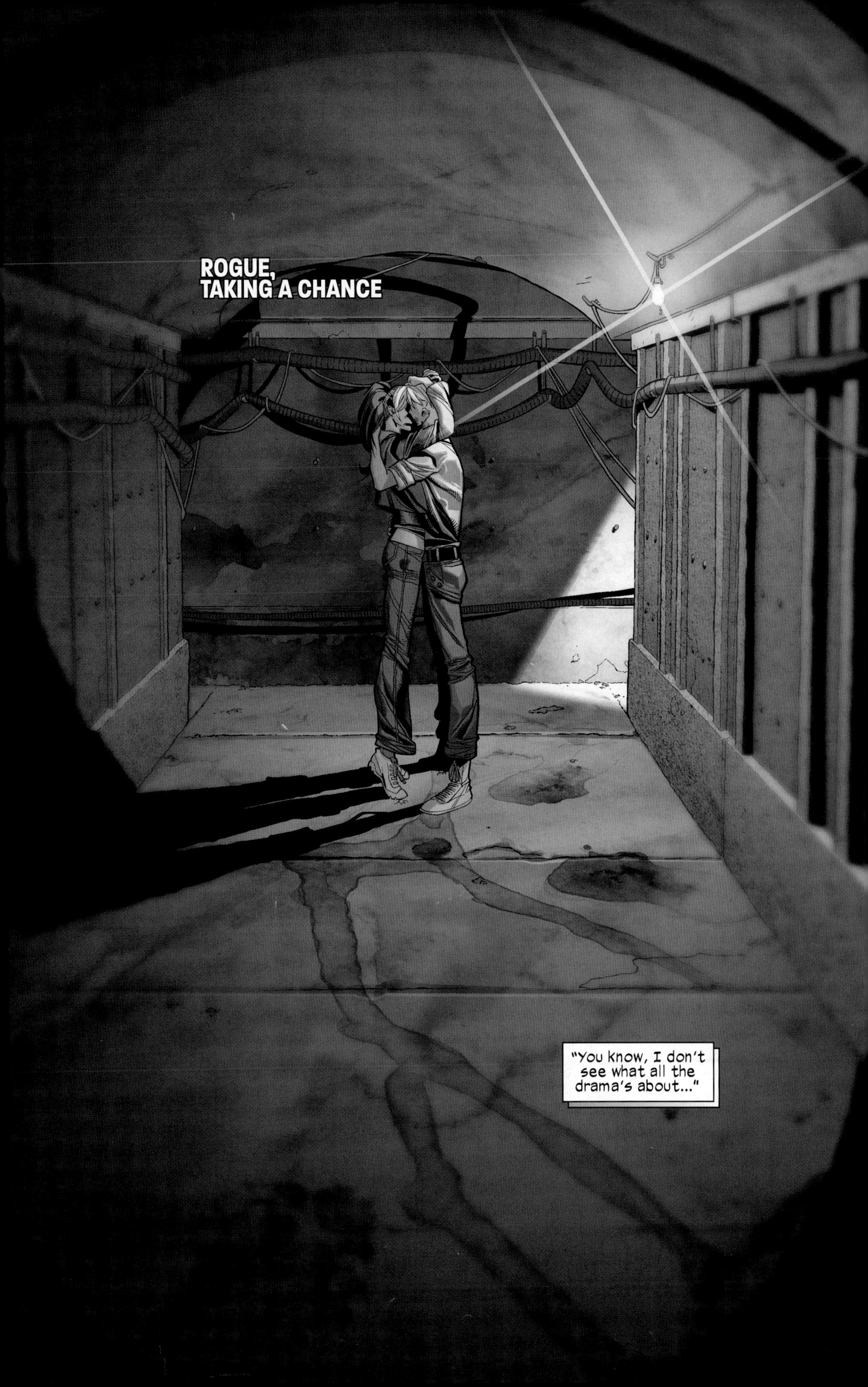
ROGUE, TAKING A CHANCE
"You know, I don't see what all the drama's about..."

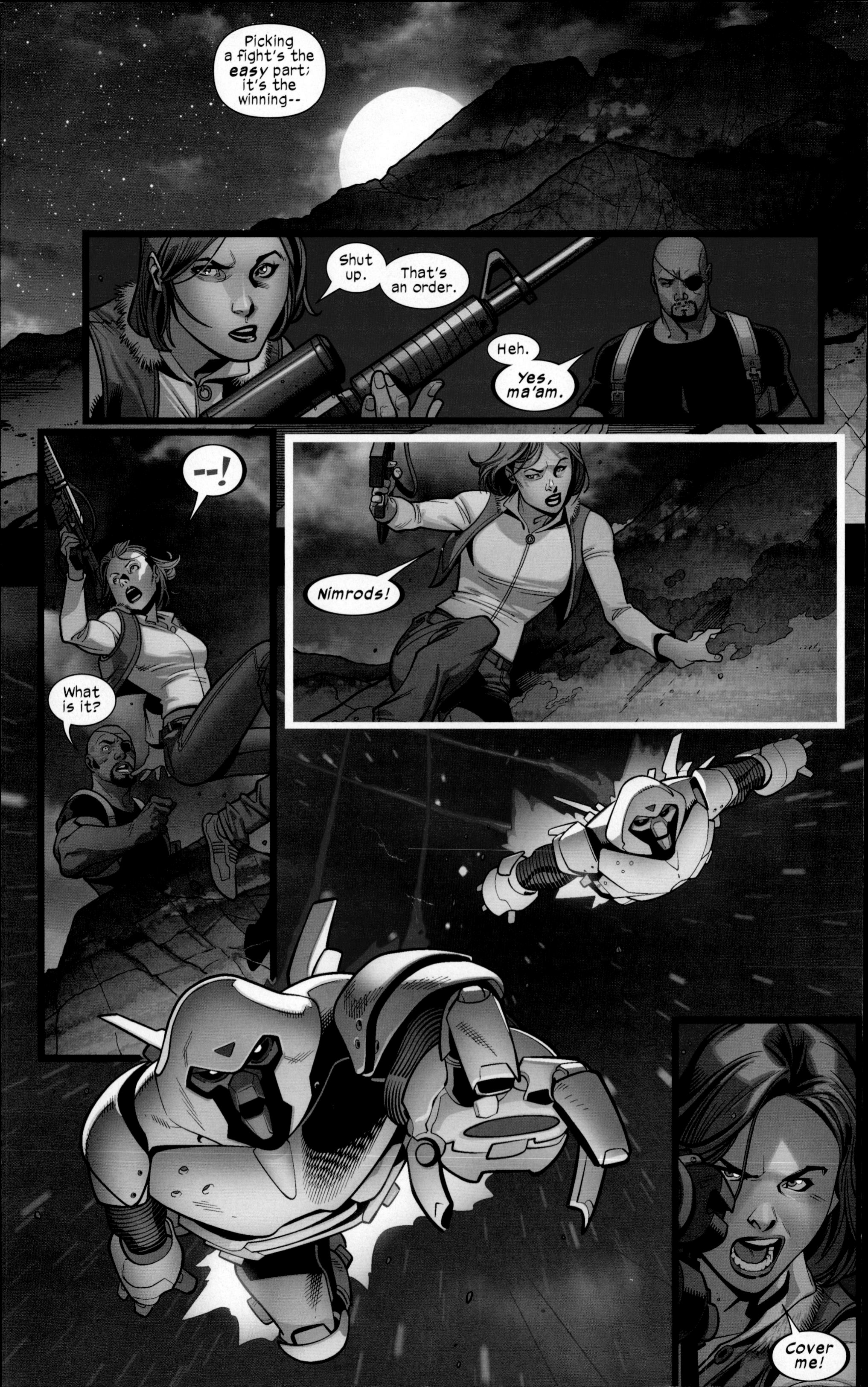
Picking a fight's the *easy* part; it's the winning--
Shut up.
That's an order.
Heh.
Yes, ma'am.
--!
What is it?
Nimrods!
Cover me!

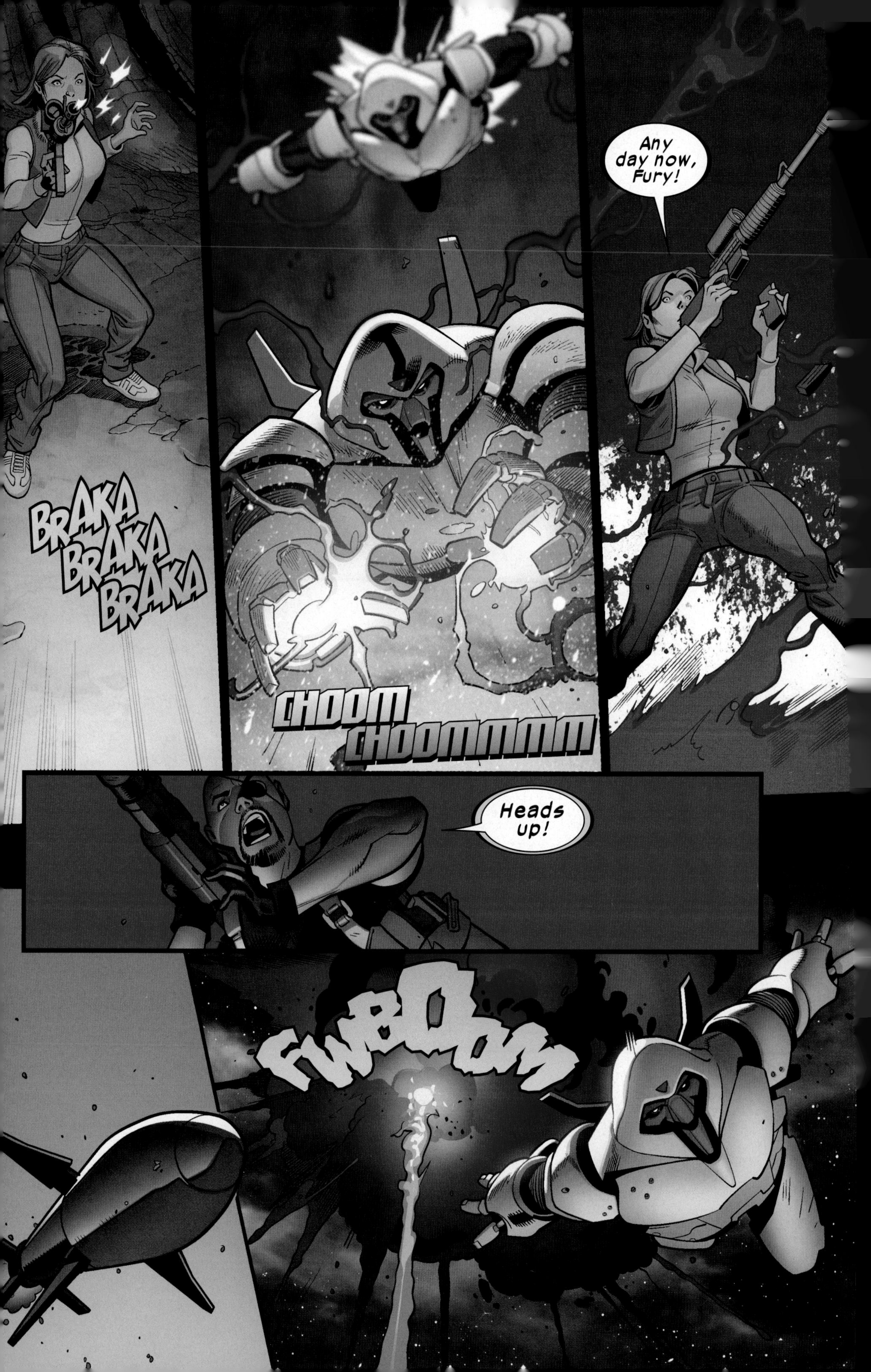

BRAKA
BRAKA
BRAKA
CHOOM
CHOOMMMMM
Any day now, Fury!
Heads up!
FWBOOM

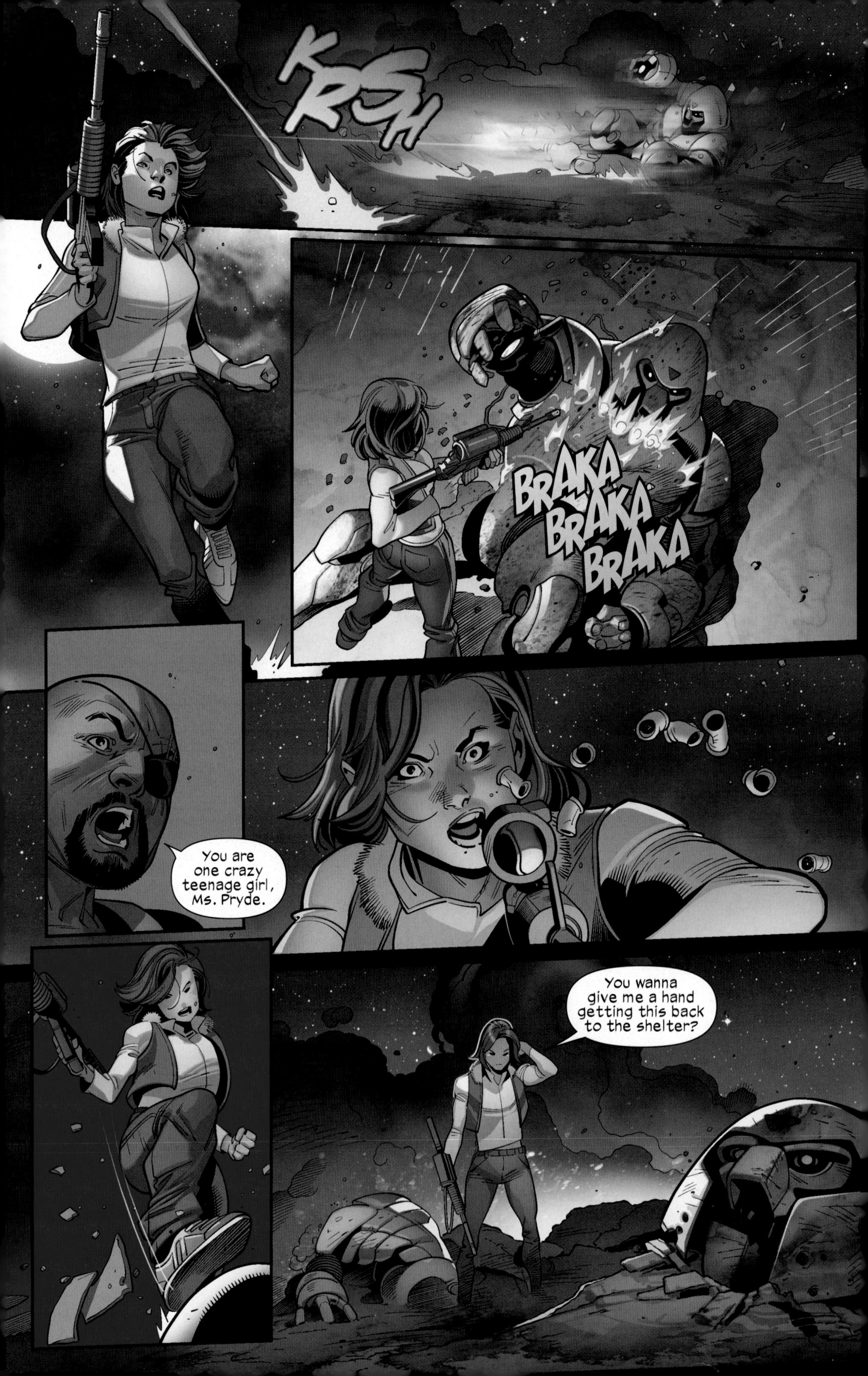
KRSH
BRAKA BRAKA BRAKA BRAKA
You are one crazy teenage girl, Ms. Pryde.
You wanna give me a hand getting this back to the shelter?

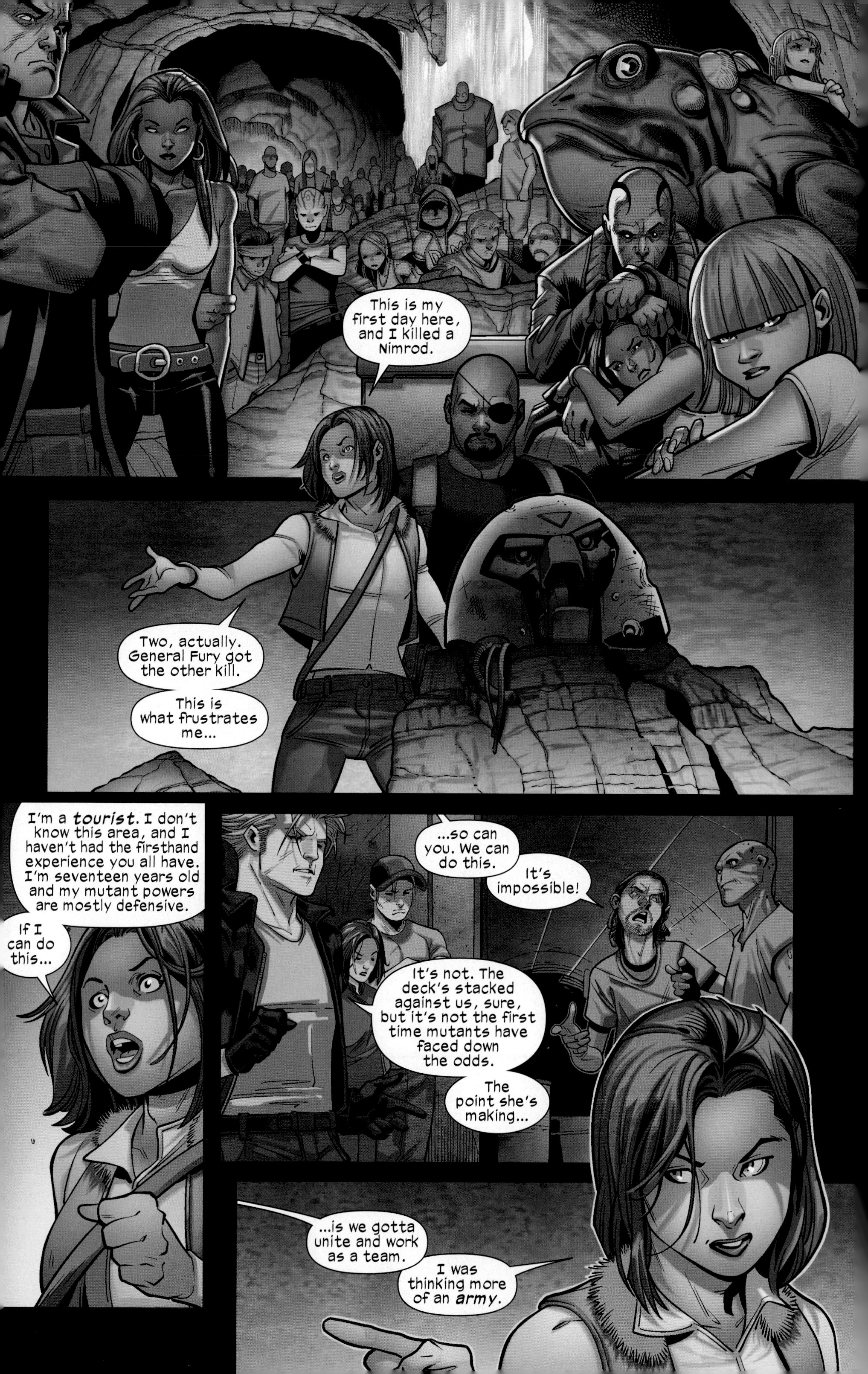

This is my first day here, and I killed a Nimrod.
Two, actually. General Fury got the other kill.
This is what frustrates me...
I'm a *tourist*. I don't know this area, and I haven't had the firsthand experience you all have. I'm seventeen years old and my mutant powers are mostly defensive.
If I can do this...
...so can you. We can do this.
It's impossible!
It's not. The deck's stacked against us, sure, but it's not the first time mutants have faced down the odds.
The point she's making...
...is we gotta unite and work as a team.
I was thinking more of an *army*.

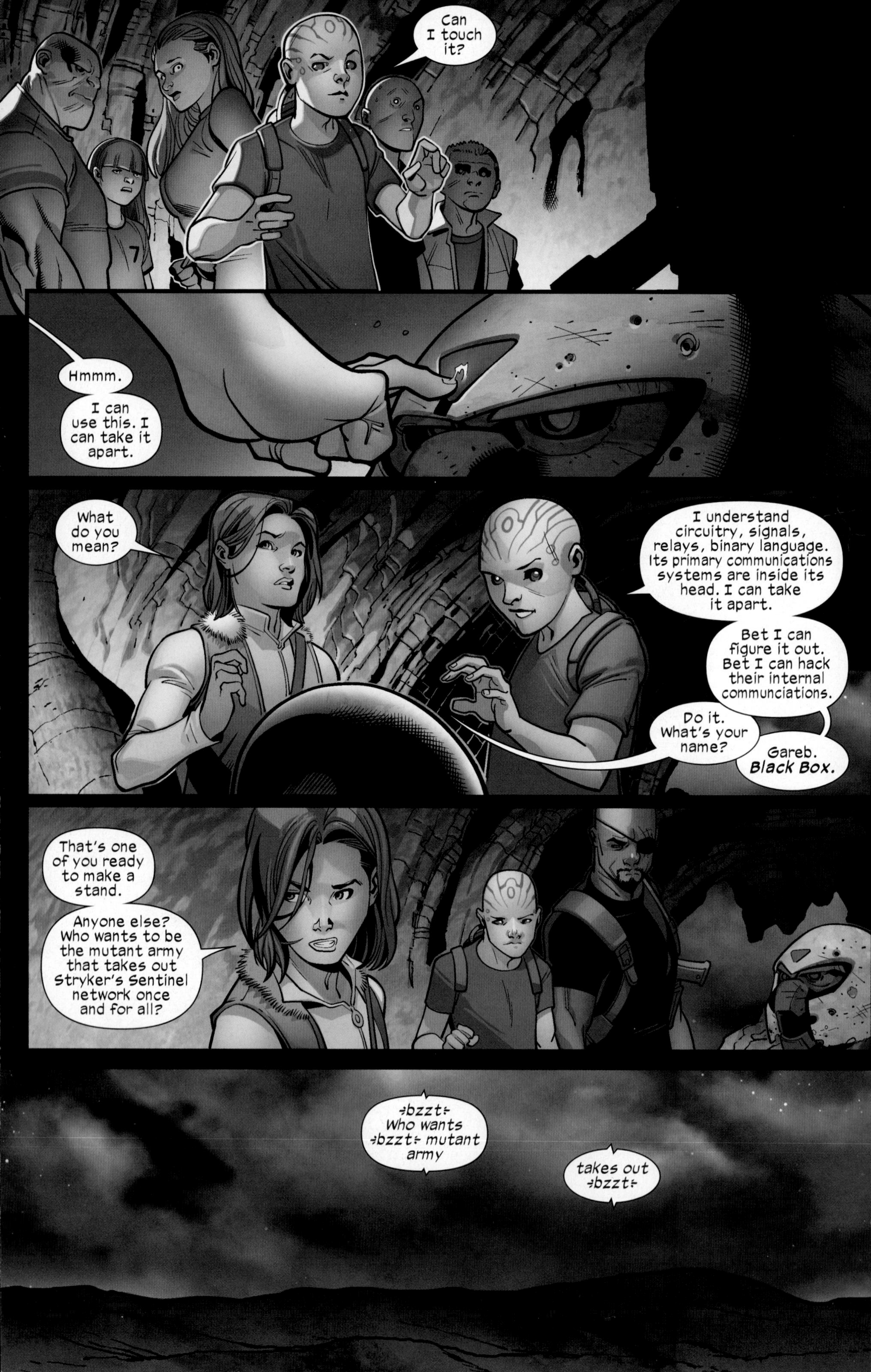

Can I touch it?
Hmmm.
I can use this. I can take it apart.
What do you mean?
I understand circuitry, signals, relays, binary language. Its primary communications systems are inside its head. I can take it apart.
Bet I can figure it out. Bet I can hack their internal communciations.
Do it. What's your name?
Gareb. *Black Box.*
That's one of you ready to make a stand.
Anyone else? Who wants to be the mutant army that takes out Stryker's Sentinel network once and for all?
-bzzt- Who wants -bzzt- mutant army
takes out -bzzt-

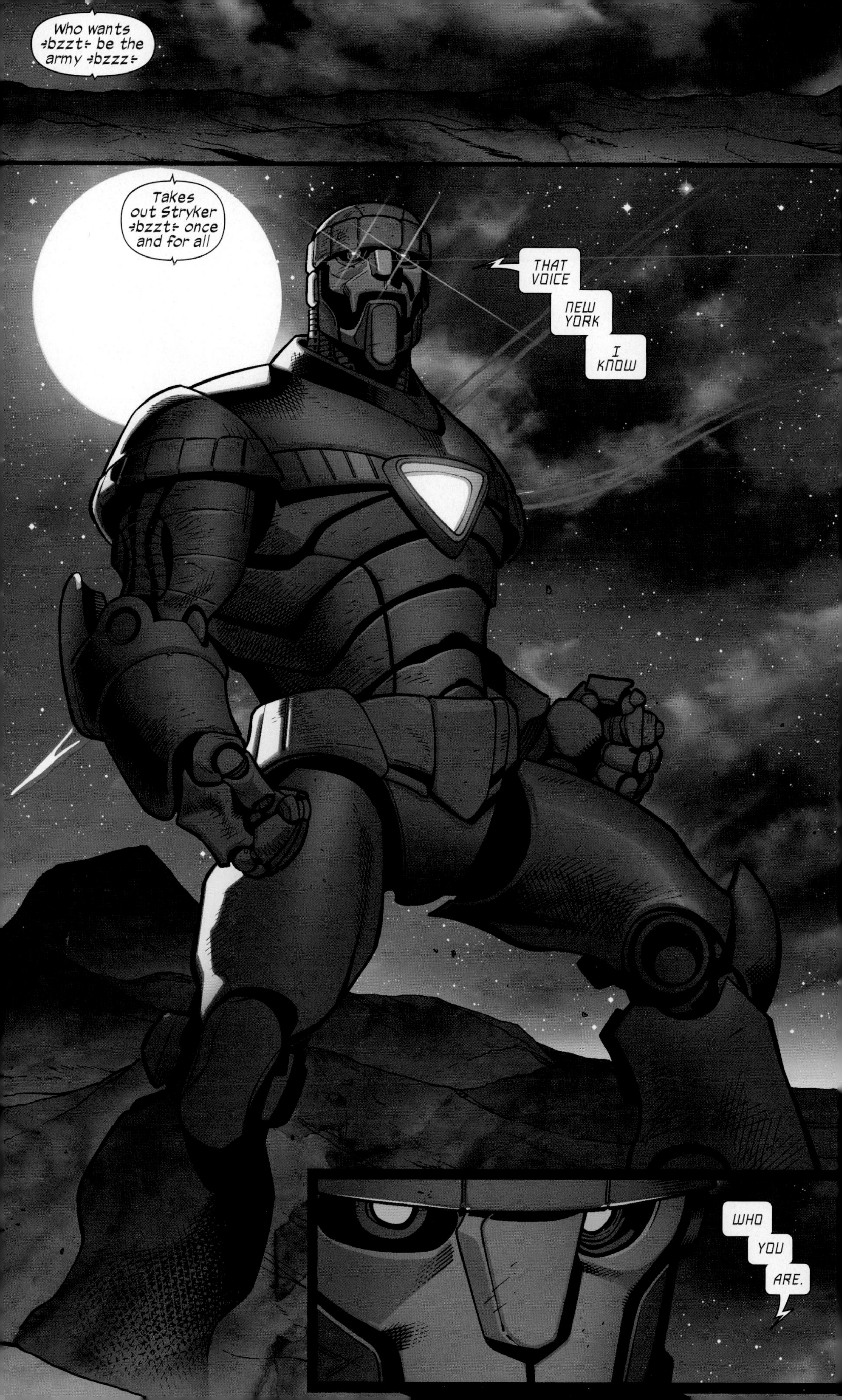
Who wants ⇢bzzt⇠ be the army ⇢bzzz⇠
Takes out Stryker ⇢bzzt⇠ once and for all
THAT VOICE
NEW YORK
I KNOW
WHO YOU ARE.

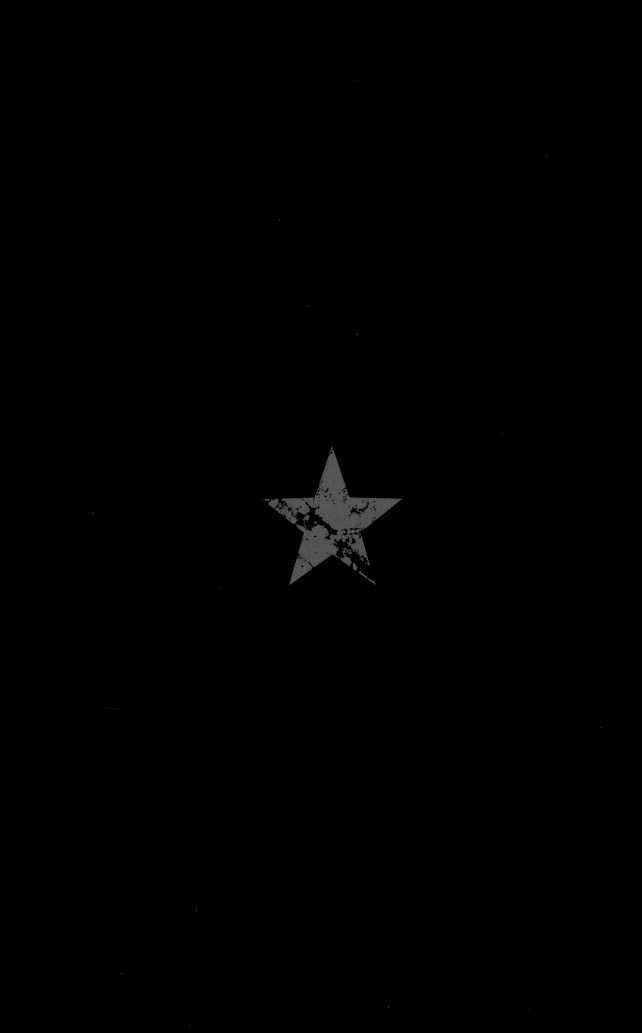

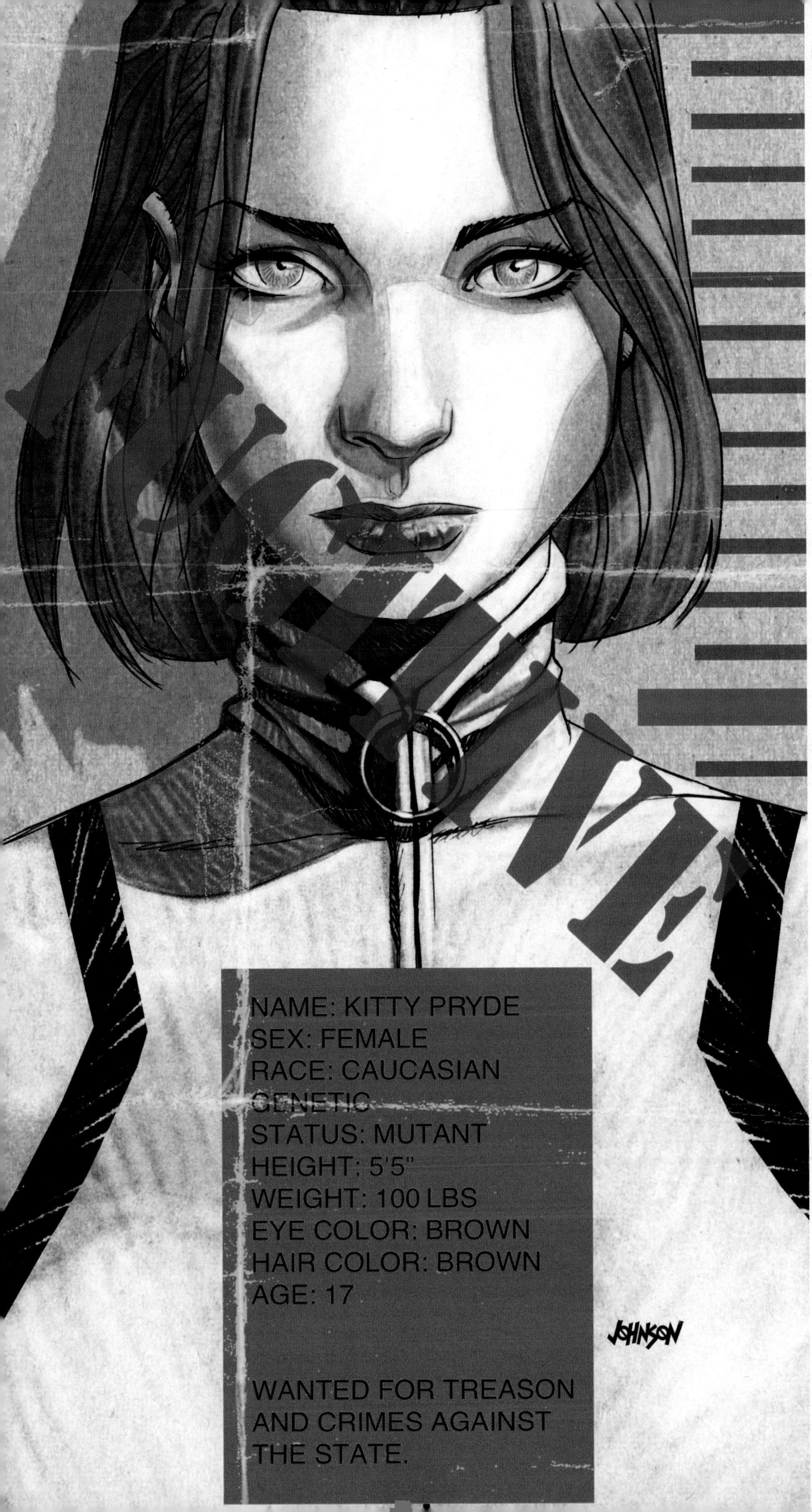
NAME: KITTY PRYDE
SEX: FEMALE
RACE: CAUCASIAN
GENETIC
STATUS: MUTANT
HEIGHT: 5'5"
WEIGHT: 100 LBS
EYE COLOR: BROWN
HAIR COLOR: BROWN
AGE: 17
WANTED FOR TREASON
AND CRIMES AGAINST
THE STATE.
JOHNSON

11

ULTIMATE COMICS **X-MEN** #17

S.H.I.E.L.D. SITUATION MAP:

[Anti-government militia hot spots]

Montana,N.Dakota,
S.Dakota,Wyoming,
Idaho,Arizona,
New Mexico,N.Carolina,
S.Carolina,Georgia

[Eastern seaboard control zone

New England,
New York,
Pennsylvania,
New Jersey,
Delaware,
Washington,D.C.,
Maryland,
Virginia

secured by
National Guard
under emergency
powers
committee

[the West Coast]

California,Oregon,
Washington

declared
independent state

[Great Lakes states]

Minnesota,
Wisconsin,
Michigan,
Illinois,
Indiana,Ohio

status unknown

ANTI-MATTE
NO FLY
ZONE

SENTINEL
PUSH

SOUTHERN
CALIFORNIA
REFUGEE ZONE

● AREA OF
URBAN
UNREST

Classified Position

Camp Hutton, secure
location of the President
of the United States

[Sentinel-controlled no-man's-land]

New Mexico,Arizona,
Utah,Oklahoma

abandoned by the
U.S. government

ALL STATES
SHOWN IN WHITE
ARE U.S. GOVERNMENT-
CONTROLLED ZONES

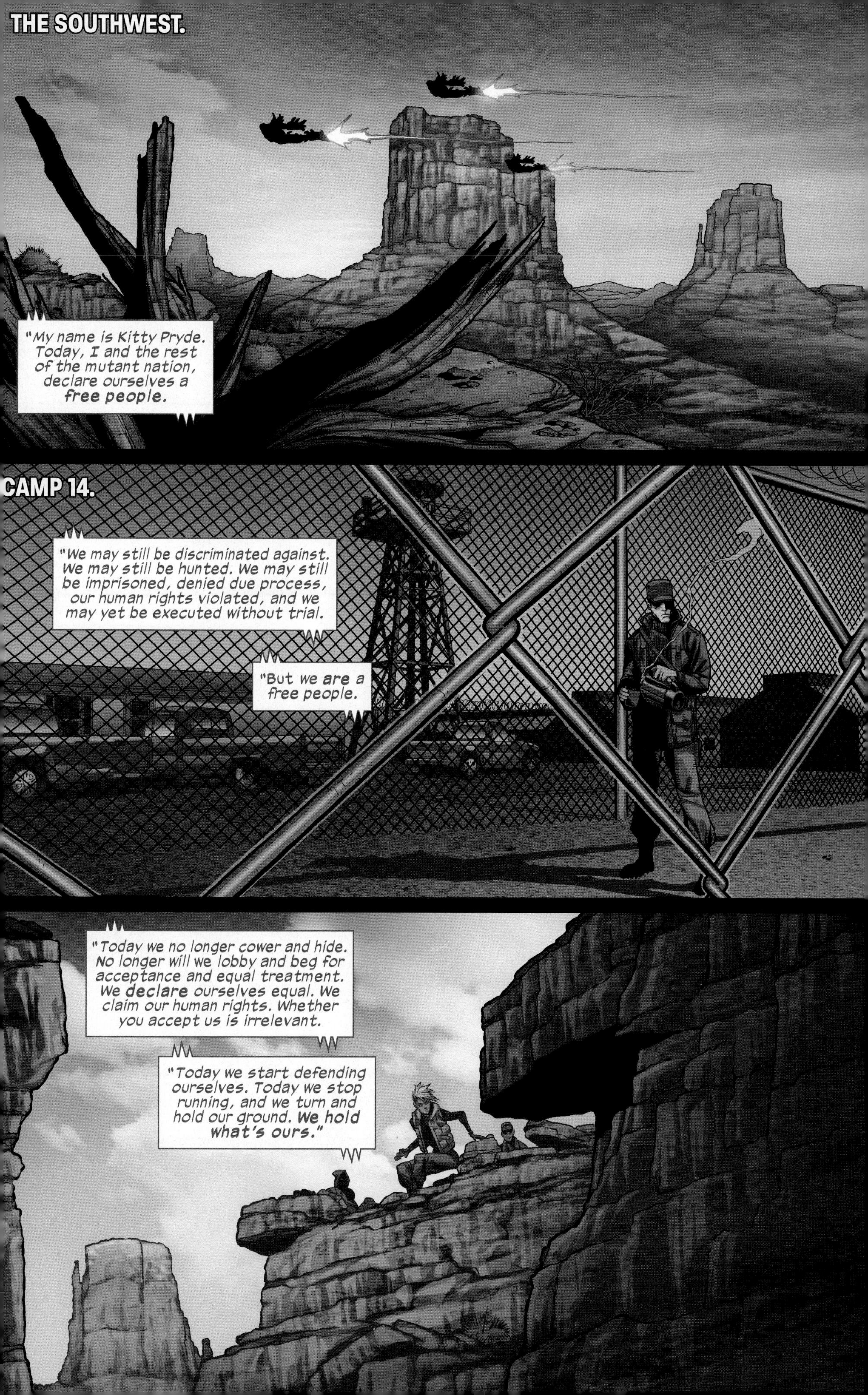
THE SOUTHWEST.
"My name is Kitty Pryde. Today, I and the rest of the mutant nation, declare ourselves a free people.
CAMP 14.
"We may still be discriminated against. We may still be hunted. We may still be imprisoned, denied due process, our human rights violated, and we may yet be executed without trial.
"But we are a free people.
"Today we no longer cower and hide. No longer will we lobby and beg for acceptance and equal treatment. We declare ourselves equal. We claim our human rights. Whether you accept us is irrelevant.
"Today we start defending ourselves. Today we stop running, and we turn and hold our ground. We hold what's ours."

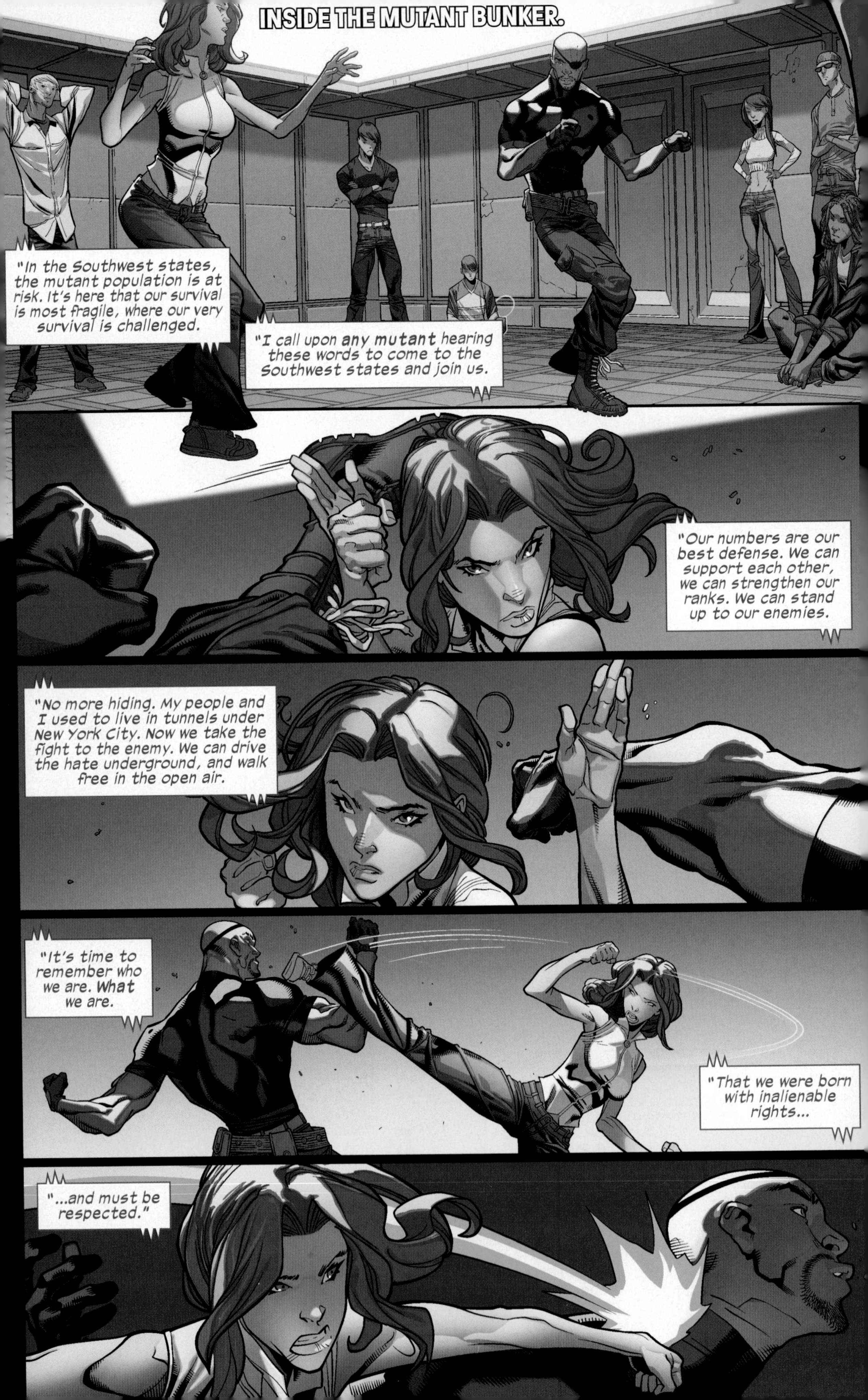
INSIDE THE MUTANT BUNKER.
"In the Southwest states, the mutant population is at risk. It's here that our survival is most fragile, where our very survival is challenged.
"I call upon any mutant hearing these words to come to the Southwest states and join us.
"Our numbers are our best defense. We can support each other, we can strengthen our ranks. We can stand up to our enemies.
"No more hiding. My people and I used to live in tunnels under New York City. Now we take the fight to the enemy. We can drive the hate underground, and walk free in the open air.
"It's time to remember who we are. What we are.
"That we were born with inalienable rights...
"...and must be respected."

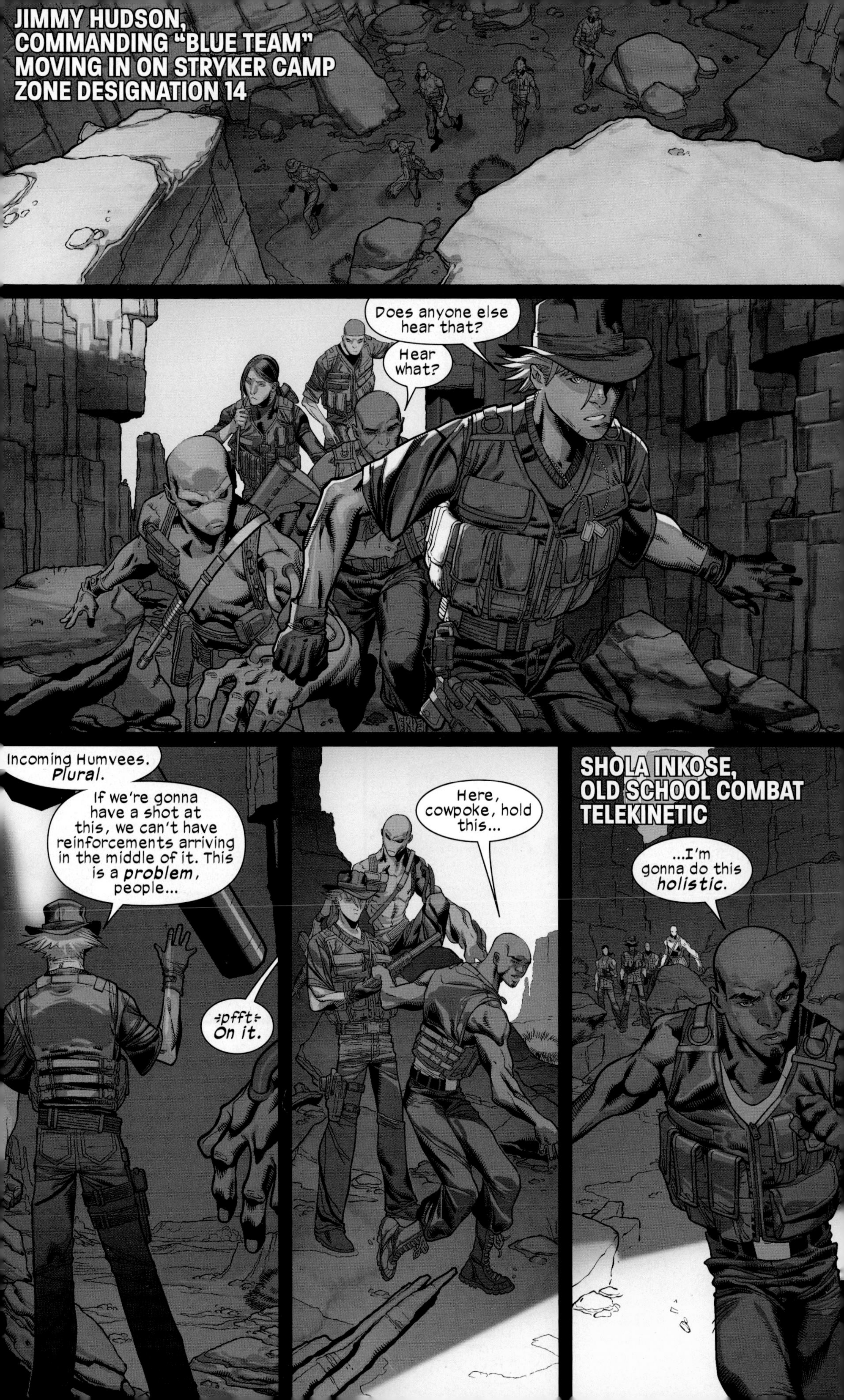

JIMMY HUDSON, COMMANDING "BLUE TEAM" MOVING IN ON STRYKER CAMP ZONE DESIGNATION 14
Does anyone else hear that?
Hear what?
Incoming Humvees. Plural.
If we're gonna have a shot at this, we can't have reinforcements arriving in the middle of it. This is a problem, people...
-pfft- On it.
Here, cowpoke, hold this...
SHOLA INKOSE, OLD SCHOOL COMBAT TELEKINETIC
...I'm gonna do this holistic.

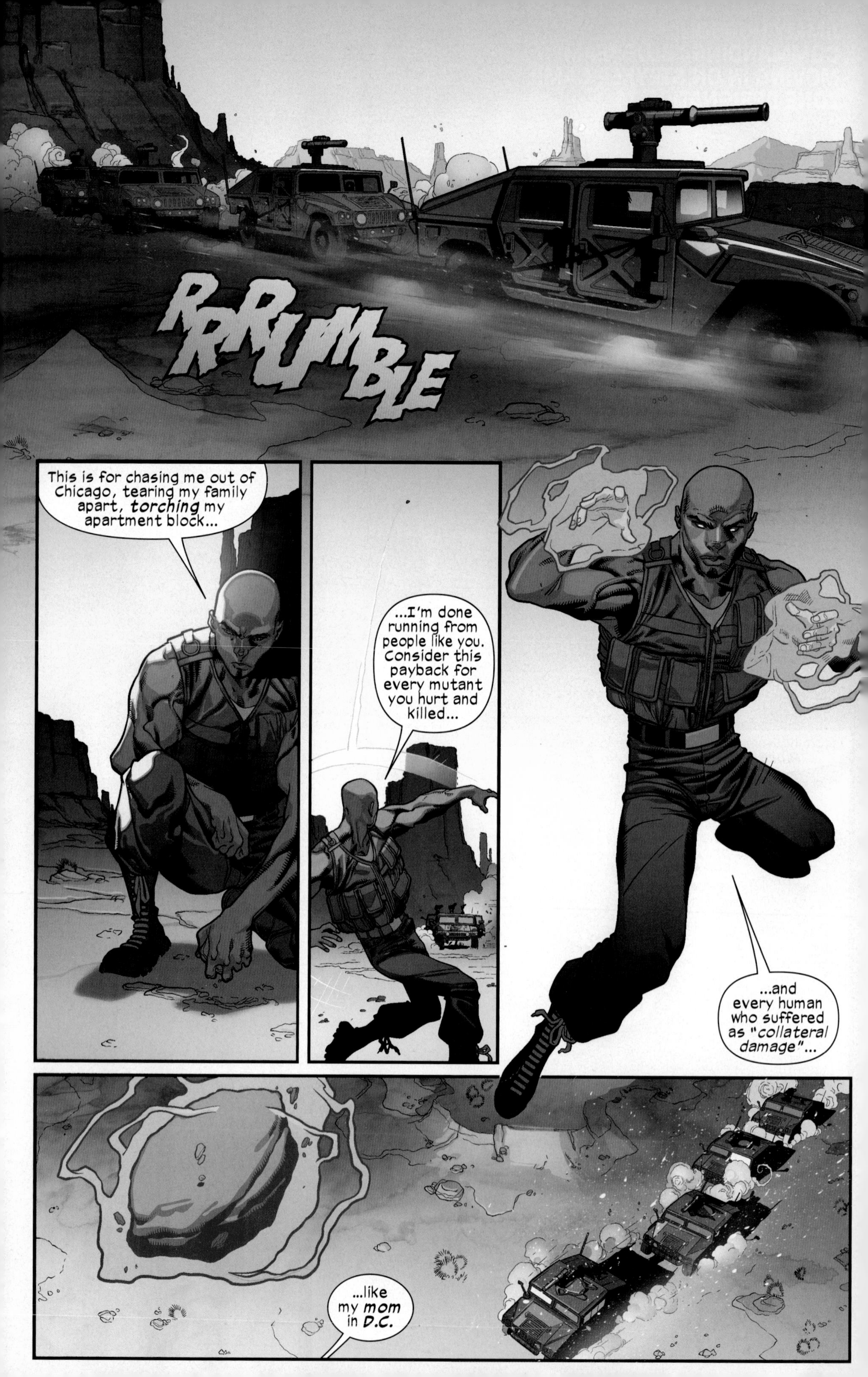
RRRUMBLE
This is for chasing me out of Chicago, tearing my family apart, *torching* my apartment block...
...I'm done running from people like you. Consider this payback for every mutant you hurt and killed...
...and every human who suffered as *"collateral damage"*...
...like my *mom* in *D.C.*

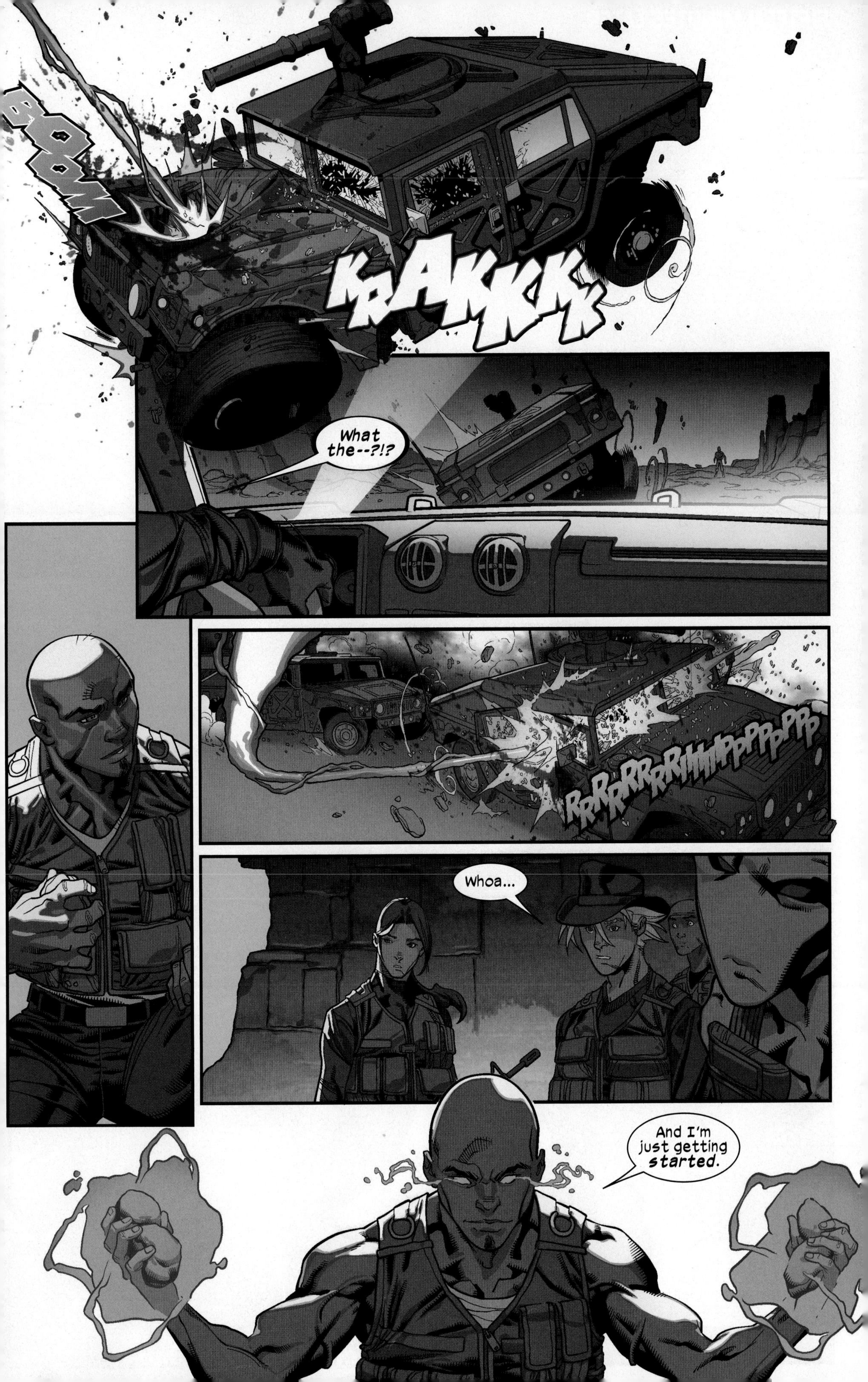
BOOM
KRAKKKK
What the--?!?
RRRRRRRRIIIIIPPPPPPPP
Whoa...
And I'm just getting started.

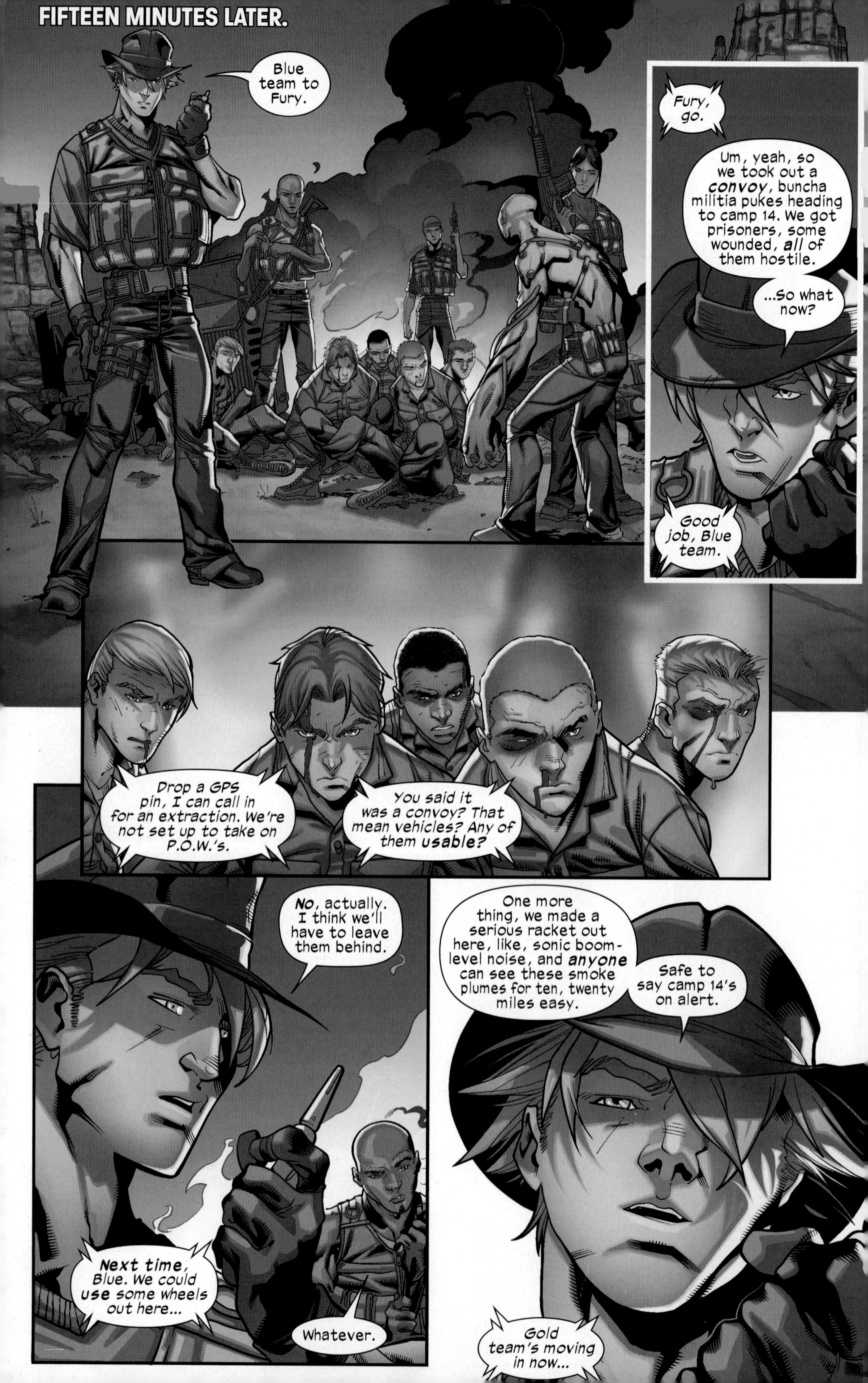
FIFTEEN MINUTES LATER.
Blue team to Fury.
Fury, go.
Um, yeah, so we took out a convoy, buncha militia pukes heading to camp 14. We got prisoners, some wounded, all of them hostile.
...So what now?
Good job, Blue team.
Drop a GPS pin, I can call in for an extraction. We're not set up to take on P.O.W.'s.
You said it was a convoy? That mean vehicles? Any of them usable?
No, actually. I think we'll have to leave them behind.
Next time, Blue. We could use some wheels out here...
Whatever.
One more thing, we made a serious racket out here, like, sonic boom-level noise, and anyone can see these smoke plumes for ten, twenty miles easy.
Safe to say camp 14's on alert.
Gold team's moving in now...

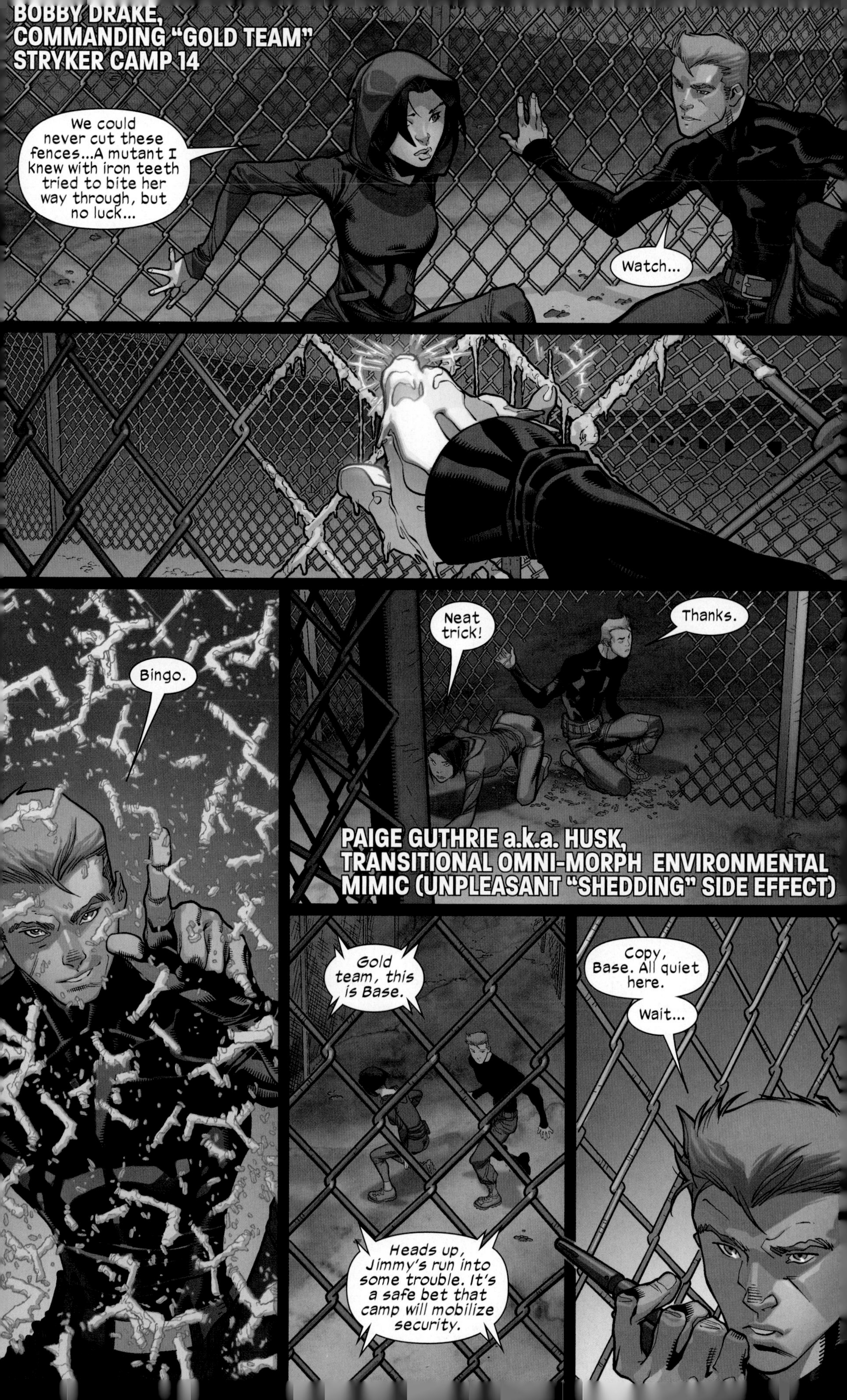
BOBBY DRAKE, COMMANDING "GOLD TEAM" STRYKER CAMP 14
We could never cut these fences...A mutant I knew with iron teeth tried to bite her way through, but no luck...
Watch...
Bingo.
Neat trick!
Thanks.
PAIGE GUTHRIE a.k.a. HUSK, TRANSITIONAL OMNI-MORPH ENVIRONMENTAL MIMIC (UNPLEASANT "SHEDDING" SIDE EFFECT)
Gold team, this is Base.
Heads up, Jimmy's run into some trouble. It's a safe bet that camp will mobilize security.
Copy, Base. All quiet here.
Wait...

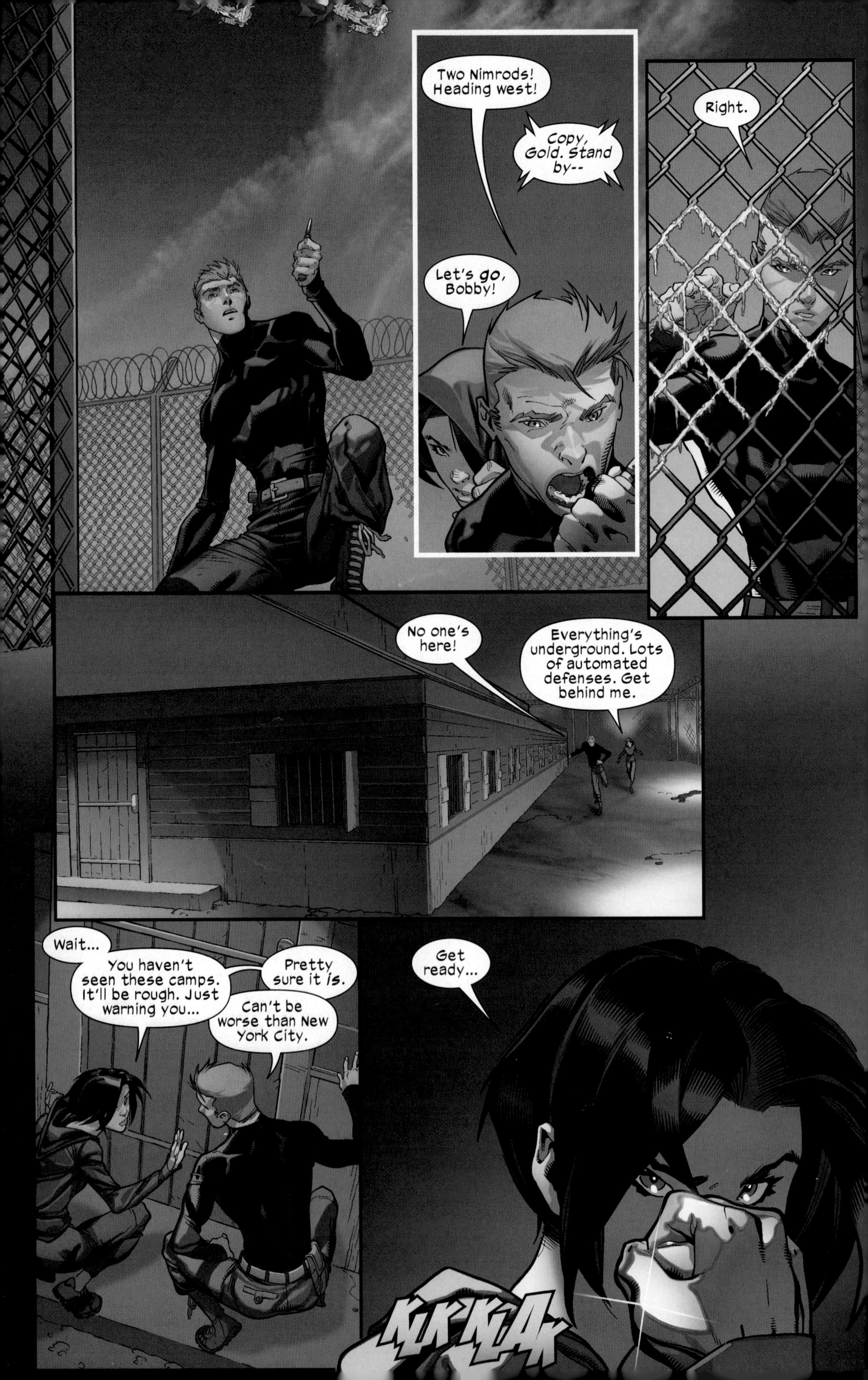

Two Nimrods! Heading west!
Copy, Gold. Stand by--
Let's go, Bobby!
Right.
No one's here!
Everything's underground. Lots of automated defenses. Get behind me.
Wait...
You haven't seen these camps. It'll be rough. Just warning you...
Pretty sure it is.
Can't be worse than New York City.
Get ready...
KLIK KLAK

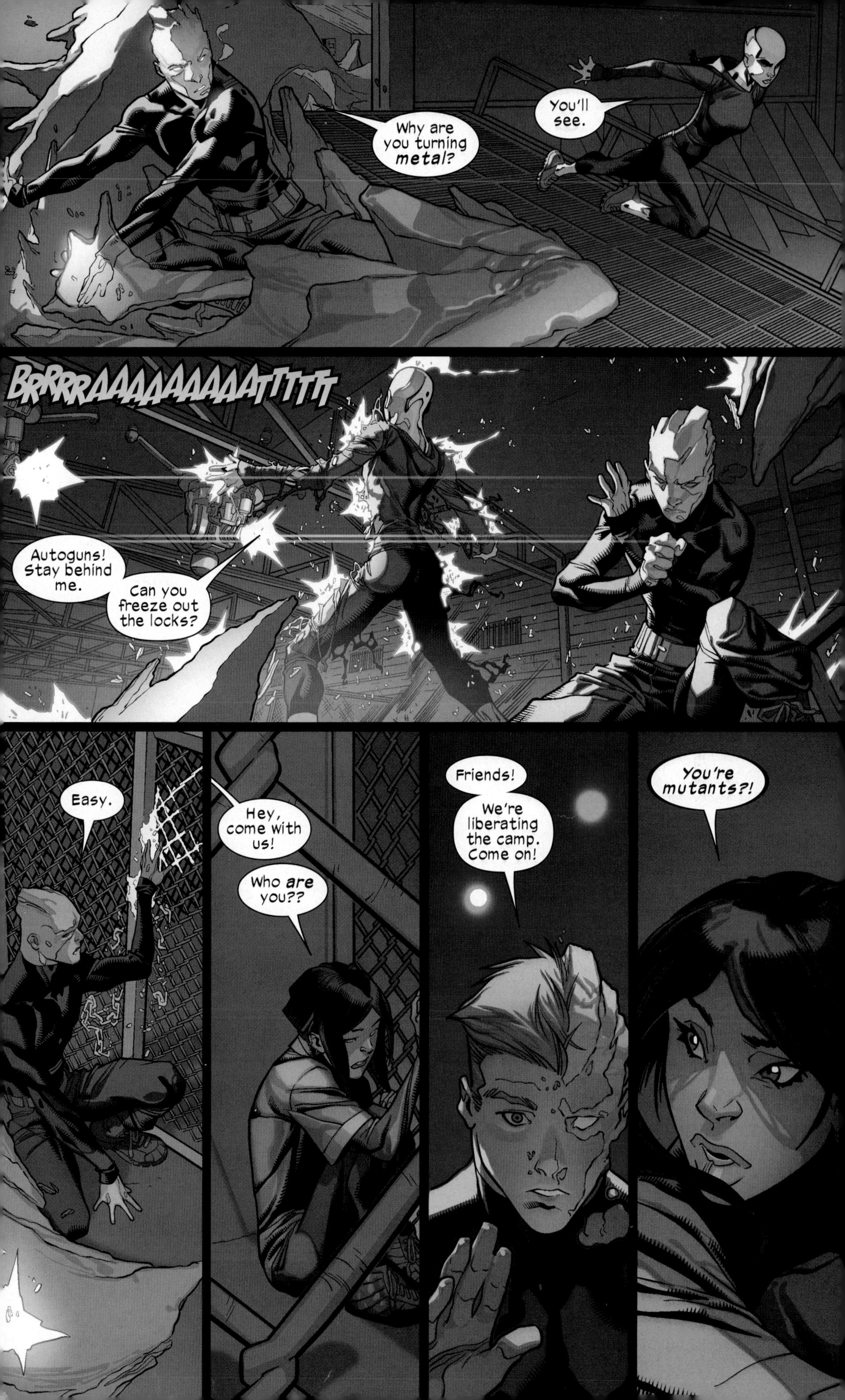
Why are you turning metal?
You'll see.
BRRRRAAAAAAAAAATTTTTT
Autoguns! Stay behind me.
Can you freeze out the locks?
Easy.
Hey, come with us!
Who are you??
Friends!
We're liberating the camp. Come on!
You're mutants?!

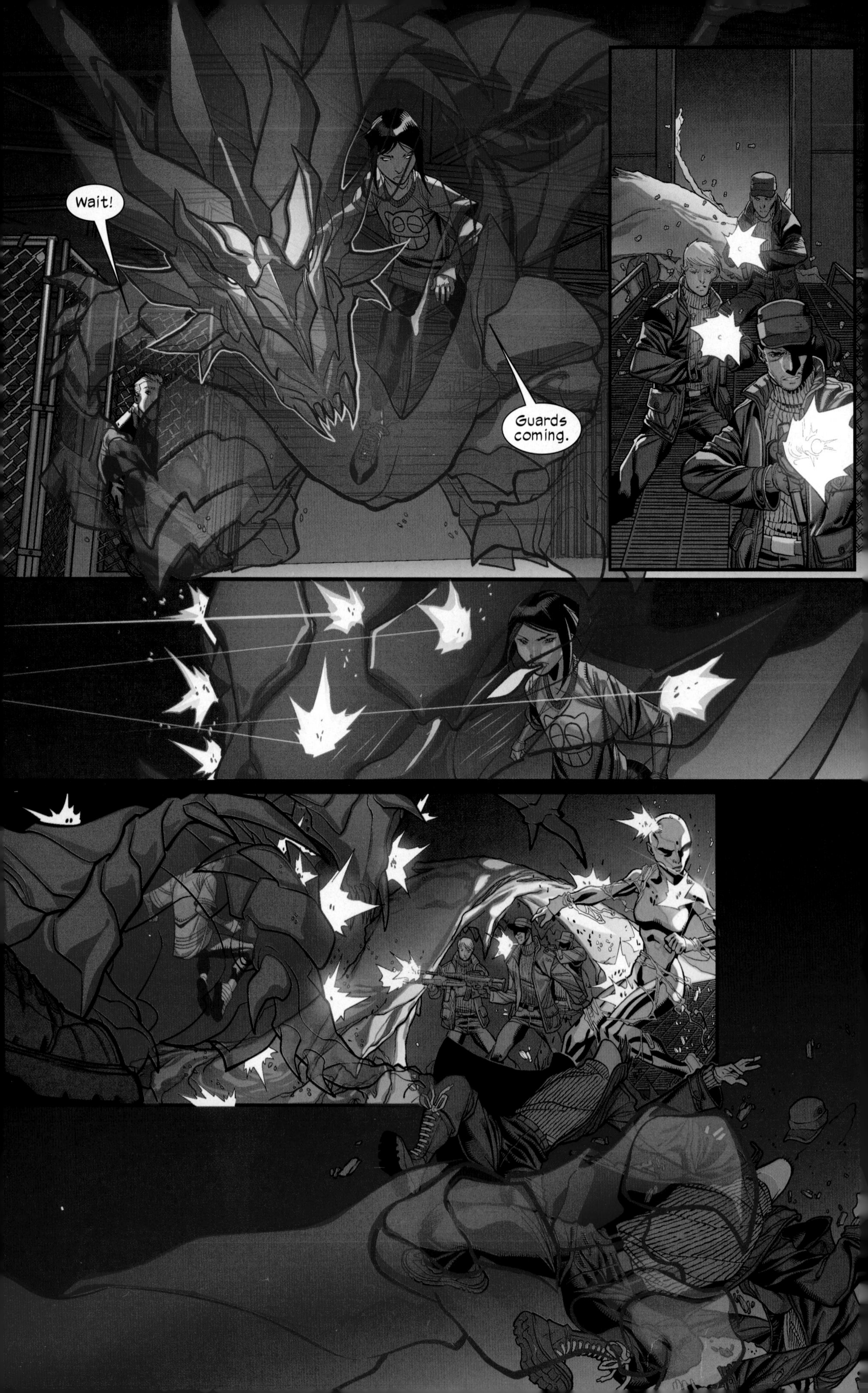
Wait!
Guards coming.

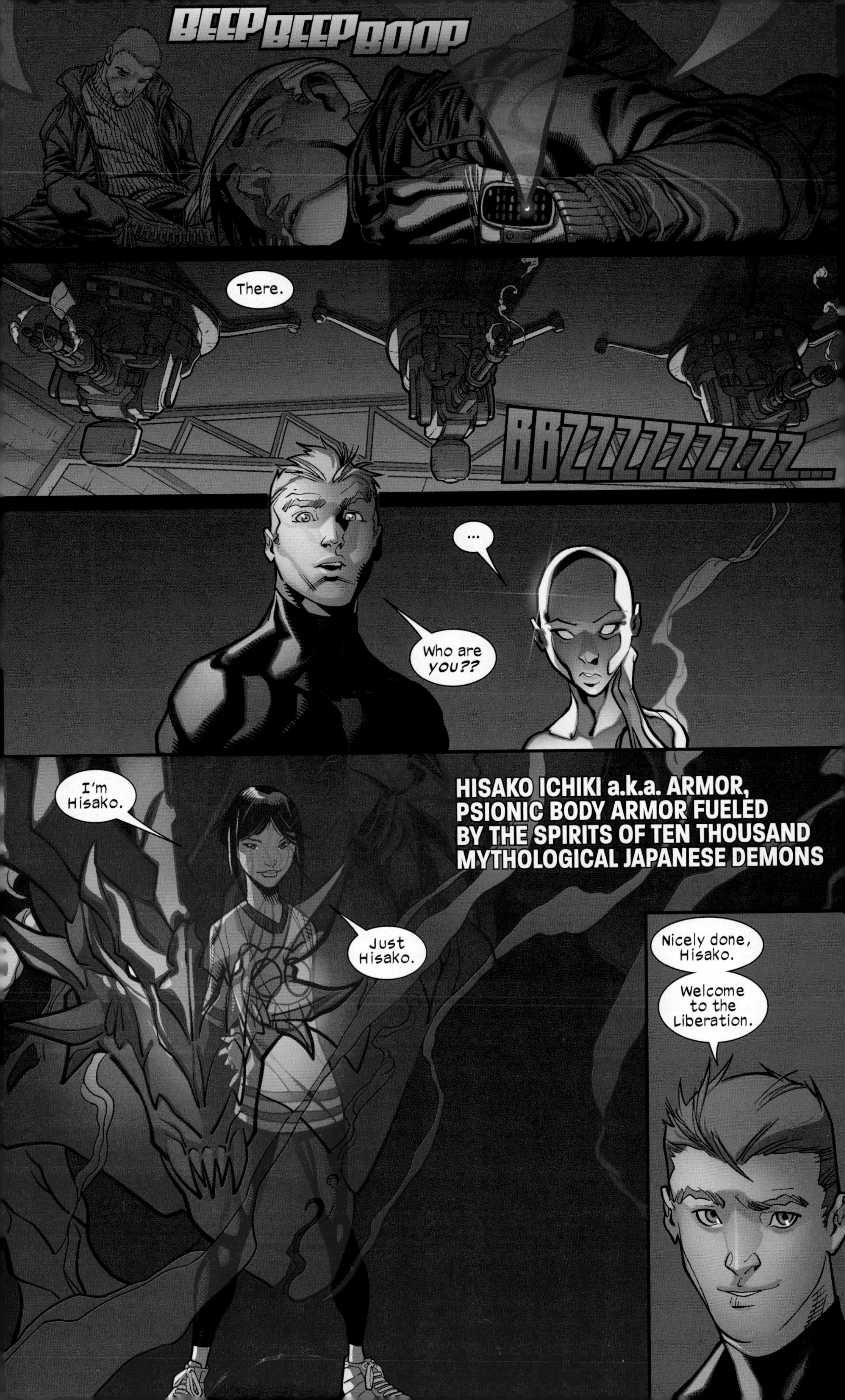
BEEP BEEP BOOP
There.
BBZZZZZZZZZZ...
...
Who are you??
I'm Hisako.
HISAKO ICHIKI a.k.a. ARMOR, PSIONIC BODY ARMOR FUELED BY THE SPIRITS OF TEN THOUSAND MYTHOLOGICAL JAPANESE DEMONS
Just Hisako.
Nicely done, Hisako.
Welcome to the Liberation.

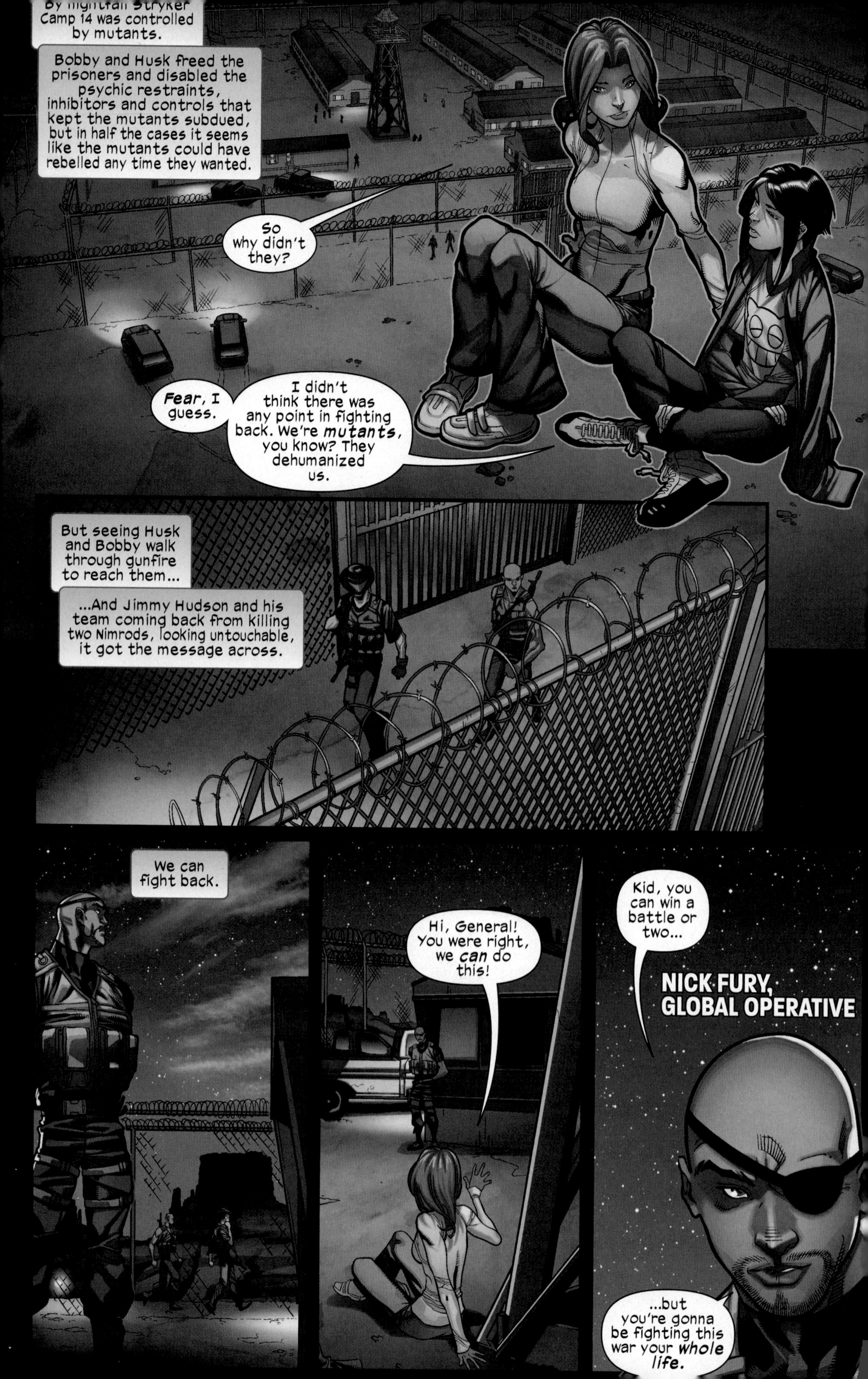

Camp 14 was controlled by mutants.
Bobby and Husk freed the prisoners and disabled the psychic restraints, inhibitors and controls that kept the mutants subdued, but in half the cases it seems like the mutants could have rebelled any time they wanted.
So why didn't they?
Fear, I guess.
I didn't think there was any point in fighting back. We're mutants, you know? They dehumanized us.
But seeing Husk and Bobby walk through gunfire to reach them...
...And Jimmy Hudson and his team coming back from killing two Nimrods, looking untouchable, it got the message across.
We can fight back.
Hi, General! You were right, we can do this!
Kid, you can win a battle or two...
NICK FURY, GLOBAL OPERATIVE
...but you're gonna be fighting this war your whole life.

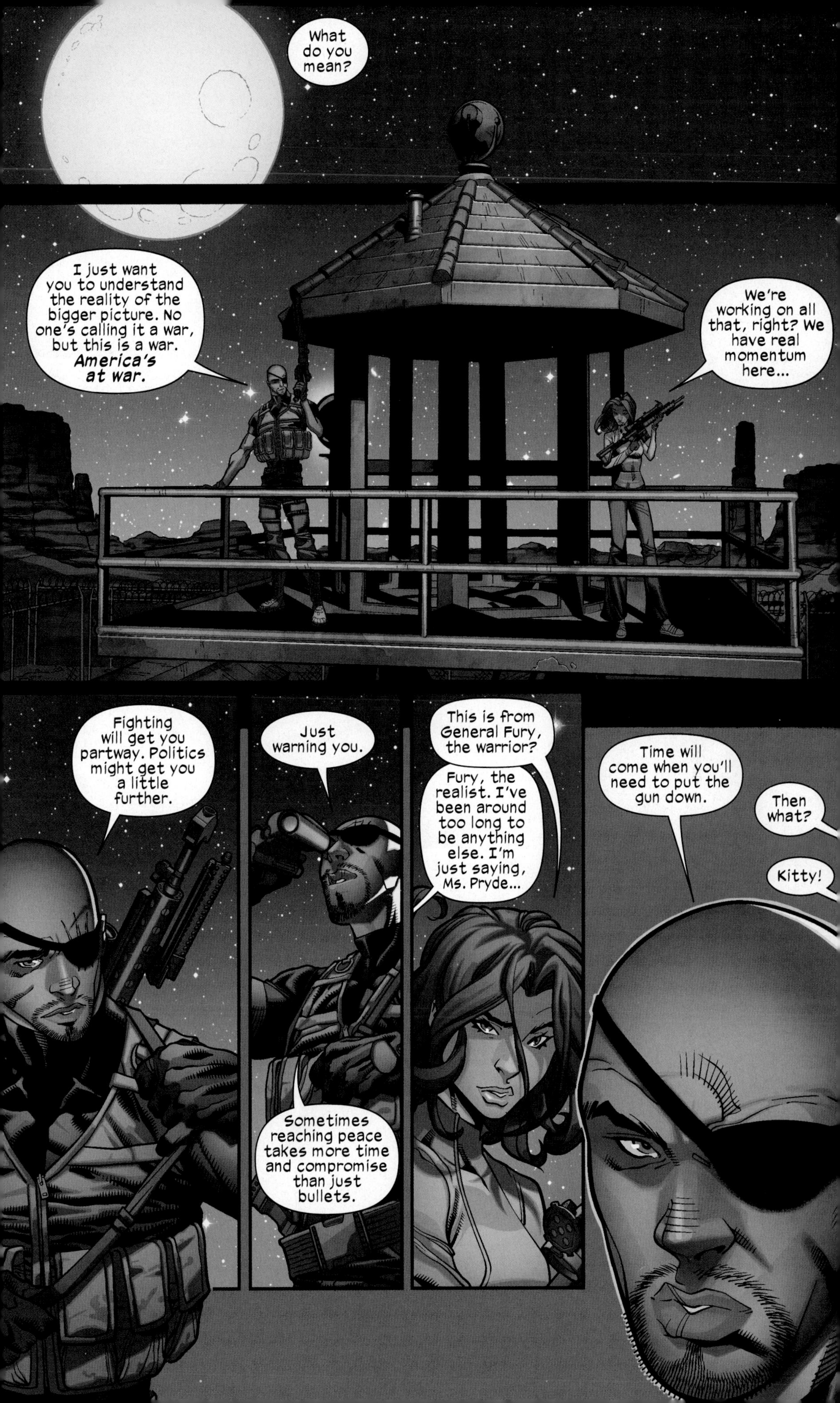
What do you mean?
I just want you to understand the reality of the bigger picture. No one's calling it a war, but this is a war. *America's at war.*
We're working on all that, right? We have real momentum here...
Fighting will get you partway. Politics might get you a little further.
Just warning you.
Sometimes reaching peace takes more time and compromise than just bullets.
This is from General Fury, the warrior?
Fury, the realist. I've been around too long to be anything else. I'm just saying, Ms. Pryde...
Time will come when you'll need to put the gun down.
Then what?
Kitty!

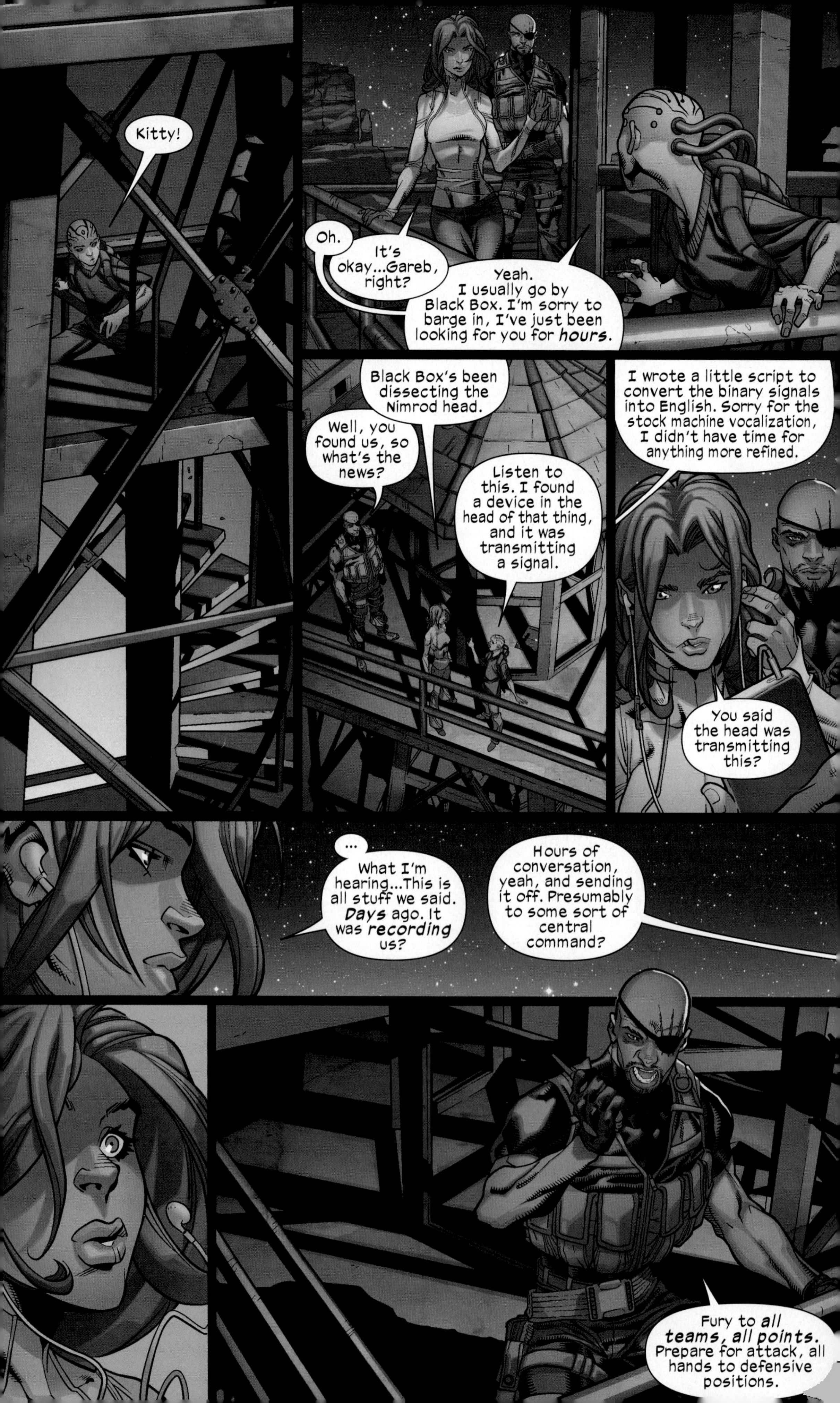
Kitty!
Oh.
It's okay...Gareb, right?
Yeah. I usually go by Black Box. I'm sorry to barge in, I've just been looking for you for *hours*.
Black Box's been dissecting the Nimrod head.
Well, you found us, so what's the news?
Listen to this. I found a device in the head of that thing, and it was transmitting a signal.
I wrote a little script to convert the binary signals into English. Sorry for the stock machine vocalization, I didn't have time for anything more refined.
You said the head was transmitting this?
...
What I'm hearing...This is all stuff we said. *Days* ago. It was *recording* us?
Hours of conversation, yeah, and sending it off. Presumably to some sort of central command?
Fury to *all teams, all points.* Prepare for attack, all hands to defensive positions.

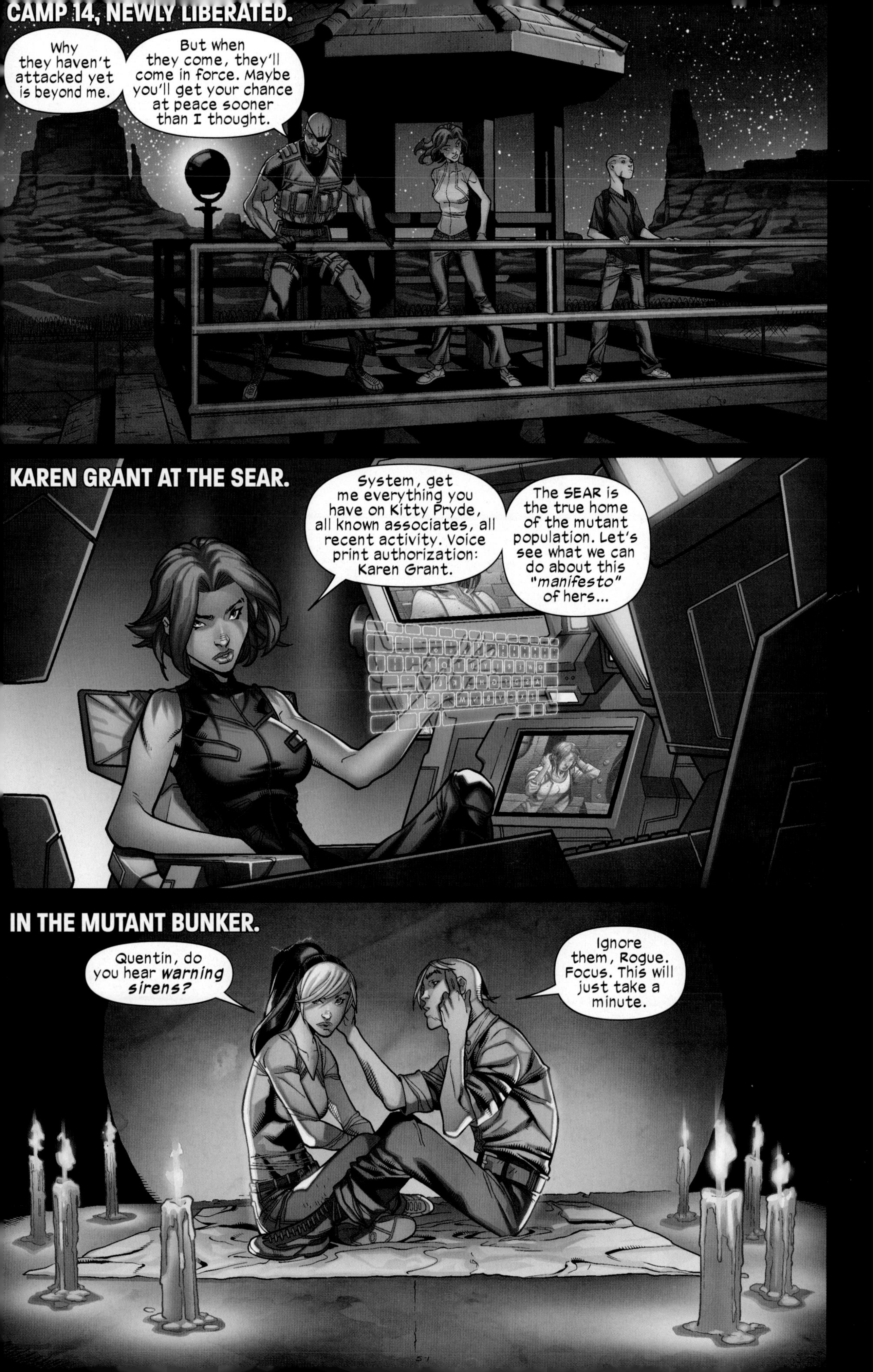

CAMP 14, NEWLY LIBERATED.
Why they haven't attacked yet is beyond me.
But when they come, they'll come in force. Maybe you'll get your chance at peace sooner than I thought.
KAREN GRANT AT THE SEAR.
System, get me everything you have on Kitty Pryde, all known associates, all recent activity. Voice print authorization: Karen Grant.
The SEAR is the true home of the mutant population. Let's see what we can do about this "manifesto" of hers...
IN THE MUTANT BUNKER.
Quentin, do you hear warning sirens?
Ignore them, Rogue. Focus. This will just take a minute.

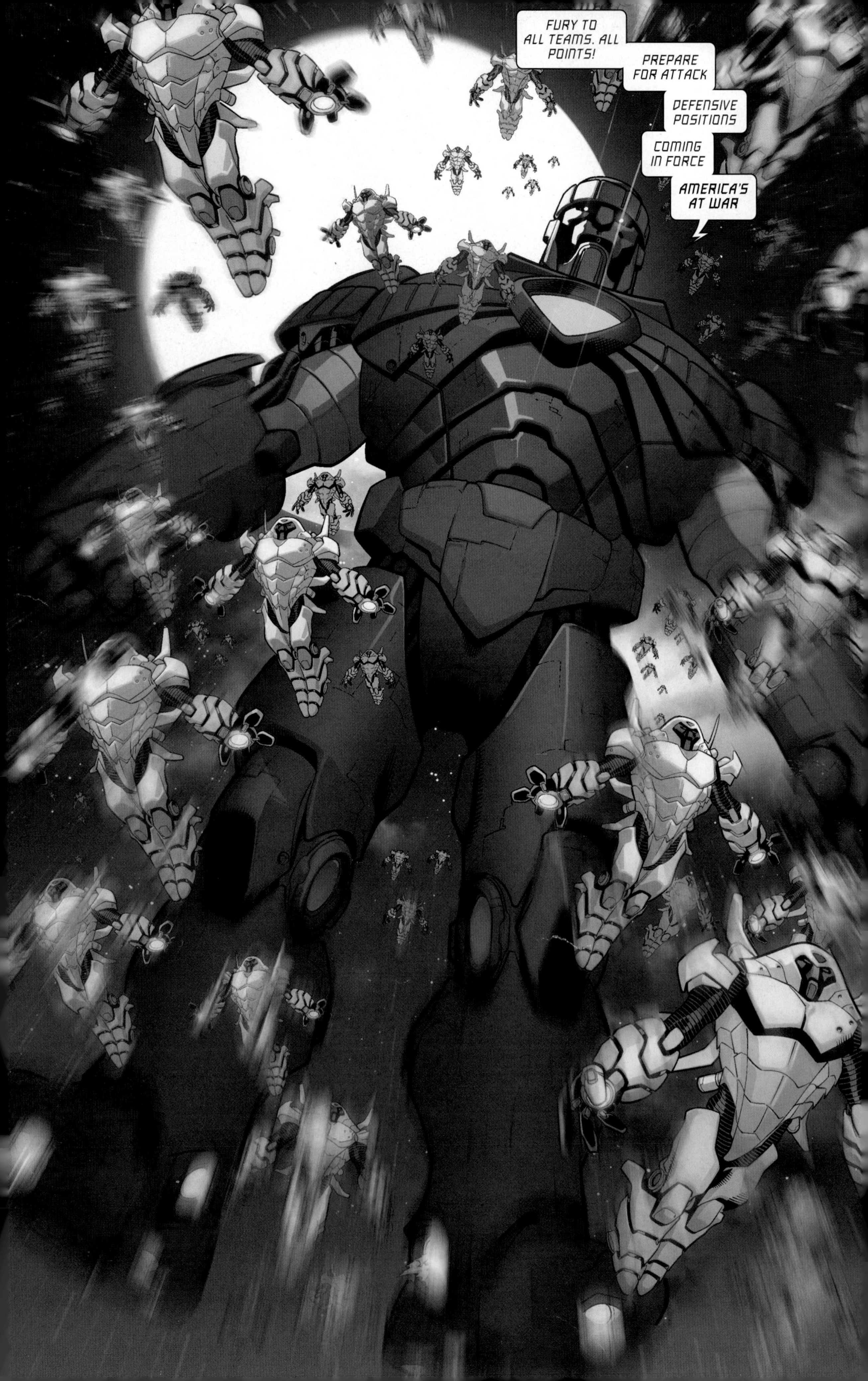
FURY TO ALL TEAMS. ALL POINTS!
PREPARE FOR ATTACK
DEFENSIVE POSITIONS
COMING IN FORCE
AMERICA'S AT WAR

12

ULTIMATE COMICS **X-MEN** #18

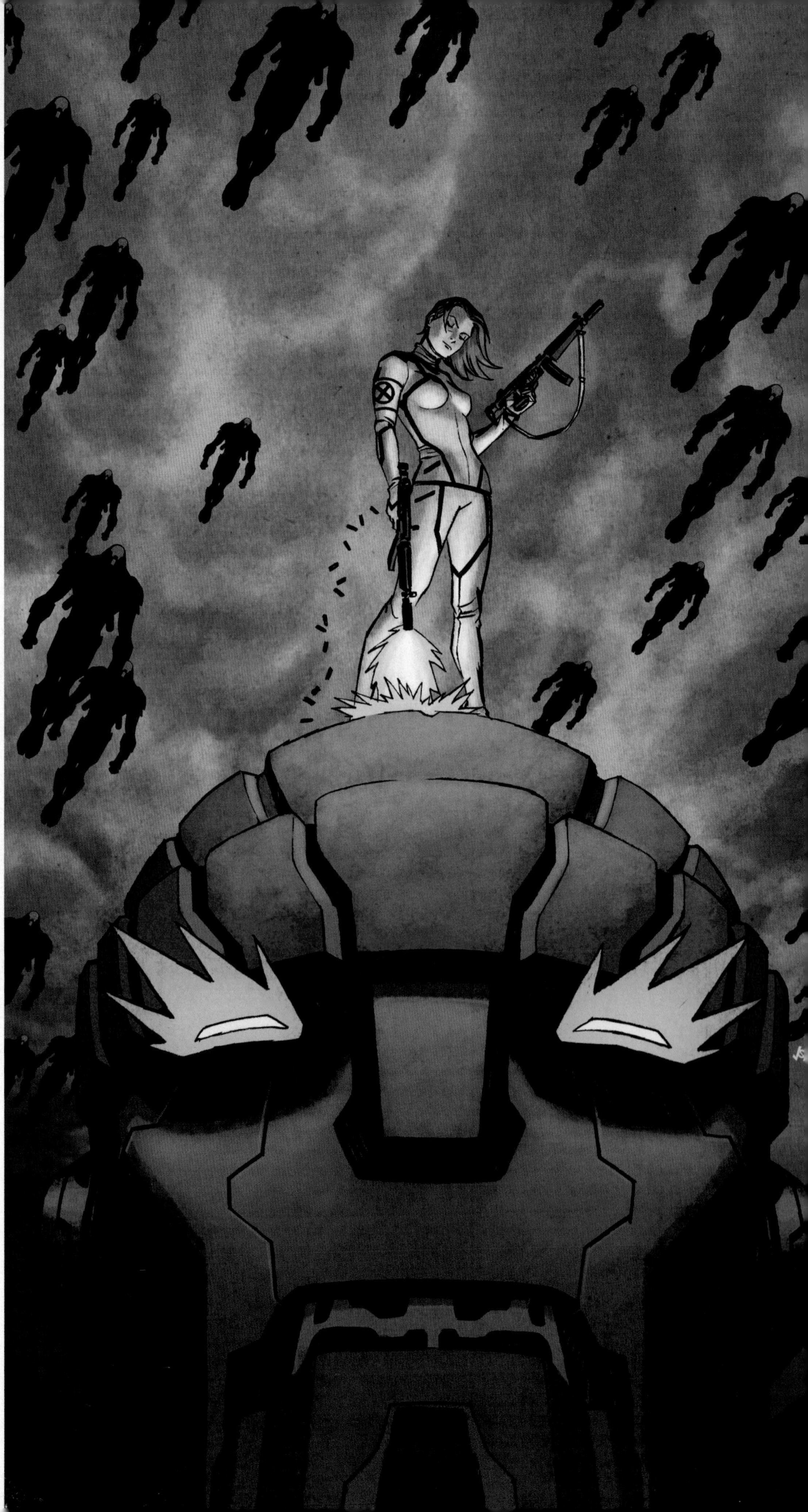

S.H.I.E.L.D. SITUATION MAP:

[Anti-government militia hot spots]

Idaho, Montana, N. Dakota, S. Dakota, Arizona, New Mexico, Wyoming

Wyoming
status unknown

[Eastern seaboard control zone]

New England, New York, New Jersey, Delaware, Washington, D.C., Maryland, Pennsylvania, Virginia

secured by National Guard under emergency powers committee

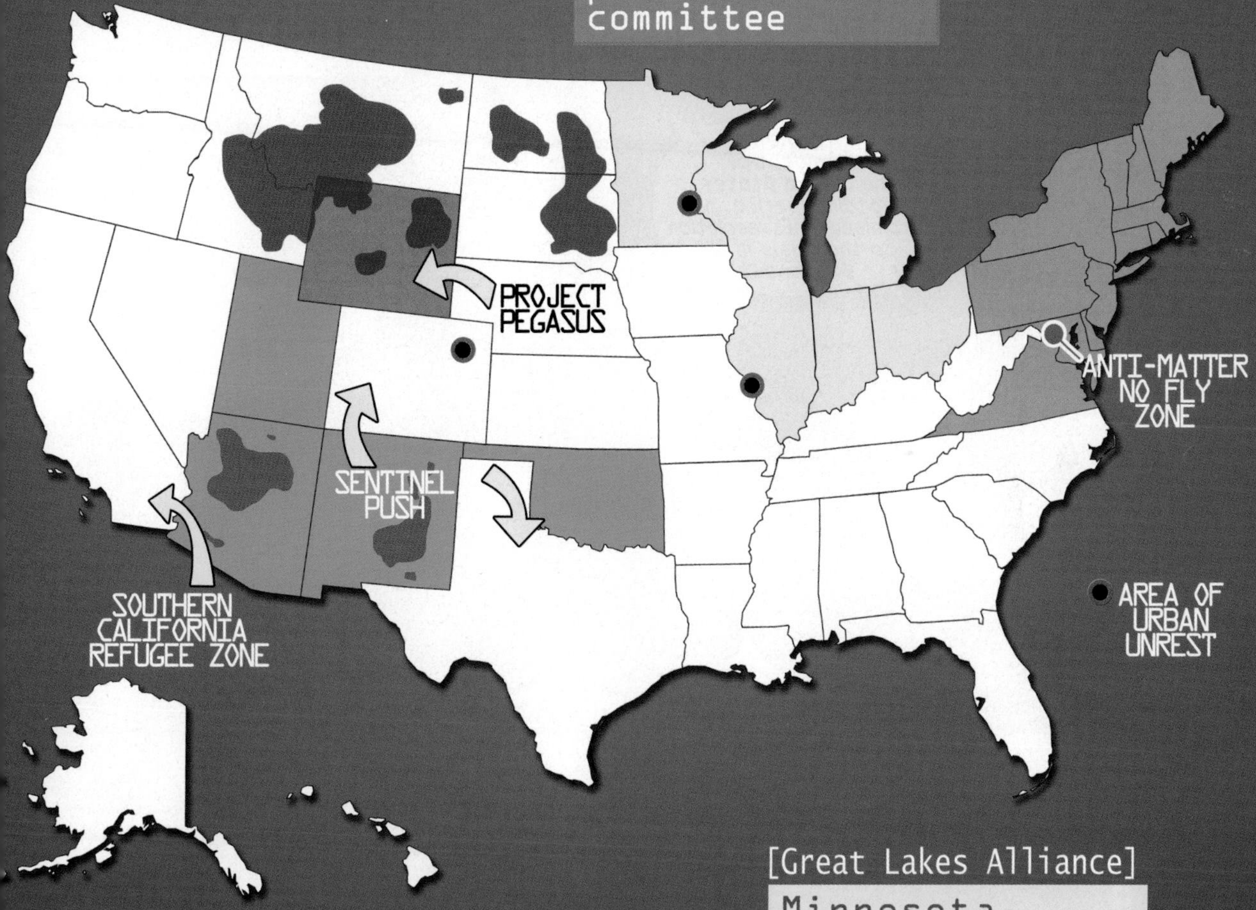
PROJECT PEGASUS
ANTI-MATTER NO FLY ZONE
SENTINEL PUSH
SOUTHERN CALIFORNIA REFUGEE ZONE
AREA OF URBAN UNREST

[Great Lakes Alliance]

Minnesota, Wisconsin, Michigan, Illinois, Indiana, Ohio

Independent nation

[Sentinel-controlled no-man's-land]

New Mexico, Arizona, Utah, Oklahoma

abandoned by the U.S. government

ALL STATES SHOWN IN WHITE ARE U.S. GOVERNMENT-CONTROLLED ZONES

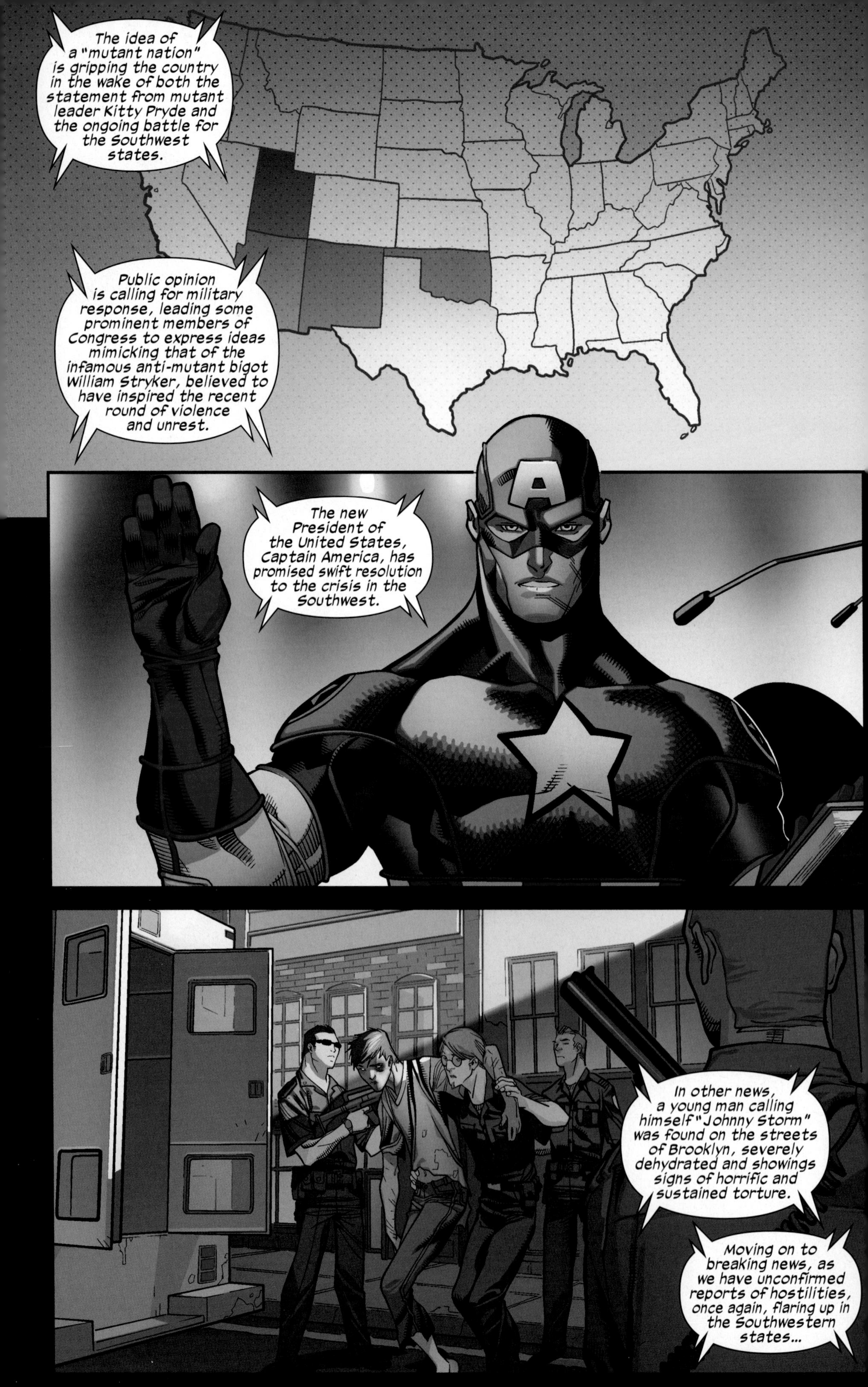

The idea of a "mutant nation" is gripping the country in the wake of both the statement from mutant leader Kitty Pryde and the ongoing battle for the Southwest states.
Public opinion is calling for military response, leading some prominent members of Congress to express ideas mimicking that of the infamous anti-mutant bigot William Stryker, believed to have inspired the recent round of violence and unrest.
The new President of the United States, Captain America, has promised swift resolution to the crisis in the Southwest.
In other news, a young man calling himself "Johnny Storm" was found on the streets of Brooklyn, severely dehydrated and showings signs of horrific and sustained torture.
Moving on to breaking news, as we have unconfirmed reports of hostilities, once again, flaring up in the Southwestern states...

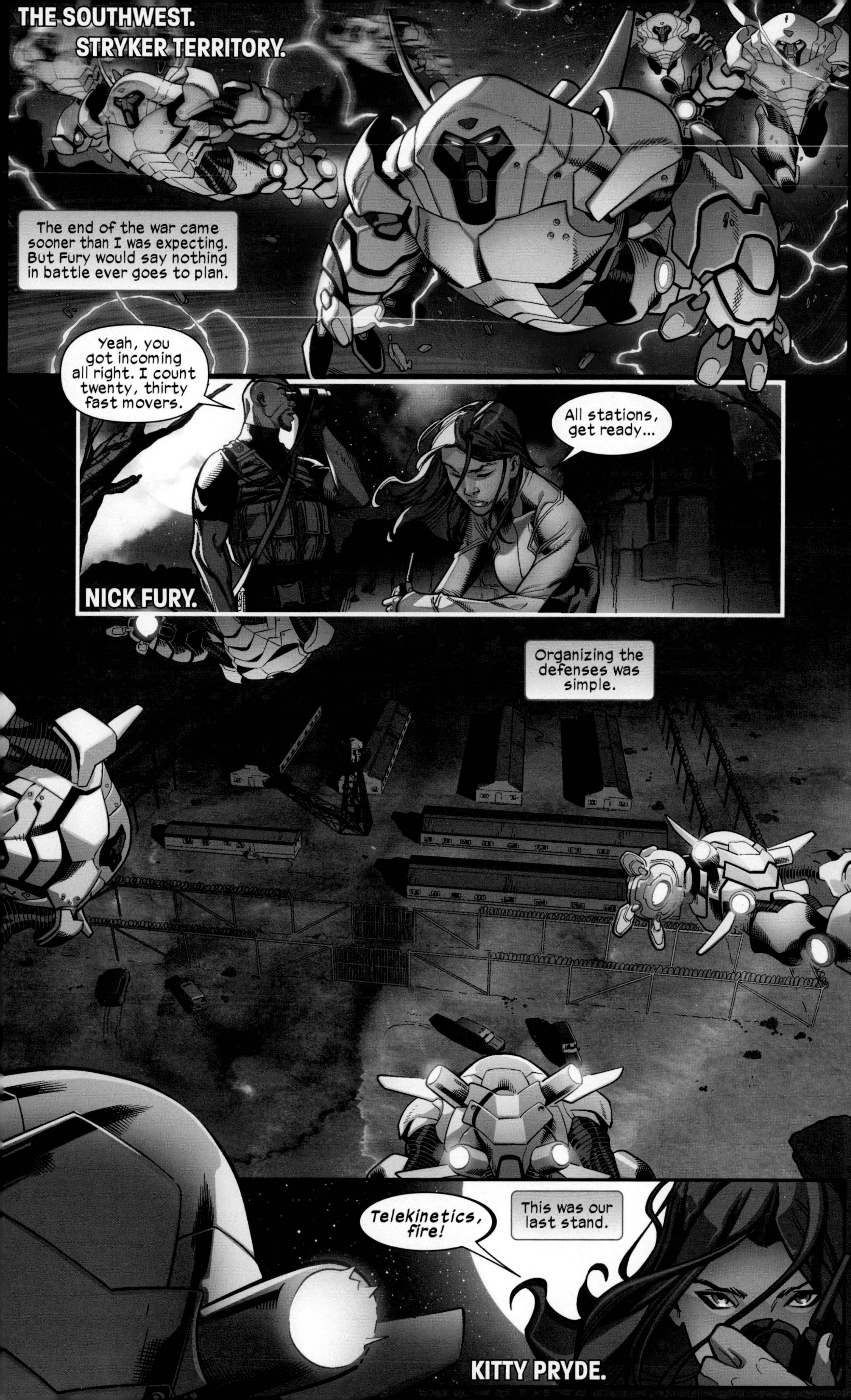
THE SOUTHWEST.
STRYKER TERRITORY.
The end of the war came sooner than I was expecting. But Fury would say nothing in battle ever goes to plan.
Yeah, you got incoming all right. I count twenty, thirty fast movers.
All stations, get ready...
NICK FURY.
Organizing the defenses was simple.
Telekinetics, fire!
This was our last stand.
KITTY PRYDE.

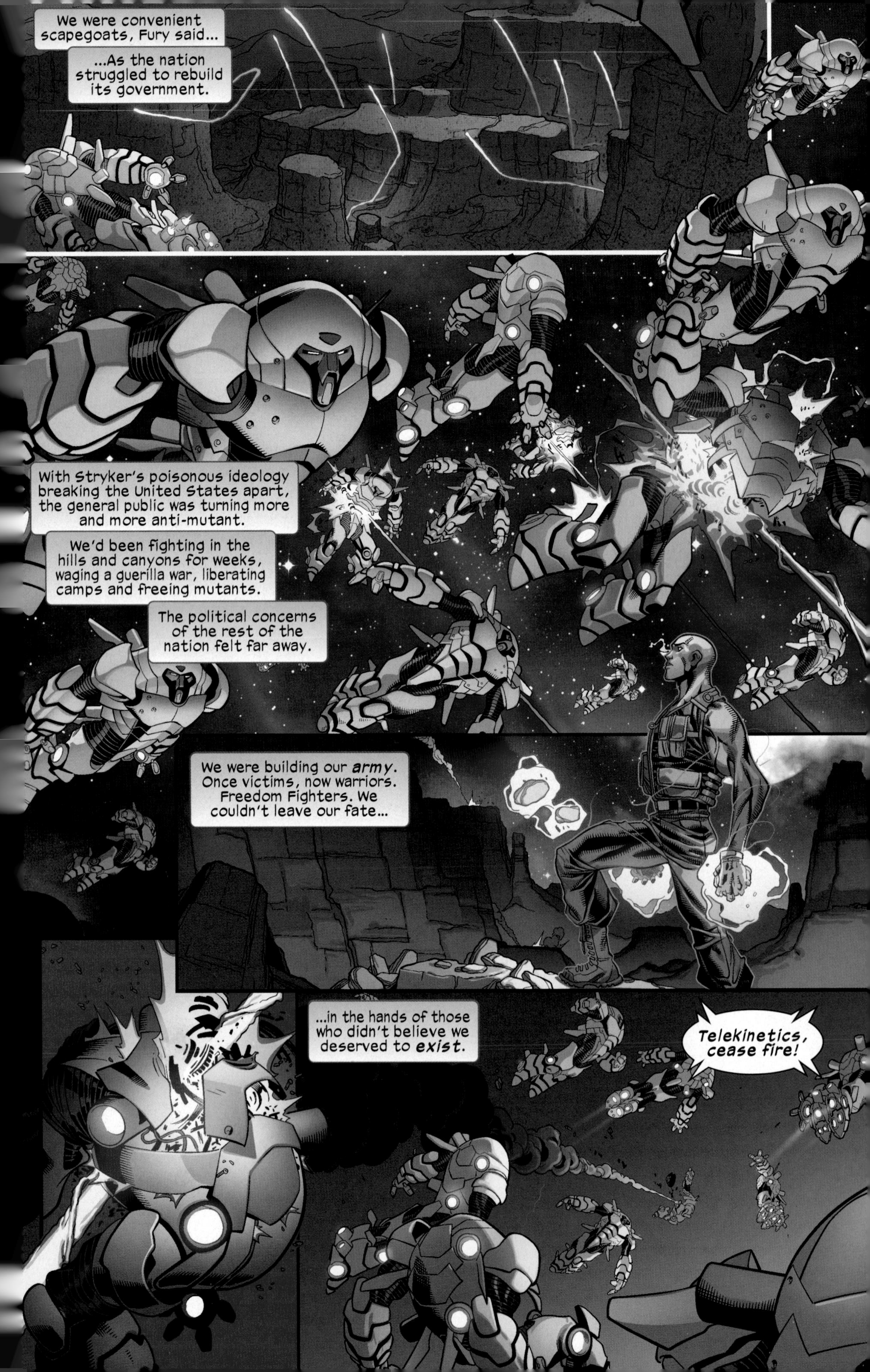
We were convenient scapegoats, Fury said...
...As the nation struggled to rebuild its government.
With Stryker's poisonous ideology breaking the United States apart, the general public was turning more and more anti-mutant.
We'd been fighting in the hills and canyons for weeks, waging a guerilla war, liberating camps and freeing mutants.
The political concerns of the rest of the nation felt far away.
We were building our *army*. Once victims, now warriors. Freedom Fighters. We couldn't leave our fate...
...in the hands of those who didn't believe we deserved to *exist*.
Telekinetics, cease fire!

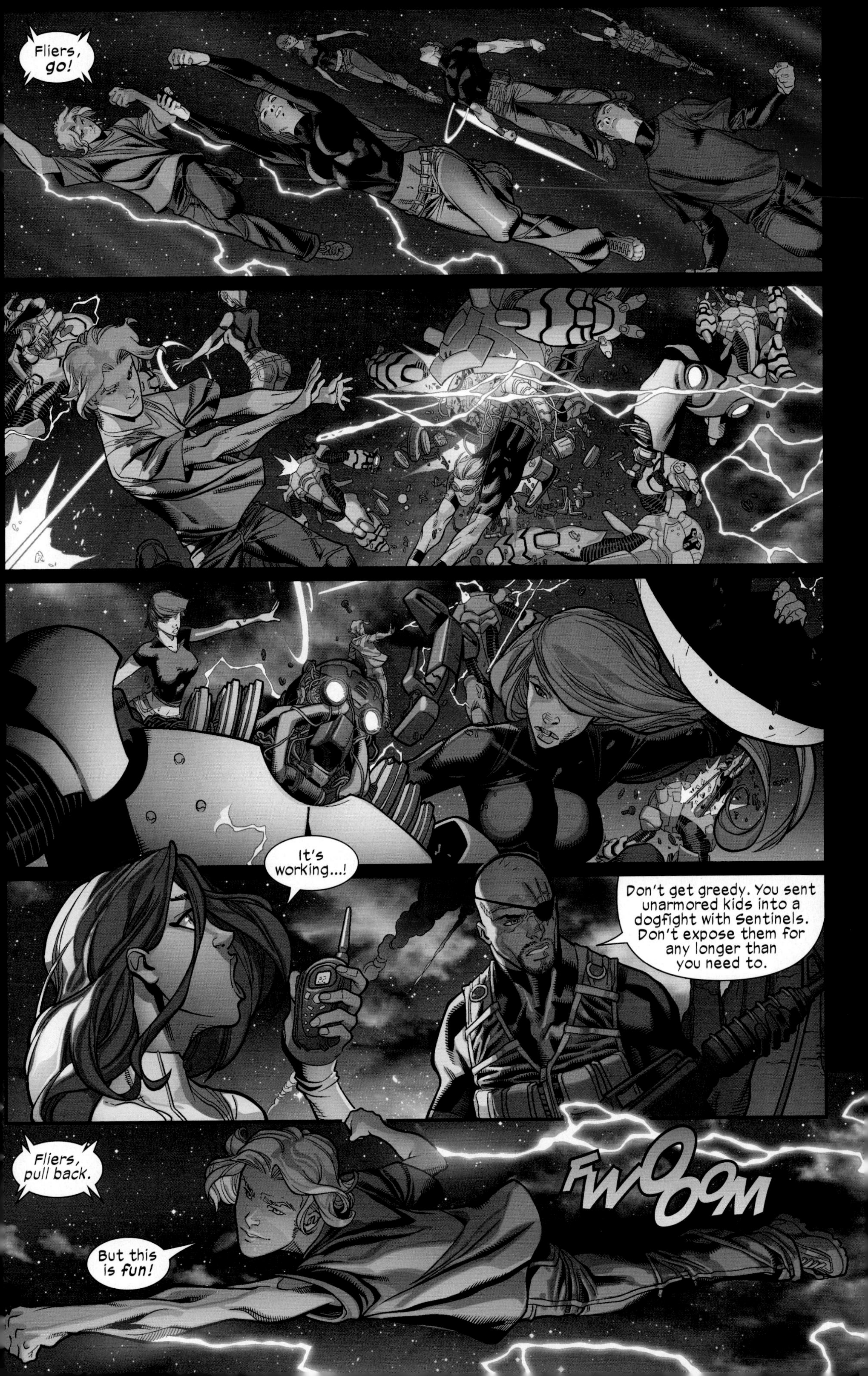

Fliers, go!
It's working...!
Don't get greedy. You sent unarmored kids into a dogfight with Sentinels. Don't expose them for any longer than you need to.
Fliers, pull back.
FWOOOM
But this is fun!

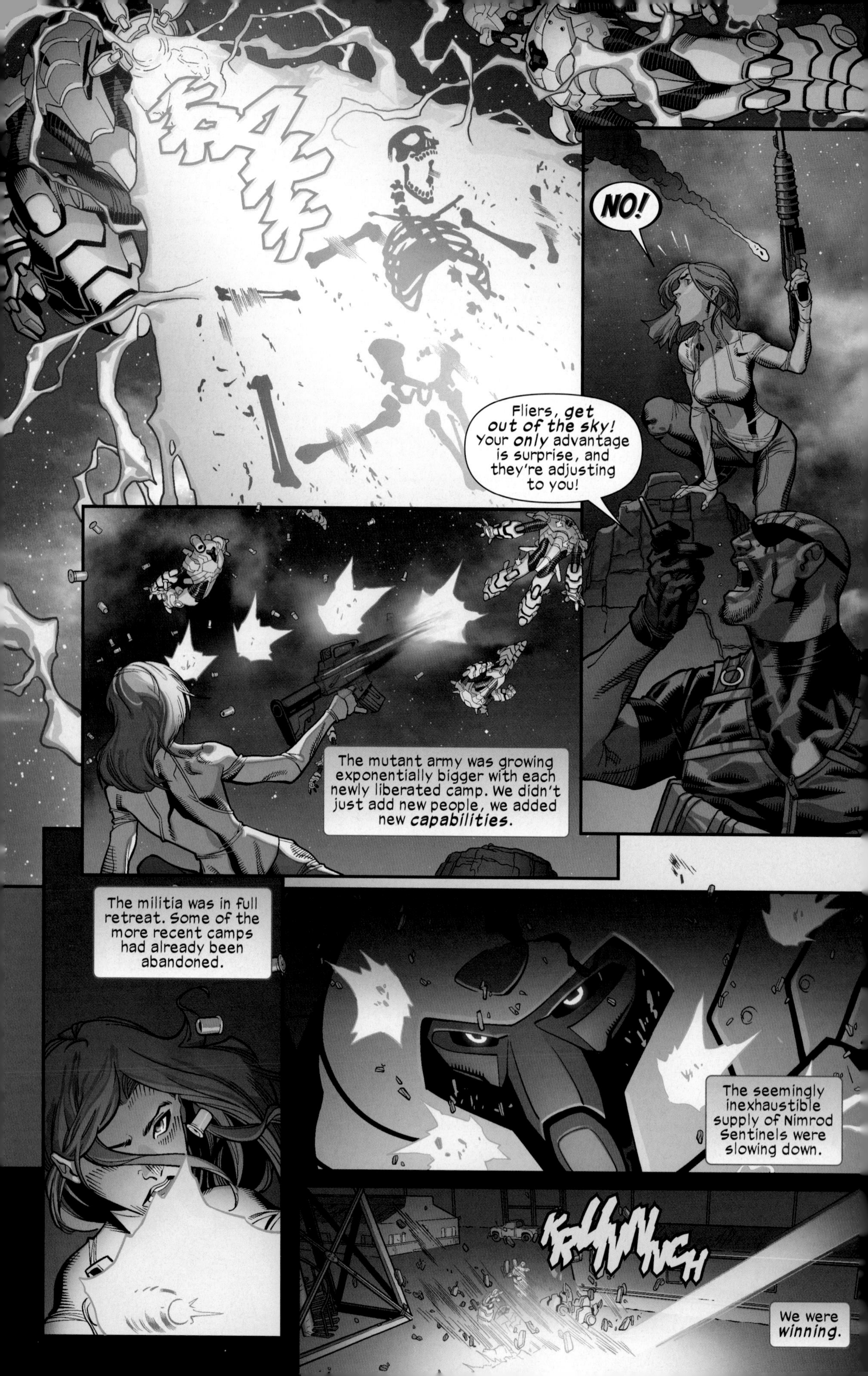
KRAK
NO!
Fliers, get out of the sky! Your only advantage is surprise, and they're adjusting to you!
The mutant army was growing exponentially bigger with each newly liberated camp. We didn't just add new people, we added new capabilities.
The militia was in full retreat. Some of the more recent camps had already been abandoned.
The seemingly inexhaustible supply of Nimrod Sentinels were slowing down.
KRUNNCH
We were winning.

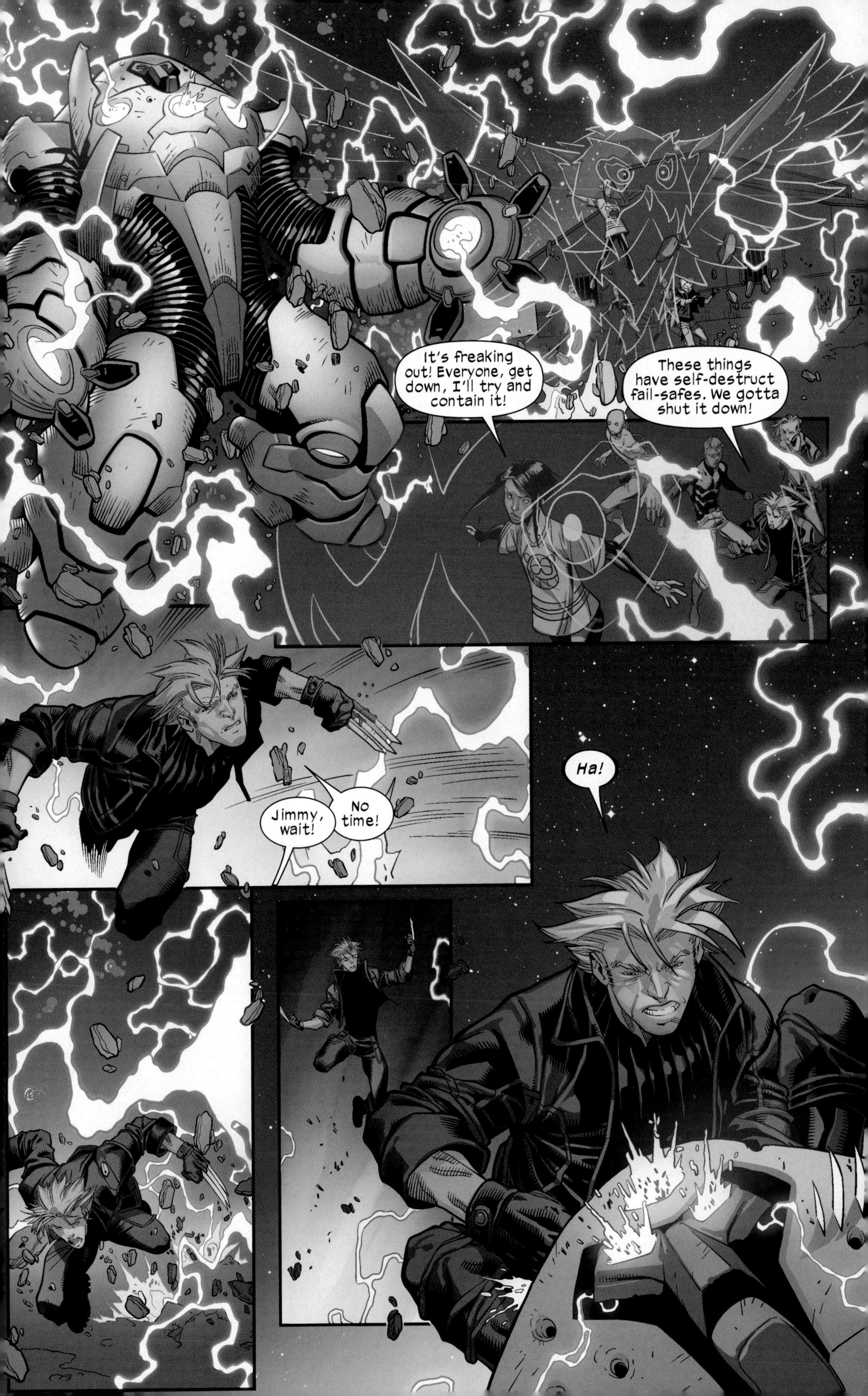
It's freaking out! Everyone, get down, I'll try and contain it!
These things have self-destruct fail-safes. We gotta shut it down!
Jimmy, wait!
No time!
Ha!

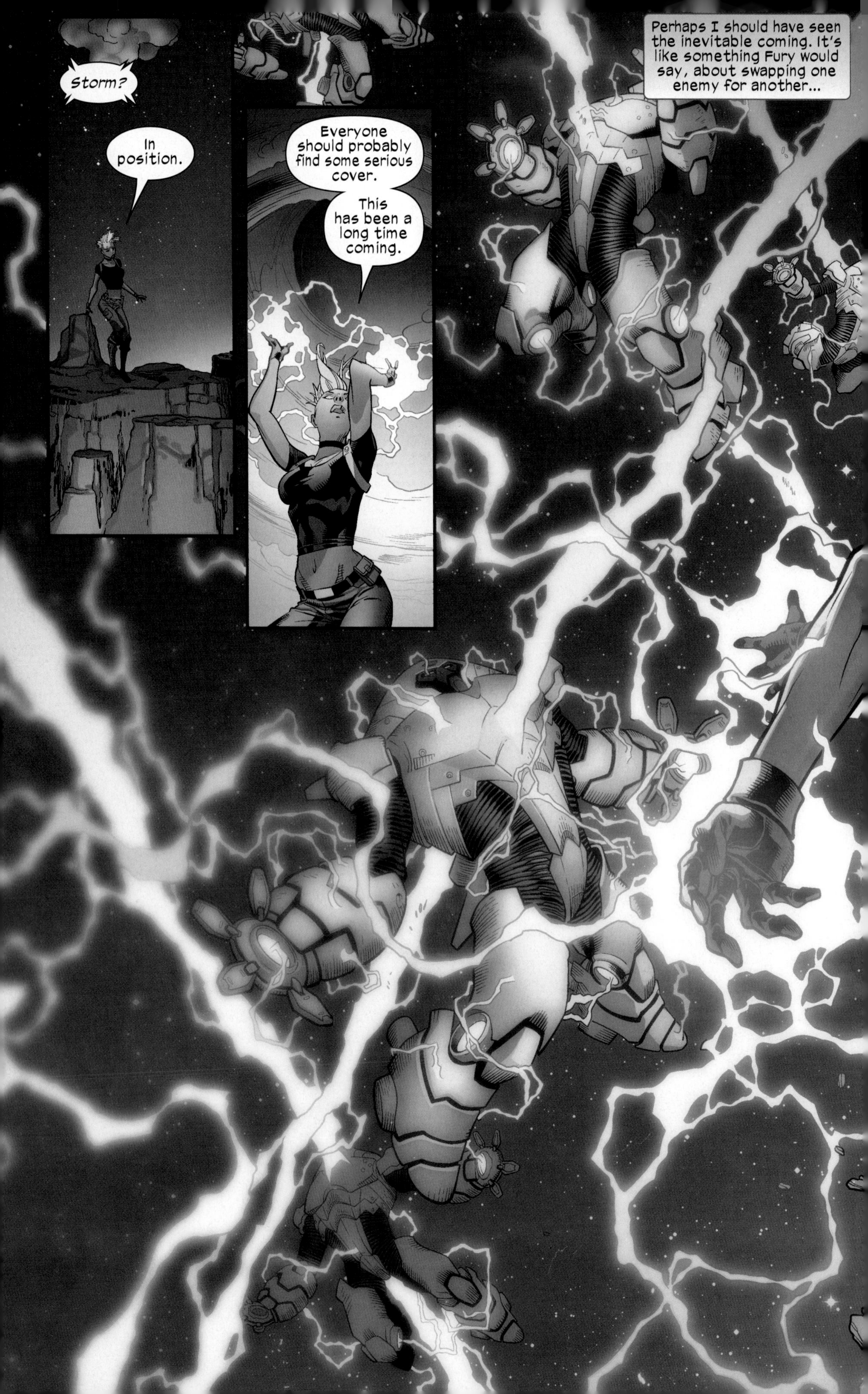
Storm?
In position.
Everyone should probably find some serious cover.
This has been a long time coming.
Perhaps I should have seen the inevitable coming. It's like something Fury would say, about swapping one enemy for another...

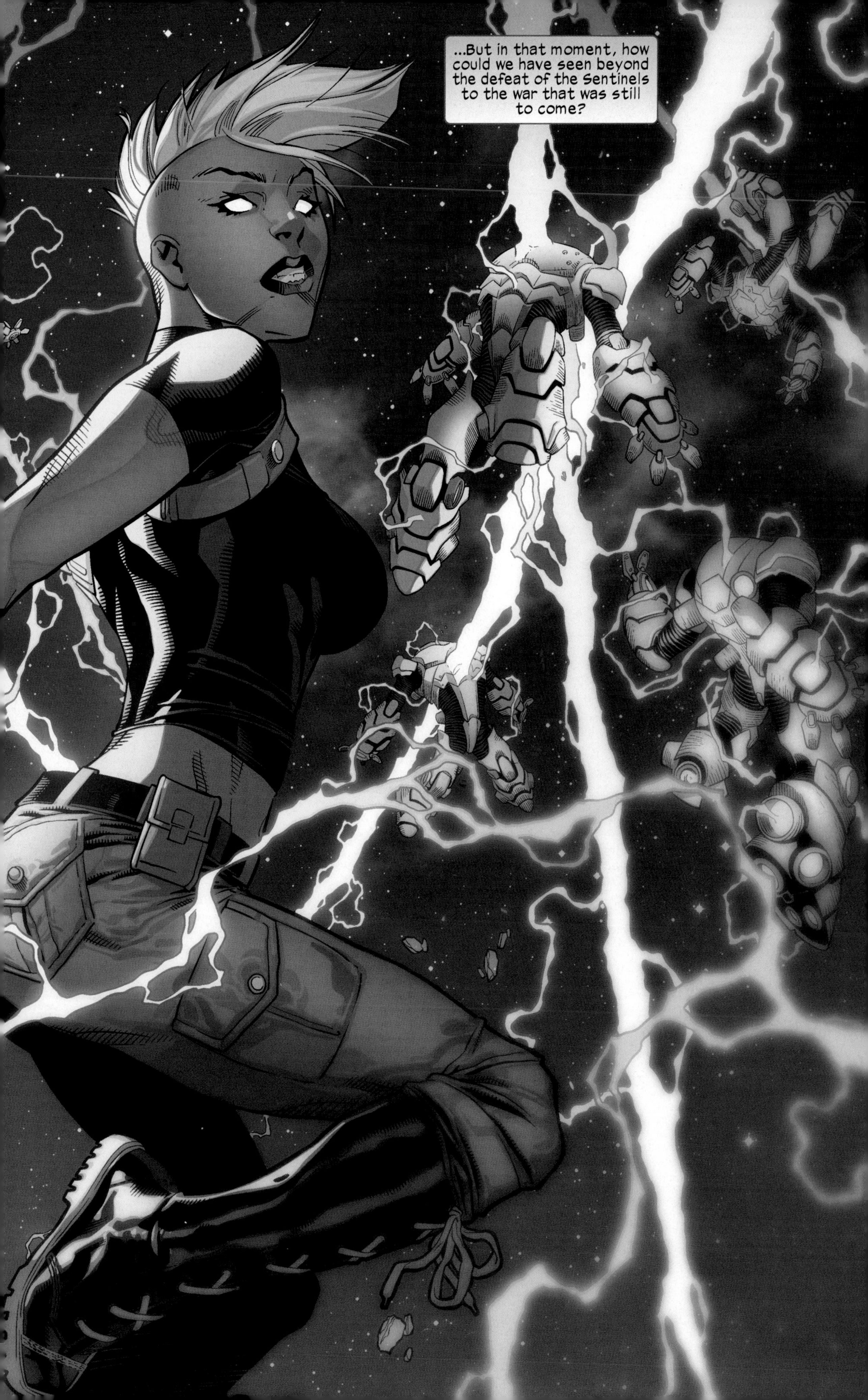
...But in that moment, how could we have seen beyond the defeat of the Sentinels to the war that was still to come?

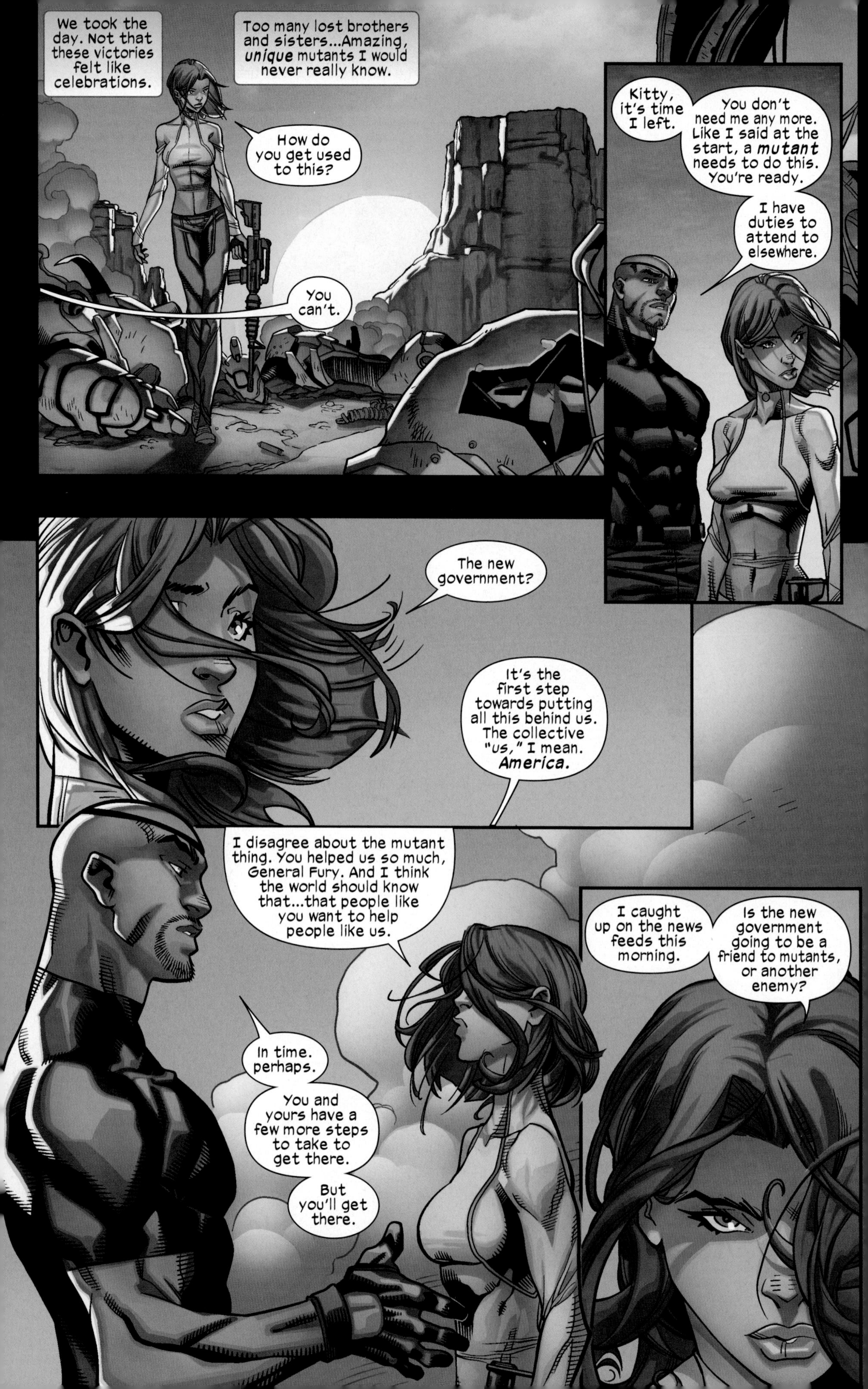
We took the day. Not that these victories felt like celebrations.
Too many lost brothers and sisters...Amazing, *unique* mutants I would never really know.
How do you get used to this?
You can't.
Kitty, it's time I left.
You don't need me any more. Like I said at the start, a *mutant* needs to do this. You're ready.
I have duties to attend to elsewhere.
The new government?
It's the first step towards putting all this behind us. The collective "*us*," I mean. ***America.***
I caught up on the news feeds this morning.
Is the new government going to be a friend to mutants, or another enemy?
I disagree about the mutant thing. You helped us so much, General Fury. And I think the world should know that...that people like you want to help people like us.
In time. perhaps.
You and yours have a few more steps to take to get there.
But you'll get there.

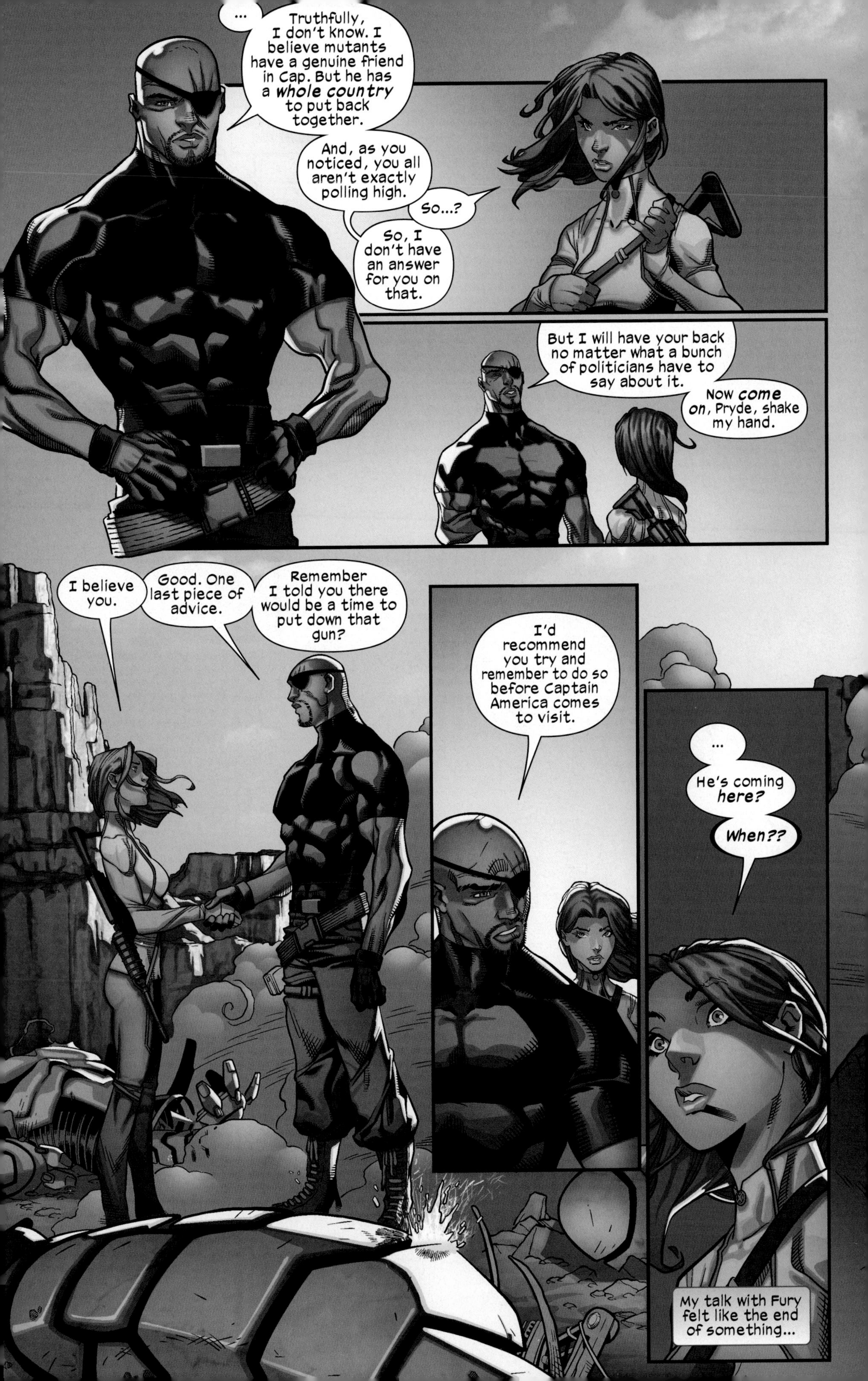
...
Truthfully, I don't know. I believe mutants have a genuine friend in Cap. But he has a *whole country* to put back together.
And, as you noticed, you all aren't exactly polling high.
So...?
So, I don't have an answer for you on that.
But I will have your back no matter what a bunch of politicians have to say about it.
Now *come on*, Pryde, shake my hand.
I believe you.
Good. One last piece of advice.
Remember I told you there would be a time to put down that gun?
I'd recommend you try and remember to do so before Captain America comes to visit.
...
He's coming *here?*
When??
My talk with Fury felt like the end of something...

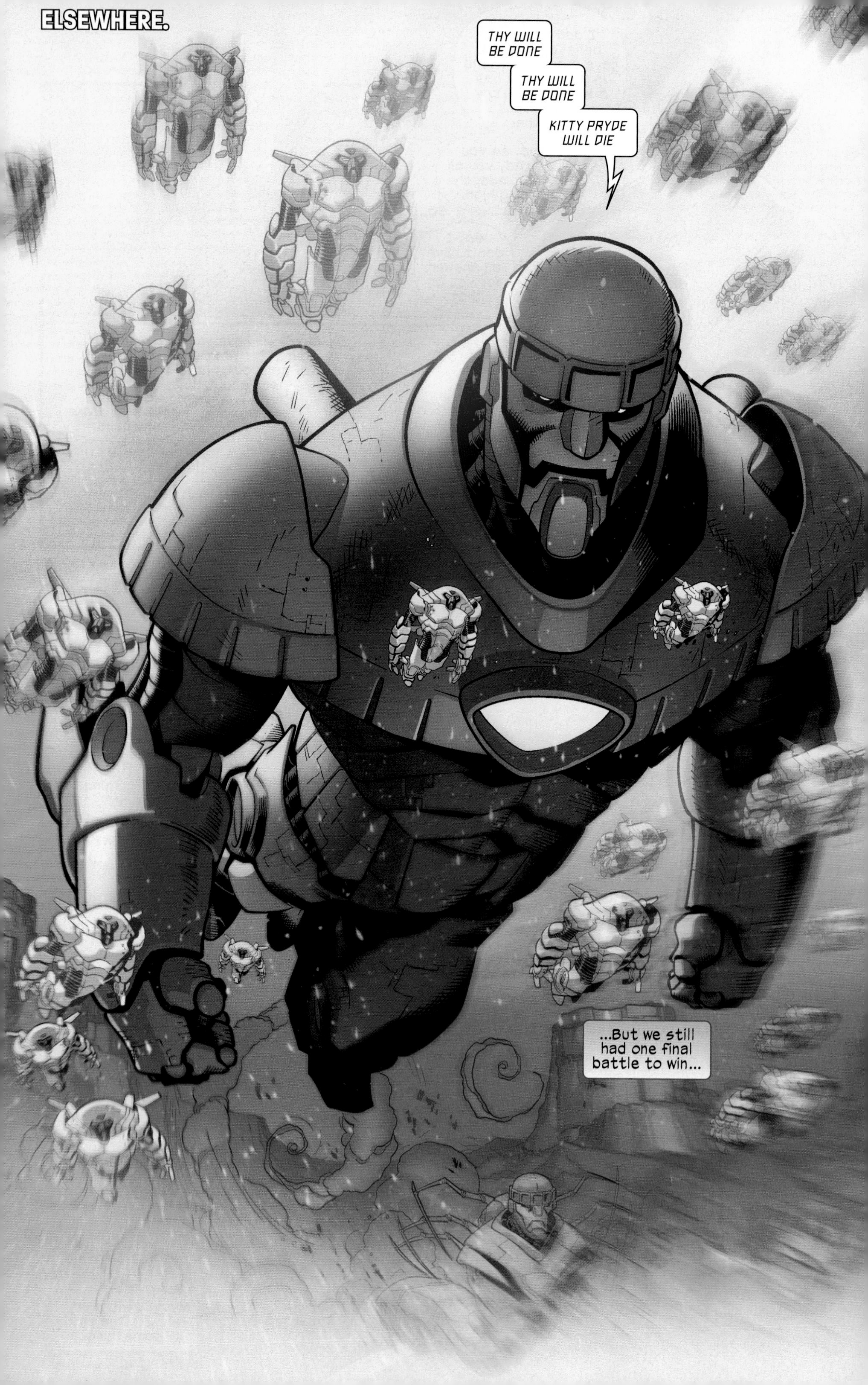
ELSEWHERE.
THY WILL BE DONE
THY WILL BE DONE
KITTY PRYDE WILL DIE
...But we still had one final battle to win...

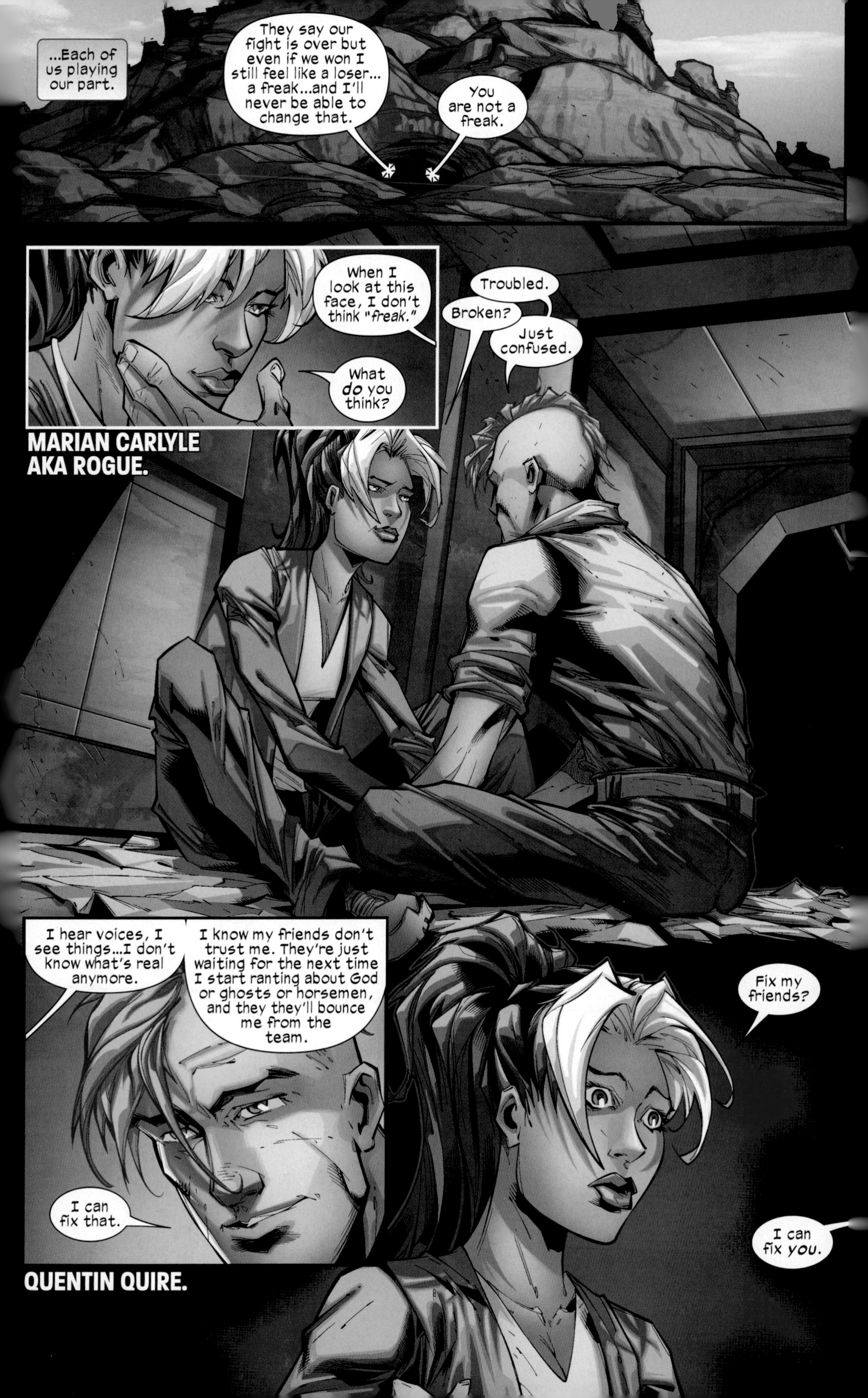
...Each of us playing our part.
They say our fight is over but even if we won I still feel like a loser... a freak...and I'll never be able to change that.
You are not a freak.
When I look at this face, I don't think "freak."
What do you think?
Troubled.
Broken?
Just confused.
MARIAN CARLYLE AKA ROGUE.
I hear voices, I see things...I don't know what's real anymore.
I know my friends don't trust me. They're just waiting for the next time I start ranting about God or ghosts or horsemen, and they they'll bounce me from the team.
I can fix that.
Fix my friends?
I can fix you.
QUENTIN QUIRE.

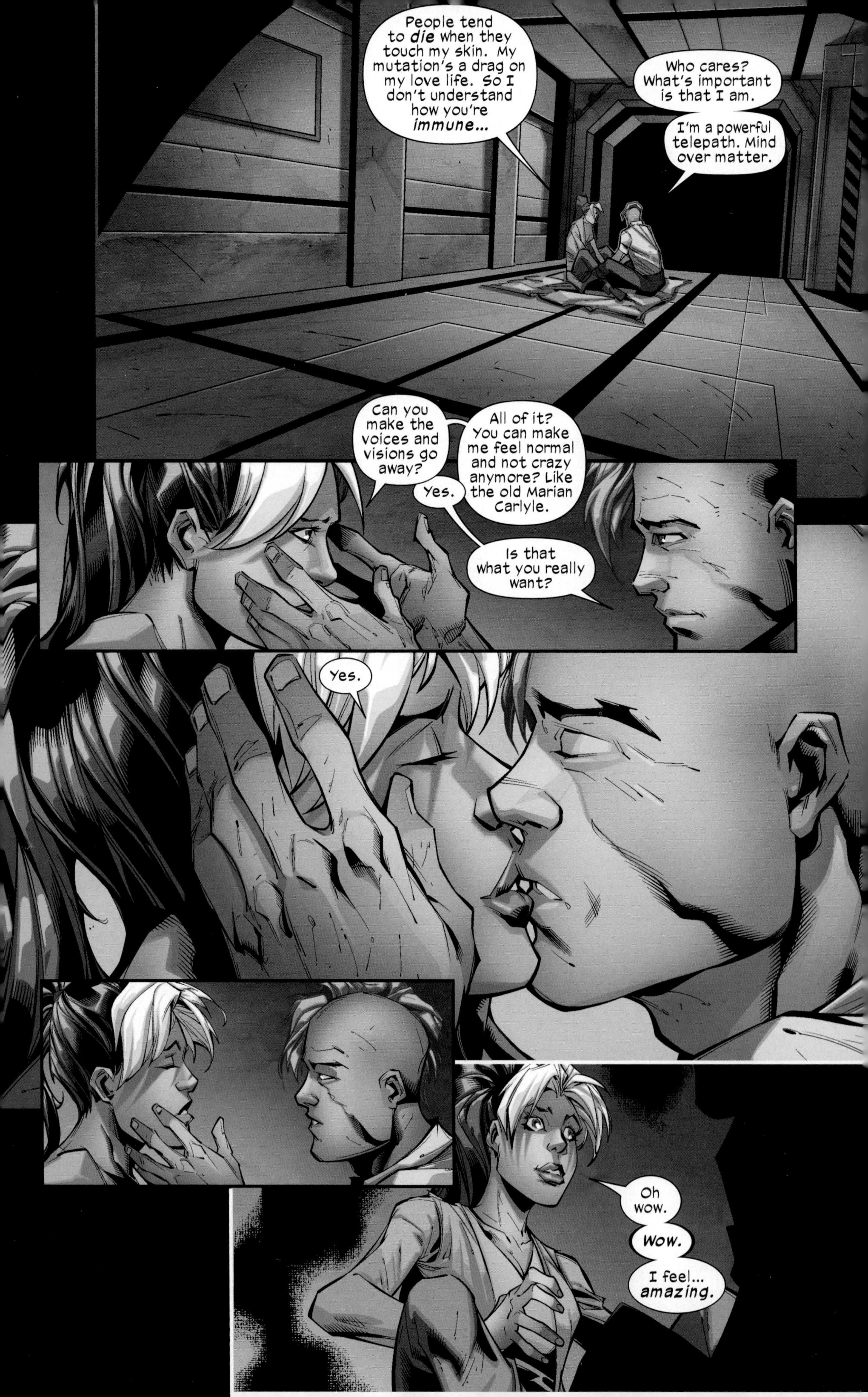
People tend to *die* when they touch my skin. My mutation's a drag on my love life. So I don't understand how you're *immune*...
Who cares? What's important is that I am.
I'm a powerful telepath. Mind over matter.
Can you make the voices and visions go away?
Yes.
All of it? You can make me feel normal and not crazy anymore? Like the old Marian Carlyle.
Is that what you really want?
Yes.
Oh wow.
Wow.
I feel... *amazing.*

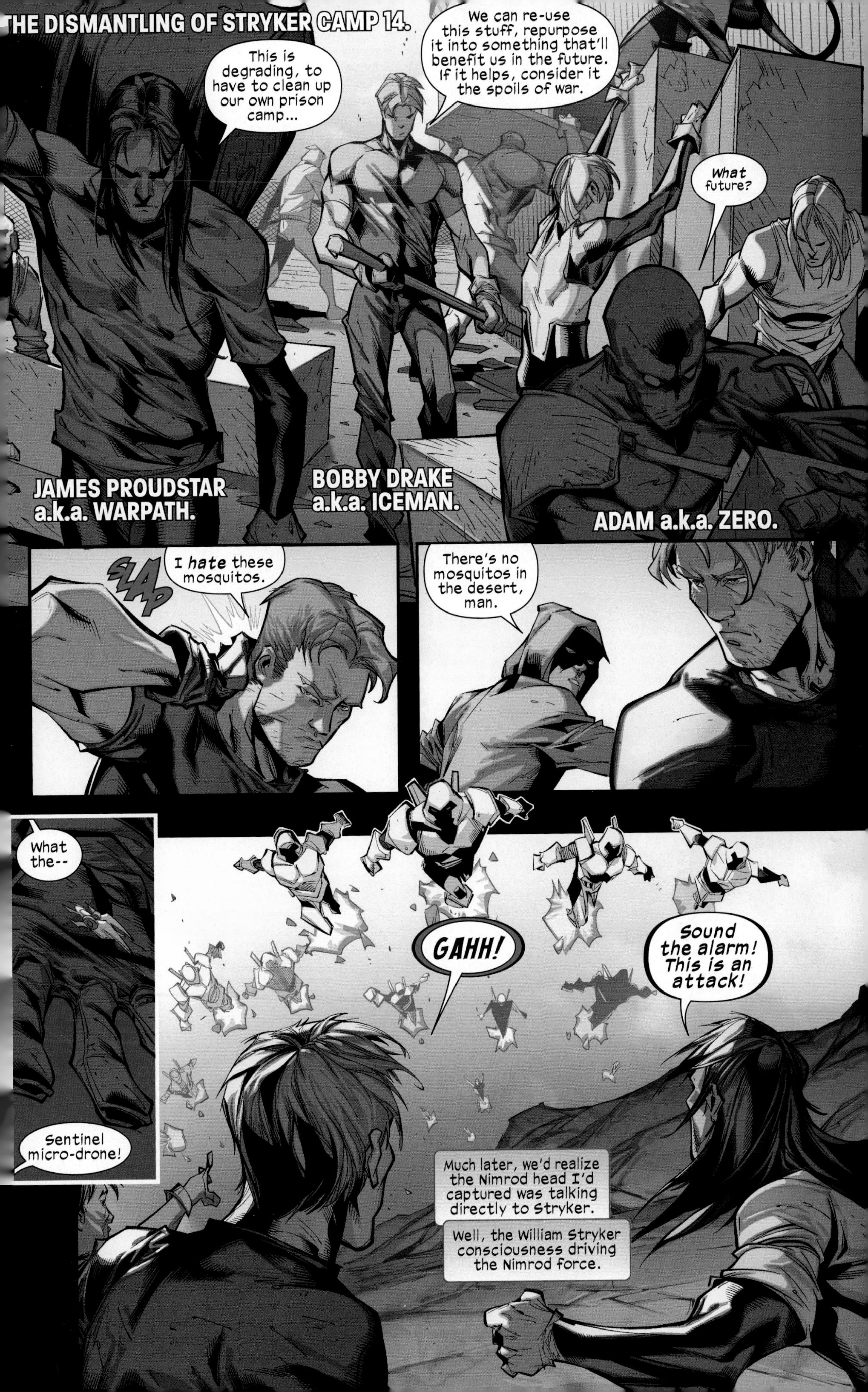
THE DISMANTLING OF STRYKER CAMP 14.
This is degrading, to have to clean up our own prison camp...
We can re-use this stuff, repurpose it into something that'll benefit us in the future. If it helps, consider it the spoils of war.
What future?
JAMES PROUDSTAR a.k.a. WARPATH.
BOBBY DRAKE a.k.a. ICEMAN.
ADAM a.k.a. ZERO.
SLAP
I hate these mosquitos.
There's no mosquitos in the desert, man.
What the--
Sentinel micro-drone!
GAHH!
Sound the alarm! This is an attack!
Much later, we'd realize the Nimrod head I'd captured was talking directly to Stryker.
Well, the William Stryker consciousness driving the Nimrod force.

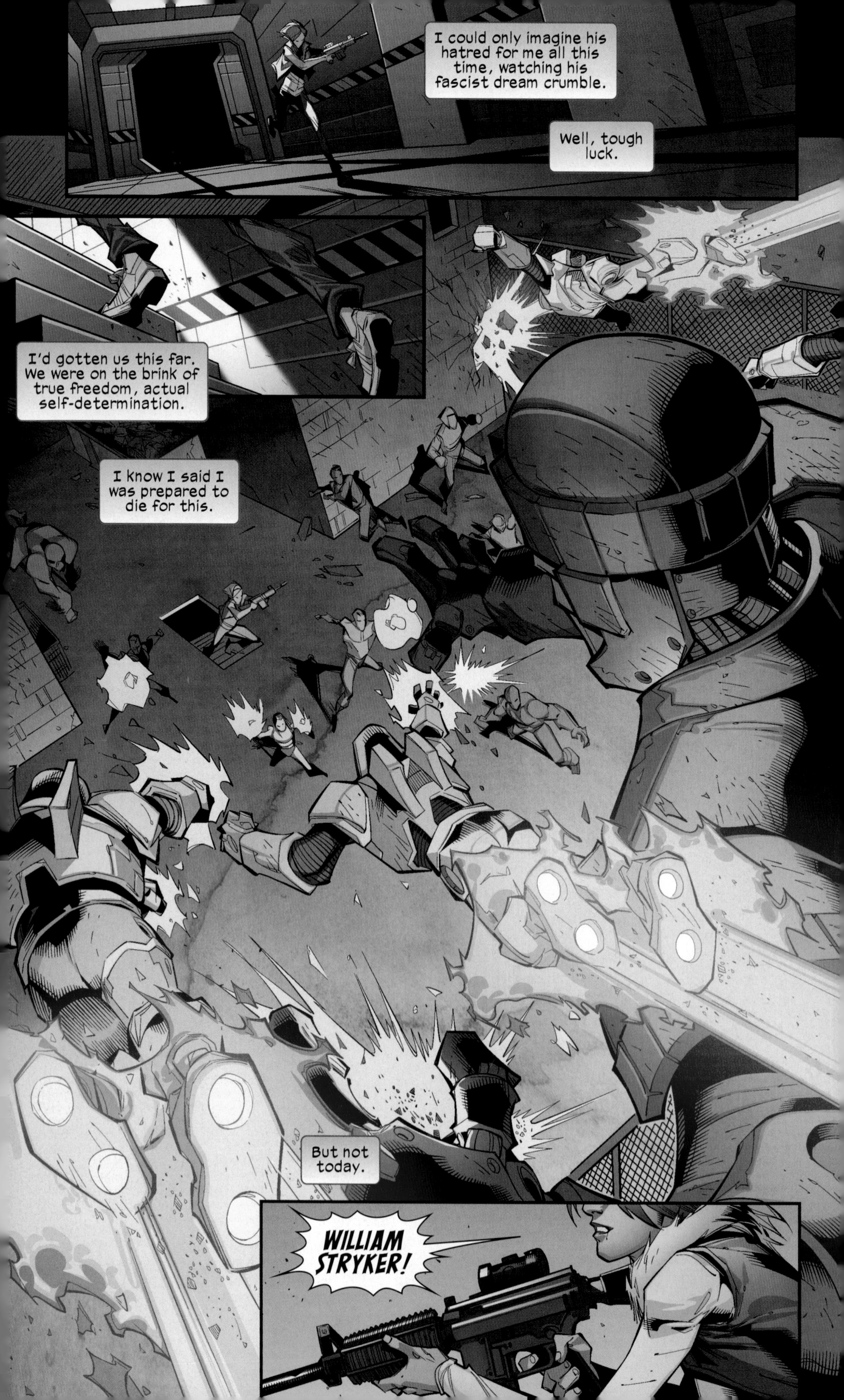
I could only imagine his hatred for me all this time, watching his fascist dream crumble.
Well, tough luck.
I'd gotten us this far. We were on the brink of true freedom, actual self-determination.
I know I said I was prepared to die for this.
But not today.
WILLIAM STRYKER!

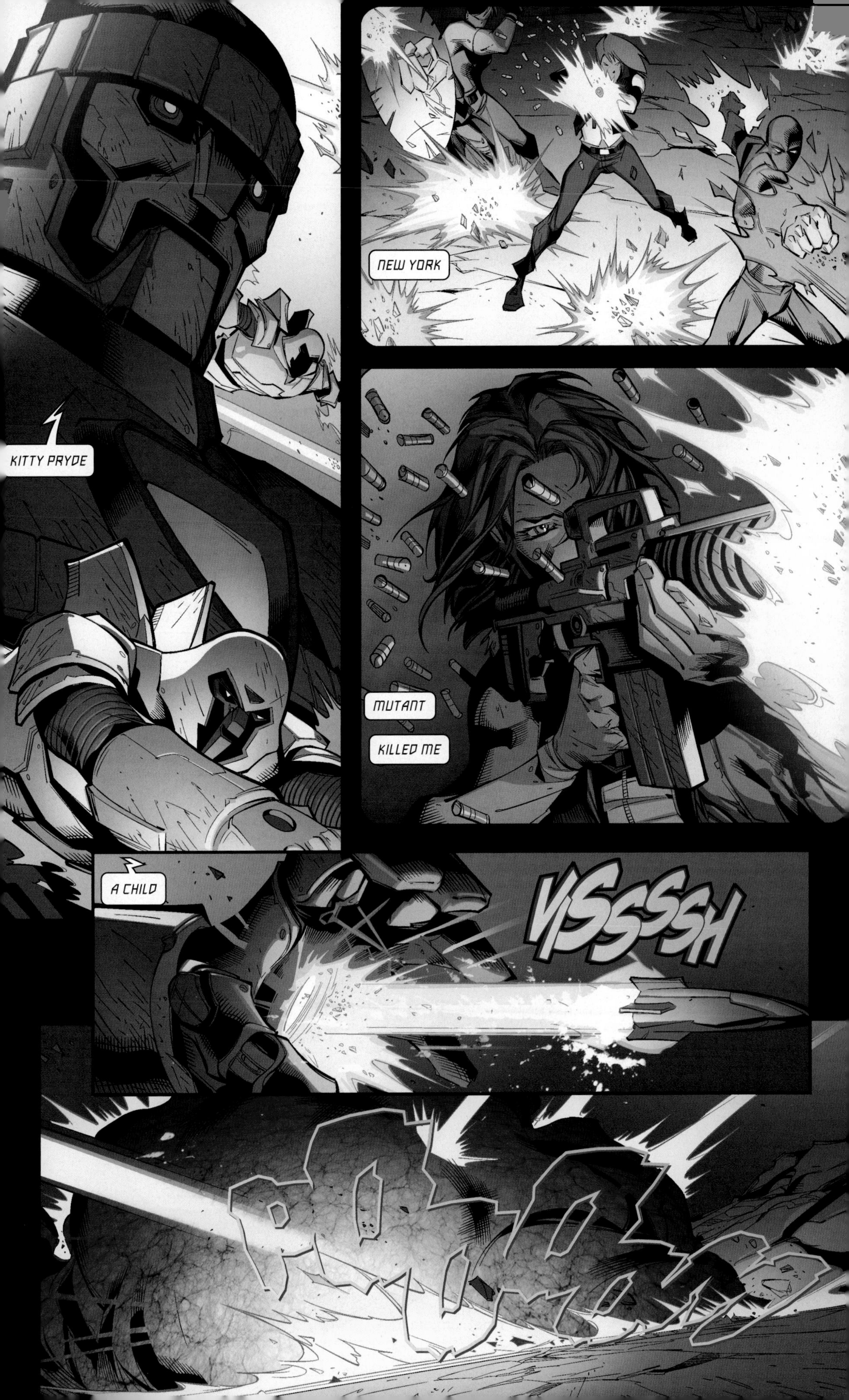
NEW YORK
KITTY PRYDE
MUTANT
KILLED ME
A CHILD
VISSSSH

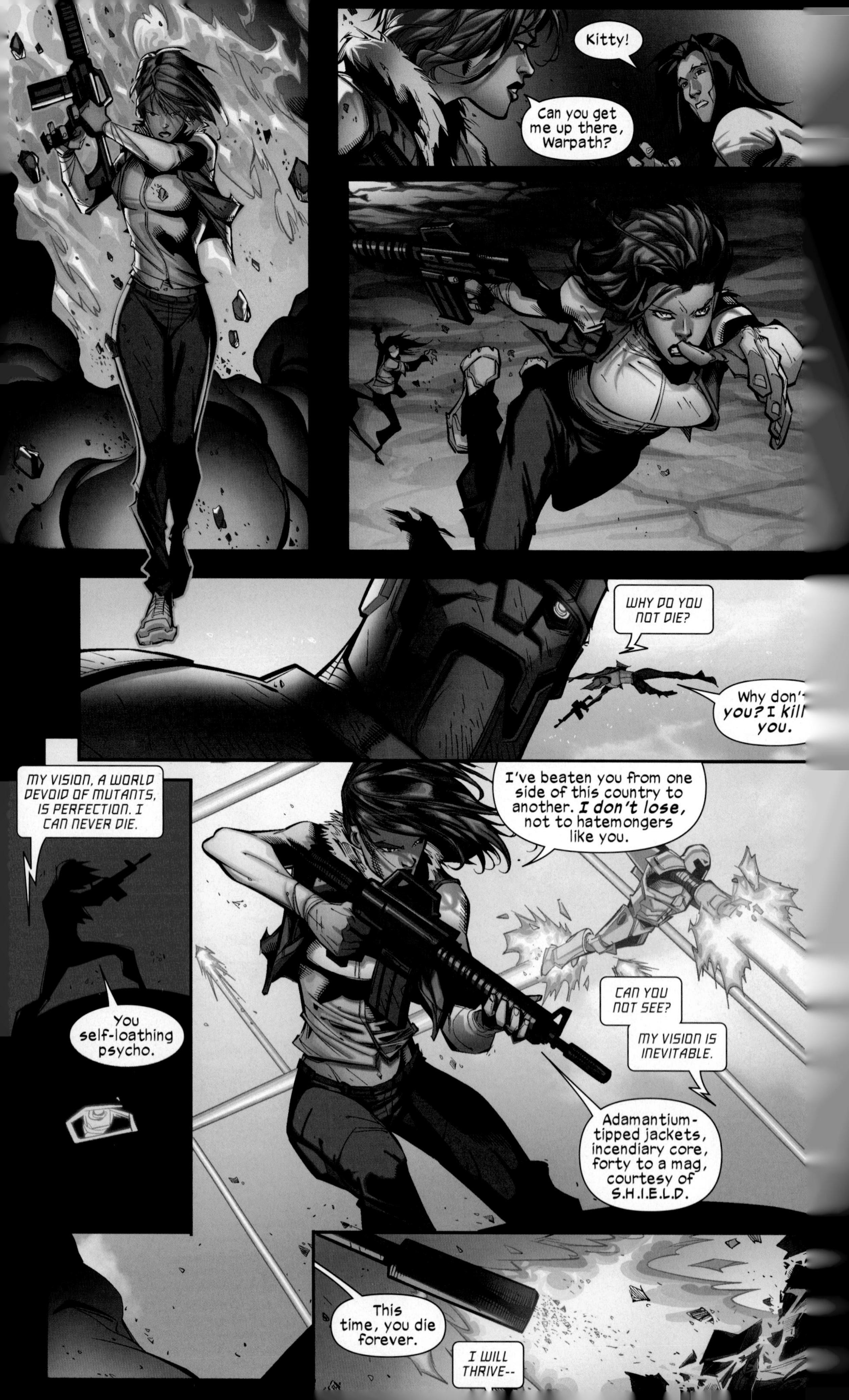
Kitty!
Can you get me up there, Warpath?
WHY DO YOU NOT DIE?
Why don't you? I kill you.
MY VISION, A WORLD DEVOID OF MUTANTS, IS PERFECTION. I CAN NEVER DIE.
You self-loathing psycho.
I've beaten you from one side of this country to another. I don't lose, not to hatemongers like you.
CAN YOU NOT SEE?
MY VISION IS INEVITABLE.
Adamantium-tipped jackets, incendiary core, forty to a mag, courtesy of S.H.I.E.L.D.
This time, you die forever.
I WILL THRIVE--

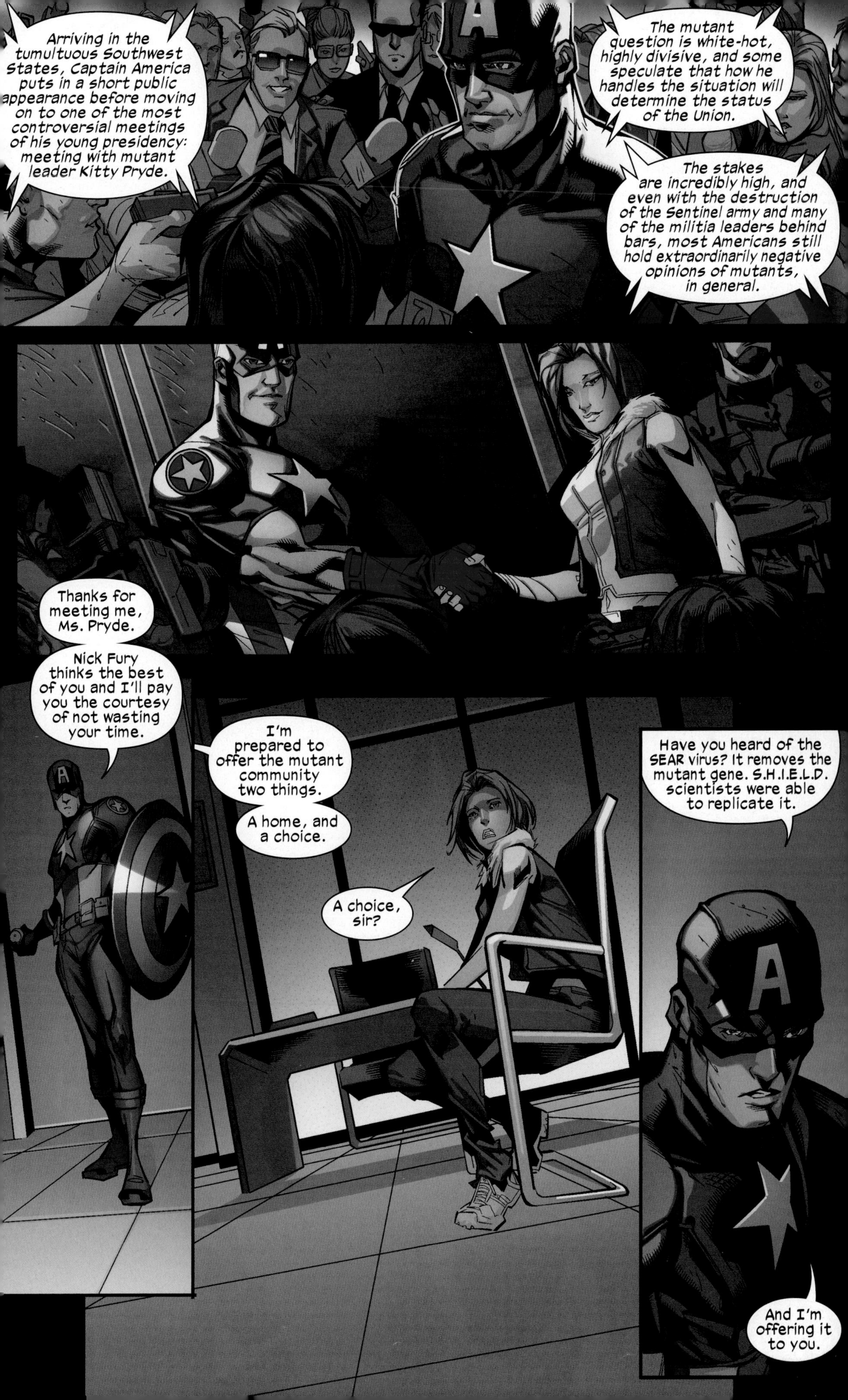
Arriving in the tumultuous Southwest States, Captain America puts in a short public appearance before moving on to one of the most controversial meetings of his young presidency: meeting with mutant leader Kitty Pryde.
The mutant question is white-hot, highly divisive, and some speculate that how he handles the situation will determine the status of the Union.
The stakes are incredibly high, and even with the destruction of the Sentinel army and many of the militia leaders behind bars, most Americans still hold extraordinarily negative opinions of mutants, in general.
Thanks for meeting me, Ms. Pryde.
Nick Fury thinks the best of you and I'll pay you the courtesy of not wasting your time.
I'm prepared to offer the mutant community two things.
A home, and a choice.
A choice, sir?
Have you heard of the SEAR virus? It removes the mutant gene. S.H.I.E.L.D. scientists were able to replicate it.
And I'm offering it to you.

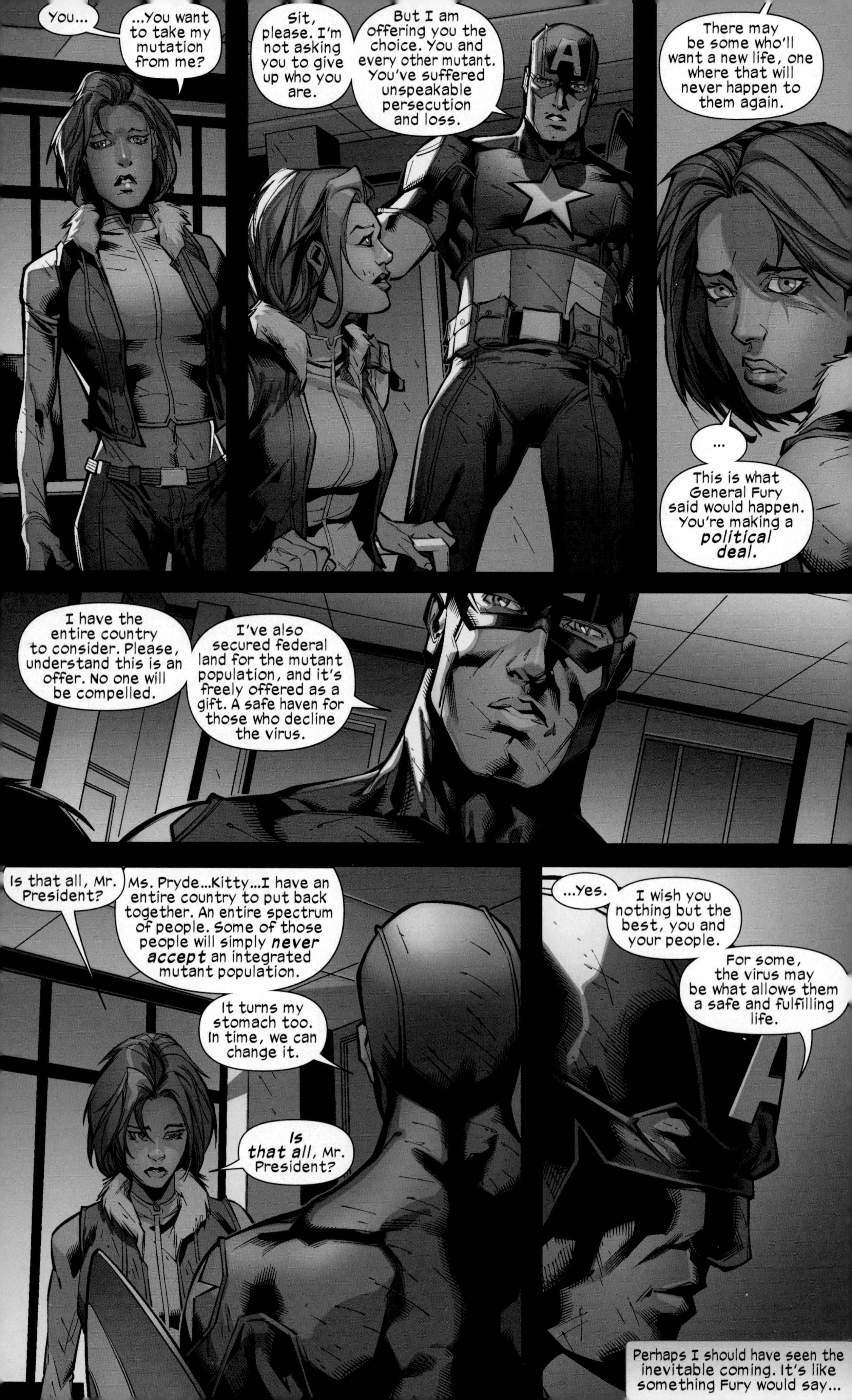

You...
...You want to take my mutation from me?
Sit, please. I'm not asking you to give up who you are.
But I am offering you the choice. You and every other mutant. You've suffered unspeakable persecution and loss.
There may be some who'll want a new life, one where that will never happen to them again.
...
This is what General Fury said would happen. You're making a *political deal.*
I have the entire country to consider. Please, understand this is an offer. No one will be compelled.
I've also secured federal land for the mutant population, and it's freely offered as a gift. A safe haven for those who decline the virus.
Is that all, Mr. President?
Ms. Pryde...Kitty...I have an entire country to put back together. An entire spectrum of people. Some of those people will simply *never accept* an integrated mutant population.
It turns my stomach too. In time, we can change it.
Is that all, Mr. President?
...Yes.
I wish you nothing but the best, you and your people.
For some, the virus may be what allows them a safe and fulfilling life.
Perhaps I should have seen the inevitable coming. It's like something Fury would say...

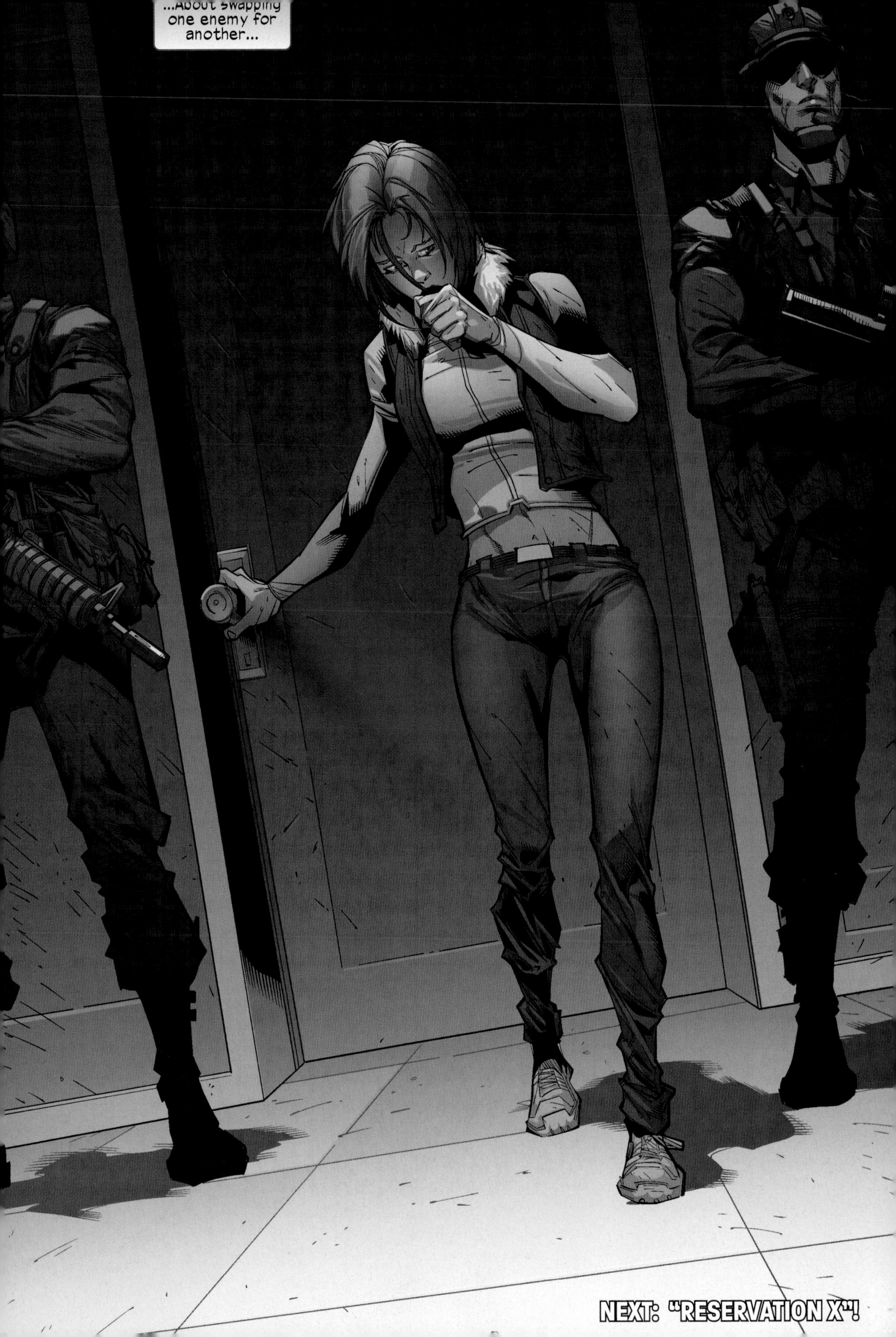
...About swapping one enemy for another...
NEXT: "RESERVATION X"!

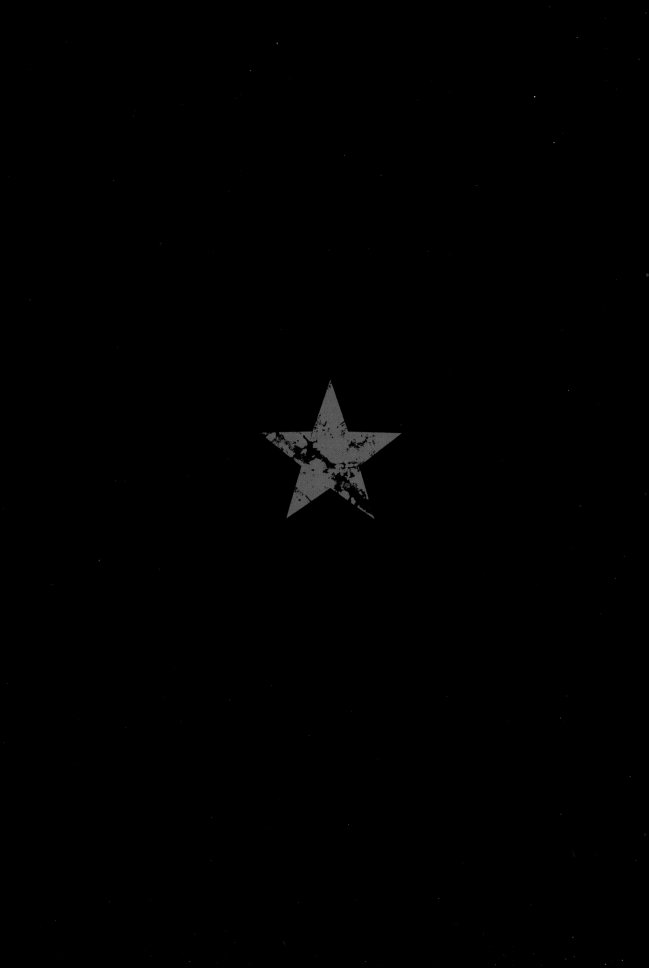

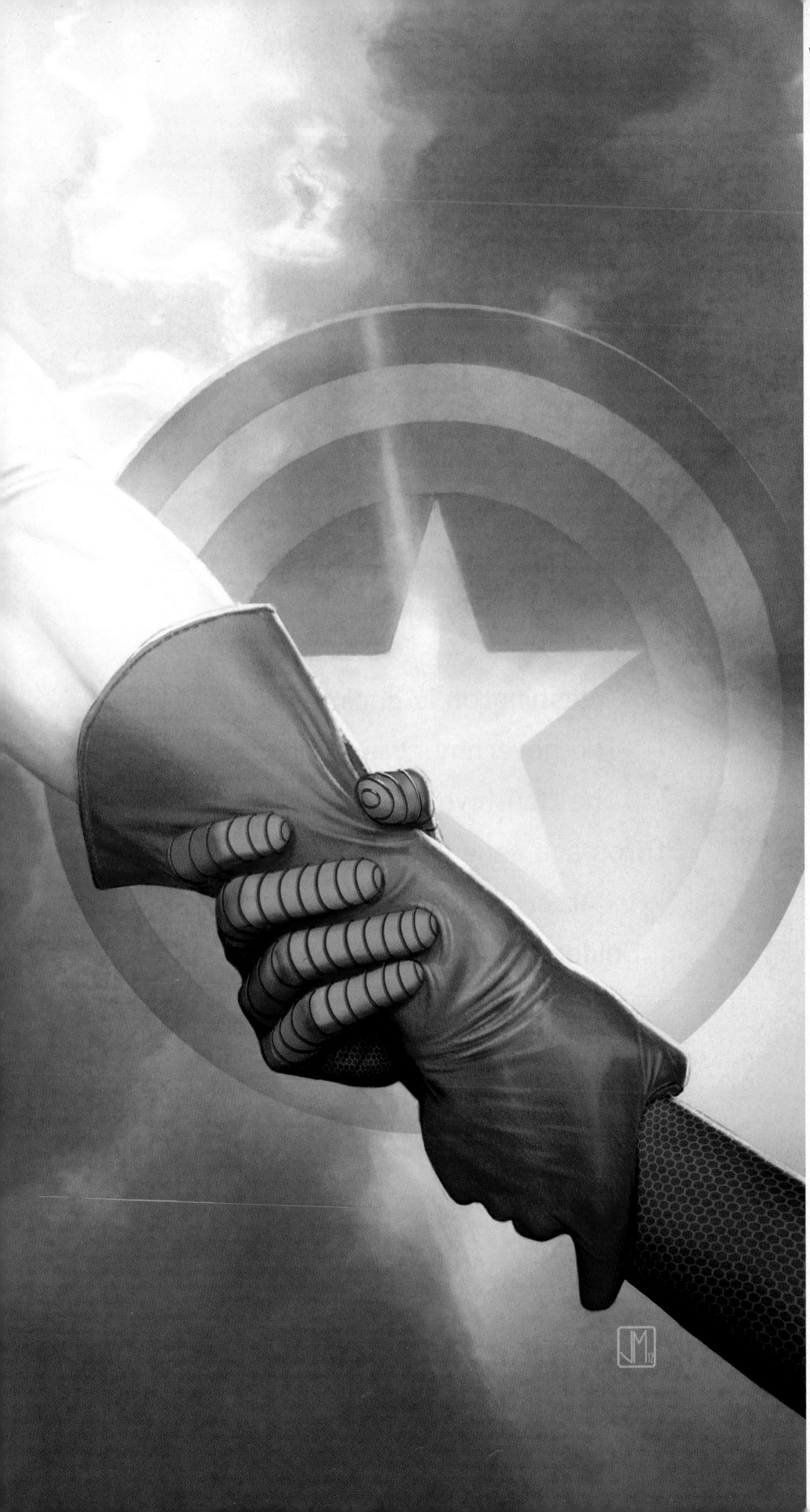

13

ULTIMATE COMICS SPIDER-MAN #13

MONTHS BEFORE PETER PARKER WAS SHOT AND KILLED, GRADE-SCHOOLER MILES MORALES WAS ABOUT TO START A NEW CHAPTER IN HIS LIFE AT A NEW SCHOOL--WHEN HE WAS SUDDENLY BITTEN BY A STOLEN, GENETICALLY ALTERED SPIDER THAT GAVE HIM INCREDIBLE ARACHNID-LIKE POWERS.

ULTIMATE COMICS ALL NEW SPIDER-MAN

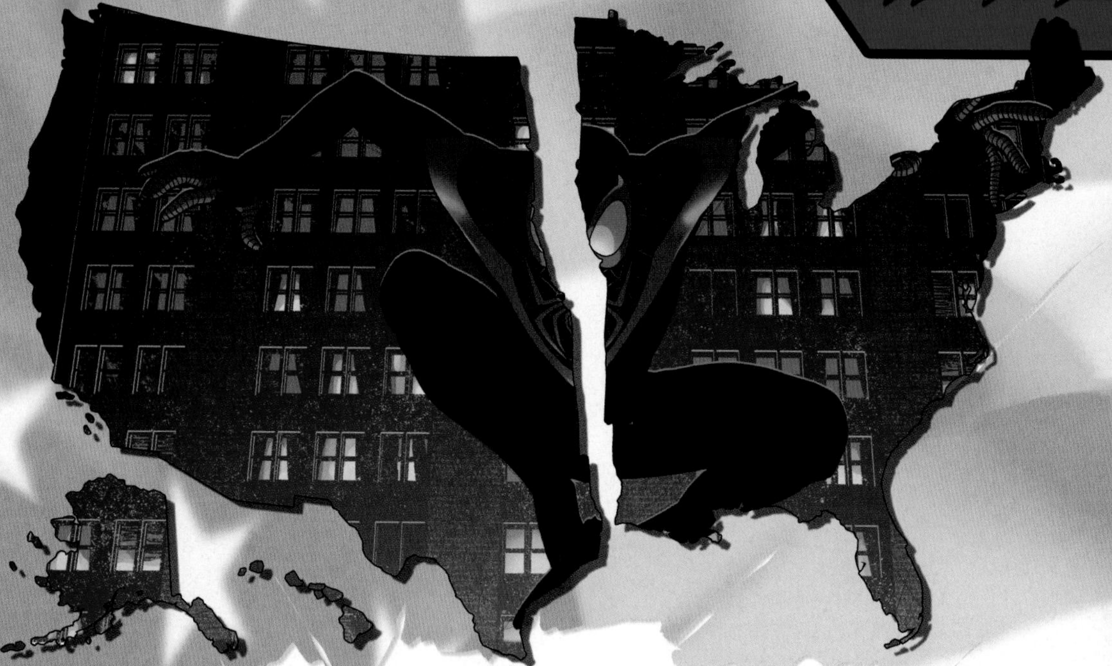

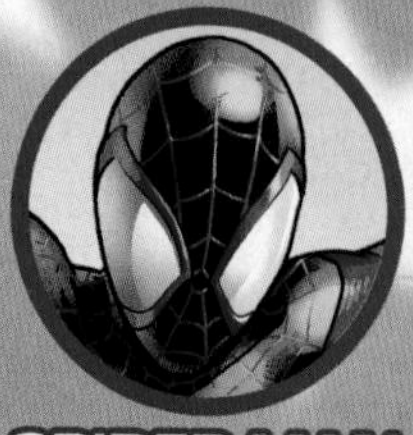
SPIDER-MAN

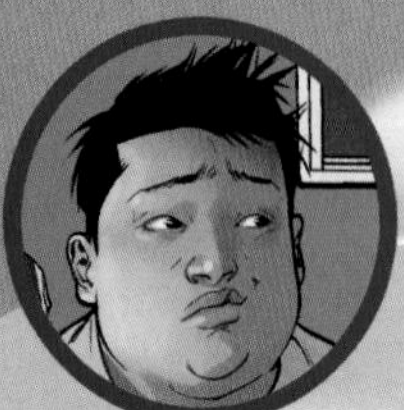
GANKE

Washington is decimated.
The government is a mess.
The Southwest is in chaos.
States are seceding from the union.
America is falling apart.
Spider-Man commits murder?

DIVIDED WE FALL

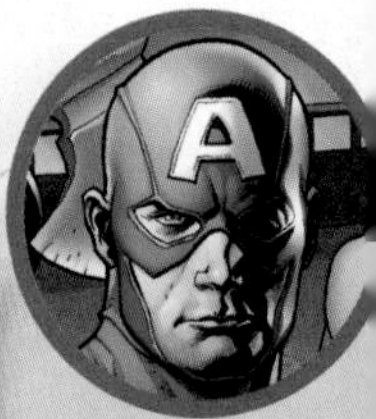
CAPTAIN AMERICA

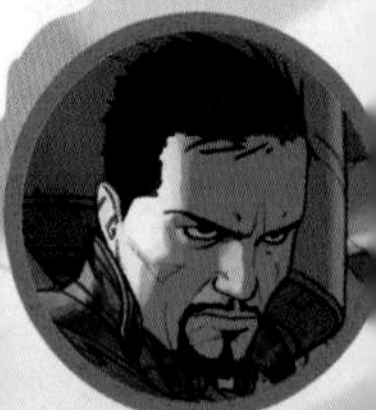
IRON MAN

S.H.I.E.L.D. SITUATION MAP:

[Anti-government militia hot spots]

Montana,N.Dakota
S.Dakota,Wyoming
Arizona,New Mexico
N.Carolina,S.Carolina,
Georgia

[Eastern seaboard control zone]

New England,
New York,
New Jersey,
Delaware,
Washington,D.C.,
Maryland,
Virginia

secured by
National Guard
under emergency
powers
committee

[the West Coast]

California,Oregon
Washington
status unknown

[Great Lakes states]

Minnesota,
Wisconsin,
Michigan,
Illinois,
Indiana,Ohio
status unknown

ANTI-MATTER
NO FLY
ZONE

SENTINEL
PUSH

SOUTHERN
CALIFORNIA
REFUGEE ZONE

NUCLEAR-ARMED
NATION

DALLAS:
CAPITAL CITY OF
THE NEW REPUBLIC
OF TEXAS

Classified Position

Camp Hutton, secure
location of the President
of the United States

[Sentinel-controlled no-man's-land]

New Mexico,Arizona
Utah,Oklahoma
abandoned by the
U.S. government

[The New Republic of Texas]

Texas
declared state
independence

ALL STATES
SHOWN IN WHITE
ARE U.S. GOVERNMENT-
CONTROLLED ZONES

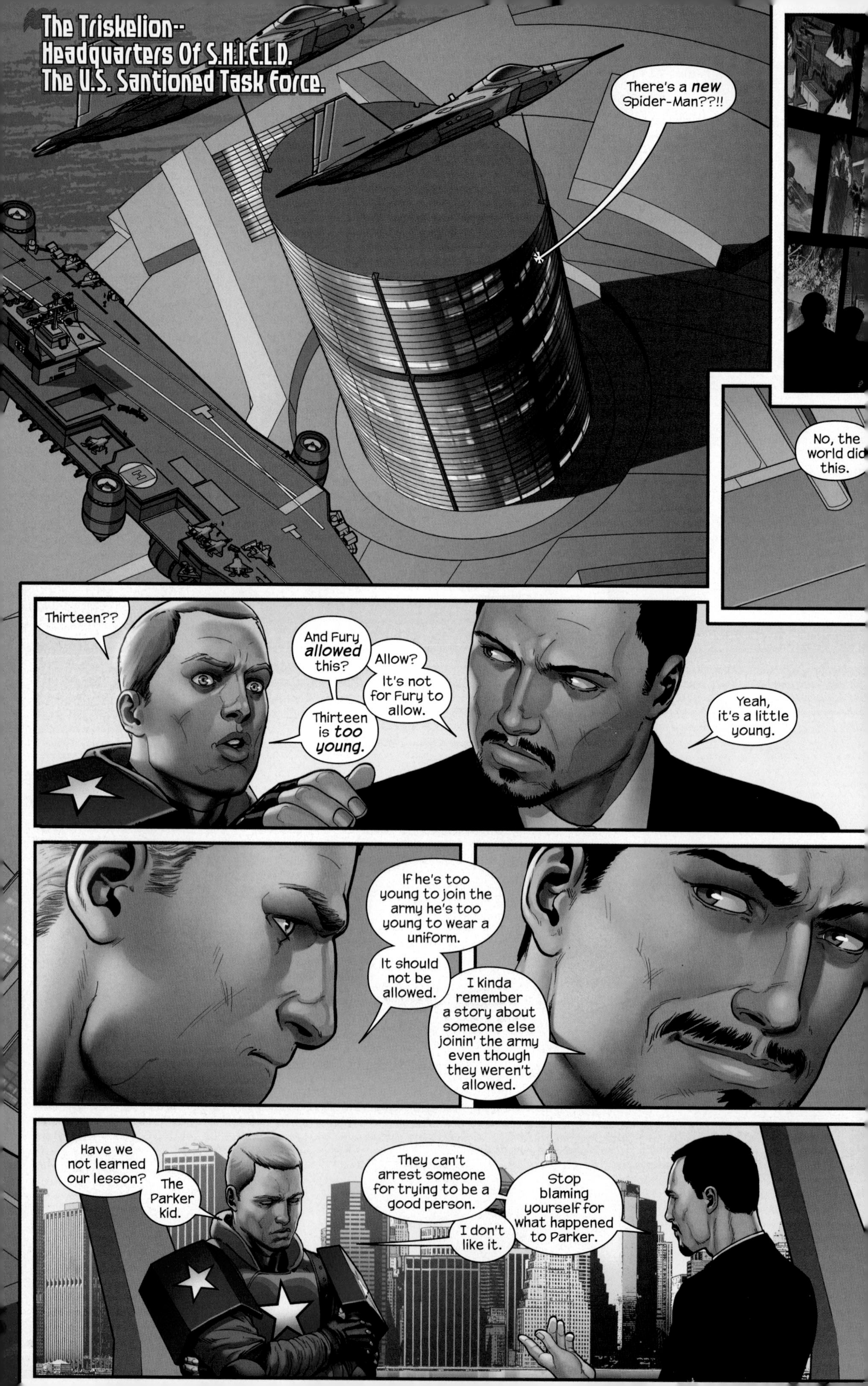
The Triskelion--
Headquarters Of S.H.I.E.L.D.
The U.S. Santioned Task Force.
There's a new Spider-Man??!!
No, the world did this.
Thirteen??
And Fury allowed this?
Allow? It's not for Fury to allow.
Thirteen is too young.
Yeah, it's a little young.
If he's too young to join the army he's too young to wear a uniform.
It should not be allowed.
I kinda remember a story about someone else joinin' the army even though they weren't allowed.
Have we not learned our lesson?
The Parker kid.
They can't arrest someone for trying to be a good person.
I don't like it.
Stop blaming yourself for what happened to Parker.

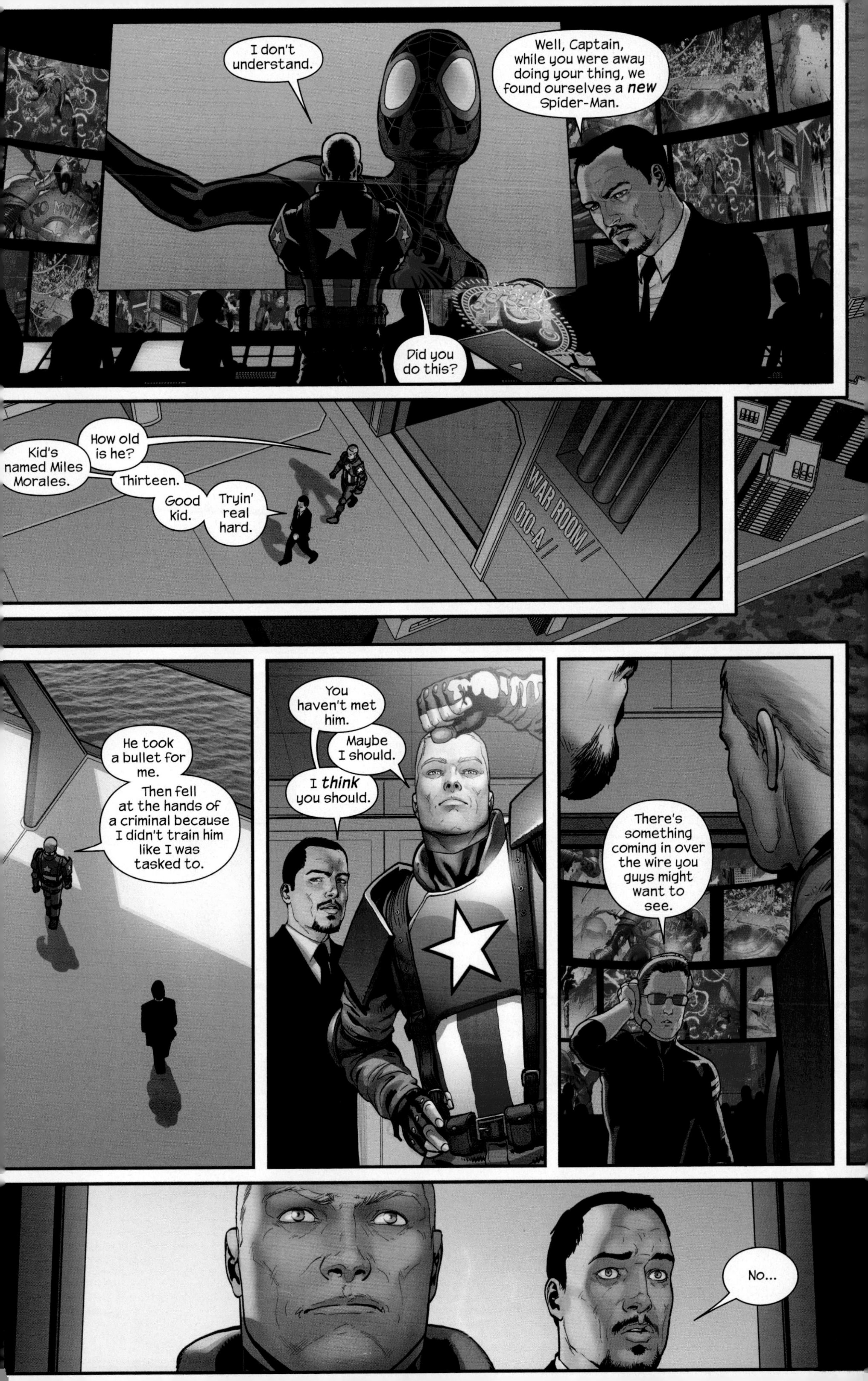
I don't understand.
Well, Captain, while you were away doing your thing, we found ourselves a *new* Spider-Man.
Did you do this?
How old is he?
Kid's named Miles Morales.
Thirteen.
Good kid.
Tryin' real hard.
WAR ROOM// 010-A//
He took a bullet for me.
Then fell at the hands of a criminal because I didn't train him like I was tasked to.
You haven't met him.
Maybe I should.
I *think* you should.
There's something coming in over the wire you guys might want to see.
No...

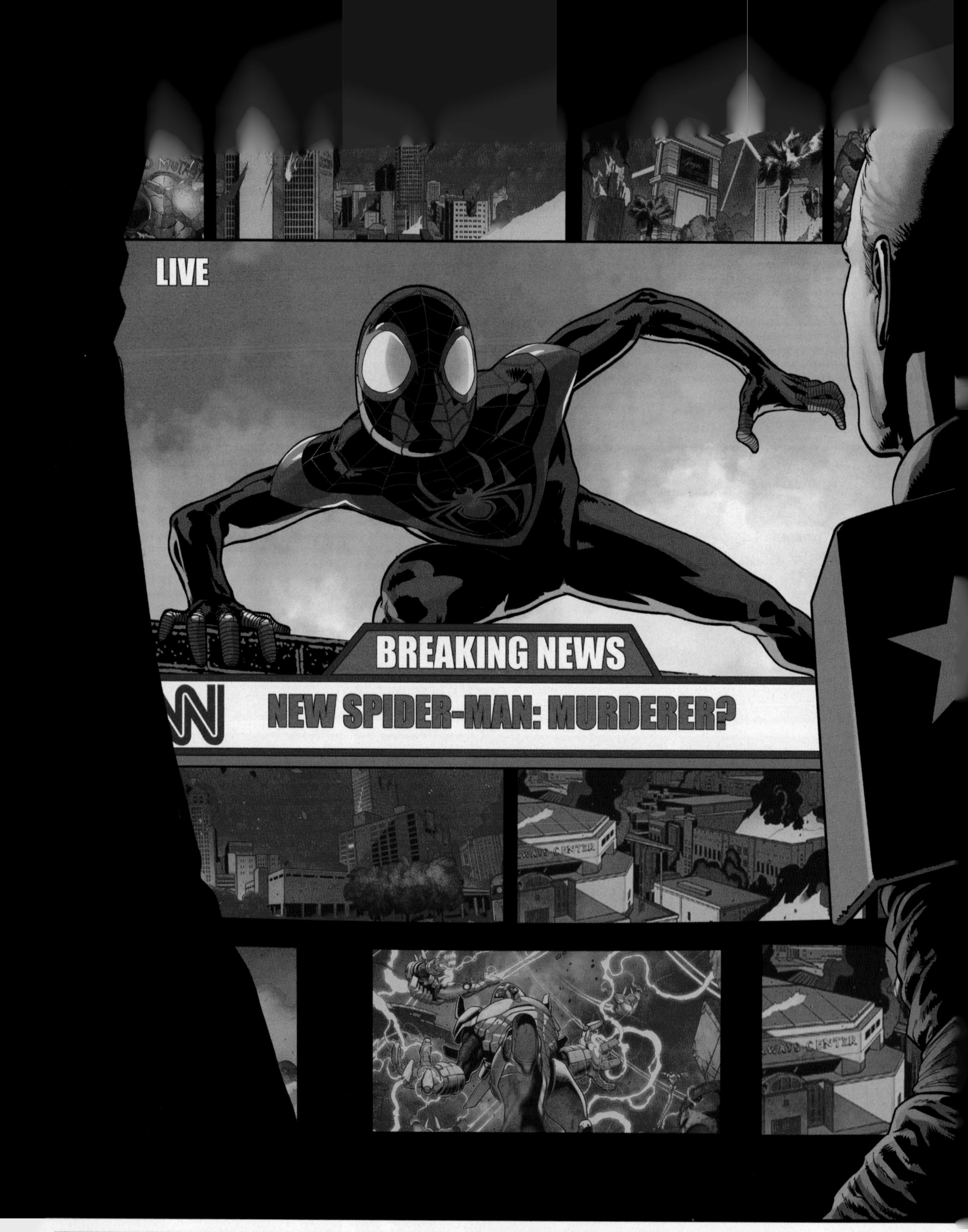
LIVE
BREAKING NEWS
NEW SPIDER-MAN: MURDERER?

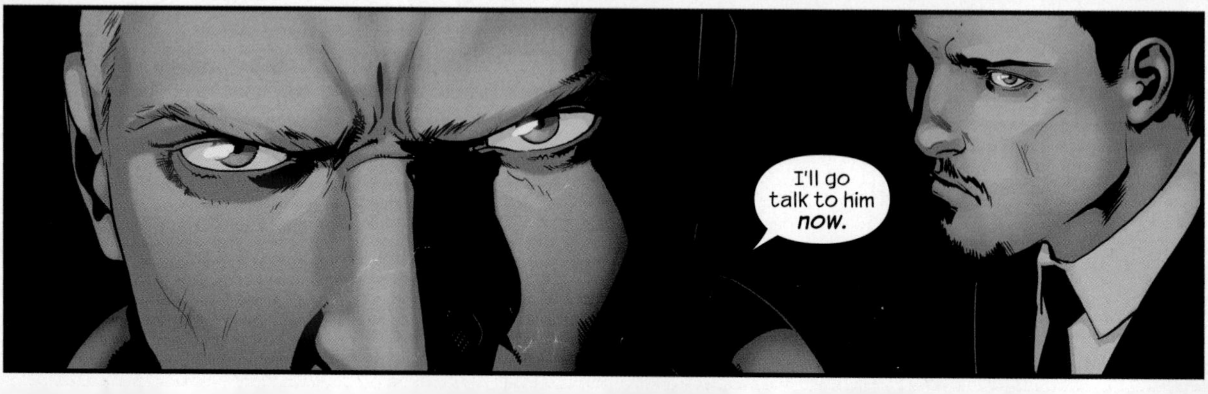
I'll go talk to him *now*.

Hey, Miles.

Hey, dad.

I-uh-I have some bad news.

Your Uncle Aaron is dead.

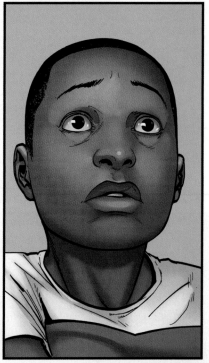

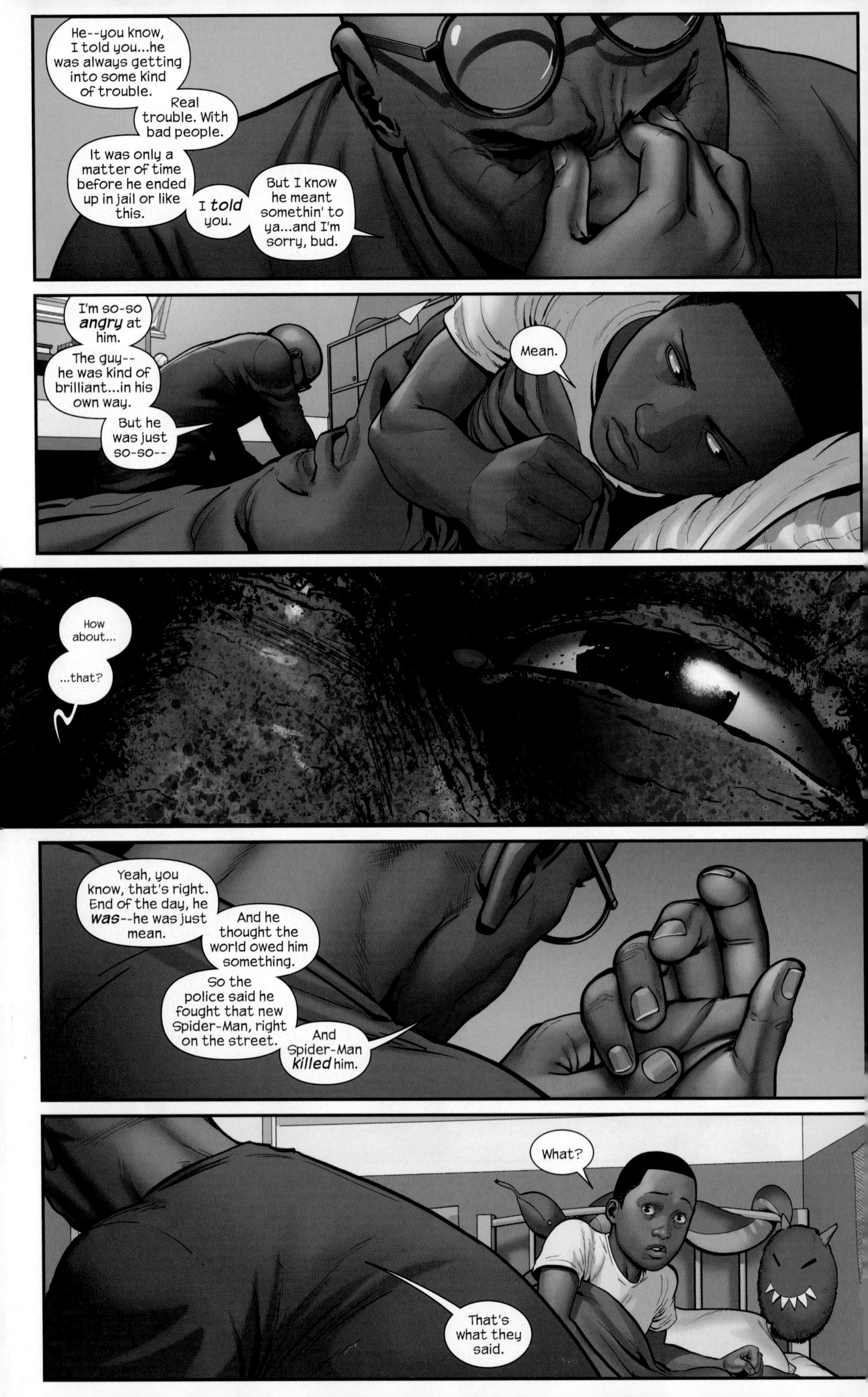
He--you know, I told you...he was always getting into some kind of trouble.
Real trouble. With bad people.
It was only a matter of time before he ended up in jail or like this.
I *told* you.
But I know he meant somethin' to ya...and I'm sorry, bud.
I'm so-so *angry* at him.
The guy--he was kind of brilliant...in his own way.
But he was just so-so--
Mean.
How about...
...that?
Yeah, you know, that's right. End of the day, he *was*--he was just mean.
And he thought the world owed him something.
So the police said he fought that new Spider-Man, right on the street.
And Spider-Man *killed* him.
What?
That's what they said.

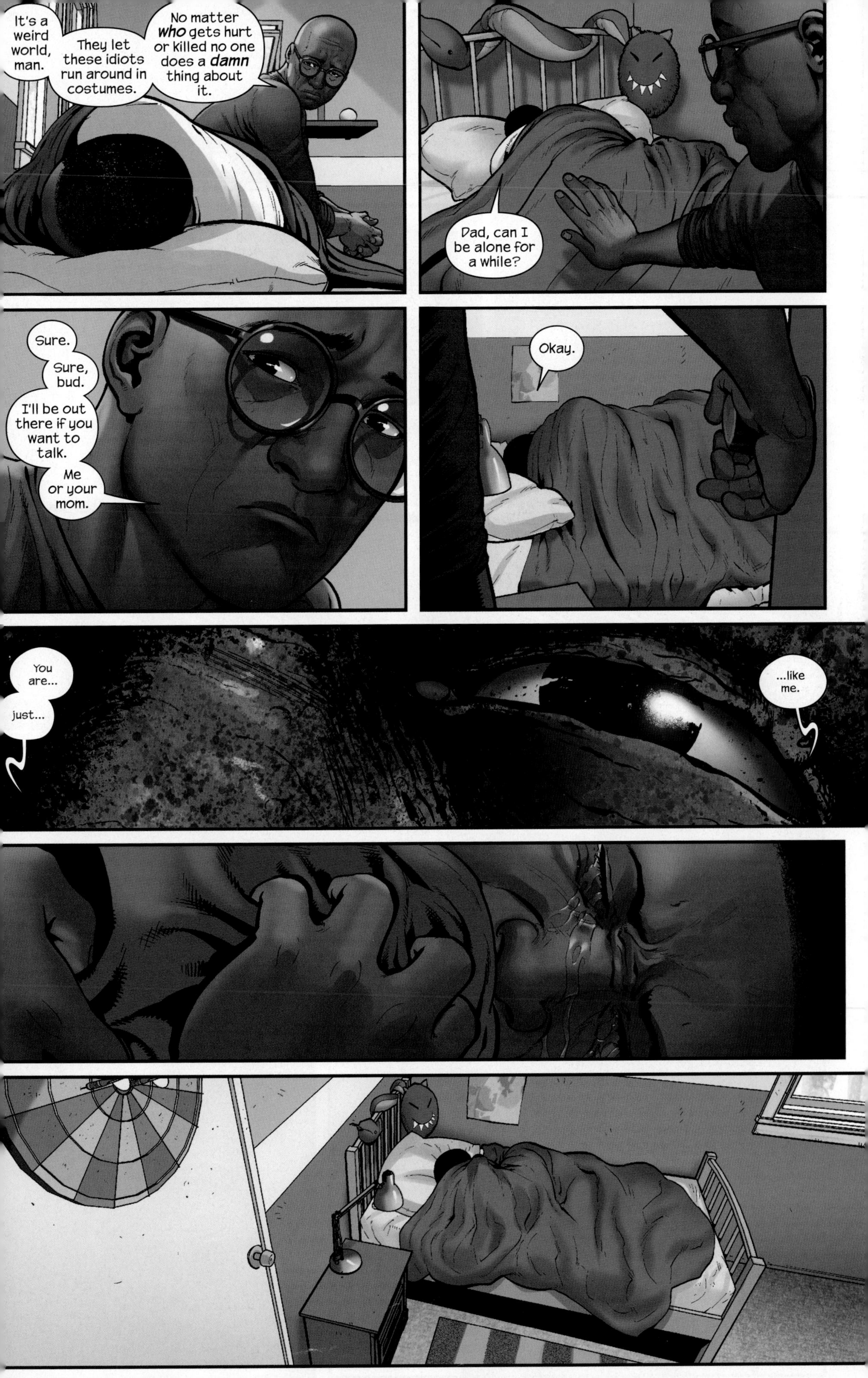
It's a weird world, man.
They let these idiots run around in costumes.
No matter *who* gets hurt or killed no one does a *damn* thing about it.
Dad, can I be alone for a while?
Sure.
Sure, bud.
I'll be out there if you want to talk.
Me or your mom.
Okay.
You are...
just...
...like me.

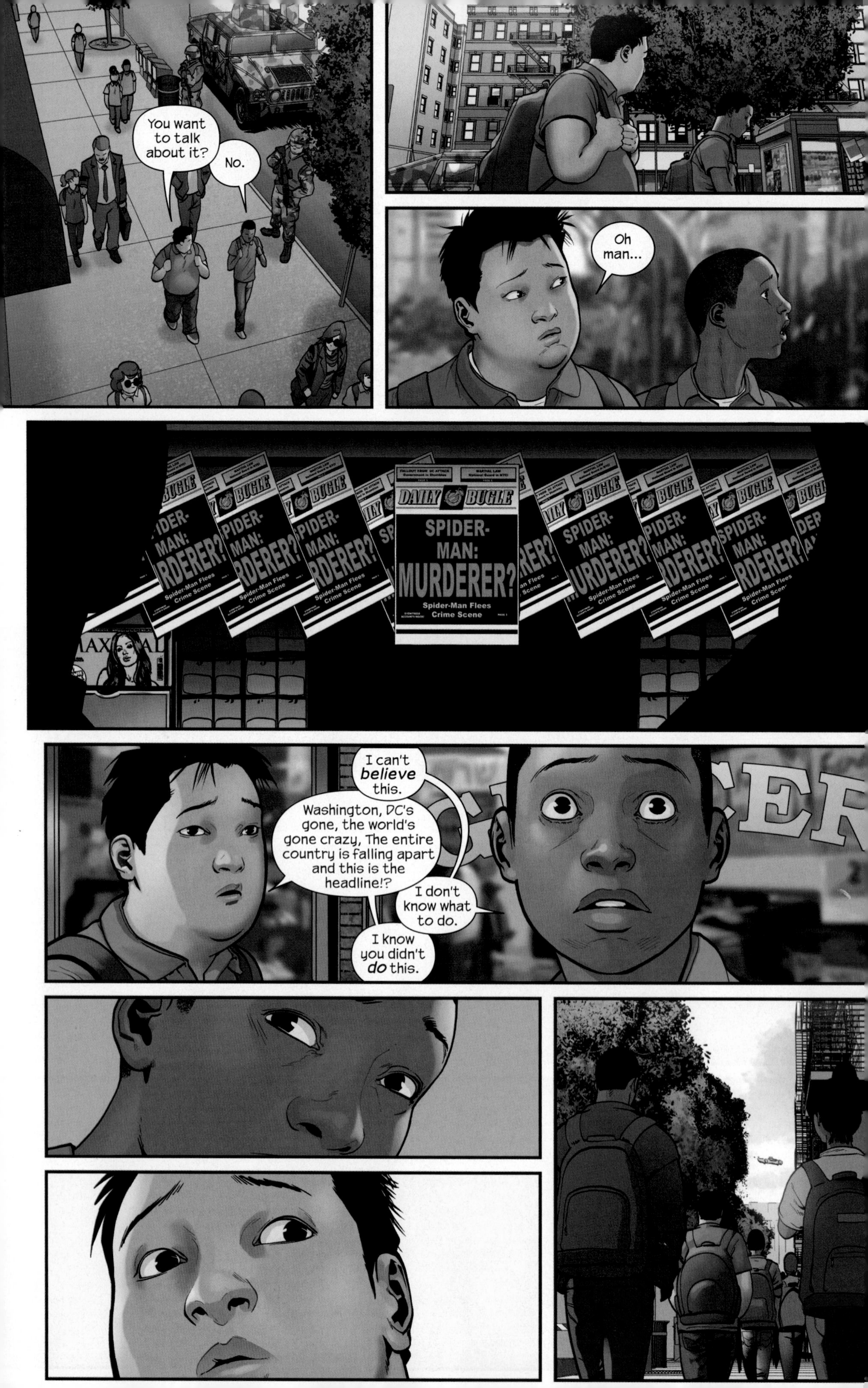
You want to talk about it?
No.
Oh man...
DAILY BUGLE
SPIDER-MAN: MURDERER?
Spider-Man Flees Crime Scene
I can't **believe** this.
Washington, DC's gone, the world's gone crazy, The entire country is falling apart and this is the headline!?
I don't know what to do.
I know you didn't **do** this.

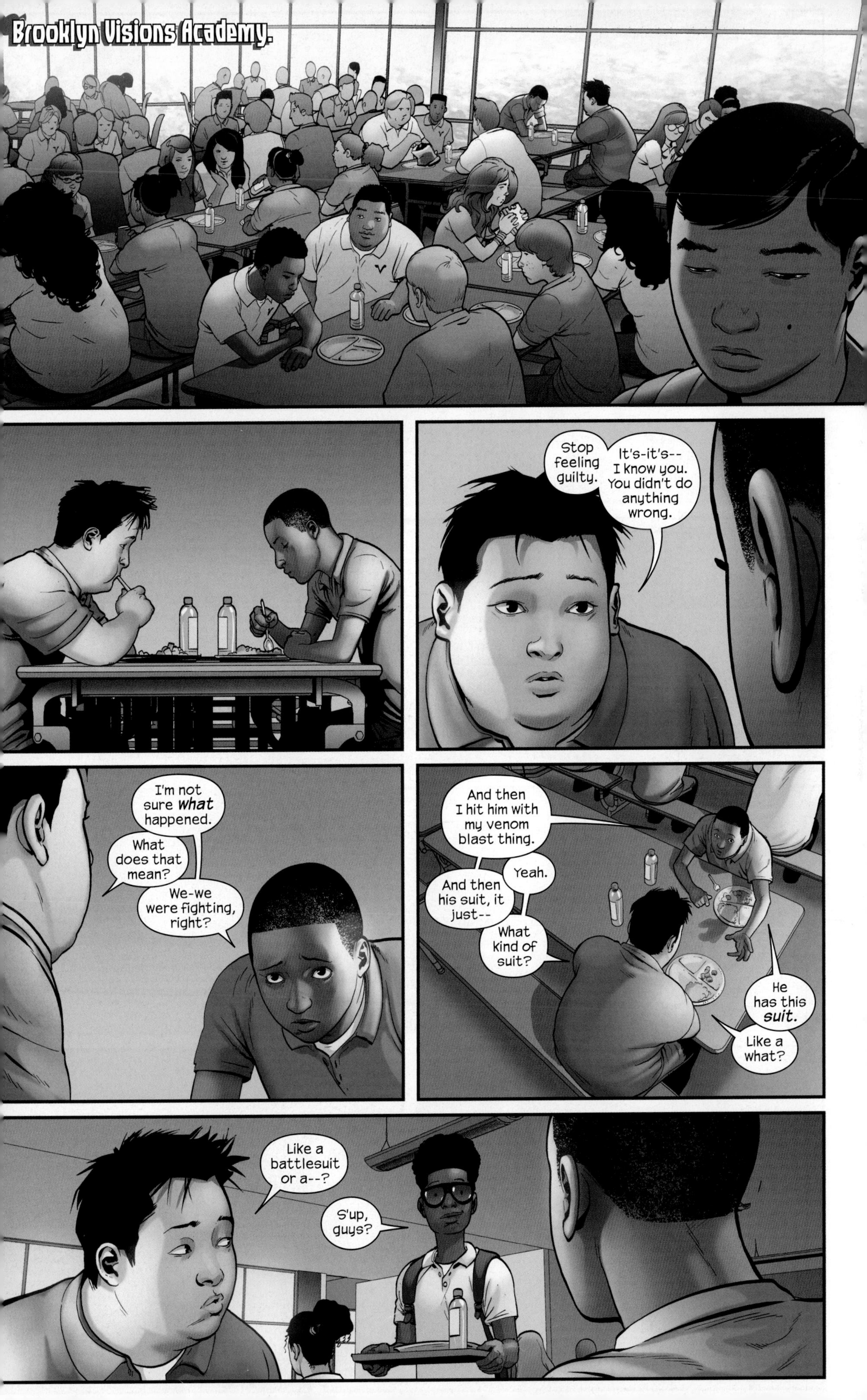
Brooklyn Visions Academy.
Stop feeling guilty.
It's-it's-- I know you. You didn't do anything wrong.
I'm not sure *what* happened.
What does that mean?
We-we were fighting, right?
And then I hit him with my venom blast thing.
Yeah.
And then his suit, it just--
What kind of suit?
He has this *suit.*
Like a what?
Like a battlesuit or a--?
S'up, guys?

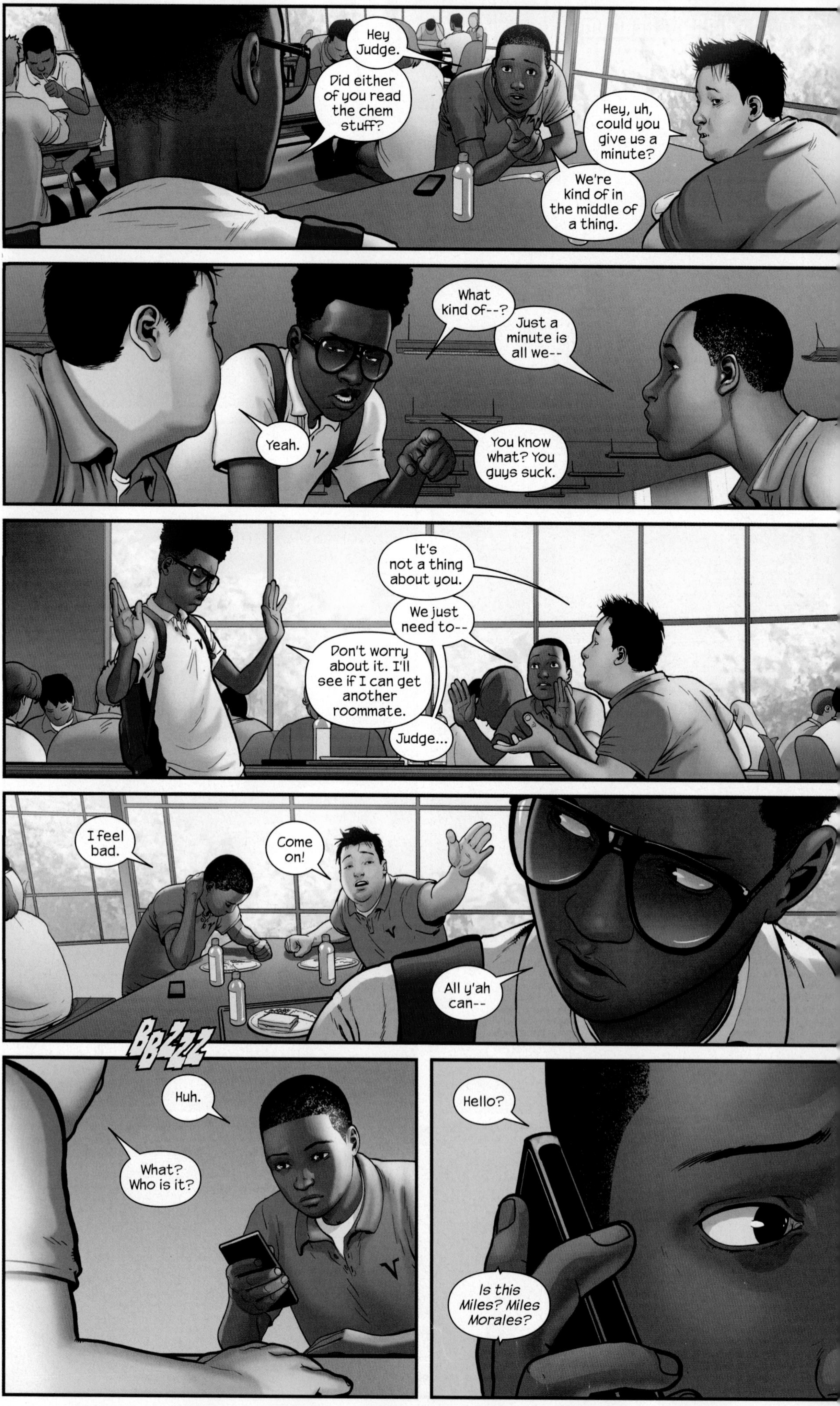
Hey Judge.
Did either of you read the chem stuff?
Hey, uh, could you give us a minute?
We're kind of in the middle of a thing.
What kind of--?
Just a minute is all we--
Yeah.
You know what? You guys suck.
It's not a thing about you.
We just need to--
Don't worry about it. I'll see if I can get another roommate.
Judge...
I feel bad.
Come on!
All y'ah can--
BBZZZ
Huh.
What? Who is it?
Hello?
Is this Miles? Miles Morales?

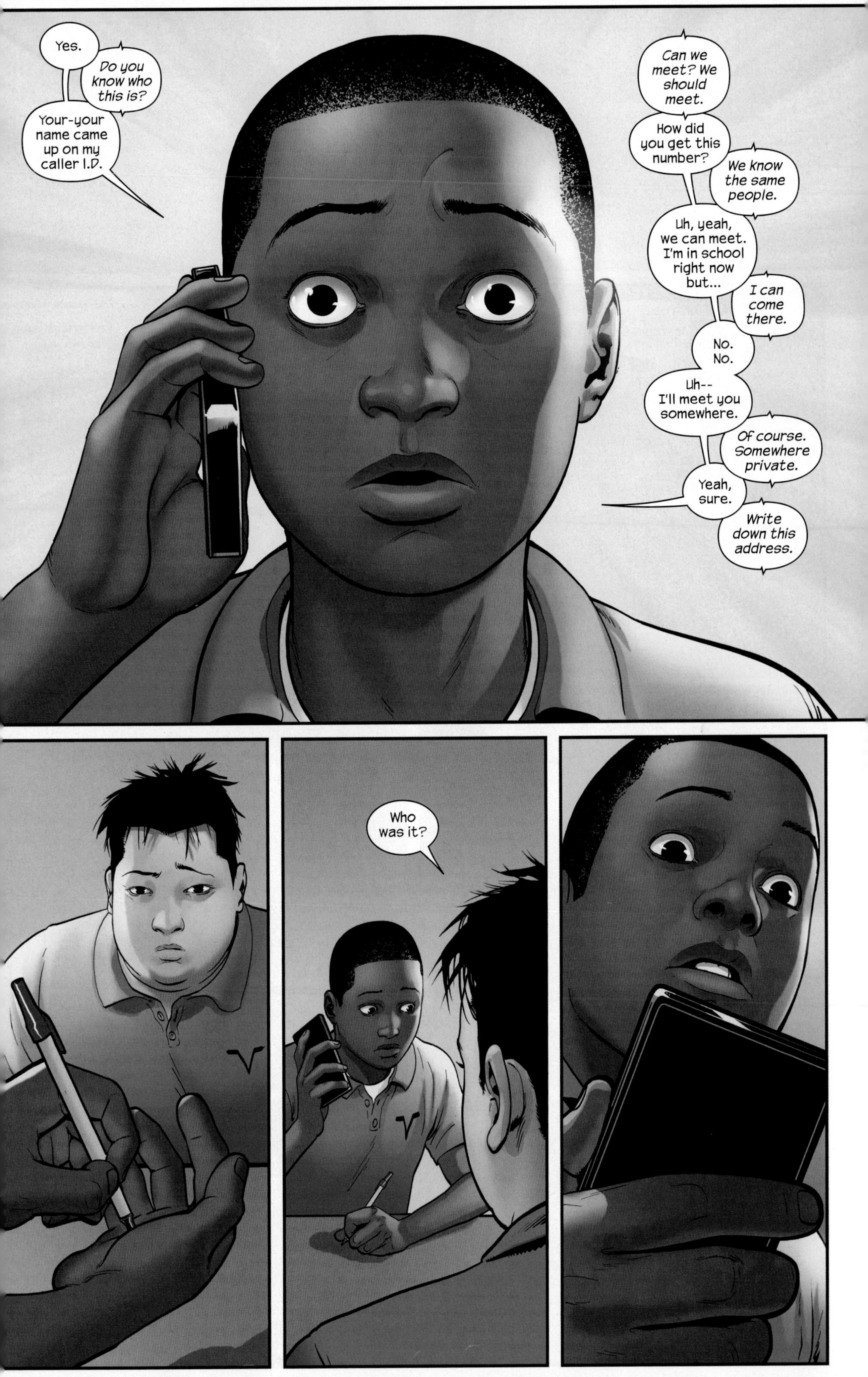
Yes.
Do you know who this is?
Your-your name came up on my caller I.D.
Can we meet? We should meet.
How did you get this number?
We know the same people.
Uh, yeah, we can meet. I'm in school right now but...
I can come there.
No. No.
Uh-- I'll meet you somewhere.
Of course. Somewhere private.
Yeah, sure.
Write down this address.
Who was it?

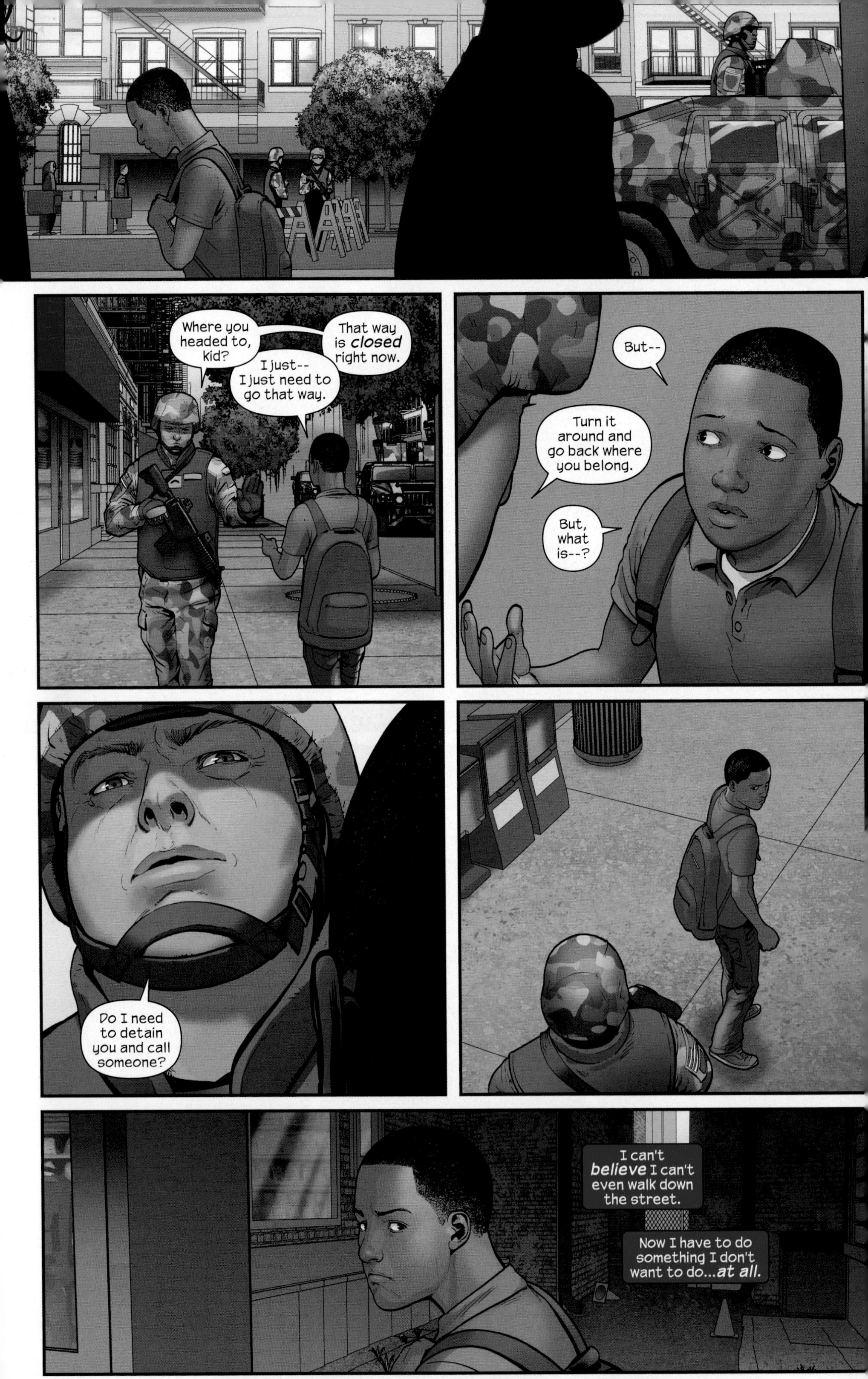
Where you headed to, kid?
That way is *closed* right now.
I just-- I just need to go that way.
But--
Turn it around and go back where you belong.
But, what is--?
Do I need to detain you and call someone?
I can't *believe* I can't even walk down the street.
Now I have to do something I don't want to do...*at all.*

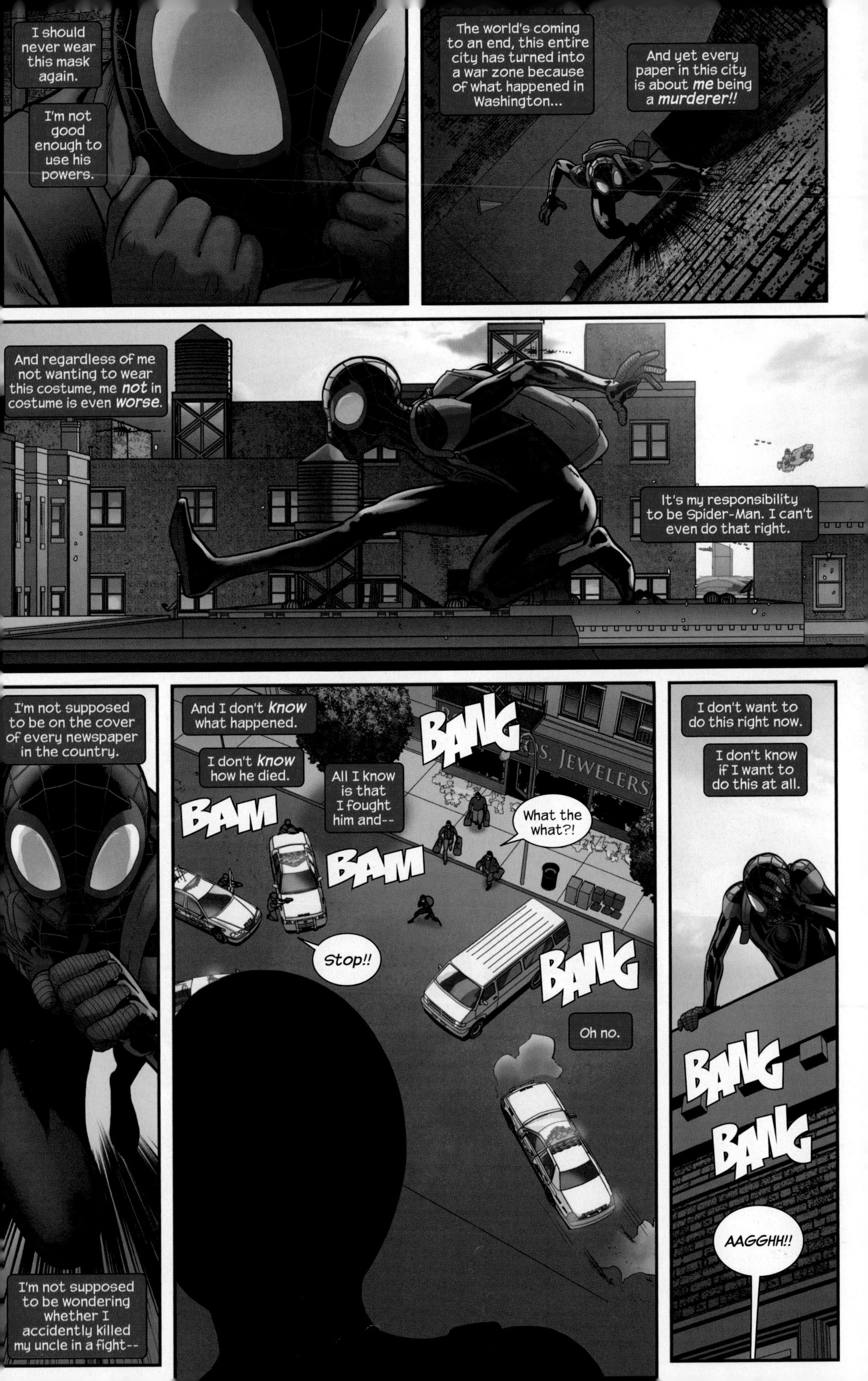

I should never wear this mask again.
I'm not good enough to use his powers.
The world's coming to an end, this entire city has turned into a war zone because of what happened in Washington...
And yet every paper in this city is about *me* being a *murderer!!*
And regardless of me not wanting to wear this costume, me *not* in costume is even *worse*.
It's my responsibility to be Spider-Man. I can't even do that right.
I'm not supposed to be on the cover of every newspaper in the country.
I'm not supposed to be wondering whether I accidently killed my uncle in a fight--
And I don't *know* what happened.
BANG
I don't *know* how he died.
All I know is that I fought him and--
S. JEWELERS
BAM
What the what?!
BAM
Stop!!
BANG
Oh no.
I don't want to do this right now.
I don't know if I want to do this at all.
BANG
BANG
AAGGHH!!

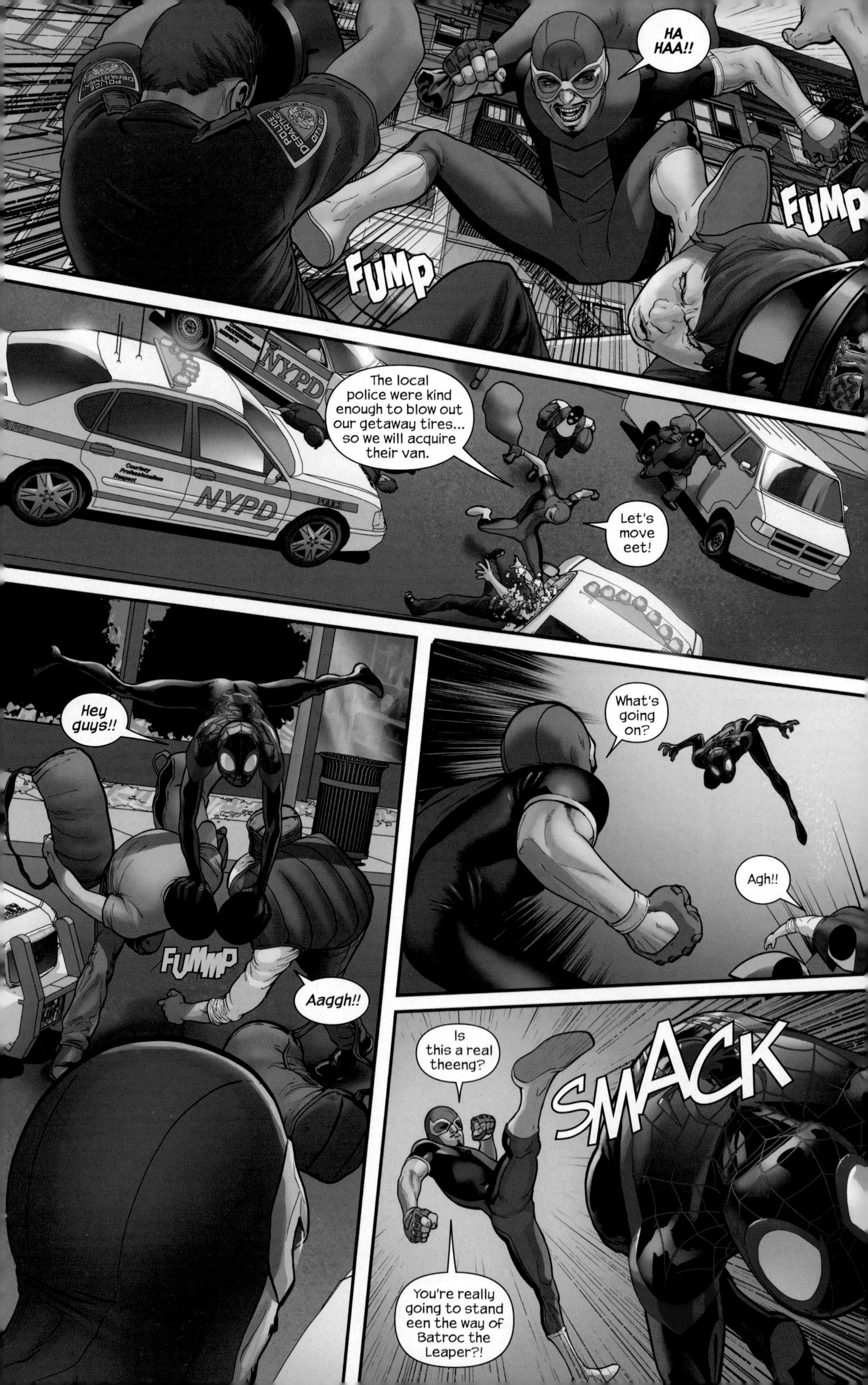
HA HAA!!
FUMP
FUMP
The local police were kind enough to blow out our getaway tires... so we will acquire their van.
Let's move eet!
Hey guys!!
FUMMP
Aaggh!!
What's going on?
Agh!!
Is this a real theeng?
SMACK
You're really going to stand een the way of Batroc the Leaper?!

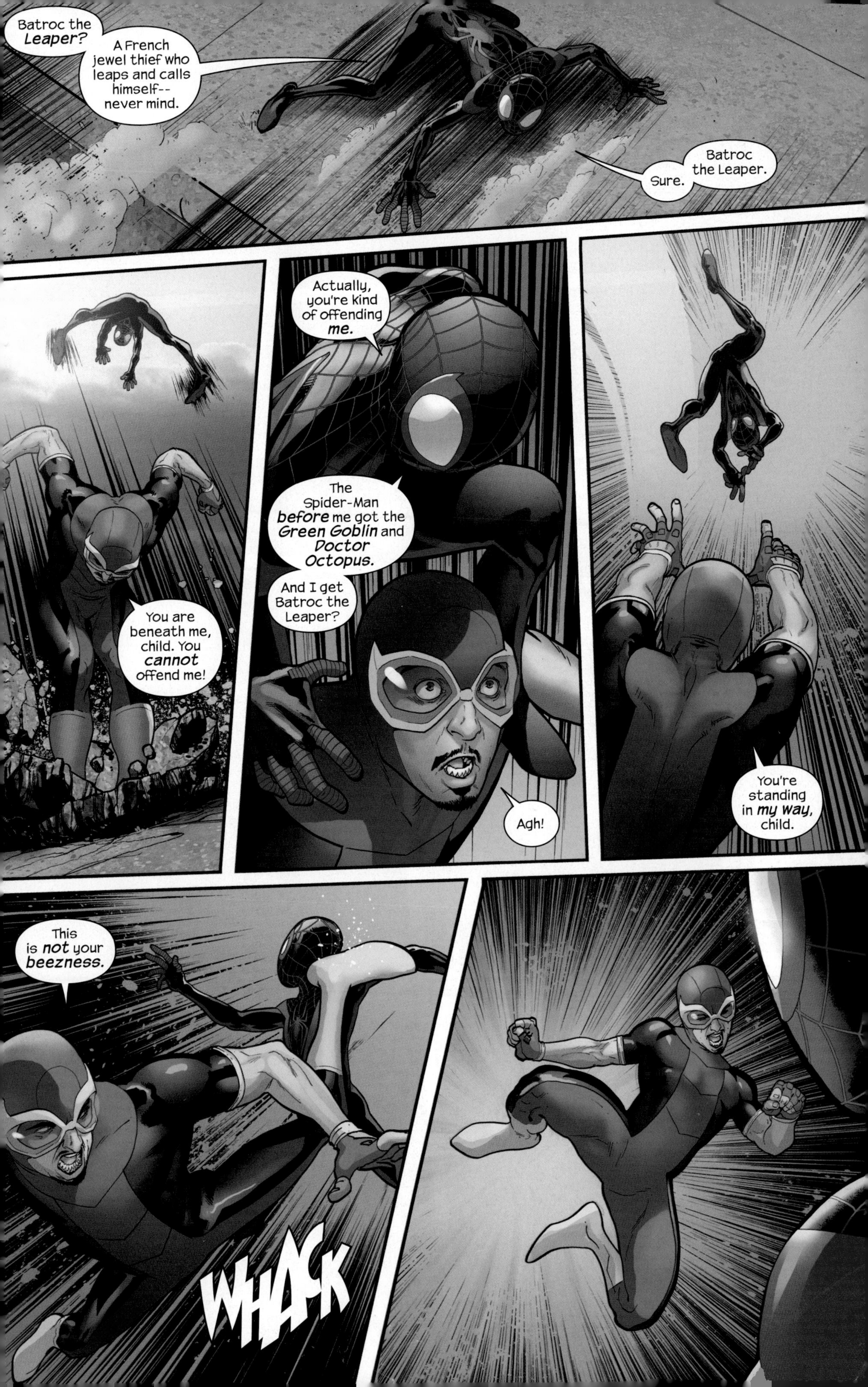

Batroc the *Leaper?*
A French jewel thief who leaps and calls himself-- never mind.
Sure.
Batroc the Leaper.
You are beneath me, child. You *cannot* offend me!
Actually, you're kind of offending *me.*
The Spider-Man *before* me got the *Green Goblin* and *Doctor Octopus.*
And I get Batroc the Leaper?
Agh!
You're standing in *my way,* child.
This is *not* your *beezness.*
WHACK

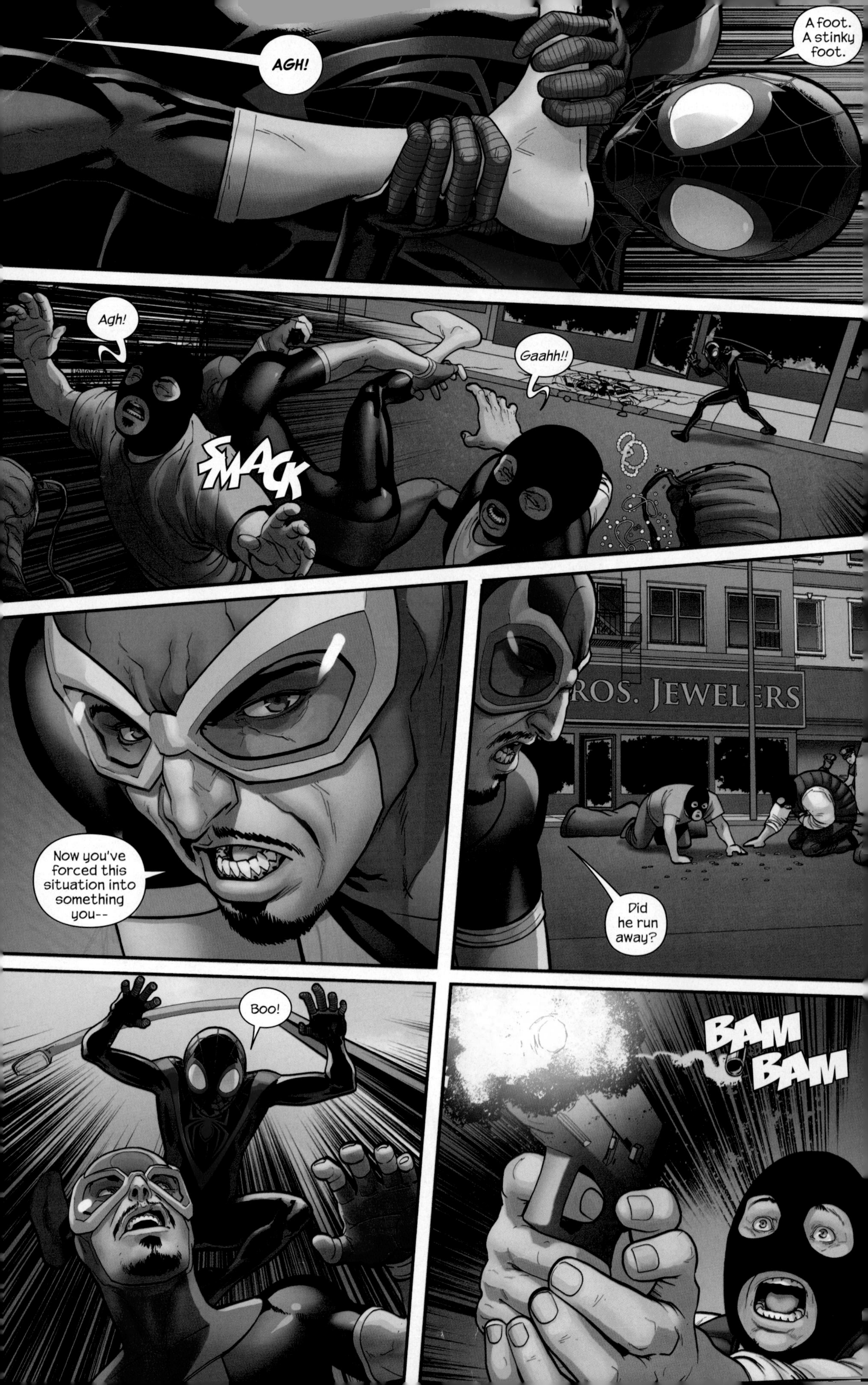

AGH!
A foot. A stinky foot.
Agh!
SMACK
Gaahh!!
Now you've forced this situation into something you--
ROS. JEWELERS
Did he run away?
Boo!
BAM BAM

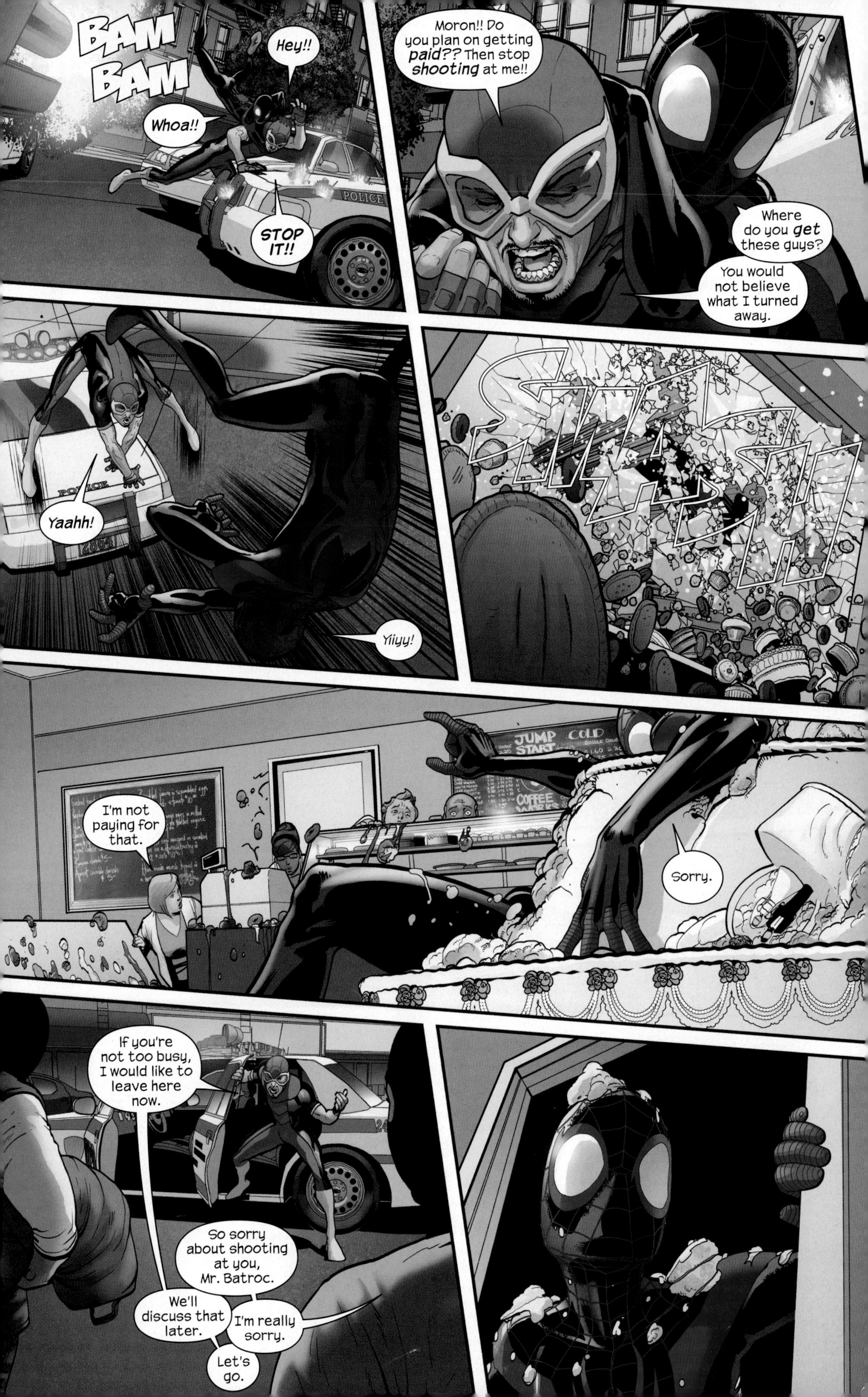
BAM
BAM
Hey!!
Whoa!!
STOP IT!!
POLICE
Moron!! Do you plan on getting paid?? Then stop shooting at me!!
Where do you get these guys?
You would not believe what I turned away.
POLICE
Yaahh!
Yiiyy!
JUMP START
COLD
COFFEE WORKS
I'm not paying for that.
Sorry.
If you're not too busy, I would like to leave here now.
So sorry about shooting at you, Mr. Batroc.
I'm really sorry.
We'll discuss that later.
Let's go.

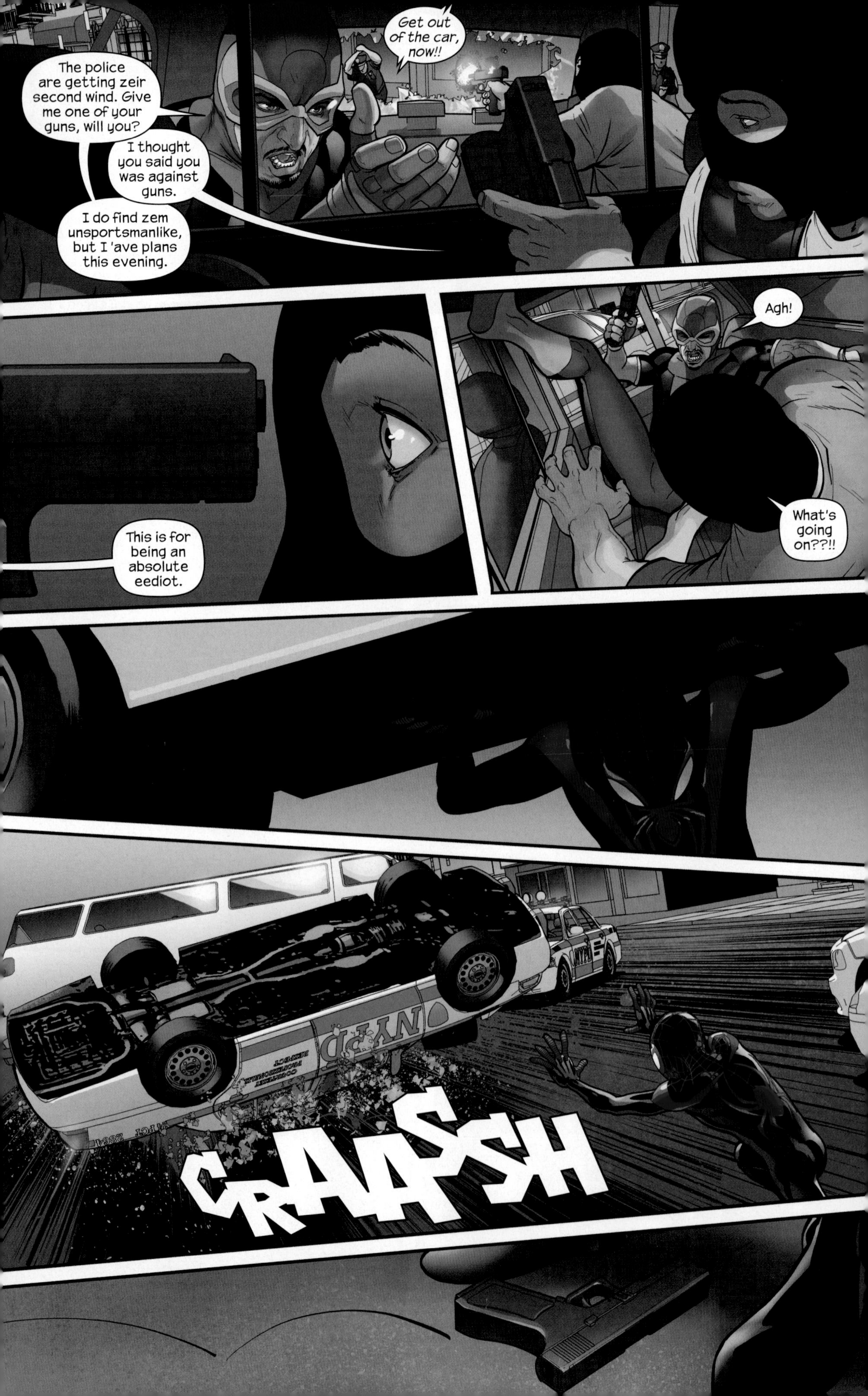
The police are getting zeir second wind. Give me one of your guns, will you?
Get out of the car, now!!
I thought you said you was against guns.
I do find zem unsportsmanlike, but I 'ave plans this evening.
This is for being an absolute eediot.
Agh!
What's going on??!!
CRAASH

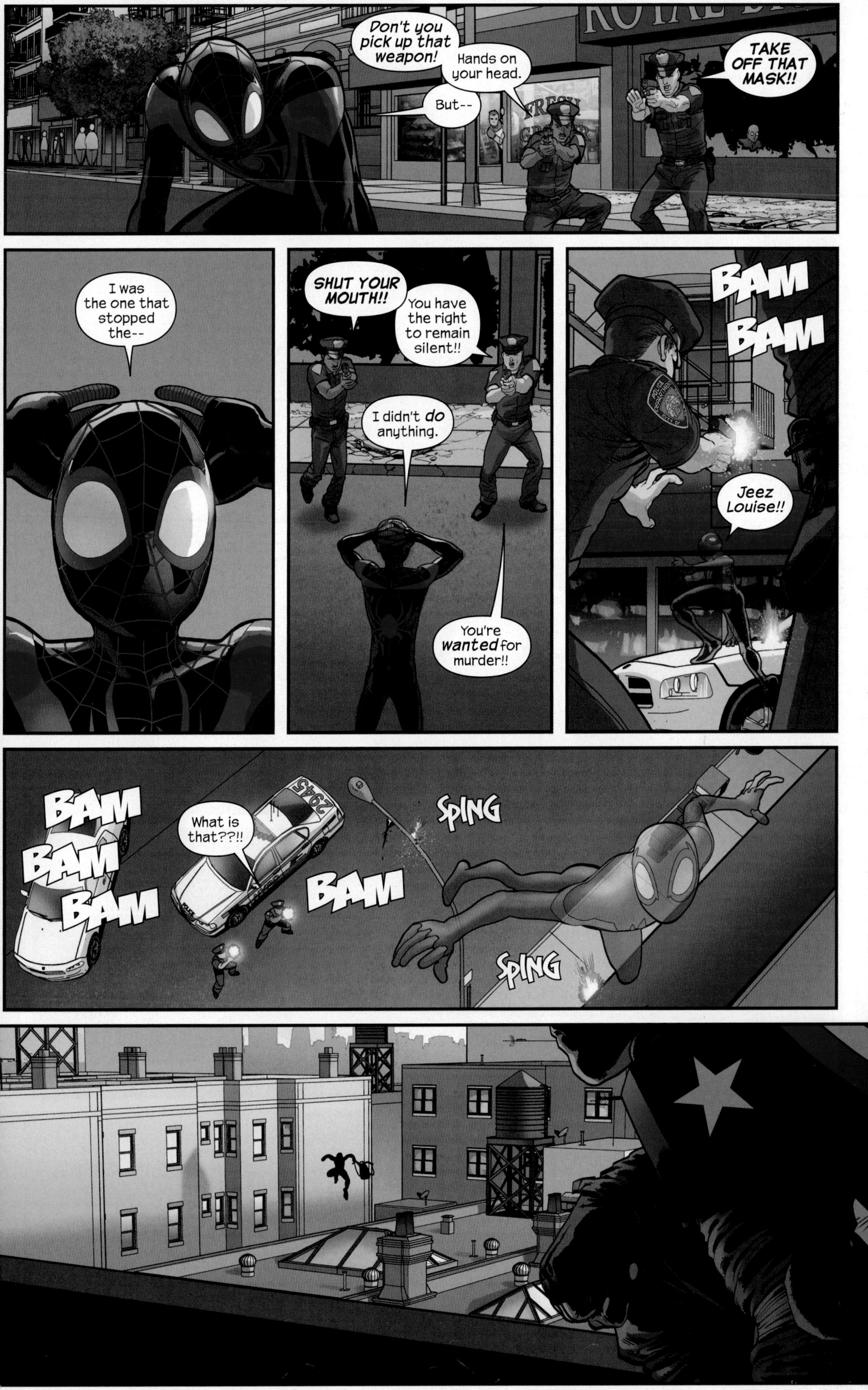
Don't you pick up that weapon!
Hands on your head.
But--
TAKE OFF THAT MASK!!
I was the one that stopped the--
SHUT YOUR MOUTH!!
You have the right to remain silent!!
I didn't do anything.
You're wanted for murder!!
BAM
BAM
Jeez Louise!!
BAM
BAM
BAM
What is that??!!
BAM
SPING
SPING

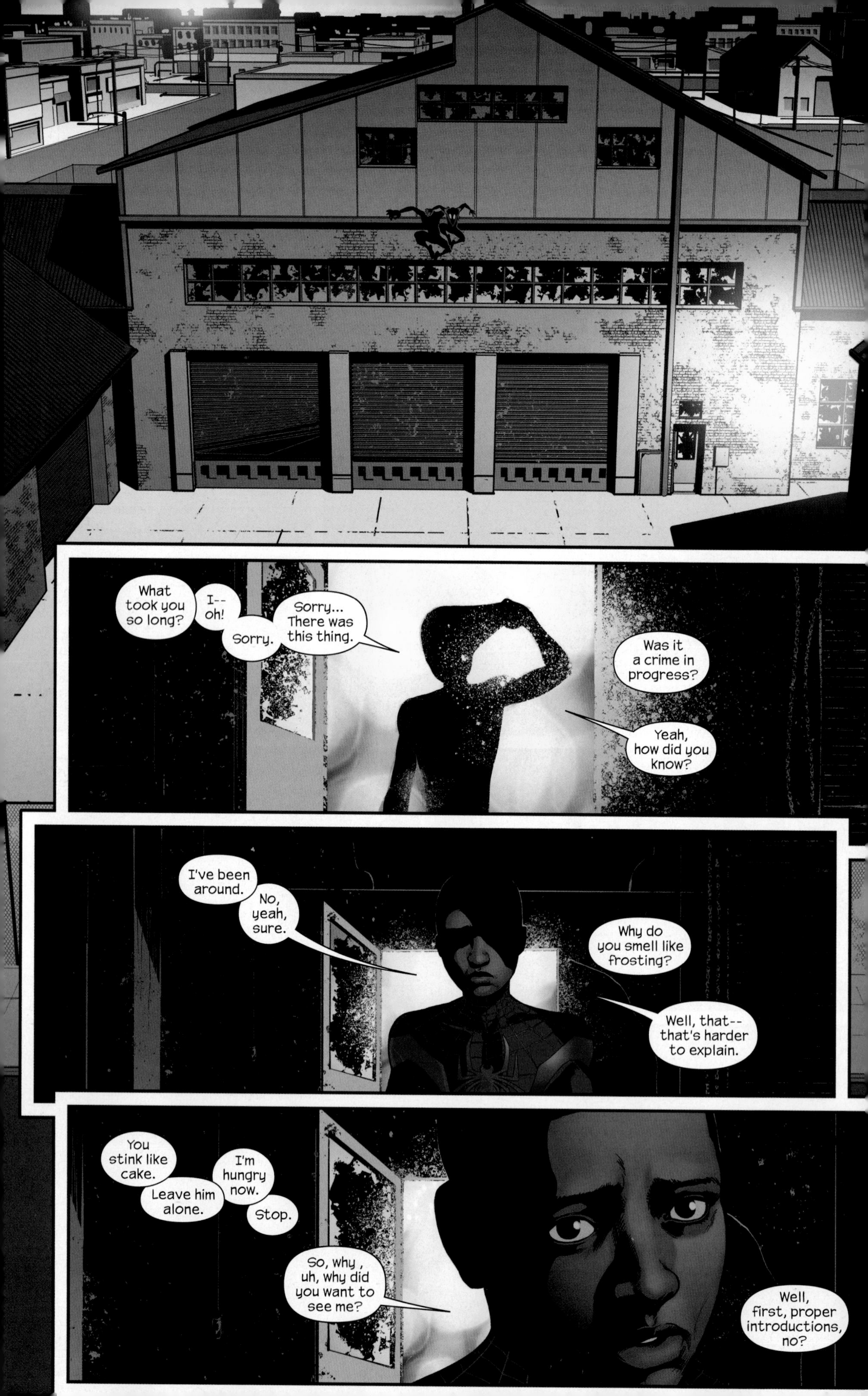

What took you so long?
I-- oh!
Sorry.
Sorry... There was this thing.
Was it a crime in progress?
Yeah, how did you know?
I've been around.
No, yeah, sure.
Why do you smell like frosting?
Well, that-- that's harder to explain.
You stink like cake.
Leave him alone.
I'm hungry now.
Stop.
So, why , uh, why did you want to see me?
Well, first, proper introductions, no?

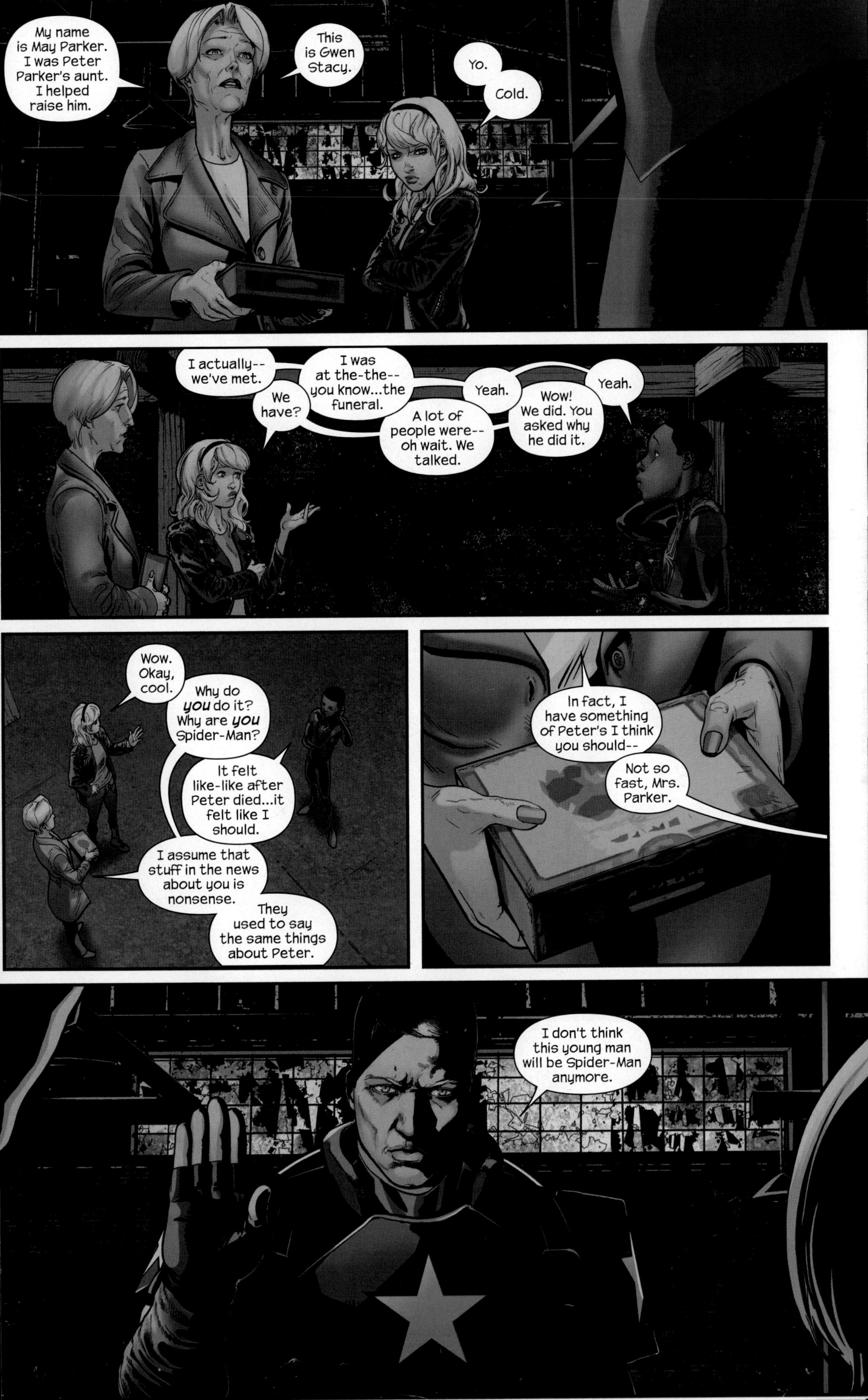

My name is May Parker. I was Peter Parker's aunt. I helped raise him.
This is Gwen Stacy.
Yo.
Cold.
I actually-- we've met.
We have?
I was at the-the-- you know...the funeral.
A lot of people were-- oh wait. We talked.
Yeah.
Wow! We did. You asked why he did it.
Yeah.
Wow. Okay, cool.
Why do *you* do it? Why are *you* Spider-Man?
It felt like-like after Peter died...it felt like I should.
I assume that stuff in the news about you is nonsense.
They used to say the same things about Peter.
In fact, I have something of Peter's I think you should--
Not so fast, Mrs. Parker.
I don't think this young man will be Spider-Man anymore.

14

ULTIMATE COMICS **SPIDER-MAN** #14

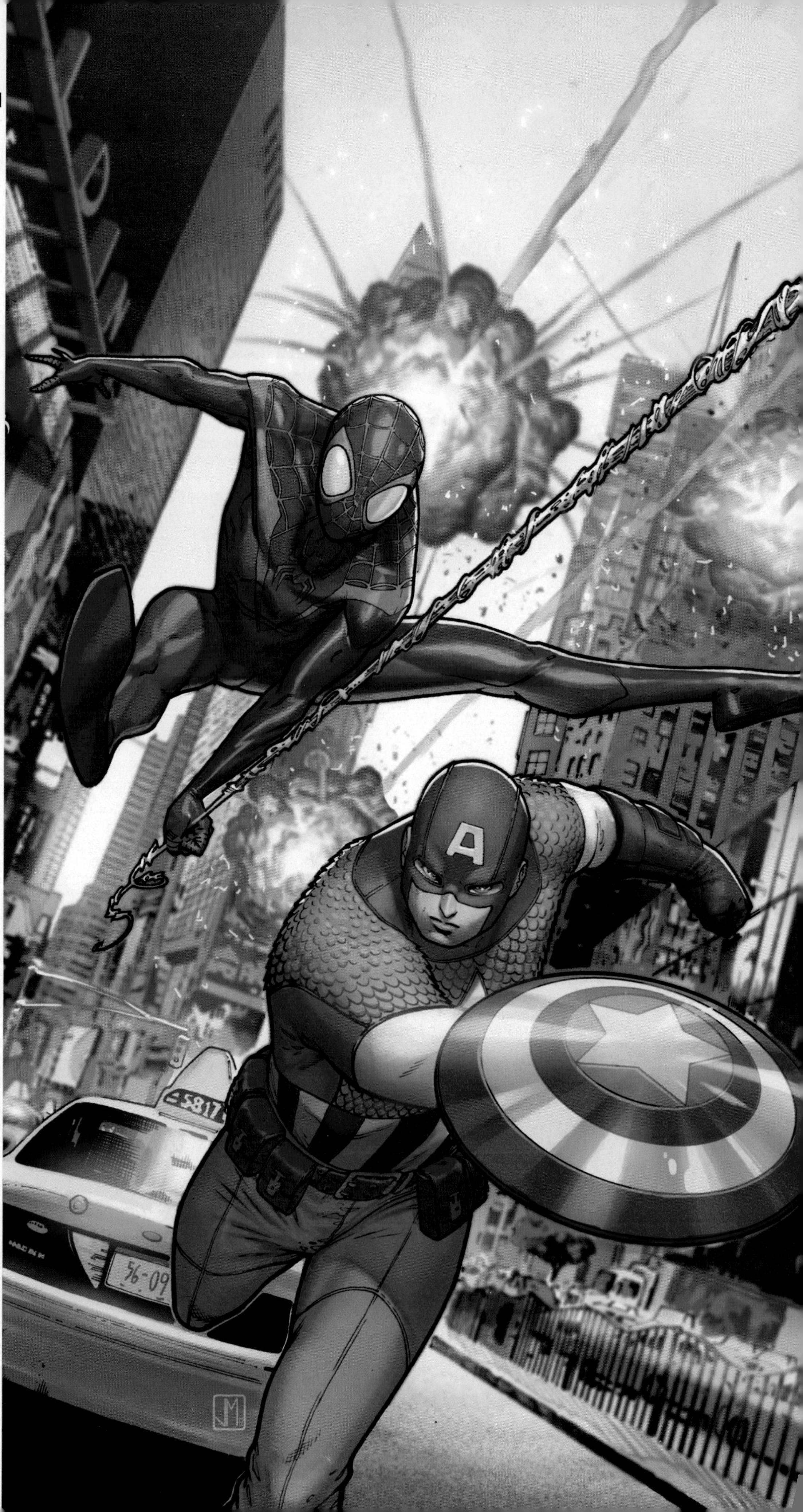

5817
56-09

S.H.I.E.L.D. SITUATION MAP:

[Anti-government militia hot spots]

Montana, N.Dakota,
S.Dakota, Wyoming,
Arizona, New Mexico,
N.Carolina, S.Carolina,
Georgia

[Eastern seaboard control zone]

New England,
New York,
New Jersey,
Delaware,
Washington D.C.,
Maryland,
Virginia

secured by
National Guard
under emergency
powers
committee

[the West Coast]

California, Oregon,
Washington
status unknown

[Great Lakes states]

Minnesota,
Wisconsin,
Michigan,
Illinois,
Indiana, Ohio
status unknown

ANTI-MATTER
NO FLY
ZONE

SENTINEL
PUSH

SOUTHERN
CALIFORNIA
REFUGEE ZONE

NUCLEAR-ARMED
NATION

AREA OF
URBAN
UNREST

DALLAS:
CAPITAL CITY OF
THE NEW REPUBLIC
OF TEXAS

Classified Position

Camp Hutton, secure
location of the President
of the United States

[Sentinel-controlled no-man's-land]

New Mexico, Arizona,
Utah, Oklahoma
abandoned by the
U.S. government

[The New Republic of Texas]

Texas
declared state
independence

ALL STATES
SHOWN IN WHITE
ARE U.S. GOVERNMENT-
CONTROLLED ZONES

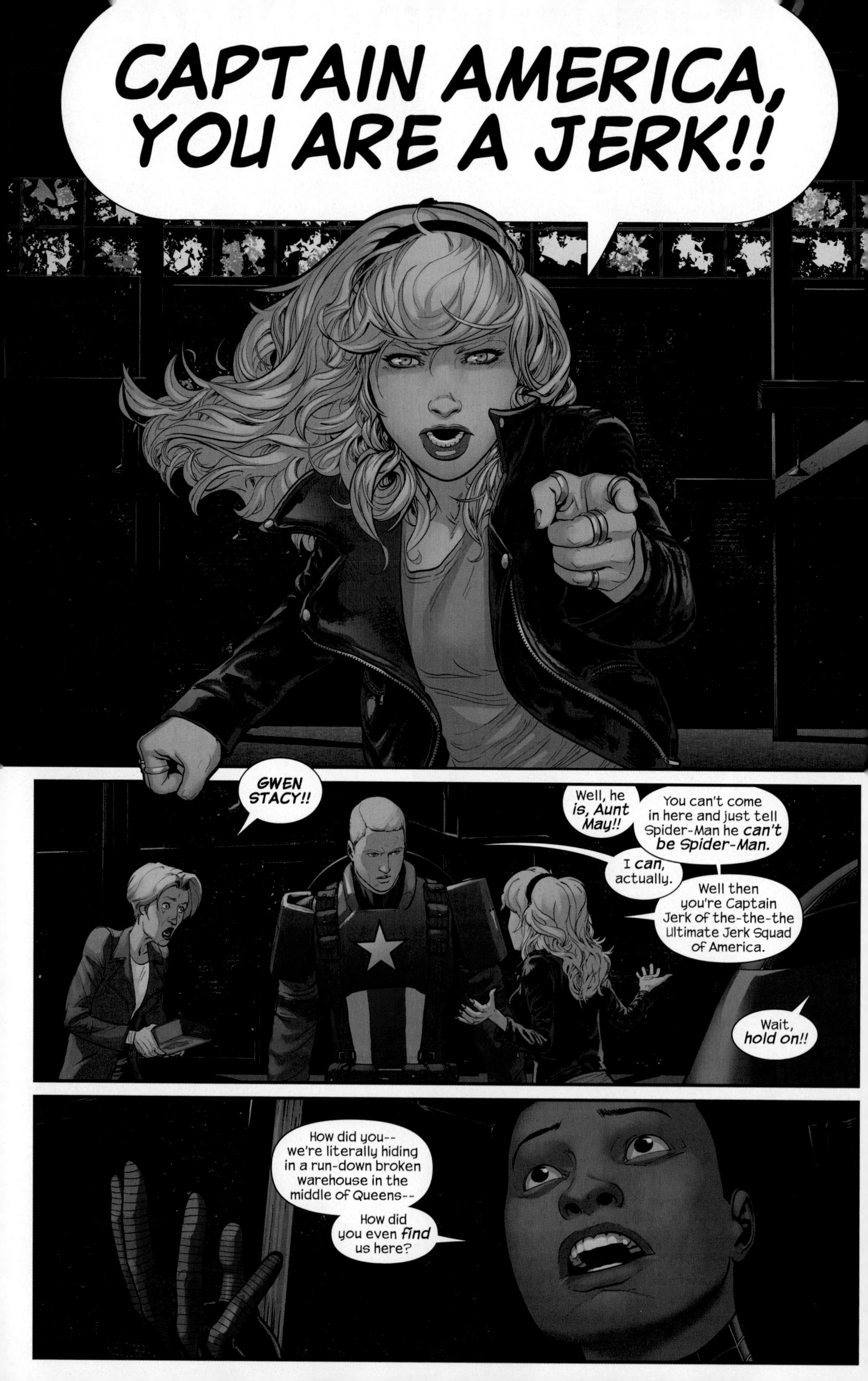
CAPTAIN AMERICA, YOU ARE A JERK!!
GWEN STACY!!
Well, he is, Aunt May!!
You can't come in here and just tell Spider-Man he can't be Spider-Man.
I can, actually.
Well then you're Captain Jerk of the-the-the Ultimate Jerk Squad of America.
Wait, hold on!!
How did you-- we're literally hiding in a run-down broken warehouse in the middle of Queens--
How did you even find us here?

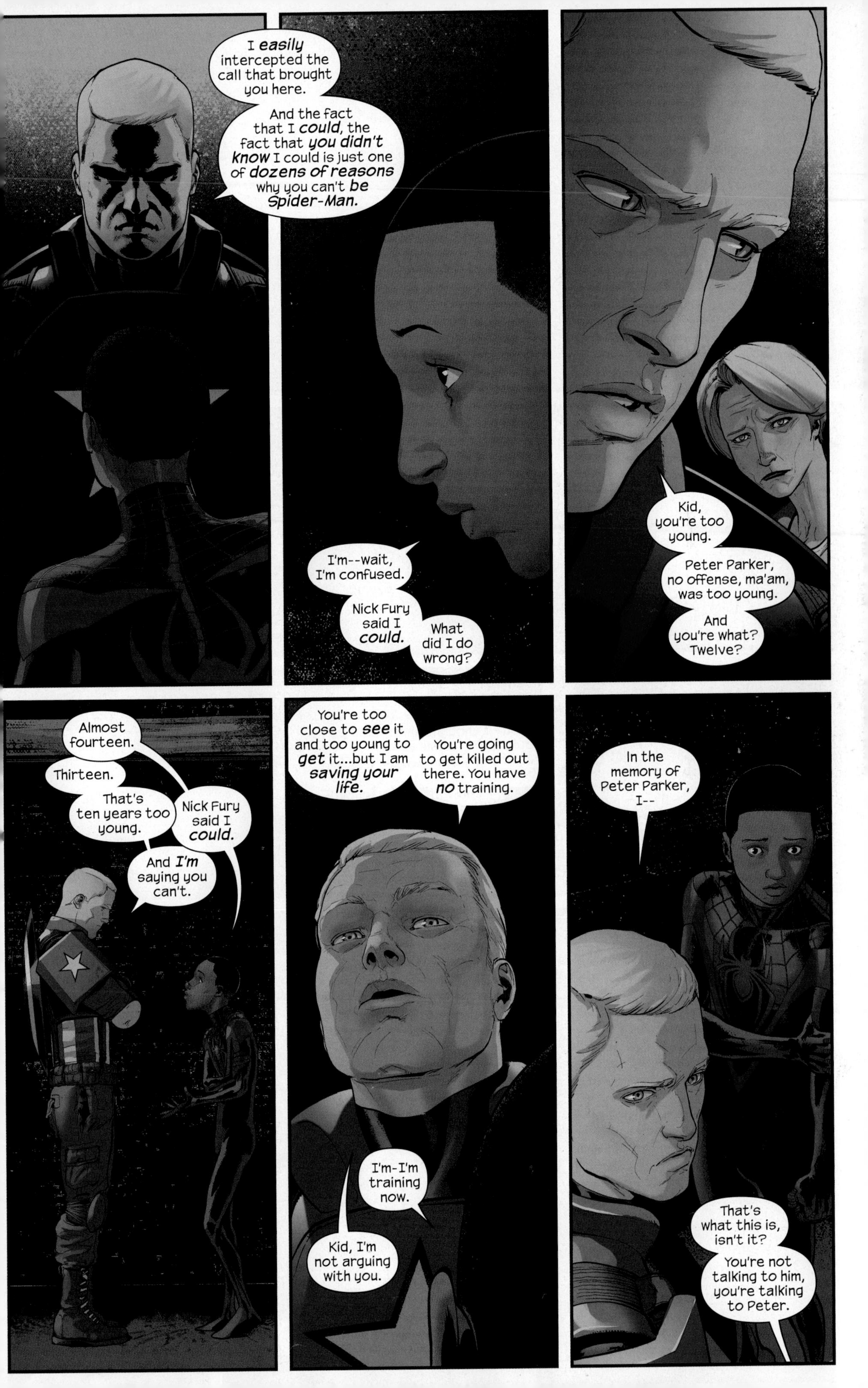
I easily intercepted the call that brought you here.
And the fact that I could, the fact that you didn't know I could is just one of dozens of reasons why you can't be Spider-Man.
I'm--wait, I'm confused.
Nick Fury said I could.
What did I do wrong?
Kid, you're too young.
Peter Parker, no offense, ma'am, was too young.
And you're what? Twelve?
Almost fourteen.
Thirteen.
That's ten years too young.
Nick Fury said I could.
And I'm saying you can't.
You're too close to see it and too young to get it...but I am saving your life.
You're going to get killed out there. You have no training.
I'm-I'm training now.
Kid, I'm not arguing with you.
In the memory of Peter Parker, I--
That's what this is, isn't it?
You're not talking to him, you're talking to Peter.

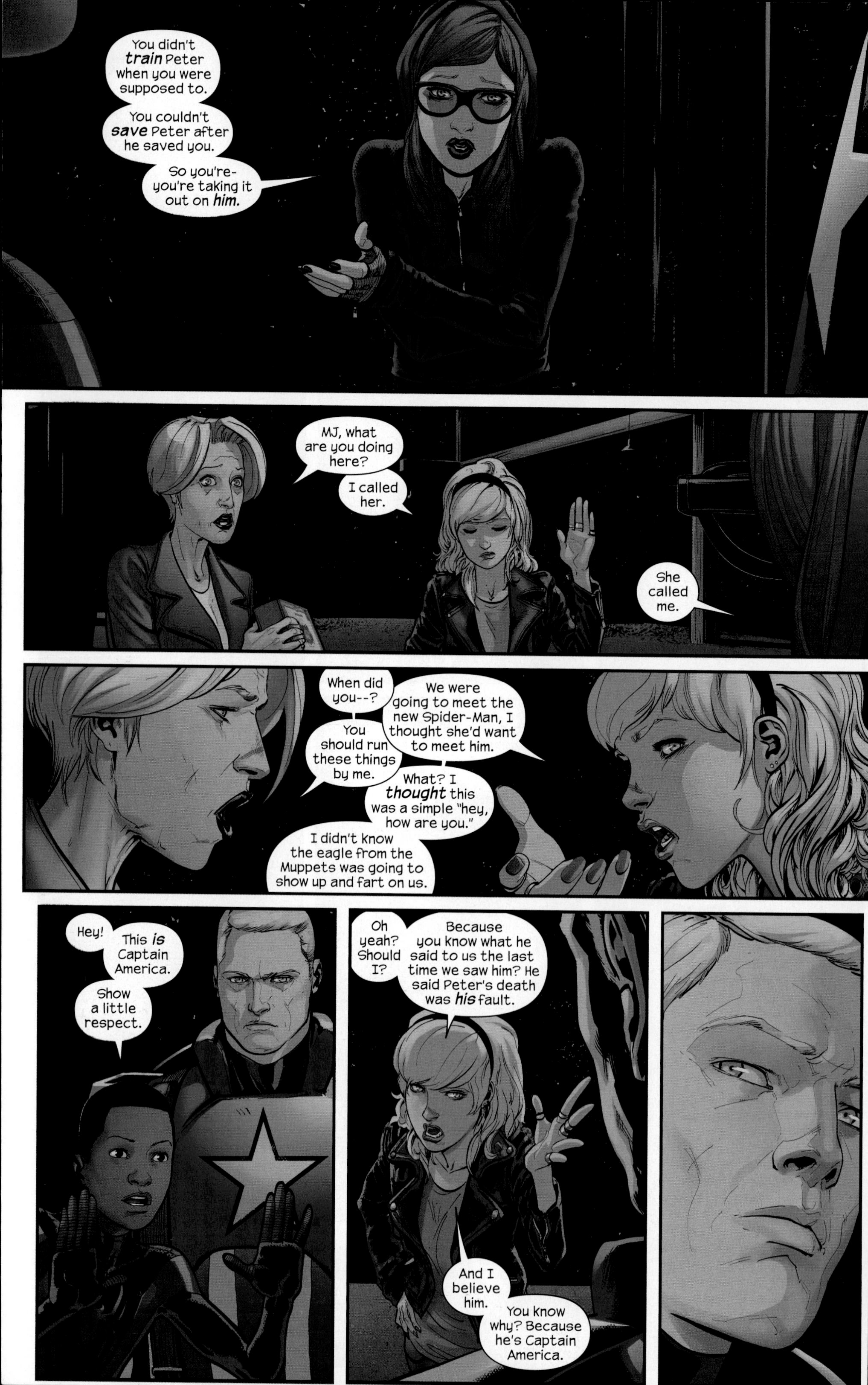

You didn't train Peter when you were supposed to.
You couldn't save Peter after he saved you.
So you're- you're taking it out on him.
MJ, what are you doing here?
I called her.
She called me.
When did you--?
We were going to meet the new Spider-Man, I thought she'd want to meet him.
You should run these things by me.
What? I thought this was a simple "hey, how are you."
I didn't know the eagle from the Muppets was going to show up and fart on us.
Hey!
This is Captain America.
Show a little respect.
Oh yeah? Should I?
Because you know what he said to us the last time we saw him? He said Peter's death was his fault.
And I believe him.
You know why? Because he's Captain America.

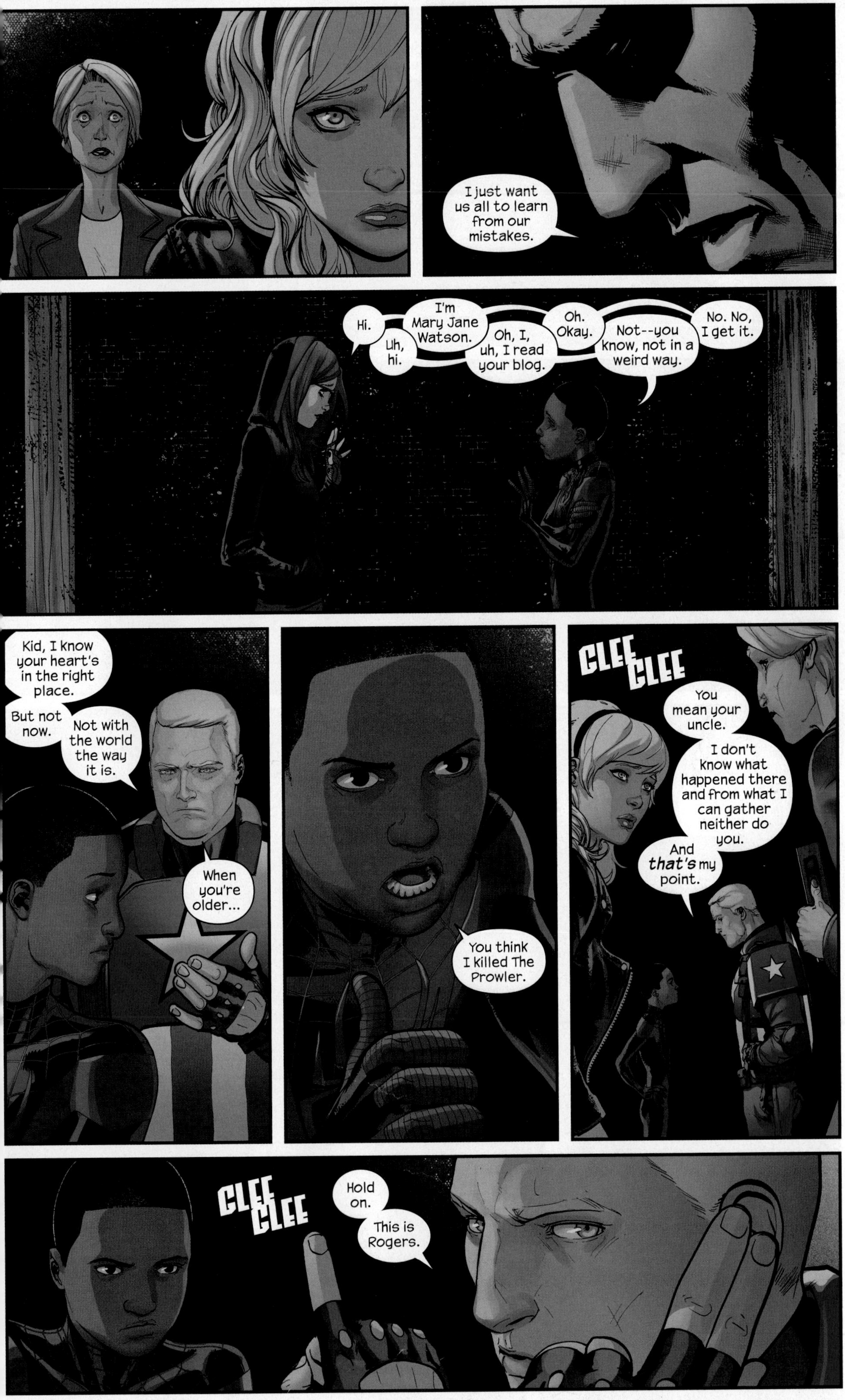
I just want us all to learn from our mistakes.
Hi.
Uh, hi.
I'm Mary Jane Watson.
Oh, I, uh, I read your blog.
Oh. Okay.
Not--you know, not in a weird way.
No. No, I get it.
Kid, I know your heart's in the right place.
But not now.
Not with the world the way it is.
When you're older...
You think I killed The Prowler.
CLEE CLEE
You mean your uncle.
I don't know what happened there and from what I can gather neither do you.
And that's my point.
CLEE CLEE
Hold on.
This is Rogers.

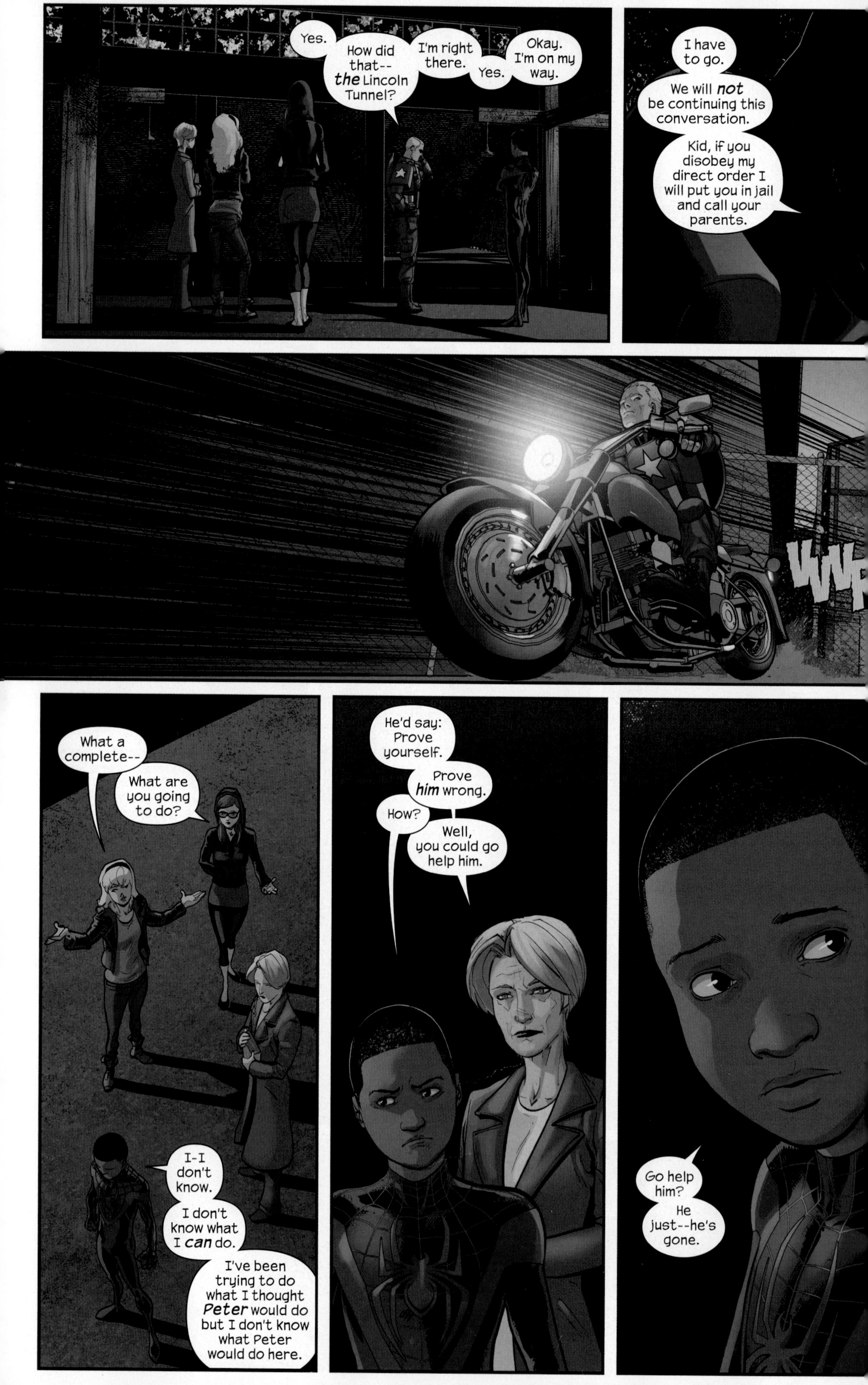
Yes.
How did that-- the Lincoln Tunnel?
I'm right there.
Yes.
Okay. I'm on my way.
I have to go.
We will not be continuing this conversation.
Kid, if you disobey my direct order I will put you in jail and call your parents.
What a complete--
What are you going to do?
I-I don't know.
I don't know what I can do.
I've been trying to do what I thought Peter would do but I don't know what Peter would do here.
He'd say: Prove yourself.
Prove him wrong.
How?
Well, you could go help him.
Go help him?
He just--he's gone.

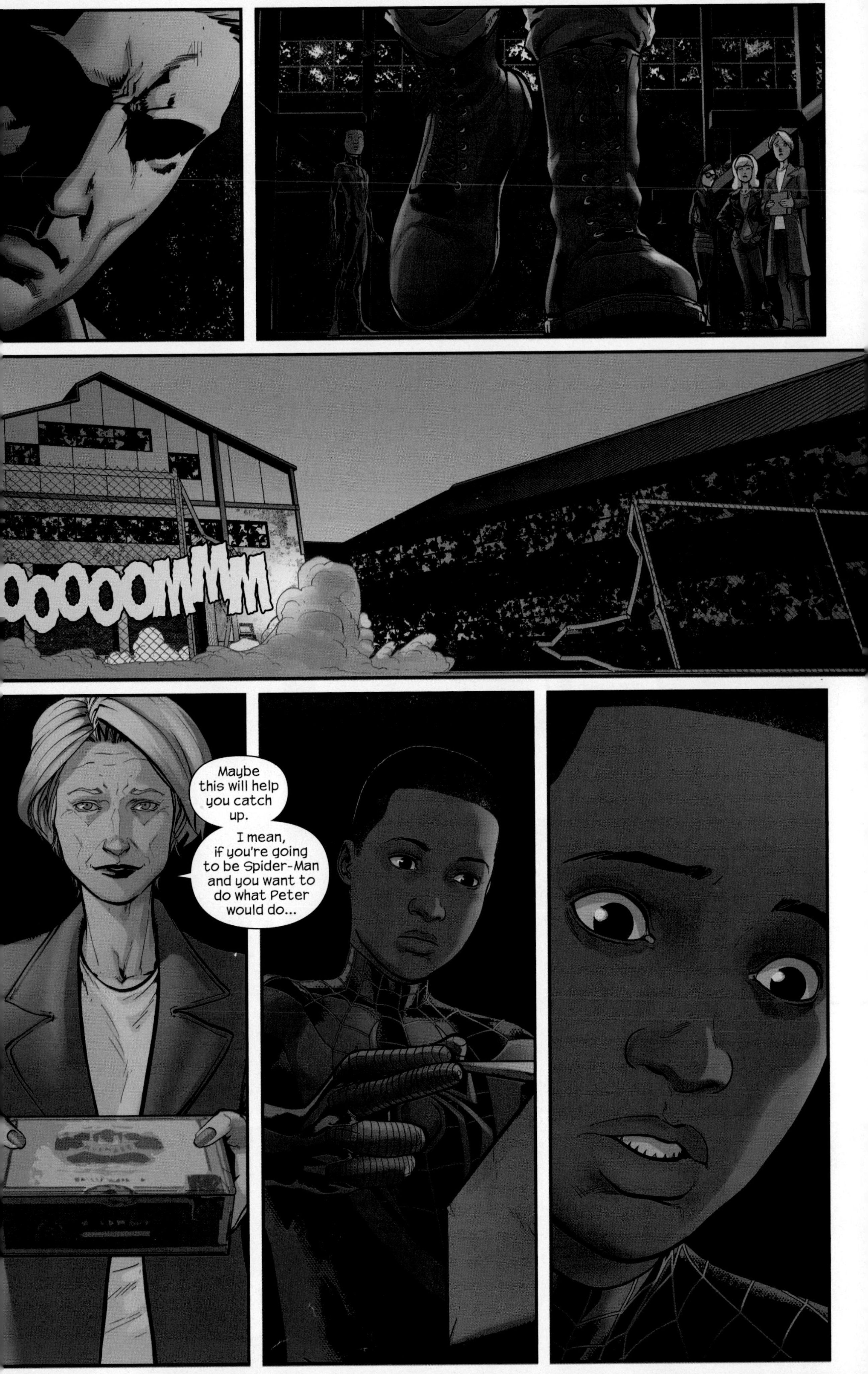

OOOOOOMMMM
Maybe this will help you catch up.
I mean, if you're going to be Spider-Man and you want to do what Peter would do...

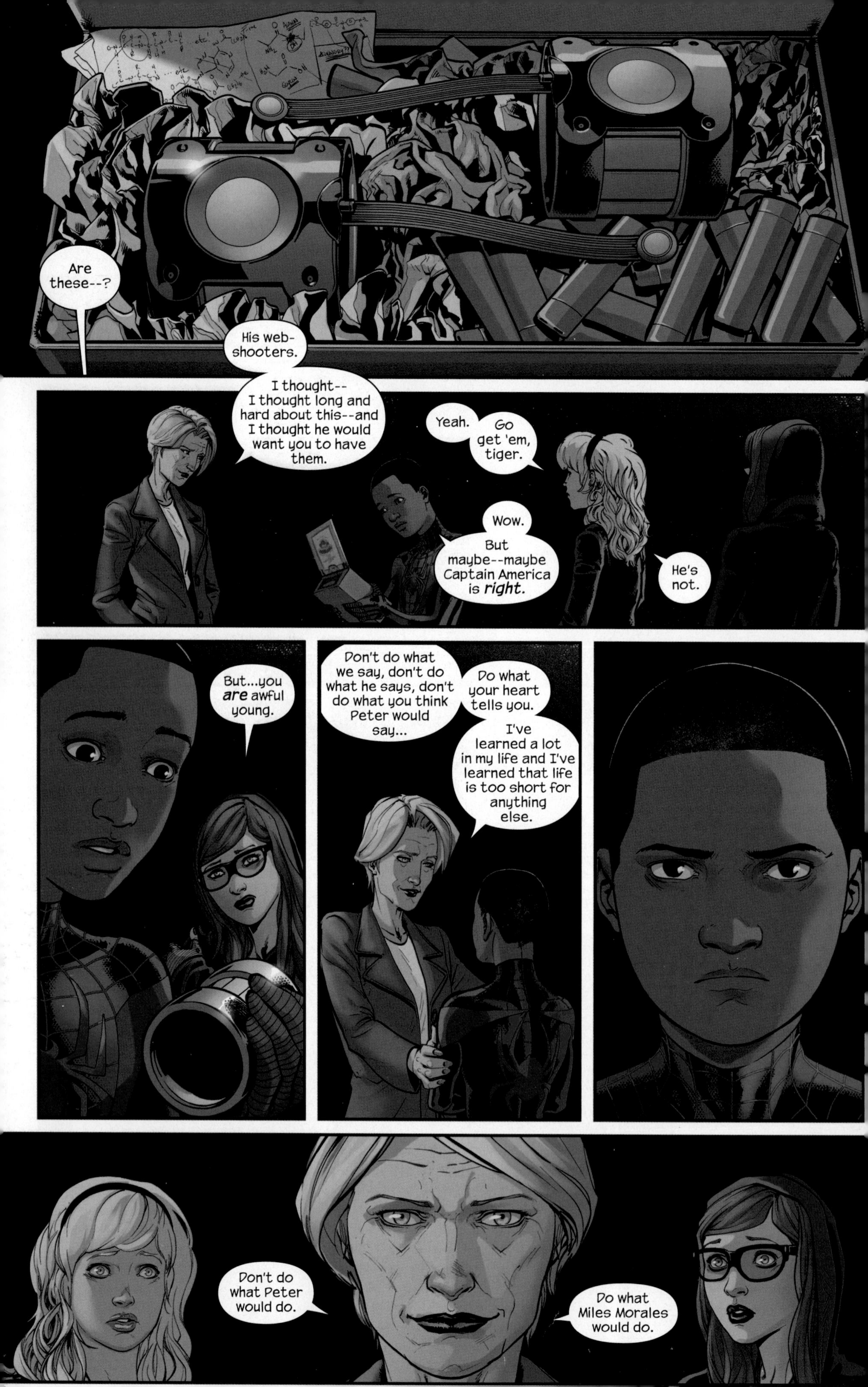
Are these--?
His web-shooters.
I thought--I thought long and hard about this--and I thought he would want you to have them.
Yeah.
Go get 'em, tiger.
Wow.
But maybe--maybe Captain America is *right.*
He's not.
But...you *are* awful young.
Don't do what we say, don't do what he says, don't do what you think Peter would say...
Do what your heart tells you.
I've learned a lot in my life and I've learned that life is too short for anything else.
Don't do what Peter would do.
Do what Miles Morales would do.

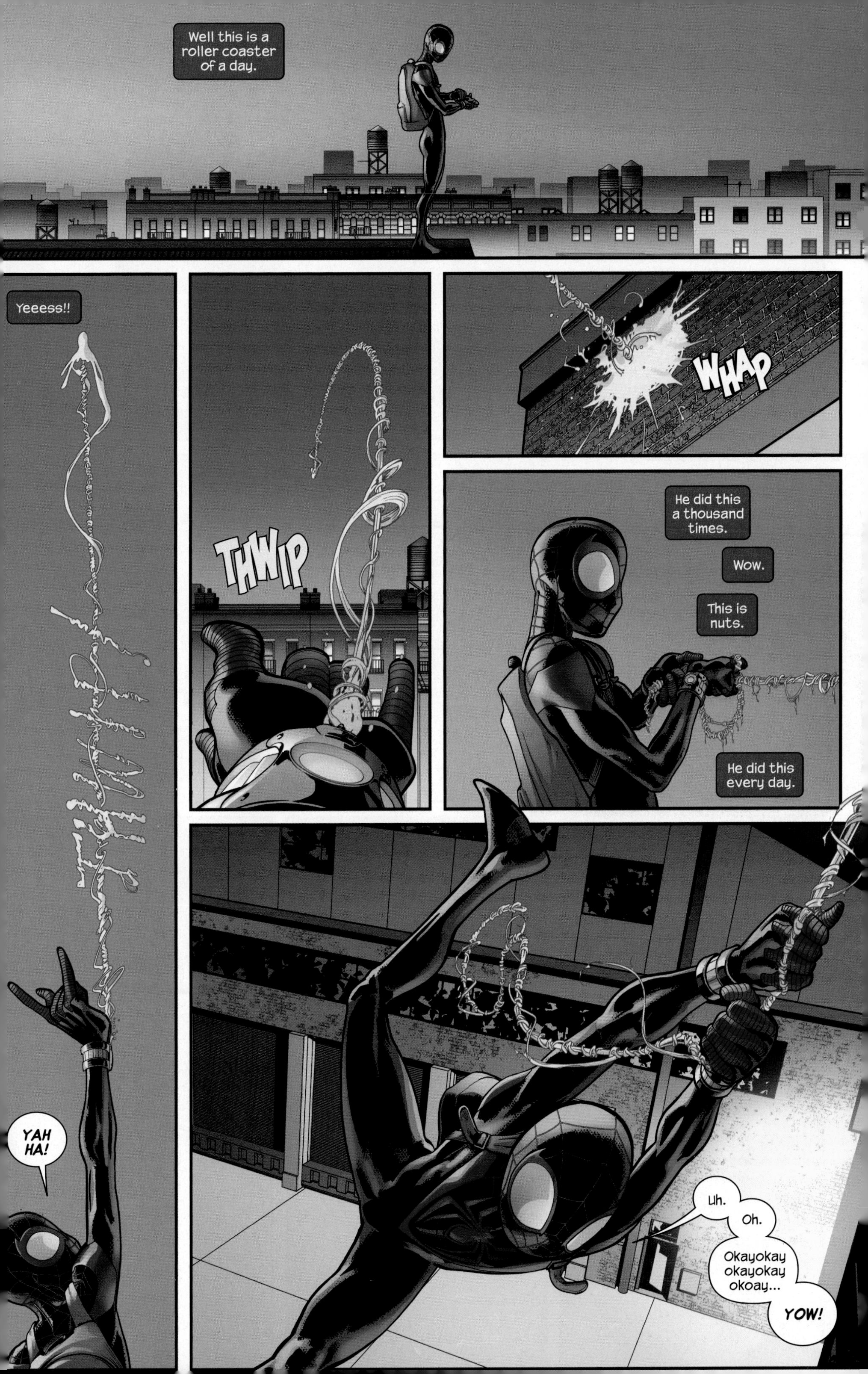

Well this is a roller coaster of a day.
Yeeess!!
THWIP
WHAP
He did this a thousand times.
Wow.
This is nuts.
He did this every day.
YAH HA!
Uh.
Oh.
Okayokay okayokay okoay...
YOW!

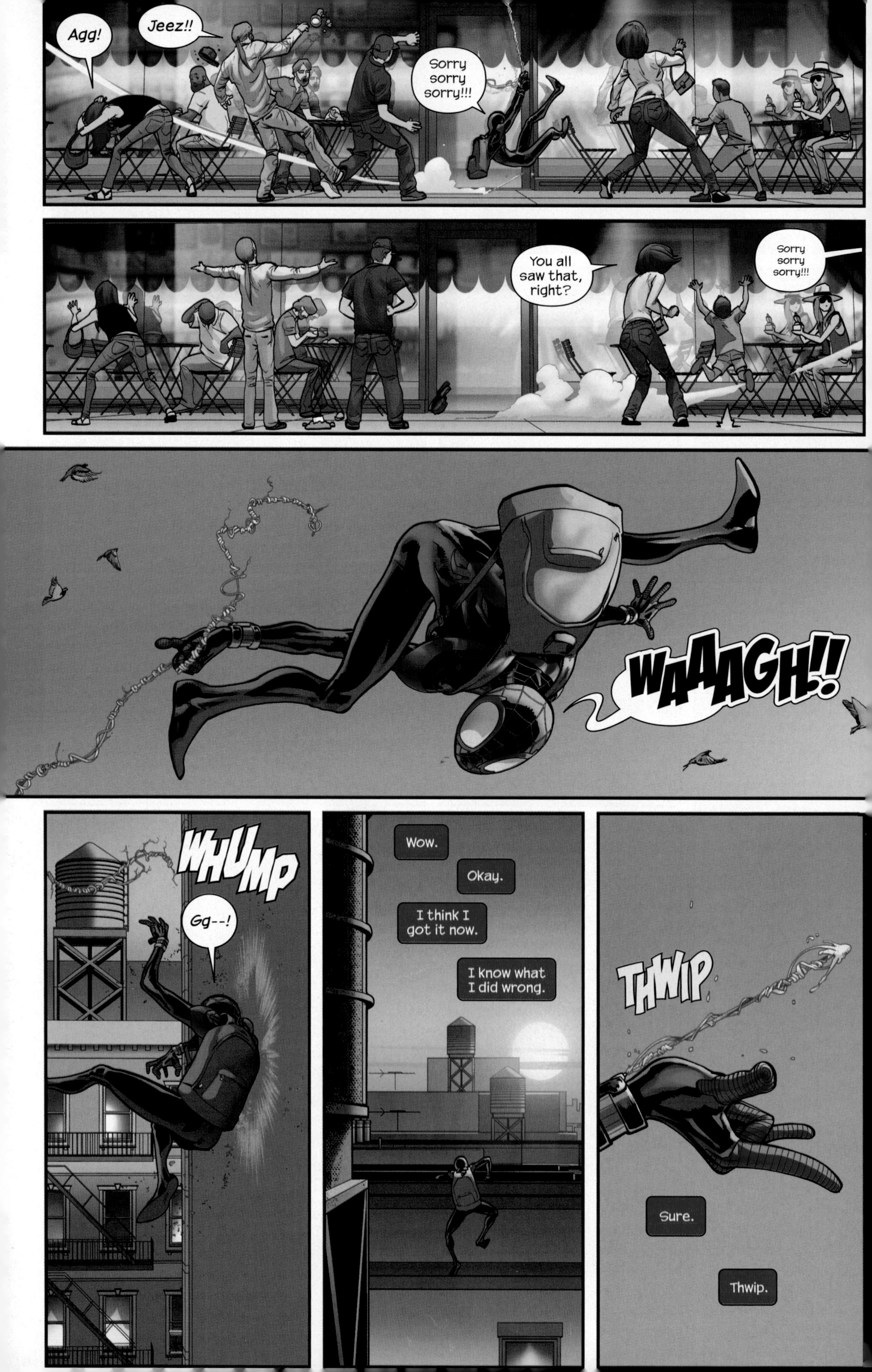

Agg!
Jeez!!
Sorry sorry sorry!!!
You all saw that, right?
Sorry sorry sorry!!!
WAAAGH!!
WHUMP
Gg--!
Wow.
Okay.
I think I got it now.
I know what I did wrong.
THWIP
Sure.
Thwip.

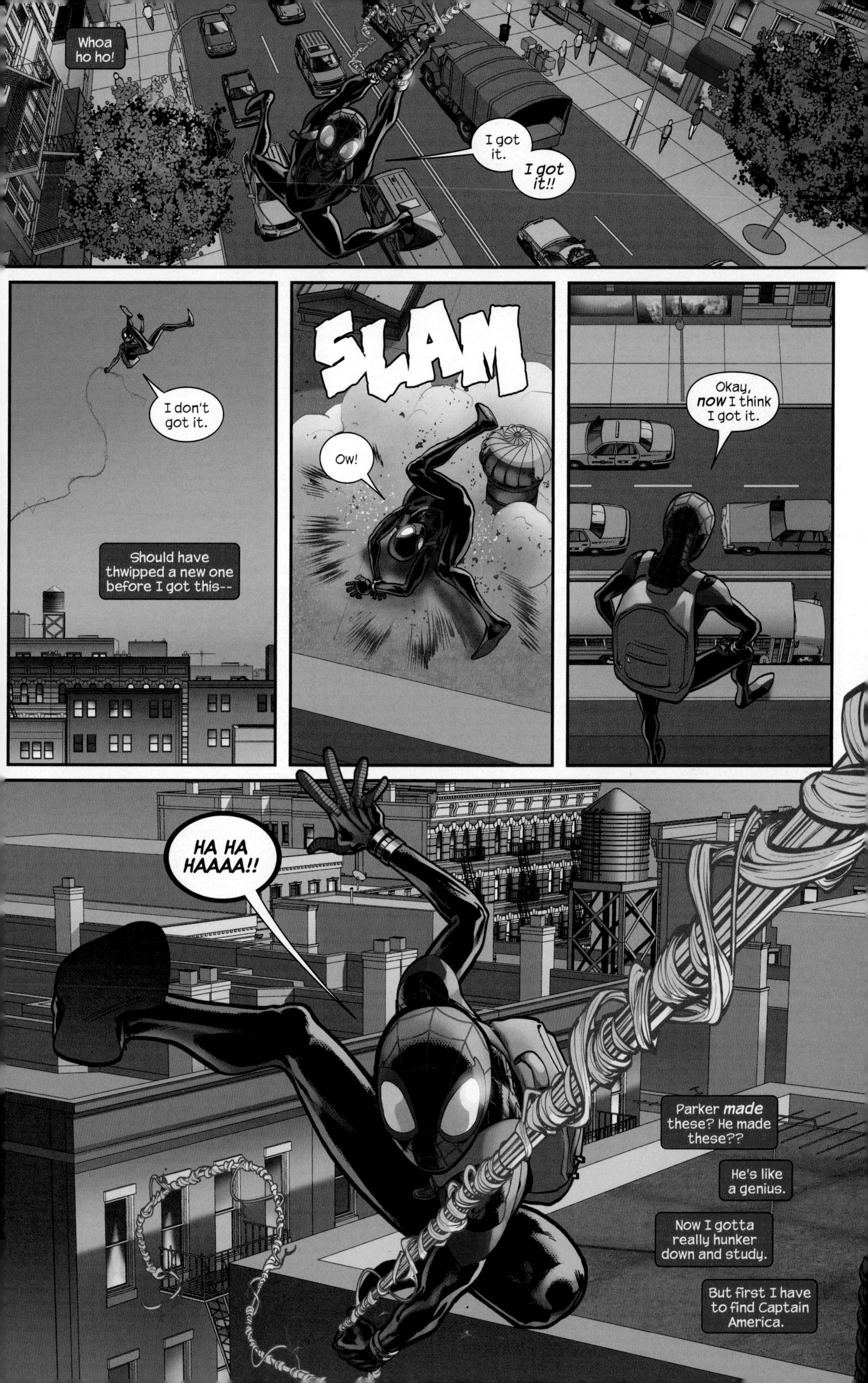
Whoa ho ho!
I got it.
I got it!!
I don't got it.
Should have thwipped a new one before I got this--
SLAM
Ow!
Okay, *now* I think I got it.
HA HA HAAAA!!
Parker *made* these? He made these??
He's like a genius.
Now I gotta really hunker down and study.
But first I have to find Captain America.

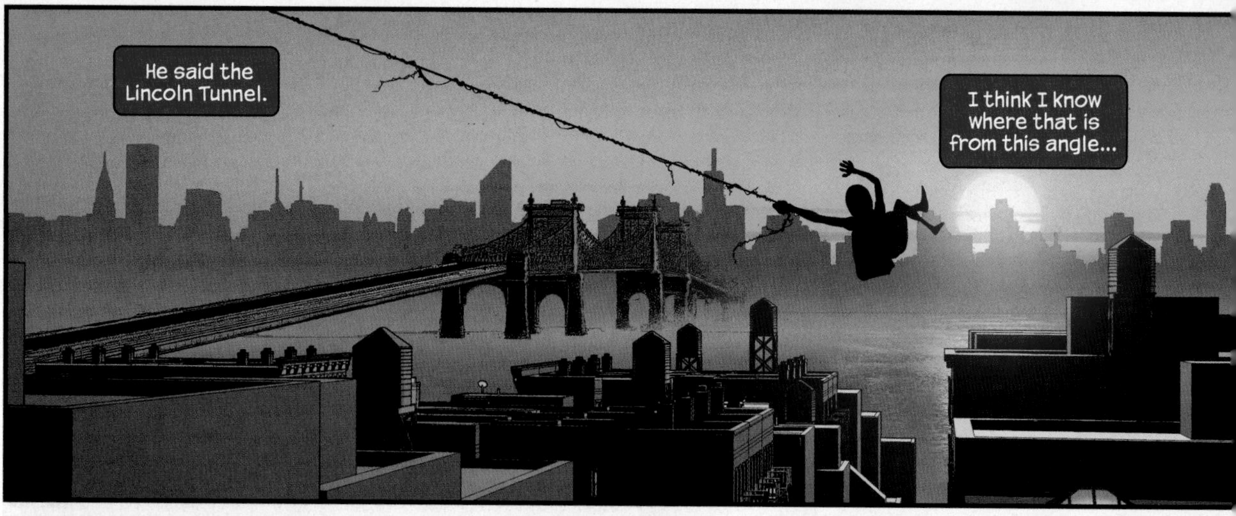
He said the Lincoln Tunnel.
I think I know where that is from this angle...
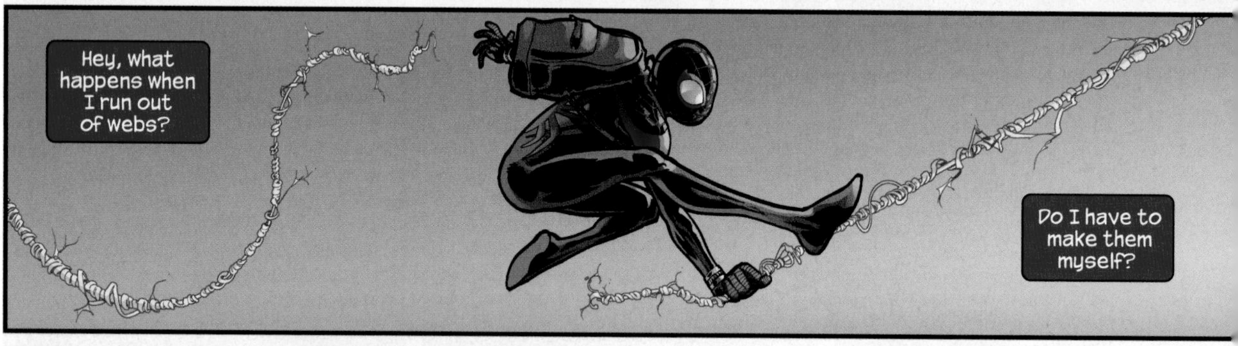
Hey, what happens when I run out of webs?
Do I have to make them myself?
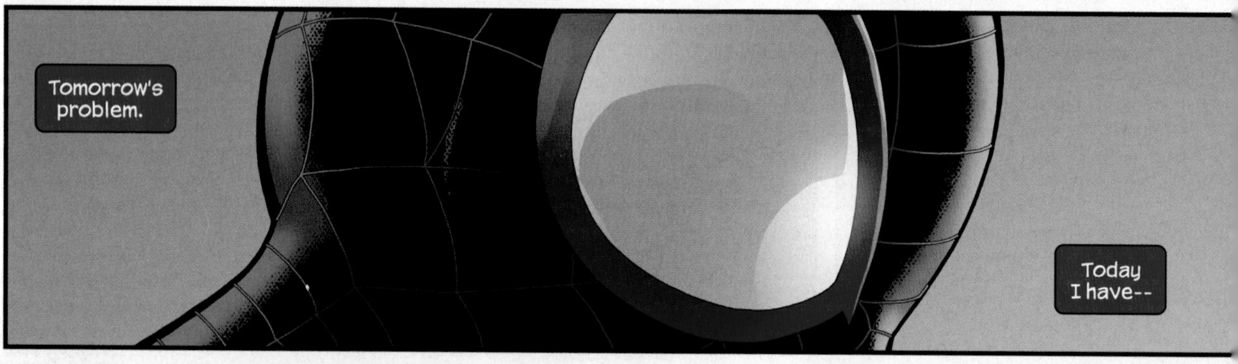
Tomorrow's problem.
Today I have--
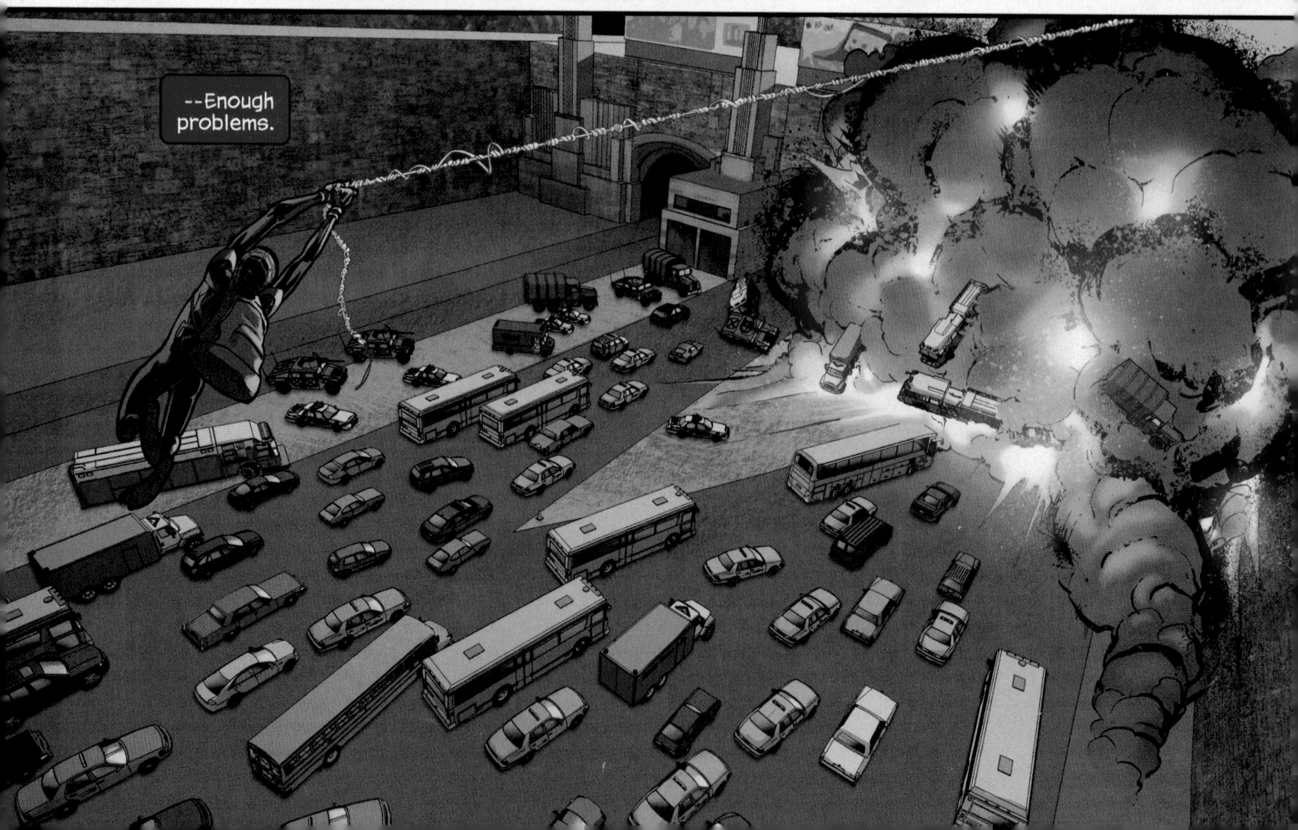
--Enough problems.

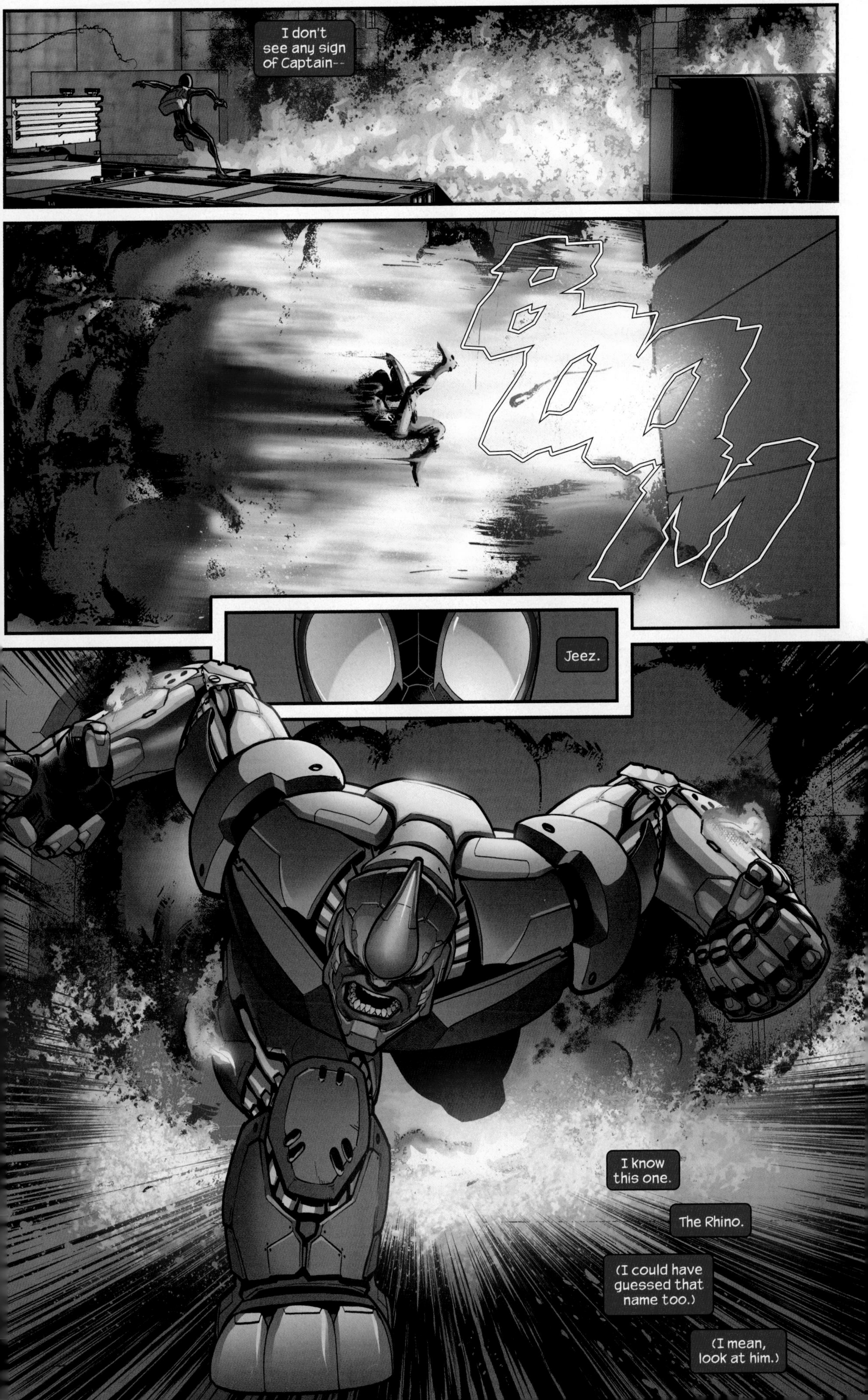
I don't see any sign of Captain--
BAM
Jeez.
I know this one.
The Rhino.
(I could have guessed that name too.)
(I mean, look at him.)

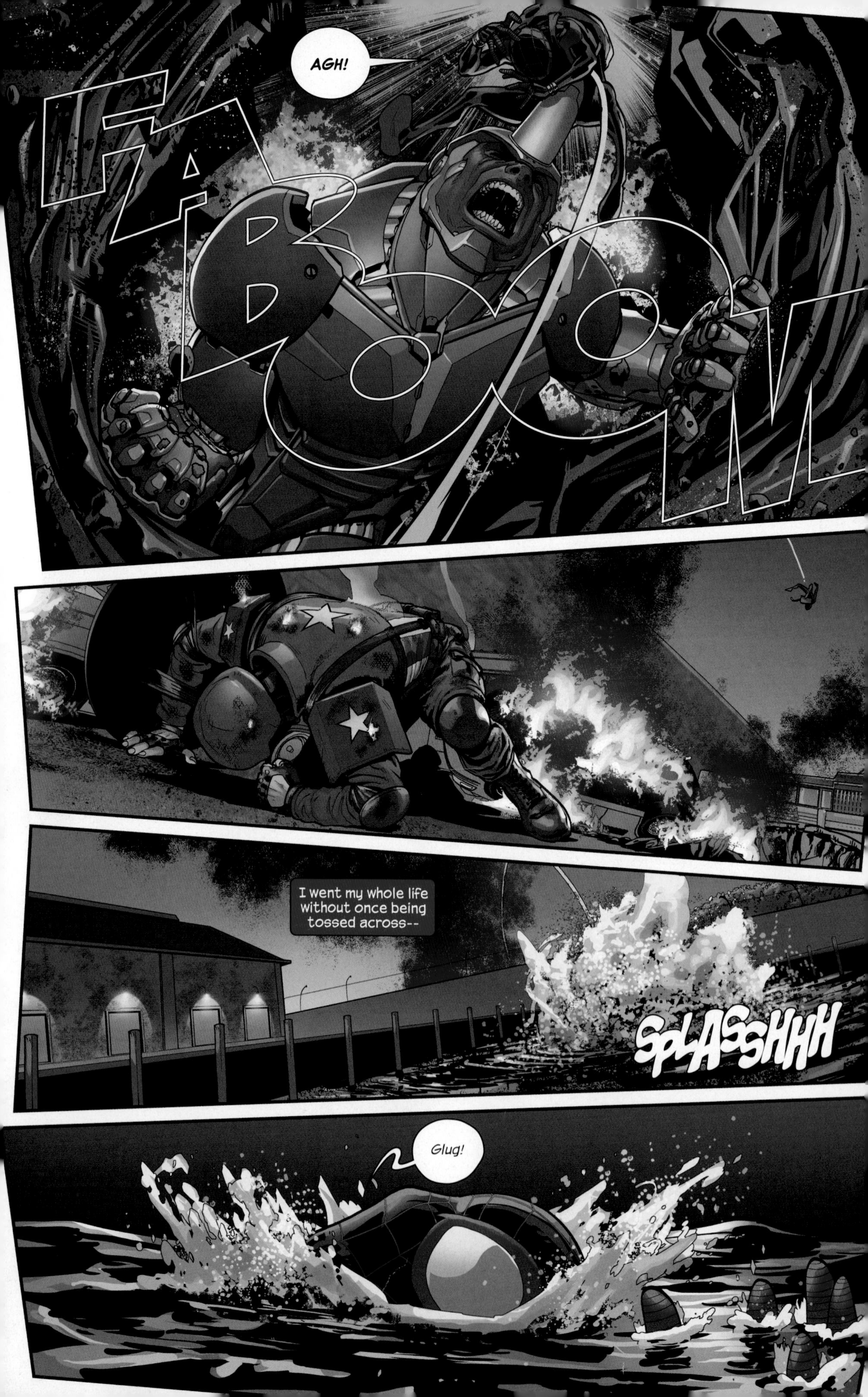
AGH!
FABOOM
I went my whole life without once being tossed across--
SPLASSHHH
Glug!

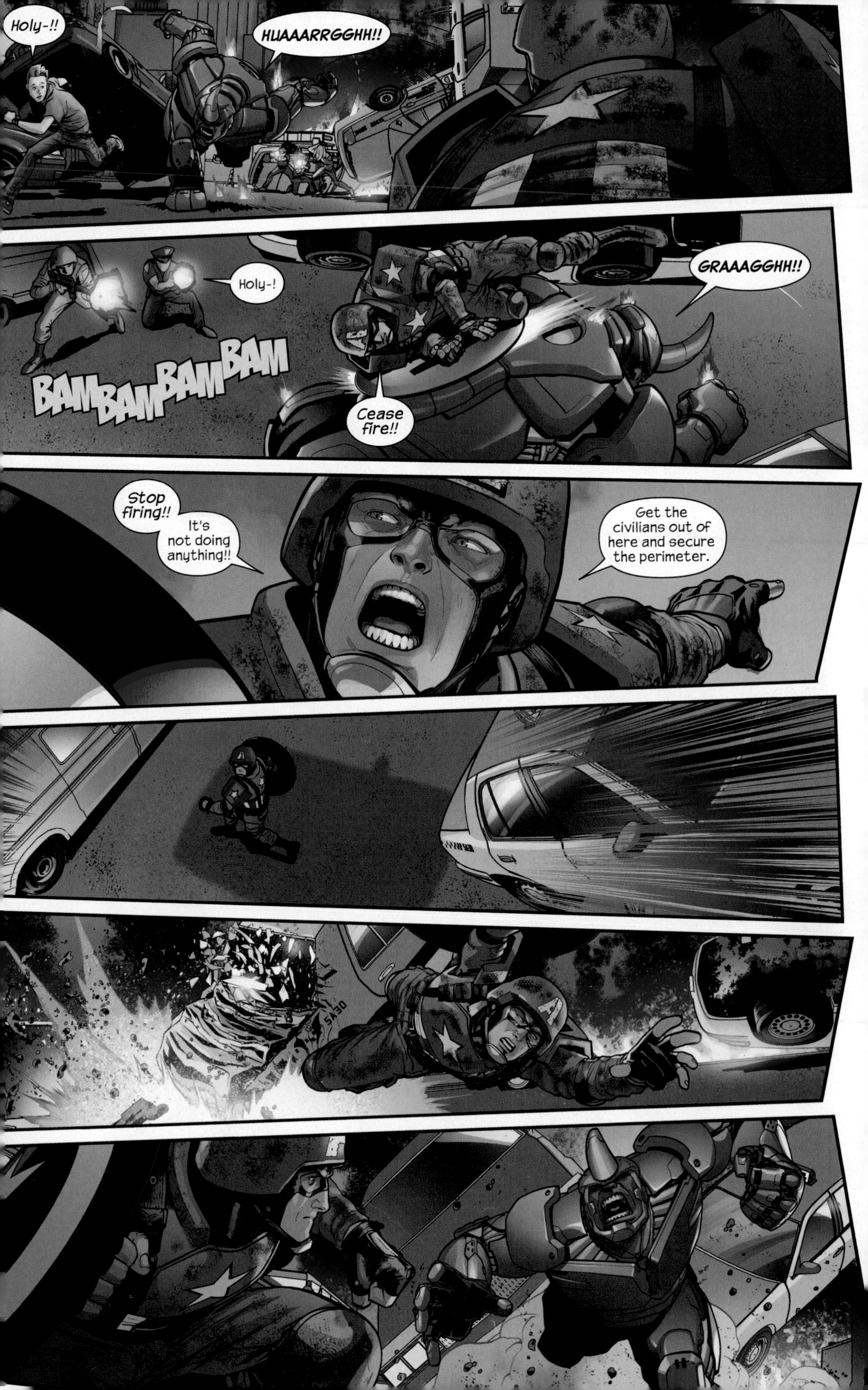

Holy-!!
HUAAARRGGHH!!
Holy-!
GRAAAGGHH!!
BAMBAMBAMBAM
Cease fire!!
Stop firing!!
It's not doing anything!!
Get the civilians out of here and secure the perimeter.

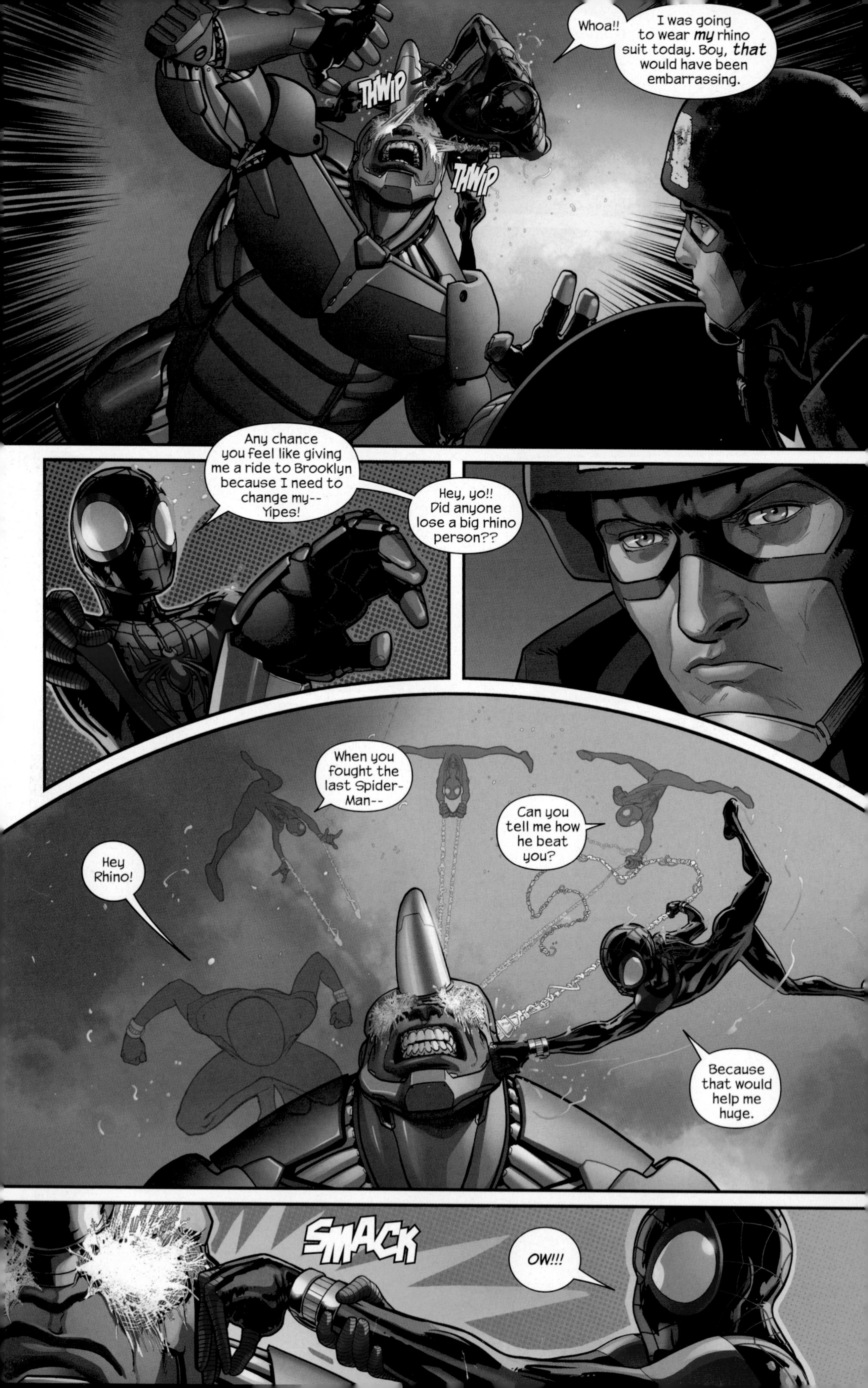
Whoa!!
I was going to wear *my* rhino suit today. Boy, *that* would have been embarrassing.
THWIP
THWIP
Any chance you feel like giving me a ride to Brooklyn because I need to change my-- Yipes!
Hey, yo!! Did anyone lose a big rhino person??
When you fought the last Spider-Man--
Can you tell me how he beat you?
Hey Rhino!
Because that would help me huge.
SMACK
OW!!!

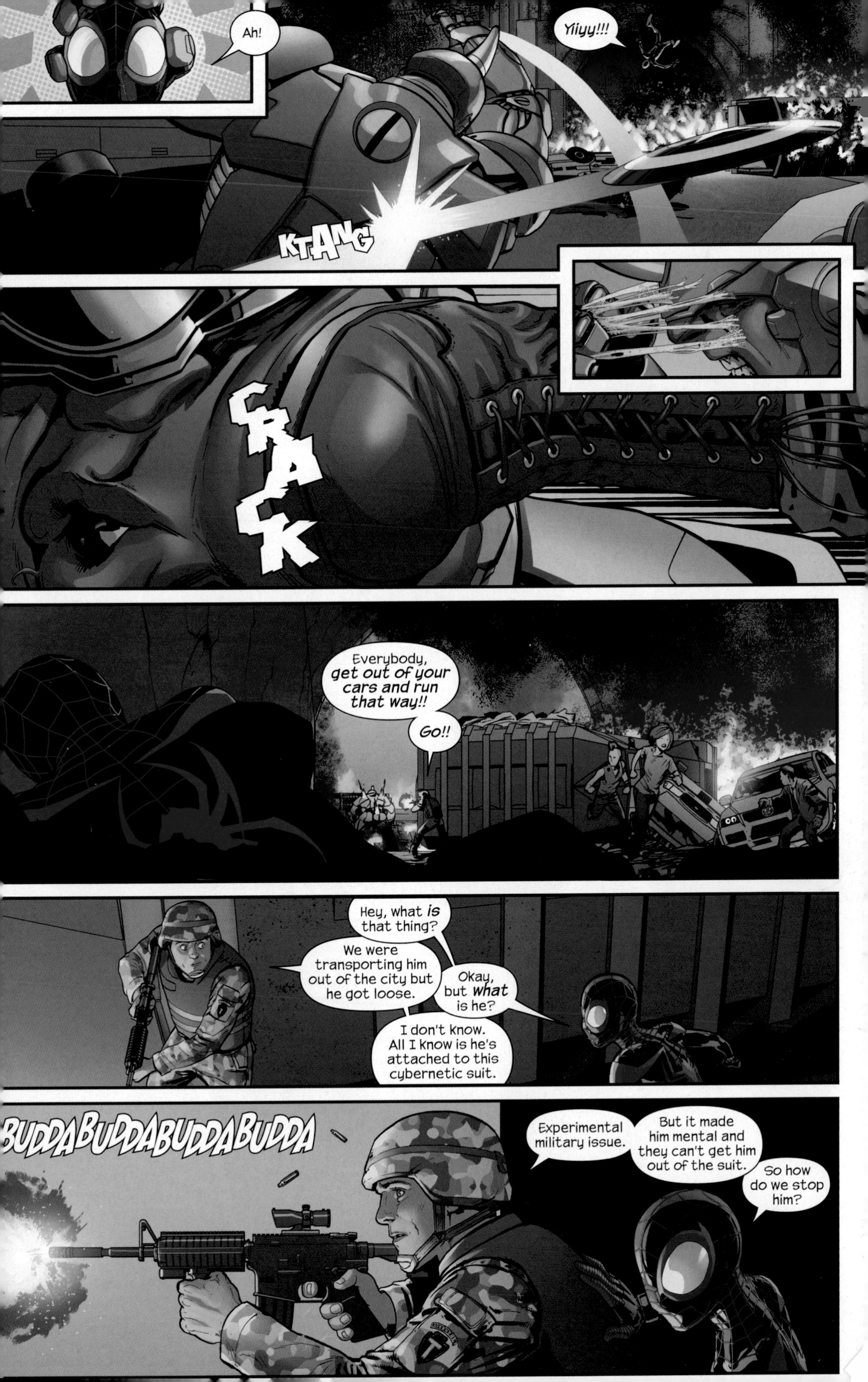
Ah!
Yiiyy!!!
KTANG
CRACK
Everybody, get out of your cars and run that way!!
Go!!
Hey, what is that thing?
We were transporting him out of the city but he got loose.
Okay, but what is he?
I don't know. All I know is he's attached to this cybernetic suit.
BUDDABUDDABUDDABUDDA
Experimental military issue.
But it made him mental and they can't get him out of the suit.
So how do we stop him?

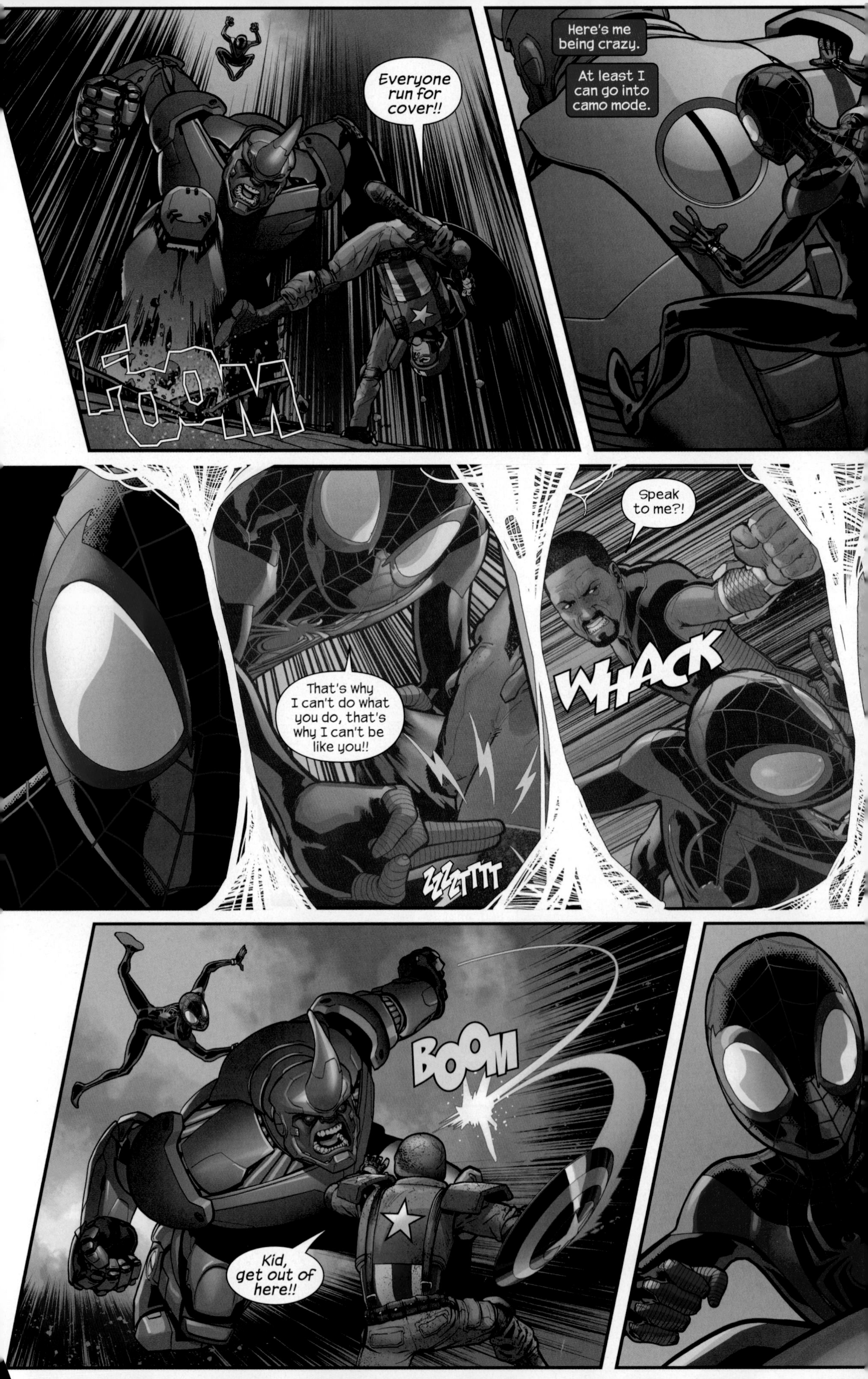
Everyone run for cover!!
FOOM
Here's me being crazy.
At least I can go into camo mode.
That's why I can't do what you do, that's why I can't be like you!!
ZZZZTTTTT
Speak to me?!
WHACK
BOOM
Kid, get out of here!!

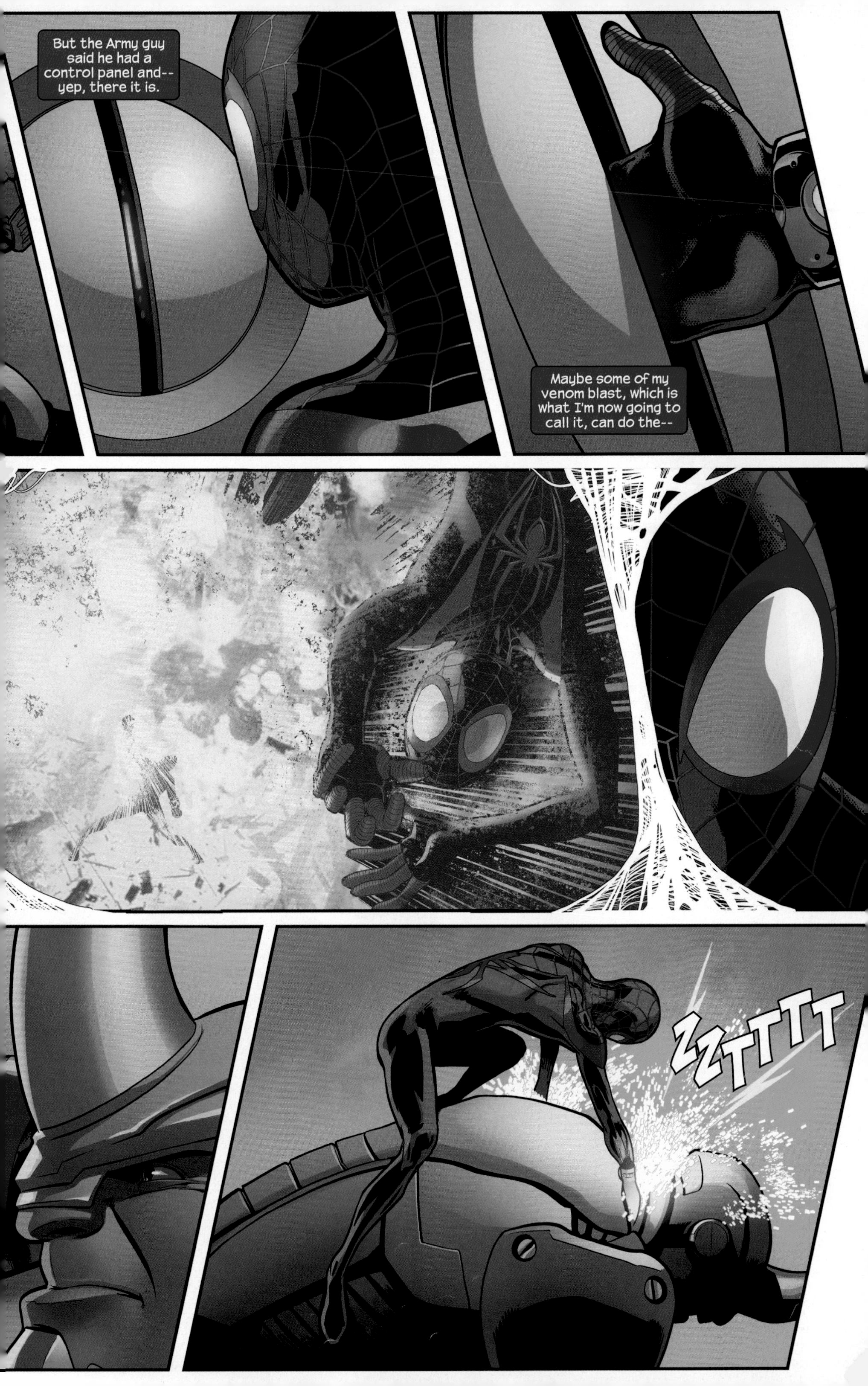
But the Army guy said he had a control panel and-- yep, there it is.
Maybe some of my venom blast, which is what I'm now going to call it, can do the--
ZZTTTTT

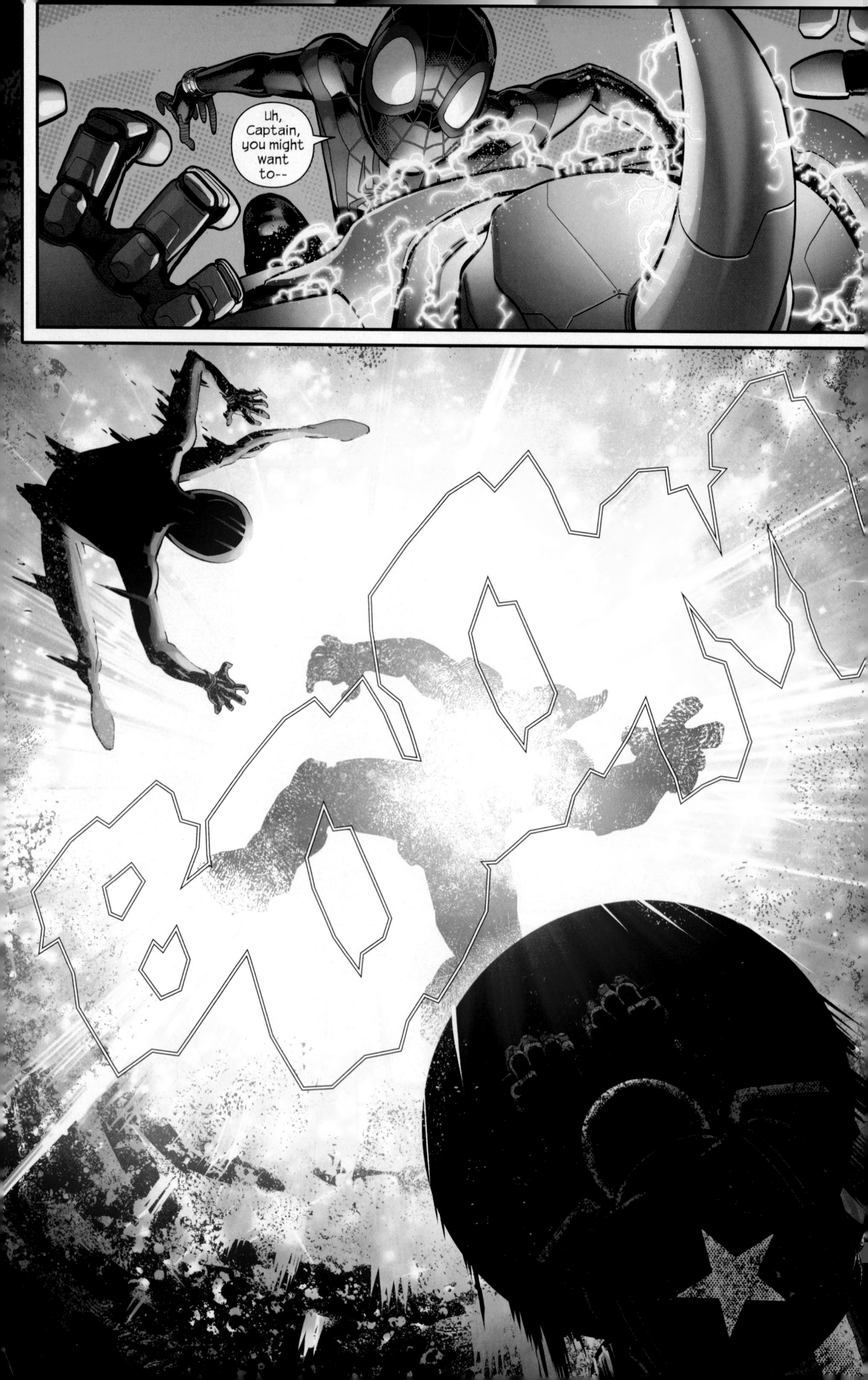
Uh, Captain, you might want to--

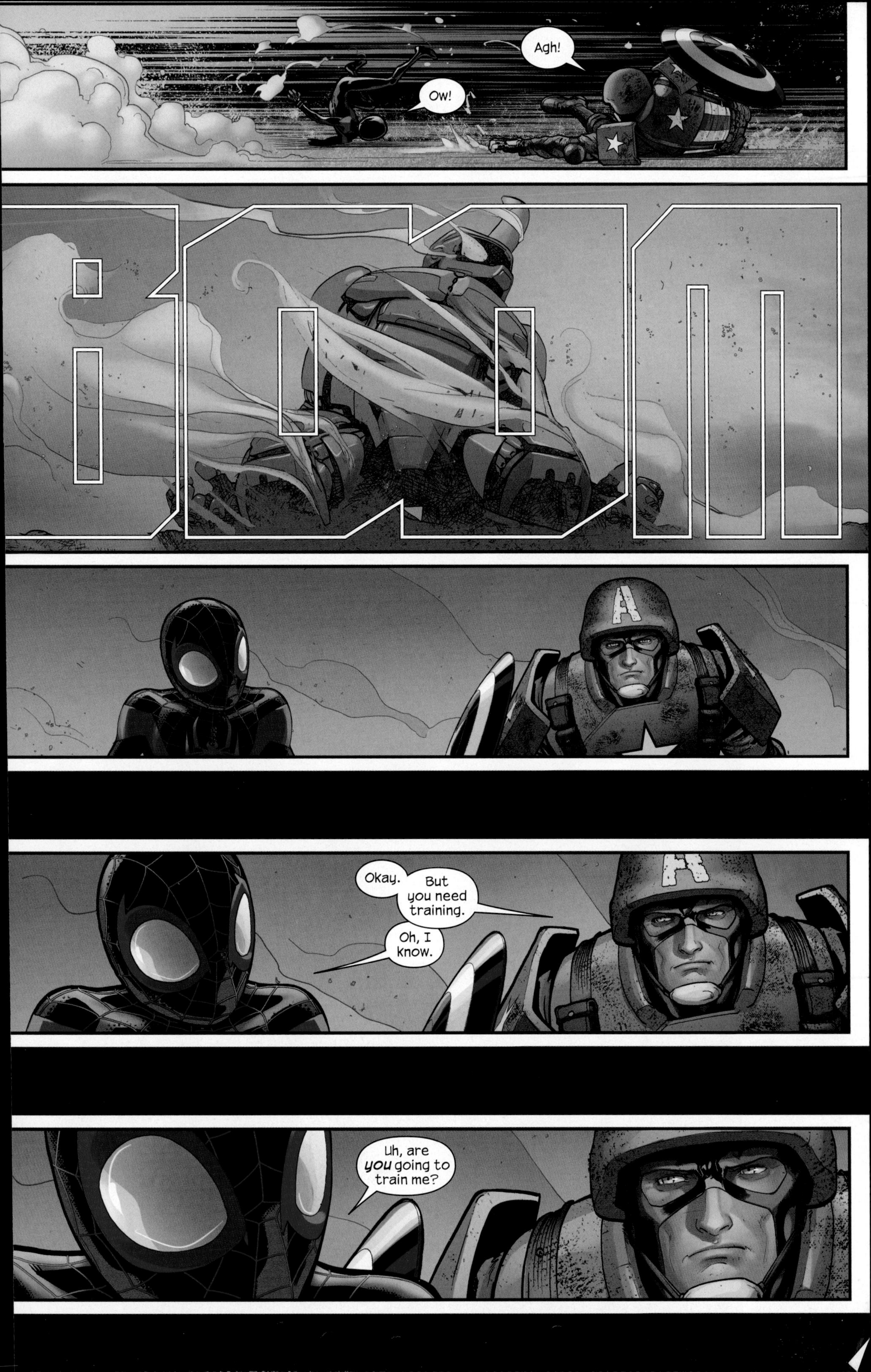
Agh!
Ow!
BOOM
Okay.
But you need training.
Oh, I know.
Uh, are *you* going to train me?

15

★

ULTIMATE COMICS **SPIDER-MAN** #15

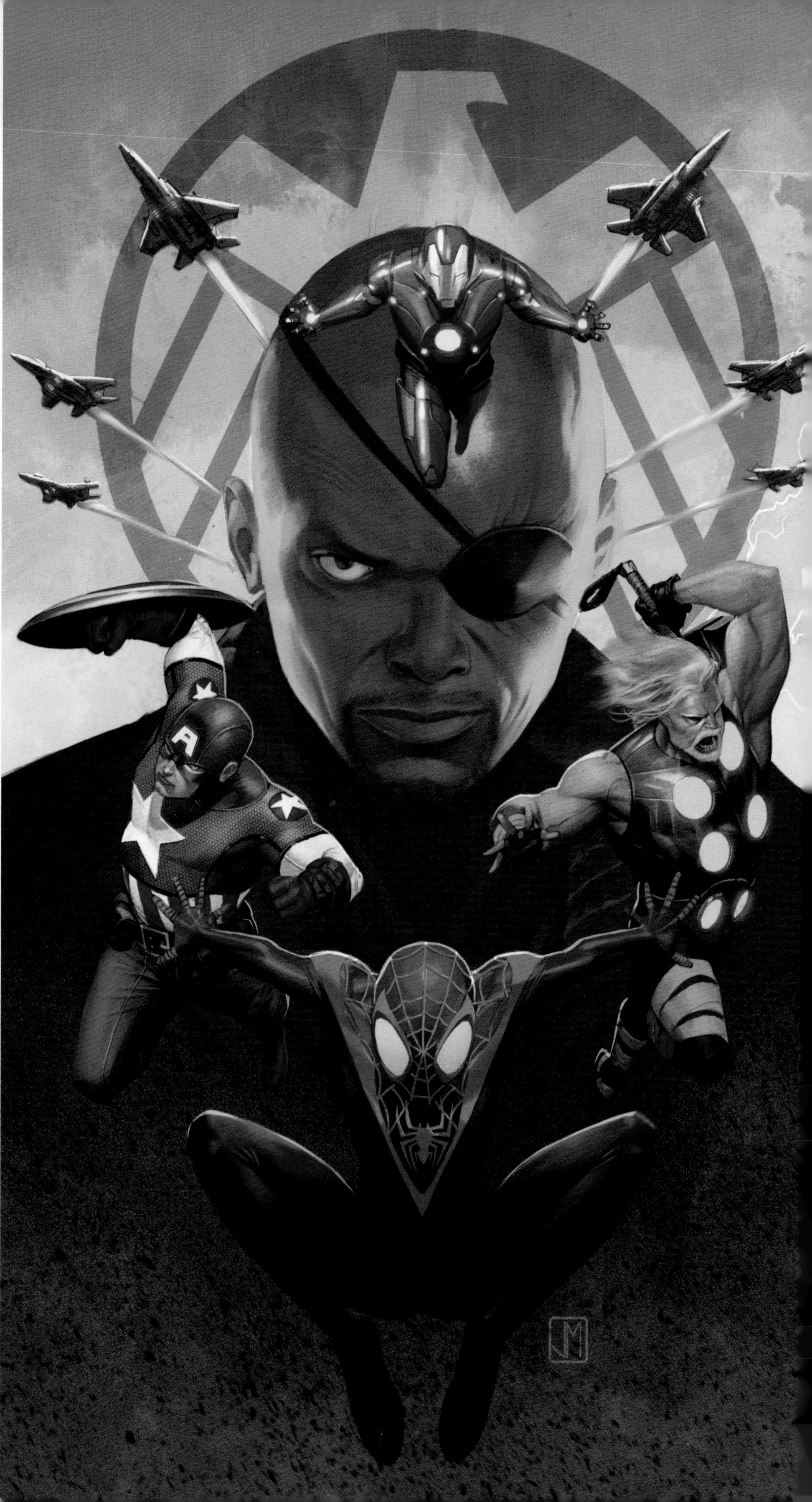

S.H.I.E.L.D. SITUATION MAP:

[Anti-government militia hot spots]

Montana,N.Dakota,
S.Dakota,Wyoming,
Arizona,New Mexico,
N.Carolina,S.Carolina,
Georgia, Idaho

[Eastern seaboard control zone]

New England,
New York,
New Jersey,
Delaware,
Washington D.C.,
Maryland,
Virginia,
Pennsylvania

secured by
National Guard
under emergency
powers
committee

[the West Coast]

California,Oregon,
Washington
status unknown

[Great Lakes states]

Minnesota,
Wisconsin,
Michigan,
Illinois,
Indiana,Ohio
status unknown

ANTI-MATTER
NO FLY
ZONE

AREA OF
URBAN
UNREST

SENTINEL
PUSH

SOUTHERN
CALIFORNIA
REFUGEE ZONE

Classified Position

Camp Hutton, secure
location of the President
of the United States

[Sentinel-controlled no-man's-land]

New Mexico,Arizona,
Utah,Oklahoma
abandoned by the
U.S. government

ALL STATES
SHOWN IN WHITE
ARE U.S. GOVERNMENT-
CONTROLLED ZONES

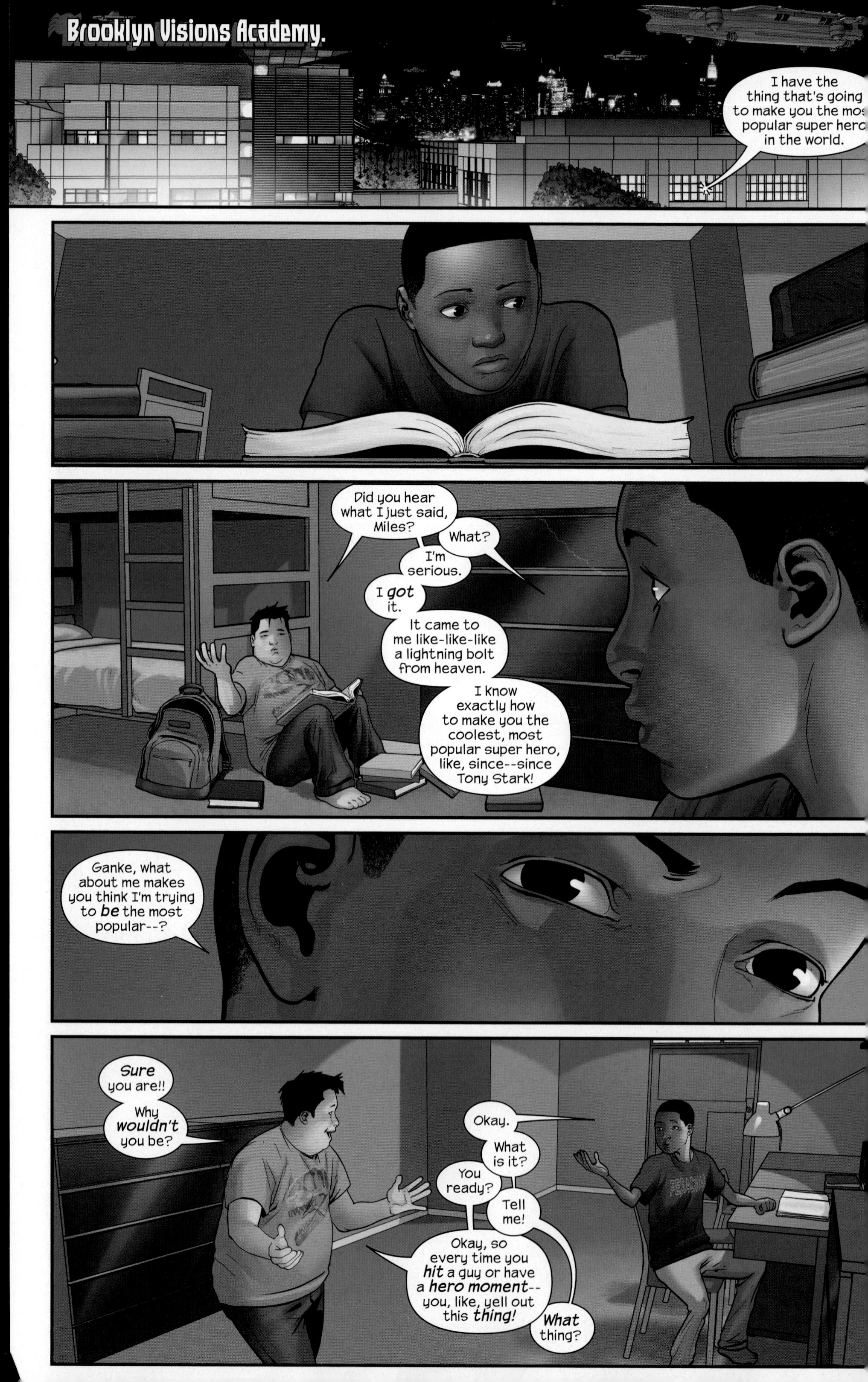
Brooklyn Visions Academy.
I have the thing that's going to make you the mos popular super herc in the world.
Did you hear what I just said, Miles?
What?
I'm serious.
I got it.
It came to me like-like-like a lightning bolt from heaven.
I know exactly how to make you the coolest, most popular super hero, like, since--since Tony Stark!
Ganke, what about me makes you think I'm trying to be the most popular--?
Sure you are!!
Why wouldn't you be?
Okay.
What is it?
You ready?
Tell me!
Okay, so every time you hit a guy or have a hero moment-- you, like, yell out this thing!
What thing?

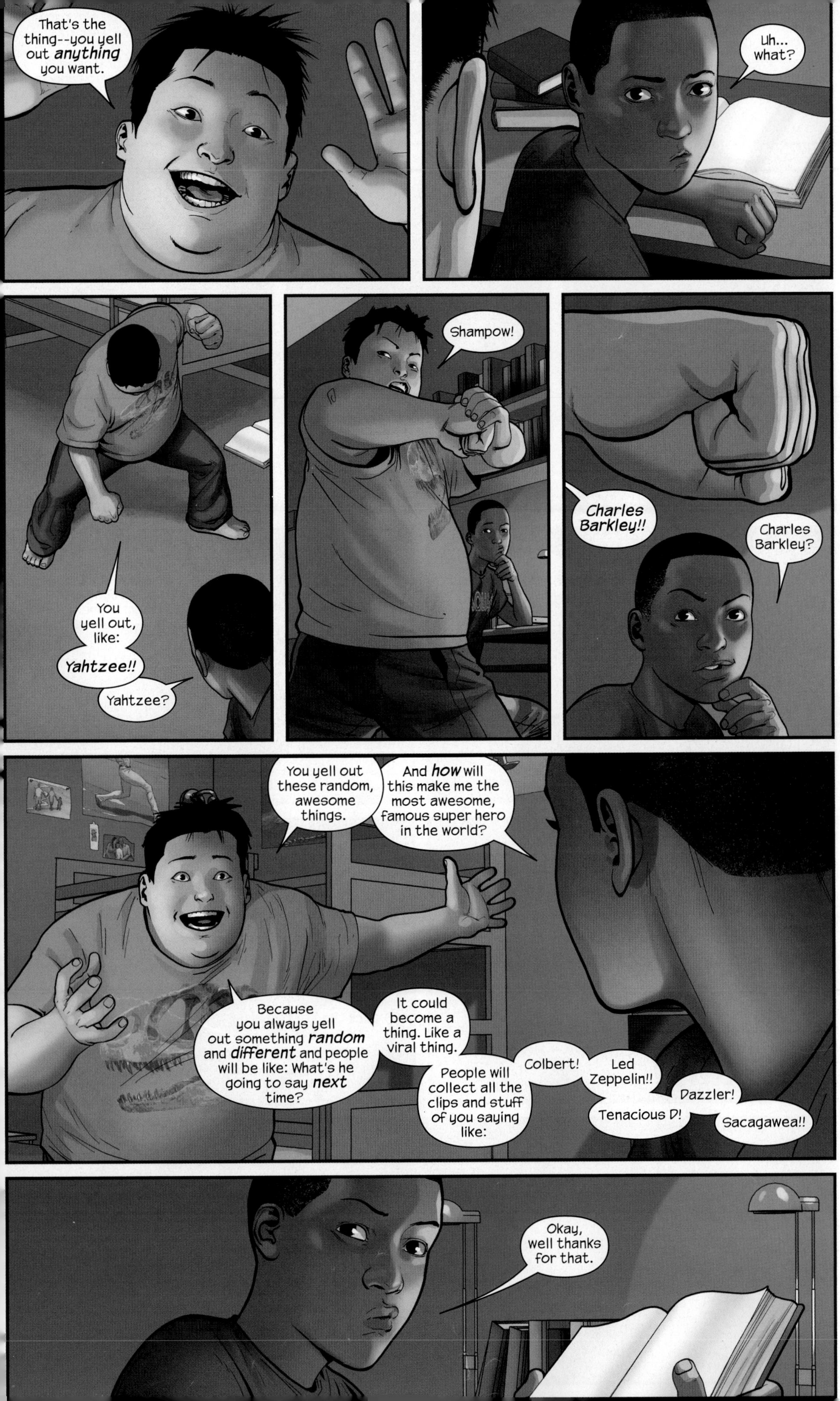
That's the thing--you yell out *anything* you want.
Uh... what?
You yell out, like:
Yahtzee!!
Yahtzee?
Shampow!
Charles Barkley!!
Charles Barkley?
You yell out these random, awesome things.
And *how* will this make me the most awesome, famous super hero in the world?
Because you always yell out something *random* and *different* and people will be like: What's he going to say *next* time?
It could become a thing. Like a viral thing.
People will collect all the clips and stuff of you saying like:
Colbert!
Led Zeppelin!!
Tenacious D!
Dazzler!
Sacagawea!!
Okay, well thanks for that.

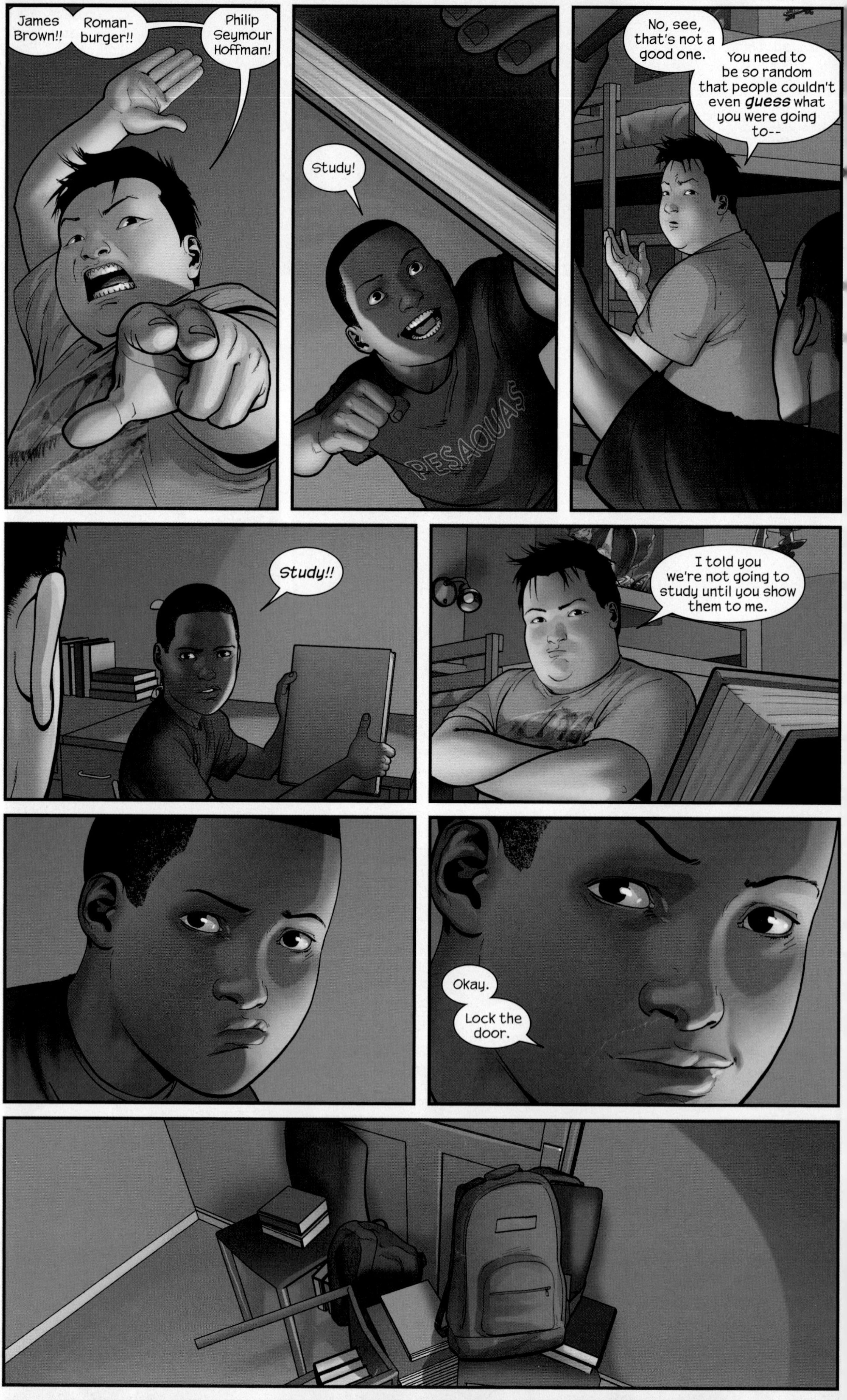

James Brown!!
Roman-burger!!
Philip Seymour Hoffman!
Study!
No, see, that's not a good one.
You need to be so random that people couldn't even *guess* what you were going to--
Study!!
I told you we're not going to study until you show them to me.
Okay.
Lock the door.

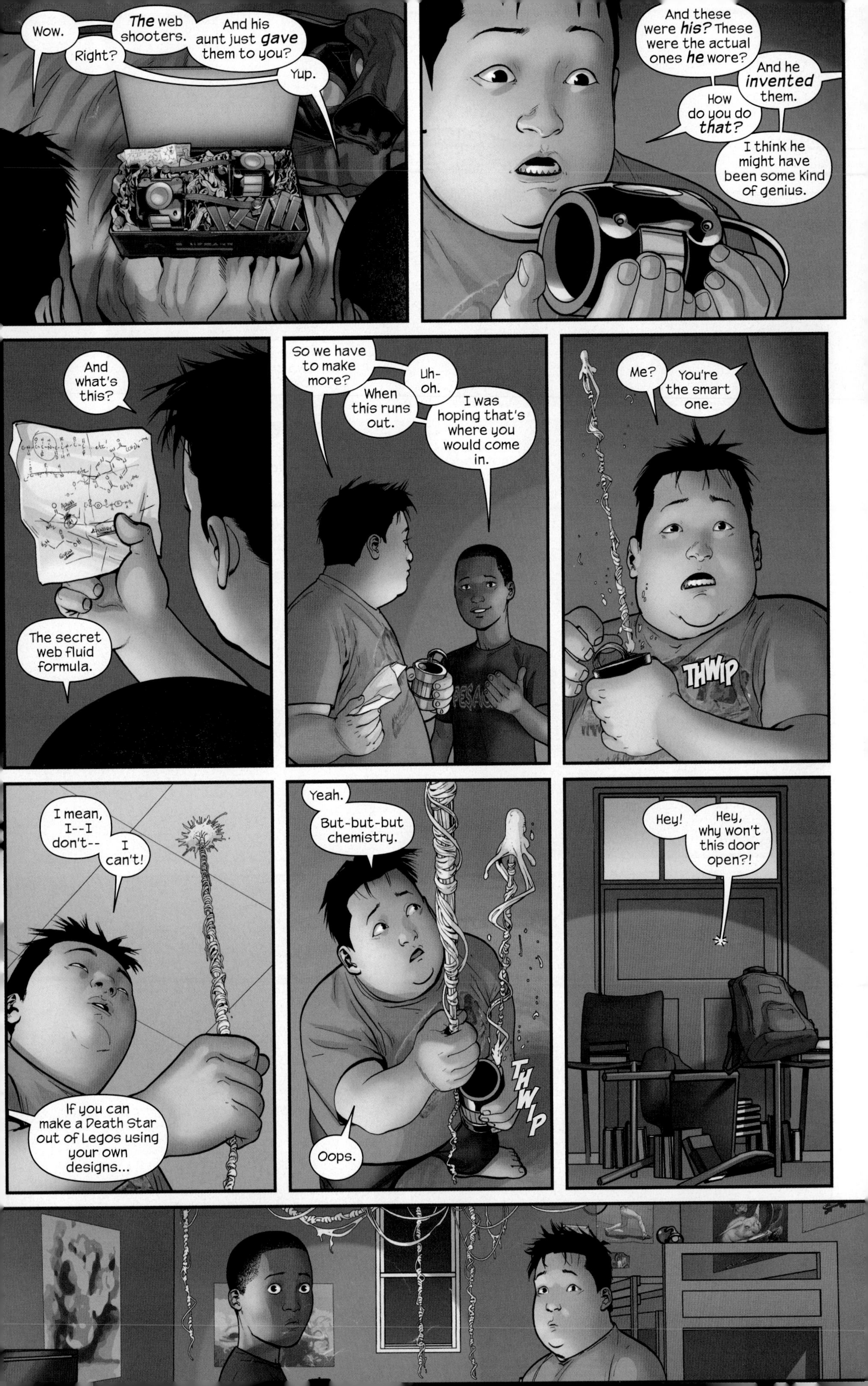
Wow.
The web shooters.
Right?
And his aunt just gave them to you?
Yup.
And these were his? These were the actual ones he wore?
How do you do that?
And he invented them.
I think he might have been some kind of genius.
And what's this?
The secret web fluid formula.
So we have to make more?
Uh-oh.
When this runs out.
I was hoping that's where you would come in.
Me?
You're the smart one.
THWIP
I mean, I--I don't--
I can't!
If you can make a Death Star out of Legos using your own designs...
Yeah.
But-but-but chemistry.
THWIP
Oops.
Hey!
Hey, why won't this door open?!

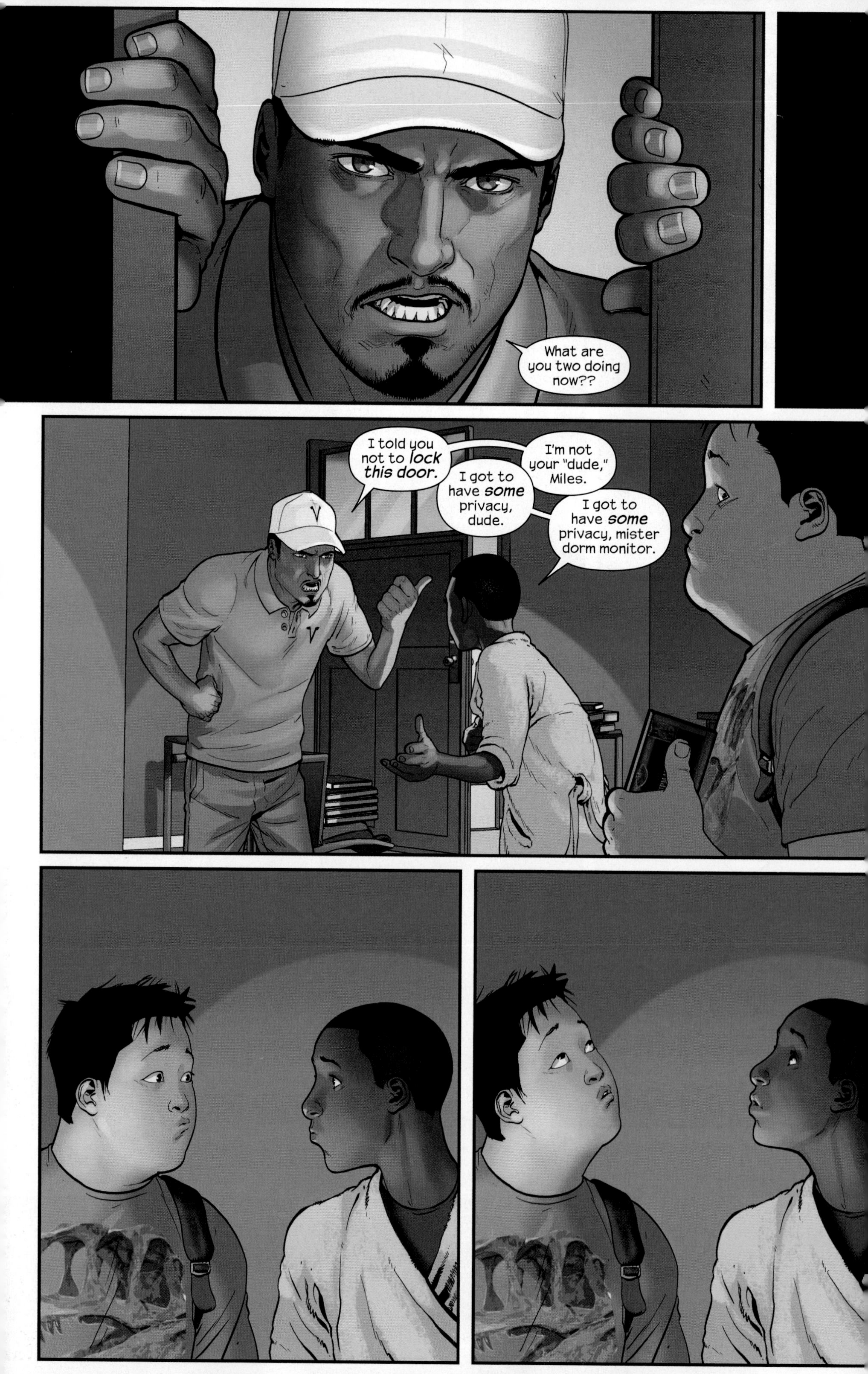
What are you two doing now??
I told you not to *lock this door.*
I got to have *some* privacy, dude.
I'm not your "dude," Miles.
I got to have *some* privacy, mister dorm monitor.

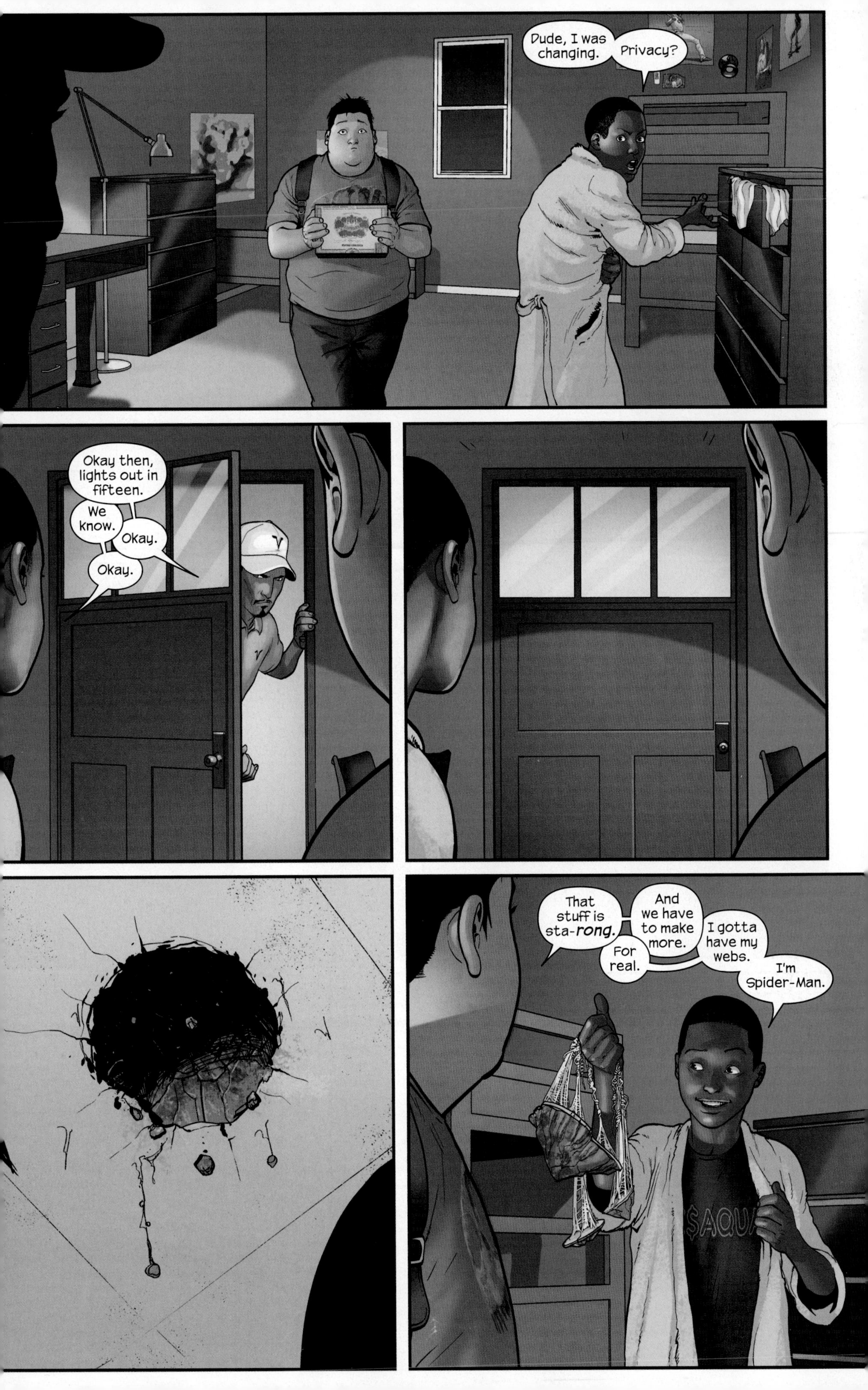
Dude, I was changing.
Privacy?
Okay then, lights out in fifteen.
We know.
Okay.
Okay.
That stuff is sta-*rong.*
For real.
And we have to make more.
I gotta have my webs.
I'm Spider-Man.

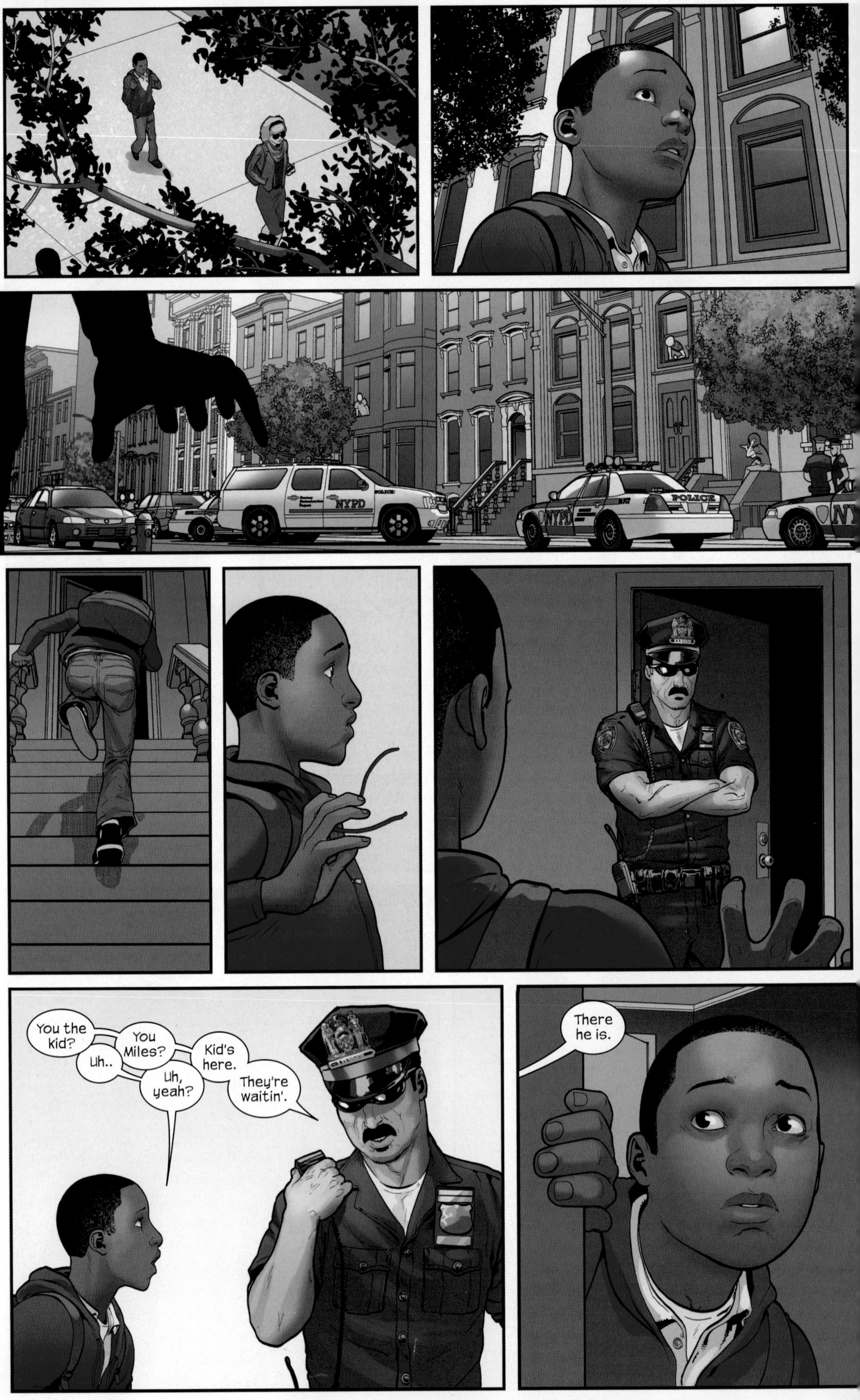
You the kid?
Uh..
You Miles?
Uh, yeah?
Kid's here.
They're waitin'.
There he is.

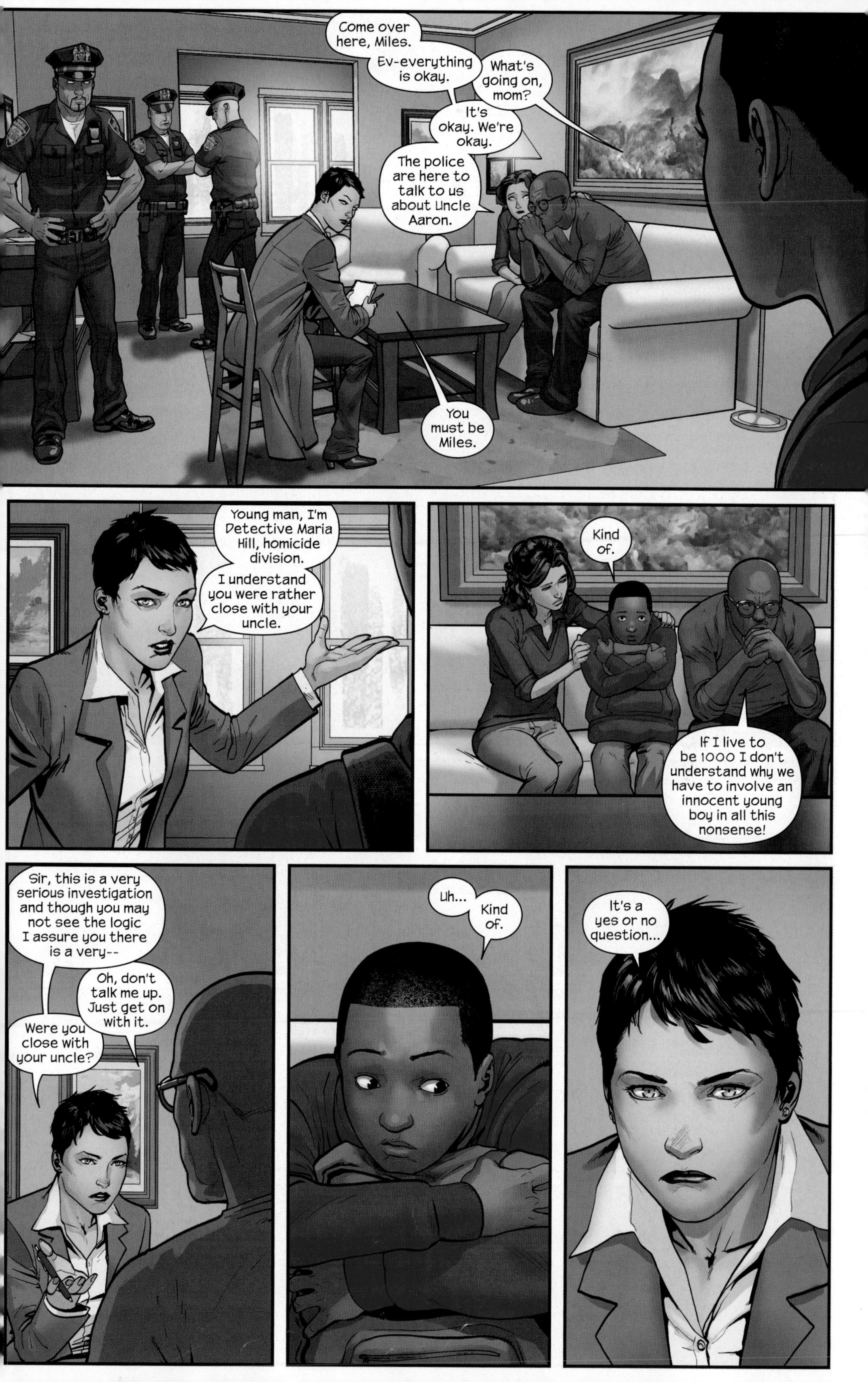
Come over here, Miles.
Ev-everything is okay.
What's going on, mom?
It's okay. We're okay.
The police are here to talk to us about Uncle Aaron.
You must be Miles.
Young man, I'm Detective Maria Hill, homicide division.
I understand you were rather close with your uncle.
Kind of.
If I live to be 1000 I don't understand why we have to involve an innocent young boy in all this nonsense!
Sir, this is a very serious investigation and though you may not see the logic I assure you there is a very--
Oh, don't talk me up. Just get on with it.
Were you close with your uncle?
Uh...
Kind of.
It's a yes or no question...

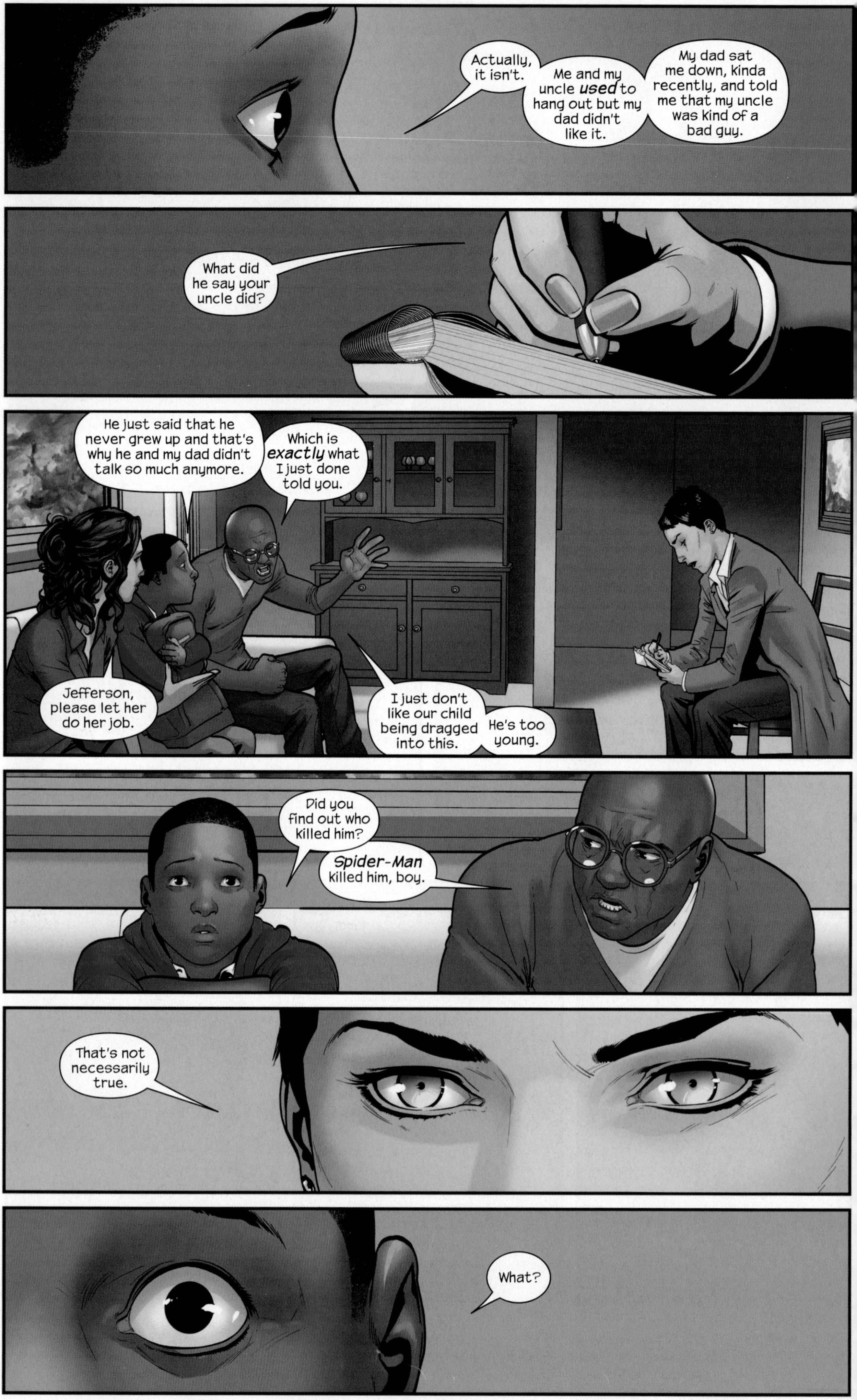

Actually, it isn't.
Me and my uncle *used* to hang out but my dad didn't like it.
My dad sat me down, kinda recently, and told me that my uncle was kind of a bad guy.
What did he say your uncle did?
He just said that he never grew up and that's why he and my dad didn't talk so much anymore.
Which is *exactly* what I just done told you.
Jefferson, please let her do her job.
I just don't like our child being dragged into this.
He's too young.
Did you find out who killed him?
Spider-Man killed him, boy.
That's not necessarily true.
What?

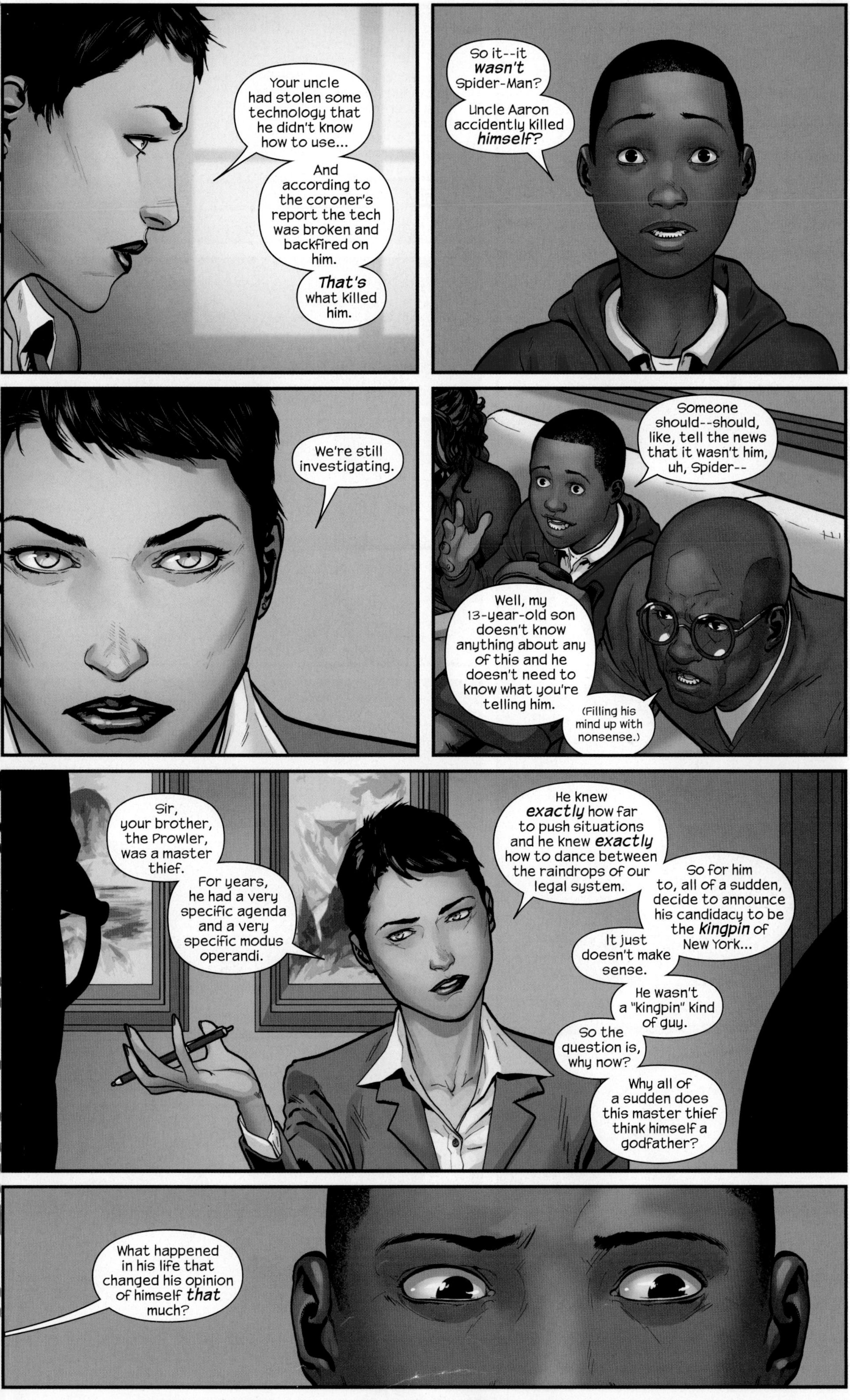
Your uncle had stolen some technology that he didn't know how to use...
And according to the coroner's report the tech was broken and backfired on him.
That's what killed him.
So it--it wasn't Spider-Man?
Uncle Aaron accidently killed himself?
We're still investigating.
Someone should--should, like, tell the news that it wasn't him, uh, Spider--
Well, my 13-year-old son doesn't know anything about any of this and he doesn't need to know what you're telling him.
(Filling his mind up with nonsense.)
Sir, your brother, the Prowler, was a master thief.
For years, he had a very specific agenda and a very specific modus operandi.
He knew exactly how far to push situations and he knew exactly how to dance between the raindrops of our legal system.
So for him to, all of a sudden, decide to announce his candidacy to be the kingpin of New York...
It just doesn't make sense.
He wasn't a "kingpin" kind of guy.
So the question is, why now?
Why all of a sudden does this master thief think himself a godfather?
What happened in his life that changed his opinion of himself that much?

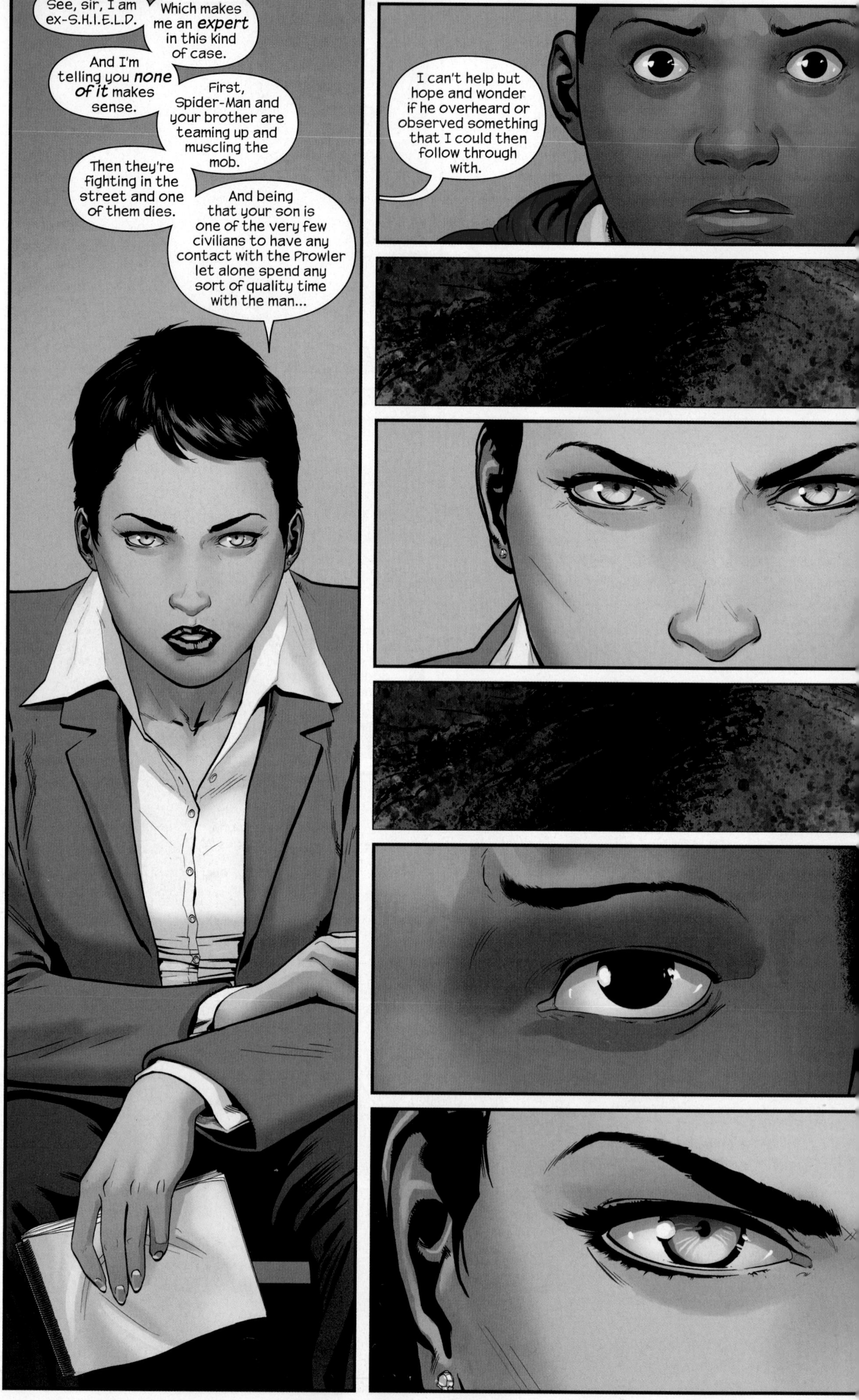

See, sir, I am ex-S.H.I.E.L.D.
Which makes me an *expert* in this kind of case.
And I'm telling you *none of it* makes sense.
First, Spider-Man and your brother are teaming up and muscling the mob.
Then they're fighting in the street and one of them dies.
And being that your son is one of the very few civilians to have any contact with the Prowler let alone spend any sort of quality time with the man...
I can't help but hope and wonder if he overheard or observed something that I could then follow through with.

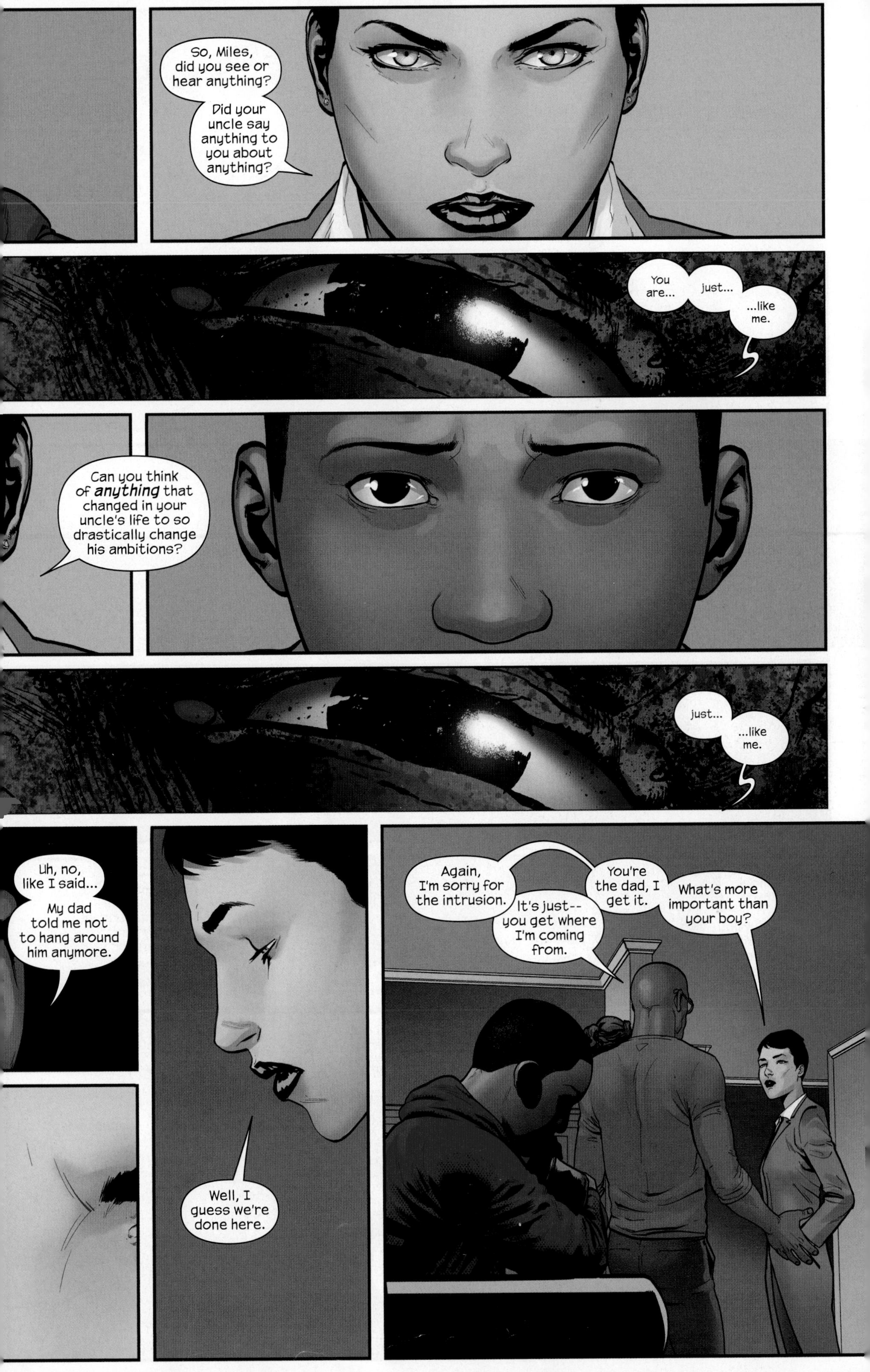
So, Miles, did you see or hear anything?
Did your uncle say anything to you about anything?
You are...
just...
...like me.
Can you think of *anything* that changed in your uncle's life to so drastically change his ambitions?
just...
...like me.
Uh, no, like I said...
My dad told me not to hang around him anymore.
Well, I guess we're done here.
Again, I'm sorry for the intrusion.
It's just-- you get where I'm coming from.
You're the dad, I get it.
What's more important than your boy?

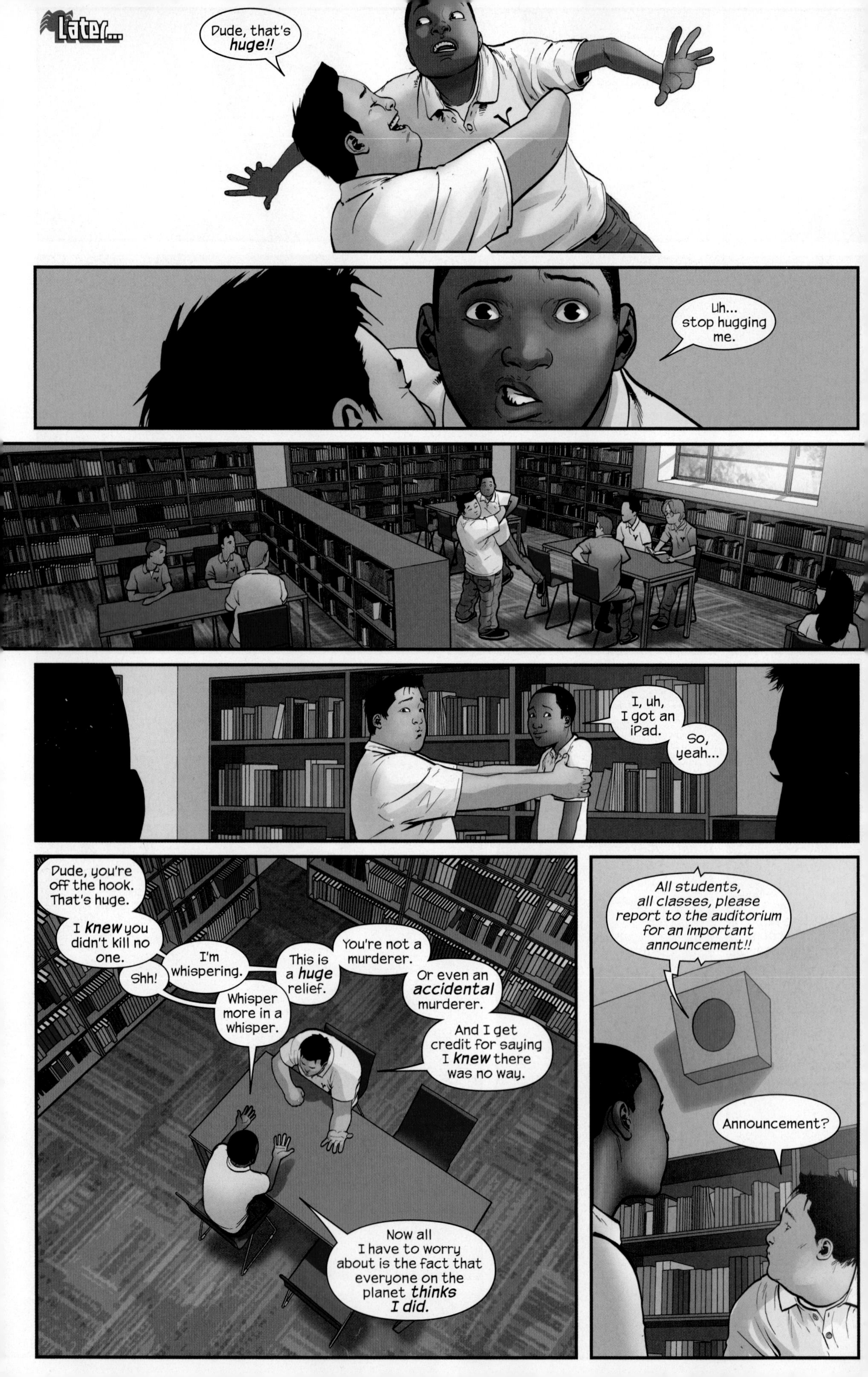

Later...
Dude, that's *huge!!*
Uh... stop hugging me.
I, uh, I got an iPad.
So, yeah...
Dude, you're off the hook. That's huge.
I *knew* you didn't kill no one.
I'm whispering.
Shh!
Whisper more in a whisper.
This is a *huge* relief.
You're not a murderer.
Or even an *accidental* murderer.
And I get credit for saying I *knew* there was no way.
Now all I have to worry about is the fact that everyone on the planet *thinks I did.*
All students, all classes, please report to the auditorium for an important announcement!!
Announcement?

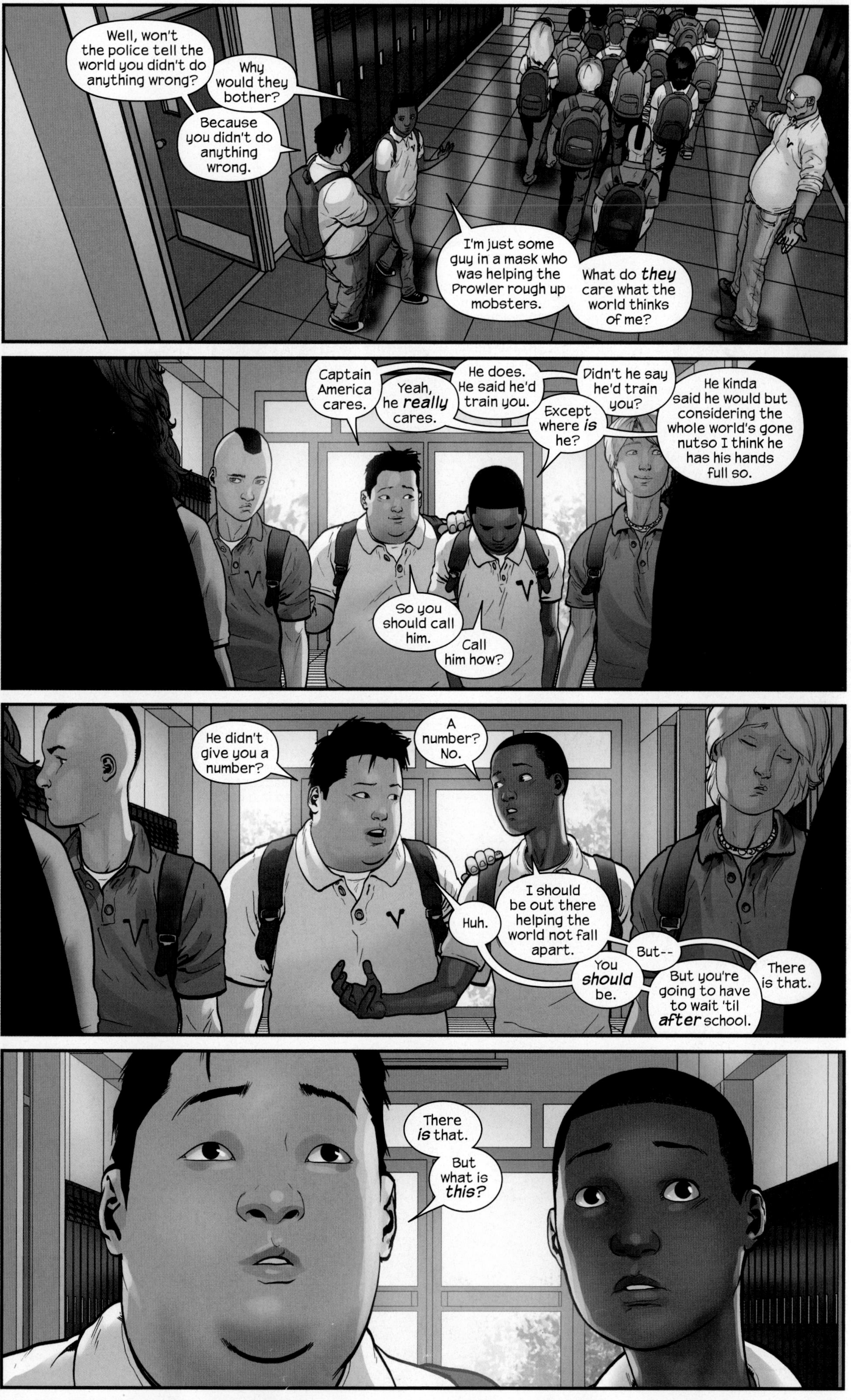
Well, won't the police tell the world you didn't do anything wrong?
Why would they bother?
Because you didn't do anything wrong.
I'm just some guy in a mask who was helping the Prowler rough up mobsters.
What do *they* care what the world thinks of me?
Captain America cares.
Yeah, he *really* cares.
He does. He said he'd train you.
Didn't he say he'd train you?
Except where *is* he?
He kinda said he would but considering the whole world's gone nutso I think he has his hands full so.
So you should call him.
Call him how?
He didn't give you a number?
A number? No.
Huh.
I should be out there helping the world not fall apart.
But--
You *should* be.
But you're going to have to wait 'til *after* school.
There is that.
There *is* that.
But what is *this?*

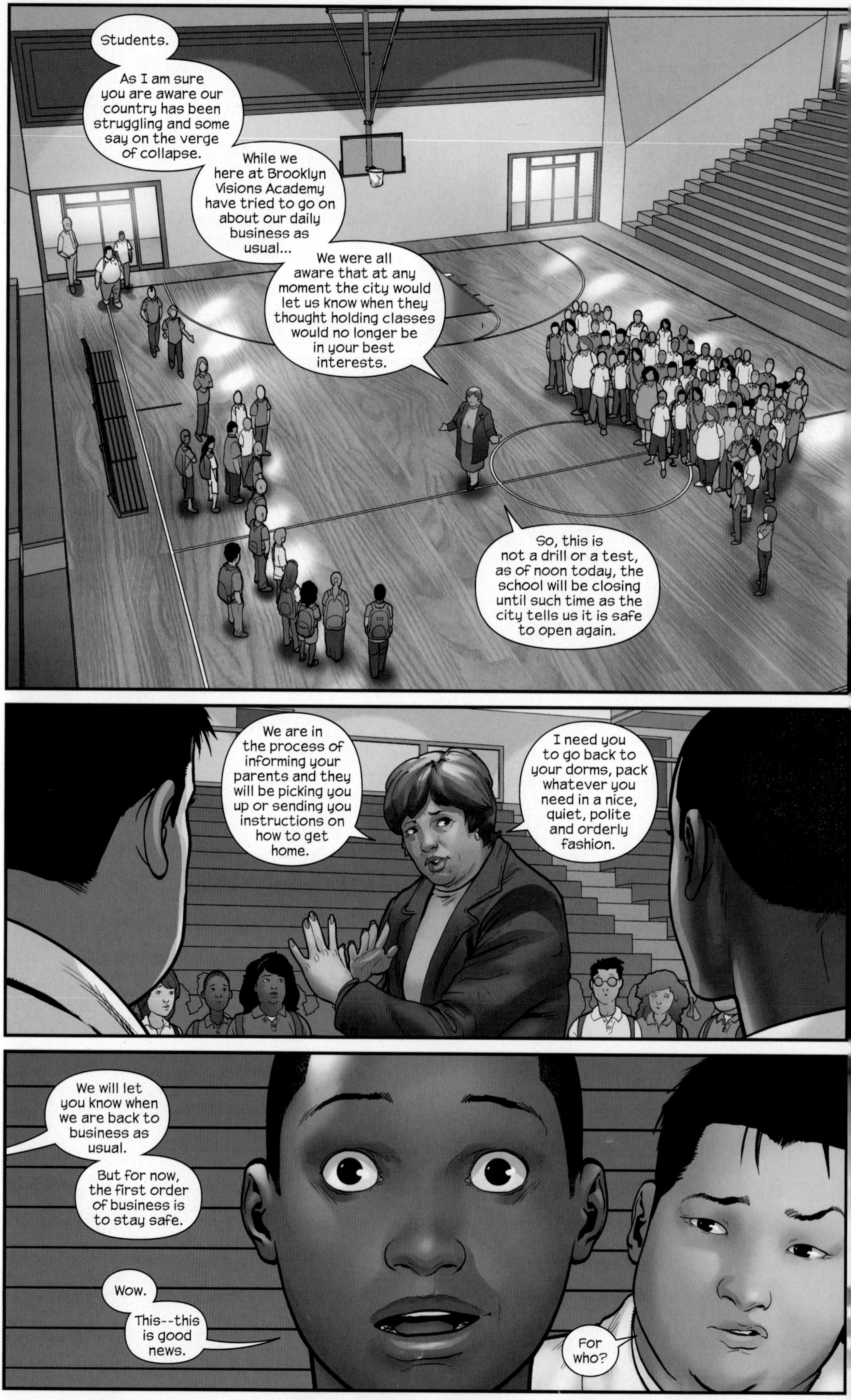
Students.
As I am sure you are aware our country has been struggling and some say on the verge of collapse.
While we here at Brooklyn Visions Academy have tried to go on about our daily business as usual...
We were all aware that at any moment the city would let us know when they thought holding classes would no longer be in your best interests.
So, this is not a drill or a test, as of noon today, the school will be closing until such time as the city tells us it is safe to open again.
We are in the process of informing your parents and they will be picking you up or sending you instructions on how to get home.
I need you to go back to your dorms, pack whatever you need in a nice, quiet, polite and orderly fashion.
We will let you know when we are back to business as usual.
But for now, the first order of business is to stay safe.
Wow.
This--this is good news.
For who?

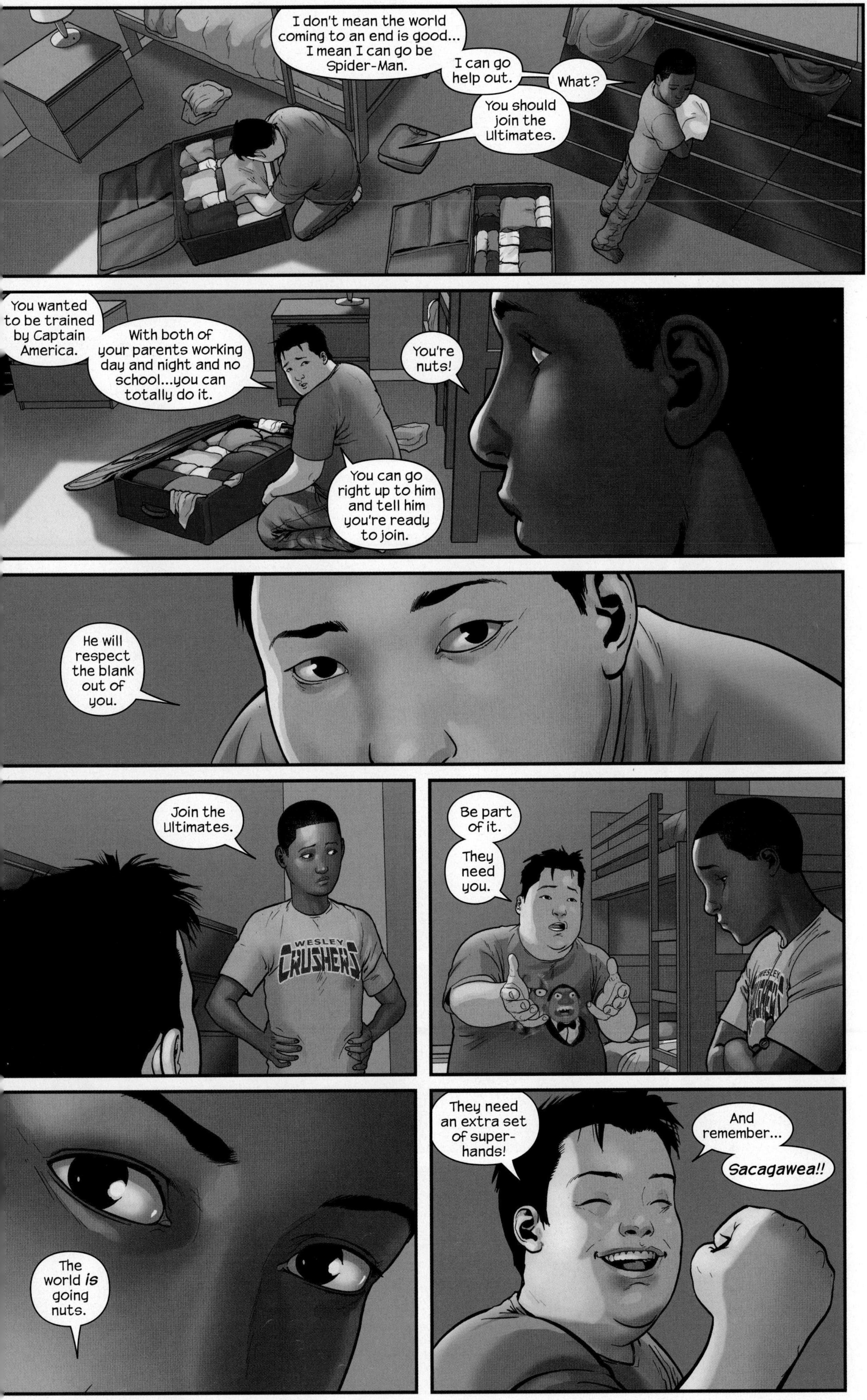

I don't mean the world coming to an end is good... I mean I can go be Spider-Man.
I can go help out.
What?
You should join the Ultimates.
You wanted to be trained by Captain America.
With both of your parents working day and night and no school...you can totally do it.
You're nuts!
You can go right up to him and tell him you're ready to join.
He will respect the blank out of you.
Join the Ultimates.
WESLEY CRUSHERS
Be part of it.
They need you.
The world *is* going nuts.
They need an extra set of super-hands!
And remember...
Sacagawea!!

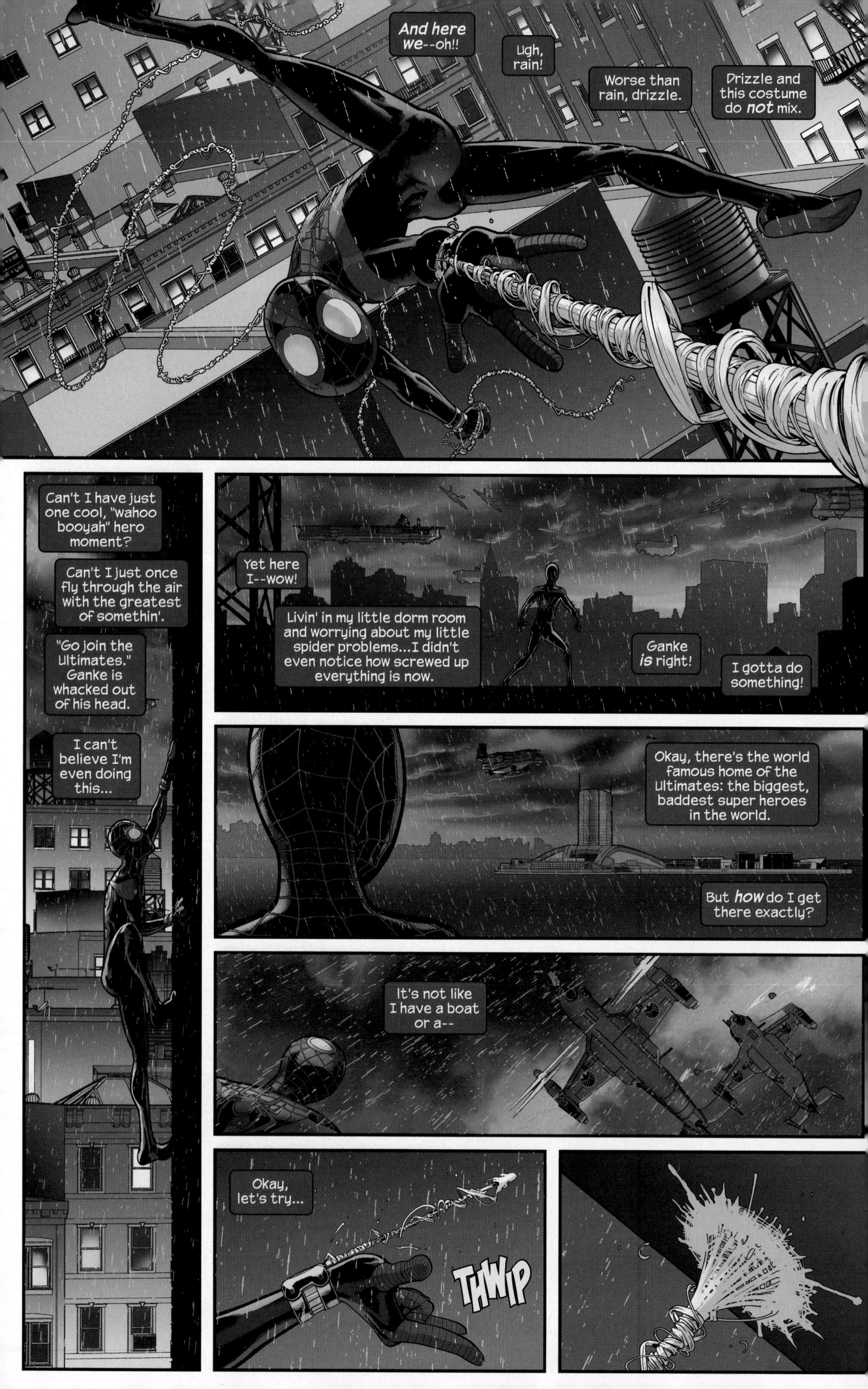
And here we--oh!!
Ugh, rain!
Worse than rain, drizzle.
Drizzle and this costume do *not* mix.
Can't I have just one cool, "wahoo booyah" hero moment?
Can't I just once fly through the air with the greatest of somethin'.
"Go join the Ultimates." Ganke is whacked out of his head.
I can't believe I'm even doing this...
Yet here I--wow!
Livin' in my little dorm room and worrying about my little spider problems...I didn't even notice how screwed up everything is now.
Ganke *is* right!
I gotta do something!
Okay, there's the world famous home of the Ultimates: the biggest, baddest super heroes in the world.
But *how* do I get there exactly?
It's not like I have a boat or a--
Okay, let's try...
THWIP

Whaaaattttt was I thinking??

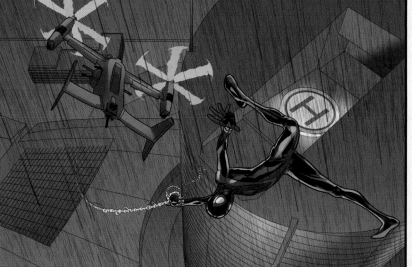

Whoa! Wahhaa!!

SSQQQQQQAAAAAAAAA

Whoa, sorry!!

Sorry everyone, I just wanted to--

We have a breach.

Um...

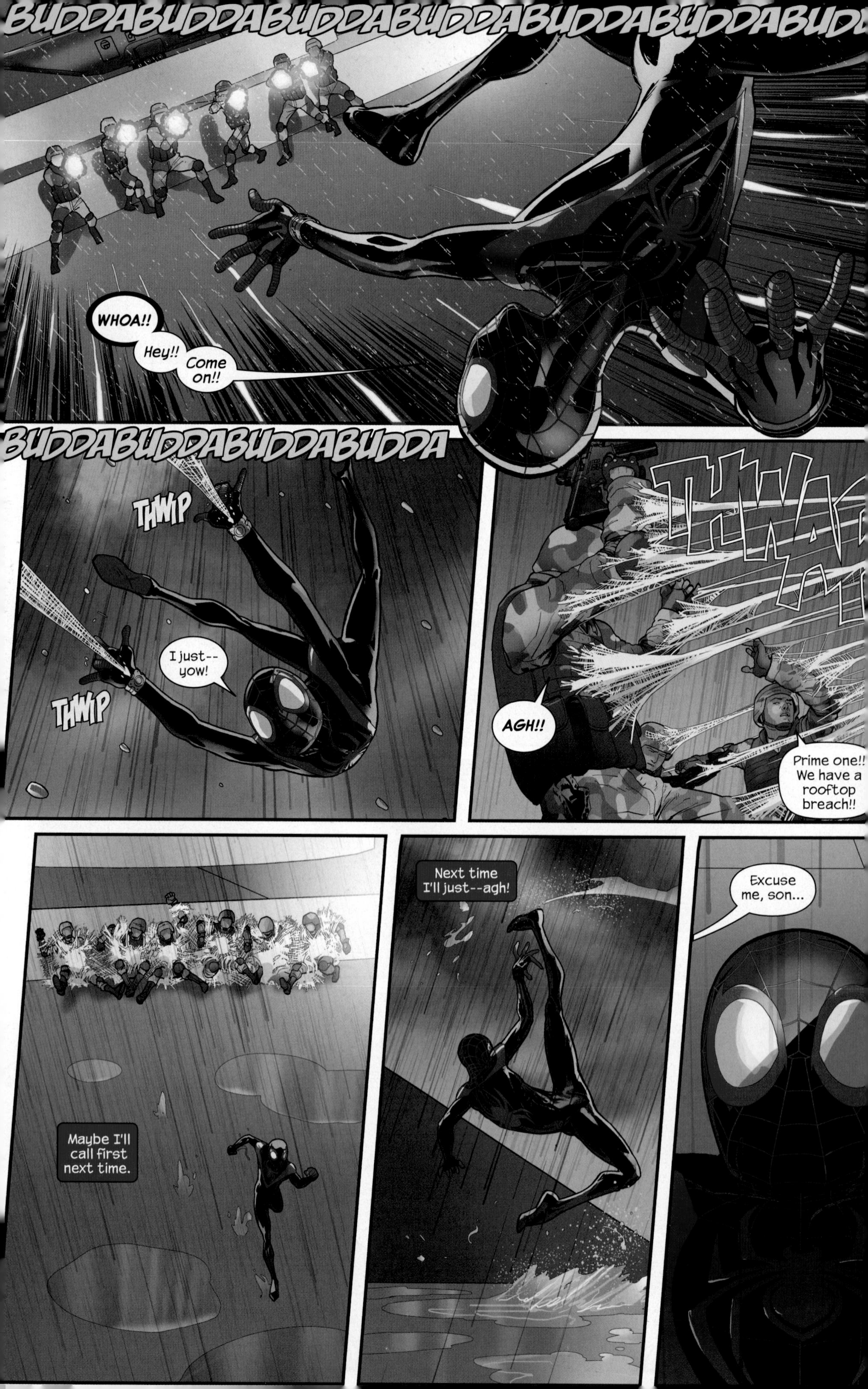
BUDDABUDDABUDDABUDDABUDDABUDDABUDD
WHOA!!
Hey!!
Come on!!
BUDDABUDDABUDDABUDDA
THWIP
I just-- yow!
THWIP
AGH!!
Prime one!! We have a rooftop breach!!
Maybe I'll call first next time.
Next time I'll just--agh!
Excuse me, son...

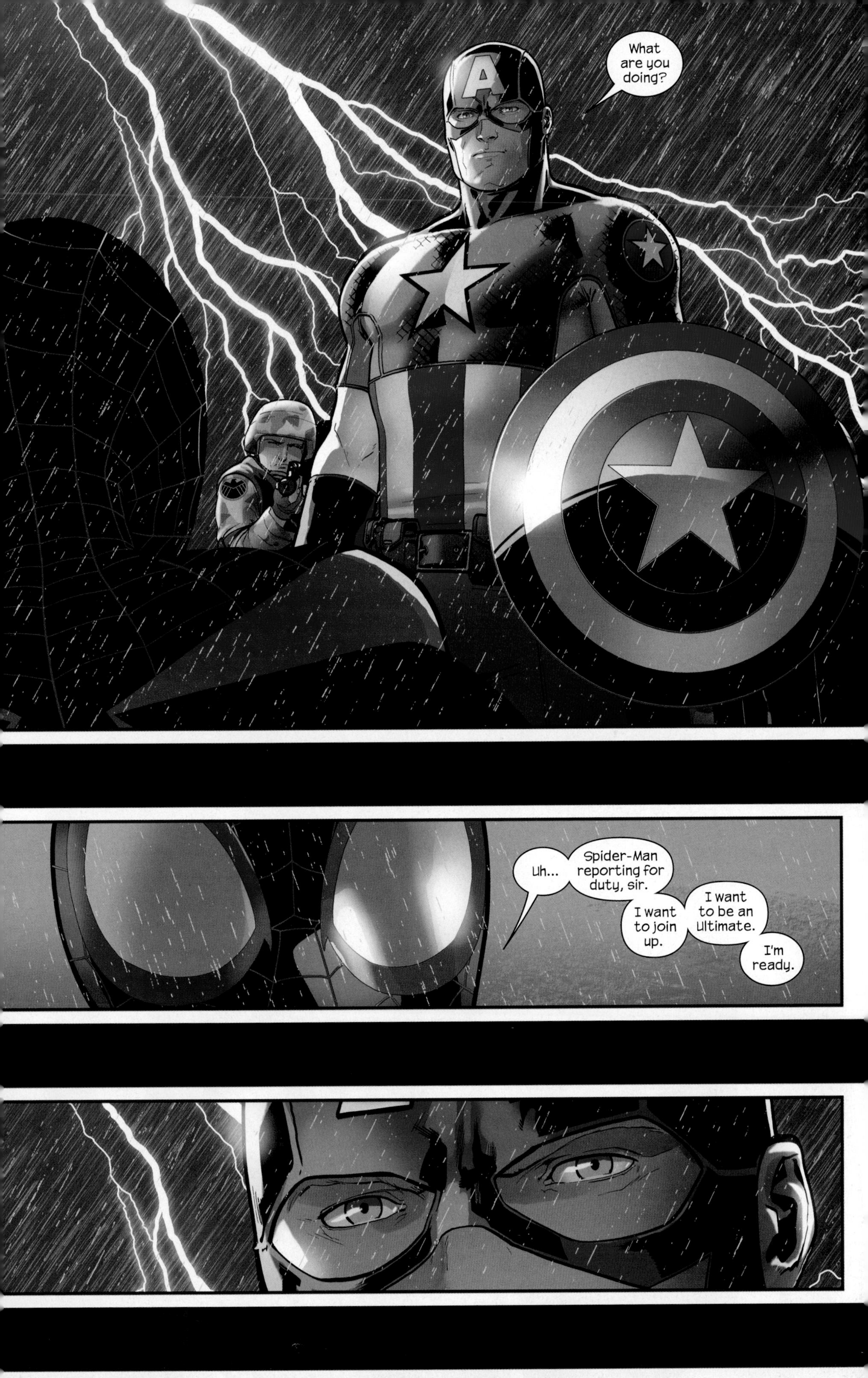
What are you doing?
Uh...
Spider-Man reporting for duty, sir.
I want to join up.
I want to be an Ultimate.
I'm ready.

16

ULTIMATE COMICS **SPIDER-MAN** #16

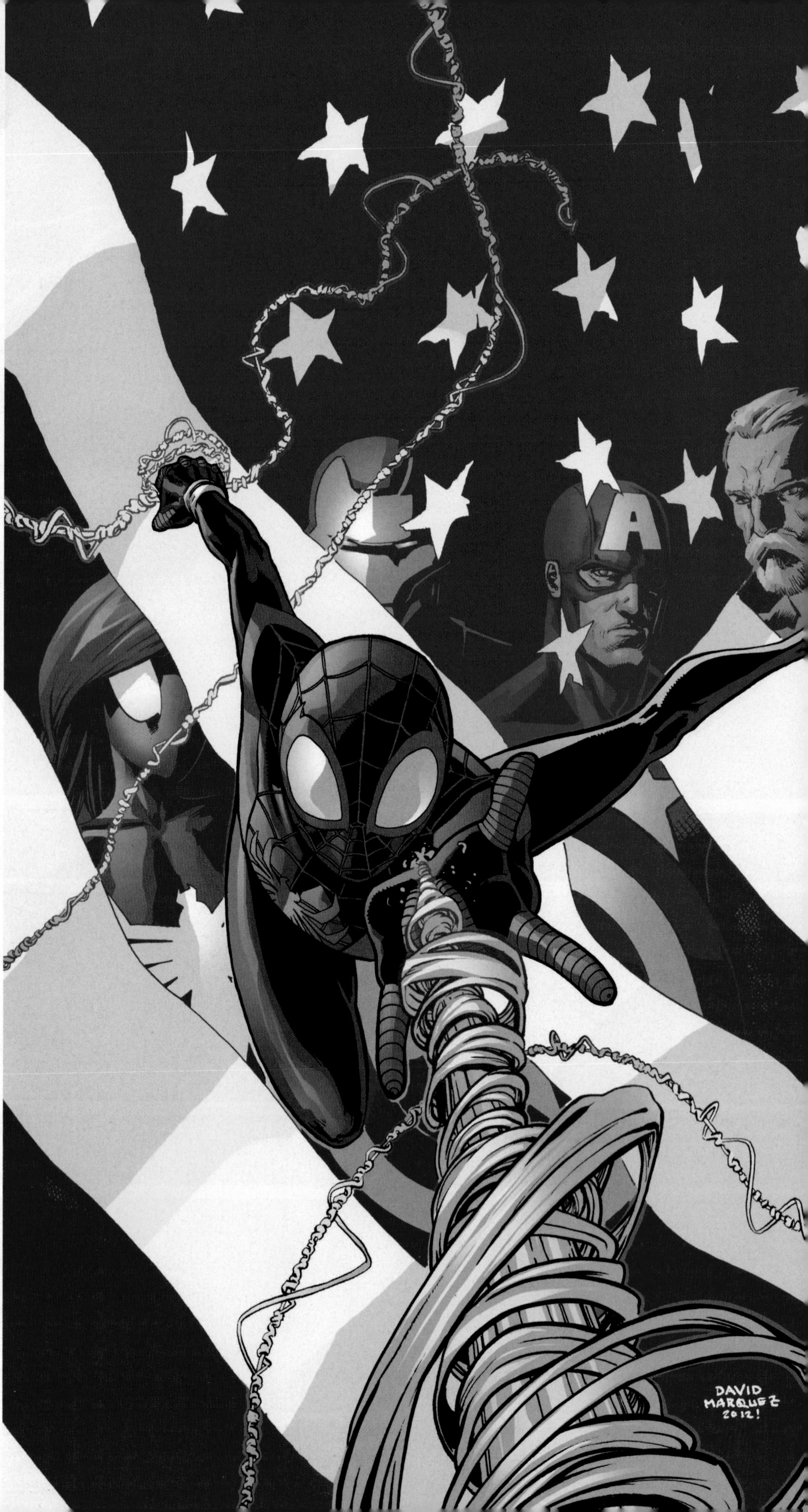
DAVID MARQUEZ 2012!

S.H.I.E.L.D. SITUATION MAP:

[Anti-government militia hot spots]

Idaho, Montana, N. Dakota, S. Dakota, Arizona, New Mexico, N. Carolina, S. Carolina, Georgia

[Eastern seaboard control zone]

New England, New York, New Jersey, Delaware, Washington, D.C., Maryland, Pennsylvania, Virginia

secured by National Guard under emergency powers committee

[The West Coast Nation]

California, Oregon, Washington

Independent nation

Wyoming

status unknown

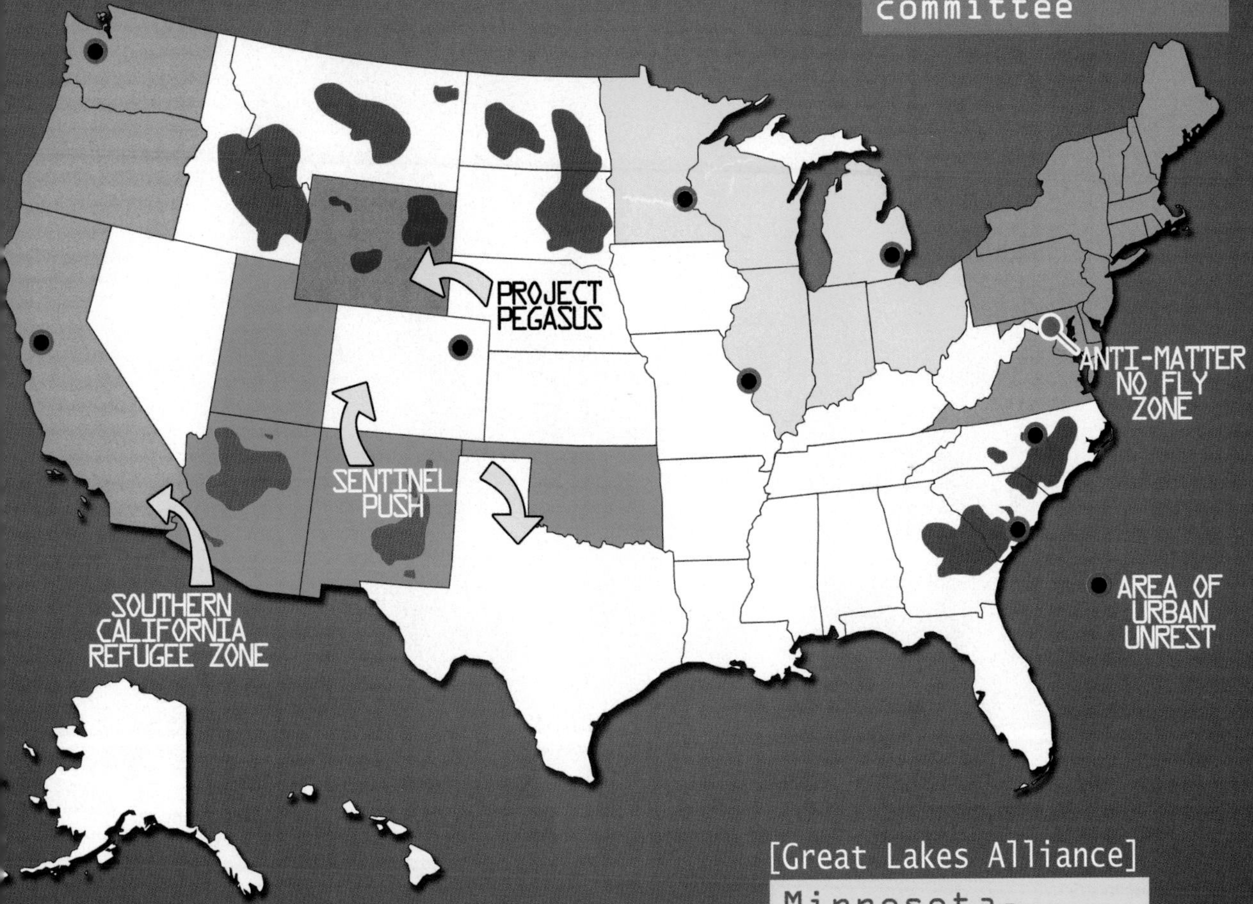
PROJECT PEGASUS
ANTI-MATTER NO FLY ZONE
SENTINEL PUSH
SOUTHERN CALIFORNIA REFUGEE ZONE
AREA OF URBAN UNREST

[Sentinel-controlled no-man's-land]

New Mexico, Arizona, Utah, Oklahoma

abandoned by the U.S. government

[Great Lakes Alliance]

Minnesota, Wisconsin, Michigan, Illinois, Indiana, Ohio

Independent nation

ALL STATES SHOWN IN WHITE ARE U.S. GOVERNMENT-CONTROLLED ZONES

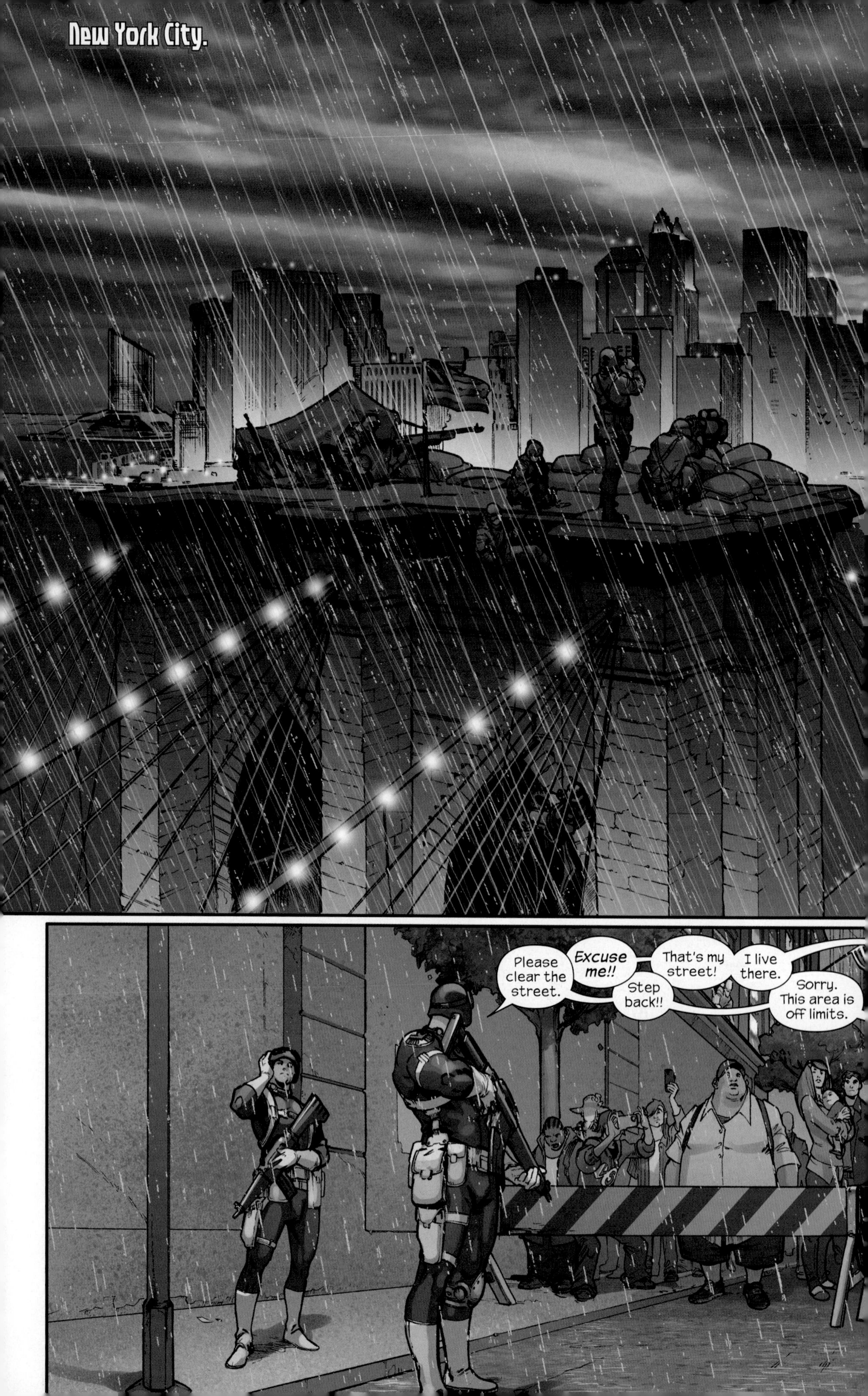
New York City.
Please clear the street.
Excuse me!!
Step back!!
That's my street!
I live there.
Sorry. This area is off limits.

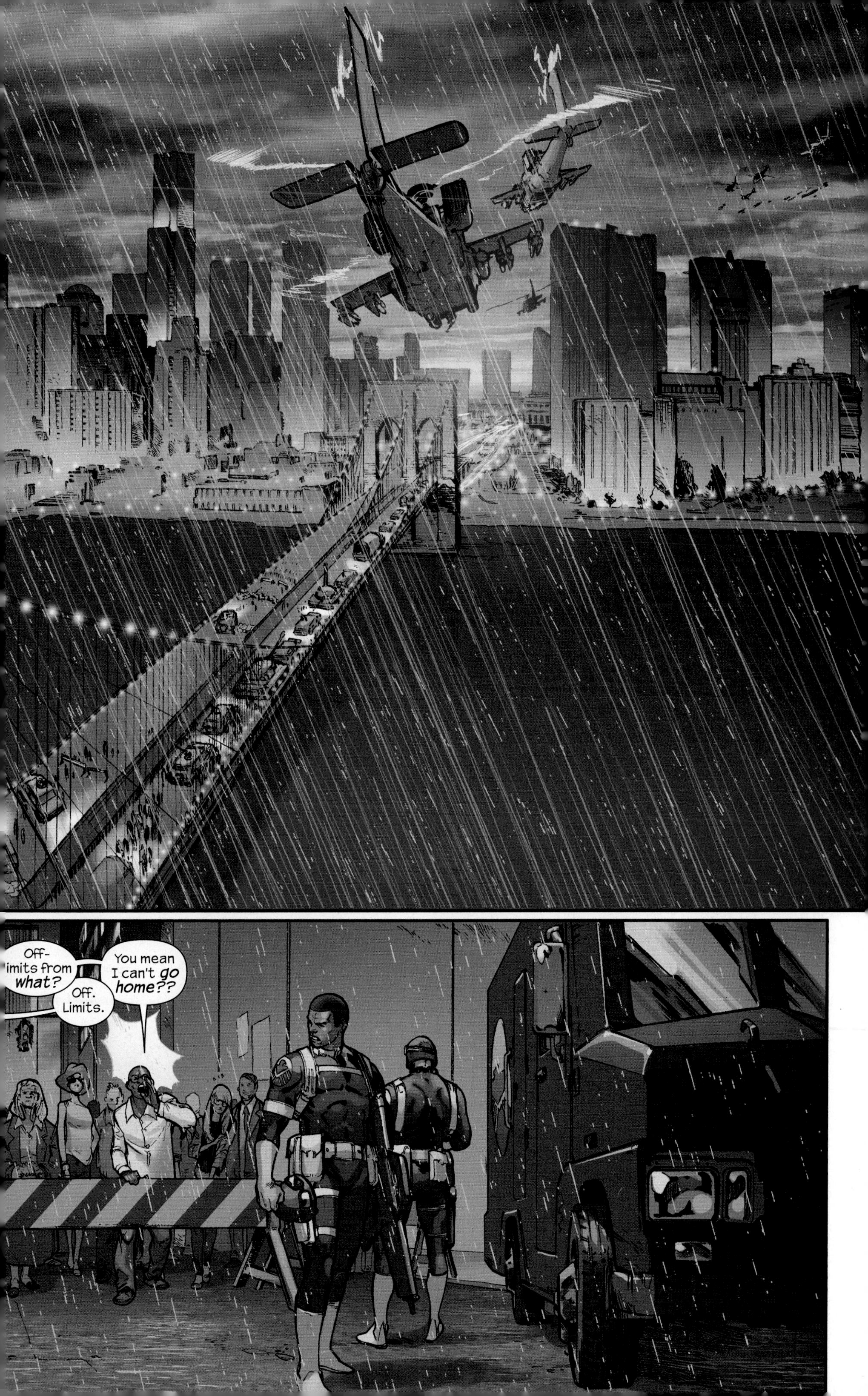
Off-limits from what?
Off. Limits.
You mean I can't go home??

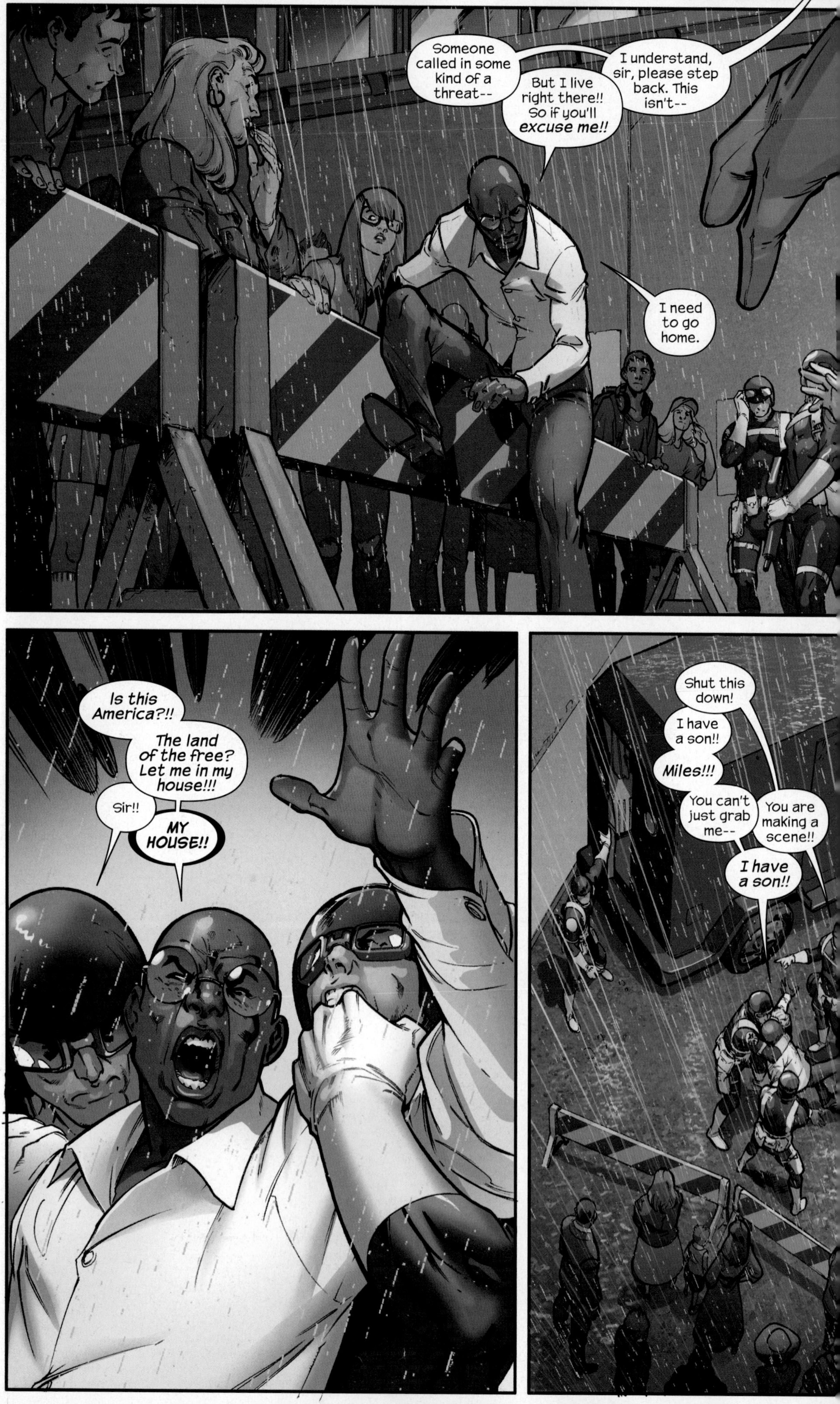
Someone called in some kind of a threat--
I understand, sir, please step back. This isn't--
But I live right there!! So if you'll *excuse me!!*
I need to go home.
Is this America?!!
The land of the free? Let me in my house!!!
Sir!!
MY HOUSE!!
Shut this down!
I have a son!!
Miles!!!
You can't just grab me--
You are making a scene!!
I have a son!!

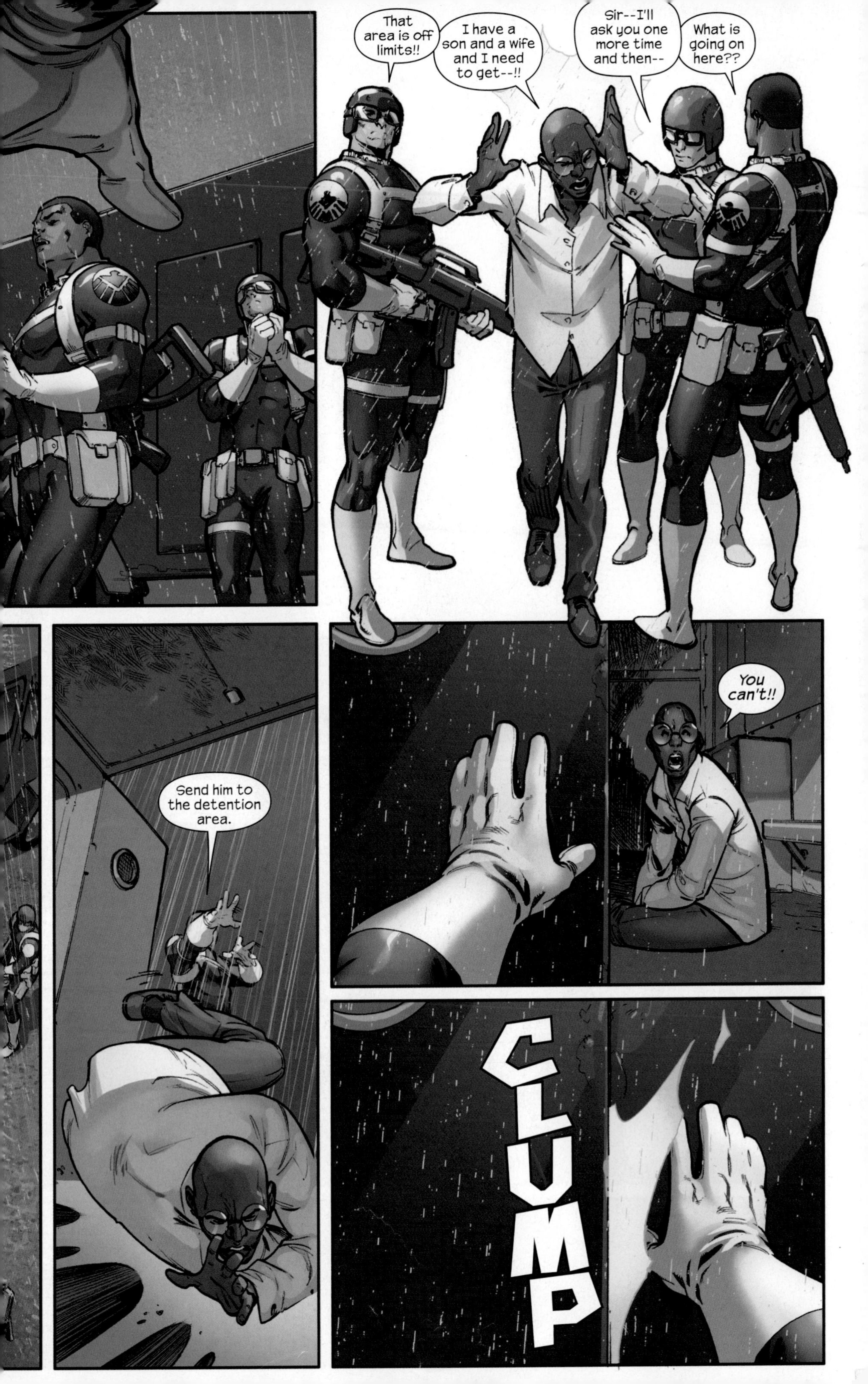
That area is off limits!!
I have a son and a wife and I need to get--!!
Sir--I'll ask you one more time and then--
What is going on here??
Send him to the detention area.
You can't!!
CLUMP

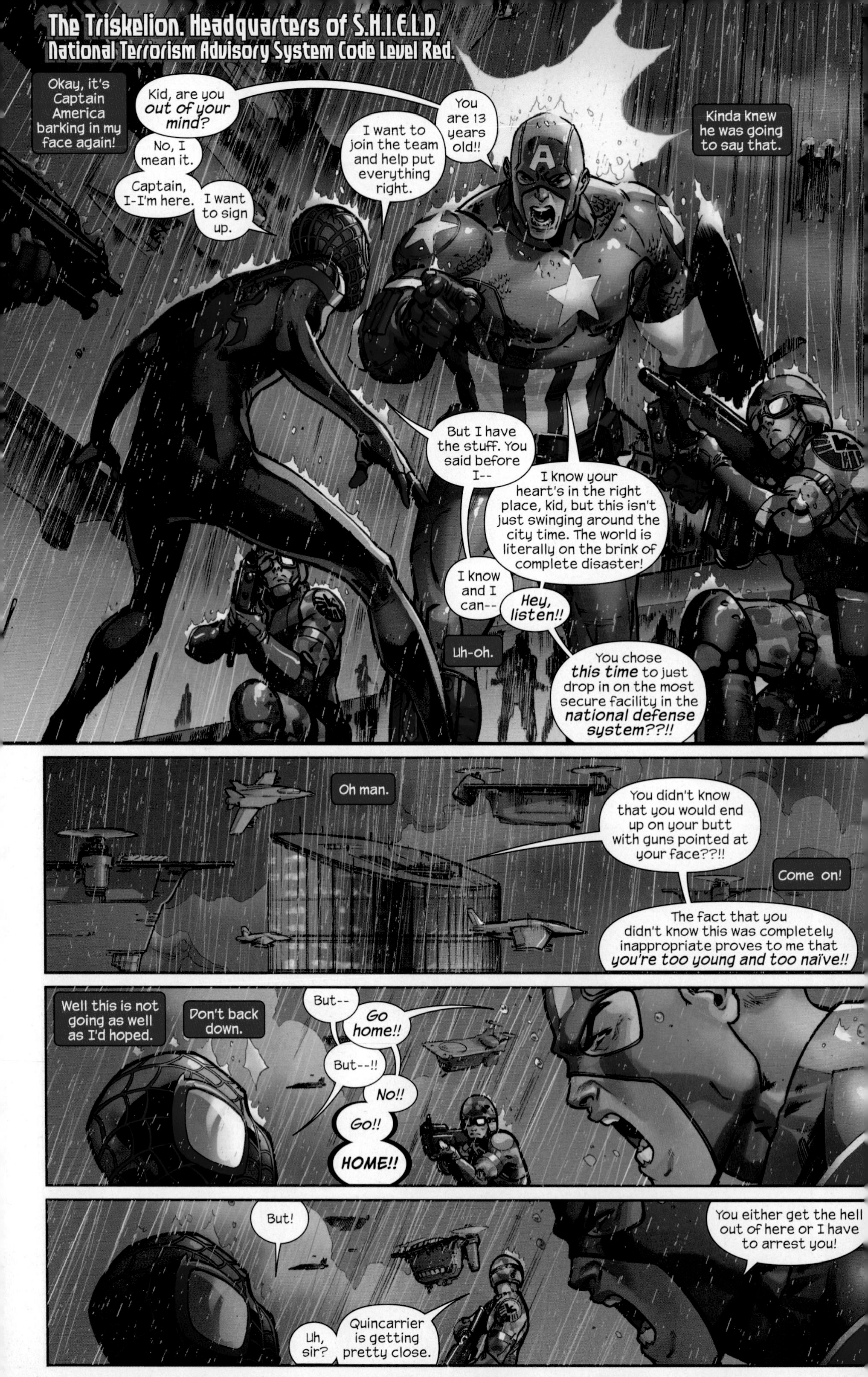
The Triskelion. Headquarters of S.H.I.E.L.D.
National Terrorism Advisory System Code Level Red.
Okay, it's Captain America barking in my face again!
Kid, are you out of your mind?
No, I mean it.
Captain, I-I'm here.
I want to sign up.
I want to join the team and help put everything right.
You are 13 years old!!
Kinda knew he was going to say that.
But I have the stuff. You said before I--
I know your heart's in the right place, kid, but this isn't just swinging around the city time. The world is literally on the brink of complete disaster!
I know and I can--
Hey, listen!!
Uh-oh.
You chose this time to just drop in on the most secure facility in the national defense system??!!
Oh man.
You didn't know that you would end up on your butt with guns pointed at your face??!!
Come on!
The fact that you didn't know this was completely inappropriate proves to me that you're too young and too naïve!!
Well this is not going as well as I'd hoped.
Don't back down.
But--
Go home!!
But--!!
No!!
Go!!
HOME!!
But!
You either get the hell out of here or I have to arrest you!
Uh, sir?
Quincarrier is getting pretty close.

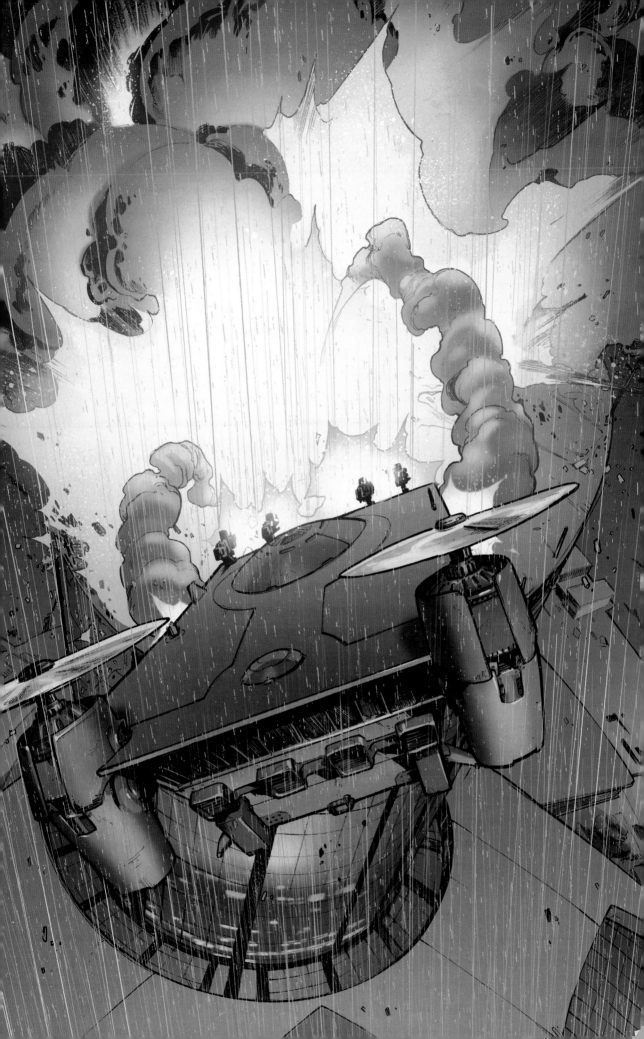

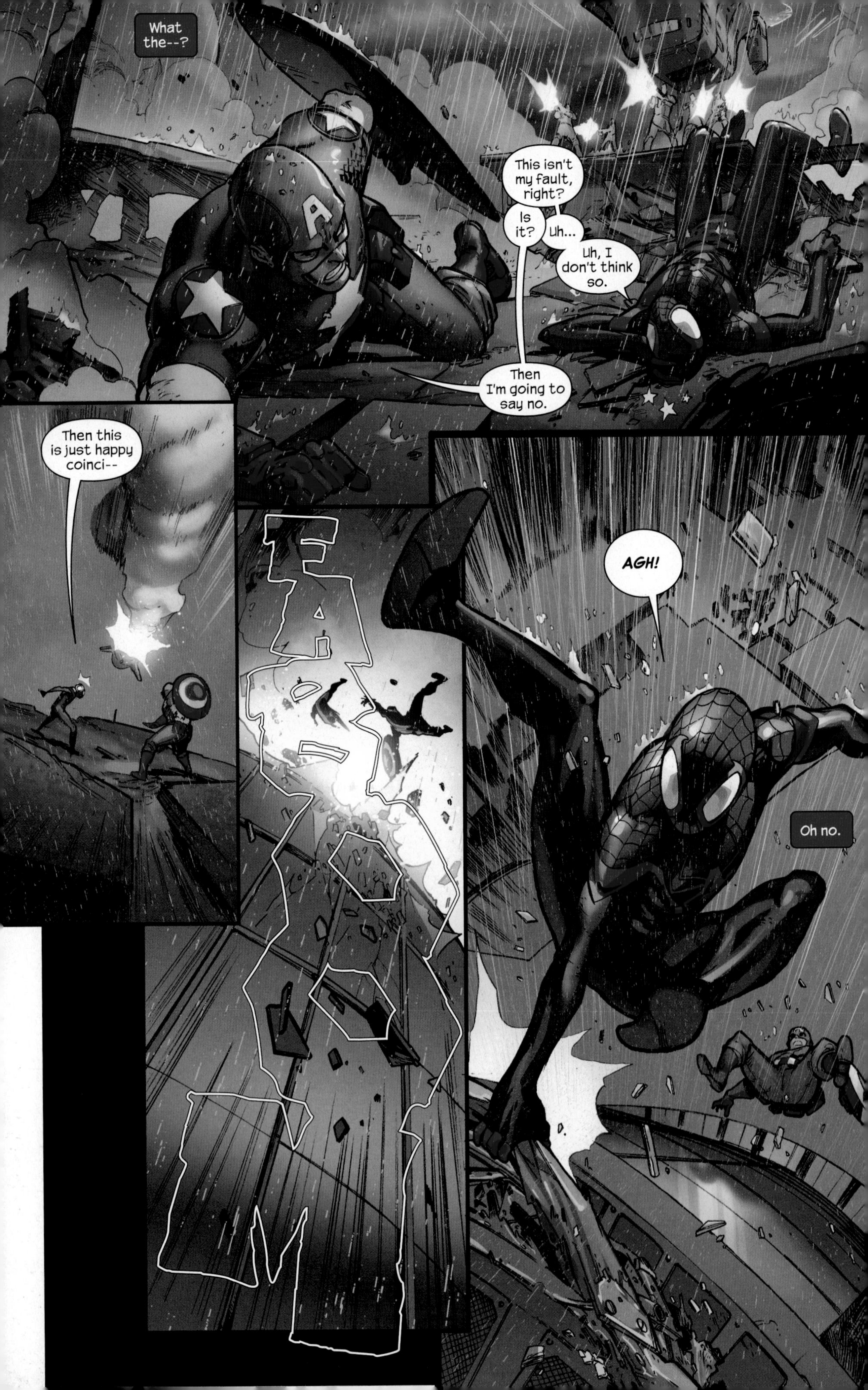
What the--?
This isn't my fault, right?
Is it?
Uh...
Uh, I don't think so.
Then I'm going to say no.
Then this is just happy coinci--
AGH!
Oh no.

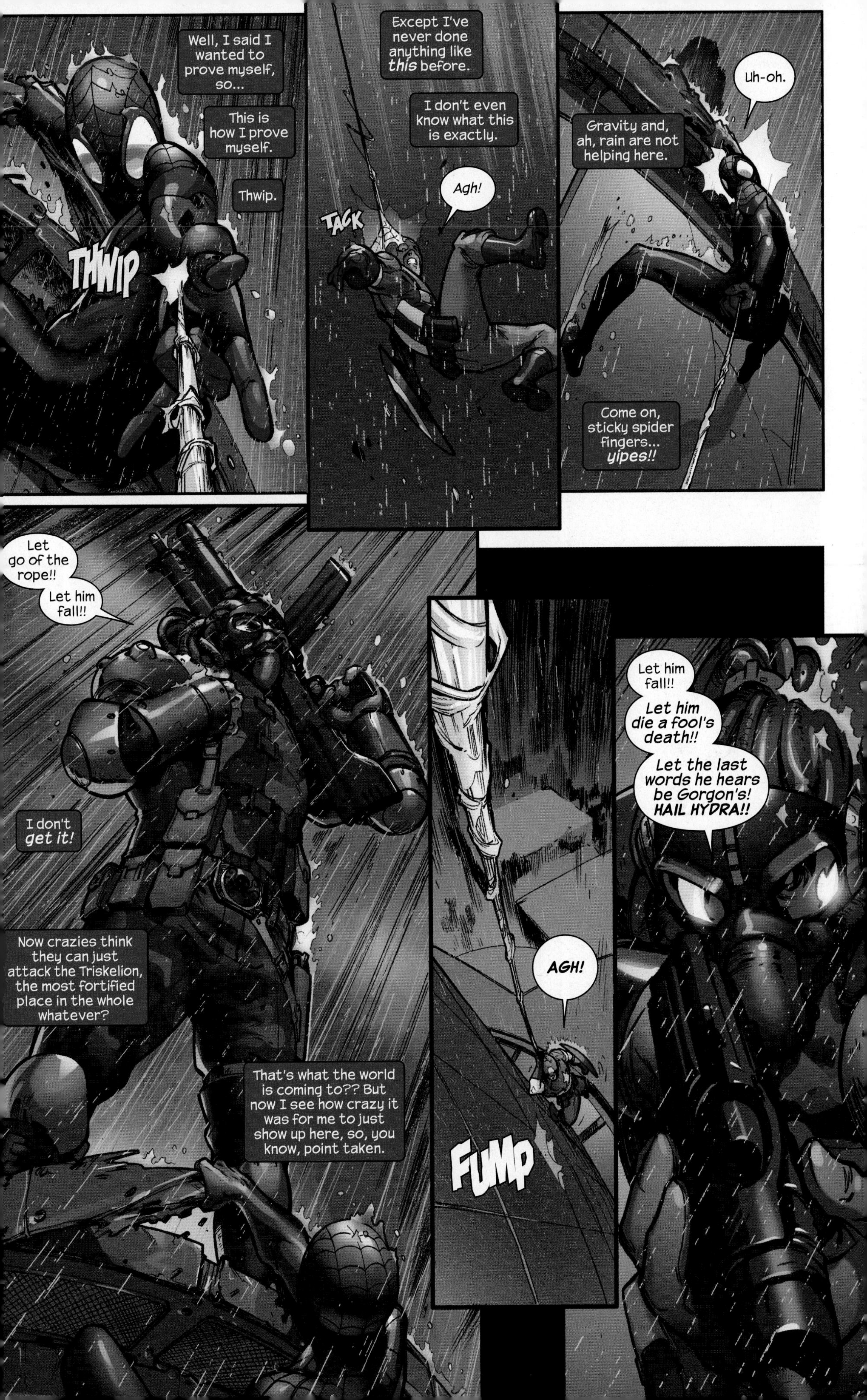
Well, I said I wanted to prove myself, so...
This is how I prove myself.
Thwip.
THWIP
Except I've never done anything like *this* before.
I don't even know what this is exactly.
TACK
Agh!
Uh-oh.
Gravity and, ah, rain are not helping here.
Come on, sticky spider fingers... *yipes!!*
Let go of the rope!!
Let him fall!!
I don't *get it!*
Now crazies think they can just attack the Triskelion, the most fortified place in the whole whatever?
That's what the world is coming to?? But now I see how crazy it was for me to just show up here, so, you know, point taken.
AGH!
FUMP
Let him fall!!
Let him die a fool's death!!
Let the last words he hears be Gorgon's! HAIL HYDRA!!

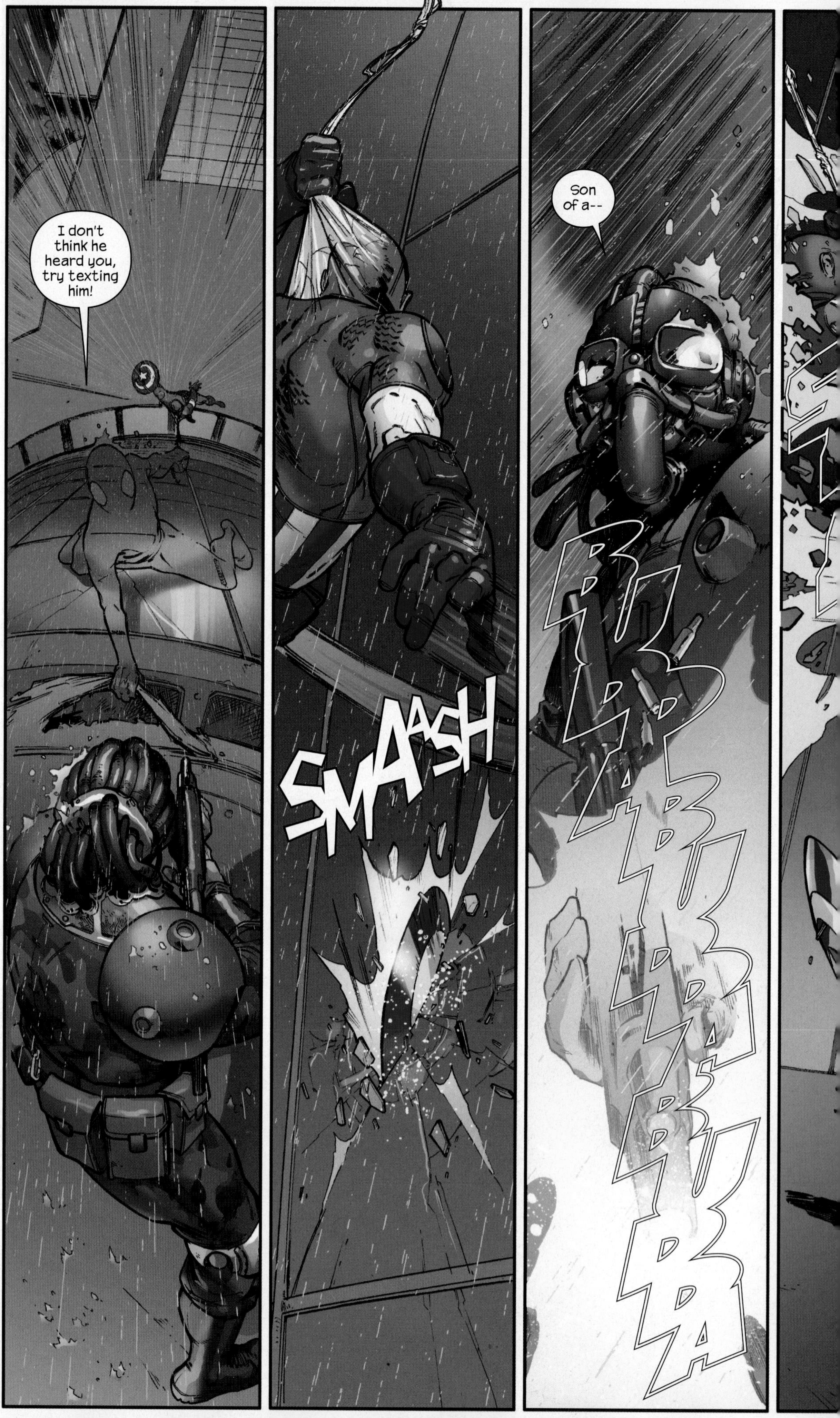
I don't think he heard you, try texting him!
SMAASH
Son of a--
BUDDA BUDDA BUDDA BUDDA

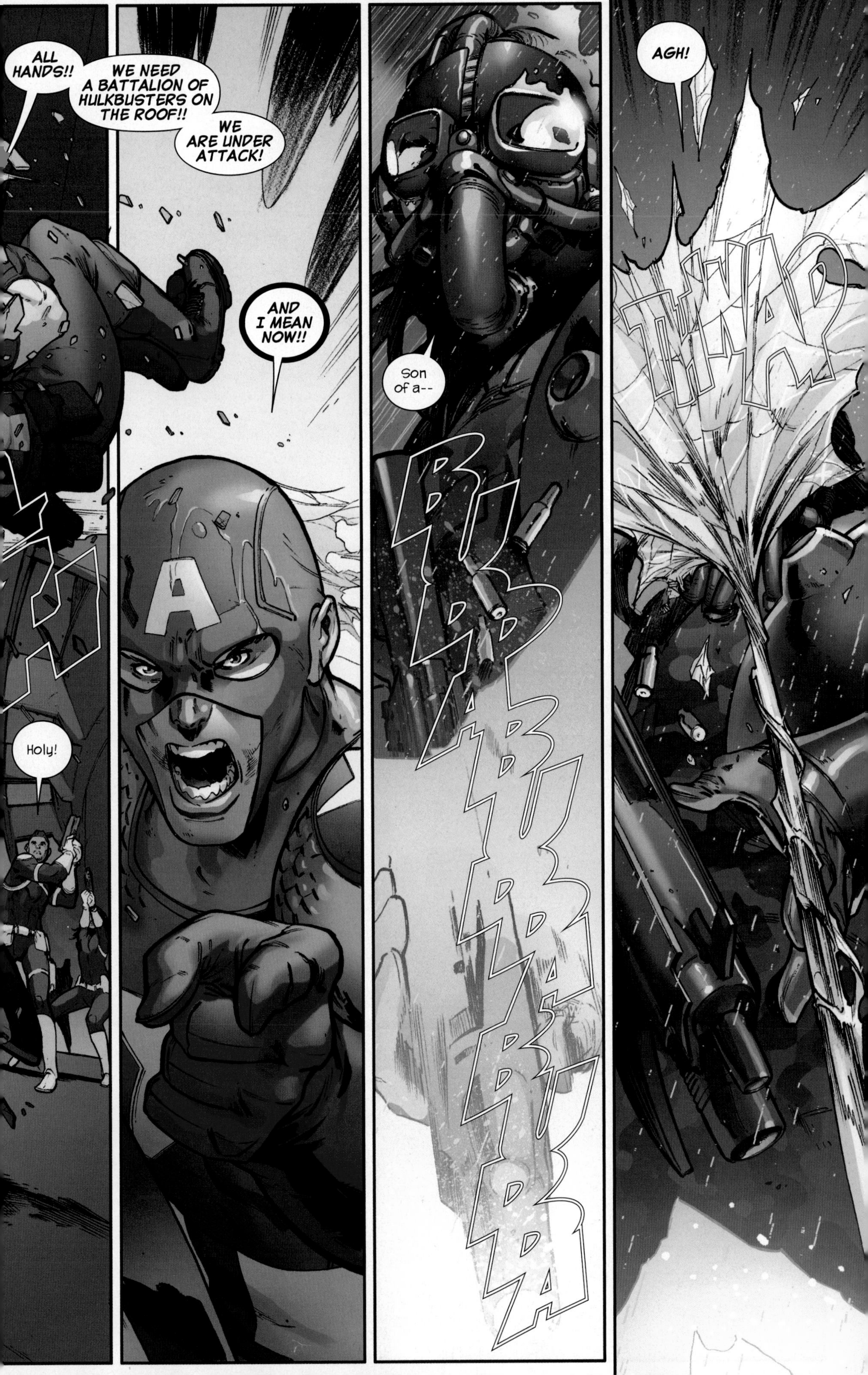
ALL HANDS!!
WE NEED A BATTALION OF HULKBUSTERS ON THE ROOF!!
WE ARE UNDER ATTACK!
AND I MEAN NOW!!
Holy!
Son of a--
AGH!

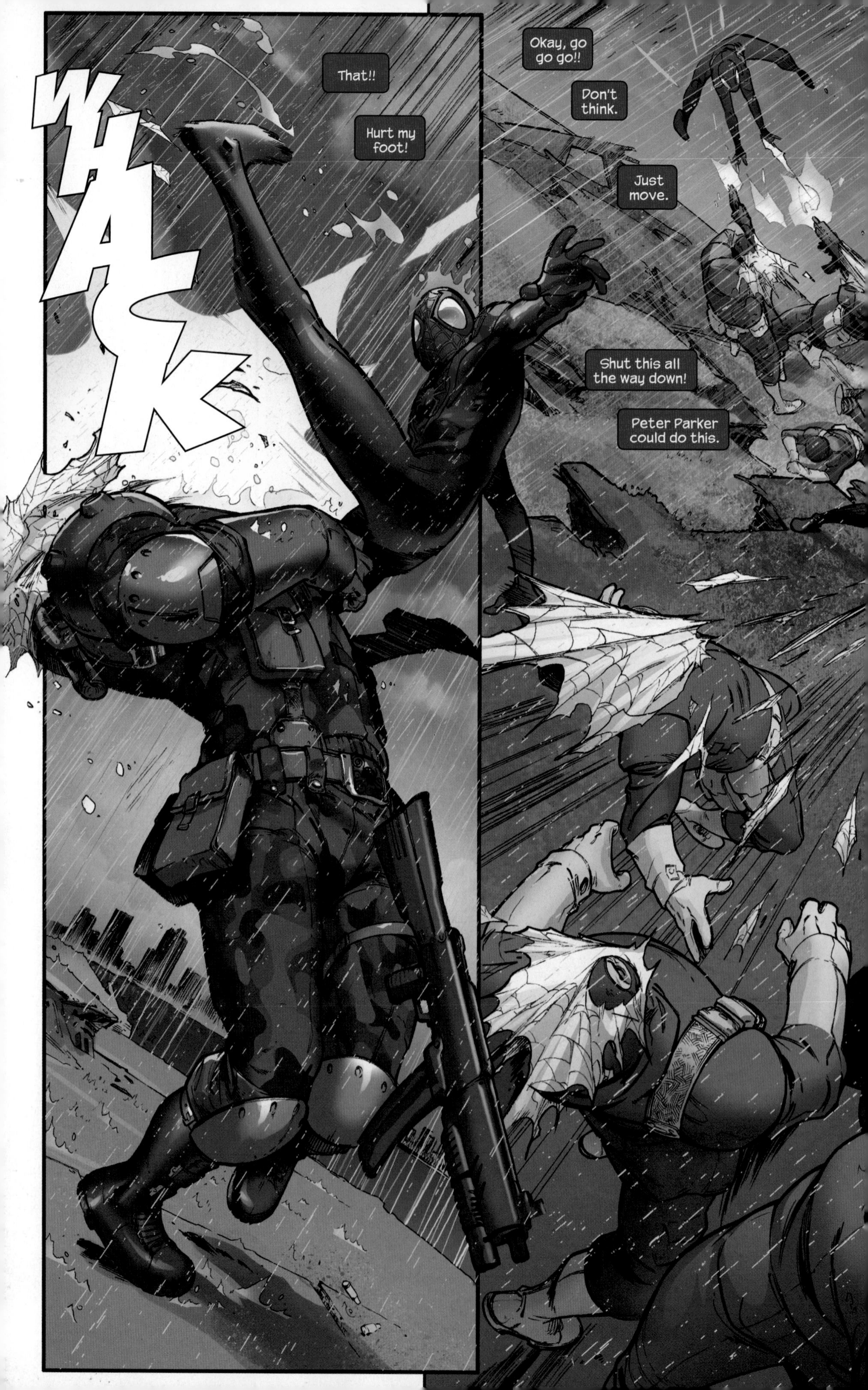
WHACK
That!!
Hurt my foot!
Okay, go go go!!
Don't think.
Just move.
Shut this all the way down!
Peter Parker could do this.

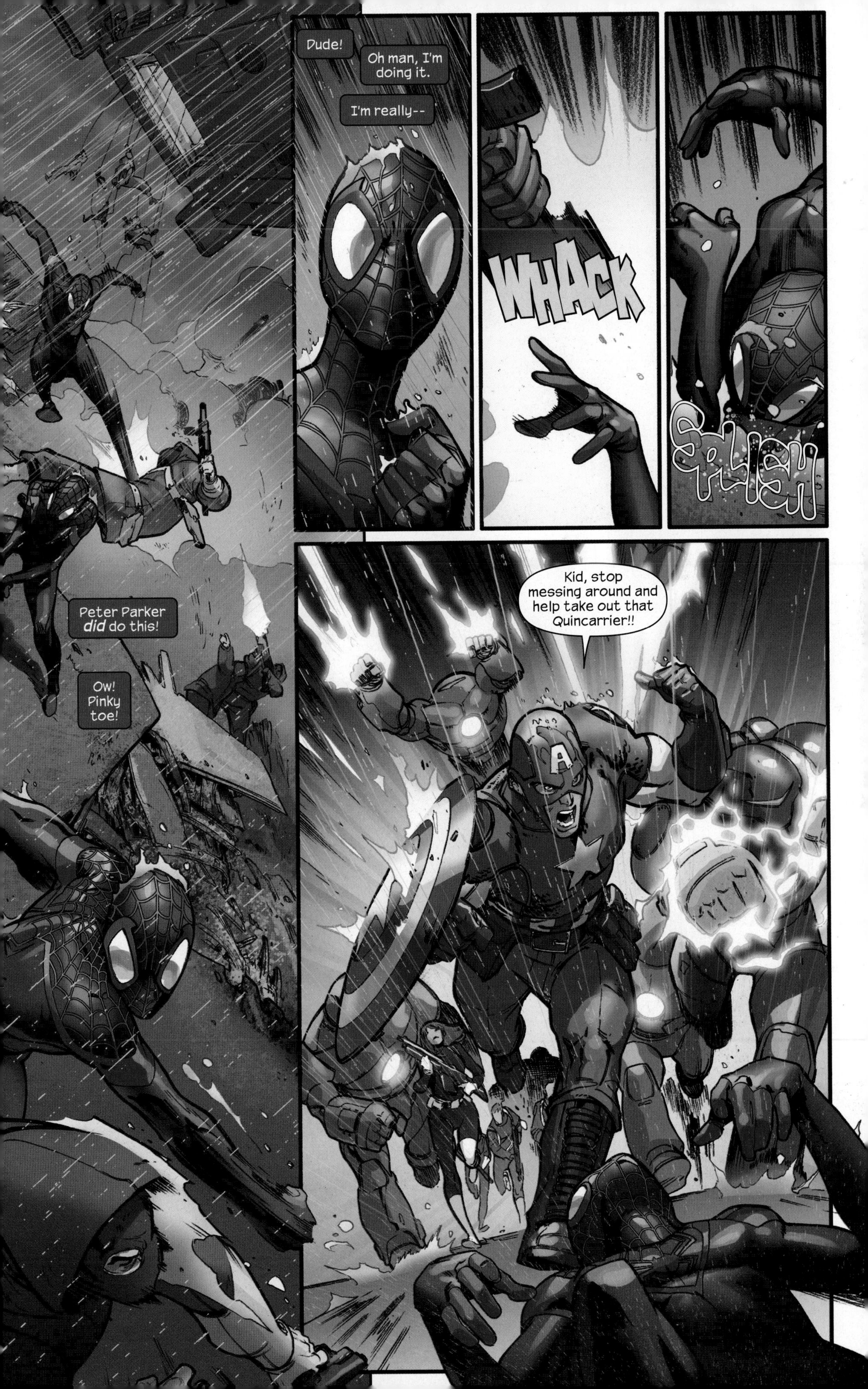

Peter Parker *did* do this!
Ow! Pinky toe!
Dude!
Oh man, I'm doing it.
I'm really--
WHACK
SPLISH
Kid, stop messing around and help take out that Quincarrier!!

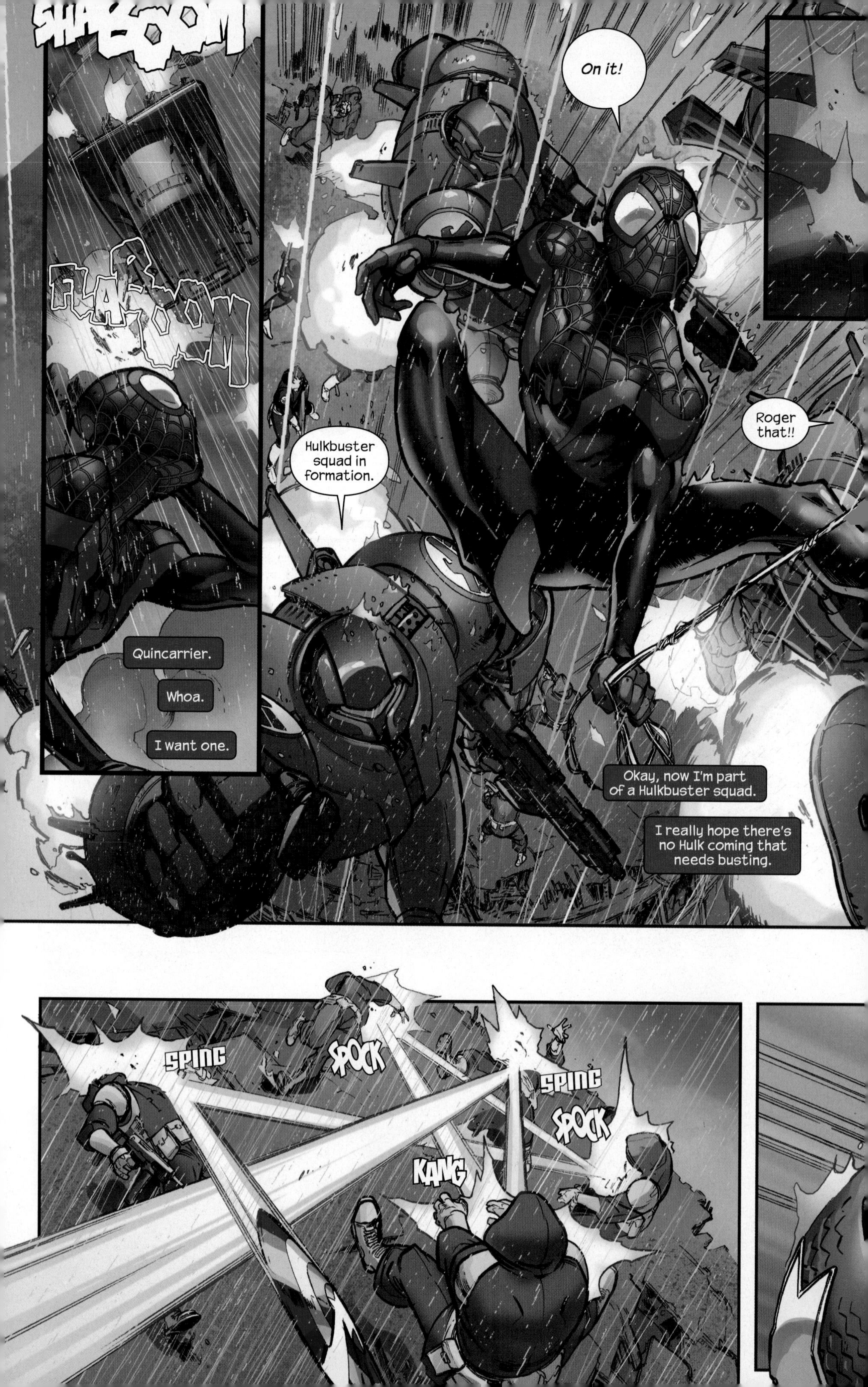
SHABOOM
Quincarrier.
Whoa.
I want one.
On it!
Hulkbuster squad in formation.
Roger that!!
Okay, now I'm part of a Hulkbuster squad.
I really hope there's no Hulk coming that needs busting.
SPING
SPOCK
SPING
SPOCK
KANG

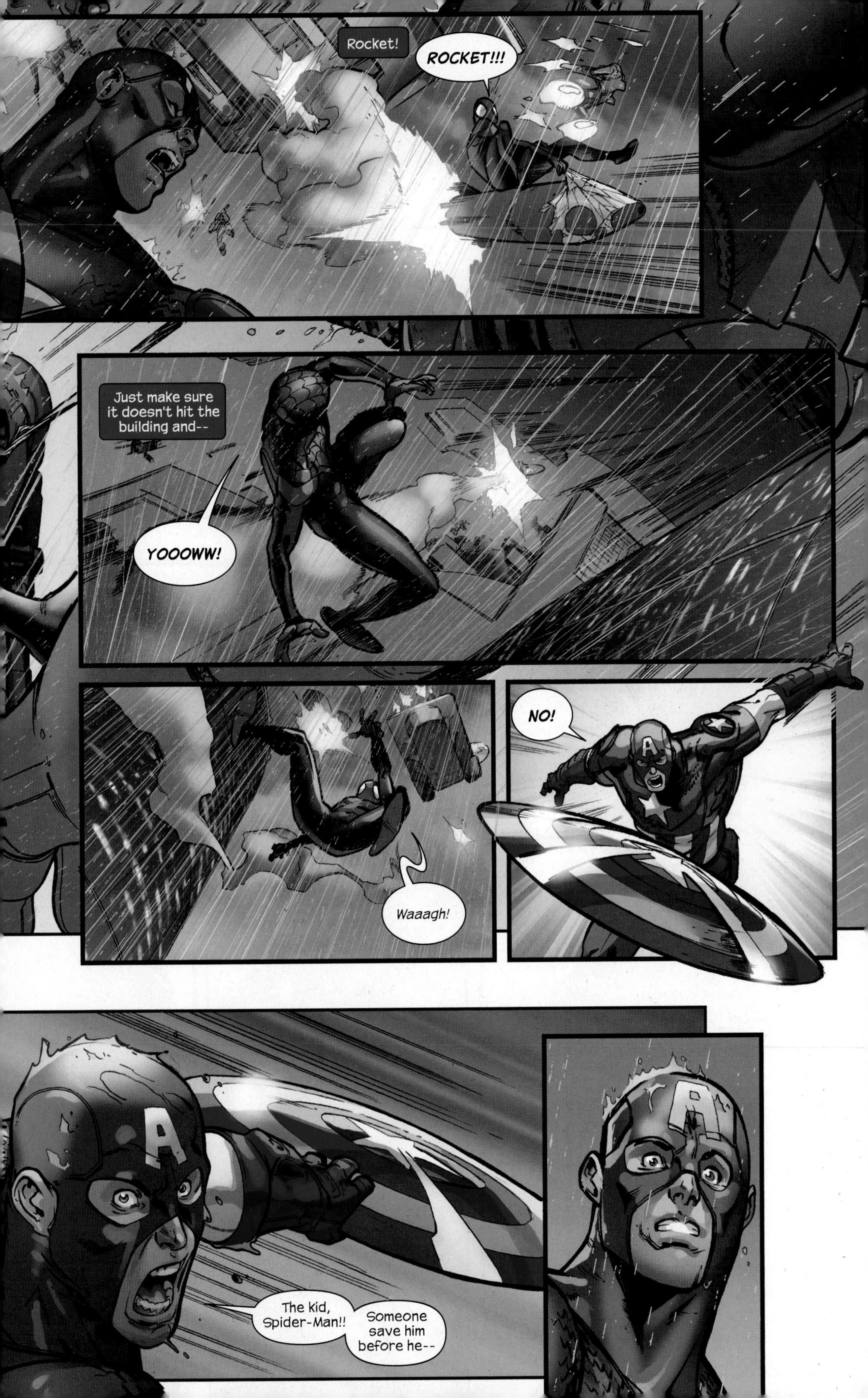
Rocket!
ROCKET!!!
Just make sure it doesn't hit the building and--
YOOOWW!
Waaagh!
NO!
The kid, Spider-Man!!
Someone save him before he--

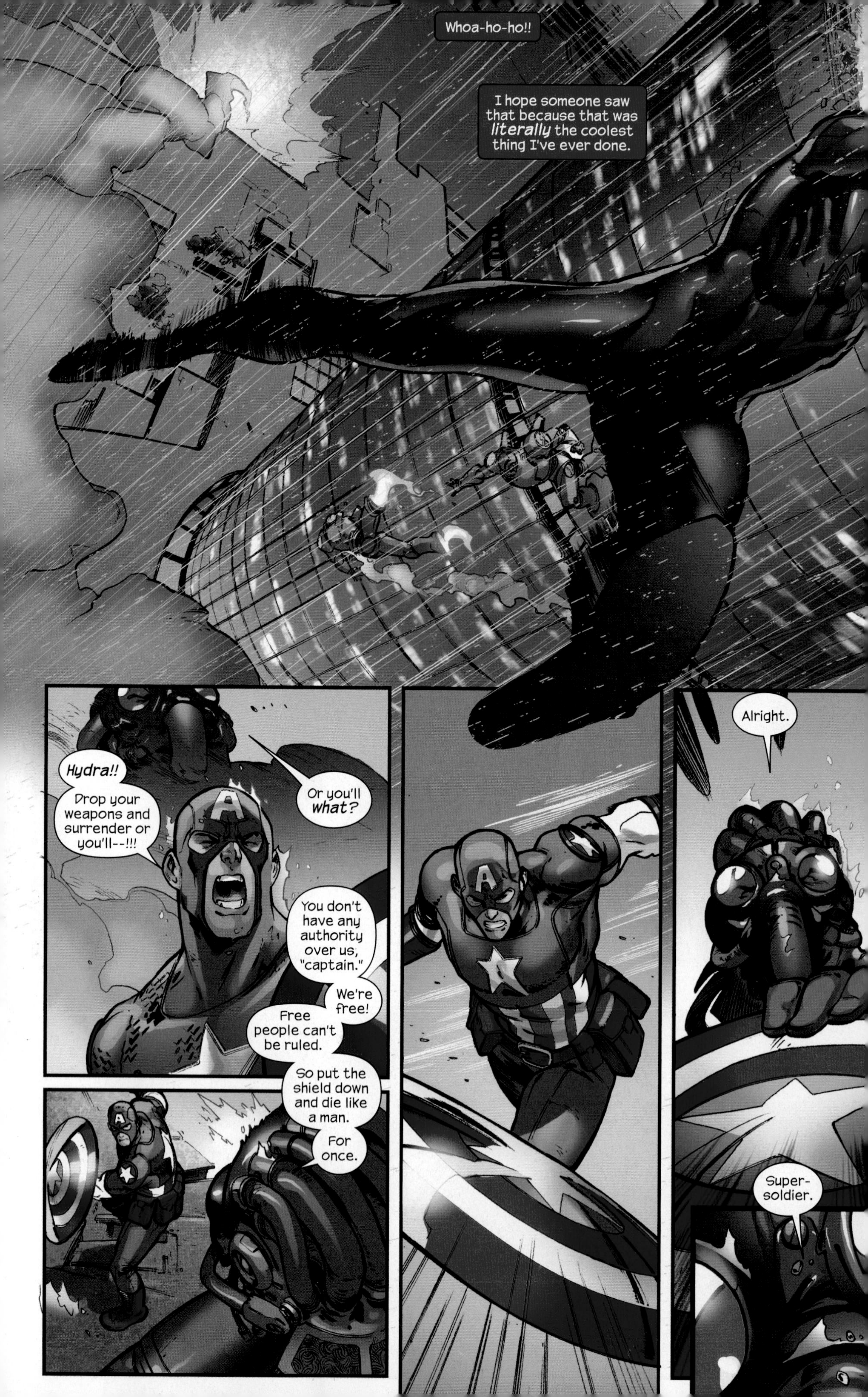
Whoa-ho-ho!!
I hope someone saw that because that was *literally* the coolest thing I've ever done.
Hydra!!
Drop your weapons and surrender or you'll--!!!
Or you'll *what?*
You don't have any authority over us, "captain."
We're free!
Free people can't be ruled.
So put the shield down and die like a man.
For once.
Alright.
Super-soldier.

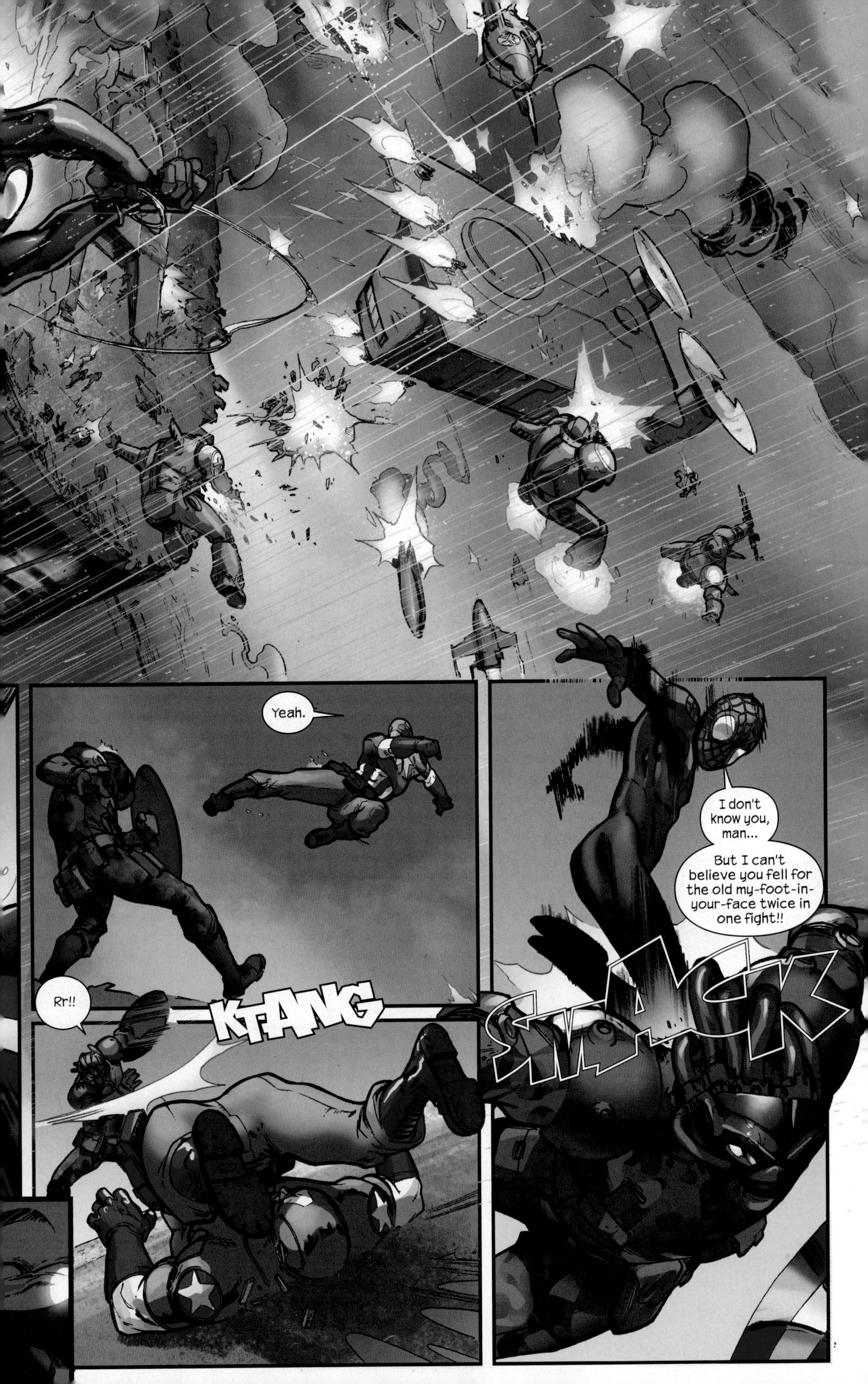
Yeah.
Rr!!
KTANG
I don't know you, man...
But I can't believe you fell for the old my-foot-in-your-face twice in one fight!!
SMACK

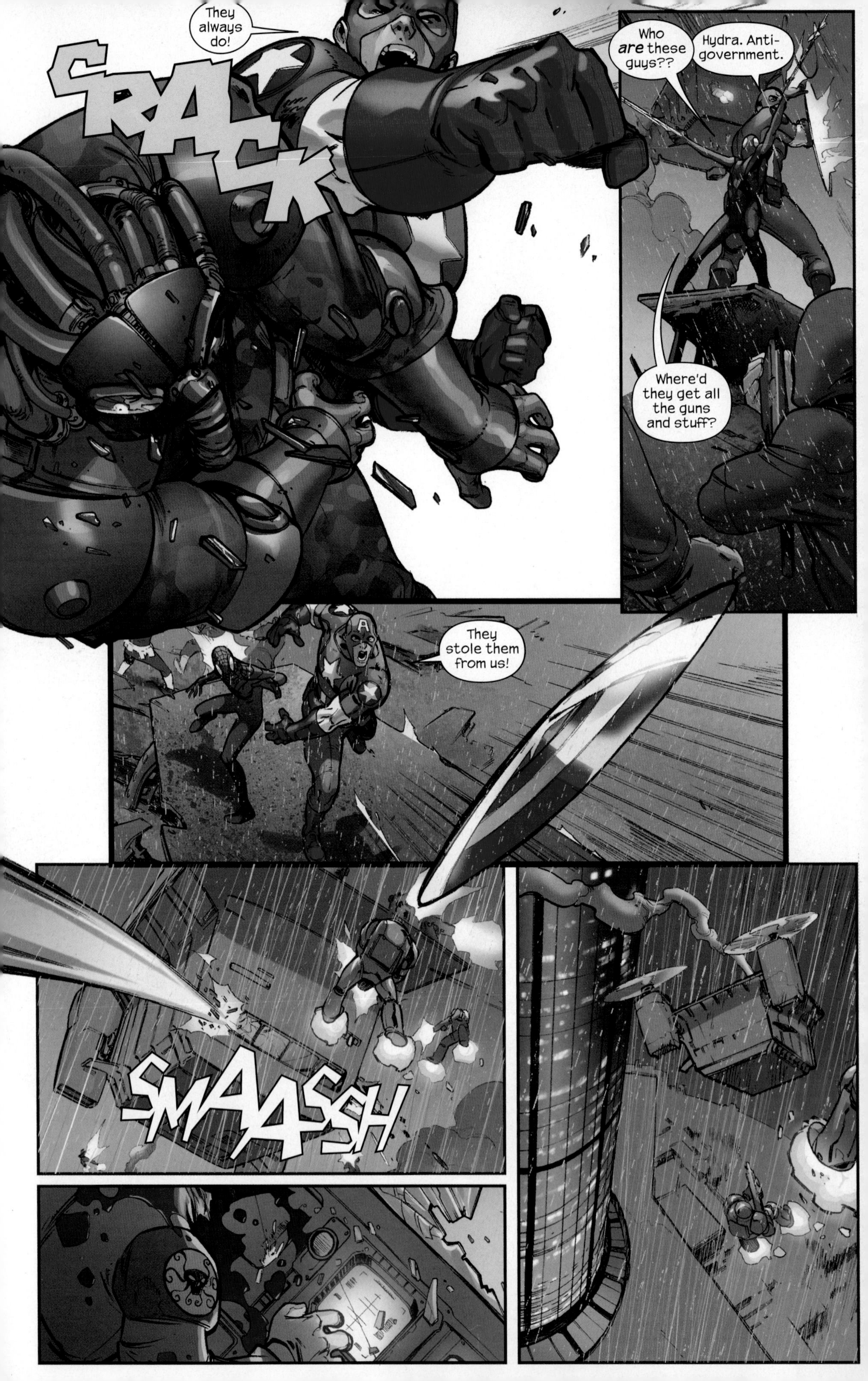
They always do!
CRACK
Who are these guys??
Hydra. Anti-government.
Where'd they get all the guns and stuff?
They stole them from us!
SMAASSH

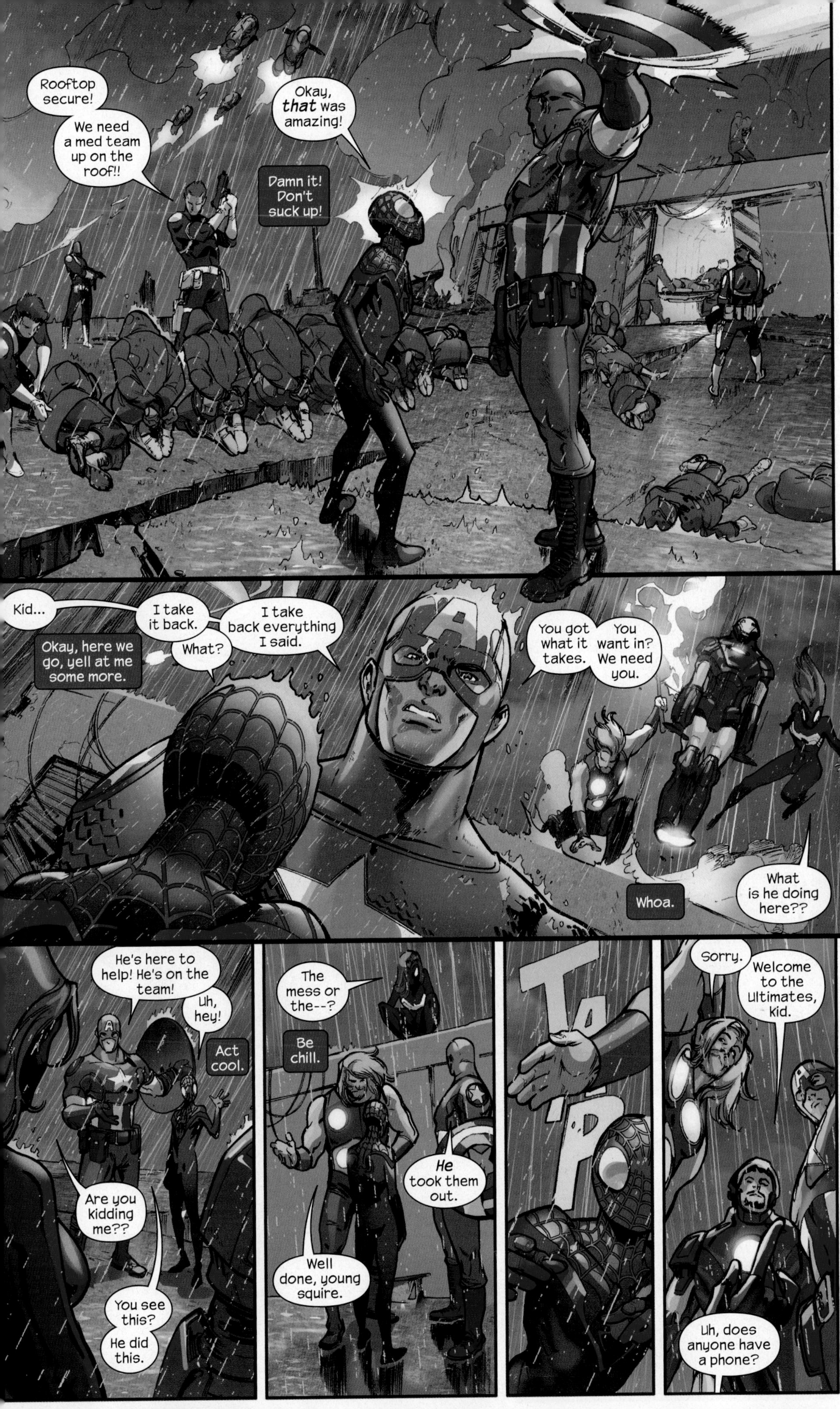
Rooftop secure!
We need a med team up on the roof!!
Okay, that was amazing!
Damn it! Don't suck up!
Kid...
I take it back.
I take back everything I said.
Okay, here we go, yell at me some more.
What?
You got what it takes.
You want in? We need you.
Whoa.
What is he doing here??
He's here to help! He's on the team!
Uh, hey!
Act cool.
Are you kidding me??
You see this?
He did this.
The mess or the--?
Be chill.
He took them out.
Well done, young squire.
TAP
Sorry.
Welcome to the Ultimates, kid.
Uh, does anyone have a phone?

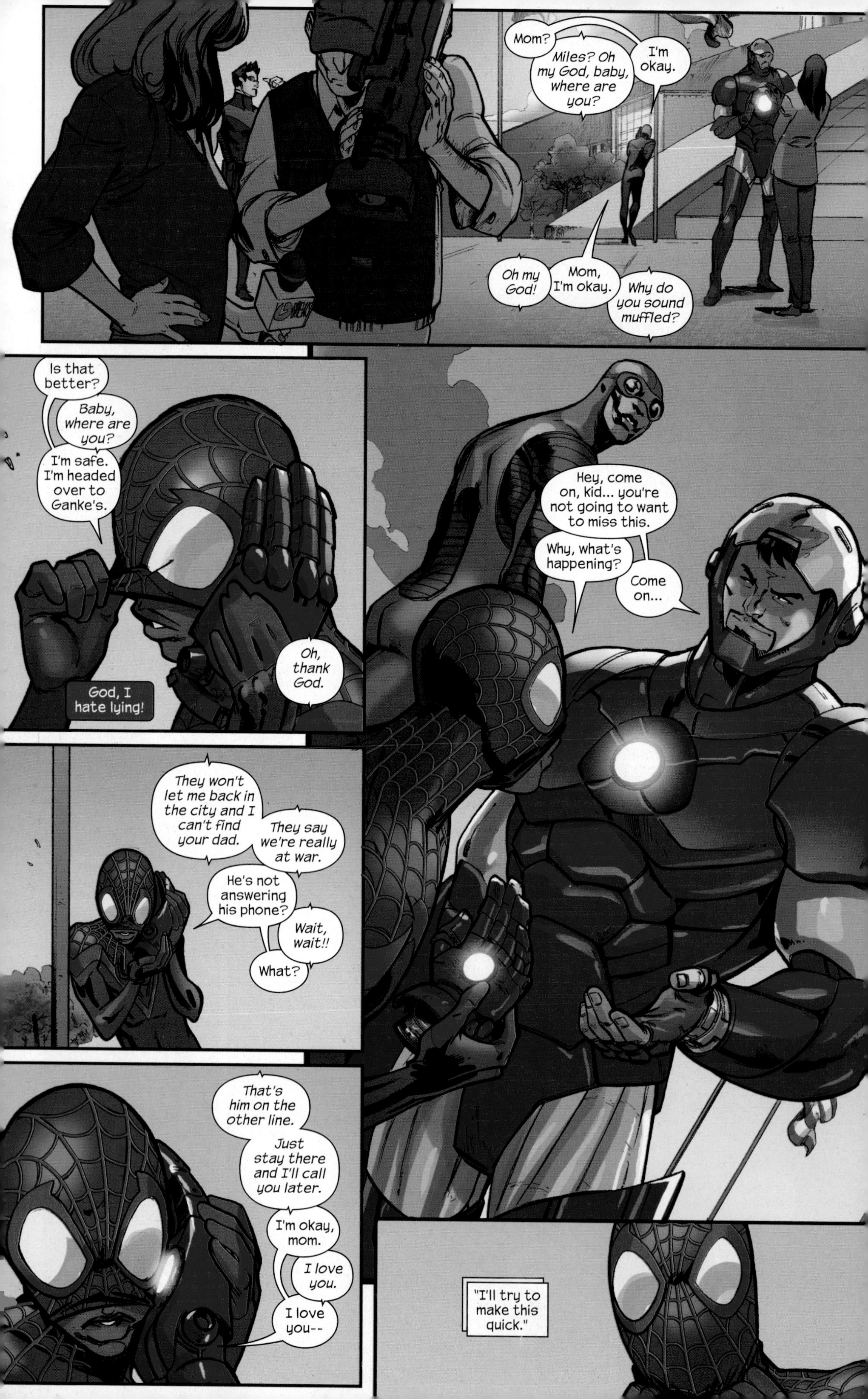
Mom?
Miles? Oh my God, baby, where are you?
I'm okay.
Oh my God!
Mom, I'm okay.
Why do you sound muffled?
Is that better?
Baby, where are you?
I'm safe. I'm headed over to Ganke's.
Oh, thank God.
God, I hate lying!
Hey, come on, kid... you're not going to want to miss this.
Why, what's happening?
Come on...
They won't let me back in the city and I can't find your dad.
They say we're really at war.
He's not answering his phone?
Wait, wait!!
What?
That's him on the other line.
Just stay there and I'll call you later.
I'm okay, mom.
I love you.
I love you--
"I'll try to make this quick."

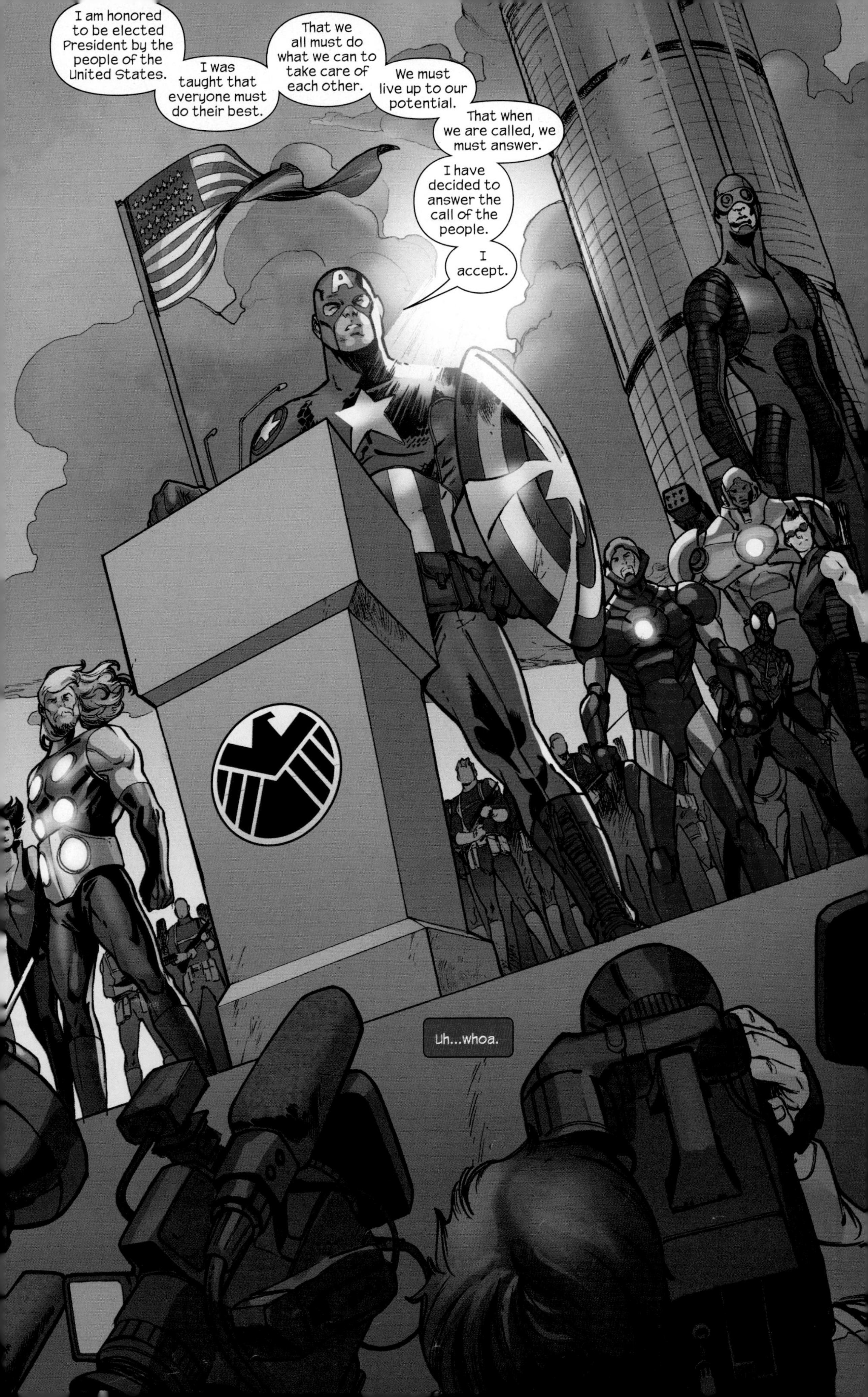
I am honored to be elected President by the people of the United States.
I was taught that everyone must do their best.
That we all must do what we can to take care of each other.
We must live up to our potential.
That when we are called, we must answer.
I have decided to answer the call of the people.
I accept.
Uh...whoa.

17

★

ULTIMATE COMICS **SPIDER-MAN** #17

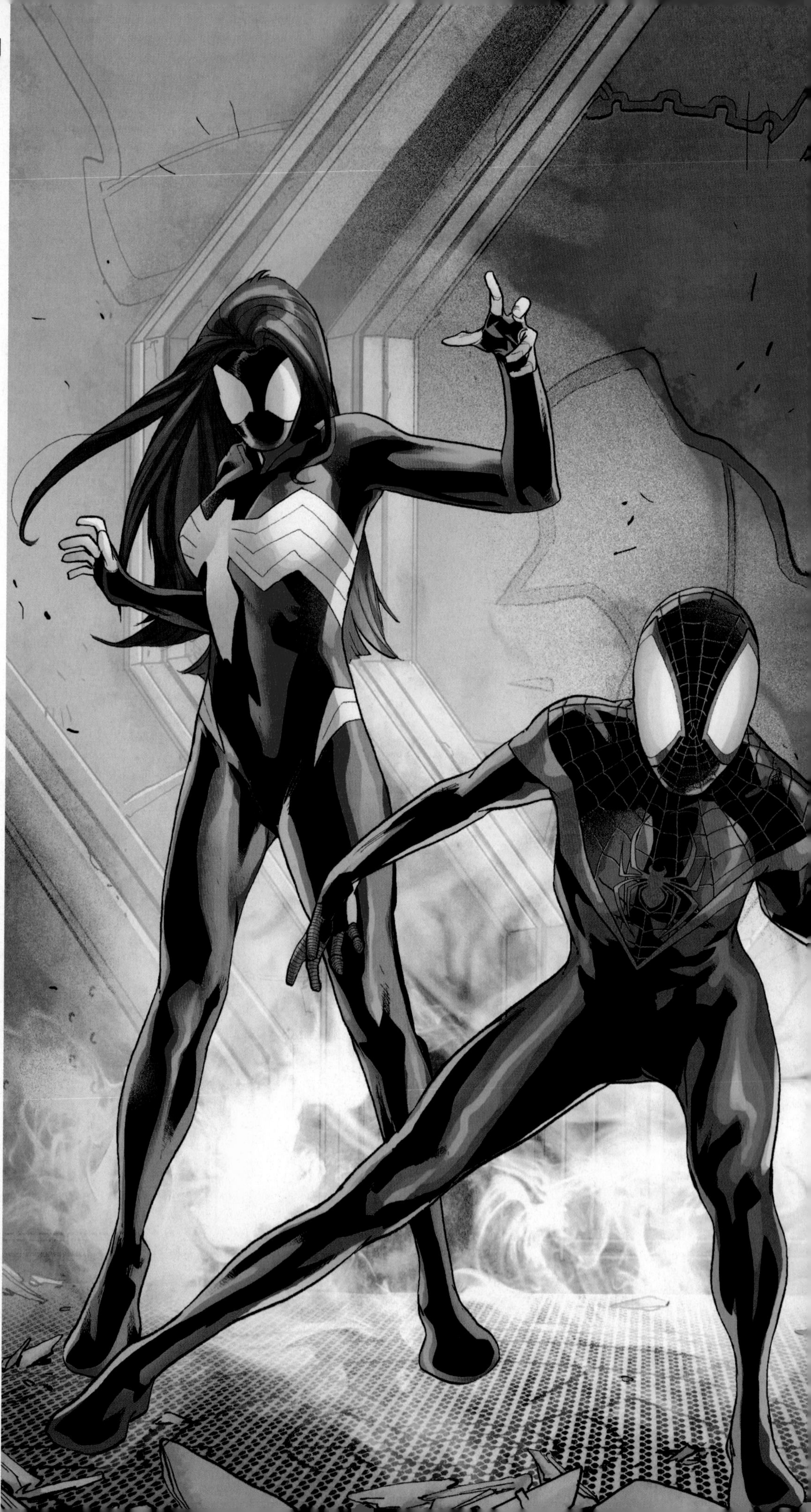

S.H.I.E.L.D. SITUATION MAP:

[Anti-government militia hot spots]

Idaho, Montana,
N. Dakota, S. Dakota,
Arizona, Wyoming

Wyoming
status unknown

[Eastern seaboard control zone]

New England,
New York,
New Jersey,
Delaware,
Washington, D.C.,
Maryland,
Pennsylvania,
Virginia

secured by
National Guard
under emergency
powers
committee

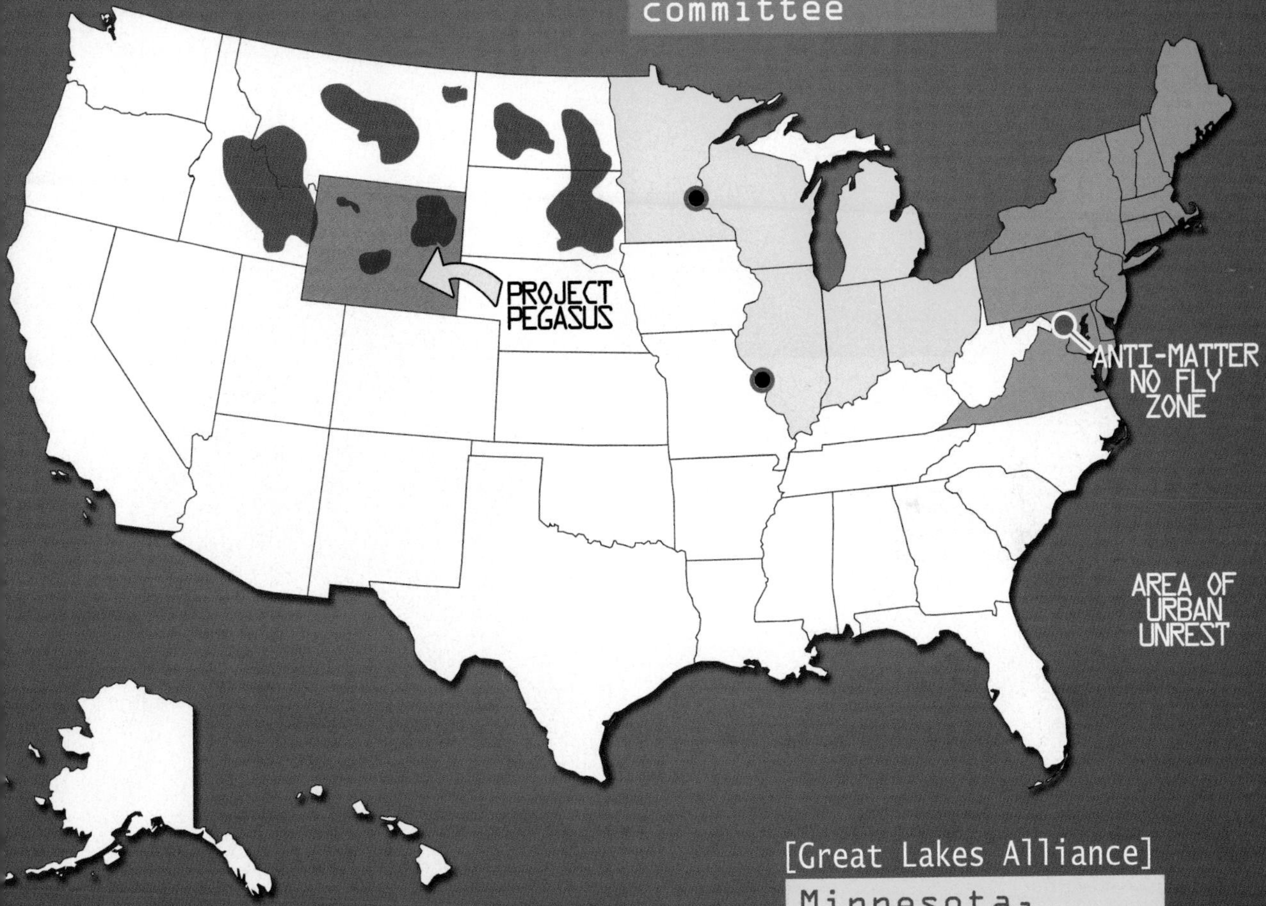
PROJECT PEGASUS
ANTI-MATTER NO FLY ZONE
AREA OF URBAN UNREST

[Great Lakes Alliance]

Minnesota,
Wisconsin,
Michigan,
Illinois,
Indiana, Ohio

Independent
nation

ALL STATES
SHOWN IN WHITE
ARE U.S. GOVERNMENT-
CONTROLLED ZONES

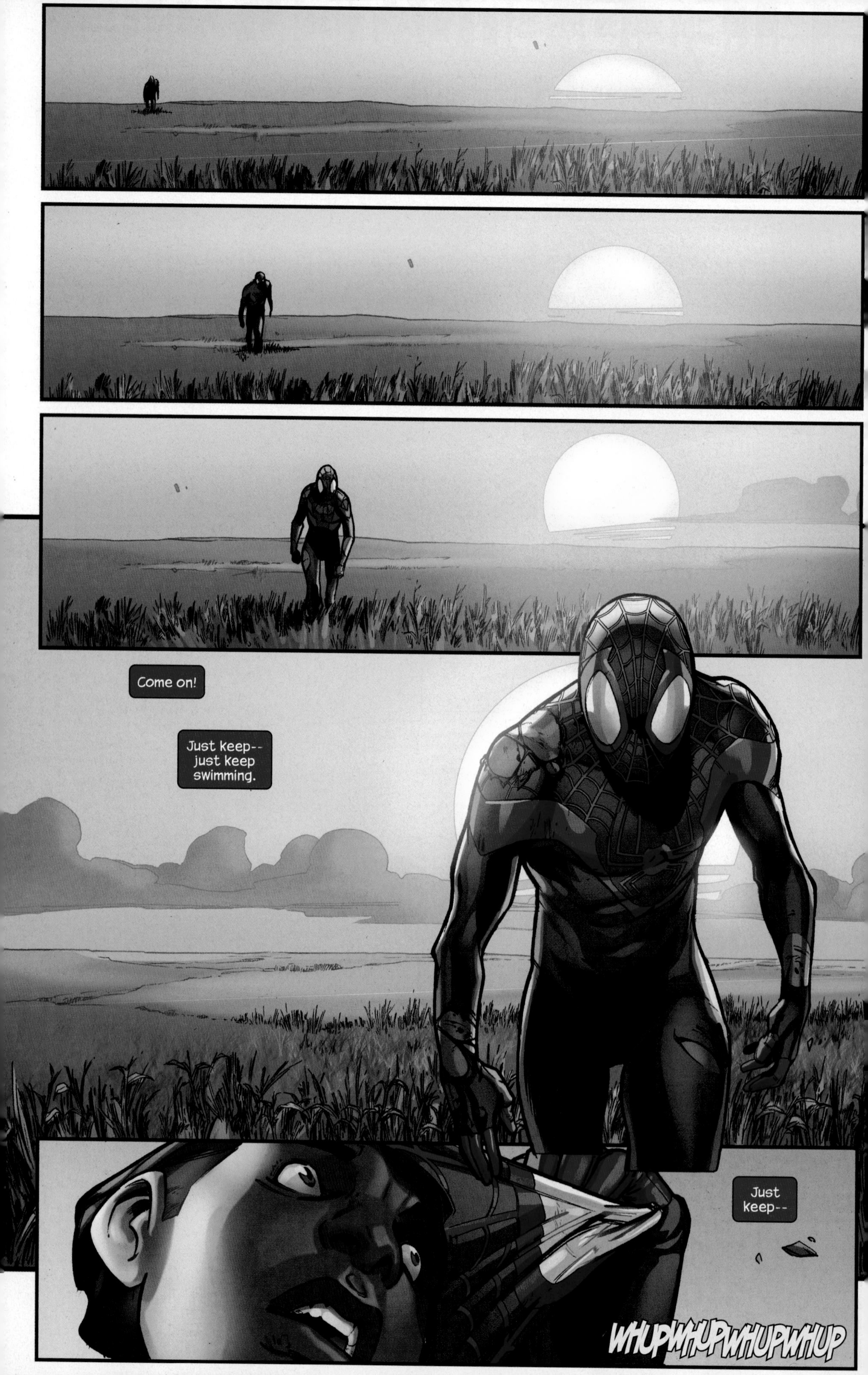

Come on!
Just keep--
just keep
swimming.
Just
keep--
WHUPWHUPWHUPWHUP

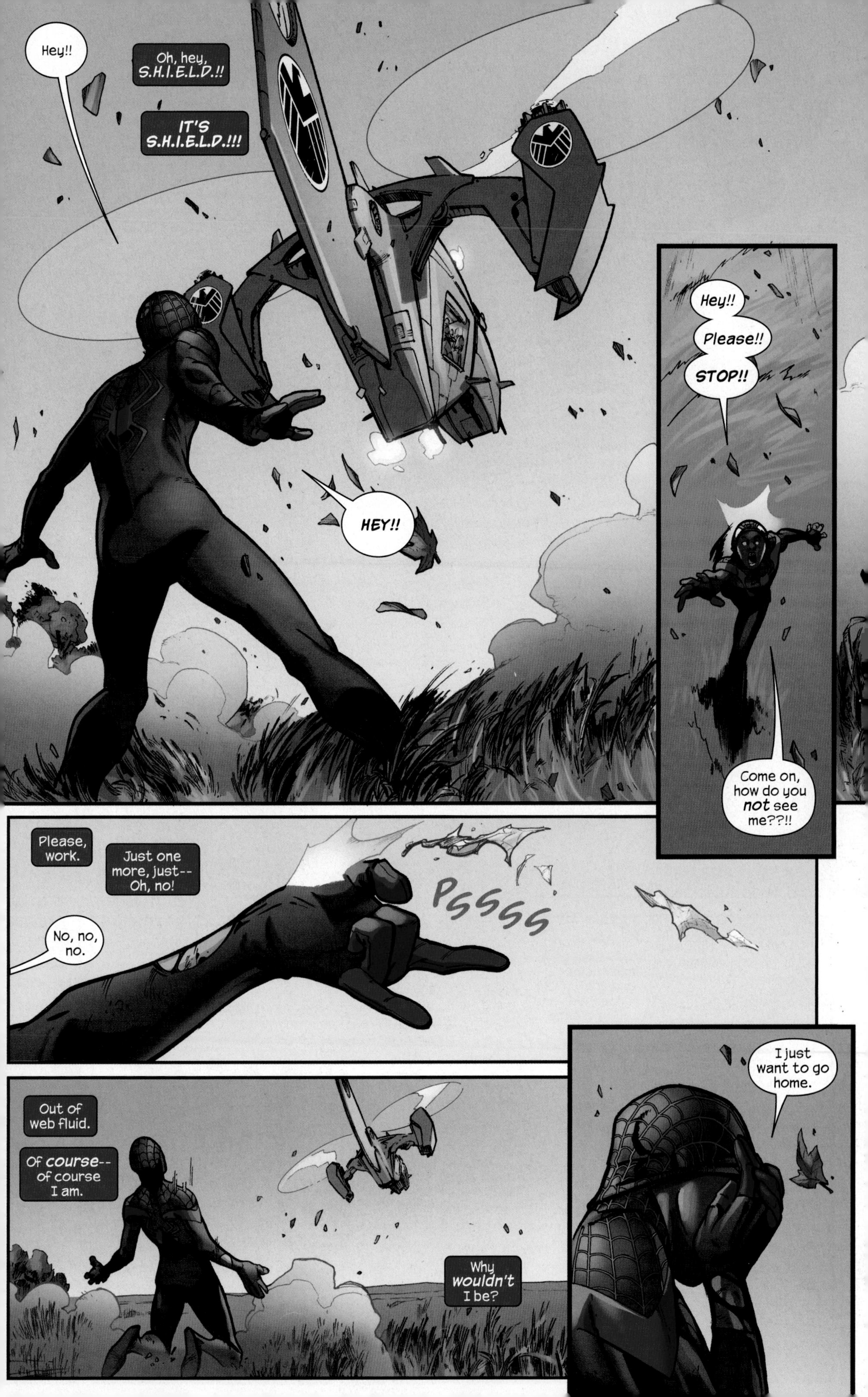
Hey!!
Oh, hey, S.H.I.E.L.D.!!
IT'S S.H.I.E.L.D.!!!
HEY!!
Hey!!
Please!!
STOP!!
Come on, how do you not see me??!!
Please, work.
Just one more, just-- Oh, no!
No, no, no.
PSSSS
Out of web fluid.
Of course-- of course I am.
Why wouldn't I be?
I just want to go home.

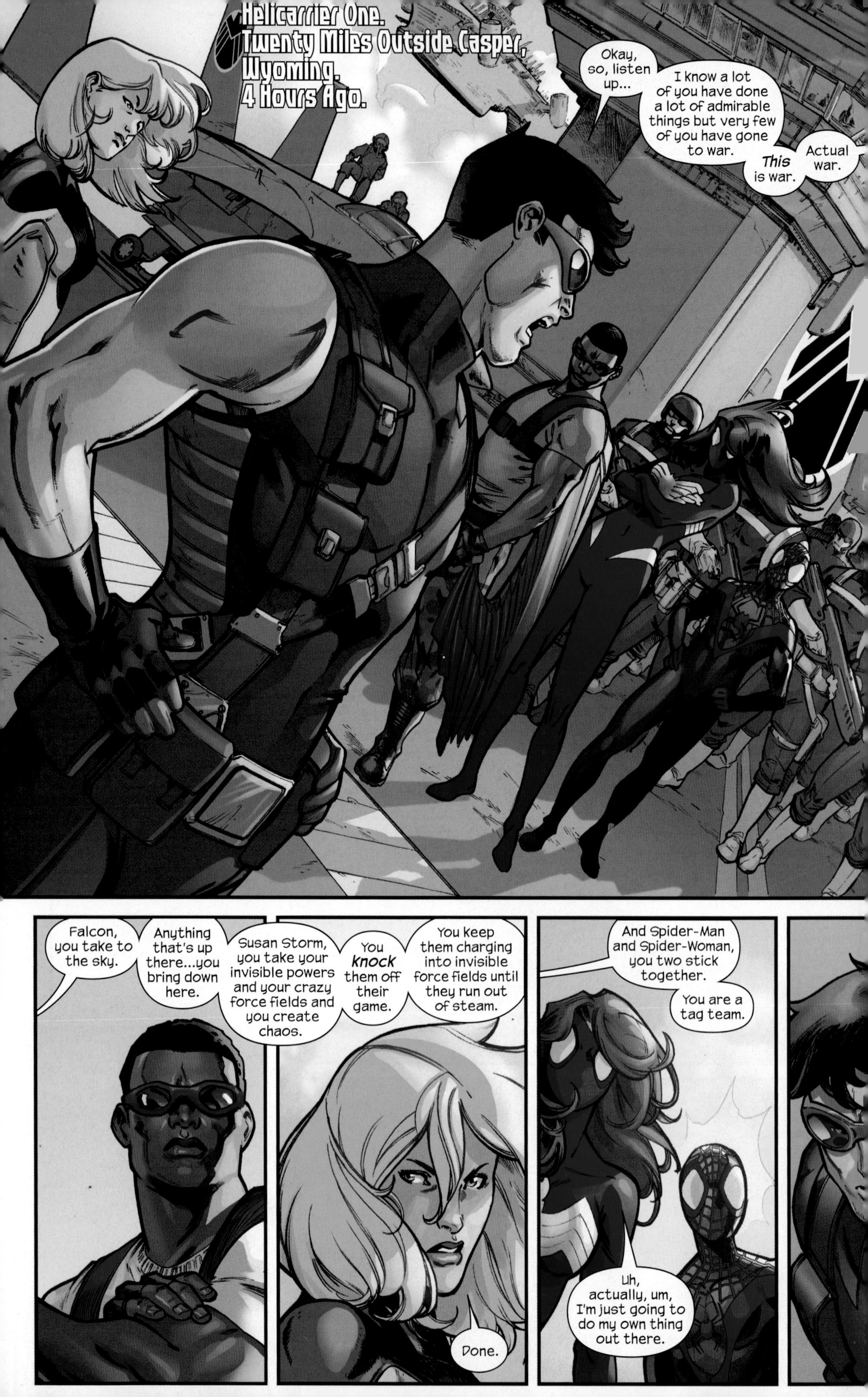

Helicarrier One.
Twenty Miles Outside Casper, Wyoming.
4 Hours Ago.
Okay, so, listen up...
I know a lot of you have done a lot of admirable things but very few of you have gone to war.
This is war.
Actual war.
Falcon, you take to the sky.
Anything that's up there...you bring down here.
Susan Storm, you take your invisible powers and your crazy force fields and you create chaos.
You knock them off their game.
You keep them charging into invisible force fields until they run out of steam.
Done.
And Spider-Man and Spider-Woman, you two stick together.
You are a tag team.
Uh, actually, um, I'm just going to do my own thing out there.

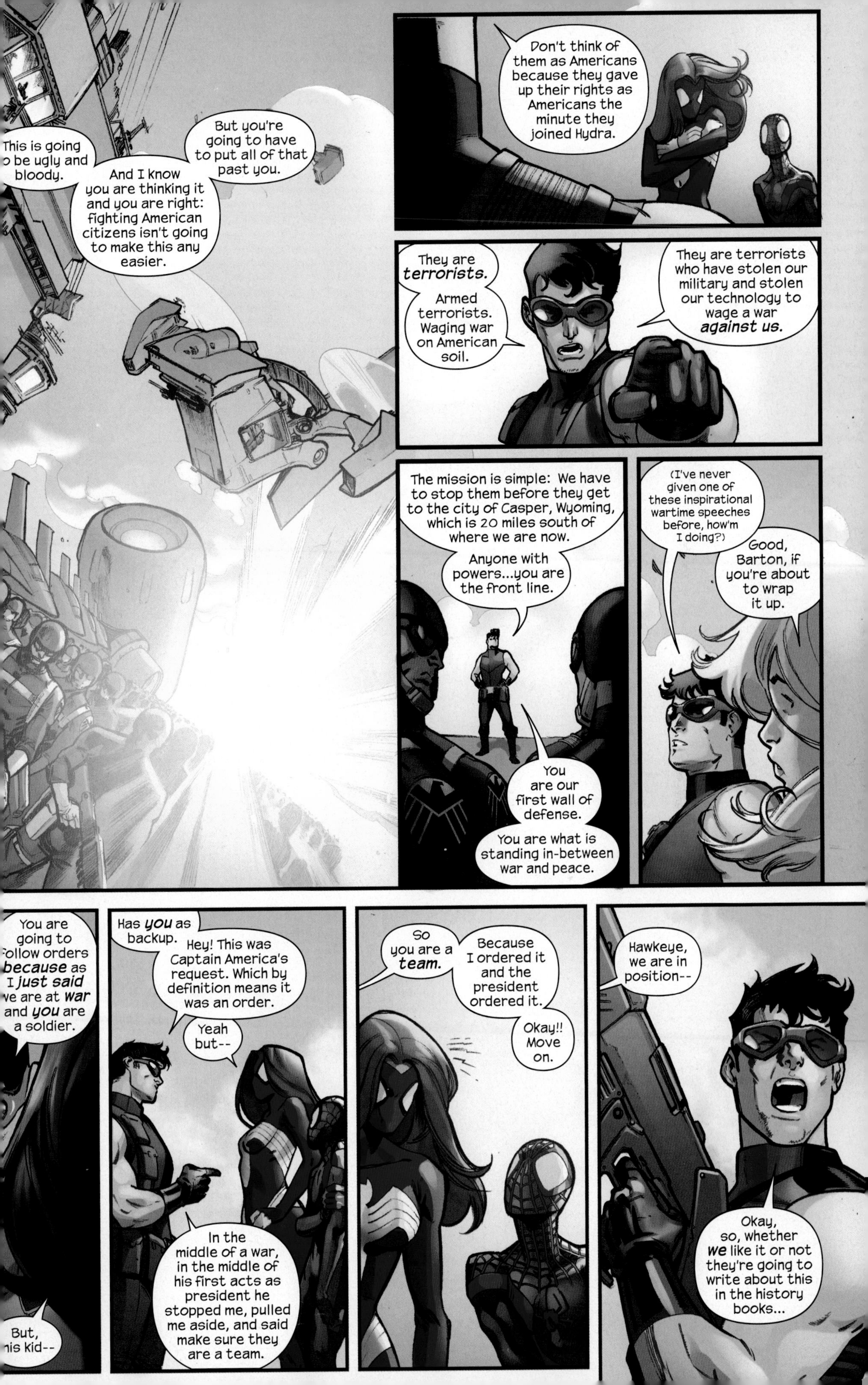

This is going
o be ugly and bloody.
And I know you are thinking it and you are right: fighting American citizens isn't going to make this any easier.
But you're going to have to put all of that past you.
Don't think of them as Americans because they gave up their rights as Americans the minute they joined Hydra.
They are *terrorists.*
Armed terrorists. Waging war on American soil.
They are terrorists who have stolen our military and stolen our technology to wage a war *against us.*
The mission is simple: We have to stop them before they get to the city of Casper, Wyoming, which is 20 miles south of where we are now.
Anyone with powers...you are the front line.
You are our first wall of defense.
You are what is standing in-between war and peace.
(I've never given one of these inspirational wartime speeches before, how'm I doing?)
Good, Barton, if you're about to wrap it up.
You are going to
ollow orders *because* as I *just said*
ve are at *war* and *you* are a soldier.
But,
is kid--
Has *you* as backup.
Hey! This was Captain America's request. Which by definition means it was an order.
Yeah but--
In the middle of a war, in the middle of his first acts as president he stopped me, pulled me aside, and said make sure they are a team.
So you are a *team.*
Because I ordered it and the president ordered it.
Okay!! Move on.
Hawkeye, we are in position--
Okay, so, whether *we* like it or not they're going to write about this in the history books...

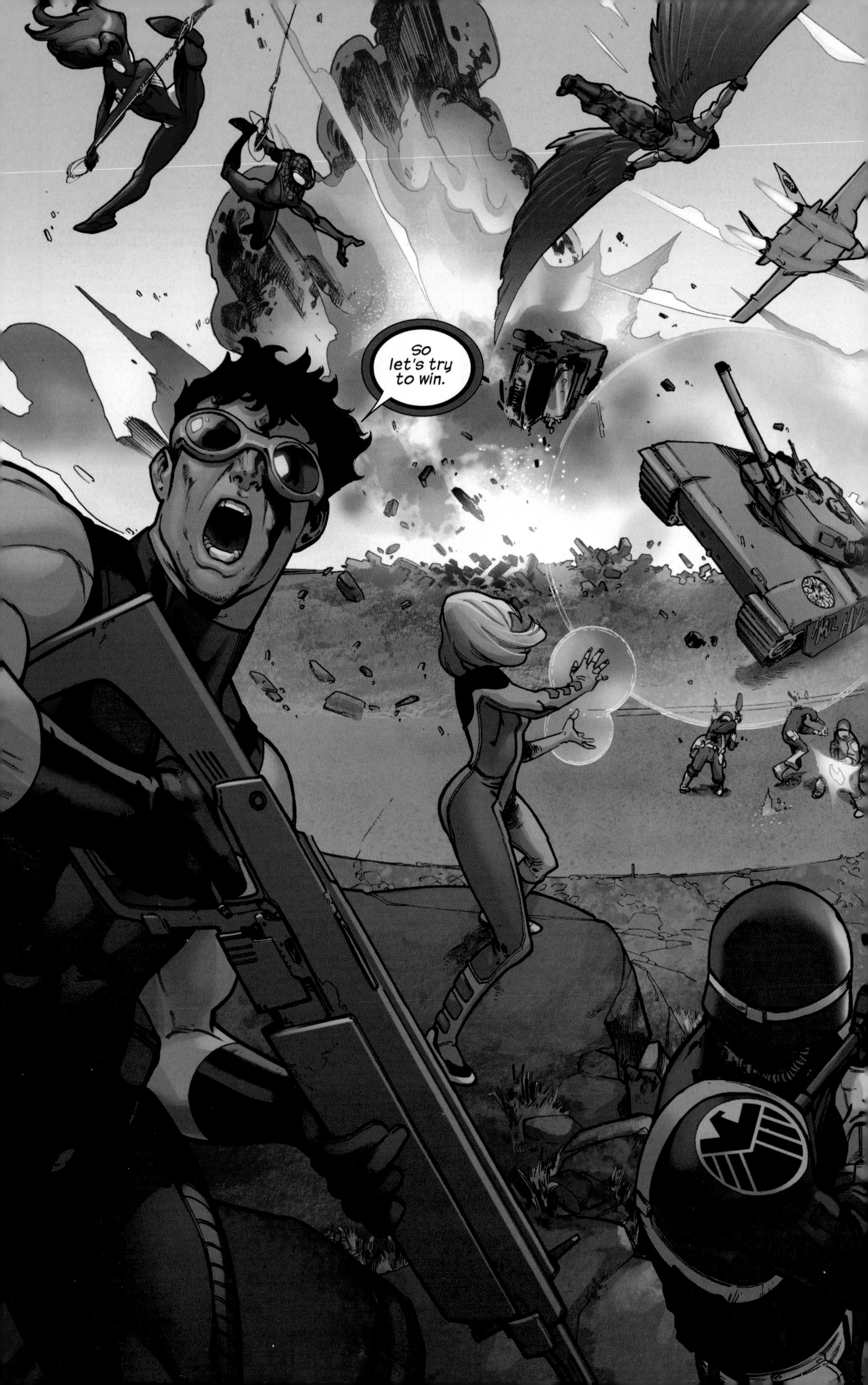
So let's try to win.

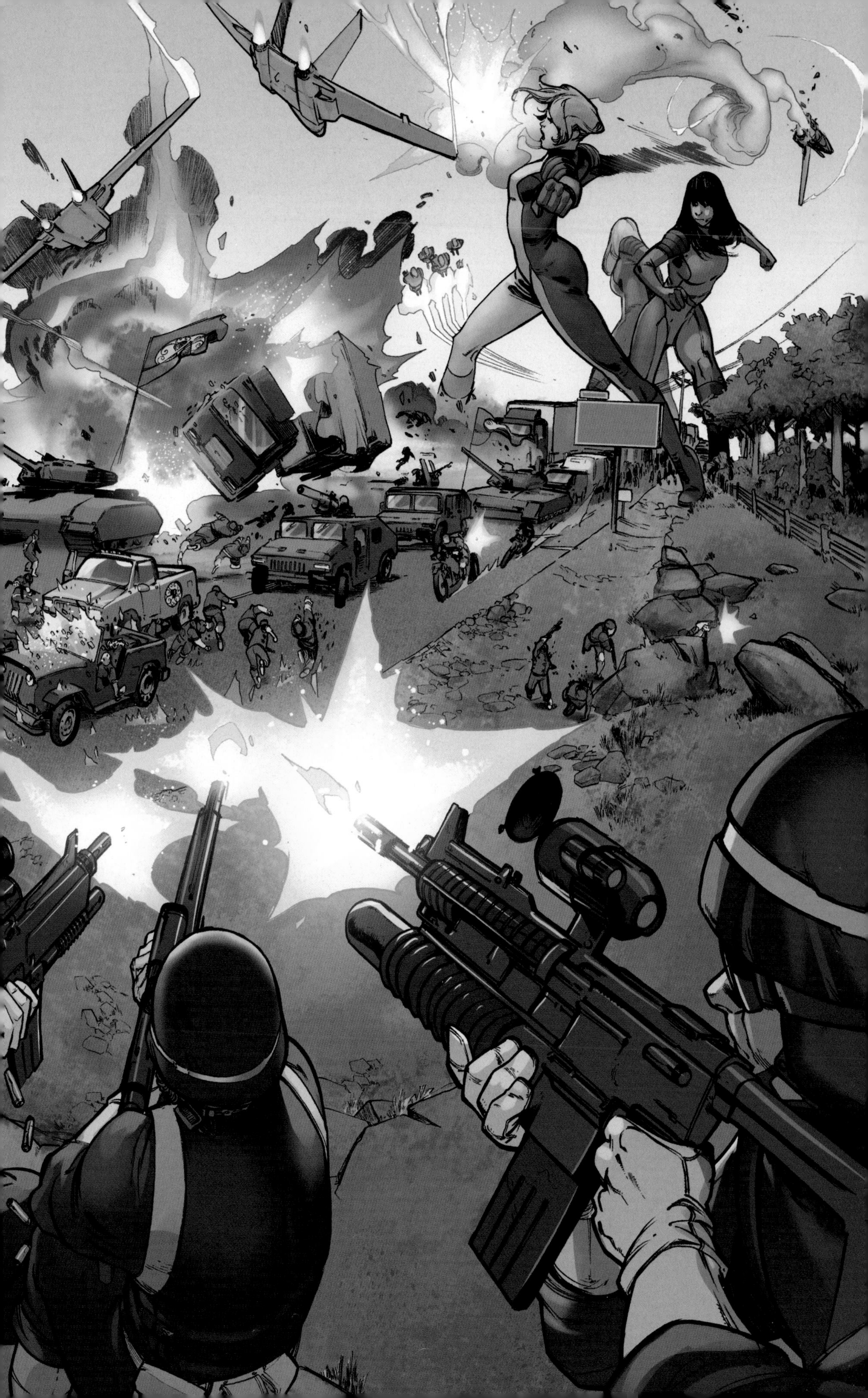

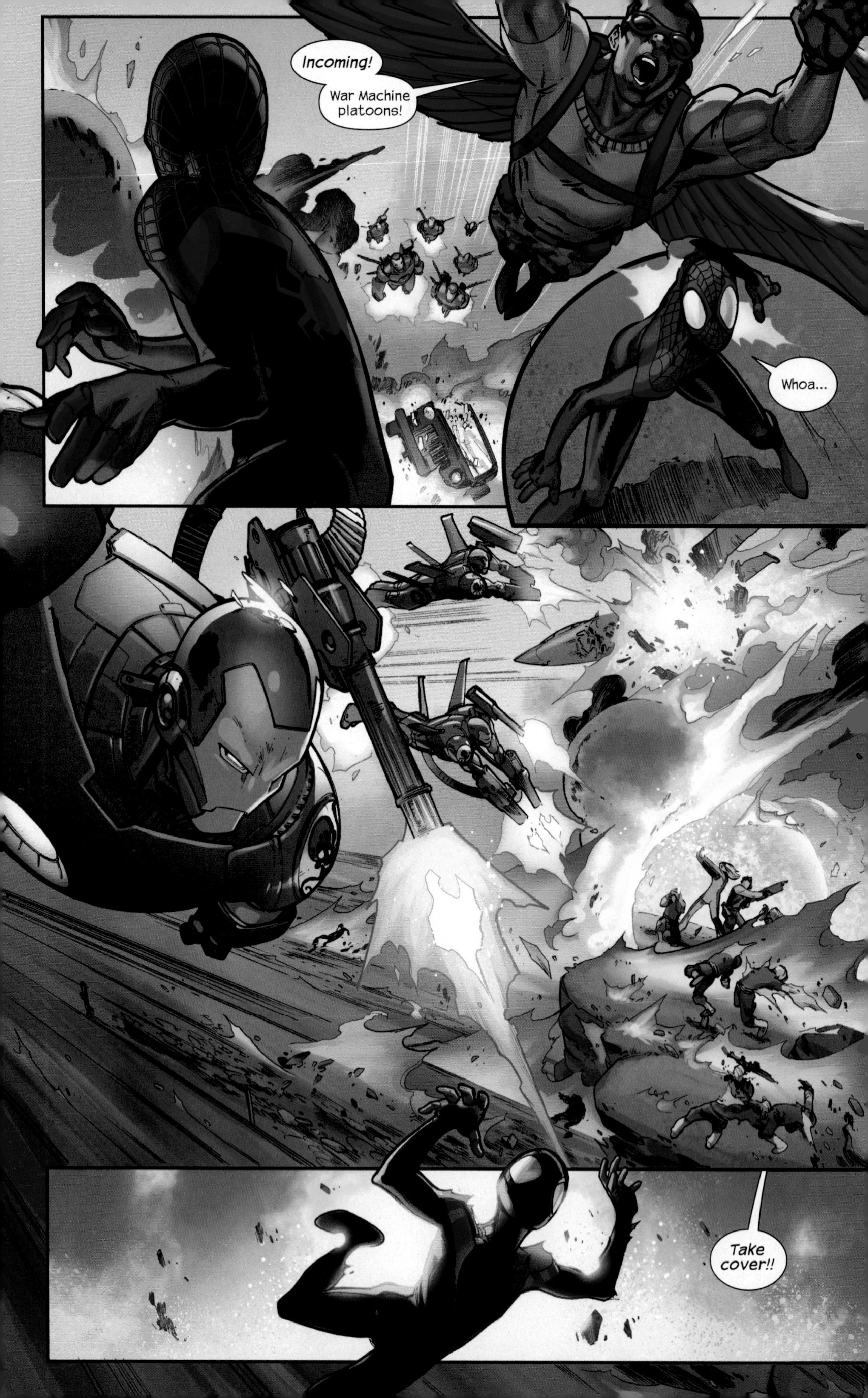
Incoming!
War Machine platoons!
Whoa...
Take cover!!

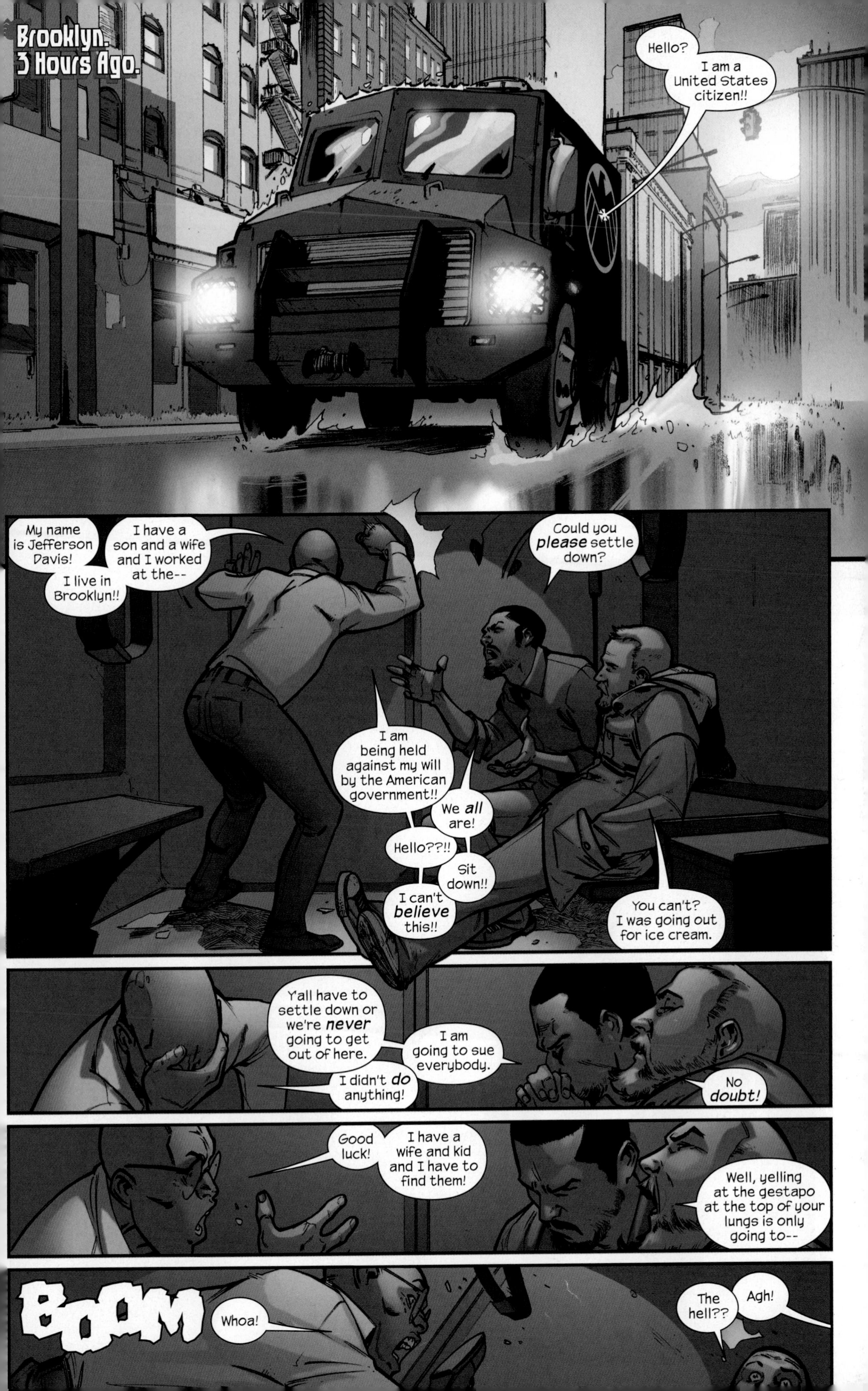
Brooklyn.
3 Hours Ago.
Hello?
I am a United States citizen!!
My name is Jefferson Davis!
I live in Brooklyn!!
I have a son and a wife and I worked at the--
Could you please settle down?
I am being held against my will by the American government!!
We all are!
Hello??!!
Sit down!!
I can't believe this!!
You can't? I was going out for ice cream.
Y'all have to settle down or we're never going to get out of here.
I am going to sue everybody.
I didn't do anything!
No doubt!
Good luck!
I have a wife and kid and I have to find them!
Well, yelling at the gestapo at the top of your lungs is only going to--
BOOM
Whoa!
The hell??
Agh!

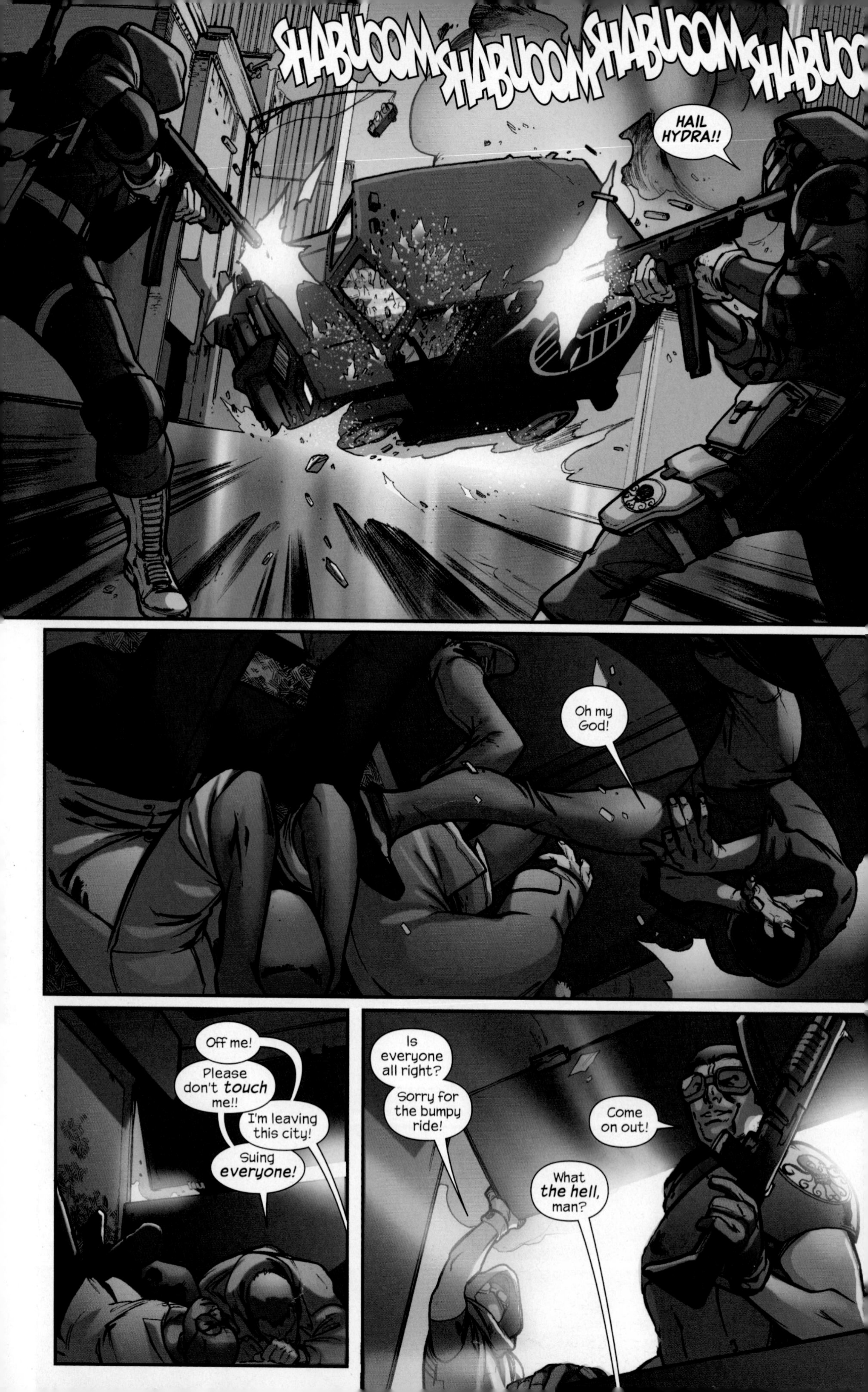
SHABUOOM SHABUOOM SHABUOOM SHABUO
HAIL HYDRA!!
Oh my God!
Off me!
Please don't *touch* me!!
I'm leaving this city!
Suing *everyone!*
Is everyone all right?
Sorry for the bumpy ride!
Come on out!
What *the hell,* man?

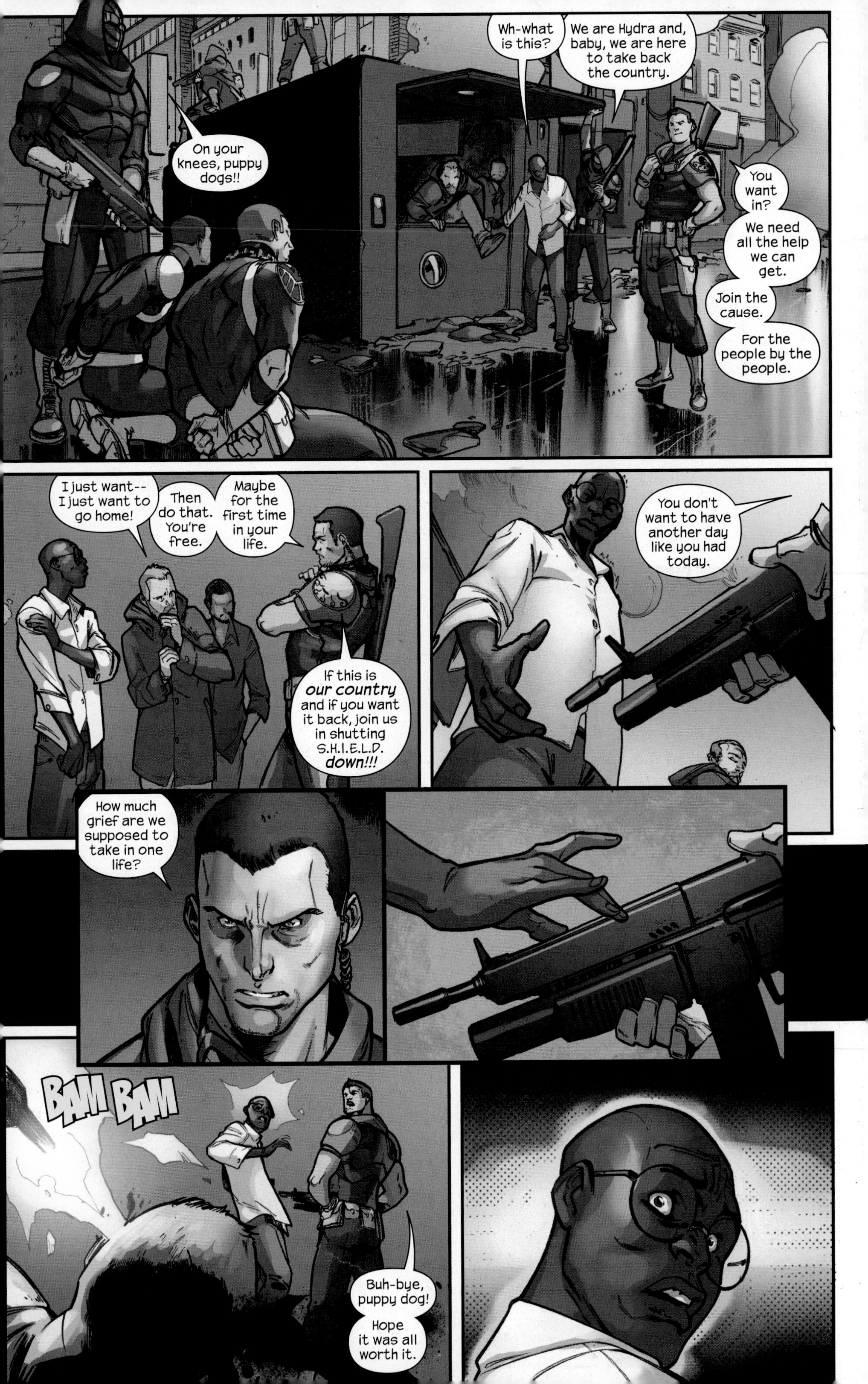
On your knees, puppy dogs!!
Wh-what is this?
We are Hydra and, baby, we are here to take back the country.
You want in?
We need all the help we can get.
Join the cause.
For the people by the people.
I just want-- I just want to go home!
Then do that. You're free.
Maybe for the first time in your life.
If this is *our country* and if you want it back, join us in shutting S.H.I.E.L.D. *down!!!*
You don't want to have another day like you had today.
How much grief are we supposed to take in one life?
BAM BAM
Buh-bye, puppy dog!
Hope it was all worth it.

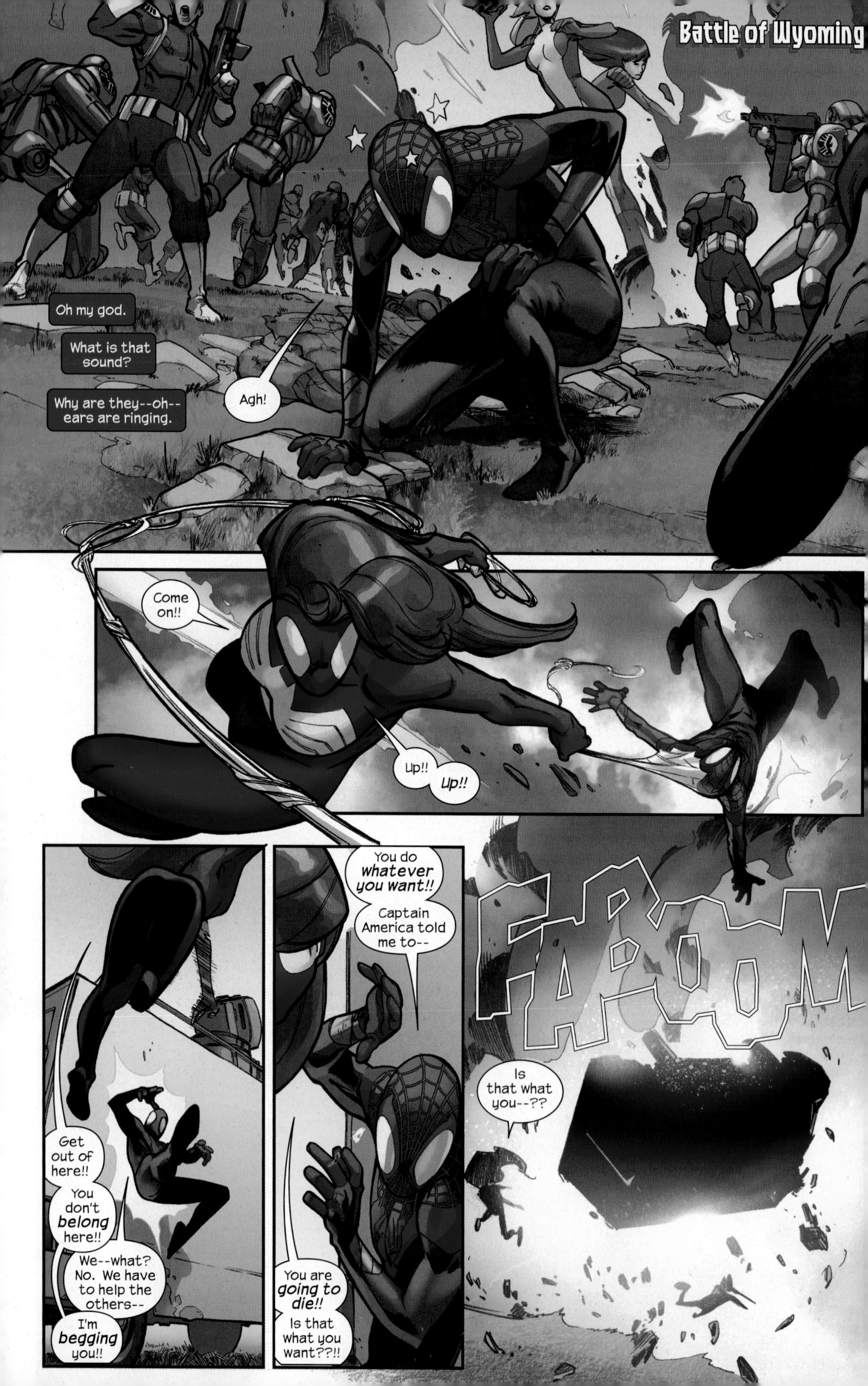
Battle of Wyoming
Oh my god.
What is that sound?
Why are they--oh-- ears are ringing.
Agh!
Come on!!
Up!!
Up!!
Get out of here!!
You don't *belong* here!!
We--what? No. We have to help the others--
I'm *begging* you!!
You do *whatever you want!!*
Captain America told me to--
You are *going to die!!*
Is that what you want??!!
FAROOM
Is that what you--??

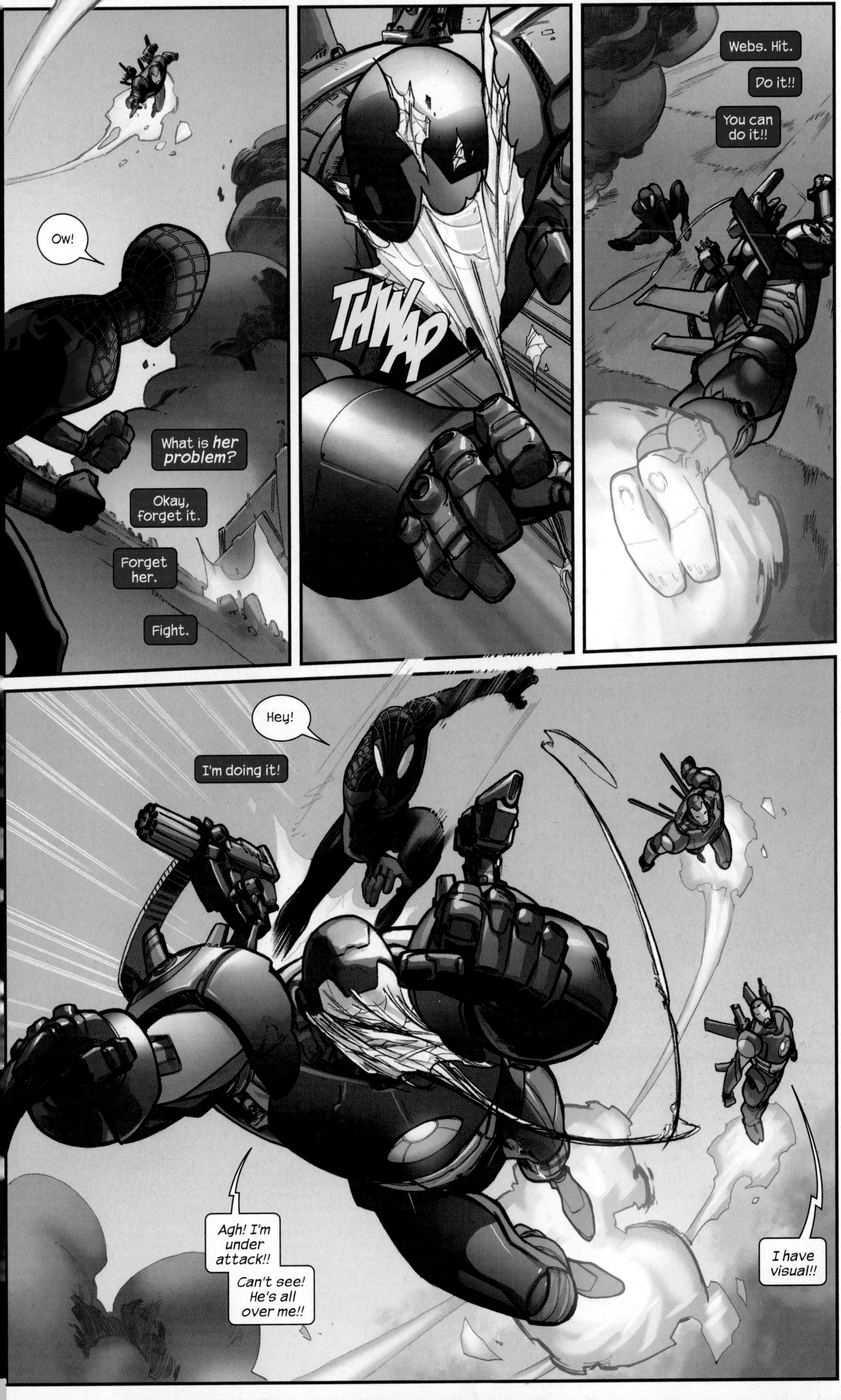
Ow!
What is her problem?
Okay, forget it.
Forget her.
Fight.
THWAP
Webs. Hit.
Do it!!
You can do it!!
Hey!
I'm doing it!
Agh! I'm under attack!!
Can't see! He's all over me!!
I have visual!!

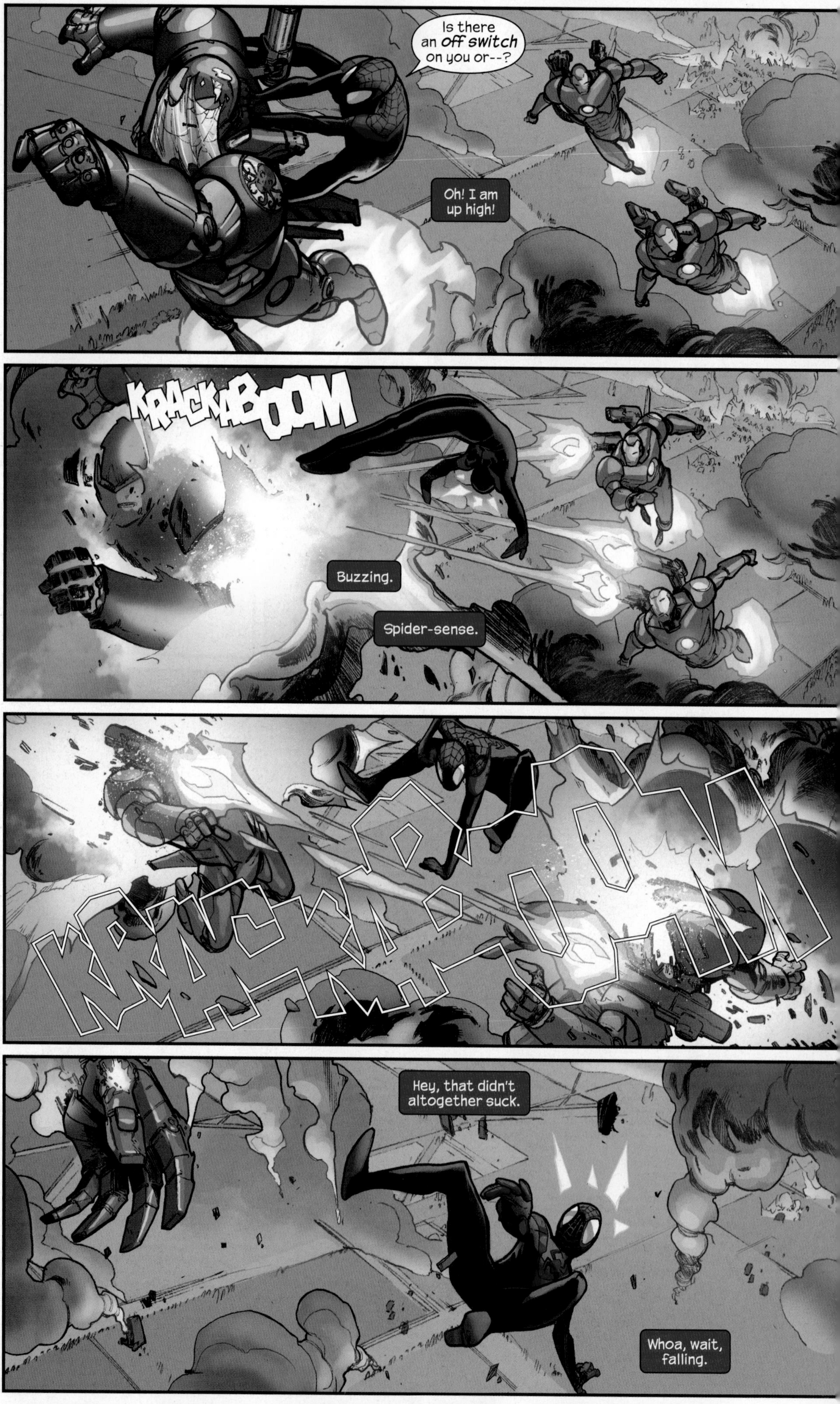
Is there an *off switch* on you or--?
Oh! I am up high!
KRACKABOOM
Buzzing.
Spider-sense.
KRACKABOOM
Hey, that didn't altogether suck.
Whoa, wait, falling.

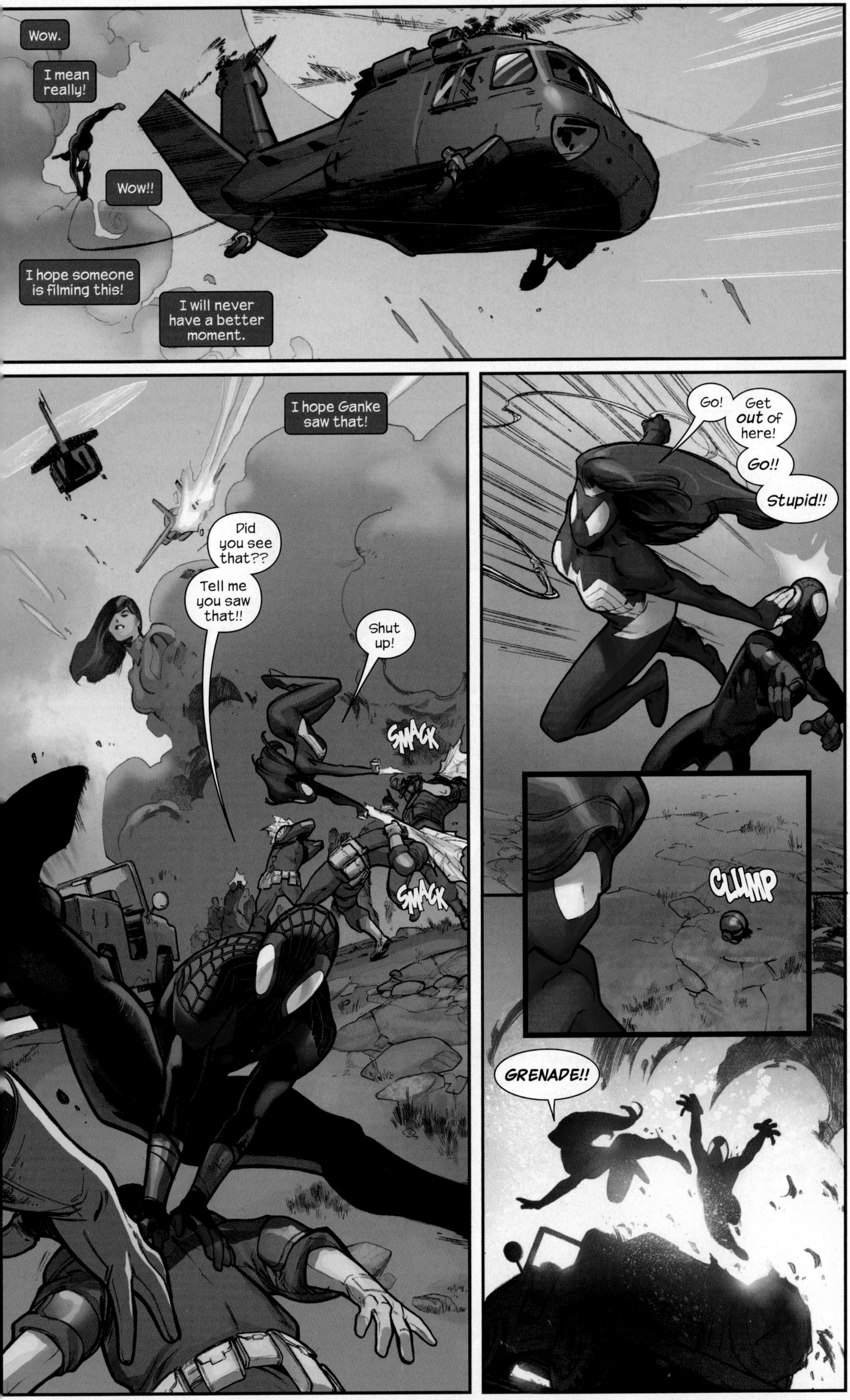
Wow.
I mean really!
Wow!!
I hope someone is filming this!
I will never have a better moment.
I hope Ganke saw that!
Did you see that??
Tell me you saw that!!
Shut up!
SMACK
SMACK
Go!
Get out of here!
Go!!
Stupid!!
CLUMP
GRENADE!!

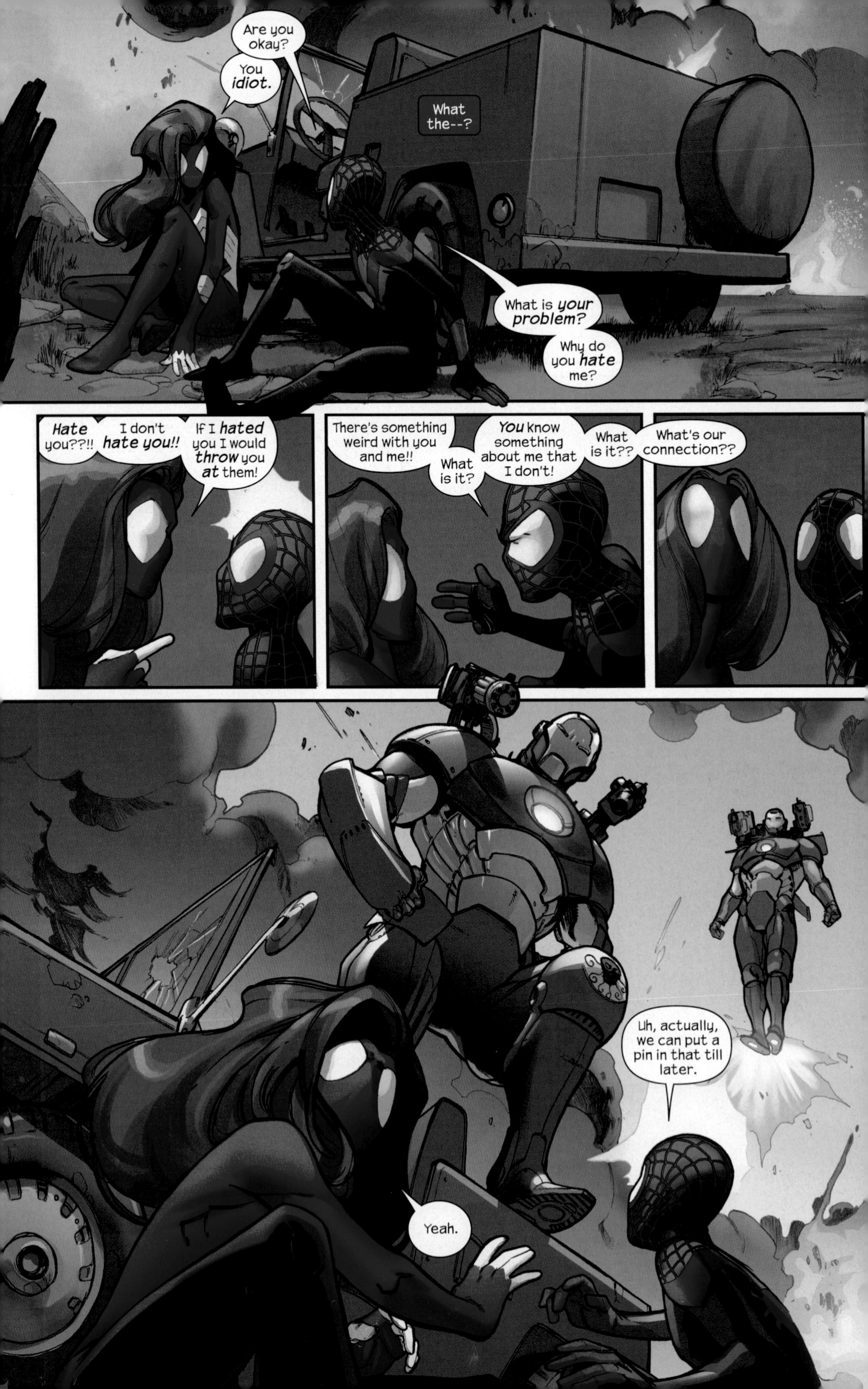
Are you okay?
You idiot.
What the--?
What is your problem?
Why do you hate me?
Hate you??!!
I don't hate you!!
If I hated you I would throw you at them!
There's something weird with you and me!!
What is it?
You know something about me that I don't!
What is it??
What's our connection??
Uh, actually, we can put a pin in that till later.
Yeah.

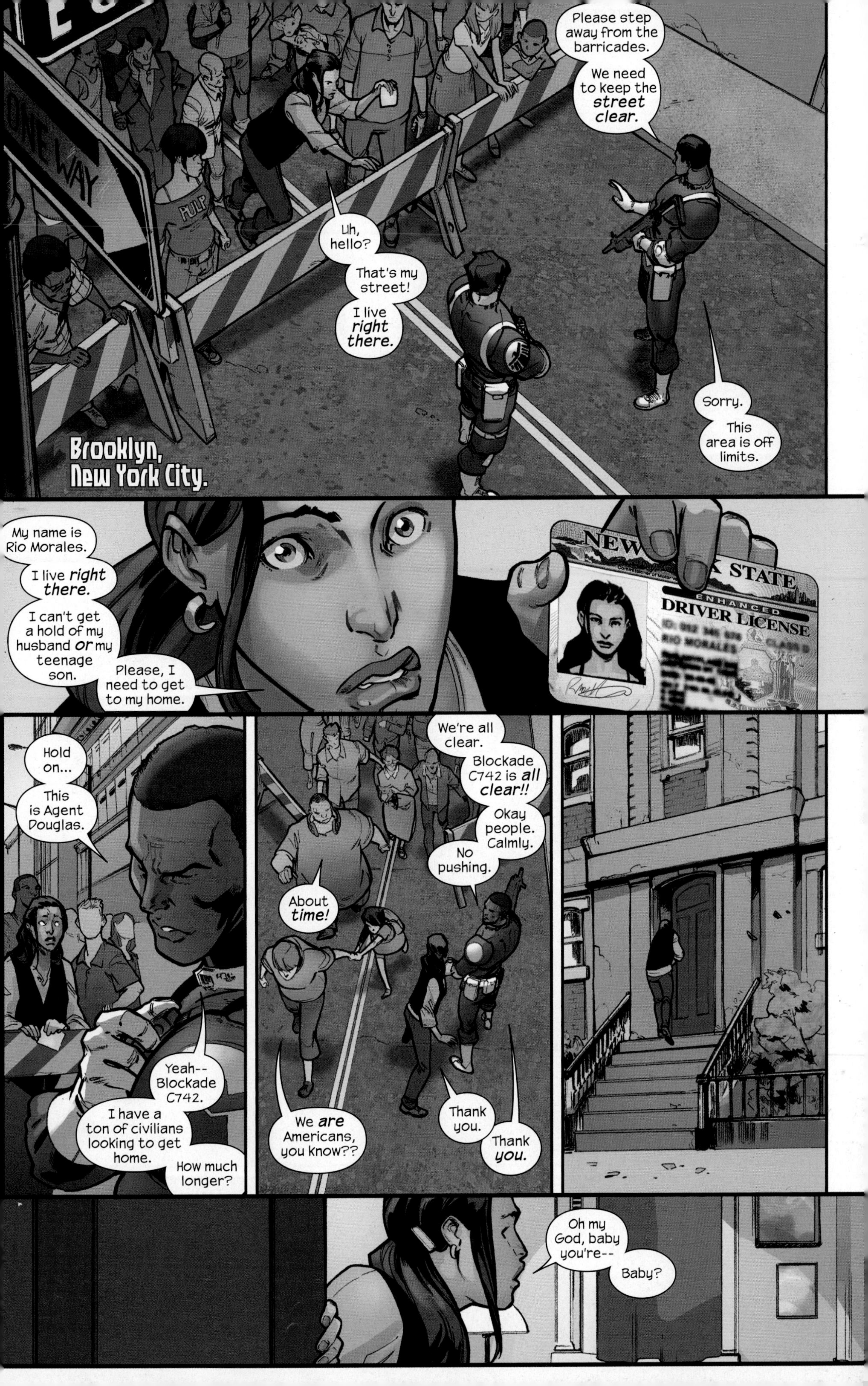

Please step away from the barricades.
We need to keep the *street clear.*
ONE WAY
PULP
Uh, hello?
That's my street!
I live *right there.*
Sorry.
This area is off limits.
Brooklyn, New York City.
My name is Rio Morales.
I live *right there.*
I can't get a hold of my husband *or* my teenage son.
Please, I need to get to my home.
ENHANCED
DRIVER LICENSE
Hold on...
This is Agent Douglas.
Yeah-- Blockade C742.
I have a ton of civilians looking to get home.
How much longer?
We're all clear.
Blockade C742 is *all clear!!*
Okay people. Calmly.
No pushing.
About *time!*
We *are* Americans, you know??
Thank you.
Thank *you.*
Oh my God, baby you're--
Baby?

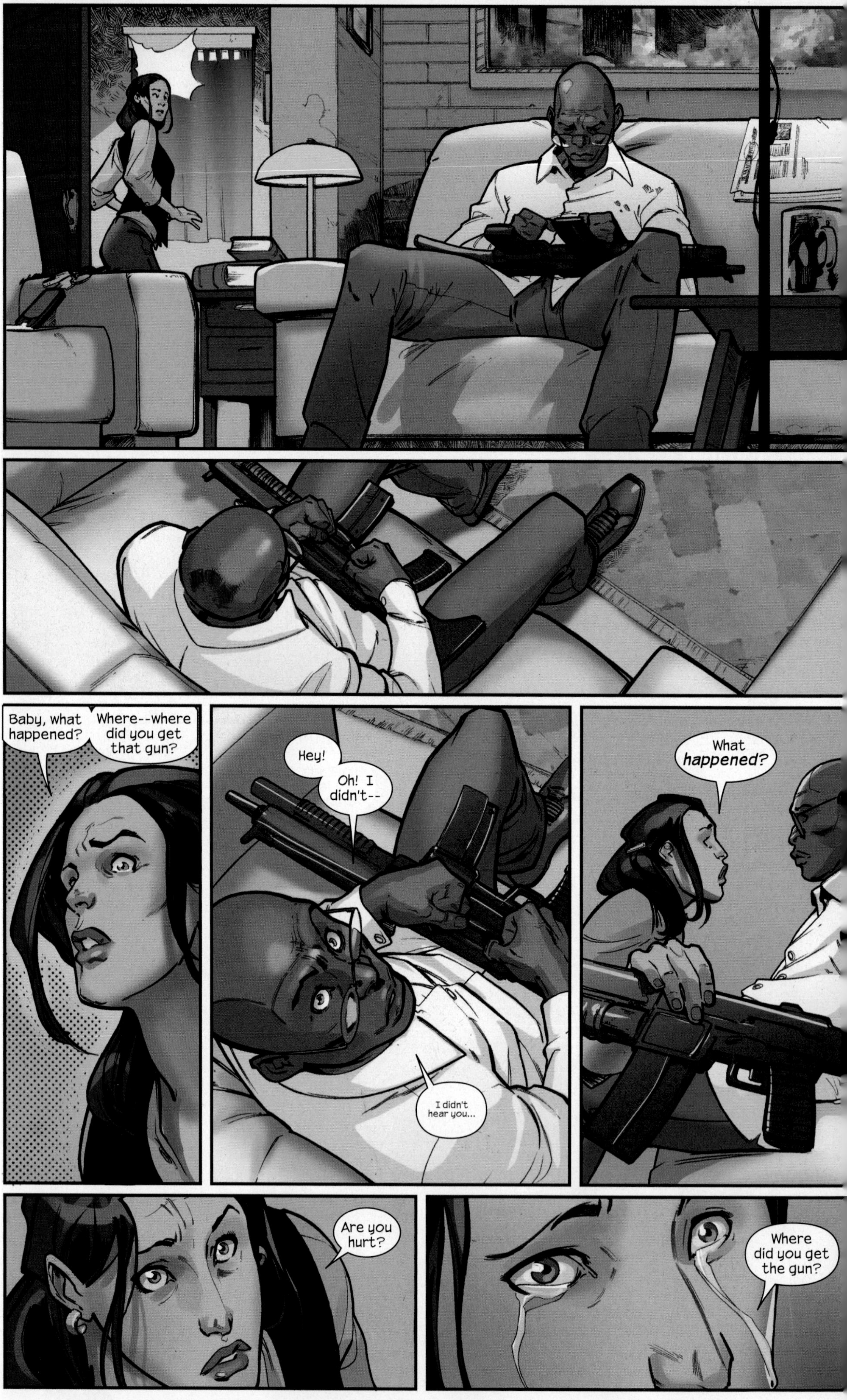
Baby, what happened?
Where--where did you get that gun?
Hey!
Oh! I didn't--
I didn't hear you...
What happened?
Are you hurt?
Where did you get the gun?

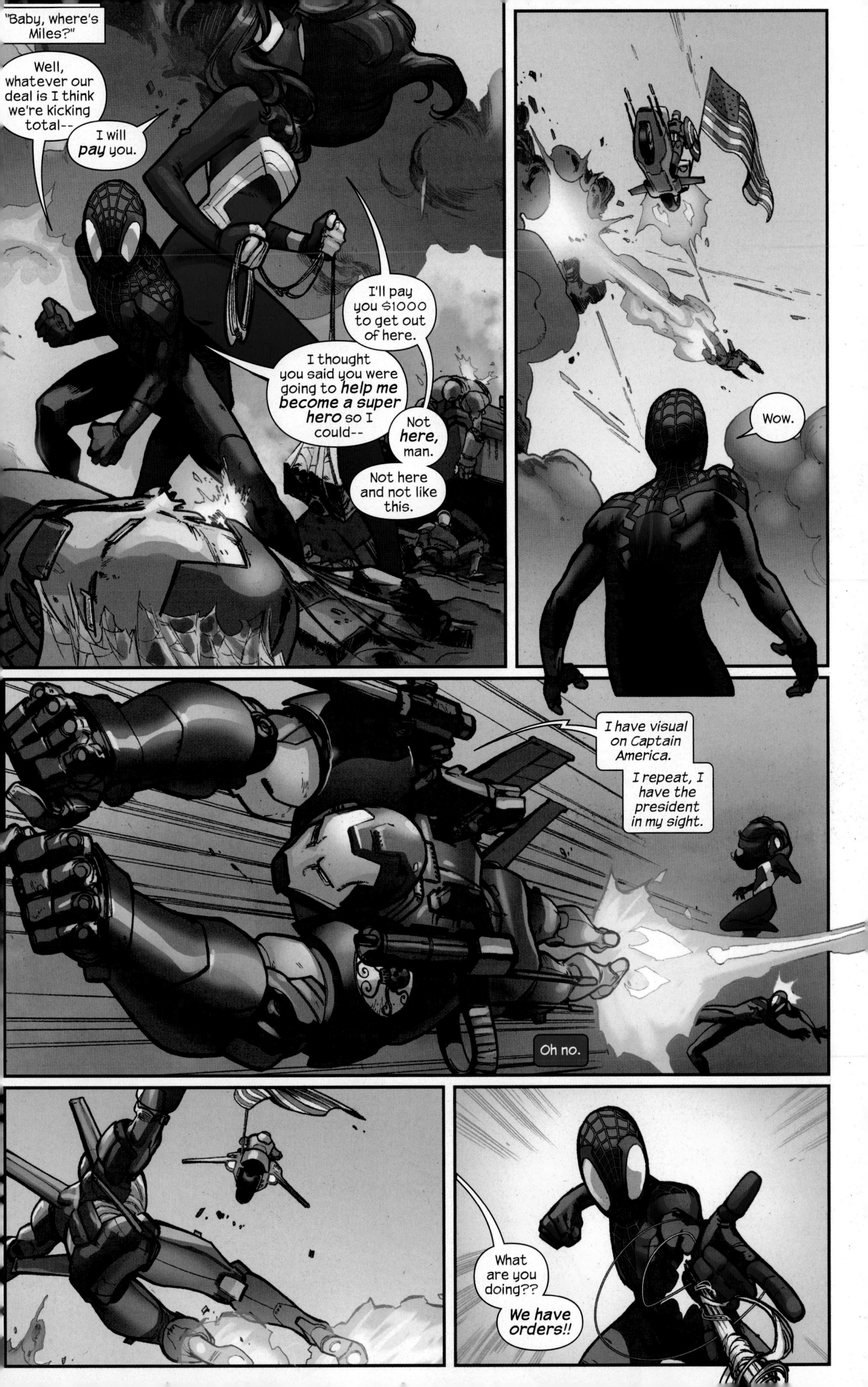
"Baby, where's Miles?"
Well, whatever our deal is I think we're kicking total--
I will *pay* you.
I'll pay you $1000 to get out of here.
I thought you said you were going to *help me become a super hero* so I could--
Not *here,* man.
Not here and not like this.
Wow.
I have visual on Captain America.
I repeat, I have the president in my sight.
Oh no.
What are you doing??
We have orders!!

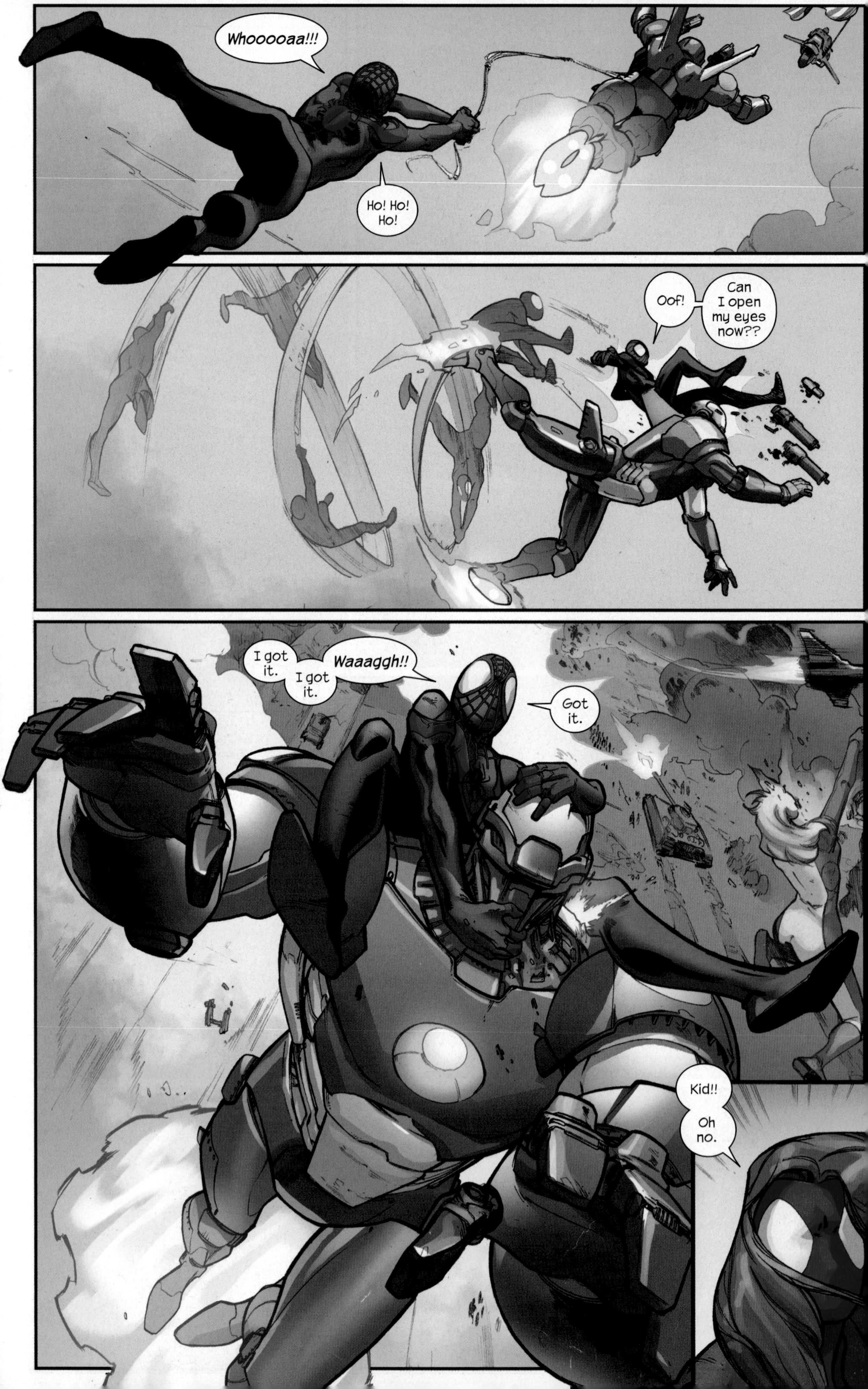

Whoooooaa!!!
Ho! Ho! Ho!
Oof!
Can I open my eyes now??
I got it.
I got it.
Waaagh!!
Got it.
Kid!!
Oh no.

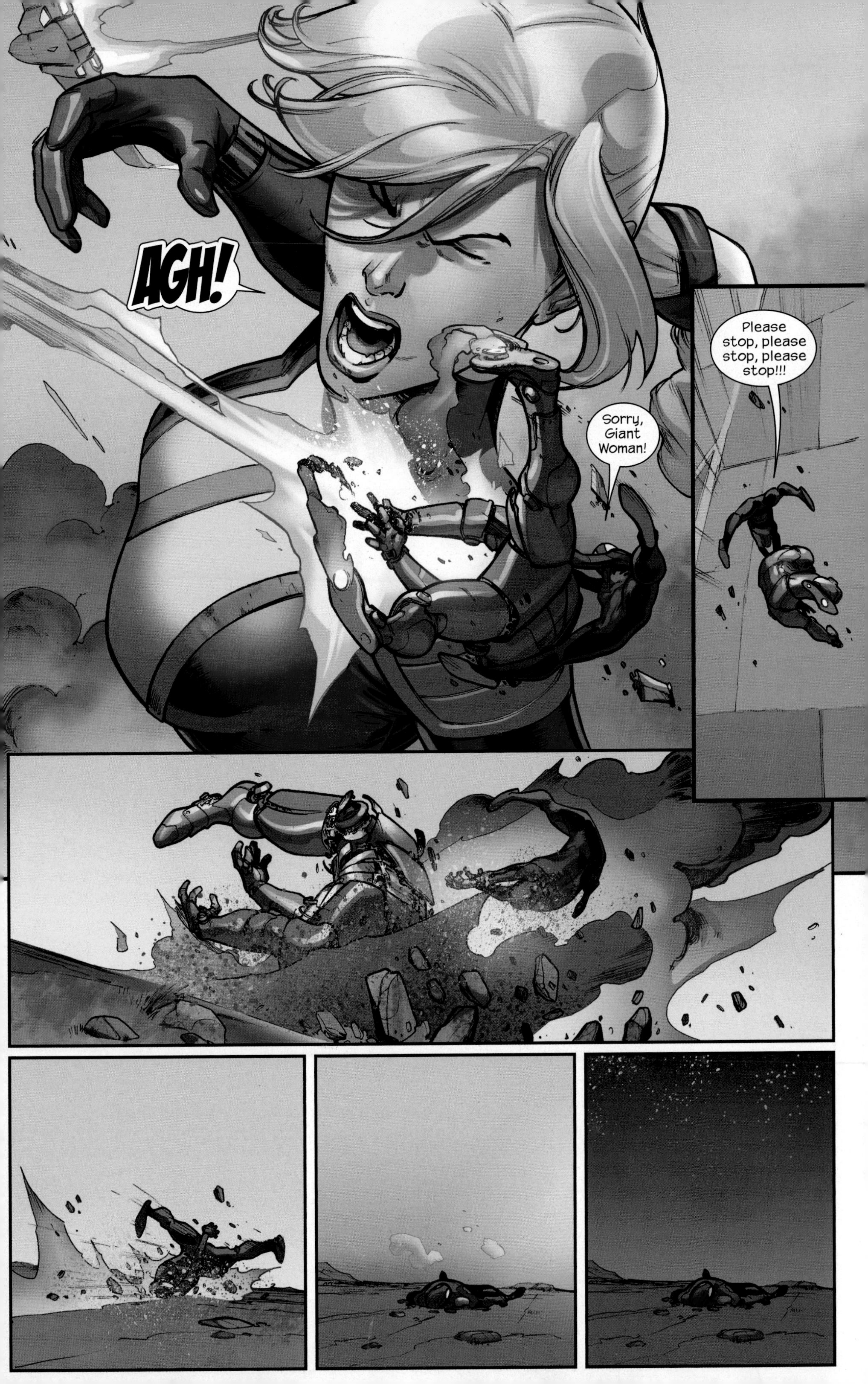
AGH!
Sorry, Giant Woman!
Please stop, please stop, please stop!!!

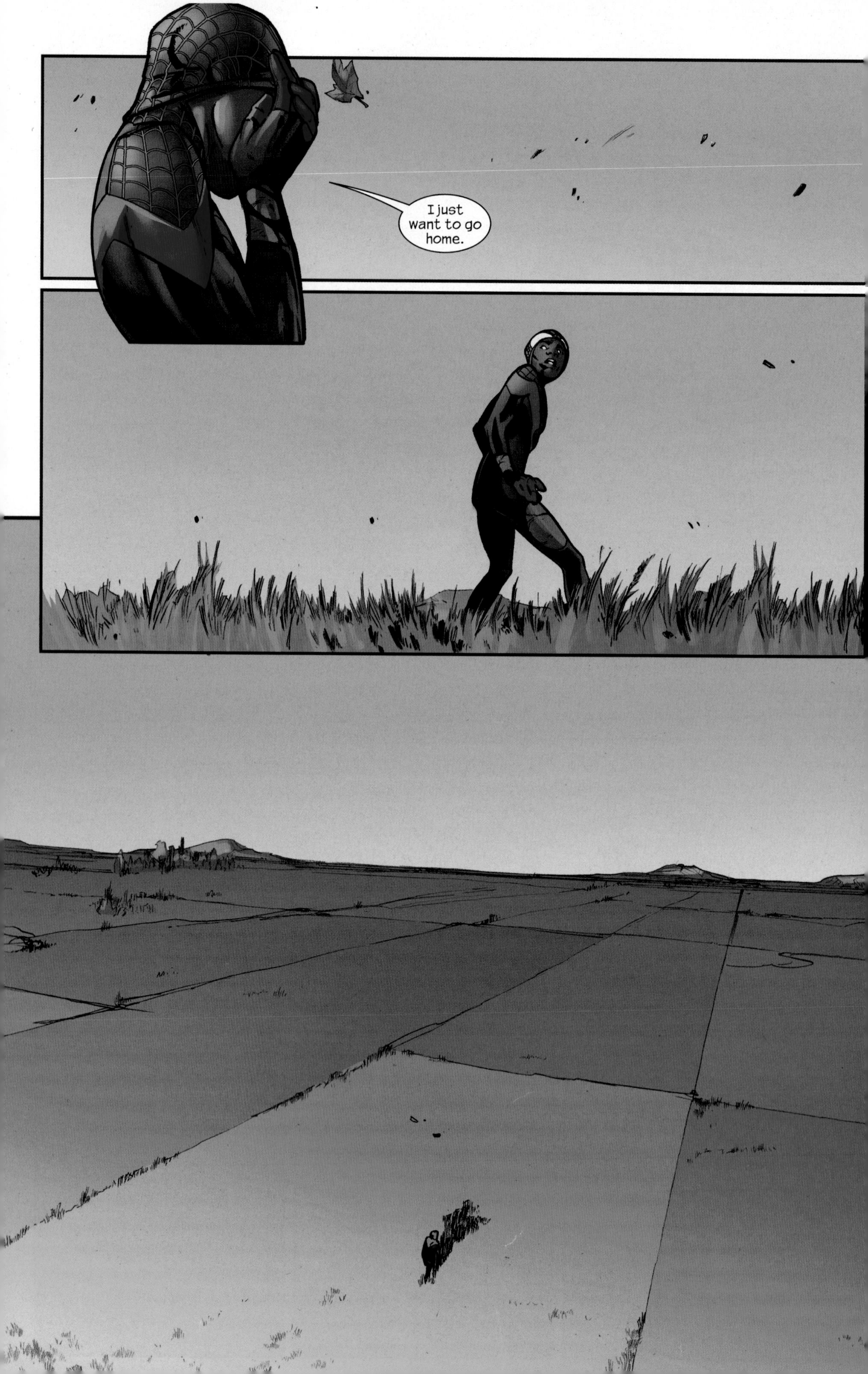
I just want to go home.

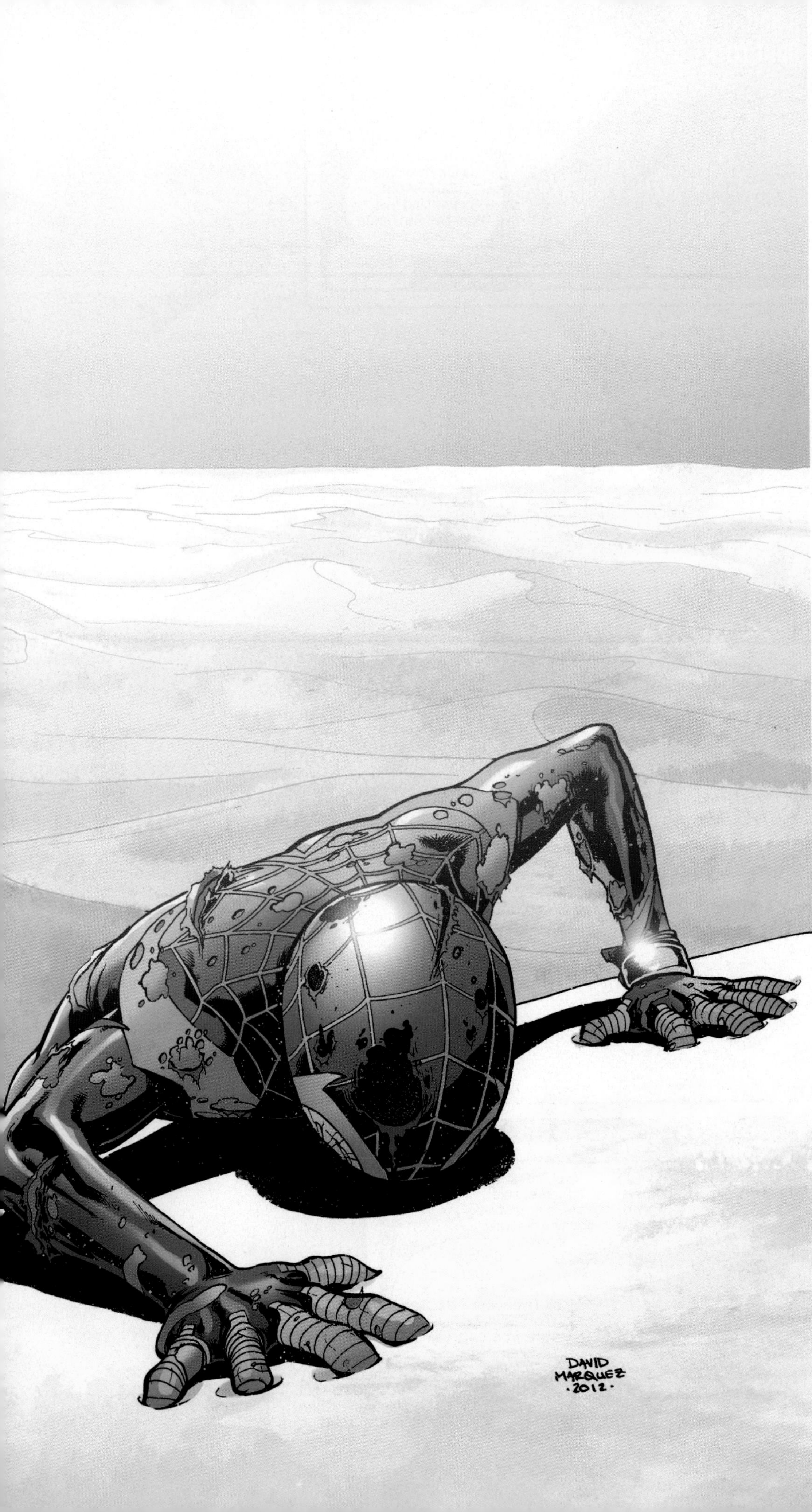
DAVID MARQUEZ ·2012·

18

ULTIMATE COMICS **SPIDER-MAN** #18

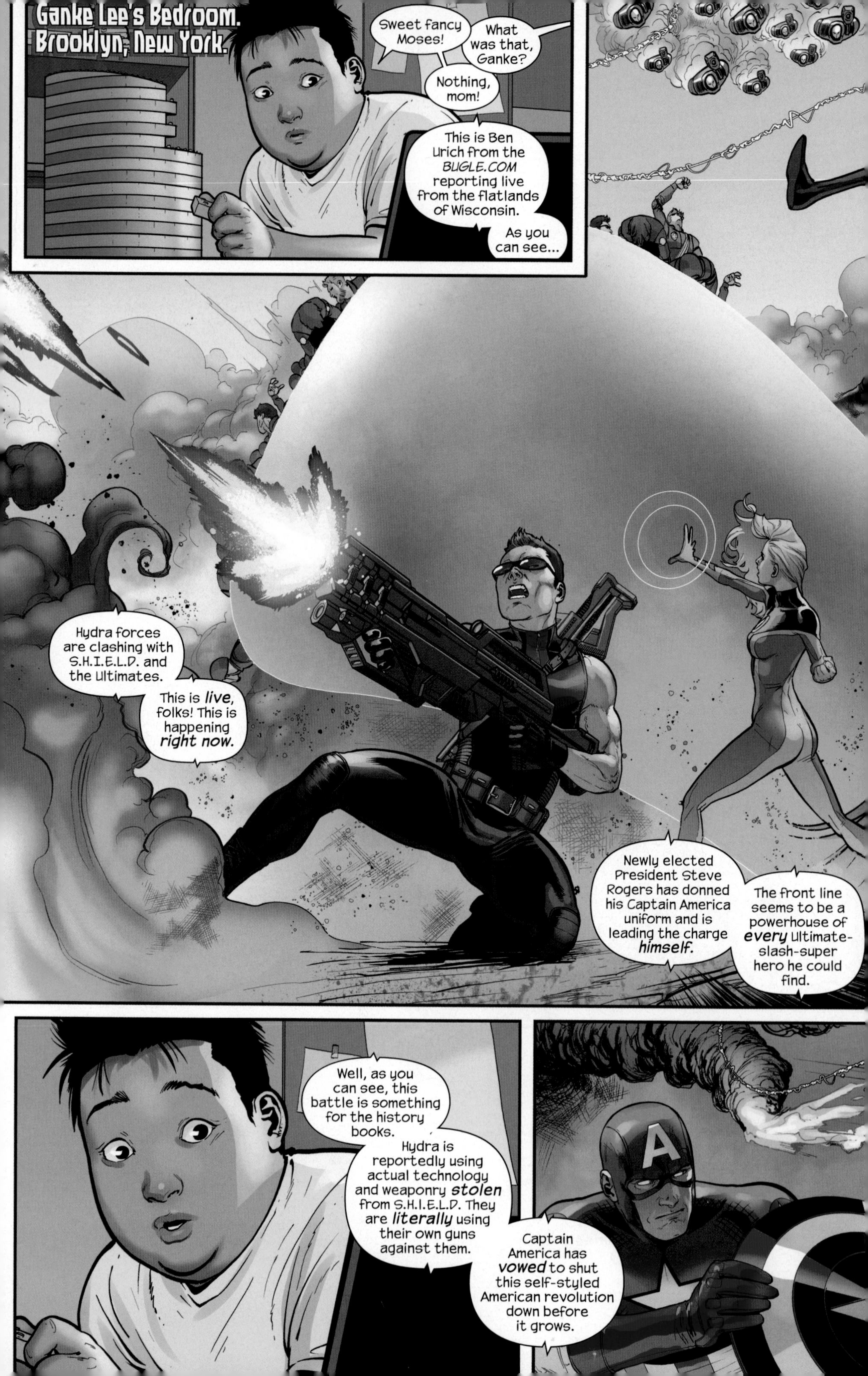
Ganke Lee's Bedroom. Brooklyn, New York.
Sweet fancy Moses!
What was that, Ganke?
Nothing, mom!
This is Ben Urich from the BUGLE.COM reporting live from the flatlands of Wisconsin.
As you can see...
Hydra forces are clashing with S.H.I.E.L.D. and the Ultimates.
This is live, folks! This is happening right now.
Newly elected President Steve Rogers has donned his Captain America uniform and is leading the charge himself.
The front line seems to be a powerhouse of every Ultimate-slash-super hero he could find.
Well, as you can see, this battle is something for the history books.
Hydra is reportedly using actual technology and weaponry stolen from S.H.I.E.L.D. They are literally using their own guns against them.
Captain America has vowed to shut this self-styled American revolution down before it grows.

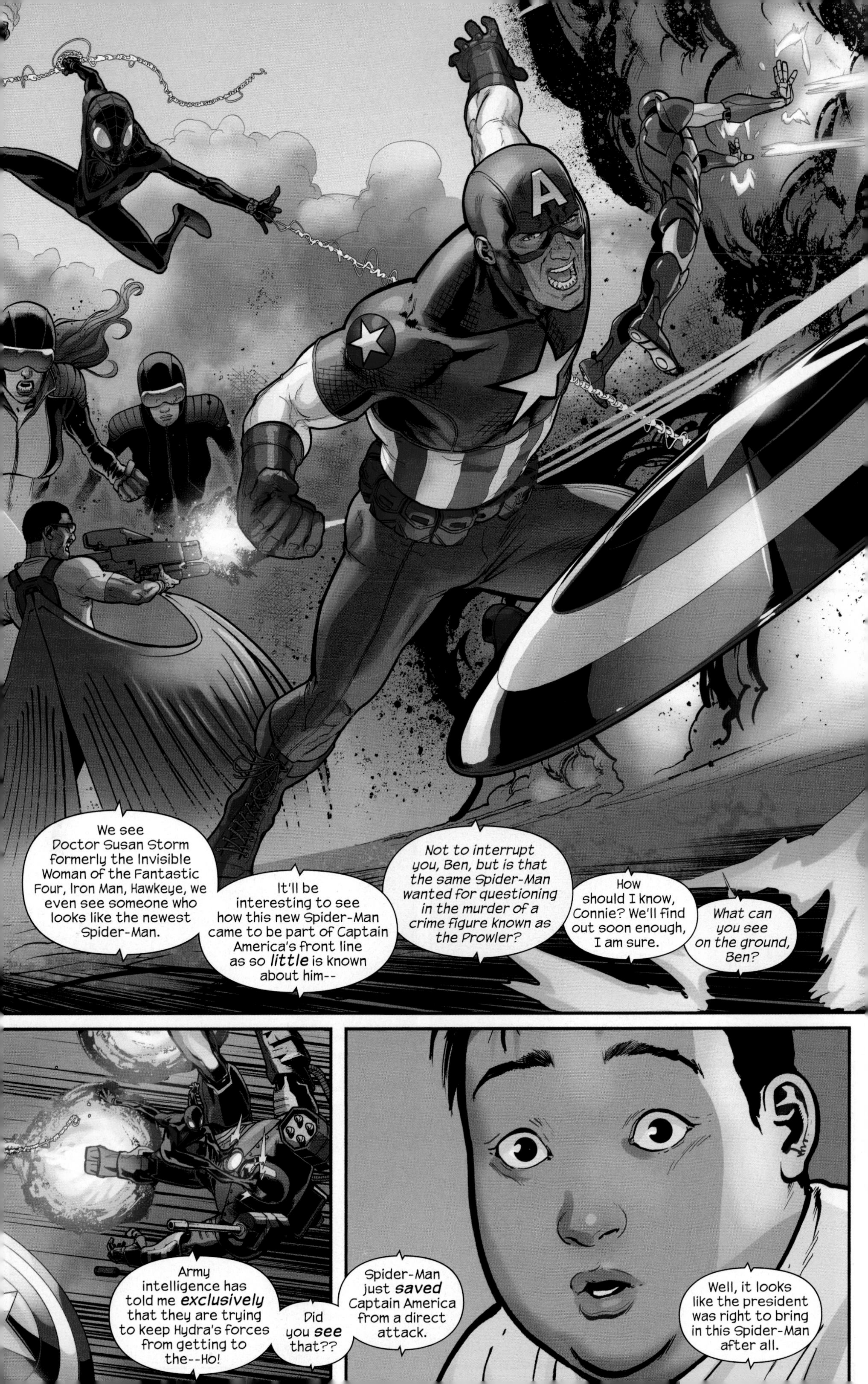
We see Doctor Susan Storm formerly the Invisible Woman of the Fantastic Four, Iron Man, Hawkeye, we even see someone who looks like the newest Spider-Man.
It'll be interesting to see how this new Spider-Man came to be part of Captain America's front line as so *little* is known about him--
Not to interrupt you, Ben, but is that the same Spider-Man wanted for questioning in the murder of a crime figure known as the Prowler?
How should I know, Connie? We'll find out soon enough, I am sure.
What can you see on the ground, Ben?
Army intelligence has told me ***exclusively*** that they are trying to keep Hydra's forces from getting to the--Ho!
Did you ***see*** that??
Spider-Man just ***saved*** Captain America from a direct attack.
Well, it looks like the president was right to bring in this Spider-Man after all.

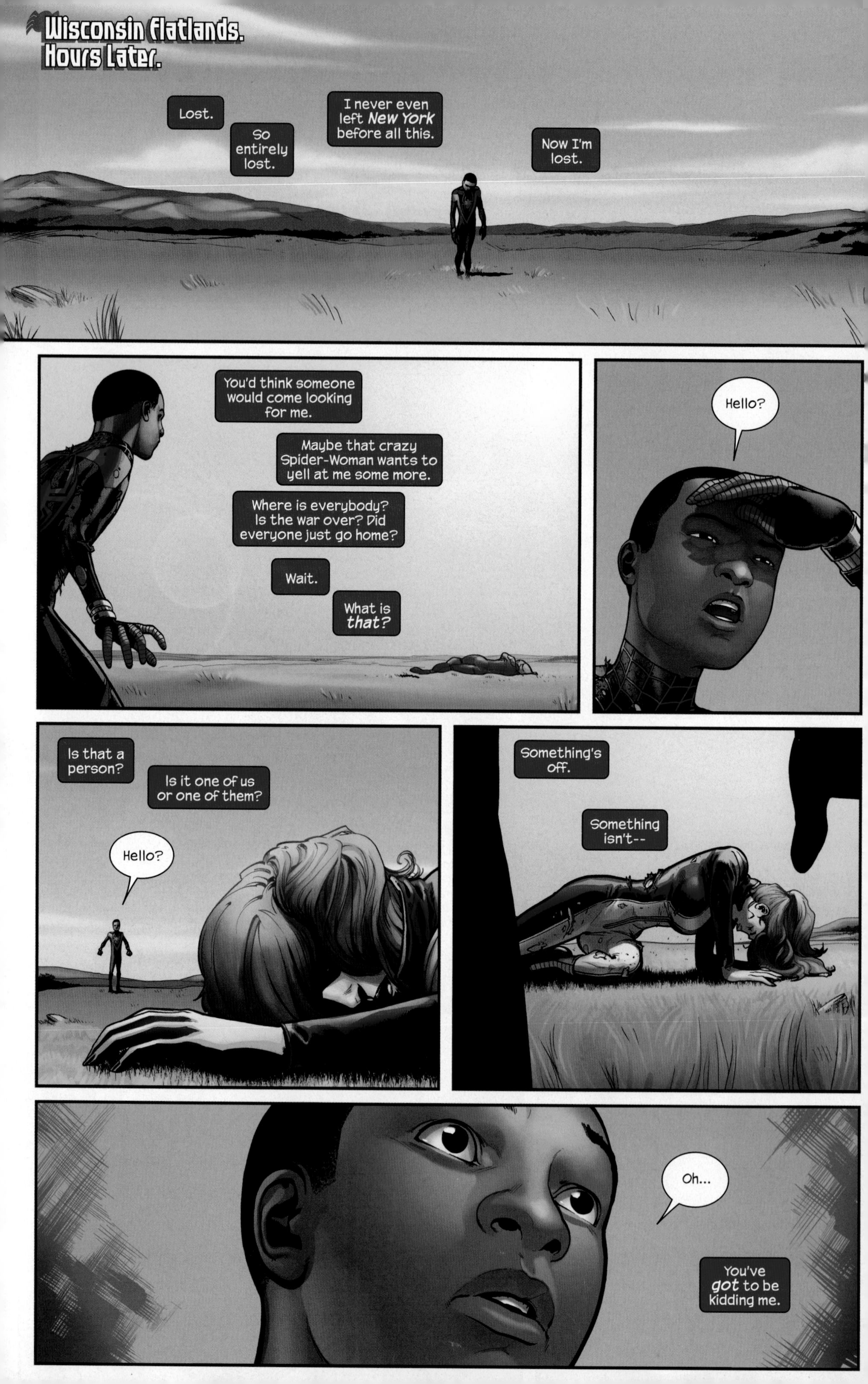
Wisconsin Flatlands.
Hours Later.
Lost.
So entirely lost.
I never even left New York before all this.
Now I'm lost.
You'd think someone would come looking for me.
Maybe that crazy Spider-Woman wants to yell at me some more.
Where is everybody? Is the war over? Did everyone just go home?
Wait.
What is that?
Hello?
Is that a person?
Is it one of us or one of them?
Hello?
Something's off.
Something isn't--
Oh...
You've got to be kidding me.

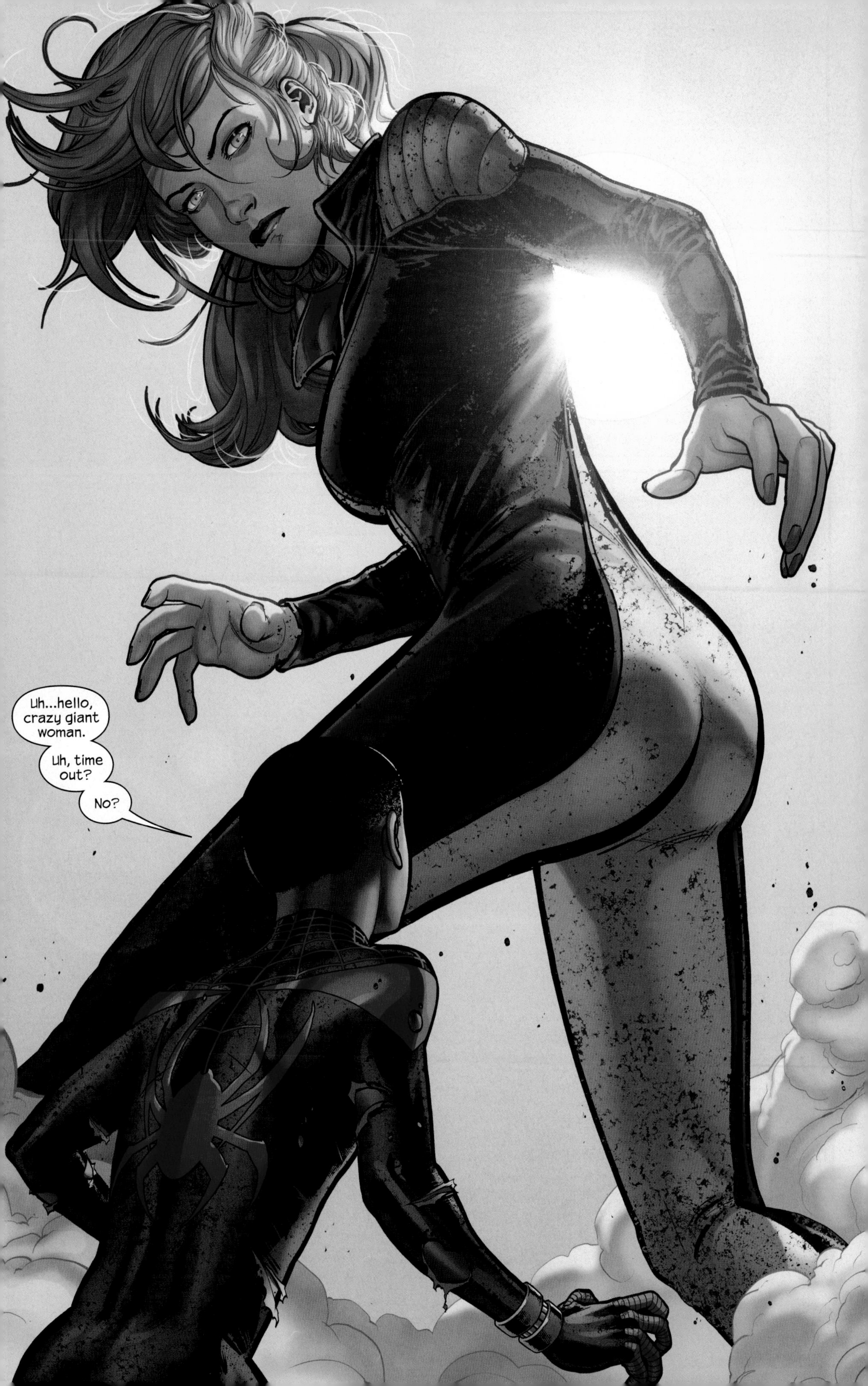
Uh...hello, crazy giant woman.
Uh, time out?
No?

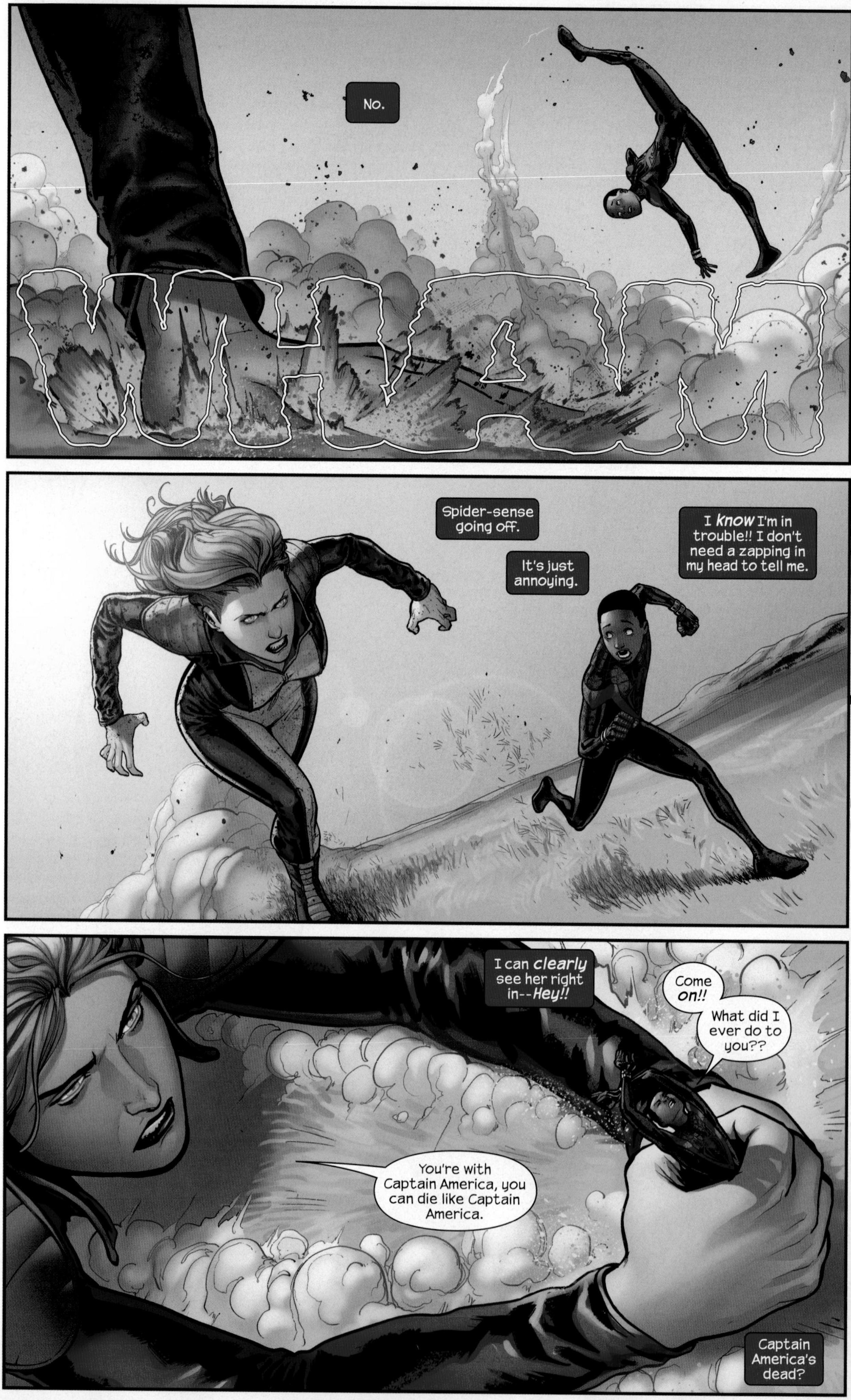
No.
WHAM
Spider-sense going off.
It's just annoying.
I *know* I'm in trouble!! I don't need a zapping in my head to tell me.
I can *clearly* see her right in--*Hey!!*
Come *on!!*
What did I ever do to you??
You're with Captain America, you can die like Captain America.
Captain America's dead?

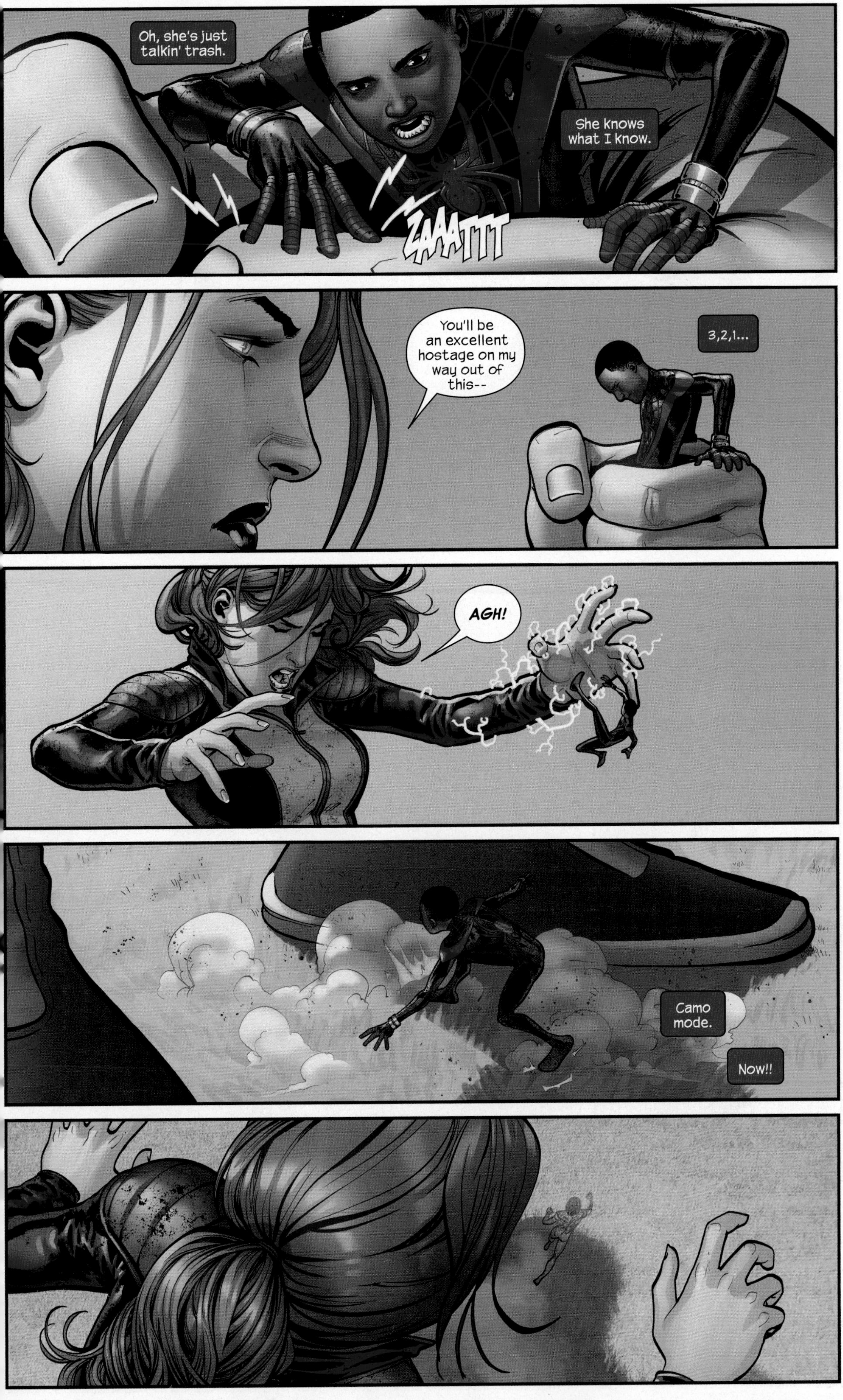
Oh, she's just talkin' trash.
She knows what I know.
ZAAATTT
You'll be an excellent hostage on my way out of this--
3,2,1...
AGH!
Camo mode.
Now!!

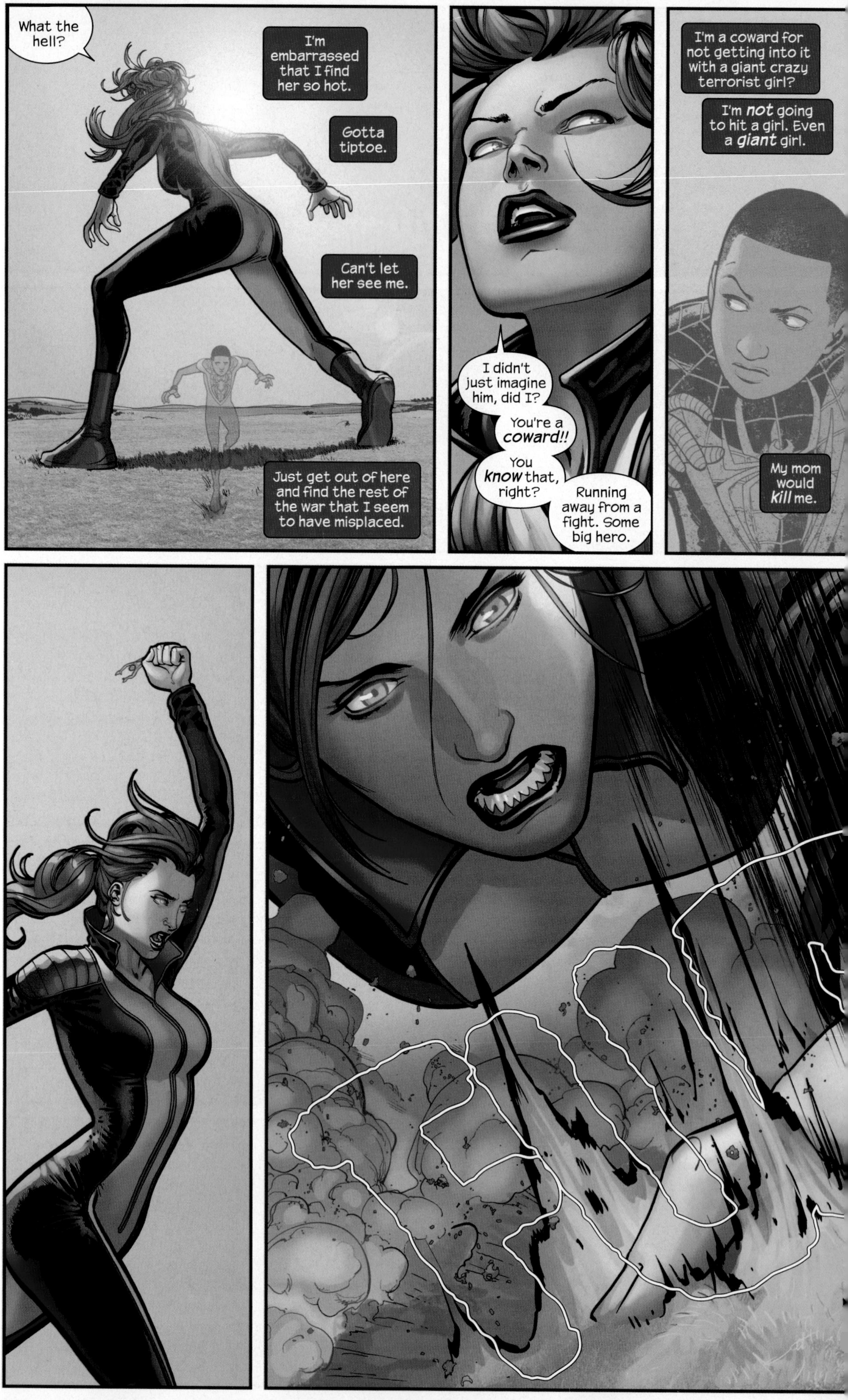
What the hell?
I'm embarrassed that I find her so hot.
Gotta tiptoe.
Can't let her see me.
Just get out of here and find the rest of the war that I seem to have misplaced.
I didn't just imagine him, did I?
You're a *coward!!*
You *know* that, right?
Running away from a fight. Some big hero.
I'm a coward for not getting into it with a giant crazy terrorist girl?
I'm *not* going to hit a girl. Even a *giant* girl.
My mom would *kill* me.

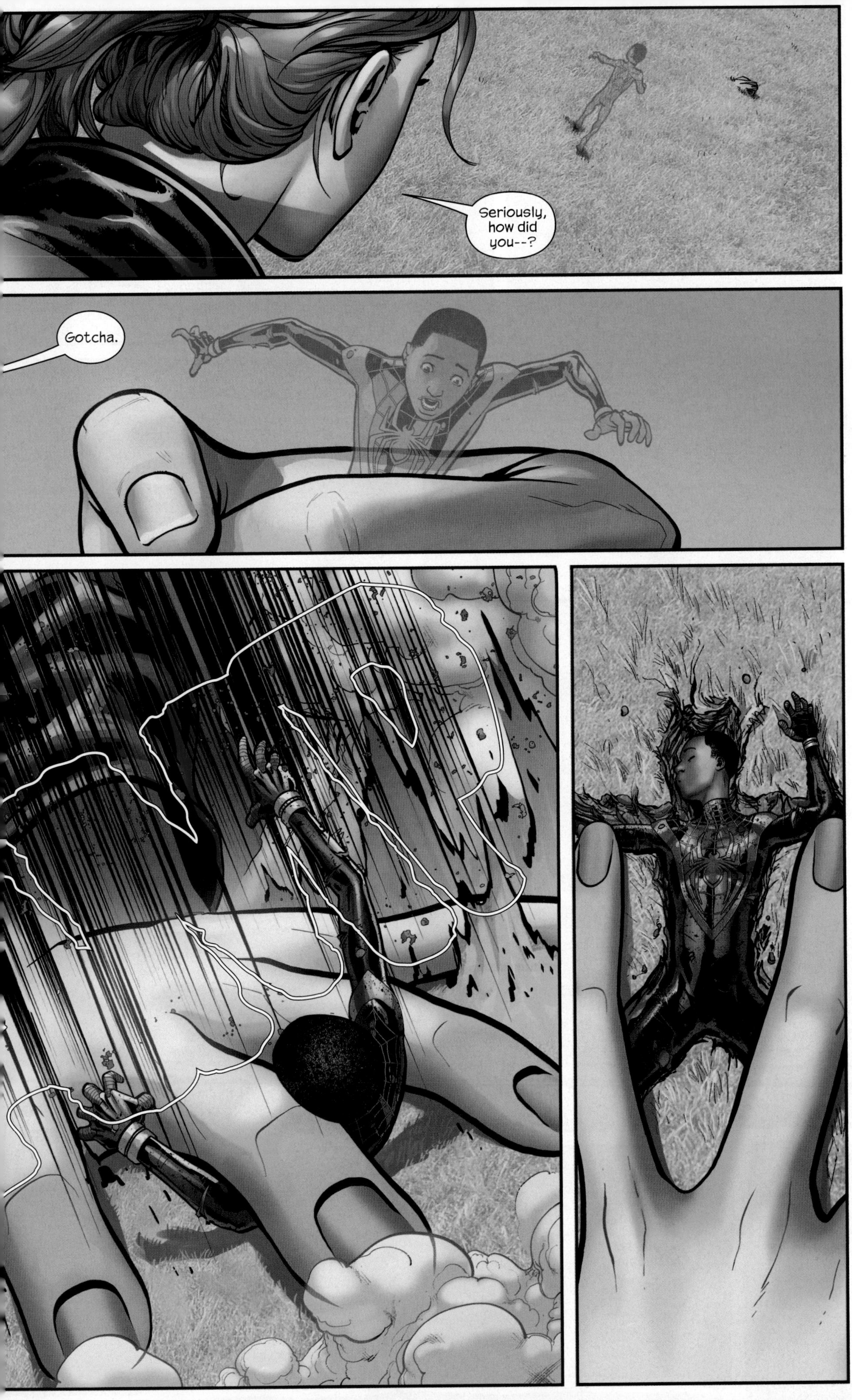
Seriously, how did you--?
Gotcha.

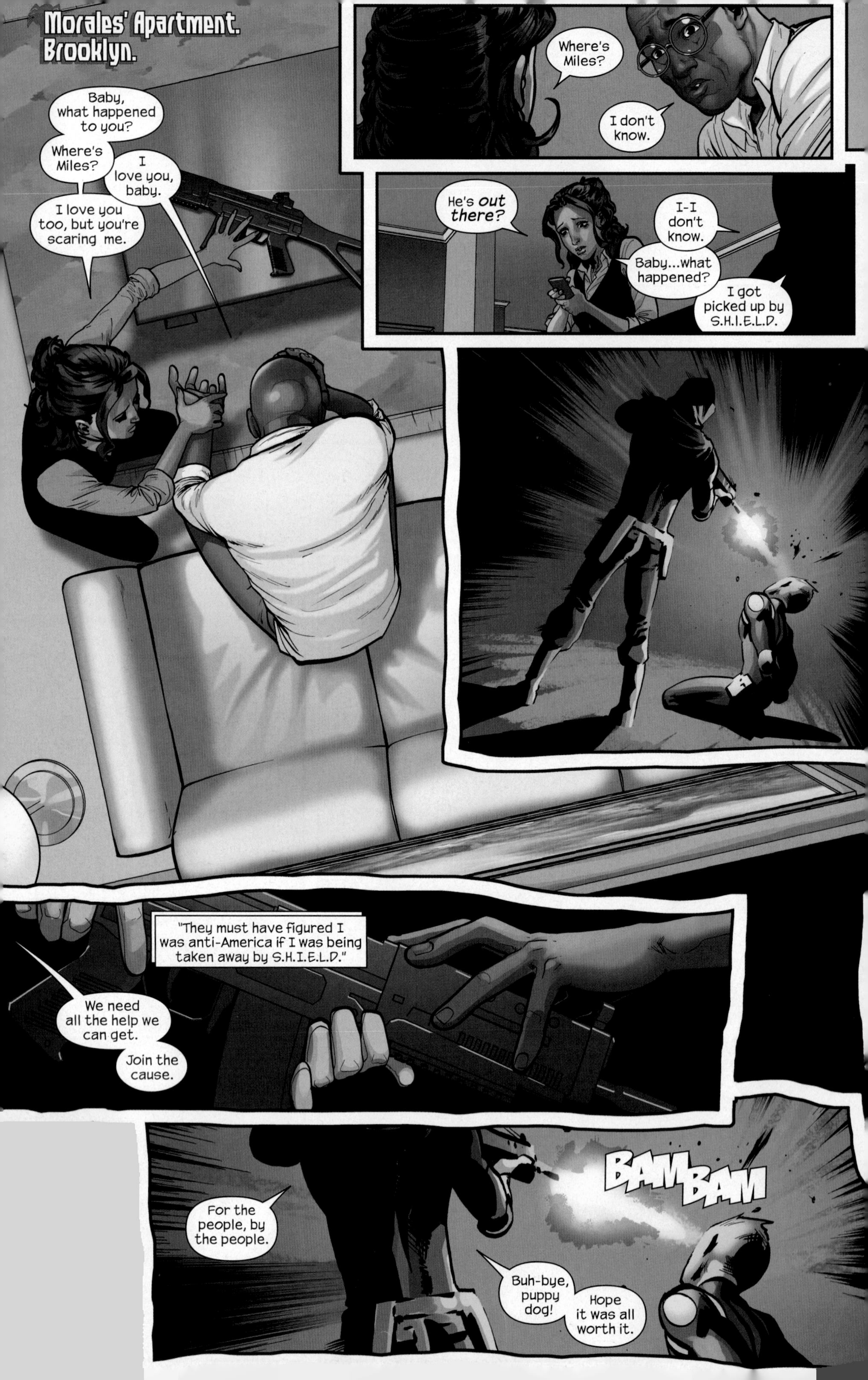
Morales' Apartment. Brooklyn.
Baby, what happened to you?
Where's Miles?
I love you, baby.
I love you too, but you're scaring me.
Where's Miles?
I don't know.
He's *out there?*
I-I don't know.
Baby...what happened?
I got picked up by S.H.I.E.L.D.
"They must have figured I was anti-America if I was being taken away by S.H.I.E.L.D."
We need all the help we can get.
Join the cause.
For the people, by the people.
BAM BAM
Buh-bye, puppy dog!
Hope it was all worth it.

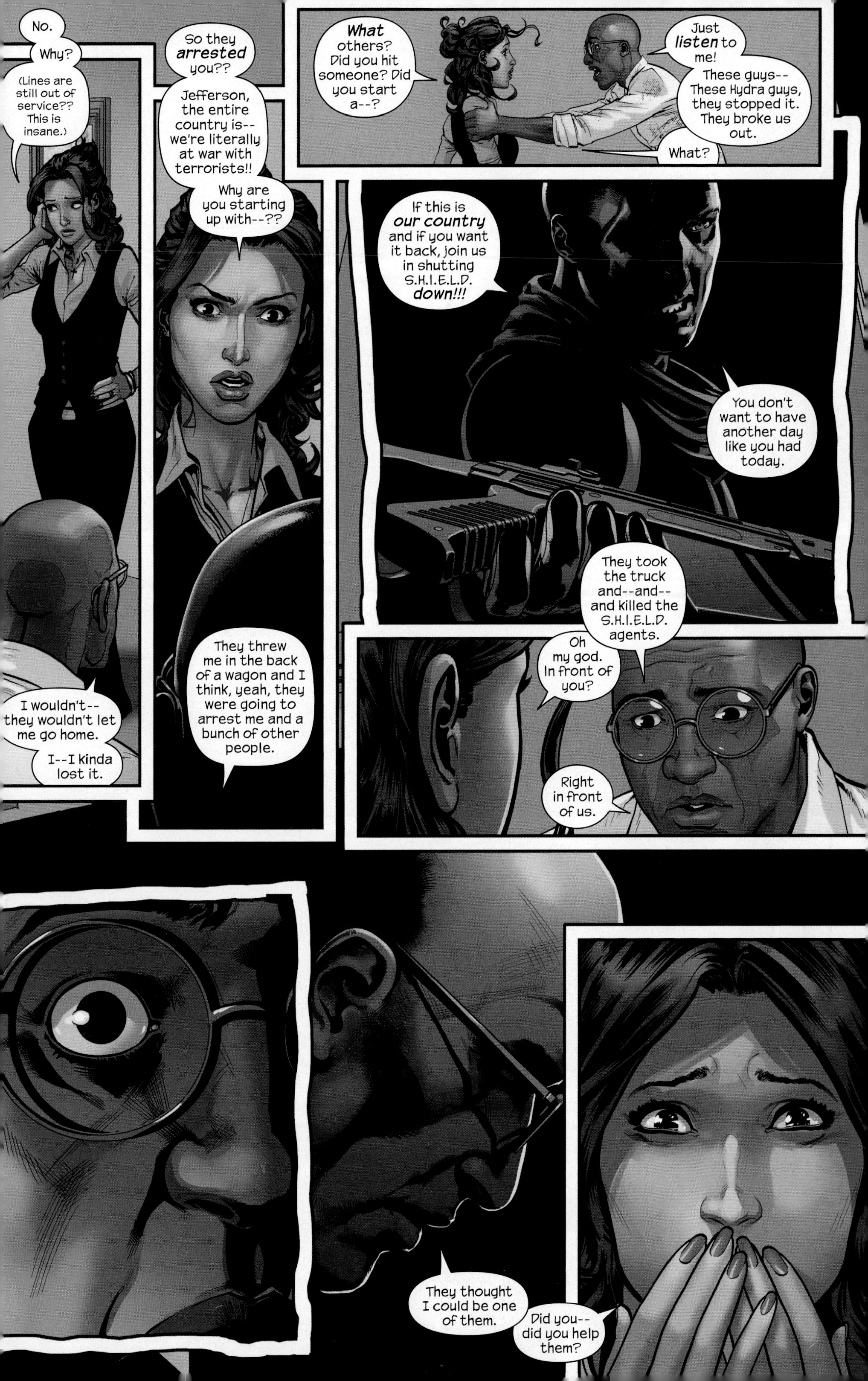

No.
Why?
(Lines are still out of service?? This is insane.)
So they arrested you??
Jefferson, the entire country is-- we're literally at war with terrorists!!
Why are you starting up with--??
I wouldn't-- they wouldn't let me go home.
I--I kinda lost it.
They threw me in the back of a wagon and I think, yeah, they were going to arrest me and a bunch of other people.
What others? Did you hit someone? Did you start a--?
Just listen to me!
These guys-- These Hydra guys, they stopped it. They broke us out.
What?
If this is our country and if you want it back, join us in shutting S.H.I.E.L.D. down!!!
You don't want to have another day like you had today.
They took the truck and--and-- and killed the S.H.I.E.L.D. agents.
Oh my god. In front of you?
Right in front of us.
They thought I could be one of them.
Did you-- did you help them?

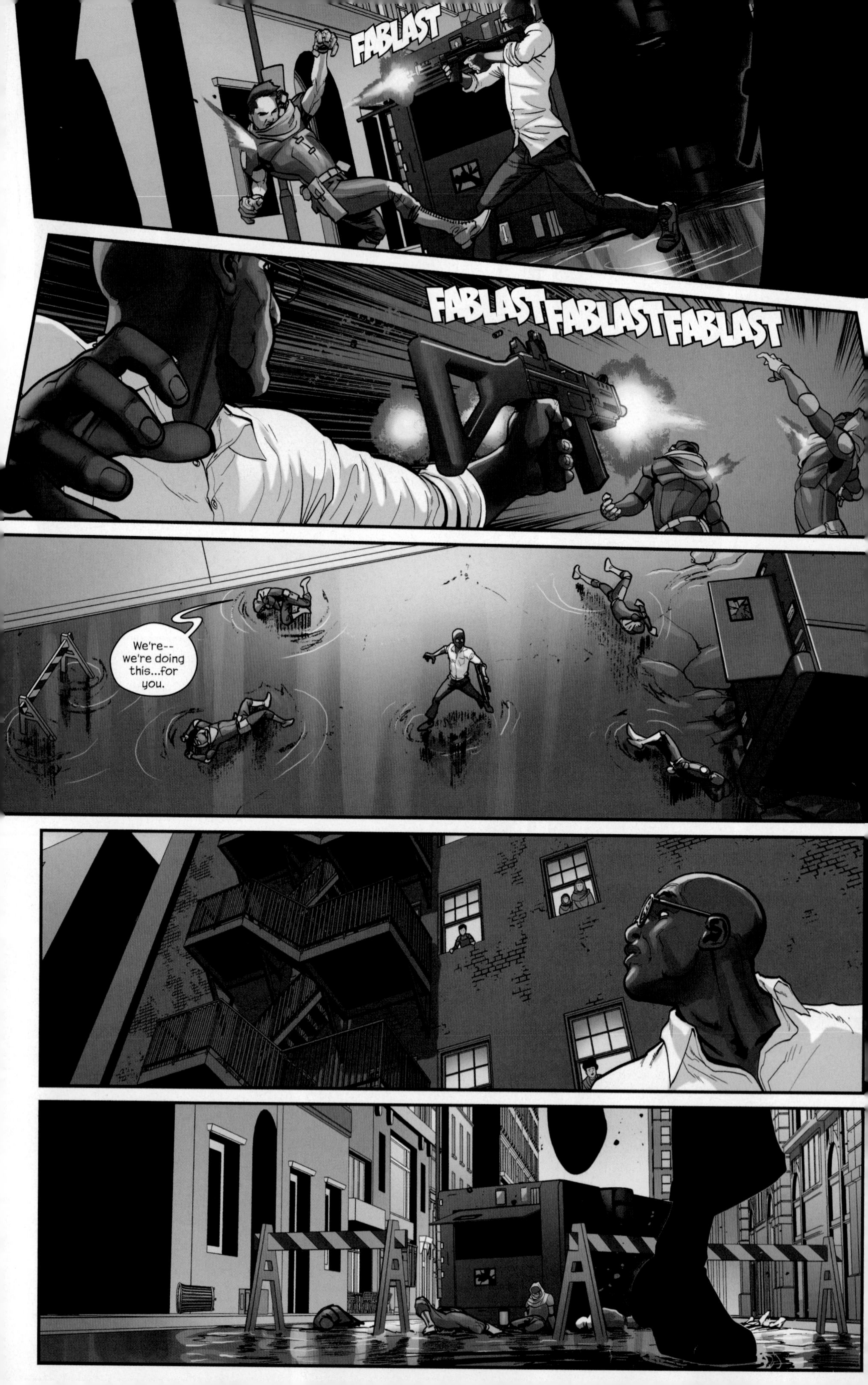
FABLAST
FABLAST FABLAST FABLAST
We're-- we're doing this...for you.

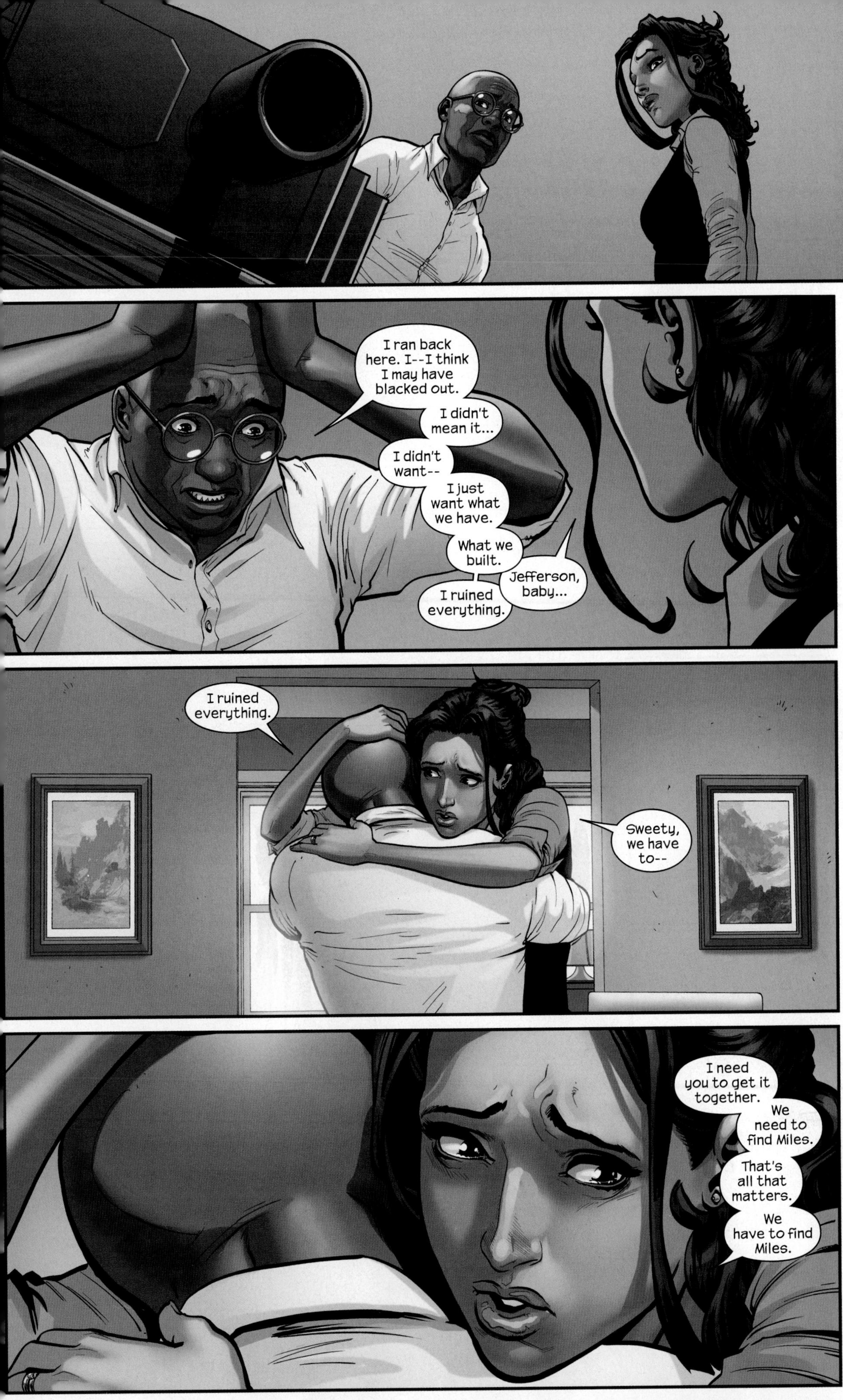
I ran back here. I--I think I may have blacked out.
I didn't mean it...
I didn't want--
I just want what we have.
What we built.
I ruined everything.
Jefferson, baby...
I ruined everything.
Sweety, we have to--
I need you to get it together.
We need to find Miles.
That's all that matters.
We have to find Miles.

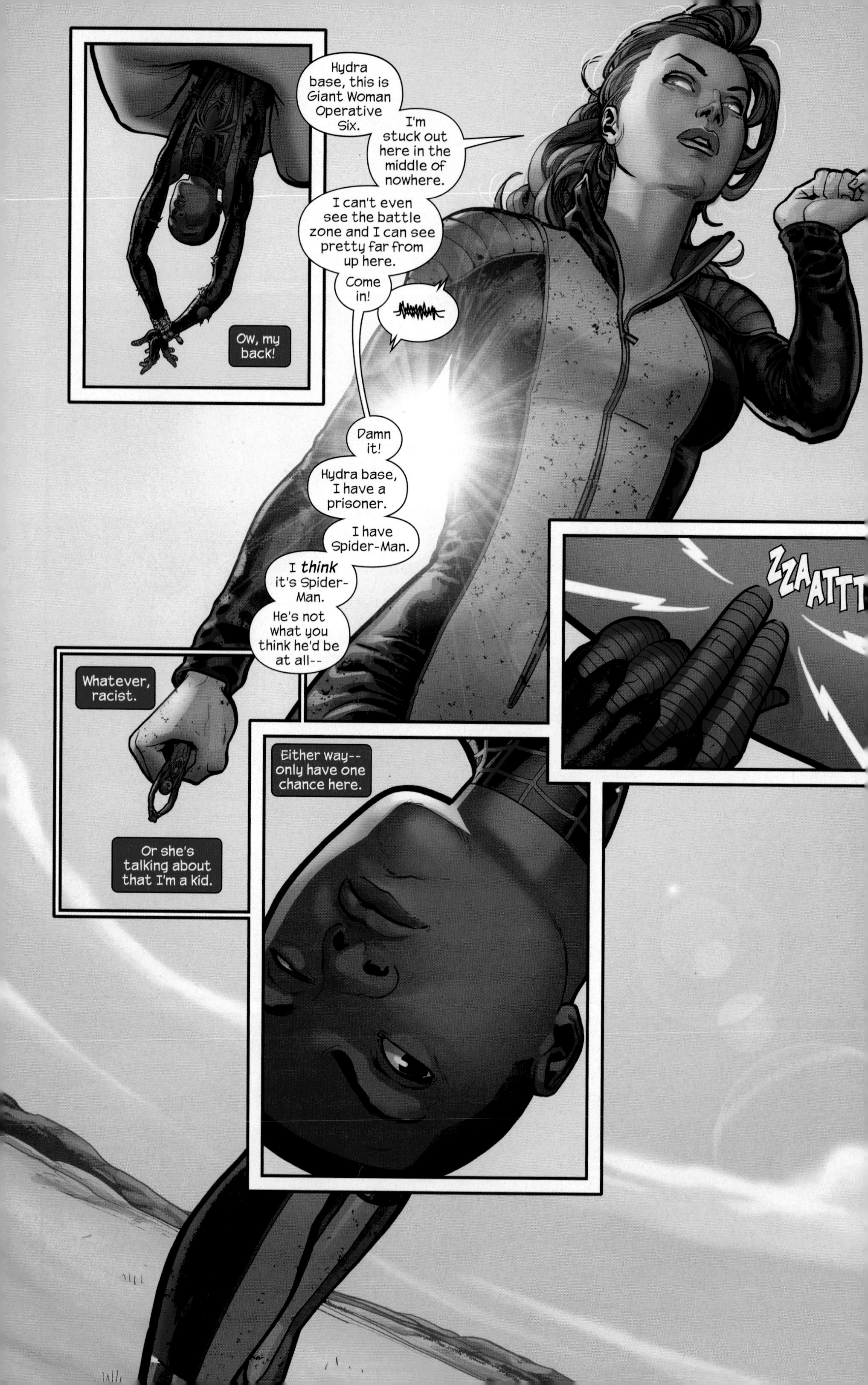
Ow, my back!
Hydra base, this is Giant Woman Operative Six.
I'm stuck out here in the middle of nowhere.
I can't even see the battle zone and I can see pretty far from up here.
Come in!
Damn it!
Hydra base, I have a prisoner.
I have Spider-Man.
I *think* it's Spider-Man.
He's not what you think he'd be at all--
Whatever, racist.
Or she's talking about that I'm a kid.
Either way-- only have one chance here.
ZZAATTT

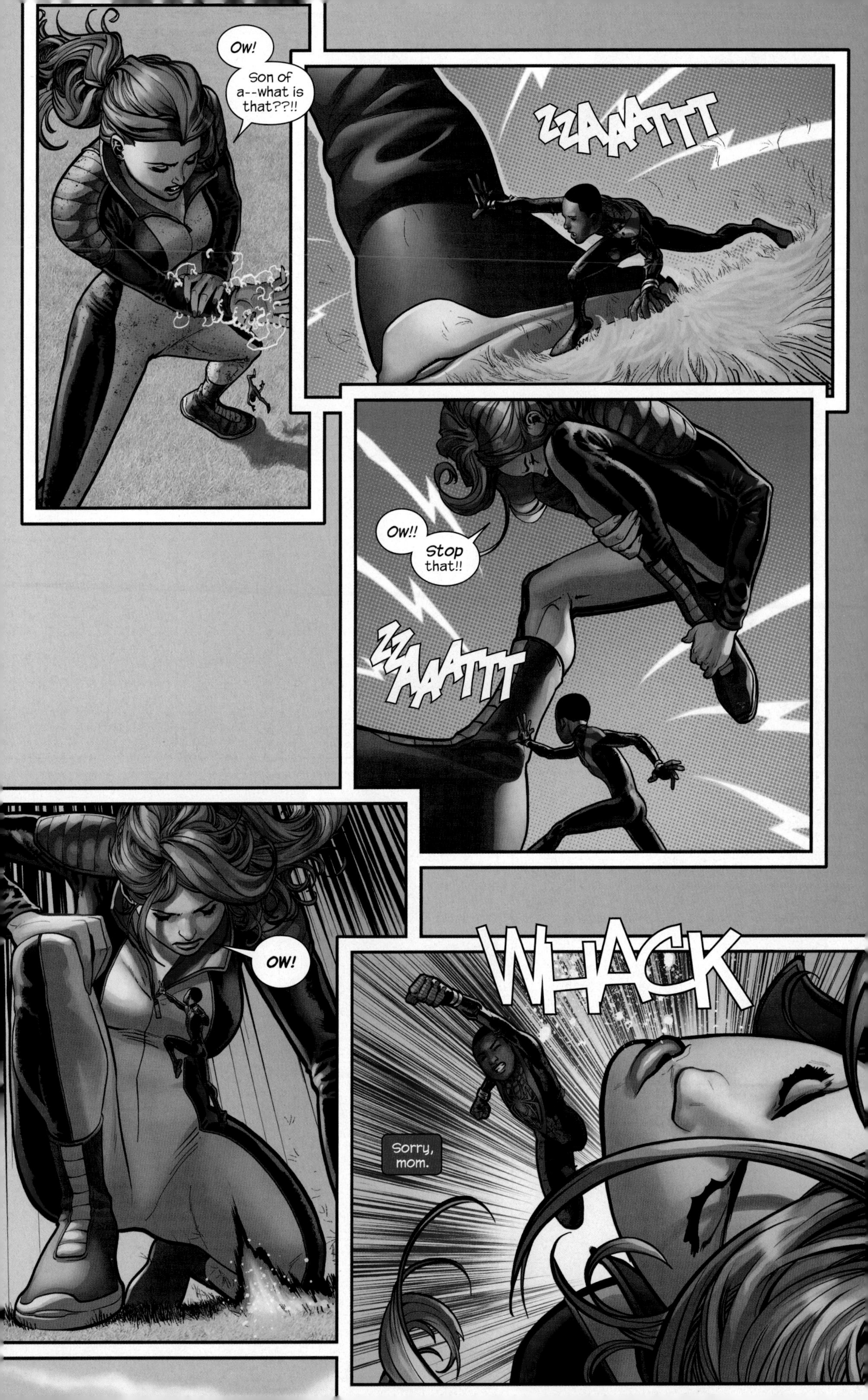

OW!
Son of a--what is that??!!
ZZAAATTT
OW!! Stop that!!
ZZAAATTT
OW!
WHACK
Sorry, mom.

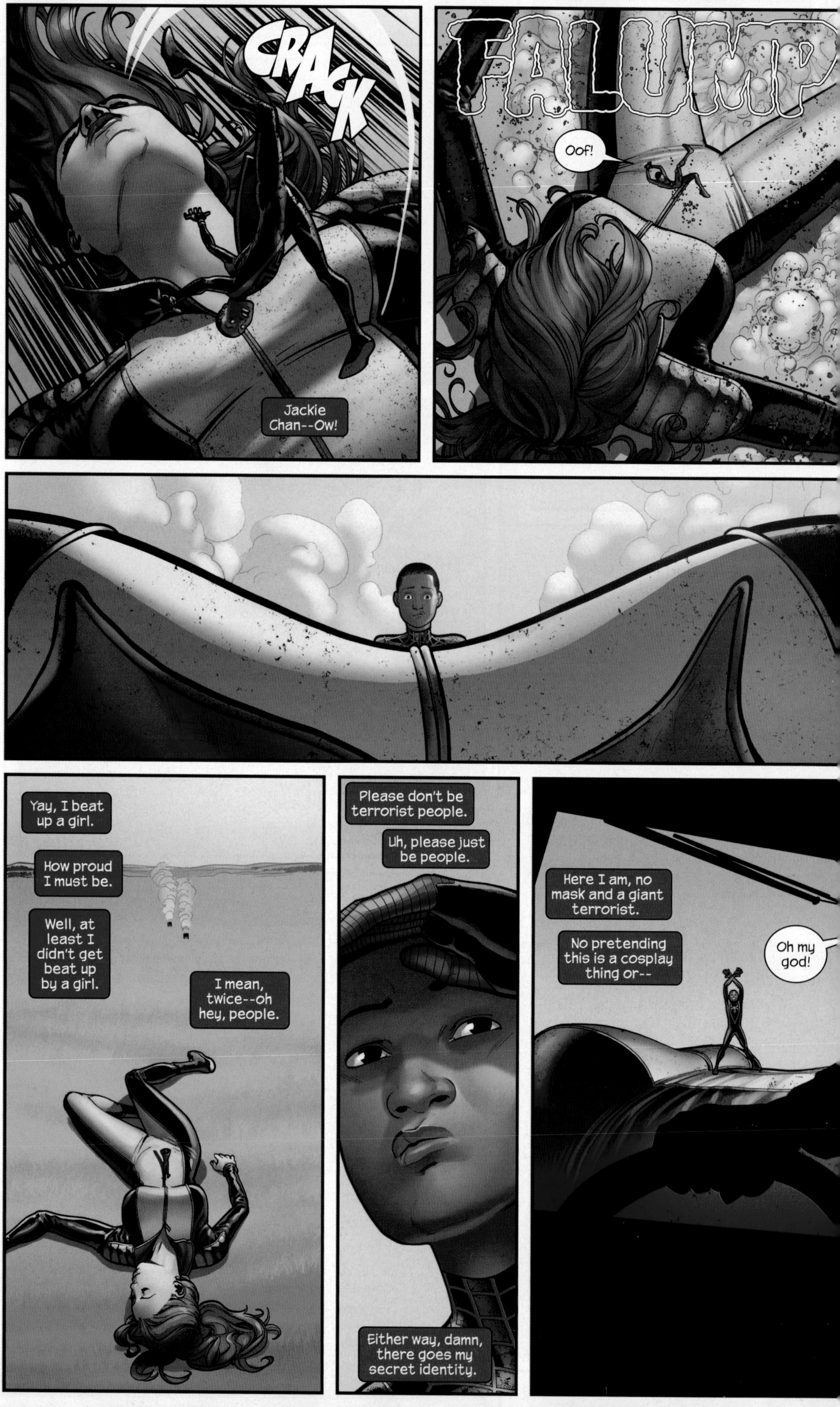
CRACK
Jackie Chan--Ow!
FALUMP
Oof!
Yay, I beat up a girl.
How proud I must be.
Well, at least I didn't get beat up by a girl.
I mean, twice--oh hey, people.
Please don't be terrorist people.
Uh, please just be people.
Either way, damn, there goes my secret identity.
Here I am, no mask and a giant terrorist.
No pretending this is a cosplay thing or--
Oh my god!

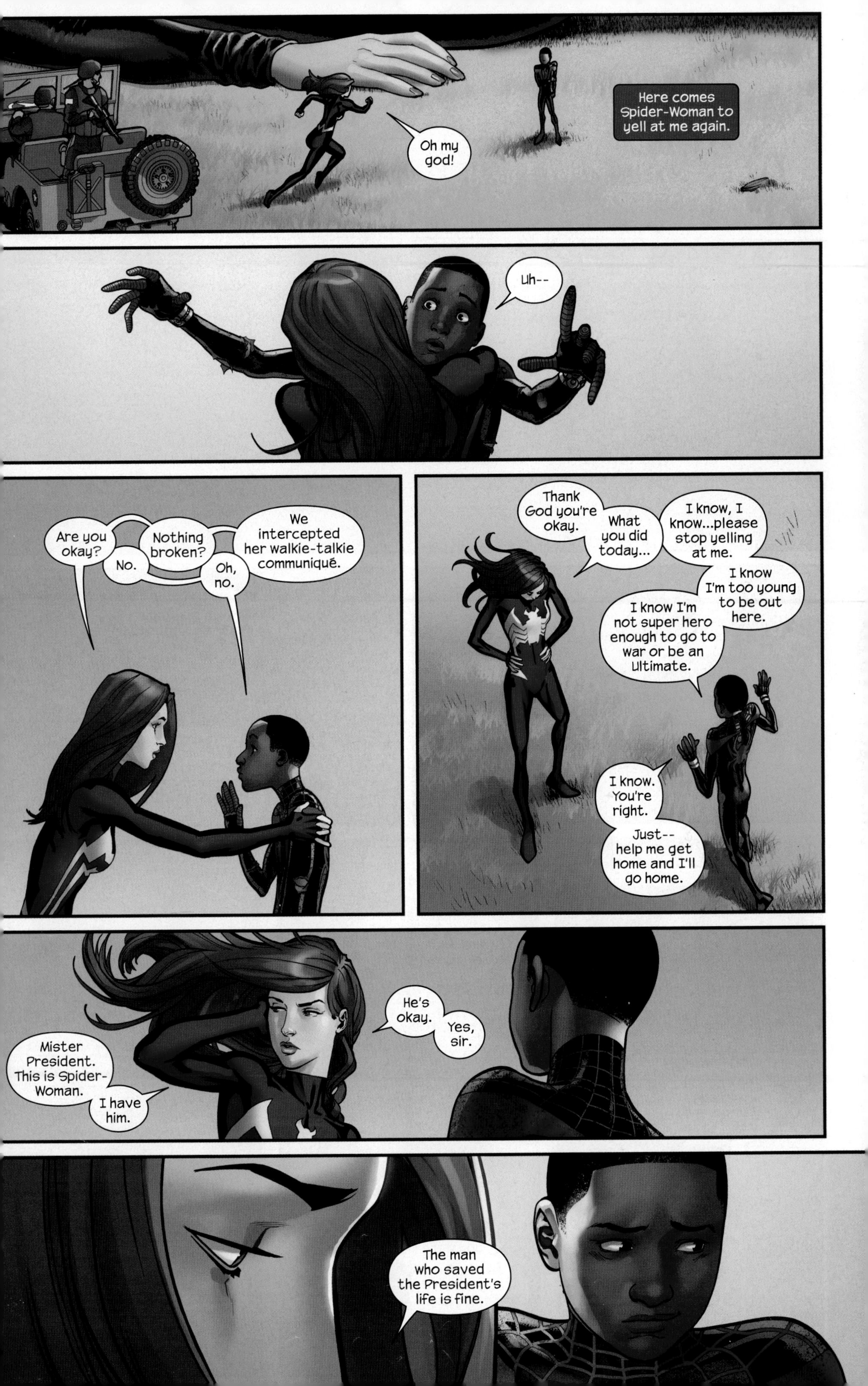
Here comes Spider-Woman to yell at me again.
Oh my god!
Uh--
Are you okay?
No.
Nothing broken?
Oh, no.
We intercepted her walkie-talkie communiqué.
Thank God you're okay.
What you did today...
I know, I know...please stop yelling at me.
I know I'm too young to be out here.
I know I'm not super hero enough to go to war or be an Ultimate.
I know. You're right.
Just-- help me get home and I'll go home.
Mister President. This is Spider-Woman.
I have him.
He's okay.
Yes, sir.
The man who saved the President's life is fine.

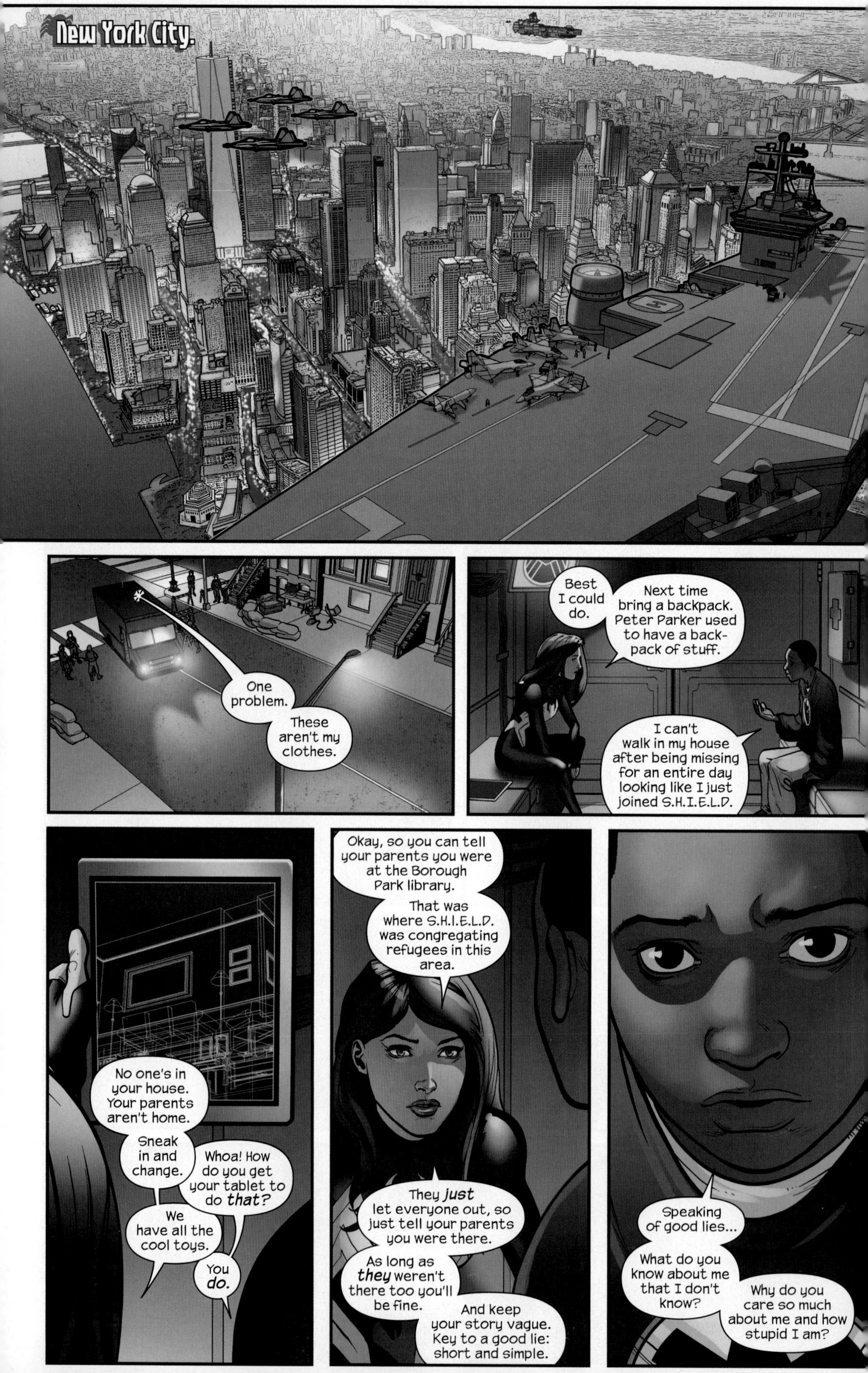
New York City.
One problem.
These aren't my clothes.
Best I could do.
Next time bring a backpack. Peter Parker used to have a back-pack of stuff.
I can't walk in my house after being missing for an entire day looking like I just joined S.H.I.E.L.D.
No one's in your house. Your parents aren't home.
Sneak in and change.
Whoa! How do you get your tablet to do *that?*
We have all the cool toys.
You *do.*
Okay, so you can tell your parents you were at the Borough Park library.
That was where S.H.I.E.L.D. was congregating refugees in this area.
They *just* let everyone out, so just tell your parents you were there.
As long as *they* weren't there too you'll be fine.
And keep your story vague. Key to a good lie: short and simple.
Speaking of good lies...
What do you know about me that I don't know?
Why do you care so much about me and how stupid I am?

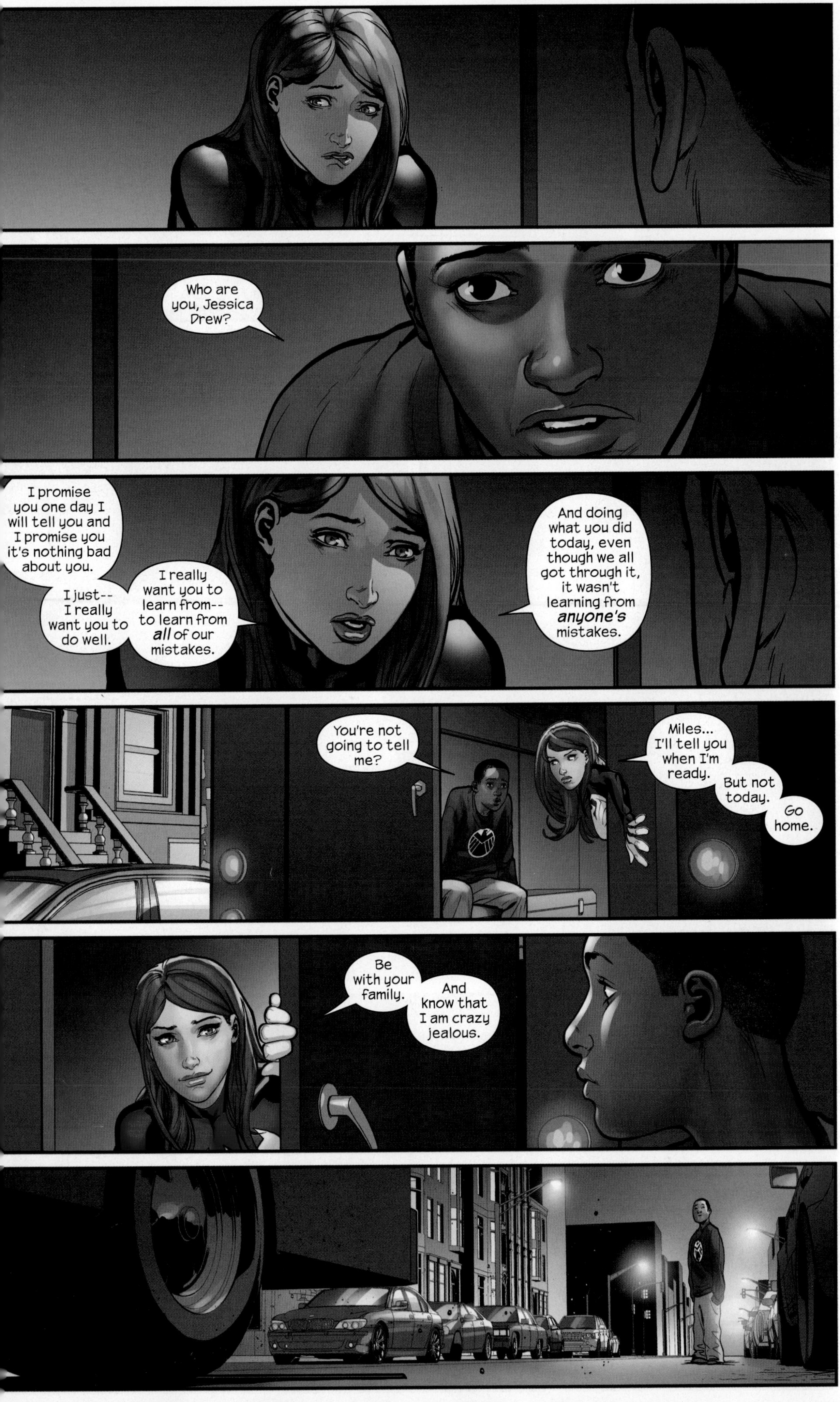
Who are you, Jessica Drew?
I promise you one day I will tell you and I promise you it's nothing bad about you.
I just-- I really want you to do well.
I really want you to learn from-- to learn from *all* of our mistakes.
And doing what you did today, even though we all got through it, it wasn't learning from *anyone's* mistakes.
You're not going to tell me?
Miles... I'll tell you when I'm ready.
But not today.
Go home.
Be with your family.
And know that I am crazy jealous.

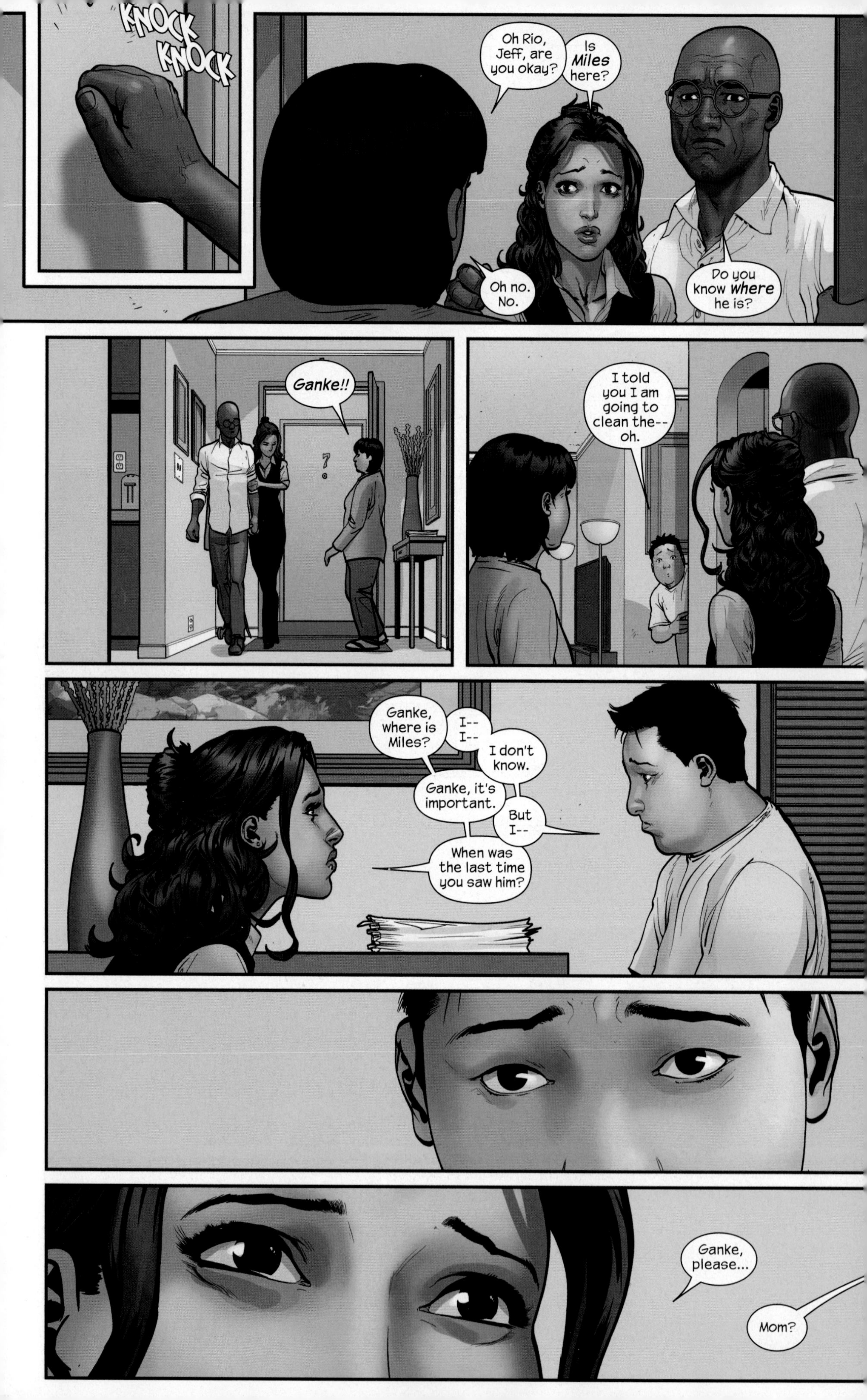
KNOCK
KNOCK
Oh Rio, Jeff, are you okay?
Is Miles here?
Oh no. No.
Do you know where he is?
Ganke!!
I told you I am going to clean the-- oh.
Ganke, where is Miles?
I-- I--
I don't know.
Ganke, it's important.
But I--
When was the last time you saw him?
Ganke, please...
Mom?

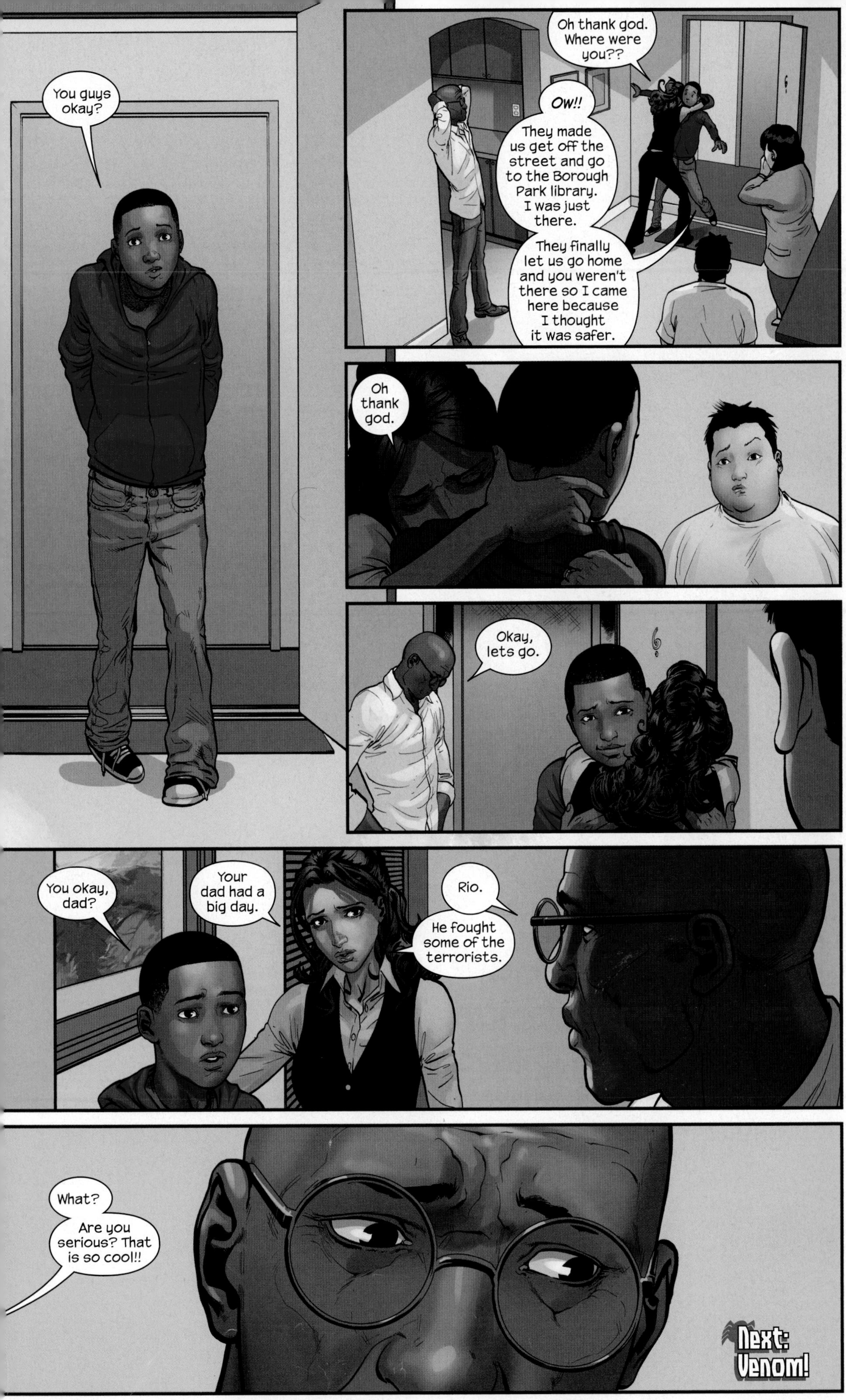
You guys okay?
Oh thank god. Where were you??
OW!!
They made us get off the street and go to the Borough Park library. I was just there.
They finally let us go home and you weren't there so I came here because I thought it was safer.
Oh thank god.
Okay, lets go.
You okay, dad?
Your dad had a big day.
Rio.
He fought some of the terrorists.
What?
Are you serious? That is so cool!!
Next: Venom!

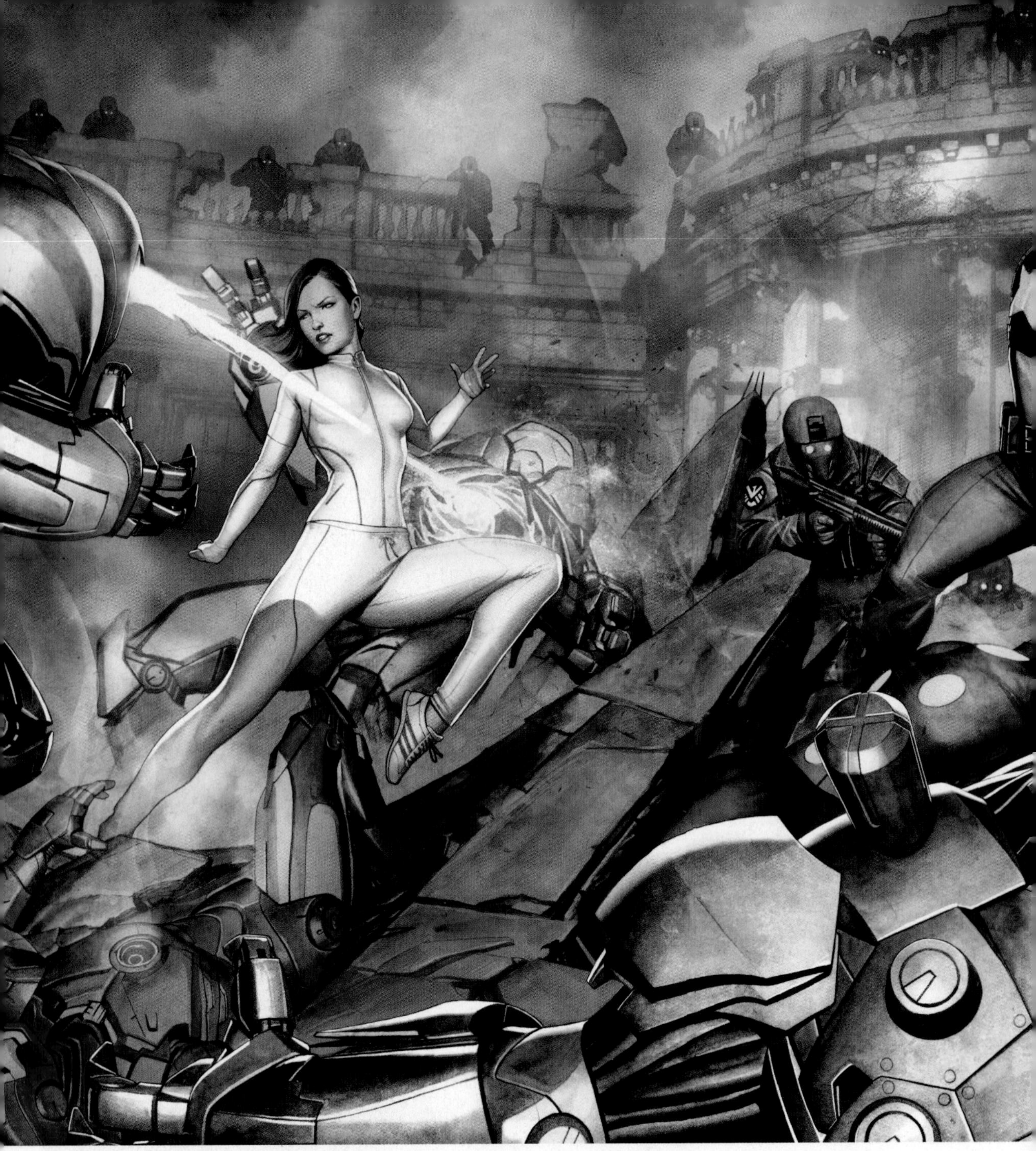

★ ULTIMATE COMICS X-MEN #14,
ULTIMATE COMICS ULTIMATES #13
ULTIMATE COMICS SPIDER-MAN#13
COMBINED VARIANT COVERS BY ADI GRANOV

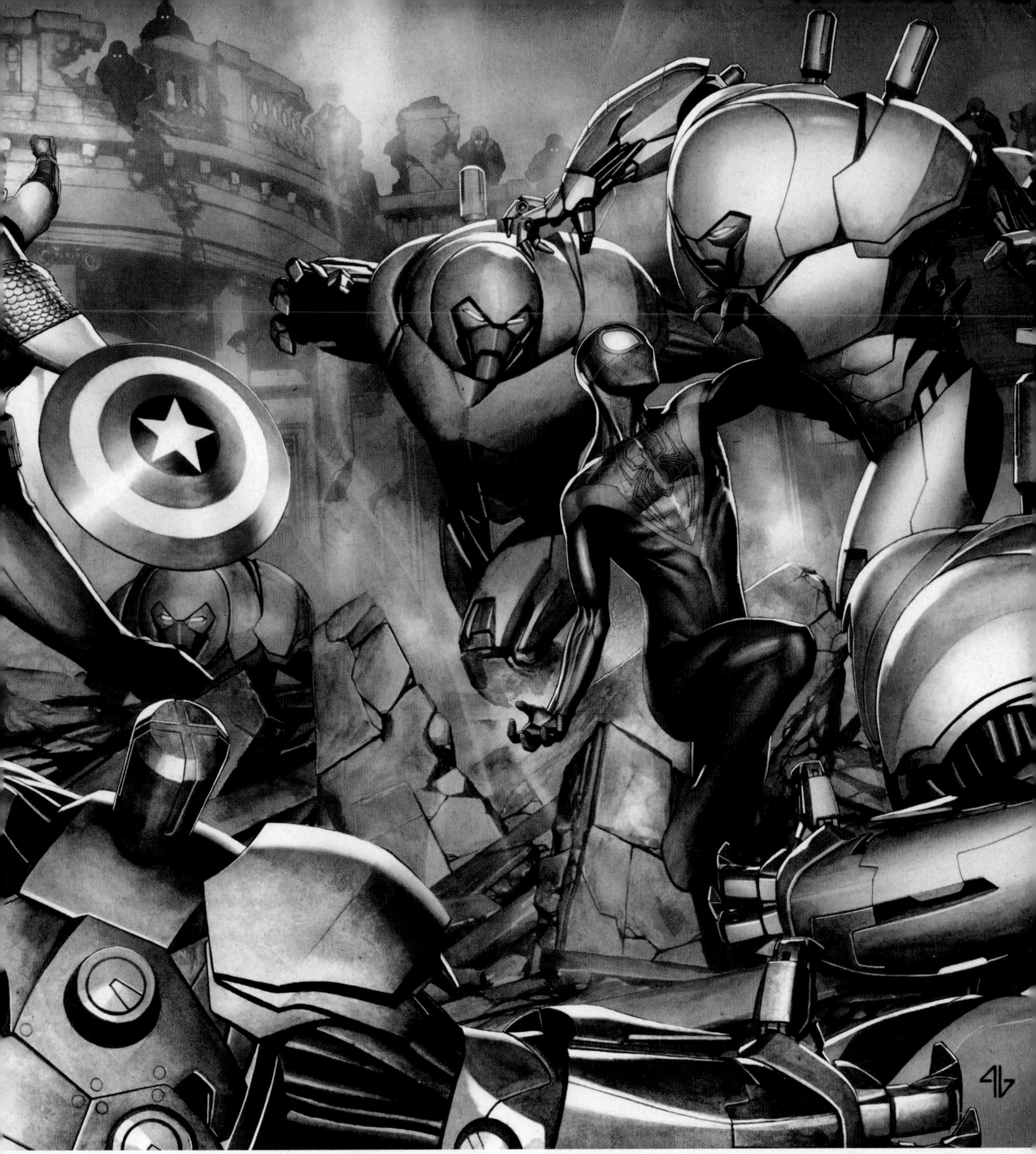

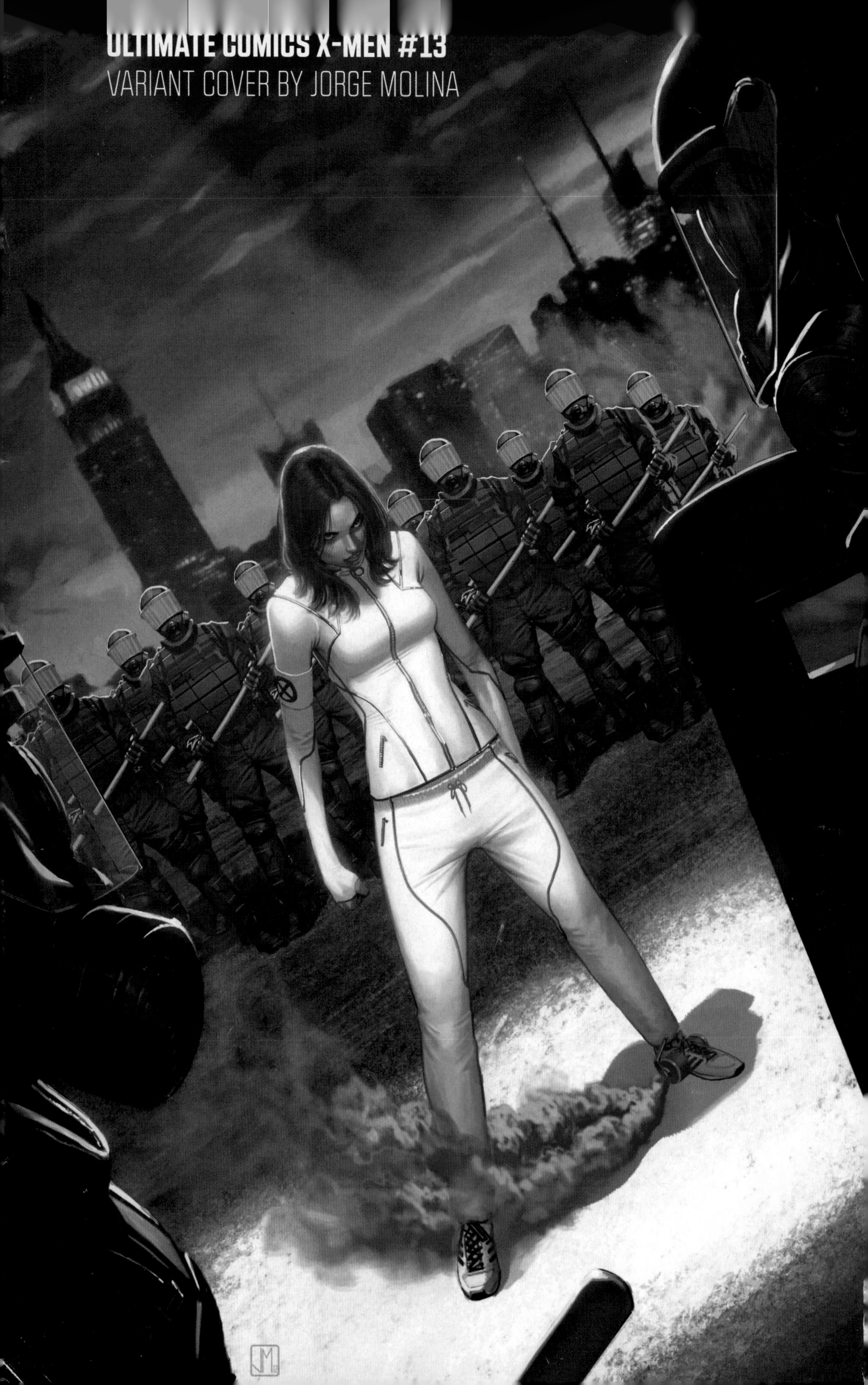

ULTIMATE COMICS X-MEN #13
VARIANT COVER BY JORGE MOLINA